**W9-CBL-342**

LANGENSCHEIDT'S
UNIVERSAL DICTIONARIES

# THE UNIVERSAL
# WEBSTER

*An English Dictionary*
*Completely revised edition*

# LANGENSCHEIDT
NEW YORK

*Webster's Universal Dictionary*
*was originally compiled by*
*Sidney Fuller, M. A., & R. Fuller*

© 1958, 1992 Langenscheidt KG, Berlin and Munich
Printed in Germany by
Druckhaus Langenscheidt, Berlin-Schöneberg

# PREFACE

This revised, updated and expanded edition of the Webster's Universal Dictionary includes the language of everyday life as well as the names of plants, animals and minerals. Besides the updated and enlarged general vocabulary the reader will also find important technical terms in current usage from such fields as space travel, engineering and medicine. Appropriate attention has also been paid to words that are not part of day-to-day English, but which the user might come across in newspapers or books. The definitions of such fundamental words as main verbs, conjunctions, prepositions, etc. have been expanded by adding illustrations of the specific ways in which the word in question is used. In this way the dictionary aims to improve students' overall linguistic competence by widening their vocabulary and giving them clear and thorough guidance as to the meaning and usage of the word they look up.

In revising the dictionary we have also tried to avoid giving mere synonyms as explanations, as this would make further reference necessary. Instead great importance has been attached to giving explanations that are easy to understand and to follow thus rendering the "Universal Webster" a highly useful and practical English reference work.

# Abbreviations

| | | | |
|---|---|---|---|
| *a* | adjective | *mus* | music |
| *Abbr.* | abbreviation | N. | North |
| *adv* | adverb | *n* | noun |
| Afr. | African | *o.s., o.s.* | oneself |
| Amer. | America, American | *pl* | plural |
| *art* | article | *poet* | poetic |
| a.th, *a.th* | anything | *prep* | preposition |
| Brit. | British | *pron* | pronoun |
| *CAN* | Canada | S. | South |
| *conj* | conjunction | Scot. | Scottish |
| E. | East | *sing* | singular |
| *esp.* | especially | *sl* | slang |
| *etc* | et cetera, and so on | s.o., *s.o.* | someone |
| Eur. | European | sth, *sth* | something |
| *f* | feminine | *TM* | trademark |
| *hist* | historical | *UK* | United Kingdom |
| *indef* | indefinite | *US* | United States |
| *infml* | informal | *usu* | usually |
| *interj* | interjection | *v* | verb |
| *m* | masculine | W. | West |

# Explanatory Notes

The arrangement of the entries is as follows:

1. The Vocabulary Entry is printed in bold-face type. The spelling, accent, syllabic division and hyphenation are shown in this entry. If the entry is a word of more than one syllable, the syllabic division is indicated either by a centered period (·) or by an accent (ʹ), each of which indicates the end of a syllable.

2. The Pronunciation is added in parentheses, and may be omitted either wholly or in part where a word offers no special difficulties in this respect.

3. The name of the Part of Speech is given in italics (see abbreviations), as in abode or will.

4. Inflectional Forms are given in parentheses and in bold-face type when they are irregular or present difficulties. The first form after the infinitive of an irregular verb is the past tense, the second the past participle. If the past participle is the same as the past tense only one form is given. Alternative forms are distinguished from one another by the word "or".

5. The Definitions are separated by semicolons. Geographical labels (*UK*, *US*, *etc*) indicate the area in which a word (only or chiefly) is used. Examples, in italics, illustrate the specific ways in which the word in question is used.

6. Run-on Entries are placed at the end of the definition(s). Such entries are usually derivative adjectives, adverbs, and nouns; their meaning can easily be inferred from the definition. If a run-on entry is stressed on the same syllable as the vocabulary entry, a bold-face hyphen replaces the vocabulary entry or the part before the vertical bar (|).

# Pronunciation Key

| Symbol | Example | Symbol | Example |
|--------|---------|--------|---------|
| ā | date | m | man |
| a | fat | n | not |
| ah | father | ng | ring |
| ãr | care | ō | old |
| aw | horn | o | top |
| b | bed | oo | foot |
| ch | chin | ou | out |
| d | day | p | put |
| dh | that | r | red |
| ē | meet | s | sun |
| e | ten | sh | she |
| e | account, over | t | to |
| | | th | thin |
| f | fill | ū | rule |
| g | go | u | cut |
| h | hat | ur | turn |
| ī | ice | v | have |
| i | hit | w | win |
| j | just | y | yes |
| k | keep | z | zone |
| l | let | zh | measure |

Foreign sounds are represented by the nearest English equivalents. The accent is indicated by ´ at the end of the syllable.

# A

**a** *n* first letter of English alphabet: *a* or *indef art* some (referring to one of group): *a flower*; one like: *a devil*; one: *a million*; any: *not a soul*; each: *once a day*

**a·back'**: **taken a.** shocked

**a·ban'don** give up entirely. **-ment**

**a·base'ment** humiliation

**a·bashed'** ashamed; confused

**a·bate'** lessen. **-ment**

**ab·bre'vi·ate** shorten

**ABC'** (ābēsē) the (Roman) alphabet; the basic facts or sth, which are learned first

**ab'di·cate** renounce formally, as throne, *etc*

**ab'do·men** part of body between chest and legs. **abdom'inal**

**ab·duct'** kidnap. **-ion**

**ab·er·ra'tion** deviation

**a·bet'** help in doing sth wrong. **-ment, -tor**

**a·bey'ance** temporary state of not being in use

**ab·hor'** loathe. **-rence, -rent**

**a·bide'** (**a·bode'**) put up with; dwell; **a. by** observe (rules, *etc*)

**a·bil'i·ty** (enough) power or skill ( to do sth)

**ab'ject** wretched; miserable

**a·blaze'** burning; excited

**a'|ble** having means or power ( to do): talented. **-bly**

**a'ble-bod'ied** having a strong healthy body

**ab·ne·ga'tion** self-denial

**ab·nor'mal** different from what is usual or expected. **abnormal'ity**

**a·board'** on or into a ship, train, *etc*

**a·bode'** *n* dwelling; see **abide**

**a·bol'ish** do away with. **aboli'tion**

**A'-bomb** atom bomb

**a·bom'i·nate** detest

**ab·o·rig'i·ne** (-rijinē) native inhabitant, *esp.* of Australia

**a·bor't** expel human fetus prematurely; cancel (mission, *etc*). **-tion, -tive**

**a·bound'** be plentiful

**a·bout'** *prep* on the subject of; here and there in: *we walked a. the city*; near (in number, *etc*): *a. fifty, a. two dozen*; on one's person; in the character of: *there's sth a. him that I like*; concerned or busy with; *adv* here and there; around; almost

**a·bove** *adv* at a higher point; overhead; higher than (in number, rank, *etc*); beyond: *his behavior was a. reproach*; upstream, *etc*; earlier (in book)

**a·bove'board** open and honest

**ab·rade'** wear away by rubbing. **abra'sion**

**a·bra'sive** rough (substance for cleaning or polishing); rude in behavior

**a·breast'** side by side and facing the same way; **a. of** keeping up with

**a·bridge'** shorten. **-ment**

**a·broad'** in or to another country; around: *There's a feeling a. that ...*

**ab'ro·gate** repeal

**ab·rupt'** sudden and *usu* unexpected; impolite. **-ness**

**ab'scess** collection of pus in body

**ab·scond'** go away secretly

**ab'|sent** not present. **-sence**

**ab·sen·tee'** one who is not where he should be. **-ism**

**ab·sent-mind'ed** forgetful

**ab'so·lute** complete; unlimited

**ab·solve'** pardon; free from guilt. **absolu'tion**

**ab·sor·b'** suck up. **-bent**; interest very much. **absorp'-tion**

**ab·stain'** refrain from (alcohol, voting, *etc*). **ab'sti-nence, ab'stinent**

**ab·stract'** *a* existing in the mind only; theoretical; *n* summary

**ab·struse'** hard to understand

**ab·surd'** ridiculous; unreasonable. **-ity**

**abun'|dant** plentiful. **-dance**

**abuse'** *v* (-z) misuse; insult; *n* (-s) misuse; insulting language

**abut'ment** support of an arch or bridge

**abyss'** immeasurably deep chasm

**ac·a·dem'ic** concerning education; theoretical

**acad'e·my** high school or school for special training; society for furthering the arts or sciences

**ac·cede'** agree (*usu* reluctantly); take over (a high post or position)

**ac·cel'er·a|te** speed up. **-tor**

**ac'cent** characteristic pronunciation; emphasis

**ac·cen'tu·ate** emphasize

**ac·cept'** receive; agree to; approve; recognize as true. **-able, -ance**

**ac'cess** *n* approach or entry (to place); right to use, get to or be with; *v* obtain, as information from computer

**ac·ces'sion** act of taking over (high post or position); addition

**ac·ces'so·ry** *a* aiding or contributing sth extra, as car radio, woman's handbag, *etc*; *n law* accomplice not present at crime

**ac·ci·dent** unexpected event; chance; mishap. **acciden'tal**

**ac·claim'** (express) praise or approval

**ac·cli'mate, ac·cli'ma·tize** accustom to new climate or situation

**ac·com'mo·date** have or get room for; adjust; help

**ac·com'pa·ny** go with. **-niment**

**ac·com'plice** partner in crime

**ac·com'plish** finish; carry out. **-ment**

**ac·cord'** agree(ment); give

**ac·cord'ing·ly** consequently; correspondingly

**ac·cord'ing to** as stated or shown by; in agreement with

**ac·cor'di·on** small portable musical instrument with bellows, reeds and keys

**ac·cost'** approach s.o. with (*usu* unpleasant) remark

**ac·count'** *n* arrangement allowing one to deposit or withdraw money from bank or to buy on credit; financial statement; report; consideration; **on a. of** because of; **on no a.** under no circumstances; *v* **a. for** explain

**ac·count'ant** account keeper

**ac·cred'it·ed** authorized

**ac·crue'** accumulate

**ac·cu'mu·late** collect; grow

in size or number

**ac·cu·ra|te** precise; correct. **-cy**

**ac·cuse'** charge with an offense. **accusa'tion**

**ace** playing card with one spot; skilled person; unreturnable tennis serve

**a·cer'bic** bitter

**a·cet'y·lene** a gas used for lighting and welding

**ache** (-k) dull continued pain

**a·chieve'** accomplish; obtain. **-ment**

**A·chil·les' heel** vulnerable point, *esp.* in person's character

**ac·id** *n* sour, *usu* corrosive substance; *sl* the drug LSD; *a* sour; (of remarks, *etc*) bitter. **acid'ity**

**ac·id rain'** rain polluted with acids from industry, cars *etc*

**ac·knowl'edge** (-nol-) admit; recognize; thank for. **-ment**

**ac·me** highest point

**ac·ne** skin disease causing pimples, *esp.* on face

**a·corn** fruit of the oak

**a·cous'tic** of sound or hearing

**a·cous'tics** science of sound; *pl* features affecting way in which sound can be heard in theater, *etc*

**ac·quaint'** make familiar with; inform. **-ance**

**ac·qui·es|ce'** accept passively or without complaint. **-cence**

**ac·quire'** get; gain. **acquisi'-tion**

**ac·quis'i·tive** eager to acquire

**ac·quit'** declare not guilty. **-tal**

**a'cre** measure of land. **-age**

**ac'rid** biting; sharp

**ac'ri·mo·ny** bitterness of temper or language

**ac'ro·bat** performer of gymnastic feats and tricks. **acrobat'ic**

**ac'ro·nym** word formed from first letters of other words, *usu* an organization, as NATO

**a·cross'** crosswise; to or on the opposite side (of); **come a.** meet with

**a·cryl'ic** chemical used in paint and fibers

**act** *v* do sth; behave; perform; have an effect; *n* deed; division of a play; law; pretense; **a. of God** natural disaster

**ac'tion** doing; deed; (interesting) events; fighting; lawsuit; mechanism; movement

**ac'tive** energetic; busy; lively; involved (in). **activ'ity**

**ac'tiv·ist** person very involved in sth, *esp.* political movement

**ac'tor** performer in plays, movies etc. **-tress**

**ac'tu·al** existing; real; present. **actual'ity**

**ac·u·punc·ture** piercing of body with needles to treat illness

**a·cute'** sharp; keen; not chronic

**ad'age** proverb

**ad'a·mant** immovable; obstinate

**Ad'am's ap'ple** projecting cartilage at front of neck which moves up and down

**a·dapt'** make suitable; adjust; modify. **adapta'tion**

**add** join (one thing to another); unite two (or more) numbers to make one sum; state further

**ad·den'dum** (*pl* **-da**) thing to be added

**ad'der** small poisonous snake

**ad·dict'** *n* one addicted

**ad·dic'ted** dependent on sth, *esp.* drugs. **-tion**

**ad·di'tion** adding; thing added. **-al** added; extra

**ad'di·tive** substance added to food, *etc* to improve taste, color, *etc*

**ad·dress'** *n* number, street, city, *etc* where person lives, *esp.* used to show destination of mail; speech; *v* write name and address on mail; speak or write to; direct (speech, *etc*) to; tackle, as problem, *etc*

**ad·dress·ee'** person to whom mail is addressed

**ad·duce'** bring forward as proof or explanation. **-ible**

**ad'e·noids** *pl* sponge-like growth at back of nose

**a·dept'** highly skilled

**ad'e·qua|te** sufficient. **-cy**

**ad·here'** stick fast

**ad·her'ent** follower

**ad·he'|sive** (substance capable of) sticking fast. **-sion**

**ad'i·pose** fatty

**ad·ja·cen|t** lying near or next (to). **-cy**

**ad'jec·tive** word used with noun to describe it more fully

**ad·join'** be situated next to

**ad·journ'** stop, *usu* for short time; move to another room, *etc.* **-ment**

**ad·judge'** decide officially; declare; award

**ad·ju'di·cate** decide by law; act as judge

**ad·just'** change to make fit or suitable; arrange. **-ment**

**ad'ju·tant** military officer who does office work

**ad·lib'** improvise

**ad·min'is·ter** manage; dispense; give. **administra'tion**

**ad·mi'ra·ble** worth admiring; excellent

**ad'mi·ral** high naval officer; kind of butterfly

**ad·mire'** regard with wonder; have high opinion of. **admira'tion**

**ad·mis'sion** act of admitting

**ad·mit'** acknowledge; say rather unwillingly; let in. **-tance**

**ad·mon'ish** warn. **admoni'-tion**

**a·do'** (-ū) stir; fuss

**ad·o·les'cent** (person) between childhood and adulthood; immature, as of behavior. **-cence**

**a·dopt'** take as one's own; take on

**a·dore'** admire greatly; love; worship. **adora'tion**

**a·dorn'** decorate. **-ment**

**a·dren'a·lin** hormone secreted in moments of fear, anger, *etc* to stimulate circulation and muscles

**a·drift'** floating uncontrolled; without purpose or plan

**a·droit'** skillful

**a·dult'** mature (person)

**a·dul'ter·ate** debase by mixture

**a·dul'ter·y** sex between married person and s.o. other than spouse. **-er**, *f* **-ess**, **-ous**

**ad·vance'** *v* move or put forward; promote; pay *money* before usual time; *n* progress; forward movement; prepayment; increase (in bid, *etc*); *a* early, as payment, warning, *etc*

**ad·vanced'** ahead of; progressive

**ad·van'tage** favorable circumstance; positive result. **advanta'geous** superiority

**ad·ven'ture** exciting experience

**ad'ver·sar·y** opponent; enemy

**ad·verse'** unfavorable;
opposing

**ad·ver'si·ty** misfortune

**ad·ver·tis|e** give public
notice of; place announcement in newspaper, *etc.* **-ing,
advertise'ment**

**ad·vice'** opinion given as to
what action to take

**ad·vis|e'** give advice to; rec-
ommend; inform. **-er**

**ad·vi'so·ry** acting as adviser
or containing advice

**ad'vo·cate** *n* (-kit) supporter;
*v* (-kāt) plead in favor of

**ae'on** see **eon**

**aer'i·al** (ār-) *a* of or in the air;
*n* antenna

**aer'o·bics** strenuous exercise
(*usu* to music) to strengthen
heart and lungs

**aer'o·drome** (ār-) *UK* air-
field

**aer·o·dy·nam'ic** (ār-) of aer-
odynamics; moving through
the air quickly and with little
resistance

**aer·o·dy·nam'ics** (ār-) science of how solid bodies
move through air

**aer·o·naut'ics** (ār-) science
of aircraft

**aer'o·plane** (ār-) see airplane

**aer'o·sol** (ār-) pressurized
container of liquid which
can be sprayed out

**aer'o·space** (ār-) having to

do with space aviation: *the a.
industry*

**aes'thete** (esthēt) one sensitive to beauty. **aesthet'ic**

**aes·thet'ics** (es-) philosophy
of the beautiful

**a·far'** at or to a great distance

**af'fa·ble** friendly

**af·fair'** event; matter; business of any kind; love affair

**af·fect'** influence; touch; pretend

**af·fec·ta'tion** artificial behavior

**af·fect'ed** artificial

**af·fec'tion** tenderness. **-ate**

**af·fi·da'vit** sworn written
statement

**af·fil'i·ate** associate; connect

**af·fin'i·ty** relationship; natural attraction

**af·firm'** state positively; confirm. **affirma'tion**

**af·firm'a·tive** answering yes;
agreeing. **a. action** policy of
favoring minorities in hiring

**af·fix'** attach; stick; add

**af·flic|t'** distress; affect;
trouble. **-tion**

**af'flu|ent** wealthy. **-ence**

**af·ford'** have the means for;
do, *etc* without fear of con-
sequences: *I can't afford to
be seen there*; provide

**af·front'** (efrunt) insult

**a·field'** away from home; at
or to a distance

**a·fire'** on fire

**a·flame'** burning brightly;
glowing

**a·float'** floating (in water or air); flooded; out of debt

**a·fore'said** said or named earlier

**a·fraid'** filled with fear; frightened; uneasy; sorry

**a·fresh'** again

**aft** in or near back of ship or plane

**af'ter** behind in place or order; later in time than; in search of; in imitation of; according to

**af'ter·ef·fect** result or consequence

**af'ter·math** aftereffect

**af'ter·noon** time between sun's highest point and about six o'clock

**af'ter·shave** liquid rubbed on face after shaving

**af'ter·thought** sth occurring to one or added later

**af'ter·ward(s)** later

**a·gain'** (-gen, -gān) once more; further; on the other hand

**a·gainst'** (-genst, -gānst) in opposition to; in contact with; in opposite direction to; touching; in contrast to; in preparation for; facing

**a·gape'** wide open; in state of wonder

**age** *n* length of life or being (from beginning to any given time); any specific period of life or history; latter part of life; **of a.** grown-up in legal sense; *v* grow old; (wine) mature

**a·ged** (ājd) of the age of; (ājid) old

**age·less** never seeming old

**a·gen·cy** business or institution providing a specific service; government department; means

**a·gent** one who acts for another; active power

**ag·gran·dize** increase; exaggerate. **-ment**

**ag·gra·vate** make worse; *infml* annoy

**ag·gre·gate** *v* collect into a mass; total; *n* sum total

**ag·gres'|sion** unprovoked attack. **-sive**

**ag·grieved'** (feeling) hurt because of wrong suffered

**a·ghast'** filled with sudden surprise, fright or horror

**ag'ile** (-j-) nimble; lively

**ag'i·ta|te** shake, disturb; arouse public feeling. **-tion, -tor**

**a·glow'** glowing; eager

**ag·nos'tic** one who believes that nothing can be known of the existence of God

**a·go'** in the past

**ag'o·nize** worry intensely and for a long time

**ag'o·ny** extreme bodily or mental suffering

**a·grar'i·an** relating to the cultivation of land

**a·gree'** be of same opinion as or in harmony with; consent; concede; come to an understanding; suit or fit, *esp.* one's constitution. **-ment**

**a·gree·a·ble** pleasing

**ag'ri·cul·ture** farming

**a·ground'** on the ground in shallow water

**a·head'** in front; forward; at an earlier time (than); in advance; in the (near) future

**aid** help

**AIDS** (Acquired Immune Deficiency Syndrome) a fatal viral infection attacking body's natural defense system

**ai'ler·on** movable control flap on airplane wing

**ail'ing** unwell; in a poor state: *the a. economy*

**ail'ment** mild illness

**aim** point (weapon, *etc*) at; direct efforts toward; intend

**aim'less** without purpose. **-ly**

**ain't** *infml* short form for *am not, is not, are not, has not, have not*

**air** *n* atmosphere; open space overhead; appearance; tune; *pl* affected manners; *v* expose to the air; make known

**air'borne** in the air; (of troops) transported by airplane

**air'brake** brake worked by air pressure

**air'·con·di·tion·ing** means of tempering and refreshing air in rooms

**air'craft** machine(s) for air travel

**air'field** place where planes can take off and land

**air'lane** flight path

**air'lift** transportation by air to or from blocked or unreachable place

**air'line** company operating planes for passengers and goods

**air'lin·er** large passenger plane

**air'mail** letters, *etc* sent by air by air

**air'plane** machine for travel by air

**air'port** place with facilities for the public where airplanes land, start, and undergo repairs

**air'space** open sky above a country and subject to its laws

**air'tight** closed so that no air can get in or out

**air'y** of or like air; light in movement or appearance; breezy; impractical; not earnest

**aisle** (īl) passage between row of seats

**a·jar'** partly open

**a·kin'** related; similar

**a·lac'ri·ty** quick and ready willingness

**a·larm'** danger signal; fright

**al·be'it** (-bē-) although

**al·bi'no** person or animal lacking coloring matter in skin, hair, and eyes

**alliance**

**al'bum** book for holding photographs, stamps, *etc*; long-playing record

**al·bu·men** substance forming white or colorless part of egg

**al'che·my** (-k-) medieval chemistry, aimed at changing metals into gold

**al'co·hol** colorless liquid, the intoxicating main element of fermented liquors; any liquor containing this. **-ism, al·cohol'ic**

**al'cove** recess in a room, *etc*

**al'der·man** high city official

**ale** type of beer

**a·lert'** *a* watchful; perceptive; *n* alarm; **on the a.** ready to act; *v* warn

**al'ge·bra** branch of mathematics using letters and signs and dealing with negative as well as real numbers. **alge·bra'ic**

**al'go·rithm** procedure involving pattern of repetition, used in (computer) calculation

**a'li·as** *adv* also called; *n* assumed name

**al'i·bi** (-bī) plea of having been elsewhere; excuse

**al'ien** (-yen) *n* foreigner; creature from outer space; *a* foreign; strange and different

**al'ien·ate** estrange

**a·light'** *v* dismount; come down; *a* lighted up; burning

**a·lign'** (līn) bring into line. **-ment**

**a·like'** similar; in the same manner, form, *etc*

**al'i·mo·ny** allowance paid by divorced husband or wife to former spouse

**a·live'** living; active; full of life

**al'ka·li** any of group of substances which, when united with acids, give salts. **-ine, -oid**

**all** *a* the whole (amount, number) of; the greatest possible; every; any whatever; *adv* wholly; *pron* everything; **a. in** a. taking everything together; **a. clear** signal that danger is over; permission (to do sth.); **a. in** extremely tired; **a.(-)out** using all one's strength, *etc*; **a. right** satisfactory; safe and sound; *as phrase* okay; **a. the same** nevertheless; making no difference; **on a. fours** on one's hands and knees

**Al'lah** Muslim name for God

**al·lay'** relieve; calm; reduce

**al·lege'** (-lej) assert without proof. **allega'tion**

**al·le'giance** (-lējens) loyalty (to government)

**al'le·go·ry** portrayal by symbol. **allegor'ical**

**al'ler·gy** sensitiveness to certain substances. **aller'gic**

**al·le'vi·ate** relieve; lessen

**al'ley** narrow passage

**al·li'ance** union by treaty for marriage; parties united in this way

**al·li·ga·tor** (leather from) crocodile-like reptile found in US and China

**al·lit·er·a'tion** use of same sound at beginning of two or more words in close succession

**al·lo·cate** set apart for particular purpose; give as share

**al·lot'** give as share. **-ment**

**al·low'** let do or have; permit; admit; **a. for** take into account

**al·low'ance** sum of money given for expenses; money in consideration given under certain circumstances

**al'loy** metallic compound

**al·lu|de'** refer indirectly (to). **-sion**

**al·lure'** charm; tempt

**al·ly'** *n* unite by agreement

**al·ly'** *n* person, country, *etc* allied

**al'ma·nac** yearbook

**al·might'y** having all power

**al'mond** (ahmend) (nut of) fruit tree

**al'most** very nearly

**alms** (ahmz) gift of charity

**a·loft'** high up

**a·lone'** apart from or without all others; only

**a·long'** from one end to the other of; lengthwise; onward; together with; **all a.** all the time

**a·loof'** distant (in manner, *etc*)

**a·loud'** in natural tone of voice, not whispering

**alp** high mountain, *esp.* one of range (the Alps) stretching from France to Austria. **-pine**

**al·pac'a** (cloth made from hair of) woolly camel-like animal

**al'pha** (alfe) first letter of Greek alphabet

**al'pha·bet** the letters of a language in their usual order. **alphabet'ical**

**al·pha·nu·mer'ic** using both letters and numbers (as symbols)

**al·read'y** by this time; before a given time; in the past

**al·right'** see **all**

**al'so** too; besides; in addition

**al'tar** table used in religious service

**al'ter** (awl-) change. **altera'tion**

**al'ter·nate** (-nit) *a* being by turns; every second (of two); alternative; *v* (-neit) happen by turns; change (from one state, *etc* to another)

**al·ter'na·tive** *a* other (of two or more); not traditional or usual; *n* choice between things

**al·though'** (-dhō) in spite of the fact that

**al'ti·tude** height above sea level

**al'to** female voice of low range

**al·to·geth'er** in all; wholly; on the whole

**al'tru·ism** unselfish concern for welfare of others

**a·lu'mi·num**, *UK* **al·u·min'i·um** white metal of very light weight

**a·lum'|nus**, *f* **-na** (*pl* **-ni, -nae**) graduate of a college

**al'ways** all the time; every time; for ever

**am** see **be**

**a·mal'gam·ate** combine

**a·mass'** collect or accumulate

**am'a·teur** (-tur) one who does a thing as a pastime without pay. **-ish**

**a·maze'** strike with wonder. **-ment**

**a·maz'ing** unbelievable; wonderful

**am·bas'sa·dor** highest official representing a nation in a foreign state; person sent as (official) representative: *goodwill a.*

**am'ber** (made of) yellowish brown resin; (of) this color

**am·bi·dex'trous** able to use both hands equally well

**am'bi·ence** atmosphere (of a place)

**am·big'u·ous** unclear; of double meaning; uncertain

**am·bi'|tion** desire for fame or success; aspiration. **-tious**

**am·biv'a·lent** having conflicting feelings, attitudes, *etc*

**am'ble** walk at an easy pace

**am'bu·lance** vehicle for transporting sick or wounded persons

**am'bush** *n* surprise attack; *v* attack from hiding

**a·me'|ba**, *UK* **-moe-** (-mē-) (*pl* **-as** or **-ae**) tiny single-celled creature. **-bic**

**a·mel'io·rate** (emēl-) make better; ease

**a'men** so be it (said after prayers)

**a·me'na·ble** (-ē-) easily managed; responsive (to)

**a·mend'** change; improve. **-ment; make amends for** make up for

**a·men'i·ty** pleasant convenience

**A·mer'i·can** *a* of America, *esp.* of USA; *n* citizen of USA

**am'e·thyst** precious purple stone of crystallized quartz

**a'mi·a·ble** good-natured; likable. **amiabil'ity**

**am'i·ca·ble** friendly. **amicabil'ity**

**a·mid(st)'** in the middle of; among

**a·miss'** wrong(ly); improper(ly); **take a.** be offended at

**am'i·ty** friendship

**am·mo'ni·a** colorless strong-smelling gas used to make fertilizers, cleaning substances, *etc*

**am·mu·ni'tion** bullets, shells, *etc* for weapons

**am·ne'si·a** loss of memory

**am'nes·ty** act of general pardon

**a·moe'ba** see **ameba**

**a·mok'** see **amuck**

**a·mong(st)'** surrounded by; in the group of; between; being one of

**a·mor'al** non-moral

**am'o·rous** expressing (sexual) love; in love

**a·mor'phous** without fixed shape or form

**am'or·tize** gradually pay off, as a debt

**a·mount'** *n* total of two or more sums; quantity; *v* **a. to** add up to; to be equal in number, effect, *etc*

**am'pere** (-pēr) unit of electric current (amp.)

**am'per·sand** sign "&", meaning "and"

**am·phib'i·an** animal that can live both on land and in water

**am·phib'i·ous** living or functioning on land or in water

**am'phi·the·a·ter** UK sth round structure with rising rows of seats around central stage

**am'ple** quite enough, large

**am'pli·fy** expand; increase volume (of sound) or strength (of electronic signal). **-fier, amplifica'tion**

**am'pu·tate** cut off (limb, *etc*)

**a·muck'** *used in phrase* **run a.** run about in violent and uncontrolled fit, *esp.* with desire to murder

**amuse'** entertain; cause to laugh. **-ment**

**an** form of **a** used before vowels or silent letter h

**a·nach'ro·nism** (-nak-) sth or s.o. placed in the wrong period of time

**an·a·con'da** large S. Amer. snake that crushes its prey

**an'a·gram** word formed from letters of another by changing their order

**a·nal'o·gy** comparison. **-gous**

**a·nal'y·sis** (*pl* **-ses**) examination; evaluation; psychoanalysis

**an'a·lyze**, *UK* **-lyse** examine (by separating into individual elements). **-lyst, analyt'ic(al)**

**an'ar·chy** (-kē) social state of lawlessness; disorder and chaos. **-chism, -chist**

**a·nat'o·my** science of bodily structure. **-mist**

**an'ces·tor** forefather. **-try**

**an'chor** (angker) heavy metal device dropped to hold ship in place. **-age**

**an·cho'vy** (-chō-) small fish of herring family

**an'cient** (ānshent) of former times; very old

**and** word used to join words, phrases, *etc*, expressing addition or continuation

**an·drog'y·nous** (-droj-) having both male and female qualities

**an'ec·dote** brief story about incident. **anecdot'al**

**a·ne'|mi·a**, UK **-nae-** lack of red blood corpuscles. **-mic**

**an·es·thet'ic**, UK **-aes-** (substance) making insensible to pain

**an'gel** (ānjel) divine attendant; guiding spirit; kind and helpful person. **angel'ic**

**an'|ger** (angger) strong feeling of annoyance. **-gry**

**an·gi'na pec'to·ris** painful disease of heart causing suffocating feeling in chest

**an'|gle** n corner; point of view; v fish. **-gler;** slant

**an·go'ra** goat or rabbit with silky hair; soft wool made from this

**angst** general feeling of anxiety or dread

**an'guish** extreme pain or grief

**an'gu·lar** having angles

**an'i·mal** (of or concerning) any being that can move and feel; (of or like a) beast

**an'i·mate** give life to; encourage

**an·i·mos'i·ty** hostility

**an'ise** herb with aromatic seeds

**an'kle** joint connecting foot with leg

**an'nals** pl historical records

**an·nex'** v take possession of. **annexa'tion**

**an'nex,** UK **-nexe** n addition to building

**an·ni'hi·late** destroy completely

**an·ni·ver'sa·ry** date of some notable event remembered each year, as wedding, etc

**an'no·tate** add notes to

**an·nounce'** make known publicly. **-ment**

**an·noy'** irritate. **-ance**

**an'nu·al** occurring, done, etc once a year

**an·nu'i·ty** fixed yearly allowance

**an·nul'** make void

**an'ode** positive electrode

**a·nom'a·|lous** abnormal; irregular. **-ly**

**a·non'y·mous** of unknown name or authorship

**an'o·rak** short weatherproof jacket

**an·o·rex'i·a** illness marked by refusal to eat. **-ic**

**an·oth'er** one more; one different; one just like; **one a.** each other

**an'swer** (anser) v reply (to); correspond to or fulfill; n sth done or said in return; solution to a problem

**ant** small insect living in highly organized communities

**an·tag'o·|nis·m** active opposition. **-nist**

**an·tag'o·nize** make hostile

**Ant·arc'tic** (of or near) the area around the South Pole

**ant·eat·er** animal which feeds on ants

**an·te·ced·ent** preceding (event); *pl* person's past life or family

**an·te·cham·ber** room leading to main room

**an·te·date** date earlier

**an·te·lope** graceful deerlike cud-chewing animal

**an·ten·na** device for sending or receiving radio or television signals; feeler on head of insect

**an·te·ri·or** situated or coming before

**an'·them** hymn; song of praise

**an·thol'o·gy** collection of writings

**an'·thrax** disease of cattle. *etc* dangerous to humans

**an'·thro·poid** *a* resembling man in shape: *n* any of the higher apes

**an·thro·pol'o·gy** scientific study of man

**an·ti·bi·ot'ic** (-bi-) substance used to kill harmful bacteria

**an·ti·bod·y** substance formed in the blood to fight disease

**an'·tic** (*usu pl*) silly behavior; caper

**an·tic'i·pate** expect; foresee; look forward to; forestall

**an·ti·cli'max** let-down

**an'·ti·dote** remedy (against poison)

**an·ti·freeze'** substance that lowers freezing point of

cooling liquid in engine

**an·ti·he·ro** main character in novel, *etc* who lacks qualities of traditional hero

**an·ti·his'ta·mine** drug used to treat allergies and colds

**an·tip'a·thy** intense dislike

**an·ti·quar·y** student or collector of antiques

**an·ti·quat·ed** out of date

**an·tique'** (-tēk) *a* of old times; *n* valuable object, as vase, *etc*, made in earlier times

**an·ti·Sem'i|te** one hostile to Jews. **-tism**

**an·ti·sep'tic** (substance) preventing infection

**an·ti·so'cial** against the interests of society; not social

**an·tith'e·sis** (*pl* -ses) opposite; contrast

**ant'·ler** branched horn of deer

**an'·to·nym** word opposite in meaning to another word

**a'·nus** (ā-) opening at lower end of intestine through which solid waste material passes out of the body

**an'·vil** block on which metal is worked

**anx·i'e·ty** (angzī-) uneasiness of mind

**anx'·ious** (angkshs) worried; eagerly desiring

**an'·y** (eni) every; some; one out of many; in whatever quantity or number; (*with negative*) none at all

**an'·y·bod·y** any person

**an'y·how** in any way whatever; nevertheless

**an'y·one** any person

**an'y·thing** a thing, no matter what; a thing of any kind

**an'y·way** anyhow

**an'y·where** to, in or at any place

**a·or'ta** main artery from heart

**a·part'** away from each other; in or into pieces; to or at one side

**a·part'heid** system in S. Africa used to keep people from different races apart

**a·part'ment** (*US*) room(s) used as dwelling place

**ap'a·thy** lack of feeling or interest. **apathet'ic**

**ape** *n* large monkey with no tail; *v* imitate

**ap'er·ture** opening

**a'pex** (ā-) (*pl* **a'pi·ces** [āpisēz]) top; highest point

**aph'o·rism** short phrase expressing general truth or observation

**aph·ro·dis'i·ac** (substance) arousing sexual desire

**a·piece'** each

**a·plomb'** self-assurance

**a·poc'a·lypse** the end of the world. **apocalyp'tic**

**a·pol'o·gy** expression of regret; justification. **-gist, -gize**

**ap'o·plex·y** illness arresting powers of sense and motion. **apoplec'tic**

**a·pos'tle** (-sl) any of Christ's twelve disciples; follower; admirer

**a·pos'tro·phe** sign (') used to show possession or to indicate omission of letter(s) in word: *Tom's book, didn't*

**ap·pal'** *UK* **-pall** (-awl) fill with fear; dismay

**ap·pa·ra'tus** (*pl* **-tuses**) equipment for specific task

**ap·par'el** *n* clothing

**ap·par'ent** plain to see; seeming

**ap·pa·ri'tion** (-rishen) ghost

**ap·peal'** *v* earnestly request; be attractive: apply to a higher court; *n* act or right of appealing

**ap·pear'** come into sight; seem; present o.s.; perform, as in play, *etc*; be published. **-ance**

**ap·pease'** placate; satisfy. **-ment**

**ap·pel'lant** one who appeals

**ap·pel·la'tion** name; title

**ap·pend'** add; attach. **-age**

**ap·pen·di·ci'tis** (-sī-) inflammation of the appendix

**ap·pen'dix** something added, *esp.* to a book; narrow worm-shaped outgrowth from intestine

**ap·per·tain'** belong to

**ap'pe·tite** desire, *esp.* for food and drink

**ap·pe·tiz'ing** (of food) having quality that stimulates the appetite. **-er**

**ap·|plaud'** express approval (by clapping). **-plause**

**ap'ple** (tree bearing) fleshy round edible (*usu* red) fruit

**ap·pli'ance** electrical household device

**ap'pli·cant** one who applies

**ap·pli·ca'tion** act of applying; written request; diligence

**ap·ply'** ask formally; put on; put to use; be suitable or relevant; devote

**ap·point'** name for a position; set time, place, *etc*. **-ment**

**ap·prais|e'** estimate value of. **-al**

**ap·pre'ci·a·ble** (-shi-) enough to be estimated or seen

**ap·pre'ci·a|te** (-shi-) think highly of; recognize; be thankful for. **-tive, ap·precia'tion**

**ap·pre·hend'** arrest; understand

**ap·pre·hen'|sive** fearful; worried. **-sion**

**ap·pren'tice** learner of craft; beginner. **-ship**

**ap·proach'** *v* come near (to); deal with; talk to (s.o.), *esp*. about a request; *n* path or method leading to sth

**ap·pro·ba'tion** approval

**ap·pro'pri·ate** *v* (-eit) take for o.s.; set apart, as funds, *etc*; *a* (-it) suitable; proper

**ap·prove'** (-prüv) accept;

consent to; **a. of** find good. **-al**

**ap·prox'i·mate** *v* (-meit) come near (to); *a* (-mit) nearly correct

**a'pri·cot** (tree bearing) round orange-pink fruit

**A'pril** fourth month of year

**a'pron** garment worn in front of clothing to protect it; advanced platform

**apt** likely (to do); suitable; quick to learn

**ap'ti·tude** natural ability

**aq·ua·ma·rine'** blue-green gem

**a·quar'i·um** tank in which living fish, *etc* are kept; public exhibit of such tanks

**a·quat'ic** living in or near water; having to do with water

**aq'ue·duct** large pipe for carrying water

**ar·a·besque'** style of ornament

**Ar'a·bic numeral** one of the figures 1, 2, 3, 4, 5, 6, 7, 8, 9, 0

**ar'a·ble** (of land) suitable for farming

**ar'bi·ter** one empowered to decide points at issue

**ar'bi·trar·y** random; despotic

**ar'bi·tra|te** settle (labor) dispute. **-tor**

**arc** part of a cirle; curve

**ar·cade'** covered passage; series of arches

**ar·cane'** mysterious and secret

**arch** curved structure sup-

porting bridge, *etc*; sth like
an a. in shape or function

**ar·chae·ol·o·gy** (-k-) study of
(buried) remains of earlier
cultures

**ar·cha·ic** (-kā-) antiquated

**arch'|er** one who shoots with
bow and arrow. **-ery**

**ar'che·type** (-ketīp) original
idea or model; typical example

**ar·chi·pel·a·go** (-kipelegō)
group of many islands

**ar'chi·tect** (-ki-) person who
designs buildings, *etc*

**ar'chi·tec·ture** (-ki-) science
or style of building

**ar'chives** (-kīvz) *pl* public records; place for these

**Arc'tic** (of or near) area
around the North Pole

**ar'dent** eager; passionate

**ar'dor,** *UK* **-dour** enthusiasm

**ar'du·ous** hard to do; strenuous

**are** see **be**

**ar'e·a** district; total surface
size; field (of study, *etc*); **a.
code** telephone number of
district, *etc* used in long distance calls

**a·re'na** place used for sports,
concerts, *etc*

**ar·gu·men'ta·tive** fond of ar-
guing

**a'ri·a** solo song, as in opera

**ar'id** dry; barren. **arid'ity**

**a·rise'** (**a·rose',** **a·ris'en**)
come into being; get up;
happen; result

**ar·is·toc'ra·cy** nobility

**a·rith'me·tic** science of
numbers; reckoning, *esp.*
adding, subtracting, multi-
plying and dividing. **arith-
met'ical**

**arm** *n* human upper limb
from hand to shoulder; anything that resembles this;
(*usu pl*) weapon; *v* equip for
fighting by giving weapons to

**ar'ma·ment** military equipment

**ar'ma·ture** part of a dynamo

**arm'chair** comfortable chair
with arm rests

**ar'mi·stice** truce

**ar'mor,** *UK* **-mour** metal covering for body, ships, *etc* as
protection during fighting

**ar'mor·y,** *UK* **-mour-** place
where weapons are kept or
made

**arm'pit** hollow under arm
where it joins shoulder

**ar'my** organized body of
people (trained and
equipped for war); great
number

**a·ro'ma** fragrance

**a·rose'** see **arise**

**a·round'** on every side (of); in
every direction; here and
there; about; near

**a·rouse'** excite; awaken

**ar·raign'** (erān) *Law* try before a court

**ar·range'** put in order; settle;
form plans (for); (music)
adapt. **-ment**

**ar·ray'** n impressive group; (battle) order; v arrange; dress

**ar·rears'** pl unpaid debts

**ar·rest'** make prisoner of (by authority of law); stop (progress of); catch (attention of)

**ar·rive'** come to place, esp. one's destination; (of time) come, **-al**; **a. at** reach (decision, etc)

**ar·ro·gance** unpleasant pride and self-importance. **-gant**

**ar·row** slender pointed rod shot from bow; sign (→) showing direction

**ar·se·nal** place for storing or making war material

**ar·se·nic** poisonous chemical element

**ar·son** criminal setting fire to (other's) property

**art** (man's ability to make) things of beauty, such as paintings, etc; skill: the a. of writing novels

**ar·ter·y** vessel carrying blood from heart. **arte'rial** main traffic channel

**art·ful** sly; cunning

**ar·thri'tis** inflammation of joint(s)

**ar·ti·choke** (tall herb with) flower eaten as vegetable

**ar·ti·cle** short piece of writing; object; Law paragraph of treaty, etc

**ar·tic·u·late** (-it) a able to express ideas clearly; able to

pronounce words clearly; v (-āt) express (ideas) clearly; speak distinctly

**ar'ti·fice** device; trickery

**ar·ti·fi'cial** not natural

**ar·til'ler·y** (part of army trained to use) large guns

**ar·ti·san** craftsman

**art'ist** person creating art, esp. painting, sculpture, etc; gifted performer. **artis'tic**

**art'less** free from deceit

**arts** pl non-scientific branches of learning, as literature, music, etc; drama, ballet, music, etc as expressions of cultural life

**as** to the same extent, equally: a. good a.; for instance: wild animals, a. the tiger; in the same way that: do a. I do; in view of the fact that: I cannot come, a. I am sick; in one's function, role, etc of: a. chairman of the board; while: he entered a. I left; though: weak a. I am; which: a. was clear; **a. regards, a. to** in connection with; **a. well (a.)** in addition to; **a. yet** up to now

**as·bes'tos** dangerous fibrous substance that does not burn

**as·cend'** move upward; rise; go up

**as·cend'an·cy** controlling influence

**as·cent'** upward movement; upward slope

**as·cer·tain'** find out. **-ment**

**ASCII** (askē) American standard Code for Information Interchange, used to exchange information between diverse computer sytems

**as·cribe'** consider as due or belonging to

**a·sep'tic** free from harmful bacteria

**ash** tree of olive family with tough wood used for furniture, *etc*; (*often pl*) powdery substance left when material is burned; *pl* remains of corpse after burning

**a·shamed'** feeling shame or guilt

**ashore'** on or to the shore

**aside'** *adv* to or on the side; out of the way; *n* words spoken to the side, so as (supposedly) not to be heard by others

**as'i·nine** stupid; foolish. **asinin'ity**

**ask** put a question to; request; expect; invite

**a·skance'** with mistrust

**a·skew'** not straight; not level

**a·sleep'** sleeping; (of legs and arms) without feeling due to lack of circulation

**as·par'a·gus** (plant with) young shoots used as vegetable

**as'pect** detail or side (of a subject); direction in which a window, *etc* faces

**as·per'sion** insulting or slanderous remark

**as'phalt** black substance used to make roads, *etc*

**as·phyx'i·ate** (asf-) suffocate

**as'pic** clear meat jelly

**as·pire'** desire earnestly; seek to attain. **aspira'tion**

**as·pi'rin** drug taken to relieve pain, fever, *etc*

**ass** long-eared animal of horse family, donkey; foolish person

**as·sail'** attack violently. **-ant**

**as·sas'si·n** (hired) murderer. **-ate**

**as·sault'** attack

**as·say'** test (metals); attempt

**as·sem'ble** gather; fit together

**as·sem'bly** gathering; legislative body; fitting together; **a. line** factory system in which workers and machines contribute in a fixed sequence to the completion of a product

**as·sent'** agree

**as·sert'** declare; insist on (claim). **-tion**; show (authority)

**as·ser'tive** forceful; self-confident

**as·sess'** evaluate (situation, *etc*); estimate value of; impose tax or fine on. **-ment**

**as'set** sth useful or beneficial; *pl* resources of a person or business

**as·sid'u·ous** persevering; diligent. **assidu'ity**

**as·sign'** give as a task or share; appoint; make over (property *etc*). **-ment**

**as·sim'i·late** absorb; make or become like

**as·sist'** help; aid. **-ance, -ant**

**as·so'ci·ate** (-shi-) *v* join or unite (with); connect in thought; *n* partner

**as·so·ci·a'tion** organization of people to further common interest; link; connection in the mind

**as·sort'** sort out; classify. **-ment**

**as·sort'ed** of various sorts or types

**as·|sume'** suppose; take (responsibility, *etc*); take on (significance, *etc*); pretend to have. **-sumption**

**as·sur'ance** (-shoor-) promise; self-confidence

**as·sure'** guarantee; state positively

**as'ter** any of group of plants with star-shaped flowers

**as'ter·isk** star used as reference mark

**a·stern'** at, to or behind the back part of a ship

**as'ter·oid** small planet

**asth'ma** (azme) disease causing breathing difficulties

**a·stig'ma·tism** defect of eye or lens

**a·stir'** in motion; excited

**as·ton'ish** amaze; surprise. **-ment**

**as·tound'** astonish

**as'tral** of, like or about the stars

**a·stray'** out of the right way

**as·trin'gent** causing contraction (of skin tissue); severe

**as·trol'o·gy** study of supposed influence of stars, *etc* on human life

**as'tro·naut** person who travels through space in a spacecraft

**as·tron'o·my** scientific study of heavenly bodies

**a·stute'** shrewd

**a·sun'der** apart

**a·sy'lum** (political) refuge or protection; hospital for mentally ill

**a·sym'me·try** lack of symmetry. **asym·met'ric(al)**

**at** in or near to: *a. the house*; in the direction of: *throw/ shoot a*; describing a certain condition: *a. work, a. war*; expressing degree, rate, *etc*: *a. a high speed*; expressing time: *a. seven o'clock, a. night*; **a. all** to any extent (*usu* with "not"); **a. that** moreover: *she tore her dress, and her best one a. that*

**ate** see **eat**

**a'the·ism** belief that there is no God

**ath'lete** (-lēt) person trained (to compete) in sports, such as running, jumping, *etc*. **athlet'ic(s)**

**at'las** book of maps

**at'mos·pher|e** air (surrounding earth). **-ic;** mood

**at·mos·pher'ics** noises in radio reception due to electrical disturbances in atmosphere; static

**at'oll** ring-shaped coral island

**at'om** smallest particle of element. **atom'ic**

**at'om** or **a·tom'ic bomb** bomb using the splitting of atoms to cause a tremendous explosion

**at'om·iz·er** instrument for spraying liquids

**a·tone'** make amends for. **-ment**

**a·tro'cious** (-shes) extremely wicked. **-ity**

**at'tro·phy** waste away through lack of use or food

**at·tach'** fasten; *Law* seize; **a. to** belong to. **-ment**

**at·ta·ché'** (ateshā) specialist attached to embassy

**at·tack'** *v* set upon with force or words; start to work vigorously on; *n* act of violence; fit of illness

**at·tain'** reach; gain. **-ment**

**at·tempt'** try

**at·tend'** be present at; pay attention; wait on. **-ant**

**at·tend'ance** attending; number of people present

**at·ten'tion** (-shen) act of concentrating the mind. **-tive**

**at·test'** testify to; certify

**at·tire'** dress; array

**at'ti·tude** way of thinking or acting; posture

**at·tor'ney** (-tur-) lawyer

**at·tract'** excite interest, feelings; draw to, as magnet. **-tion, -tive**

**at·trib'ute** *v* regard as belonging or due to; ascribe to. **-tive**

**at'tri·bute** *n* characteristic quality

**at·tri'tion** *n* wearing away

**a·typ'i·cal** out of the ordinary

**au'burn** reddish brown

**auc'tio|n** public sale by bid. **-neer**

**au·da'cious** daring; impudent. **-ity**

**au'di·ble** able to be heard

**au'di·ence** group of listeners; official interview

**au'di·o** of or related to sound

**au·di·o·vi'su·al** combining sound and sight

**au'dit** examine, as accounts; *US* attend (lectures)

**au·di'tion** hearing to try out singer, actor, *etc*

**au'di·tor** one who examines accounts; hearer. **-ry**

**au·di·to'ri·um** hall for concerts, lectures, *etc*

**aug·ment'** increase; enlarge

**au·gust'** *a* venerable; majestic

**Au'gust** *n* eighth month of year

**aunt** sister of one's father or mother; wife of one's uncle

**au'ra** atmosphere around a person or place

**au'ral** (aw-) of the ear or sense of hearing

**au'ri·cle** outer part of ear;

heart chamber receiving blood from veins. **auric'ular**

**aus'pice** omen; *pl* patronage

**aus·pi'cious** favorable; promising

**aus·ter|e'** stern; severe. **-ity**

**au·then'tic** genuine

**au·then'ti·cate** establish as true or authentic

**au'thor** writer of book, *etc*; originator, creator. **-ess, -ship**

**au·thor'i·tar·i·an** imposing or expecting obedience

**au·thor'i·ty** (legal) power; influence; source of correct information. **-tative**

**au'thor·ize** empower

**au'tis·m** mental illness marked by withdrawal from reality. **autis'tic**

**au'to** automobile

**au·to·bi·og'ra·phy** one's life written by oneself. **autobiograph'ical**

**au'to·crat** absolute ruler. **autoc'racy**

**au'to·graph** one's own signature

**au·to·mat'ic** able to function or operate without outside influence

**au·to·ma'tion** use of automatic equipment to save time and labor

**au·to·mo·bile** car driven by motor

**au·ton'o·mous** selfgoverning. **-my**

**au'top·sy** medical examination of dead body

**au'tumn** season between summer and winter. **autum'nal**

**aux·il'ia·ry** helping; supporting

**a·vail'** be of use or benefit

**a·vail'a·ble** at one's disposal

**av'a·lanche** sliding mass of snow, *etc*

**av'a·rice** greed. **avari'cious**

**a·venge'** get revenge for

**av'e·nue** wide street, *usu* lined with trees; way of reaching or escaping from sth

**a·ver'** declare positively

**av'er·age** *n* amount found by dividing the sum of a series by the number of items in the series; *a* ordinary; usual

**a·verse'** unwilling; opposed

**a·ver'sion** strong dislike

**a·vert'** prevent; turn away

**a·vi·a'tion** flying by plane; aircraft industry. **a'viator**

**av'id** eager; enthusiastic

**av·o·ca'do** pear-shaped tropical fruit

**a·void'** keep away from; refrain from doing. **-able**

**a·vow'** declare openly. **-al**

**a·wait'** wait for; be in store for

**a·wake'** *v* (**a·woke'** or **a·waked'**, **a·waked'** or **a·wok'en**) stop sleeping; become conscious of; wake s.o. up; also **a·wak'en;** *a* not sleeping; alert

**a·ward**[1] v grant; n judgment
**a·ware**[1] knowing; conscious of. **-ness**
**a·way**[1] adv to or at a distance; without stopping; without delay; **do, make a. with** kill; get rid of; a absent
**awe** respect mixed with fear
**awe·some** filling with awe
**aw·ful**[1] very bad or unpleasant; very great; inspiring awe
**a·while**[1] for a time
**awk·ward** clumsy; difficult to use or handle; embarrassing. **-ness**
**awl** tool to pierce holes, esp. in leather
**awn·ing** rooflike canvas cover

**AWOL** (ā'wol) absent without leave (or permission)
**a·wry**[1] (-rī) twisted; wrong; amiss
**ax**, UK **axe** tool with sharp metal blade and wooden handle, used for chopping; **get the a.** be removed from office, etc
**ax·i·om** established principle; self-evident truth. **axiomat·ic**
**ax·is** (pl **ax·es**) line about which a thing revolves
**ax·le** bar on which a wheel or pair of wheels turns
**a·ya·tol·lah** Muslim religious leader
**ay(e)** yes
**az·ure** (azhər) sky-blue

# B

**b** second letter of English alphabet
**bab·ble** talk unclearly; talk foolishly; of stream, etc murmur; US reveal information. **-bler**
**babe** baby; US inexperienced person
**ba·boon** large monkey with doglike muzzle and short tail
**ba·by** very young child; childish person; small thing of its kind. **-ish**
**ba·by-sit** take care of children while parents are away. **-ter**

**bac·ca·lau·re·ate** bachelor's degree
**bach·e·lor** unmarried man; (holder of) lowest university degree
**back** n rear part of human body or, in animals, part corresponding to it; spine; rear part of a. th.; **behind one's b.** without one's knowledge; **turn one's b.** on turn away from; avoid; v support; (cause to) move backwards; approve of or support, as candidate; **b. down** accept defeat; admit error; **b. out (of)** withdraw; a

lying behind or far away; of or from the past; overdue; *adv* flowing or moving to the rear; in return or reply

**back'bit·ing** spiteful remark(s). **-er**

**back'bone** spine; main support; firmness of character

**back'break·ing** very hard or strenuous

**back'drop** painted cloth at rear of stage; background

**back'fire** produce (too early explosion of gas in engine); go wrong, as plan, *etc*

**back'ground** scenery behind sth seen or depicted; circumstances or information explaining sth; sum of one's experience and education

**back'ing** aid or support; body of supporters; musical accompaniment

**back'lash** strong negative reaction

**back'log** work not yet done

**back'pack** rucksack with metal frame

**back'ped·al** pedal backwards on bicycle; retreat

**back'slide** become less good; work less. **-er, -ing**

**back'ward** *a* shy; behind in development. **-ness**

**back'ward(s)** *adv* toward the back; with the back foremost; in reverse of the usual way; toward the past; toward a worse state

**back'wa·ter** water held back

by dam, *etc*; place marked by lack of development

**ba'con** salted or smoked back and sides of pig, *usu* in thin slices

**bac·te·ri·ol'o·gy** science dealing with bacteria. **-gist**

**bac·te'ri·um** (*pl* **-ia**) microscopic plant organism

**bad (worse, worst)** not good; below standard; incorrect; not valid; unfavorable; wicked; painful; rotten; **feel b.** be ill; **feel b. about** regret

**bade** see **bid**

**badge** emblem worn as sign of office, membership, *etc*

**badg'er** burrowing animal; *v* pester

**baf'fle** be too hard to understand

**bag** *n* container made of soft material with opening at top, used for carrying things; *v* kill or capture in hunting; hang loosely. **-gy**

**bag'gage** (-gij) the trunks, suitcases with which one travels; portable equipment of an army

**bag'pipe(s)** musical wind instrument

**bail** *n* money paid as security for prisoner's appearance; *v* dip water from; free on security

**bait** *n* tempting thing, *esp.* food; *v* put b. in trap, on hook, *etc.*; lure; torment

**bank**

**bake** cook by dry heat, *esp.* in oven; dry or harden by heating

**bak'er** one who makes bread and cakes. **-y**

**bal'ance** *n* steady or even distribution of weight, amount, *etc*; difference between positive and negative (aspects, *etc*); weighing instrument; *v* make equal; settle an account

**bal'ance of trade** difference between a country's exports and imports

**bal'co·ny** platform projecting from wall of building; interior gallery in public building, *esp.* theater

**bald** lacking natural covering, such as hair; plain

**bale** *n* large bundle, as hay; *v* pack closely

**balk** (bawk) *n* hindrance; *v* block; refuse to go on

**ball** any round body; round body of leather, *etc* used in games; missile for cannon, *etc*; a large formal dance; *infml* good time

**bal'lad** simple song; poem, *esp.* one that tells a story

**bal'last** weight carried to steady ship

**bal'let** (-lā) theatrical group dance with fixed poses and steps; music for this dance

**bal·lis'tic mis'sile** missile guided while rising, but falling freely

**bal·loon'** *n* bag of light material filled with gas or hot air so that it rises; *v* swell out when filled with air

**bal'lot** voting ticket; system of secret voting

**balm** (bahm) soothing ointment or lotion

**bal·us·trade'** railing

**bam·boo'** tropical reed

**ban** *v* prohibit; *n* prohibition

**ba·nal'** commonplace

**ba·na'na** (yellow finger-shaped fruit of) large-leaved tropical plant

**band** *n* something that holds things together; flat narrow strip; group of persons who are together for some purpose; group of musicians playing together; *radio* a group of wavelengths; *v* tie with a band; **b. together** join together in a group

**ban'dage** (-ij) strip of material used to dress wounds

**ban'dit** armed robber. **-ry**

**bane** poison; harm. **-ful**

**bang** *v* hit sharply; beat, shut, *etc* with loud noise; *n US usu pl* fringe of hair across forehead

**ban'ish** exile. **-ment**

**ban'is·ter** handrail

**ban'jo** stringed musical instrument with long neck and round body

**bank** *n* business which holds money for its customers, gives credit, *etc* **-er;** mound or pile, *esp.* of earth; ground along edge of lake or river; shelf on floor of sea; mass of clouds, snow, *etc;* group of objects arranged in order; *v* carry on business of a bank; put money in bank; raise or heap up in a bank; cover (fire) with fresh fuel and reduce draft of air; slope an airplane sideways when turning

**bank'note** paper money printed for central bank as legal tender

**bank'rupt** unable to pay debts. **-cy**

**ban'ner** piece of cloth, ended with a sign or an emblem, symbolizing group, country, *etc*

**ban'quet** (-kwet) feast; formal dinner with speeches

**ban'tam-weight** boxer weighing up to 118 lbs.

**ban'ter** tease playfully

**bap'tism** ceremony of admittance to Christian church. **baptize'**

**bar** *n* long narrow piece of wood or metal; band or stripe, as of color; anything that stands in the way or prevents; court, system of courts, or the legal profession; counter at which food or liquor is served; line dividing written music into measures; *v* fasten or close with bars; prohibit or pre-

vent; block

**barb** point on hook curving backward; cruel remark. **-ed**

**bar·bar'i·an** uncivilized or brutal person. **-ic**

**bar'be·cue** frame for roasting food, *esp.* over open fire; outdoor party where such food is served

**bar'ber** one who cuts hair, shaves beards, *etc*

**bar·bit'u·rate** drug to calm or put to sleep

**bar'code** system of coding information (*esp.* price, *etc*) in thick and thin vertical bars which can be read by computer

**bare** *a* without clothing or covering; empty; having just enough; plain. **-ly;** *v* uncover; reveal

**bare'back** without a saddle

**bare'faced** shameless

**bar'gain** *n* agreement; thing bought cheap; *v* haggle over or come to terms

**barge** large freight-boat

**bar'i·tone** male voice of middle range

**bar'i·um** tracer metal used in X-rays

**bark** *n* tough outside covering of tree, bush, *etc;* short sharp noise made by dogs, seals, *etc; v* peel bark from tree; rub skin from (by bumping, *etc*); issue cry of dog

**bar'ley** cereal used for food and in making liquors

**barn** building on farm for keeping cattle, storing grain, farm tools, *etc*

**bar·na·cle** kind of shellfish

**ba·rom·e·ter** instrument for measuring atmospheric pressure

**bar·racks** *pl* soldiers' quarters

**bar·rel** (amount contained by) round bulging container, longer than it is wide, with flat ends, for beer, food, *etc*; metal tube of gun

**bar·rage** (-rahzh) barrier of shellfire; rapid series of questions, *etc*

**bar·ren** unfruitful; sterile

**bar·ri·cade** hasty defense barrier

**bar·ri·er** obstacle; boundary

**bar·ring** except for

**bar·ris·ter** *UK* lawyer entitled to plead cases before court (see **solicitor**)

**bar·tend·er** one who mixes and serves drinks at a bar

**bar·ter** trade by exchange

**base** *n* part on which sth stands or rests; bottom; main part or principle; starting-point; military center; chemical substance which combines with acid to form salt; *v* found on; *a* morally low; selfish; mean; of little value; (of coins) false

**base·ball** (ball used in) American team sport played on field with four bases arranged in diamond shape

**base·ment** lowest floor below ground level

**bash·ful** very shy

**bas·ic** fundamental

**BASIC** widespread computer language used by non-specialists

**ba·sil** (-z-) herb of mint family used in cooking

**ba·sin** (bā-) shallow round container for holding water, *etc*; natural hollow in land, containing water; area drained by river

**ba·sis** (*pl* **-ses**) foundation; main ingredient

**bask** bathe in pleasant warmth

**bas·ket** container made of thin strips of wood, reeds, or other flexible material woven together

**bas·ket·ball** (large ball used in) team sport played on court with basketlike goals

**bas-re·lief** (bah-) shallow sculpture on wall, *etc*

**bass** (bas) kind of food fish; (bās) male voice; musical instrument of lowest range

**bas·si·net** an infant's bed

**bas·soon** musical wind instrument of low register

**bas·tard** illegitimate (child)

**baste** sew loosely; moisten roasting meat

**bas·tion** stronghold

**bat** (wooden) club, *esp.* one used in various games for

**batch**                                            34

striking the ball; nocturnal
flying mammal with fore-
limbs shaped like wings
**batch** quantity of similar
things
**bath** (bath) container for
bathing; washing of the
body with water, *etc*; water
or other liquid used in bathing; liquid used for some
special purpose, as dye b.
**bathe** (bādh) wash, as in a
bath; apply water or other
liquid to; surround with water; go swimming; (of light,
*etc*) envelop
**ba·ton'** orchestra leader's
stick; thin rod passed to next
runner in relay race
**bat·tal'ion** body of troops
**bat'ter** *v* beat violently; *n* cake
mixture
**bat'ter·y** portable cells for
producing electricity; artillery unit; beating
**bat'tle** large-scale fight between armed forces; any
contest
**bat'tle-ship** warship of largest and most heavily armed
class
**bau'ble** trinket; trifle
**bawl** cry or shout with full,
loud sound
**bay** *n* inlet of the sea; laurel
tree, whose dried leaves are
used in cooking; *v* bark; *a*
reddish
**bay'o·net** blade attachable to
rifle

**bay'ou** (biū) inlet from river
**bay'win·dow** projecting window forming alcove
**ba·zaar'** Oriental market;
sale, *esp.* to raise money for
charity
**be** (am, is, are, was, were,
been) exist; have reality;
happen: *the wedding was last
week;* keep a certain position
or condition: *he is in the garden;* belong to class of: *I am a
man;* have same meaning or
identity as, amount to: *you
are my friend*
**beach** shore of sea or lake,
*esp.* one with sand or pebbles
**bea'con** signal light
**bead** small ball with hole
through it for stringing or
sewing in decorative pattern;
any small round body, as of
liquid, oil, *etc*. **-ed;** small
bump on barrel of gun, used
for aiming; **draw a b. on**
aim at
**bea'dy** (of eyes) small and
bright
**bea'gle** small hunting dog
**beak** bill of bird or noselike
part of turtle, *etc*
**beam** *n* timber; ray; radio signal guiding airplanes; *v* shine
**bean** smooth kidney-shaped
seed of certain plants, growing in pods and eaten as
food; similar seed of other
plants, such as coffee
**bear** *v* (bore, borne) carry;
support, as load; endure;

give, as testimony; hold (in the mind); produce; give birth to; move in a certain direction; **b. on** relate or refer to; **b. out** confirm or prove (sth) to be true; **b. up** keep up one's courage; **b. with** suffer patiently; *n* large omnivorous mammal with heavy fur; surly or ill-tempered person

**beard** (bērd) hair growing on chin and cheeks; any similar growth. **-ed**

**bear'ing** behavior; influence on; direction; part of machine in which a pin revolves

**beast** any four-footed animal; any brutal or unpleasant person. **-ly**

**beat** *v* (**beat, beat'en**) strike or pound again and again with force; make (path) by treading; overcome or surpass (s. o. or sth); mark off by strokes; strike underbrush so as to rouse wild animals; throb; *n* accent in music or poetry; heavy rhythm of popular music; course or path that is gone over regularly

**beau'ty** (byūti) combination of qualities which causes admiring pleasure, *esp.* to sense of sight; exceptionally good one of its kind; lovely woman. **-tiful, -tify**

**bea'ver** (fur of) large rodent with broad flat tail, which builds dams to protect its underwater house

**be·came'** see **become**

**be·cause'** for the reason that; as a result of

**beck** silent signal or call, by nodding or motioning; **at one's b. and call** ready to obey

**beck'on** call by gesture

**be·come'** (**be·came'**, **be·come'**) come to be; suit; **b. of** be the fate of

**be·com'ing** attractive; suitable

**bed** piece of furniture, *usu* of framework with springs and mattress, to sleep on; level piece of ground prepared for plants; bottom, *esp.* of river; layer, as of rock

**bed'bug** wingless blood-sucking insect often found in beds

**bed'ding** coverings for a bed

**be·dev'il** cause trouble for; upset

**bed'lam** madhouse

**bed'pan** portable device used by bedridden persons for bodily wastes

**be·drag'gled** dirty and limp

**bed'rid·den** kept in bed by illness

**bed'rock** solid layer of rock supporting soil above it; facts, principles, *etc* upon which sth is based

**bed'sore** sore on body of sick

person due to constant pressure against bed

**bed'stead** (-sted) framework of a bed

**bee** stinging insect, which produces wax and honey and lives in highly organized groups

**beech** (valuable hardwood of) tree with edible nut

**beef** meat of ox, cow or bull used as food

**beef'y** fleshy; big and meaty

**bee'hive** container or box in which bees live

**bee'line** direct course

**been** (bin, *UK* bēn) see **be**

**beer** fermented alcoholic liquor made of hops, malt, *etc*

**beet** plant with oval leaves and juicy root used as food and as source of sugar

**bee'tle** kind of insect

**be·fall'** (-fell, -fallen) happen (to)

**be·fore'** *prep* at an earlier time; ahead of in order, importance or time; in the presence of; in front of; *adv* already; previously; in the past; ahead; *conj* sooner than; rather than

**be·fore'hand** in advance

**be·friend'** act as friend to

**be·fud'dle** confuse

**beg** ask for, *esp.* gifts of food or money; ask very earnestly (for a favor, *etc*); **b. the question** assume that sth still to be proved is true

**be·gan'** see **begin**

**beg'gar** one who lives by begging; poor person

**be·gin'** (be·gan', be·gun') start; do the first part of some act; come into existence; be the first to do something. **-ner**

**be·gin'ning** start; first part, source

**be·grudge'** envy possession of; give unwillingly

**be·guile'** deceive; charm

**be·gun'** see **begin**

**be·half':** **on b. of** in the interest of

**be·hav|e'** act (in a particular way); conduct o. s. (properly). **-io(u)r**

**be·head'** cut off the head of

**be·held'** see **behold**

**be·hind'** in or to rear of (in place, time or direction); on the farther side of; slow or backward in progress; late; in a place or time which has been left; below in worth or position; supporting

**be·hold'** (be·held') see

**beige** (bāzh) pale yellowish brown color

**be'ing** existence; true nature (of sth); a. th that is alive

**be·la'bor,** *UK* **-bour** repeat the obvious

**be·lat'ed** delayed

**belch** eject gas from stomach through mouth

**be·lea'guer** besiege

**bel'fry** bell tower

**beret**

**be·lie'** show to be false; create false impression

**be·lief'** acceptance as true, *esp.* of a religion; trust

**be·lie|ve** accept (statement, *etc*) as true; trust in. **-vable;** be of opinion; **make b.** pretend, act as if

**be·lit'tle** make appear unimportant

**bell** metal cup-shaped musical instrument, sounded by striking; a. th of a similar shape; signal to attract attention, as doorbell

**bel·la·don'na** (drug prepared from) poisonous plant of nightshade family

**bell'boy** hotel servant

**bel'li·cose** inclined to fighting. **bellicos'ity**

**bel·lig'er|ent** aggressive; carrying on war. **-ence**

**bel'low** roar

**bel'lows** device for blowing air onto fire, *etc*

**bel'ly** *n* abdomen

**be·long'** be in proper place; **b.** to be a member of or connected with; be owned by

**be·long'ings** *pl* personal property or goods

**be·lov'ed** (one) dearly loved

**be·low'** at or to a lower place; downstairs; at foot of page or later in book, *etc*; lower in rank, amount, *etc*

**belt** *n* strip of leather or other flexible material worn around waist; strip of color,

land, *etc*, stretching around or across; strap, ends of which are joined together, connecting wheels, *etc* in machine; *v* put strap around; fasten by means of strap; beat with a strap

**bench** long seat; body of judges

**bend (bent)** force from straight or upright state into curved or crooked position; curve; turn in new direction; direct one's efforts

**be·neath'** (directly) under; in a lower position; unworthy of

**ben'e·fac·tor** one who gives friendly aid. **benefac'tion**

**ben·e·fi'ci·ar·y** (-fishi-) receiver of a benefit

**ben'e·fit** advantage; favor. **benefi'cial;** concert, *etc* to raise money for a good cause

**be·nev'o·|lence** good will; charitableness, **-lent**

**be·nign'** (-nīn) gentle; kindly; not dangerous

**bent** *n* tendency; bias; *v* see **bend**

**be·numb'** (-num) deaden

**ben·zine'** (-zēn) chemical cleaning fluid

**be·queath'** give by will

**be·quest'** thing bequeathed

**be·rate'** scold

**be·reave (be·reaved'** or **bereft')** deprive (of hope, *etc*); sadden by loss. **-ment**

**be·ret'** (-rā) soft round cap

**ber'ry** small juicy fruit with seeds enclosed in pulp

**berth** ship's anchorage place; sleeping-place in ship, *etc*

**be·seech'** (**be·sought'** or **be·seeched'**) ask earnestly

**be·set'** hem in; assail; harass

**be·side'** close to; at the side of; compared with; **b. oneself** greatly excited; hysterical

**be·sides'** in addition (to)

**be·siege'** surround with army; beset (with requests, *etc*)

**be·sought'** see **beseech**

**best** *a* (see **good**) of or to the highest quality, degree, amount, *etc*; *adv* (see **well**) in the most excellent way; *n* that which is best; **at b.** at most; **get or have the b. of** win; **make the b. of** manage as well as one can (under bad circumstances); *v* defeat; do better than; outwit

**bes'tial** like a beast. **bestial'ity**

**best man** chief attendant of bridegroom at wedding

**be·stow'** confer as gift. **-al**

**best-sell'er** book with very large sale

**bet** (**bet** or **bet'ted**) risk one's money, *etc* on outcome of an event, correctness of a statement, *etc*; wager

**be·to'ken** give evidence of

**be·tray'** give up or reveal treacherously; be disloyal to. **-al**

**bet'ter** *a* (see **good**) of, in a more excellent kind, way, *etc*; larger; improved in health; **b. off** in more favorable (financial) circumstances; *adv* (see **well**) in a more effective way; to a greater degree; **get the b. of** outwit; **think b. of** change one's mind; **know b. than** not be so foolish as to (do, think, *etc*); **had b.** would be wiser, safer, *etc* to; *v* improve. **-ment**

**be·tween'** in the space or time which separates; connecting; (as choice) one or the other of; (as share) among; **be·twixt' and b.** undecided

**bev'el** (tool for making) sloping edge or surface

**bev'er·age** liquid for drinking, other than water

**bev'y** flock; company

**be·ware'** be cautious of

**be·wil'der** confuse. **-ment**

**be·witch'** charm; enchant

**be·yond'** farther away; at or to the farther side of; out of the reach of; above as in excellence

**bi'as** prejudice; diagonal across fabric

**bib** small cloth tied under child's chin to protect clothes from food, *etc*; top part of apron, overalls, *etc*

**Bi'ble** book of writings believed by Jews and Christians to be inspired by God; **b.** any very important book

**bib·li·og·ra·phy** history or list of books. **-pher**

**bib'li·o·phile** lover of books

**bi·cen·te·nar·y** two hundredth anniversary

**bi'ceps** upper arm muscle

**bick'er** quarrel; wrangle

**bi'cy·cle** (bisikel) light two--wheeled vehicle with pedals

**bid** (bid) offer as a price; **b. up** (at an auction) raise price by repeated bids

**bid** (bade or bid, bid'den) order; invite; say (greeting or farewell)

**bide: b.** one's time wait for the right moment

**bi·en'ni·al** lasting, happening every, two years

**bier** support for coffin

**bi·fo'cals** glasses with two portions, one for near, one for far vision

**big** large in size or importance; swelling; pregnant; grown up

**big'a·my** having two wives or husbands at once

**big'ot** one blindly devoted to a (wrong) belief. **-ry**

**bike** short for **bicycle, motorcycle**

**bi·ki'ni** very brief two-piece bathing suit for women

**bi·lat'er·al** of or between two nations, groups, *etc*

**bile** liver secretion; ill humor. **-ious**

**bilge** bottom part of ship

**bi·lin'gual** in or speaking two languages

**bill** *n* horny noselike part of bird's jaw; draft of law presented to body of lawmakers for enactment; poster; statement or list of items, *esp.* of goods sold, showing price due; piece of paper money; *law* a statement in writing listing complaint of wrong done; *v* make list or bill of; submit bill to; advertise by posters

**bill'board** large surface for outdoor advertising

**bill'fold** folding pocketbook for paper money; wallet

**bill'iards** game played on cloth-covered table by hitting balls into pockets with cues

**bil'lion** *US* one thousand millions; *UK* one million millions

**bil'low** big wave; sth resembling this, as smoke

**bin** large box; receptacle

**bi'na·ry** of or marked by two parts, *etc*; **b. code** system based on 0 and 1 used in computers

**bind** (bound) tie together; fasten (to sth). **-er;** unite into a solid mass; bandage (wound, *etc*); fasten book's pages into cover; oblige or force by promise, law, *etc*

**bind'ing** book cover

**bin·oc·u·lar** *a* for both eyes; *n pl* field glasses

**bi·o·chem·is·try** (study of) the chemical processes of plant and animal life

**bi·o·de·grad·a·ble** capable of being decomposed, *esp.* by bacteria

**bi·og·ra·|phy** written history of person's life. **-pher**

**bi·o·log·i·cal war'fare** warfare using deadly germs as weapons

**bi·ol·o·gy** science of life and its forms

**bi'op·sy** examination of living body tissue, *etc* for diseases

**bi·par'ti·san** representing two parties

**bi'ped** a two-footed animal

**birch** (hardwood from) tree with toothed leaves

**bird** feathered vertebrate animal with two feet and wings which can *usu* fly

**bird's'-eye** seen from above

**birth** act of being born or coming into life; beginning; descent

**birth' con·trol** use of contraceptive methods to limit the number of children born

**birth'day** day of birth; anniversary of day of birth

**birth'mark** mark on the skin from birth on

**birth'rate** number of live births per thousand people per year

**bis·cuit** (biskit) various kinds of cake or bread, usually in small pieces

**bi·sect'** divide into two parts

**bi·sex'u·al** of or involving both sexes; (person) attracted sexually by members of both sexes

**bish'op** clergyman holding the office of governor of a diocese; piece in the game of chess

**bi'son** buffalo

**bit** small piece or quantity of a. th; smallest unit of computer information; part of bridle placed in horse's mouth; a. th that holds or restrains; tool for drilling; part of key that enters and turns a lock

**bitch** *n* female dog, *etc*; insulting term for a woman; *v sl* complain

**bite** (bit, bit'ten) grab and hold or tear apart with teeth and jaws; cut or pierce; sting; cause stinging pain; eat into

**bit'ter** having a harsh or disagreeable taste; unpleasant; causing or expressing grief or pain; cruel; harsh. **-ness**

**bi·tu'men** (-tū-) any of various substances (tar, asphalt, *etc*) won from petroleum. **-minous**

**bi'valve** (bī-) marine animal with hinged shell, such as oyster, clam, *etc*

**blaze**

**biv'ouac** (bivwak) temporary camp

**bi·zarre'** odd; grotesque

**blab** tell (secrets)

**black** opposite to white; having no or unable to reflect light; dark-skinned, *esp.* Negro; gloomy; dirty; sinister; threatening

**black art** magic; witchcraft

**black'ball** exclude by vote

**black'ber·ry** (shrub with) dark purple fruit

**black'bird** common bird, the male of which is black

**black'board** dark smooth surface, *usu* of slate, for writing on with chalk

**black box'** flight recorder in airplane

**black'guard** (-aggahrd) scoundrel

**black'head** small plug of grease and dirt filling pore, *esp.* on face

**black'jack** leather-covered club; card game *usu* played for money

**black'list** list of persons, firms, *etc* considered suspicious or blameworthy

**black'mail** extortion by threats

**black mar'ket** illegal trade in controlled or rationed goods

**black'smith** person who works iron to make horseshoes, tools, *etc*

**blad'der** (in human and animal bodies) container for urine; baglike container for fluid or gas

**blade** cutting part of knife or tool; leaf, *esp.* of grass; a. th resembling this; flattened part of instrument, as of oar, *etc*; any of various flat bones of human body

**blame** find fault with; accuse; hold responsible

**blanch** turn white or pale; boil vegetable, *etc* briefly

**bland** courteous; mild in taste

**blank** *a* free of marks or writing; looking lifeless or without expression; not shaped into finished form; *n* an empty space (on paper) to be filled in; bull's-eye of a target; gun cartridge with powder but no bullet; piece of material still to be shaped, *esp.* into key, coin, *etc*

**blan'ket** *n* thick woven cloth covering; any layerlike covering, as snow; *a* all-embracing

**blare** (make) loud harsh sound

**blas'phe·my** irreverence toward God or sacred things

**blast** strong gust of wind; sound made by whistle, *etc*; explosion; charge, as of dynamite

**bla'tant** offensively showy

**blaze** *n* (brightly burning) fire; strong hot light; active outburst; white mark or stripe, *esp.* on face of animal; *v* spread (news) far and wide

**blaz'er** lightweight jacket

**bleach** whiten

**bleach'ers** *pl* roofless seats at outdoor sports

**bleak** dreary; bare

**blear'y** dim; watery

**bleat** cry like a sheep

**bleed (bled)** give out blood; be wounded; issue forth; *infml* extort money from

**blem'ish** *n* stain; *v* injure; mar

**blend** mix, *esp.* so thoroughly that different items cannot be distinguished; (of colors) merge or fade into each other; harmonize

**bless** set apart for sacred uses; make happy

**blew** see **blow**

**bless'ed** holy; happy. **-ness**

**blight** *n* plant disease; *v* wither; mar

**blimp** gas-filled, non-rigid airship

**blind** *a* not having the power to see; made or done without reason or intelligence; concealed or covered; having only one opening; *n* cover for window to keep out light; sth intended to mislead or deceive; place or means of concealment (when hunting)

**blind'er** (blind-) flap on horse's bridle to keep it from seeing objects at side

**blind'fold** cover eyes (by bandage, *etc*); prevent from seeing

**blink** lower and raise eyelids rapidly; (of a light) go on and off; twinkle; ignore

**blip** signal on radar screen

**bliss** gladness; joy. **-ful**

**blis'ter** small raised area of skin, containing watery matter and caused by burning, rubbing, *etc*; similar spot on painted wood, metal, *etc*

**blithe** gay; happy; casual

**bliz'zard** heavy snowstorm

**bloat** swell up, *esp.* unhealthily

**bloc** combination of groups united by one goal

**block** large piece of wood, *etc*; quantity or group of things treated as a unit; row of houses, seats, *etc*; area in towns enclosed by four streets; platform on which sth is sold at auction; mold or form on which articles are shaped; engraved material used for printing; cube or rectangle of wood, *etc* used as child's toy; a. th that hinders or obstructs; (in sports) obstruction of opponent

**block·ade'** barring of exit from and entrance to a place

**blond(e)** fair; light-colored; having yellowish or lightcolored hair

**blood** liquid circulating in veins and arteries of higher animals; ancestry; temper

**blood¹ count** (number of) blood cells in a quantity of blood

**blood² pres·sure** (measure of) force exerted by blood flowing through the body

**blood'shed** slaughter

**blood'shot** (of eyes) red from swollen blood vessels

**blood'stream** circulating blood

**blood ves·sel** any of the veins, etc through which the blood circulates

**bloom** flower of a plant; state of having opened buds; healthy condition; whitish powdery coating on certain fruits and leaves

**blos'som** flower, esp. of fruit trees; the state of flowering

**blot** n spot or stain, esp. of ink; blemish or defect in character or reputation; v make spot on; dry (ink, etc) with absorbent paper; **b. out** erase; hide

**blotch** inflamed spot on skin. **-y**

**blot'ter** absorbent paper for drying ink; US book in which events, such as arrests, sales, etc are noted

**blouse** loose garment for upper part of body, usu taken in at waist

**blow** (blew, blown) (of wind or air) move along; give off current of air; play musical wind instrument; (of electri-cal, etc equipment) become unusable through overloading; shape melted glass by current of air; **b. up** (cause to) explode; **b. over** pass; die down

**blow'-dry** dry and style hair with hand-dryer

**blow'out** bursting of an automobile tire

**blow'torch** device giving off intense hot flame, used in welding, etc

**blub'ber** n whale fat; v weep noisily

**bludg'eon** short thick club

**blue** having the color of the clear sky; discolored due to lack of circulation; unhappy; indecent

**blue'bell** plant with blue bell-shaped flowers

**blue'ber·ry** (shrub with) edible blue fruit

**blue'bird** small blue N. Amer. songbird

**blue'bot·tle** large buzzing fly with steel blue abdomen

**blue'fish** blue-backed sport and food fish

**blue jay** bright blue, crested N. Amer. bird of crow family

**blue'-pen·cil** edit or cross out with blue pencil

**blue'print** (photographic print of) detailed plan

**blue rib·bon** highest honor or award

**blues** pl depression of spirits; kind of jazz music

**bluff** n steep bank; v mislead

**blun·der** (make) gross mistake

**blunt** having a thick edge or point; dull or slow in understanding; outspoken or tactless

**blur** make unclear by smearing; make dim to the sight

**blurt** utter suddenly

**blush** become red, esp. in the face, from shame, etc

**blus·ter** roar; swagger

**boar** male swine

**board** n thin piece of sawed wood, longer than it is wide; square (of wood) used for games, notices, etc; pl the stage of a theater; table, esp. one for food; a group of officially-appointed persons; meals and lodging; **on b.** on(to) a ship, etc; v go onto (a ship, plane, etc); give or receive meals and lodging; **b. up** cover with boards

**boast** praise one's own ability, deeds, etc; show or announce with pride

**boat** small open craft for travel on water, driven by oars, sails, etc; any ship

**bob** ball or weight hanging from line or rod; short jerking motion; short hair cut; kind of sled

**bob·bin** spool; reel

**bode** foretell; foreshadow

**bod·ice** (-is) close-fitting top part of dress

**bod·i·ly** a having a body or material form; having to do with the (human) body; adv as one whole body; completely

**bod·y** the physical organism, esp. of man, animal or plant; main or central part; any mass of matter considered by itself; thickness or substance; any group or number of persons or things

**bod·y·guard** person(s) hired to escort and protect s. o.

**bod·y stock·ing** elastic garment which covers the body and ensures freedom of movement

**bog** marsh; swamp. **-gy**

**bo·gus** counterfeit; sham

**bo·g(e)y** specter

**boil** v be heated or heat to point where steam is formed; be in seething motion; become stirred by anger; n state of boiling; local infected swelling on skin, filled with pus

**bois·ter·ous** rough and noisy

**bold** willing to take risks; very brave; rude; clear or well-marked. **-ness**

**bo·le·ro** short jacket; Spanish dance

**boll** pod of cotton, etc

**bol·ster** n pillow; v pad; support

**bolt** n sliding bar used to lock door, etc; metal pin held by nut, used to fasten things together; sudden flash of lightning; roll of cloth, *etc*; short arrow to be shot from crossbow; *v* swallow without chewing; run away suddenly

**bomb** (bom) device set off by impact or timer to produce explosion, fire or smoke

**bom·bard'** attack with artillery; direct stream (of particles, questions, *etc*) at

**bomb'er** (bomer) one that bombs, *esp.* airplane used for dropping bombs

**bo·na fi'de** (fīde) in good faith; genuine

**bo·nan'za** rich source of profit

**bond** uniting tie; certificate of financial obligation; adhesion

**bond'age** slavery

**bone** *n* one of hard parts of skeleton of vertebrate animal; *v* remove bones from; put bones in (corset, *etc*)

**bon'fire** large open-air fire

**bon'net** head covering

**bo'nus** sth in addition, *esp* money paid beyond sum agreed on

**boo'by trap** explosive hidden in otherwise harmless object

**book** *n* number of (printed) sheets of paper bound between covers; story, *etc* printed on them; main division of a long literary work; *v* enter in a book, *esp.* to reserve a room, passage, *etc*; (of actors, *etc*) engage for a certain date

**book'case** piece of furniture with shelves for storing books

**book'keep·er** person who keeps accounts for a business

**book'worm** larva which feeds on binding and paste of books; person extremely fond of reading

**boom** deep resonant noise; rapid development

**boom'er·ang** curved Australian weapon which returns to thrower

**boon** benefit; favor

**boor** rude, clumsy person

**boost** lift or push from below; raise; support (by praise, *etc*)

**boot** *n* covering of leather, rubber, *etc* for foot and part of leg; *v* kick with foot

**booth** small covered stall

**boot'leg** make, sell or deal in (liquor) illegally

**boo'ty** plunder

**bo'rax** colorless or white crystalline chemical substance used as cleaner, in medicine, *etc*

**bor'der** outer part or edge; margin; frontier or boundary of country; ornamental strip along edge (of garment, carpet, *etc*)

**bor'der·line** boundary; dividing line

**bore** see **bear**

# bore

**bore** *v* make weary by dullness, *etc* **-dom;** make hole in, *esp.* with tool that turns; force (way through) with difficulty; *n* tiresome person or thing; hole made by boring; diameter of a hole, *esp.* in guns

**bored** tired and disinterested

**bo'ric ac'id** weak acid solution or ointment used as antiseptic

**born** brought into existence by birth; having certain characteristics from birth

**borne** see **bear**

**bor'ough** (burrō) incorporated town

**bor'row** receive sth for temporary use, with the intention of returning it to owner; take (idea, *etc*) and use as one's own

**bos'om** (boozem, būzem) human breast considered as the seat of feeling; the female breasts; part of garment covering these

**boss** *n* manager; master; *v* order about

**bot'a·ny** science of plants

**botch** bungle; repair badly

**both** the one as well as the other

**both'er** annoy; worry. **-some;** trouble o. s.

**bot'tle** narrow-necked (glass) container for liquid

**bot'tle-neck** narrow place; a. th obstructing an even

flow (of traffic, production, *etc*)

**bot'tom** lowest part; bed of a body of water; part of a. th which is underneath (and serves as support); (lowest part of) ship; heart or core of a matter

**bot'u·lis·m** food-poisoning caused by bacteria in food

**bough** (bou) (large) branch of tree

**bought** see **buy**

**bouil·lon'** (bū-, boolyon) clear raw broth

**boul'der** large detached rock

**boul'e·vard** broad street

**bounce** (of ball, *etc*) be thrown back by solid surface; burst noisily into or out of; (of check) be returned for lack of money

**bounc'ing** (of children) strong and healthy

**bound** *a* certain; on the way; *n* a jumping upward or forward; *usu pl* limits; limitations; *v* jump; set limits to; see also **bind**

**bound'a·ry** border; limit

**boun'ty** generosity; premium; reward

**bou·quet'** (būkā) bunch of flowers; aroma of wine

**bour·geois'** (-zhwah) (person of) middle class

**bout** contest; spell of illness, *etc*

**bo'vine** oxlike

**bow** (bou) *v* bend or kneel;

submit; nod head in greeting, *etc*; cause to bend; *n* front end of ship

**bow** (bō) curve; strip of wood bent by string tied to its ends, for shooting arrows; looped knot, as of ribbon; strip of wood with horsehairs stretched upon it, for playing violin, *etc*; a. th curved or arched

**bow'el** (bouel) *usu pl* part of food canal below stomach which moves waste matter out of body; inner part of a. th

**bowl** (bōl) *n* (amount contained in) deep round dish; any rounded hollow part, as of pipe, spoon, *etc*; (wooden) ball used in certain games; *v* roll (ball) along surface; **b. over** knock down; upset by surprise

**bow'leg'ged** having legs that bend outward at knee

**box** *n* (amount held by) container of wood, *etc*, *usu* with lid, for solids; enclosed space in theater, stable, *etc*; small shelter; compartment rented at post office for mail; boxwood; *v* put sth in a box; fight with fists; slap, *esp.* on ear

**box'car** enclosed railway freight car

**box'er** athlete who fights with his fists. **-ing**

**box of'fice** booth in theater, *etc* where tickets are sold

**box'wood** evergreen shrub

**boy** male child. **-hood, -ish**

**boy'cott** exclude by refusing to deal with

**bra** (brah) brassière

**brace** *n* securing band; pair; tool to hold a bit; *v* support, fasten

**brace'let** band of gold, *etc* worn around wrist

**brac'ing** invigorating

**brack'et** projecting support; income group; punctuation mark(s) to enclose letters, figures

**brack'ish** slightly salty

**brag** boast

**brag'gart** boaster

**braid** *n* plait; narrow band; *v* interweave strands (of hair, *etc*)

**braille** (brāl) system of writing for the blind using raised dots

**brain** *n* grayish-white nerve substance in skull of vertebrates, center of thought, feeling, *etc*; *usu pl* intelligence. **-y**

**brain'storm** temporary mental disturbance; sudden inspiration

**brain'wash** alter thought structure by (forcible) persuasion. **-ing**

**braise** cook (meat) in closed vessel with little water

**brake** device for stopping motion of wheel, *etc*; *v* apply b.; slow or retard

**branch** limb growing from tree; any section or part of body or system; arm of river, road, *etc*; local office of large company

**brand** *v* mark by searing; *n* trade mark to identify product; partly burned piece of wood

**bran'dish** flourish; wave

**brand-new** completely unused

**bran'dy** strong alcoholic liquor made from grapes, *etc*

**brash** rashly over-confident; impudent

**brass** alloy of copper and zinc

**bras·sière'** (brezir) woman's undergarment worn to support breasts

**brat** (used in annoyance for) child

**brave** *a* having courage; *v* meet or face with courage. **-ry;** native N. Amer. warrior

**brawl** quarrel noisily

**brawn'y** muscular; strong

**bray** (make) cry of donkey

**bra'zen** made of brass; shameless. **-ness**

**breach** (brēch) hole or gap made by breaking; breaking, as of agreement, friendship, *etc*

**bread** (bred) flour mixed with liquid and leavening, baked in loaves; food

**breadth** (bredth) distance measured from side to side; quality of being wide in range; open-mindedness

**break** (brāk) (**broke, bro'ken**) (cause to) separate or crack into two or more parts; open up (hard) surface of; defeat; crush (strength, spirit); degrade in rank; violate (law, promise); reveal (news); interrupt (electric circuit); make bankrupt; tame (horse); change (direction, pace) suddenly; change register (of voice); (prices) fall sharply. **-able**

**break'down** (mental) collapse; detailed analysis

**break'er** heavy (foaming) wave

**break'fast** (brekfest) first meal of the day

**break'neck** dangerously fast

**break'through** sudden advance in method, knowledge, *etc*

**break'wa-ter** wall to break force of waves

**breast** (brest) *n* one of the two milk-secreting organs on chest of woman; front part of body between neck and abdomen; seat of conscious feeling; *v* to meet and struggle with bravely

**breast'bone** central bone in chest connecting the ribs

**breath** (breth) air inhaled and exhaled; slight breeze; **under one's b.** in very low tones. **-less**

**bristle**

**breathe** (brēdh) take in and let out air from lungs; be alive; say softly

**breath'er** brief pause for rest

**breath'tak·ing** very delightful, exciting or surprising

**breech·es** (brichis) trousers fastened at or below knee

**breed** (bred) produce young; result in

**breed'ing** behavior; manners

**breeze** light wind

**brev'i·ty** shortness

**brew** prepare (beer, *etc*) by mixture and fermentation. **-ery**; make (tea, *etc*) by pouring boiling water on leaves, *etc*; be forming or gathering, as storm, evil, *etc*

**bri'ar** see brier

**brib|e** gift made to gain (illegal) favor for giver. **-ery**

**brick** oblong block made by moulding and baking clay, *etc*. used for building; any oblong block

**brid|e** woman just married or about to be married. **-al**

**bride'groom** man just married or about to be married

**bridge** structure built over valley, river, *etc* to permit crossing; anything resembling this, as small arch on violin that raises strings; kind of card game; device for holding artificial teeth in place; high platform on ship; upper bone of nose

**bri'dle** *n* controlling headgear

for horses, *etc*; check; *v* control; toss head in resentment

**brief** *a* short; *n* summary of legal case; *v* instruct

**brief'case** flat leather case for carrying papers

**bri'er** shrub whose woody root is used for tobacco pipes; kind of prickly bush

**bri·gade'** military unit

**bright** giving off (much) light; shining; very noticeable because of vivid color; clever; cheerful. **-en, -ness**

**bril'liant** splendid; extremely clever or capable. **-liance**

**brim** *n* edge of anything hollow; rim of (cup, hat); *v* be filled to the edge

**brine** salt water

**bring** (**brought**) cause to come with o.s. as by carrying or leading; be the cause of; persuade (to do); present (suit in law); be sold for; **b. about** or **to pass** cause to take place; **b. forth** give birth to; **b. home** prove; make realize; **b. on** lead to; cause; **b. round** cause (one) to change opinion; **b. to** make conscious again; **b. to bear** influence; **b. up** rear or educate (children)

**brink** edge; verge

**brisk** lively; quick

**bris'tle** (brisl) *n* short stiff coarse hair on back of hog, *etc* used in making brushes, *etc*; *v* rise or stand up, like bristles; show anger or defiance

**brit·tle** easily broken; fragile

**broach** begin to talk about; tap (cask)

**broad** (brawd) wide; of great extent; clear; plain; liberal in thought. **-en**

**broad·cast** send (program) by radio or television

**broad·cloth** smooth woven cloth

**bro·cade'** silk material with raised pattern

**broc·co·li** variety of green branching cauliflower

**bro·chure'** (-shoor) informative pamphlet

**brogue** dialectal accent

**broil** cook directly over fire

**broke, bro'ken** see **break**

**bro'ker** middleman in transactions

**bro'ker·age** broker's commission or business

**bro'mide** soothing drug; commonplace remark

**bron'chi·al** (-kĭel) of the (branches of the) windpipe

**bron·chi'tis** (-kī-) inflammation of bronchial tubes

**bronze** alloy of copper and tin; brown color

**brooch** ornamental pin

**brood** n offspring; v sit on (eggs to hatch them); ponder sadly and at length

**brook** n small stream; v endure

**broom** long-handled implement for sweeping, *usu* made of fibers or straw

**broth** liquid in which meat, vegetables, *etc* have been slowly boiled; thin soup

**broth'el** house of prostitution

**broth'er** male having same parents as another; fellow man; fellow-member or close companion; man who belongs to religious order but is not a priest. **-hood**

**broth'er-in-law** brother of one's husband or wife; husband of one's sister

**brought** see **bring**

**brow** (brou) eyebrow; forehead; top of hill

**brow'beat** v bully

**brown** dark color with reddish tinge

**brown'ie** chocolate nut cake

**brown'stone** reddish-brown sandstone for building

**browse** graze; look through (books)

**bruise** (brūz) (cause) discolored surface injury to flesh without breaking skin

**bru·net(te)'** dark-haired (person)

**brunt** main force or shock

**brush** n device made of bristles, hair, *etc* set in a handle, used for sweeping, scrubbing, painting, *etc*; thick tail of fox, squirrel, *etc*; small branches cut from trees; underwood; short lively fight; v rub or touch with a light quick motion

**brusque** (brusk) rough; abrupt

**brus'sels sprout** very small green head of a vegetable related to cabbage

**brute** irrational animal; cruel person. **-tal, brutal'ity**

**bub'ble** thin film of liquid filled with air; small ball of air within glass, *etc*; sth fragile or unsteady

**buc·ca·neer'** pirate

**buck** n male of certain animals, as deer; sl US dollar; v (of horse, *etc*) jump vertically; resist or unsteady

**buck'et** container for holding or carrying things, *esp*. liquids

**buck'le** n device for fastening two loose ends together, as of a belt; v fasten with buckle; (cause to) bend or crumple up; **b. down (to work)** apply o. s. with energy and will

**buck'ram** type of stiff cloth

**buck'shot** coarse shot

**buck'skin** type of soft strong leather

**buck'tooth** (front) tooth that juts out

**buck'wheat** cereal with triangular seed

**bu·col'ic** rustic

**bud** undeveloped shoot or flower growing out of plant, tree, *etc*

**budge** move slightly

**budg'et** plan of income and expenses

**buff** dull-yellow (leather)

**buf'fa·lo** any of several kinds of wild ox

**buf'fer** a. th that lessens shock of a blow

**buf'fet** v strike (repeatedly); n blow; slap

**buf·fet'** n (-fā) sideboard; refreshment counter

**buf·foon'** clown

**bug** insect, *esp*. of a kind that crawls; a bedbug; *infml* virus, *esp*. causing influenza; *infml* defect in machine, computer program, *etc*; sl hidden microphone

**bug'gy** light carriage

**bu'gle** kind of horn

**build** (bild) v (**built**) put together or construct; **b. up** produce gradually by effort; n general shape or figure; **b.-up** gradual increase

**build'ing** any structure, such as a house

**bulb** root of certain plants, as lily, onion, *etc*; electric lamp. **-bous**

**bulge** n swelling; v swell

**bulk** size, *esp*. large size; mass. **-y**

**bulk'head** partition in a ship or mine

**bull** male of certain animals; market speculator

**bull'dog** short-haired muscular dog of great courage

**bull'doz·er** large tractor for leveling earth

**bul'let** missile, *usu* of lead, to be shot from small gun

**bul'le·tin** short news report

**bull'frog** large N. Amer. frog

**bull'head·ed** stubborn

**bull'ion** uncoined gold or silver

**bull's'-eye** target's center

**bul'ly** *n* cruel blustering fellow; *v* intimidate

**bul'wark** defense; protection

**bum'ble·bee** large-sized bee

**bump** *v* strike or hit (against); *n* (dull sound of) heavy blow; swelling due to blow, *etc*; uneven area of a surface. **-y**

**bump'er** *n* protective bar mounted on front and back ends of car; *a* unusually large

**bump'tious** self-assertive

**bun** kind of sweet roll or biscuit; hair worn in knot

**bunch** cluster of grapes, *etc*, growing off one stem; number of things of the same kind (fastened together)

**bun'dle** number of things tied together to form a bunch or package; a group of things considered together

**bun'ga·low** one-story house

**bun'gle** do clumsily; fail to accomplish

**bun'ion** inflamed swelling on great toe

**bunk** berth, as in a ship

**bunk'er** place for storing fuel; underground shelter

**bunk('um)** nonsense

**bunt** *v* butt; push

**bun'ting** thin cloth for flags

**buoy** (būi, boi) floating device anchored in water as marker

**buoy'ant** floating; light. **-cy**

**bur(r)** prickly seed pod

**bur'den** something carried, as load, responsibility, debt, *etc*; main theme or content; chorus of a song. **-some**

**bu'reau** (-rō) chest of drawers; office; government department

**bu·reauc'ra·cy** administration characterized by excessive office routine. **bureaucrat'ic**

**bur'glar** person who enters illegally to steal. **-y**

**bur'gun·dy** wine from or like that of Burgundy; *a* of a dark red color

**bur'i·al** (ber-) act of putting dead body under ground

**bur'lap** type of coarse cloth

**bur·lesque'** *a* comical; *n* dramatic or literary parody; variety show

**bur'ly** strong; muscular

**burn** (burned or burnt) be on fire; destroy or damage by flame or heat; give off light; treat with heat; as clay for pottery; eat through, as acid; (of skin) redden from sun; feel or look as if greatly heated (by emotion, *etc*)

**burn'er** part of stove, *etc* that produces heat

**bur'nish** polish; make bright

**bur'ro** small donkey

**bur'row** hole dug in the ground by animal

**burst (burst)** fly apart or into pieces due to blow or pressure from within; enter or leave violently or suddenly; make one's way violently; break into (tears, laughter, *etc*); (cause to) come open, as bud, *etc*

**bur'y** (beri) place (dead body) in ground and cover with earth; hide: **b. o.s. in** become very occupied with

**bus** *n* large (public) motor vehicle for carrying passengers; *v* US transport children to distant schools to attain racial balance

**bush** thick dense shrub or group of shrubs; wild uncleared country. **-y**

**bush'el** measure = 4 pecks or 32 quarts

**busi'ness** (biznes) one's work or regular employment; affair or matter; buying and selling of goods; commercial enterprise carrying on trade

**bust** (piece of sculpture showing) head and upper part of human body; woman's breasts; clothing size (distance around woman's bosom and back)

**bus'tle** (busl) *v* hurry about; *n* noisy activity

**bus'y** (bizi) engaged in doing sth; full of activity; constantly active or meddling

**but** except: *he took all b. one*; however, nevertheless: *he is old b. strong*: on the other hand: *it costs a lot b. can be used for many things*; only: *he is still b. a child*; other than: *I cannot b. accept his offer*

**butch'er** (boo-) person who kills animals and prepares their meat for sale; person who causes cruel and unnecessary death. **-y**

**but'ler** head manservant

**butt** *n* target of ridicule; cask; thick end (of rifle, *etc*); *v* shove with head or horns

**but'ter** solid fat obtained by beating cream; butterlike substance obtained by crushing nuts, fruit, *etc*

**but'ter-cup** (wild flower with) small yellow blossom

**but'ter-fly** any of various slender-bodied insects with colored wings

**but'ter-milk** liquid remaining after making butter

**but'tocks** *pl* rump

**but'ton** small knob or disk for fastening clothes; any similar knob or disk

**but'ton-hole** *n* slit for holding button; *v* forcibly engage in conversation

**but'tress** support

**bux'om** plump; comely

**buy (bought)** get (property, etc) by paying a price. **-er**

**buzz** (make) low continuous murmuring sound. **-er**

**buz'zard** slow-flying hawk living on mice, etc

**by** prep near, beside: the house stood b. the lake; along, over or through: he came b. the woods; past: he walked b. the house; during: b. day; through the agency or means of: he went b. train, made b. hand; not later than: pay this bill b. the tenth; one after the other: step b. step; to the amount of: too long b. a foot; in respect of: noble b. birth; to the measure of: cloth b. the yard; adv past: years gone b.; aside: put money b.

**by'gone** (sth) past

**by'law** regulation of association, etc

**by'-line** line of print giving author's name in newspaper, etc

**by'pass** n road around a town; device for diverting flow of blood around heart; v go around

**by'-prod·uct** product in addition to main product; secondary result

**by'stand·er** an unengaged observer

**byte** unit of computer information equal to 8 bits

# C

**c** third letter of English alphabet

**cab** taxicab; sheltered driver's seat on train, truck, crane, etc

**cab'bage** vegetable with short stem and leaves forming a round head

**cab'in** small simple house; bedroom on ship; pilot's compartment in airplane

**cab'i·net** storage case with drawers or shelves; governing body of ministers

**ca'ble** strong thick rope of fiber or wire; combination of insulated wires for carrying electricity; (telegram sent by) wire laid on bottom of sea

**ca'ble car** car pulled up steep slope by endless cable on the ground or in the air

**ca·cao'** (tree with) bean used to make cocoa and chocolate

**cack'le** make shrill broken cry, as hen; chatter noisily

**cac'tus** juicy desert plant with thick stem and sharp spines

**ca·dav'er·ous** corpse-like

**CAD'/CAM** computer-aided design and manufacture of industrial products

**cad·dy** golf player's attendant; box for tea

**ca·dence** rhythm; fall of voice; *mus* final series of notes

**ca·det'** pupil at military or police academy

**ca·dre** active political or military core of trained people

**ca·fe'** (kafā) restaurant, often also with outdoor seating

**caf·e·te·ri·a** self-service restaurant where customers fetch their own food

**cage** boxlike prison made of wires or bars, for keeping animals; *UK* car of mine elevator

**cake** flour mixed with sugar, fat, *etc* and baked or fried; shaped or molded mass of food, *etc*

**ca·lam·i|ty** disaster; misfortune. **-tous**

**cal·ci·um** silver-white metal, found in chalk, teeth, bones, milk, *etc*

**cal·cu·late** compute mathematically; plan; reckon

**cal·cu·la·tor** small mechanical device for computing sums, now often solar-powered

**cal·dron,** *UK* **caul-** large kettle

**cal·en·dar** system for fixing beginning, length and divisions of year; table showing days and months; list of events, saints, *etc*

**calf** (kaf) (*pl* **calves**) young of cow, seal, elephant, *etc*; fleshy part at back of human leg below knee

**cal·i·ber,** *UK* **-bre** inside diameter of gun or tube; degree of ability

**cal·i·co** cotton cloth

**cal·is·then·ics,** *UK* **call-** bodily exercises for health, *etc*

**call** cry out in loud voice; make characteristic sound, as bird; announce; invite; talk with s.o. by telephone or radio; give name or description to; **c. down** scold; **c. for** go and get; request to be brought; make necessary; **c. forth** give rise to (action, memories, *etc*); **c. in** collect (loan, *etc*); ask to come; **c. into being** create; **c. on** appeal to; make visit to; **c. up** telephone to; bring to mind; summon to serve in army

**cal·lig·ra·phy** (beautiful) handwriting

**call·ing** profession or trade; summons

**cal·lis·then·iis** see **calisthenics**

**cal·lous** hardened in feeling

**cal·lus** hard thickened area of skin

**calm** without wind or motion; quiet; not excited

**cal·o·rie** unit of quantity of heat; measure of energy in food

**cal'um·ny** slander

**calve** give birth to calf

**ca·lyp'so** improvised song of the W. Indies

**cam** projection on wheel to transmit irregular motion

**cam'bric** (kām-) fine white linen

**came** see **come**

**cam'el** large four-footed animal of Africa and Asia with one or two humps, used as beast of burden

**ca·mel'li·a** (evergreen plant with) sweet-smelling roselike flower

**cam'e·o** gem carved in relief; short sketch (in film by well-known performer)

**cam'er·a** photographing apparatus

**cam'ou·flage** (-ūflahzh) disguise

**camp** place where troops, *etc* live in tents, *etc*; group of persons sharing same ideals, *etc*

**cam·paign'** (-pān) series of (military) operations

**cam'phor** (kamfer) strong-smelling gumlike substance used in medicine, *etc*

**cam'pus** college or university grounds

**can** *v* (**could**) be able to; have right to; be permitted to; preserve food; *n US* container of tin, *etc* for holding liquids, fruits, *etc*. **-nery**

**ca·nal'** pipe-like passage; channel dug in earth and filled with water to allow passage of boats, to irrigate land, *etc*

**ca·nar'y** bright yellow songbird of finch family

**ca·nas'ta** card game similar to rummy

**can'cel** cross out; make void

**can'cer** (disease marked by) dangerous growth of body cells; source of evil

**can·de·la'brum** (*pl* **-bra**) large branched candlestick

**can'did** frank. **-ness**

**can'di·da|te** person trying for office or honor. **-cy**

**can'dle** (slender) mass of tallow or wax, containing wick, burned to give light

**can'dle·pow·er** unit for measuring intensity of light

**can'dor**, *UK* **-dour** openness; frankness; honesty

**can'dy** crystals or solid mass formed by boiling sugar, with nuts, *etc* added

**cane** flexible walking stick; (hollow) stem of certain grasses, as sugar

**ca'nine** (kānin) (of or like a) dog

**can'is·ter** metal box or drum

**can'ker** spreading sore, *esp.* at mouth; plant disease

**can'na·bis** (*sl* pot) drug made from hemp plant and smoked as stimulant

**can'ni·bal** one who eats human flesh

**can·non** heavy gun mounted on wheels

**can·ny** careful; shrewd

**ca·noe'** (-nū) light narrow boat paddled by hand

**can·on** church law; fundamental principle; type of musical composition

**can·on·ize**, *UK* **-ise** declare (a person) a saint

**can·o·py** suspended rooflike cover

**cant** special idiojargon

**can't** = cannot

**can·ta·loup(e)** kind of melon

**can·tan·ker·ous** ill-natured

**can·ta·ta** choral work, *usu* of a religious nature

**can·teen'** shop at military post selling extra provisions, *etc*; company restaurant for employees; small container for water carried by soldiers, *etc*

**can·ter** (move at) easy gallop

**can·ti·le·ver** projecting beam supported at only one end

**can·to** division of long poem

**can·ton·ment** temporary quarters of troops

**can·tor** official singer, *esp.* in synagogue

**can·vas** heavy, closely woven linen fabric used for tents, sails, oil-painting, *etc*; such a painting

**can·vass** for votes, *etc*

**can·yon** deep valley with high slopes

**cap** *n* covering for head, *esp.* one without brim for informal use; a.th. of similar shape used to cover openings; *etc*; *v* equal or surpass; form a covering for

**ca·pa·ble** able; competent. **capabil'ity**

**ca·pac'i·ty** receiving power; cubic content; power

**ca·per** leap; frolic

**cap·il·lar·y** *a* hairlike; *n* fine blood vessel

**cap·i·tal** *n* town serving as seat of government; accumulated wealth; large letter, as A, B, C; top of a column; *a* punishable by death; relating to wealth; principal

**cap·i·tal·is·m** system where production is dominated by private ownership. **-ist**

**cap·i·tal·ize** *UK* **-ise** write (word) with large first letter; convert into capital; supply money for (business, *etc*)

**Cap·i·tol** *US* building where Congress meets

**ca·pit·u·late** surrender

**ca·price'** (-ēs) whim. **capri'-cious**

**cap·size'** overturn (boat)

**cap·sule** gelatin case enclosing medicine; detachable nose cone of spacecraft

**cap·tain** leader of a group; army or naval officer; master of a ship or airplane

**cap·tion** heading; writing in cartoons or at bottom of movie or television screen

**cap'ti·vate** charm

**cap'tive** prisoner. **captiv'ity**

**cap'ture** v seize; take; n seizure

**car** any vehicle moved on wheels; cage of elevator; part of balloon or airship which carries passengers

**ca·rafe'** (-rahf) wide-necked bottle for wine or water

**car'a·mel** burnt sugar, used as coloring for candies, etc; chewy candy, usu in small blocks

**car'at** unit of weight for precious stones; measure of purity of gold

**car'a·van** Oriental traveling group of merchants; UK trailer

**car'a·way** (herb bearing) small pungent seed used for flavoring

**car'bine** short rifle

**car·bo·hy'drate** energy-producing compound in sugars, starches, etc, necessary for a balanced diet

**car·bol'ic ac'id** poisonous acid obtained from coal tar, used as antiseptic

**car'bon** chemical element occurring in all organic substances

**car'bon dat'ing** method used to determine age of object by measuring amount of carbon in it

**car'bon di·ox'ide** gas formed in breathing or when oil, coal, etc are burned

**car'bon pa'per** wax-coated paper used to make copies of written or typed matter

**car'bun·cle** severe boil; red gem

**car'bu·re·tor,** UK **-ret·tor** device mixing air with fuel vapor to power an engine

**car'cass** dead body of animal

**car·cin'o·gen** substance causing cancer

**card** small flat thin piece of pasteboard used in games, for writing on, etc; wire-toothed instrument for combing wool, etc

**card'board** stiff pasteboard used for cards, boxes, etc

**car'di·ac** of the heart or heart disease

**car'di·gan** (usu collarless) sweater opening down the front

**car'di·nal** a deep red; fundamental; n Roman Catholic official ranking just below the Pope; crested Amer. bird, the male of which is bright red

**care** n anxiety; worry. **-free;** watchful attention; charge or custody; caution. **-ful, -less;** v have wish or liking for; feel interest for; provide for needs of

**ca·reen'** lean or tilt (ship) on one side

**ca·reer'** course through life; profession

**ca·ress'** fondle; stroke or touch lovingly

**care'tak·er** person hired to look after another's property

**car'go** load carried by ship

**car'i·ca·ture** ridiculously exaggerated portrayal

**car'ies** tooth decay

**car'mine** (of) crimson red

**car'nage** great slaughter

**car'nal** of the body. **car·nal'ity**

**car·na'tion** (plant with) decorative red, pink or white flower

**car'ni·val** traveling amusement show; season of merrymaking before fast

**car·niv'o·rous** flesh-eating

**car'ol** *n* song of joy; *v* sing

**ca·rouse'** drink freely

**carp** *v* complain without cease; *n* large edible freshwater fish

**car'pen·ter** workman who builds or repairs wooden structures, houses, *etc.* **-try**

**car'pet** heavy woven or felted floor covering

**car'riage** (karij) (cost of) transport, *esp.* of goods; manner of carrying or holding one's body; wheeled vehicle for carrying, *esp.* for persons; wheeled framework or support; part of machine which moves and supports some other part

**car'ri·er** person or thing, *esp.* person or company in transport business, that carries sth or s. o.; person or animal that transmits disease germs without becoming ill

**car'ri·on** dead rotting flesh

**car'rot** (plant with) orange root eaten as vegetable

**car'ry** convey from one place to another, in hand, on ship, *etc*; bear weight of; hold (body, head, *etc*) in a certain manner; take by force; win; keep on hand or in stock

**cart** vehicle, *usu* two-wheeled, for carrying goods, passengers, *etc*; any small vehicle moved by hand

**car·tel'** (illegal) group of manufacturers cooperating to regulate production and prices

**car'ti·lage** elastic connective tissue around joints in skeleton

**car·tog'ra·phy** map-making

**car'ton** cardboard box

**car·toon'** (funny) sketch or drawing, *esp.* in newspaper

**car'tridge** cylinder-shaped case for holding powder and bullet for rifle, *etc*; protected roll of film, magnetic tape, *etc*; small removable box holding the needle in a record player

**carv|e** fashion or produce by cutting into or out of (wood, stone, *etc*). **-ing;** cut meat

**cas·cade'** series of small waterfalls

**case** example of sth; actual condition or situation; statement of facts, arguments, *etc*; instance of disease or illness; suit or action at law; **in any c.** under any circumstances; anyhow; **in c.** if; if it should happen that; thing for holding or enclosing sth; box with its contents

**case'ment** window which opens on hinges

**cash** *n* money (coins or banknotes); *v* exchange check, *etc* for money

**cash·ier'** one in charge of cash; *v* dismiss in disgrace

**cash'mere** soft woolen fabric

**ca·si'no** (-sē-) public amusement or gambling room

**cask** small barrel for liquids

**cas'ket** small box; coffin

**cas'se·role** (food prepared in) covered cooking dish

**cas·sette'** container of magnetic tape, *etc* for use in video, tape recorder, *etc*

**cas'sock** long garment worn by priests, *etc*

**cast** *v* (**cast**) throw (off, away, *etc*); direct (glance, *etc*); select (actors for parts of a play); form (molten metal) in mold; **c. about** look (mentally) for idea, *etc*; **c. down** discourage; *n* act of throwing; surgical dressing of plaster; sth shaped in mold; appearance

**cast'a·way** shipwrecked person

**caste** (kahst) (Indian) hereditary social class

**cast'er** small wheel on furniture leg, *etc*

**cas'ti·gate** punish

**cas'tle** (kasl) fortified building serving as home for nobleman in feudal times; piece in chess

**cast'-off'** (sth) discarded

**cas'trate** remove reproductive glands

**cas'u·al** (kash-) informal; due to chance; occasional

**cas'u·al·ty** person injured or killed; **c. ward** section of hospital where accident victims are treated

**cat** small tame meat-eating four-footed animal, of same family as lion, tiger, *etc*; any member of this family

**cat'a·clysm** violent change or upheaval

**cat'a·comb** underground burial place

**cat'a·log(ue)** list, *usu* alphabetical, of goods, books, *etc*

**cat'a·lyst** sth which speeds chemical reaction or produces change

**cat·a·ma·ran'** boat with twin hulls

**cat'a·pult** device for launching airplane from deck of ship; *hist* apparatus for throwing stones

**cat'a·ract** large waterfall; eye ailment clouding lens

**ca·tarrh'** (-tahr) inflammation of mucous membrane

**ca·tas'tro·phe** (-fē) great disaster. **catastroph'ic**

**cat'call** (give) loud whistle or shout of disapproval in theater, etc

**catch** v (**caught**) capture, esp by hunting or fishing for; trap; overtake, as fleeing person; be in time for (train, etc); lay hold of or grasp; surprise s.o. at; check suddenly, as breath; stop motion of and hold, as ball; become entangled with, as coat on nail; be infected with (disease); take fire; take hold, as door lock; grasp with mind; arrest, as attention: n act of catching; amount caught, as fish; a.th worth having; device for checking movement of door, etc

**cat·e·gor'i·cal** absolute; unconditional

**cat'e·go·ry** division for purposes of classification

**ca'ter** provide food or services. **-er**

**cat'er·pil·lar** wormlike larva of butterfly or moth; tractor with wheels moving inside endless belt

**cat'gut** animal intestines dried and twisted to make strings of musical instruments

**ca·thar'tic** cleansing the bowels; purging strong emotions

**ca·the'dral** principal church of a diocese

**cath'e·ter** tube inserted into body to put in or drain fluids

**cath'ode** negative electric pole

**cath'o·lic** of interest to all

**Cath'o·lic church** the Christian church headed by the Pope

**cat'nap** short light sleep

**cat'sup** see **ketchup**

**cat'tle** cows, oxen, etc considered collectively

**cau'cus** policy meeting of party leaders

**caught** see **catch**

**caul'dron** see **caldron**

**caulk** (kawk) seal seam of ship, window, etc

**cau'li·flow·er** (plant with) large white flowerlike head used as vegetable

**caus'al** of, expressing or due to a cause. **causal'ity**

**cause** n that which produces an effect; ground or reason for doing, etc; matter over which person goes to law; aim or purpose which group supports; v bring about

**cause'way** raised road across low or wet ground

**caus'tic** burning or corroding; biting

**cau'tio|n** carefulness with regard to risks, danger, etc; warning. **-us**

**cav·al·cade'** procession of riders, cars, *etc*

**cav'al·ry** soldiers on horseback or in armored cars

**cave** *n* hollow in earth, *esp.* in side of mountain; *v* **c. in** fall or sink in, as ground

**cav'ern** large cave. **-ous**

**cav'i·ar(e)** salted fish eggs, eaten as expensive delicacy

**cav'i·ty** hollow place

**CD** see **compact disc**

**cease** stop. **-less**

**ce'dar** (sē-) (fragrant hardwood of) large evergreen tree

**cede** yield; give up

**ceil'ing** overhead interior surface of room; height above ground as measure of visibility or maximum height of airplane; top limit of prices, *etc*

**cel'e·brate** observe event or day with ceremonies, festivities, *etc*; praise publicly

**ce·leb'ri·ty** fame; famous person

**ce·le'ri·ac** kind of celery with edible bulblike root

**cel'e·ry** (plant with) long stalk used as vegetable

**ce·les'tial** heavenly

**cell** small simple room in convent, prison, *etc*; any small room or compartment; very small structural unit of plant or animal life; unit of electric battery; small group acting as unit within

larger organization. **-lular**

**cel'lar** room below building, used for storage, *etc*

**cel'lo·phane** (selōfān) tough transparent wrapping material

**cel'lu·loid** *n* plastic made of guncotton and camphor; *a* of or related to motion pictures

**cel'lu·lose** substance contained in solid walls of plants

**Cel'si·us** centigrade

**ce·ment'** (siment) substance of lime and clay which becomes stonelike, used for floors, *etc*; glue

**cem'e·ter·y** burial ground

**cen'sor** official inspector of printed matter, *etc*, with power to determine final form

**cen'sure** (-sher) blame; disapprove

**cen'sus** official count of population

**cent** hundredth part of dollar

**cen'te·nar·y, cen·ten'ni·al** anniversary of 100 years

**cen'ter,** *UK* **-tre** middle point, equally distant from all points on edge or surface; main point or place; person, thing, *etc* occupying middle position. **-tral**

**cen'ti·grade** of a thermometer having 100 degrees between zero and boiling point

**cen'ti·me·ter,** *UK* **-tre** hundredth part of meter

**cen·tral·ize**, *UK* **-ise** concentrate power in a central organization

**cen·trif·u·gal** tending to fly away from the center

**cen·tri·fuge** (-fūdzh) device used to separate out parts of a liquid, as blood, *etc*

**cen·trip·e·tal** tending towards the center

**cen·tu·ry** period of one hundred years

**ce·phal·ic** of or in the head

**ce·ram·ics** art of pottery

**ce·re·al** grain yielding plants, as wheat, oats, rice, *etc*; breakfast food made from this

**cer·e·bral** of the brain

**cer·e·mo·ny** formal social behavior. **ceremo·nial**

**cer·e·mo·ni·ous** careful to observe ceremony

**cer·tain** (surtn) settled; definite; reliable; sure to happen; existing but not specified. **-ty**

**cer·tif·i·cate** document formally stating fact to be true. **cer'tify**

**cer·ti·tude** feeling certain

**cer'vix** (*pl* **-vices** or **-vixes**) necklike opening into womb. **-vical**

**ces·sa'tion** ceasing; pause

**ces'sion** giving up; surrendering

**cess'pool** tank in ground for holding waste matter

**chafe** rub; make sore

**chaff** grain-husks; sth worthless

**chaf'ing dish** table vessel for cooking food

**cha·grin'** severe disappointment due to failure

**chain** *n* series of connected links or rings of metal, *etc*; series of connected things, as stores, *etc*; *v* fetter; fasten with c.

**chair** seat for one person, *usu* with back; official position of professor, *etc*; chairman

**chair'lift** endless cable from which chairs are suspended, used to move people up/down steep slope

**chair'man,      -wo·man, -per·son** one who runs meeting or acts as head

**chalk** (chawk) soft limestone; white or colored piece of such material used for writing

**chal'lenge** *n* invitation to take part as opponent in fight or contest; objection raised that sth is untrue, unjust, *etc*; *v* call to account; disagree

**cham'ber** (chām-) room in house, esp. bedroom; hall for meetings of governing body; part of governing, *etc* body; judge's room; any enclosed space

**cha·me'le·on** (ka-) small lizard with ability to change color; s.o. who adapts quickly and often

# chamois

**cham'ois** (shami) (piece of) soft leather used for cleaning and polishing, *esp.* glass, cars, *etc*

**cham·pagne'** (shampān) sparkling wine

**cham'pi·on** fighter, *esp.* one who defends person or cause; person who wins first place in some field, as sports

**chance** unforeseen way in which things happen; absence of design or cause; opportunity; risk; likelihood

**chan'cel·lor** high state or law official

**chan·de·lier'** hanging lamp with several arms

**change** alter by putting or taking one thing instead of another; make or become different; exchange; put on other clothes; re-cover, as a bed; give or receive smaller coins or bills for. **-able**

**chan'nel** bed of a stream; closed passage through which any liquid flows; long furrow or groove; any narrow waterway between two pieces of land; a television station

**chant** sing; speak or repeat rhythmically

**cha'os** (kāos) complete confusion; lack of order

**cha·ot'ic** in great disorder

**chap** *v* (of skin) crack open in small slits; *n* fellow; *usu pl* fleshy covering of jaw of animal

**chap'el** any room or building used as church

**chap'er·on(e)** (shaperōn) older woman in charge of girl in public

**chap'lain** clergyman officially serving army unit or other public institution

**chap'ter** division of book or organization

**char** burn surface of

**char'ac·ter** (kar-) letter or mark; distinguishing feature of a thing; status; sum of distinguishing mental or moral features in person or people; moral strength or excellence; reputation; person in drama or novel; odd person. **-ize, characteris'tic**

**cha·rade'** (sherād) sham; *usu pl* kind of guessing game

**char'coal** (chahr-) black, partly burned wood, used as fuel or for drawing

**charge** (chahrj) *v* make s.o. responsible for; fix price; record (in an account) as owing; accuse; rush upon or attack; load; ask payment; *n* load, burden, duty or responsibility; order; accusation of an offense; (person, thing given in) care or custody; cost; violent attack (against enemy, *etc*)

**charg'er** device for charging storage batteries

**cha·ris·ma** (ka-) ability to inspire others to loyalty or support

**char'i·ty** act or feeling of love or kindness towards others; any institution for aiding the poor. **-table**

**char'la·tan** (sháhr-) person falsely claiming knowledge or skill

**charm** any action, formula or object thought to have magic power; quality that fascinates or attracts

**chart** map, *esp.* of sea; graph

**char'ter** written grant of privileges

**char·treuse'** apple-green

**char'wom·an** *UK* woman hired to clean house

**chase** run after in order to catch; cause to flee; carve, *etc* ornaments on metal surface

**chasm** (kazm) deep gap

**chas'sis** (shasi) supporting framework of automobile, *etc*

**chaste** pure; virtuous. **-tity**

**chas'ten** (chásn) *v* correct by punishment

**chas·tise'** punish; beat

**chat** talk informally

**chat'ter** talk fast and continually

**chauf'feur** s.o. paid to drive a car for another

**chau'vin·ism** aggressive and exaggerated patriotism; male prejudice against women

**cheap** bought or selling at a low price; worth little; costing little effort to get; deserving contempt

**cheat** deceive someone (in order to get money from him, win game, *etc*)

**check** *v* bring to a sudden stop; examine, test, *etc* for accuracy; mark something so as to show that it has been examined, *etc*; deposit article for temporary safekeeping; *n* written order to bank to pay money as stated; supervision to determine accuracy, progress, *etc*; ticket *etc* to identify person or thing; sudden stopping; pattern of squares; in chess, attack on king

**check'book** folder containing blank checks from bank

**check'er** piece in game of checkers; square resembling square of checkerboard

**check'ers** game for two players, each having twelve pieces, on board with sixty-four squares of alternate colors

**check'mate** *n* final move in chess; *v* defeat; hinder

**check'-up** general (medical) examination

**cheek** fleshy part of face below eye; impudence. **-y**

**cheer** urge on, *esp.* by shouts of encouragement; (cause to) be hopeful or comforted. **-ful, -y**

**cheese** milk thickened into solid or nearly-solid mass

**chef** (shef) head cook

**chem·i·cal** substance used or obtained in chemistry

**chem·i·cal war'fare** war using poison gases, *etc*

**chem·is·try** science of the elements and their laws of combination and behavior

**cher'ish** treat tenderly; value; hold in mind

**cher'ry** (wood-bearing tree with) small edible, *usu* red fruit

**chess** game played on checkerboard by two players, each having sixteen pieces

**chest** part of body enclosed by ribs and breastbone; box with lid; (funds in) treasury of public institution

**chest'nut** (wood-bearing tree with) smooth red-brown edible nut; horse chestnut tree; red-brown color; old joke or story

**chew** bite and grind with the teeth

**chic** (shēk) fashionably elegant in style

**chick'en** young bird, *esp.* of common barnyard fowl; edible meat of this bird

**chick·en pox** contagious disease causing rash

**chide** (chīd or chid'ed, chid or chid'den or chid'ed) scold

**chief** head of tribe; highest official of department, *etc*

**chif'fon** very thin silk fabric

**child** (*pl* chil'dren) young person between ages of infancy and youth; son or daughter

**chill** *v* make cold; discourage; *n* feeling of cold, *esp.* when accompanied by feverish shivering

**chime** *v* sound harmoniously, as bells; *n* sound of bell, *etc*; *pl* set of bells in tune with each other

**chim'ney** passage of stone, metal, *etc* letting smoke escape out of stove, *etc*; glass tube placed around lamp flame

**chim·pan·zee'** African manlike ape

**chin** front of lower jaw, below mouth

**chi'na** fine porcelain

**chink** small crack or opening

**chintz** printed cotton cloth, often glazed

**chip** small piece, as of wood, cut or broken off; thin slice of potato, *etc*; counter in games of chance; small piece of silicon containing an electric circuit, used in computers, *etc*

**chi·rop'o·dist** (kīr-) person who cares for feet and treats their diseases

**chirp** short sharp note uttered by birds

**chuck**

**chis'el** metal tool with cutting edge used in shaping wood, stone, *etc*

**chiv'al·ry** gallantry; valor; medieval knightly virtues

**chive** herb related to onion

**chlo'rine** substance used for bleaching and to disinfect water

**chlo'ro·form** an anesthetic

**chlo'ro·phyl(l)** green coloring matter of plants

**choc'o·late** (chokelit) candy made from roasted cacao beans, with added sugar, *etc*

**choice** *n* (power of) choosing; alternative; number or variety to choose from; person or thing chosen; *a* worthy of being chosen; superior

**choir** (kwīr) group of singers, *esp.* of religious music

**choke** cut off breath by squeezing windpipe; be unable to breathe because of food, *etc* blocking windpipe; clog

**chol'e·ra** serious, often fatal, disease attacking stomach and bowels

**choose** (**chose, cho'sen**) select from many; take certain course of action

**chord** (k-) *mus* notes in harmony; straight line joining two points on a curve

**chore** (chōr) small (household or farm) job; unpleasant work

**chor·e·og'ra·phy** art of designing dances

**cho'rus** (kōr-) choir; group of singers or dancers in musicals; part of song repeated at regular intervals; words spoken together by group

**chose, cho'sen** see **choose**

**chow'der** soup or stew containing fish, clams, *etc*

**chris'ten** baptize; give name to

**Chris'tian** (krischn) of, believing in, or belonging to any of religions that accept teachings of Jesus Christ

**Christ'mas** church festival celebrating birth of Christ

**chro·mat'ic** of color(s); *mus* progressing by half tones

**chrome, chro'mi·um** grayish-white metal used to plate iron, *etc* to make it rust-resisting

**chron'ic** (k-) of long duration

**chron'i·cle** register of events in order of time

**chro·nol'o·gy** (k-) arrangement of events with dates. **chronolog'ical**

**chro·nom'e·ter** (k-) very accurate clock

**chrys·an'the·mum** (plant with) decorative flower

**chub'by** plump and round

**chuck** *v* throw with short jerking motion of arm; pat under chin; *n* portion of beef (neck and shoulder); device for holding work in place in machine

**chuck·le** laugh with closed mouth

**chum** close friend

**church** building for public religious services; group (*usu* of Christians) organized in religious society

**churn** *n* vessel for making butter; *v* stir up; agitate

**chute** (shūt) slide for conveying things to lower level; *infml* parachute

**ci·der** (sī-) juice pressed out of apples and fermented

**ci·gar** small roll of tobacco leaf for smoking

**cig·a·rette** roll of cut tobacco wrapped in paper for smoking

**cin·der** partly burnt piece of wood or coal, *pl* ashes

**cin·e·ma** *esp.* UK motion pictures; place where these are shown

**cin·e·ma·theque'** (-tek) *US* place where historical motion pictures are stored and shown

**cin·e·ma·tog·ra·phy** art of motion picture photography

**cin·na·mon** inner bark of Asian laurel tree, used as spice; yellow-brown color

**ci'pher** *or* **cy'pher** code

**cir'cle** *n* perfectly round closed curve, every point on which is the same distance from center; anything ring-shaped or arranged in ring form; group of people having same interests; *v* move around in circle. **-culate**

**cir'cuit** (-kit) circular course; path of electric current; group of electronic elements

**cir'cuit break·er** device to interrupt electric current

**cir·cu'i·tous** roundabout; indirect

**cir'cu·lar** in the form of a circle; round

**cir·cum·cise** cut off foreskin. **circumci'sion**

**cir·cum'fer·ence** (length of) outer boundary of circle, *etc*

**cir·cum·lo·cu'tion** use of many words where few would do

**cir·cum·nav'i·gate** sail around

**cir'cum·scribe** draw a line around; limit; confine

**cir'cum·spect** cautious

**cir'cum·stance** condition or event influencing another

**cir·cum·vent'** evade

**cir'cus** round enclosure with seats, for acrobatic shows, *etc*

**cis'tern** tank for storing water

**cite** summon officially; mention as example. **cita'tion**

**cit'i·zen** person owing allegiance to a state and entitled to protection by it

**cit'rus** (of) fruit family including lemon, orange, grapefruit, *etc*

**clay**

**cit'y** large important town

**civ'ic** of citizens and citizenship

**civ'ics** study of duties and rights of citizens

**civ'il** of, carried on by, or belonging to duties and rights of, citizens; civilized; polite; of private rights as distinguished from criminal offenses

**civ·i·li·za'tion** act of civilizing; advanced stage of social development

**civ'i·lize** bring out of barbarism

**civ·il rights'** freedom, equality, *etc* due to every citizen regardless of race, creed, sex

**claim** demand as belonging or due to o.s. by some right. **-mant;** assert a fact or right; call for attention, *etc*

**clair·voy'ance** ability to see sth in the mind that is happening out of sight. **-ant**

**clam** shellfish with hinged double shell and *usu* edible flesh

**clam'ber** climb with hands and feet

**clam'my** cold and damp

**clam'o(u)r** loud and continued noise or outcry

**clamp** device for fastening or holding things together

**clan·des'tine** secret

**clang** loud ringing metallic sound

**clap** strike (hands, *etc*) together with loud noise, *esp.* in approval; close (door, *etc*) with loud noise

**clap'trap** nonsense

**clar'et** (wine having) deep purplish red color

**clar'i·fy** make clear. **-ty**

**clar'i·on** loud and clear

**clash** come into conflict; strike together; disagree, as colors

**clasp** fasten together; take with or in the hand

**class** group of people having same social position; group of things or persons of the same kind or with the same interests, *esp.* group of students taught together; group, division, *etc* marked according to quality, price, *etc*

**clas'sic** *a* of high artistic rank; typical; simple and harmonious; *n* artist, work, *etc* of highest rank

**clas'si·fy** arrange in classes

**clat'ter** confused rattling noise

**clause** part of sentence; single provision in contract, *etc*

**claus·tro·pho'bi·a** dread of closed places

**claw** *n* sharp curved nail of animal; curved device for holding; *v* tear, grab, dig, *etc* (with claws)

**clay** kind of earth which can be molded when wet and hardened by baking

**clean** free of dirt.
**clean'liness** (klen-); free of flaws or obstructions; well--proportioned

**cleanse** (klenz) make clean

**clear** bright; light; transparent; (*color*) pure; (*complexion*) fresh; plain to hear, see, or understand; not confused or in doubt; free of guilt; free of debt, extra charges, *etc*; free of obstructions

**clear'ance** act of clearing; distance allowed between two objects passing each other; sale

**cleave (cleaved, cleft** or **clove, cleaved, cleft** or **clo'ven)** split open. **-age**

**clef** *mus* symbol showing pitch, treble or bass c.

**cleft** *v* see **cleave;** *n* crack made by splitting

**cleft pal'ate** birth defect in which roof of mouth is split

**clem'en·cy** mildness; mercy

**clench** close together tightly, as teeth, fists, *etc*

**cler'gy** (-ji) priests or ministers of a church

**cler'i·cal** of the clergy; of office workers

**clerk** (klurk, *UK* klahk) person whose job is to keep records. *etc* in an office; *US* one who serves customers in a store

**clev'er** skillful; showing mental sharpness

**clew** see **clue**

**cli·ché'** (-shā) worn-out phrase

**click** (make) slight snapping noise, as when lock catches

**cli'ent** (klī-) person who employs services of professional person such as lawyer, doctor, *etc*; customer

**cli·en·tele'** customers of doctor, shop, *etc*

**cliff** steep face of rock

**cli·mac'ter·ic** bodily changes in middle age; menopause in female, reduced sexual activity in male

**cli'mate** (klīmit) average condition of weather in any region; prevailing opinion at a given time

**cli'max** highest point in series of ideas, events, *etc*

**climb** (klīm) go up to higher point, *esp.* with support of hands and feet; rise (as prices, road, *etc*) to higher point

**clinch** fasten firmly, as with nails; make final or conclusive; (*boxing*) hold opponent firmly with arms

**cling (clung)** stick together in a stiff mass; stick to; hold fast, as by putting arms around

**clin'ic** part of hospital for treatment of outpatients

**clip** *v* cut off, as with scissors; *n* small metal device for holding papers, *etc* together; device for cutting fingernails, *etc*; fast pace

**clip'pers** shears for cutting hedge, hair, *etc*

**clique** (klēk) small exclusive set of people

**cloak** *n* loose outer coat; *v* hide, as with cloak

**clock** device for measuring time, *esp.* one not worn on body; ornament on side of stocking

**clod** lump of earth

**clog** hinder; choke up

**close** *v* (-z) stop or fill up, as an opening; shut; bring or come to an end; settle (bargain); *a* (-s) near; narrow; dense; fitting tightly; keeping to a standard or original; strict; accurate; secretive; *n* (-z) the end of sth; (-s) enclosed place, as around a cathedral

**closed shop** factory employing only union members

**clos'et** (kloz-) small room for household utensils, clothing, *etc*; small private room; small room containing toilet

**close'-up** film shot at close range

**clot** lump of thickened liquid, *esp* blood

**cloth** (piece of) woven or felted material made of cotton, silk, wool, *etc*; tablecloth

**clothe** (clothed or clad) provide with garments; put garments on

**clothes** (klōdhz, klōz) *pl* garments for the human body,

clothing

**cloud** mass of particles of water hanging in air, (*usu*) high above the earth; mass of smoke or dust; great number of insects, birds, *etc* in flight

**cloud'y** overcast; not clear; opaque

**clove** *n* dried flower bud of tropical tree used as spice; one of small bulbs of a larger bulb, as garlic

**clove, clo'ven** *v* see **cleave**

**clo'ver** (klō-) herb of pea family, used for fodder

**clown** comic character in circus, play, *etc*. **-ish**

**club** heavy wooden stick, *esp.* of kind used in playing certain games; group of persons joined together for common purpose, such as games, sport, *etc*

**club'foot** short misshapen foot as birth defect

**clue** fact or hint suggesting line of inquiry

**clump** unshaped mass, as of earth; thick group of trees

**clum'sy** without skill or grace; awkward; ill-made so as to be hard to handle

**clung** see **cling**

**clus'ter** bunch; group

**clutch** *v* seize; grasp; *n* coupling device connecting or disconnecting two working parts in machinery

**clut'ter** confused mass

**coach** (kōch) comfortable

bus for long distances; passenger car on railroad; private teacher who helps prepare students for examinations; teacher in athletics, singing, *etc*

**co·ag·u·late** change from liquid to solid; clot

**coal** black or brown solid mineral mined for fuel; ember

**co·a·lesce** come together to form one mass, *etc*

**co·a·li·tion** union formed for special purpose

**coarse** of low quality; made up of large particles; harsh; rough; vulgar

**coast** *n* shore of sea or lake; *v* move, *esp.* downhill, without effort or power

**coast'er** small mat put under glasses, *etc* to prevent stains

**coat** long-sleeved outer garment; feathers or fur on birds or animals; covering layer, as of paint

**coax** urge by flattery or gentle persuasion

**cob** male swan; corncob

**co'balt** (kō-) silverwhite metallic element used in making metals; blue pigment made from it

**co'bra** (kō-) poisonous Asiatic and African hooded snake

**cob'web** network of fine threads spread by a spider

**co·caine'** (kōkān) or *sl* **coke** habit-forming narcotic drug, used illegally as stimulant

**cock** *n* male of common barnyard fowl or of other birds; faucet, tap or valve; hammer of gun, *etc*; *v* tilt, as hat; lift (hammer of gun) for firing; lift (eye or ear)

**cock'eyed** having a squinting eye; crooked; absurd

**cock'ney** Londoner; his dialect

**cock'pit** space for pilot, *etc* in airplane

**cock'roach** large nocturnal beetle infesting kitchens, *etc*

**cock'tail** mixed alcoholic drink; small bits of food, as lobster, *etc* eaten before main course of meal

**co'coa** (kōkō) (drink made with) chocolate powder

**co'co·nut** large nutlike fruit of tropical palm, containing milky liquid and edible white flesh

**co·coon'** silky case spun by larva for protection

**cod** large food fish of North Atlantic

**cod'dle** pamper or spoil, as child; cook gently in water just below boiling

**code** system of laws; system of secret symbols

**cod'i·cil** addition to a will

**cod'i·fy** frame laws into code; arrange in system

**co·ed·u·ca'tion** education of boys and girls together

**co·er·ce'** compel by force. **-cion**

**co·ex·ist'** exist side by side. **-ence**

**cof'fee** (drink made from ground, roasted) beanlike seed of tropical shrub

**cof'fer** chest, *esp.* for valuables; *pl* funds

**cof'fin** box in which dead person is put for burial

**cog** tooth on rim of a wheel

**co'gen|t** (kōjent) convincing. **-cy**

**cog'i·tate** think; ponder

**cog'nate** similar or related in origin, nature, *etc*

**cog·ni'tion** process of knowing

**cog'ni·|zance** notice; being aware of. **-zant**

**co·here'** stick together

**co·her'ent** sticking together; logical, consistent

**co·he'sion** sticking together, *esp.* of molecules

**coil** *n* series of rings, or spirals, of rope, cable, *etc*; *v* wind in round or spiral shape

**coin** *n* piece of metal marked and issued by government to be used as money; *v* make coins; invent, as a word

**coin'age** act of coining; system of coins

**co·in·cide'** happen at same time; agree

**co'i·tus** sexual intercourse

**coke** (kōk) gray porous fuel obtained by heating coal; non-alcoholic soft drink; *sl* cocain

**col'an·der** plastic, *etc* bowl with many holes, used for draining liquid off food

**cold** *a* of low temperature; lacking warmth or feeling; unfriendly; (of color) having a bluish or greenish tint; *n* weather with low temperature; disease causing inflammation of nose and throat

**cole'slaw** salad of chopped raw cabbage

**col'ic** severe cramp in the abdomen

**col·lab'o·ra|te** work together; co-operate with enemy of one's country. **-tor**

**col·lapse'** break down; cave in

**col'lar** neckband, *esp.* as part of shirt, *etc*

**col'lar·bone** bone joining breastbone and shoulderblade

**col·late'** compare critically, as two texts

**col·lat'er·al** *n* security for a loan; *a* parallel; subordinate

**col'league** *n* associate; working partner

**col·lec't** bring or come together; get or force payment of (bill, *etc*). **-tor**; regain control of (thoughts, o.s., *etc*)

**col·lec'tive** done by or relating to a group

**col·lege** (kolij) institute for higher education, or for professional studies, as medicine. **colle·giate** (kelējit)

**col·li·de'** come together with force; be in conflict. **-sion**

**col·lie·r** coal miner; coal ship. **-ry**

**col·lo·qui·al** belonging to everyday speech. **-ism**

**col·lu·sion** secret understanding for fraudulent purposes

**co·logne'** (-lōn) a kind of light perfume

**co·lon** punctuation mark (:); lower part of large intestine

**colo·nel** (kurnel) military rank; US honorary title in Amer. South

**col·on·nade'** row of columns supporting roof

**col·o·ny** group of settlers in new country, governed by mother state. **-nist, -nize, colo·nial;** foreigners, artists, etc living in group in city

**col·or,** UK **-our** sensation caused on eye by light broken down into its spectral elements; component or mixture of components of spectrum; complexion; racial complexion; blush; vivid quality in literary work; paint; pl flag, badge, etc serving as symbol

**col·or-blind** unable to see certain colors

**col·or-fast** dyed so as not to fade or run

**co·los'sal** huge

**colt** young male horse

**col·umn** upright shaft of stone, supporting roof, etc; vertical row of lines on printed page; special section in newspaper, etc

**co·ma** state of prolonged unconsciousness

**comb** (kōm) toothed strip of bone, etc for arranging hair; similar device for smoothing wool, etc; red growth on head of fowl

**com'bat** battle; fight

**com·bine'** v join in close union. **combina'tion;** n machine for threshing and reaping

**com·bus'ti·on** n burning; oxidation. **-ble**

**come** (kum) (**came, come**) move towards, or arrive at, place, result, time; happen; be available (in certain form); issue; be result of; enter (into being); become; be brought; **c. about** happen; **c. across** meet with; **c. by** get; **c. into** get possession of; **c. off** happen; **c. round** give in; change opinion; recover; **c. to** recover consciousness; amount to

**com'e·dy** light, amusing stage play or film with happy ending; humor. **come'dian**

**come'ly** (kum-) pleasant to look at

**communicative**

**com'et** heavenly body with long tail, moving around sun

**com'fort** *v* soothe when in grief; make s.o. feel at ease in mind or body; *n* relief in grief; cause of satisfaction or well-being. **-able**

**com'fort·er** *US* quilted covering for bed; *UK* woolen scarf

**com'i|c** of comedy; causing laughter; funny. **-cal**

**com'ic strip** group of cartoons telling story

**com'ma** punctuation mark (,) used to separate parts of sentence, items on list, *etc*

**com·mand'** order; be in charge of; have at one's disposal; overlook from higher position

**com·man·deer'** seize for military or public use

**com·mem'o·rate** celebrate memory of. **commemo·ra'tion**

**com·mence'ment** beginning; graduation ceremony

**com·mend'** praise. **-able, commenda'tion;** entrust

**com·men'su·ra·ble** measurable by the same standard

**com·men'su·rate** equal in measure or extent; adequate

**com'men|t** explanatory remark; criticism. **-tary, -tator**

**com'merce** exchange of goods, *esp.* on large scale

**com·mer'cial** *a* of or engaged in commerce; *n* (radio or television) sales announcement. **-ize**

**com·mis'er·ate** feel or express pity for

**com'mis·sar·y** head of commissariat; store in army camp; deputy

**com·mis'sion** order; authority to act; document giving authority, *esp.* to military officer; sum given agent for services; act of committing. **-er**

**com·mit'** give in trust; hand over for treatment or safekeeping; do, as a crime; bind oneself. **-ment**

**com·mit'tee** body of persons appointed for special purpose

**com·mod'i·ty** article of trade; useful thing

**com'mon** shared; ordinary; vulgar; frequent

**com'mon·place** ordinary; usual

**com·mo'tion** disturbance;. violent agitation

**com·mu'nal** owned jointly by all; relating to a community

**com'mune** *n* group of people living or working together

**com·mune'** *v* share ideas or feelings; talk together

**com·mu'ni·cate** transmit; give information; be connected with. **communica'tion**

**com·mu'ni·ca·tive** ready to give information; talkative

**com·mun·ion** sharing

**com·mu·ni·que'** official bulletin

**com'mu·|nism** system in which means of production are jointly owned and products shared. **-nist**

**com·mu'ni·ty** people sharing similar interests, *etc*, or living in same area; neighborhood

**com'mu·tat·or** device for altering course of electric current

**com·mute'** travel regularly same distance between home and work, *esp.* by train; lessen punishment; exchange one (kind of payment) for another

**com'pact'** *a* closely packed; small

**com'pact** *n* small case with face powder and rouge; agreement

**com·pact disc'** digital sound recording

**com·pan'ion** person who spends time with another (for pay). **-ship;** handbook

**com'pa·ny** organization of people engaged in business, trade, *etc* for profit; visitors; companionship

**com·pa·ra·ble** that can be compared

**com·par|e'** examine for likenesses and differences. **-ative, compa'rison**

**com·part'ment** division

**com'pass** magnetic instrument for determining location; (*UK* **-es** *pl*) instrument for drawing circles; range

**com·pas'sion** pity. **-ate**

**com·pat'i·ble** able to be used together, as equipment; able to coexist; consistent. **compatibil'ity**

**com·pel'** force

**com·pen'di·|um** brief but complete summary. **-ous**

**com'pen·sate** make up (for); pay for; counterbalance

**com·pete'** engage in contest. **competi'tion**

**com'pe·|tence** sufficient ability; legal capacity. **-tent;** sufficient income

**com·pile'** collect and arrange (literary) material in book, list, *etc*. **compila'tion**

**com·pla·|cent** self-satisfied. **-cence, -cency**

**com·|plain'** express pain or dissatisfaction; make formal charge. **-plaint**

**com·plai'|sant** willing to do what others want. **-sance**

**com'ple·ment** that which completes; full number required. **complemen'tary**

**com·plete'** *a* whole; having all the necessary parts; finished; *v* finish; make whole. **-tion**

**com'plex** *a* consisting of many parts; complicated; *n* system; abnormal mental state due to suppression of emotions. **complex'ity**

**com·plex'ion** natural color of skin, *esp.* of face; character

**com·pli'ance** yielding to request or command. **-ant**

**com'pli·cate** make intricate

**com·plic'i·ty** partnership in wrongdoing

**com'pli·ment** expression of praise. **complimen'tary**

**com·ply'** act in accordance with request, *etc*

**com·po'nent** *a* forming part of; *n* part

**com·pose'** write music, *etc*; arrange or fashion; calm o.s.

**com·pos'ite** made up of various parts

**com·pos'i·tor** one who sets type

**com·po'sure** calmness

**com'pound** *a* mixed; *n* mixture; enclosure

**com·pound'** *v* combine; make sth worse

**com'pound in'ter·est** interest on interest and principal

**com·pre·hend'** understand. **-sion**; include. **-sive**

**com·press'** *v* squeeze together; condense. **-sion**

**com'press** *n* surgical pad

**com·prise'** include; consist of

**com'pro·mise** settle dispute by mutual concessions; endanger reputation of

**comp·trol'ler** (ken-) controller

**com·pul'|sion** force that makes s.o. do sth; strong (unreasonable) desire. **-sive, -sory**

**com·punc'tion** remorse

**com·pute'** calculate; use computer. **computa'tion**

**com·put'er** electronic machine (using programs (software) to control operations, *etc*

**com·put'er·ize,** UK **-ise** equip with or produce by computer; adapt material for computer

**com'rade** companion in work, play, war, *etc*

**con·cave'** curved like the inside of a circle; hollow

**con·ceal'** (-sēl) hide; keep secret

**con·cede'** grant; admit as true

**con·ceit'** (-sēt) exaggerated opinion of one's own abilities, importance, *etc*. **-ed**

**con·ceive'** imagine; become pregnant. **-ed**

**con'cen·trate** bring to one point; intensify; center attention. **concentra'tion**

**con·cen'tric** having a common center

**con'cept** general notion

**con·cep'tion** act of conceiving; thing conceived

**con·cern'** (-surn) *v* be connected with; affect; interest (oneself in); *n* matter of interest or anxiety; (large) business firm

**con·cern'ing** with regard to; about

**con·cert'** *n* musical performance; agreement

**con·cert'** *v* arrange by agreement

**con·cert'ed** combined

**con·cer'to** (kenchertō) composition for solo instrument and orchestra

**con·ces'sion** sth granted; right to use land, sell goods, *etc*

**con·cil'i·a|te** reconcile; win over. **-tory, concilia'tion**

**con·cise'** expressing much in few words

**con·clu|de'** end; settle; infer. **-sion**

**con·clu'sive** decisive; convincing

**con·coc|t'** make up of mixed ingredients; invent. **-tion**

**con·com'i·tant** accompanying

**con'cord** agreement; harmony; treaty. **concord'ant**

**con'course** coming together; open meeting space

**con'crete** (-krēt) *a* existing in material form; real; not general or abstract; *n* mixture of cement, small stones, sand and water used as building material

**con·cu·bine** woman who lives with man without being married to him. **concu'binage**

**con·cur'** agree; happen together. **-rent**

**con·cus'sion** violent shaking or shock, *esp.* of brain

**con·demn'** declare wrong; sentence; declare unfit for use. **condemna'tion**

**con·dens|e'** change gas into liquid by cooling. **-er;** reduce liquid by removing water; put into few words. **condensa'tion**

**con·de·scend'** do sth one feels is beneath one's dignity. **-sion**

**con·de·scend'ing** patronizing

**con'di·ment** seasoning

**con·di'tion** *n* situation in which person or thing exists; state of being (at any given time); thing which must occur, be done, *etc* if another is to happen; *v* make dependent on; bring into desired state; train

**con·do|le'** express sympathy. **-lence**

**con'dom** protective rubber sheath worn over penis during sexual intercourse

**con·do·min'i·um** apartment building in which each apartment is privately owned; such an apartment; control of a territory by two or more states

**con·done'** forgive; overlook

**con·du'cive** favorable; contributing to

**con'duct** *n* behavior; management

**con·duct'** v guide; direct; behave o.s.; transmit

**con·duc'tor** director of orchestra; one in charge of train, bus, *etc*; thing that conducts electricity, *etc*

**con'duit** (-dit) pipe; channel

**cone** solid figure, with round base, tapering to point; sth having this shape; fruit of pine or fir tree

**con·fed'er·a·cy** political alliance. **-ate, confedera'tion**

**con·fer'** grant; talk over together

**con'fer·ence** meeting for discussion

**con·fes|s'** admit, *esp.* guilt, secret, *etc*; declare belief, *etc*; reveal one's sins (to a priest). **-sion**

**con·fet'ti** small bits of colored paper thrown at weddings, *etc*

**con·fi·dant'**, *f* **-dante'** one to whom secrets are entrusted

**con·fide'** have trust in; tell secrets to

**con·fi·|dence** belief in one's ability. **-dent;** trust; a secret

**con·fi·den'tial** secret; private

**con·fig·u·ra'tion** shape; arrangement of parts

**con·fine'** keep within limits; imprison; be in childbirth. **-ment**

**con·firm'** establish more firmly; ratify; verify. **con·firma'tion**

**con·fis·cate** seize by authority

**con·fla·gra'tion** a large destructive fire

**con·flict'** v come into or be in opposition; struggle

**con'flict** n battle; quarrel; opposition of principles, interests, *etc*

**con·for|m'** make or be like; comply. **-mity**

**con·found'** mix up; confuse

**con·front'** bring or meet face to face

**con·fu|se'** mix up (in the mind); mistake. **-sion**

**con·fute'** prove sth wrong

**con·geal'** freeze; thicken, as blood; solidify

**con·gen'ial** sympathetic; suited to

**con·gen'i·tal** existing at, or dating from, birth

**con·ges'tion** overfullness of blood vessels, *etc*; crowdedness

**con·glom'er·ate** large corporation formed from many diverse companies; materials collected into a mass

**con·grat'u·late** express pleasure to another person on his good fortune or success

**con'gre·gate** gather in a group or crowd. **congrega'tion**

**con'gress** formal meeting of delegates; national lawmaking body of some nations

**con·gru'i·ty** agreement; suitableness. **con'gruous**

**co'ni·fer** cone-bearing, *usu* evergreen tree

**con·jec'ture** guess

**con'ju·gal** of marriage or the relationship between husband and wife

**con'ju·gate** give set of forms of a verb; join together

**con·junc'tion** union; combination of events, *etc*

**con'jure** (kunjer) practice magic; summon (spirit, *etc*); appeal solemnly to

**con·nect't** join or fasten together; unite by telephone; attach to (electric power outlet); link time schedules of trains, *etc*; bring or come into relationship. **-tive**

**con·nive'** co-operate secretly in; pretend not to see wrongdoing

**con·nois·seur'** (konisur) expert in matters of art, *etc*

**con·note'** mean; imply

**con'quer** (kongker) overcome; defeat. **con'quest**

**con'science** moral sense of right and wrong

**con·sci·en'tious** obedient to conscience; painstaking. **c. objector** person whose conscience forbids him to do military service

**con'scious** aware; knowing; intentional. **-ness**

**con'se·crate** declare sacred; dedicate to some purpose

**con·sec'u·tive** following uninterruptedly

**con·sen'sus** general agreement

**con·sent'** agreement; permission

**con'se·quence** result; importance. **con'sequently**

**con·ser·va'tion** act of conserving; protection; *esp.* of natural environment, as soil, water, *etc*

**con·ser·va'tion·ist** supporter of conservation

**con·serv'a·tive** tending to keep existing institutions; cautious: *a c. estimate.* **-tism**

**con·serv'a·to·ry** greenhouse; school of music

**con·serve'** keep from harm, decay or loss

**con·sid'er** turn over in mind; regard as; make allowance for; pay attention to (rights, *etc* of) others. **considera'·tion**

**con·sid'er·a·ble** of large extent; important

**con·sid'er·ate** thoughtful towards others

**con·sid'er·ing** in view of

**con·sign'** (-sin) deliver; send goods, *etc* to a person to sell. **-ment**

**con·sist'** be made up (of)

**con·sist'ence, con·sist'en·cy** degree of density or firmness; state of being consistent

**con·sist'ent** not contradictory; holding to the same principles

**contact**

**con·sole'** v comfort. **conso·la'tion**

**con'sole** n frame enclosing keyboard, etc of organ; floor-model television set; control panel for machinery, etc

**con·sol'i·date** solidify; combine

**con·som·mé'** (-mā) clear meat or vegetable broth

**con'so·nant** n (sound corresponding to) any letter of alphabet except a, e, i, o, u; a in agreement (with)

**con'sort** n (royal) spouse; ship sailing with another

**con·sort'** v keep company

**con·sor'tium** (international) association, esp. of companies, banks, etc allied for some purpose

**con·spic'u·ous** easy to be seen; attracting notice

**con·spire** plot (against). **-racy, -rator**

**con'sta·ble** UK policeman. **constab'ulary**

**con'stant** unchanging; steady; regular; faithful

**con·stel·la'tion** group of fixed stars

**con·ster·na'tion** amazement

**con·sti·pa'tion** blocked state of bowels

**con·stit'u·en·cy** body or district of voters

**con·stit'u·ent** a being part of a whole; having power to make or change political constitution; n component part; voter

**con·sti·tute'** establish; appoint; make up

**con·sti·tu'tion** structure of body or mind; laws and principles underlying government of state. **-al**

**con·strain'** force; restrain. **-straint**

**con·strict'** draw together; cause to contract. **-tion**

**con·struct'** build; fit together. **-tion**

**con·struc'tive** useful

**con·strue'** interpret

**con'sul** agent abroad protecting citizens of his state

**con'su·late** building or office of consul

**con·sult'** ask advice from

**con·sult'ant** one giving professional advice or services

**con·sume'** use, eat or drink up; destroy; squander; waste away (as by sickness). **-sumption**

**con·sum'er** person who purchases goods or services; **c. goods** those used by private persons as opposed to industry

**con·sum'mate** (-meit) v accomplish; complete (marriage by sexual intercourse); (-met) a highly skilled

**con'tact** n touch; connection; v get into touch with; **c. lens** thin lens fitting against eyeball to correct vision

**con·ta·|gion** passing on of disease by contact. **-gious**

**con·tain'** hold or be capable of holding within itself. **-er;** include as part; keep under control, as feelings

**con·tam'i·nate** make impure or infect by contact

**con·tem'plate** meditate on. **contem'pla·tive;** view (mentally); intend

**con·tem'po·rar·y** (one) belonging to same time or age; modern

**con·tempt'** feeling that s.o. or sth does not deserve respect; **c. of court** *law* disobedience to court. **-tuous**

**con·temp'ti·ble** deserving contempt

**con·tend'** fight; compete; argue; assert earnestly. **-er.**

**con·tent'** *a* satisfied; having desires limited to what one can have. **-ed, -ment**

**con·tent** *n* (*usu pl*) what is contained (in room, book, *etc*); (*sing*) amount which is or can be contained; main elements of book, *etc*

**con·test'** *v* dispute; challenge; compete for

**con·test** *n* competition; struggle. **contes'tant**

**con·text'** words before and after a passage, fixing its meaning

**con·tig'u·ous** touching; neighboring. **contig'uity**

**con·ti·nent** one of (six) main land masses of the earth. **continen'tal**

**con·tin'gen·cy** possible future event; chance occurrence

**con·tin'gent** (-inj-) *a* conditional; possible; accidental; *n* group of people within larger group

**con·tin'u·al** going on all the time; happening again and again

**con·tin'ue** keep on doing, being, *etc*; start again after interruption; stay on in place, position *etc*. **continua'tion**

**con·tin'u·ous** having the parts directly connected; uninterrupted

**con·tor't** twist. **-tion**

**con'tour** outline

**con'tra·band** smuggled goods

**con·tra·cep'tive** (device, *etc*) preventing conception

**con'tract** *n* legal agreement

**con·trac'|t** *v* agree by contract; get, as debt or fever; draw together. **-tion**

**con·tra·dic'|t** be contrary to; deny. **-tion**

**con·tral'to** lowest female singing voice

**con·trap'tion** *infml* gadget; device

**con'tra·ry** opposite in nature, tendency or direction; being the opposite one of two; (contra'ry) insisting unreasonably on one's own will

**cook**

con'trast n difference(s) as shown by (mentally) placing (objects, ideas) side by side and comparing them

con·trast' v show difference by comparing; set off (colors, etc)

con·trib'ute give (to common fund); supply literary article. contribu'tion

con·triv|e' invent; bring about; plan; manage. -ance

con·trol' v hold power over and direct; hold in check; check (by experiment, standard); n power of directing and checking; usu pl device for regulating speed, direction, etc of motor, airplane, etc

con·trol'ler officer who handles (public) accounts; s.o. who directs sth, as air traffic

con'tro·ver·sy dispute; debate. controver'sial

con·tu'sion bruise

co·nun'drum riddle

con·va·les|ce' recover from illness. -cence, cent

con·vene' assemble; meet

con·ve'ni·ent suited to, practical or comfortable for use; that can be easily reached, handled, etc; not troublesome. -ence

con·ven'tion formal assembly; (social) custom; agreement. -al

con·verge' tend toward one point; come together

con·ver'sant familiar (with)

con·verse' v talk with. conversa'tion

con'verse (sth) opposite or contrary

con·ver|t' change to another state, form or belief. -sion

con·vert'i·ble a able to be changed; n automobile with folding roof

con'vex curved like the outside of a circle

con·vey' carry; transfer (property); transmit. -er

con·vey'ance vehicle; document transferring property

con·vey'or (UK -er) belt endless rotating belt, used to move objects, esp. in factory

con'vict n criminal serving sentence

con·vict' v prove or declare guilty of a crime

con·vic'tion act of convincing or convicting; strong belief

con·vince' persuade by argument

con·viv'i·al sociable; merry. -ity

con·voke' call together. convoca'tion

con·vo·lut'ed twisted; difficult to follow, as argument, etc

con'voy group of ships or vehicles (with armed escort)

con·vulse' shake or tighten violently. convul'sion

cook prepare (food) by heating

**cook'book, UK cook'e·ry book** book with recipes for cooking

**cook'ie, cook'y** small flat sweet cake

**cool** moderately cold; not excited; lacking warmth or enthusiasm

**cool'ant** liquid used to cool machinery, *etc*

**coop** enclosure, *usu* with bars or wire, for chickens, *etc*

**co·op'er·ate** work together

**co·op'er·a·tive** *a* willing to cooperate; *n* society producing or distributing wares whose profits are shared by members

**co·or'di·nate** (-net) *a* equal in rank; (-neit) *v* bring into proper relation. **coordina'tion**

**cope** struggle with successfully

**cop'i·er** machine that makes photocopies

**co'pi·ous** plentiful; abundant

**cop'per** reddish metal that can be easily shaped, used to make wire, coins, *etc*

**cop'u·late** (-yū-) unite sexually

**cop'y** exact imitation of sth, as painting, or duplicate, as photocopy; specimen of book, newspaper, *etc*; matter to be printed

**cop'y·right** exclusive right to publish and sell literary, *etc* work

**co·quette'** (-ket) woman who likes to flirt

**cor'al** hard skeleton of certain sea animals; (of) deep pink or red color

**cord** thin rope made of several strands twisted together; similar structure in animal body; ribbed cloth, *esp.* corduroy; measure of cut wood

**cor'dial** *n* sweetened liquor; *a* hearty

**cor'don** line of police, *etc* guarding an area

**cor'du·roy** (-deroi) thick ribbed cotton cloth

**core** hard center of fleshy fruit, containing seeds; innermost part; center of nuclear reactor

**cork** light-weight bark of c. oak; round bottle stopper made of this material

**cork'screw** spiral steel device for pulling corks from bottles; any similar spiral

**corn** *n US* (grain plant with) ear of yellow kernels, used as vegetable or fodder; *UK* any edible cereal grain; hardened layers of skin, *esp.* on toes; *v* preserve (meat, *etc*) by salting

**corn'cob** woody center of ear of corn; an ear of corn

**cor'ne·a** transparent covering over iris and pupil of eye

**cor'ner** *n* point where two lines, edges or surfaces meet; place where two streets meet; narrow or secret place; *v* drive into corner; buy up goods so as to control prices: *c. the coffee market*

**cor·ner·stone** stone placed at bottom corner joining two walls (often in ceremony); the basis of sth

**corn'flakes** breakfast cereal *usu* eaten with milk

**corn'flour** (*UK*) see **corn-starch**

**cor'nice** ornamental band on top of wall or building

**corn'starch** starch made from maize and used to thicken puddings, *etc*

**cor·ol·la·ry** sth that follows logically from sth already proved

**cor'o·na·ry** of the heart or its blood vessels

**cor·o·na'tion** act of crowning

**cor'o·ner** official who inquires into cause of (unnatural) death

**cor'po·ral** *a* of the human body; physical

**cor·po·ra'tion** business or governmental enterprise authorized to act as a person

**cor·po're·al** bodily; tangible

**corps** (*sing* kōr, *pl* kōrz) body of troops, or the like

**corpse** dead (human) body

**cor'pu·|lence** fleshiness; fatness. **-lent**

**cor'pus** body of writings or materials

**cor'pus·cle** tiny constituent

particle, *esp.* of blood

**cor'ral** pen for animals

**cor·rect'** *v* set right; remove or mark errors; call attention to error in order to improve; counteract (harmful) effect; *a* free from error; in accordance with accepted standards (of behavior, *etc*)

**cor're·late** bring into or have mutual relation

**cor·re·spon|d'** agree; be similar; exchange letters. **-dence, -dent**

**cor'ri·dor** passage, into which rooms open, connecting parts of building

**cor·rob'o·ra|te** confirm. **-tive**

**cor·ro|de'** eat away gradually, *esp.* by chemical action. **-sion, -sive**

**cor'ru·gated** formed into folds or ridges, as metal

**cor·rupt'** *a* evil; dishonest; *v* make evil; destroy purity; bribe. **-ible**

**cor·sage'** flowers worn at waist or shoulder

**cor'set** woman's undergarment, stiffened to support and shape the figure

**cor'tex** outer gray matter of brain; plant root

**cor'ti·sone** substance used to treat arthritis and allergies

**cos·met'ic** *n* beautifying preparation; *a* serving to beautify

**cos'mic** of the universe

**cos·mo·pol'i·tan** *a* of all parts of the world; *n* person free from national prejudices; widely traveled person

**cos'mos** the universe

**cos'mo·naut** Russian astronaut

**cost** *n* price paid to get, produce or maintain thing; outlay of money, time, labor, *etc*; **c. of living** price of goods and services necessary for basic existence; *v* (**cost**) have as price; require a sacrifice, *etc*

**cost'ly** of great price or value

**cos'tume** style of dress; set of garments

**co'sy** (*UK*) see **cozy**

**cot** light portable bed; small bed for child

**cot'tage** (kotij) small house, *esp.* in the country

**cot'tage cheese** soft curded white cheese

**cot'ton** (plant with) soft white hairy substance enclosing seeds; thread or cloth made from this

**couch** *n* sofa; bed; *v* express in words

**cough** (kof) *v* expel air from lungs with effort so as to clear throat; *n* act of coughing; illness causing frequent coughing

**could** see **can**

**coun'cil** assembly for consultation, *etc.* **-lor**

**coun'sel** consultation; advice; (legal) adviser. **-or,** *UK* **-lor**

**count** *v* say numerals in order; check over one by one to determine total number; include in reckoning; consider to be; **c. on** rely on; *n* nobleman

**count'down** act of counting last few seconds, *usu* from 10 to 0, before an important operation begins

**coun'te·nance** *n* (expression of) face; support; composure; *v* encourage; permit

**count'er** *n* table over which goods are passed and on which money is counted; small piece of metal, *etc* used in board games; device for counting

**coun'ter** *adv* in the opposite direction; *a* contrary; *v* act in opposition

**coun·ter·act'** act against

**coun·ter·bal'ance** *v* offset

**coun·ter·bal'ance** *n* weight balancing another

**coun·ter·clock'wise** in a circular movement from right to left

**coun'ter·feit** forge (money, *etc*)

**coun·ter·mand'** cancel or recall previous order

**coun'ter·mea·sure** step taken to counter another

**coun'ter·part** equivalent; duplicate; natural complement

**coun'ter·point** combining of individual melodies

**coun'ter·sign** n sign in support of other signature; n password

**coun'tess** noblewoman; wife of count

**count'less** too many to be counted

**coun'try** (kun-) region; territory of a nation; land of person's birth or citizenship; (farming) area outside towns or cities

**coun'ty** administrative or political division

**coup** (kū) successful action or move; **c. d'état** sudden seizure of political power

**cou·pé'** (kūpā) automobile with two doors

**cou'ple** n two together, esp. man and woman; a small number, few; v link together

**cou'pling** connecting link

**cou'pon** (kū-) (detachable) ticket entitling holder to receive sth, as discount, etc; form for ordering sth, entering competition, etc

**cour'age** (kurij) quality that enables person to meet danger, etc firmly. **coura'geous**

**cour'i·er** messenger

**course** (kōrs) onward movement; path or direction of anything moving; area for sports, as racing, golf; progress of time, events, etc; series of lectures, etc; manner of acting or behaving; each successive part of a meal; **in due c.** in the natural order of events, etc; **of c.** certainly

**court** (kōrt) n open space enclosed by walls, etc, as for playing games; residence of king, etc and his courtiers. **-ly;** place where law cases are settled. **-house, -room;** body of judges; v try to win favor of, esp. of woman; act so as to invite (punishment, etc)

**cour'te·ous** polite

**cour'te·sy** (kurtesi) politeness; polite favor

**court'ship** wooing

**cous'in** (kuz-) child of one's uncle or aunt

**cove** small sheltered bay

**cov'e·nant** solemn agreement

**cov'er** v put something over or on to close, protect or hide; extend over; pour or scatter over; hide (feelings, etc); include; provide for; aim gun at; report news of; pass or travel over; n that which covers, as lid, book binding, blanket, etc; place of hiding or protection; plate, cutlery, etc laid out for person at table

**cov'ert** a secret; n shelter

**cov'er-up** (attempt at) concealing sth damaging or criminal from others' knowledge

**cov'et** (kuvit) desire eagerly (what belongs to another). **-ous**

**cow** n female of (domestic) cattle; female of elephant, whale, etc; v make afraid

**cow'ard** person afraid to meet danger or difficulties. **-ice**

**cow'boy,** f **-girl** US person in charge of cattle at ranch

**cow'er** cringe (esp. from fear)

**coy** (affectedly) modest

**coy'ote** (kiōt, kiōti) N. Amer. prairie wolf

**co'zy** snug; comfortable

**crab** (edible flesh of) hard-shelled sea animal with sharp pincers; grouchy person

**crab ap·ple** small sour apple

**crack** n slight opening, as between door and wall; small split in china, etc; sudden sharp sound, as of whip; v break open (without coming apart entirely); make sudden sharp noise

**crack'er** thin crisp biscuit

**cra'dle** bed for infant, built on rockers; holder for telephone receiver

**craft** trade; skill; cunning; boat, plane, etc

**craft'y** clever; sly

**crag** rough, steep rock

**cram** fill overfull; stuff into; study intensely for examination

**cramp** n sudden painful tightening of muscles due to chill, strain, etc; v restrict; crowd into small space

**cran'ber·ry** small red acid berry used in sauce, etc

**crane** tall wading bird; machine for lifting heavy weights

**cra'ni·um** skull. **-al**

**crank** device for transferring motion; eccentric or grouchy person. **-y**

**cran'ny** crevice; crack

**crash** breaking or falling to pieces with loud noise; sudden loud noise, as of thunder; sudden ruin (of business); collision that damages or wrecks automobile, etc

**crass** stupid; unfeeling

**crate** packing case made of wooden slats

**cra'ter** mouth of volcano; hollow cavity left by meteor, etc

**crave** ask or long for

**crawl** move slowly on hands and knees or by dragging body along ground; be, or feel as if, covered with crawling things

**cray'on** pencil of colored wax, chalk, etc

**craze** v make insane; n popular fashion; mania

**cra'zy** insane. **-ziness**

**creak** harsh squeaking sound

**cream** fatty part of milk; smooth fatty mass; best part of anything; light yellow color

**crease** line in cloth, *etc* caused by folding; wrinkle

**cre·ate'** cause to be or exist; give rise to. **-tion, -tor**

**crea'ture** (krēcher) any living being; contemptible person

**cre·den'tials** *pl* papers proving identity or authority

**cred'i·ble** worthy of belief

**cred'it** deferred payment; trust in person's intention or ability to pay; financial balance in a persons's favor; belief; source of honor or recognition; *US* unit of student's work

**cred'it·a·ble** praiseworthy

**cred'it card** card allowing person to buy sth and pay for it later

**cred'i·tor** one to whom a debt is owed

**cre'do** (krēdō) creed

**cred'u·lous** too ready to believe. **credu'lity**

**creed** brief formal summary of a (religious) belief

**creek** small inlet or stream

**creep** (**crept**) move along with body close to ground or on hands and knees; move slowly or stealthily; behave servilely; (of plants) grow along ground or wall; feel shivering sensation on one's skin. **-y**

**cre'mate** burn (dead body) to ashes. **crema·to'rium**

**cres'cent** moon in first or last quarter; object shaped like this

**crest** comb or tuft on animal's head; top of mountain or wave

**cret'in** mentally retarded person

**crev'ice** fissure, *esp.* in rock

**crew** (krū) group of persons with a particular job, *esp.* operating ship, train, *etc*

**crib** child's bed with enclosed sides; rack for holding fodder

**crick'et** insect that gives off chirping sound by rubbing wings together; *UK* kind of ball game

**cried** see **cry**

**crime** act punishable by law; wicked deed. **crim'inal**

**crim'son** deep red color

**cringe** bend body in crouching position, as in fear or servility

**crip'ple** person who cannot use one or more of his limbs

**cri'sis** turning-point; moment of great danger

**crisp** hard but easily broken; fresh; brisk; lively; curly or wrinkled

**criss'cross** (marked by) crossing lines

**cri·te'ri·on** (*pl* **-ria**) principle or standard used to judge sth or s.o.

**crit'i|c** person giving judgment as to merits and faults. **-cism, -cize**

**crit·i·cal** marked by careful judgement; finding fault; marking a crisis

**croak** deep, hoarse cry

**cro·chet'** kind of knitting done with hooked needle

**crock'er·y** earthenware vessels

**croc'o·dile** large, thick-skinned reptile living in tropical waters

**crone** withered old woman

**crook** hooked staff; bend or curve; *infml* dishonest person. **crook'ed**

**croon** sing in low tone. **-er**

**crop** cultivated food plants; pouch in bird's gullet; handle of whip; short haircut

**cro·quet'** (krōkā) ball game played on grass with mallets

**cross** *n* structure of one upright and one transverse piece of wood, *esp.* the one on which Christ was put to death; anything resembling this, as two lines which cut each other; suffering; mixture of breeds of animals, *etc*; *v* make sign of, or mark with, cross; cancel by drawing line through; lie or pass across; meet and pass; mix breeds; thwart; *a* passing or lying across; contrary; ill-humored

**cross'-eyed** having eye disorder in which the two eyes do not focus together

**cross'ing** place where roads, *etc* cut each other; place where river, *etc* can be crossed

**crotch** fork or place of forking, *esp.* where legs join trunk in human body

**crotch'et·y** given to odd fancies

**crouch** stoop or bend low

**crow** *n* large shiny black bird with harsh cry; cry of rooster; *v* boast

**crow'bar** heavy iron lever

**crowd** *n* large number of persons gathered together; *v* come together in large group; push; press together in narrow space

**crown** band of gold, *etc* worn by monarch as sign of power; sign of champion in sports; top part, as of hat, mountain, *etc*; (artificial covering for) visible part of tooth

**cru'cial** decisive; severe

**cru'ci·ble** melting pot; severe searching test

**cru'ci·fix** cross bearing image of Christ

**cru'ci·fy** kill by fastening to a cross; torment. **crucifix'ion**

**crude** raw; unripe; lacking finish; blunt. **-dity**

**cru'el** taking pleasure in making others suffer; indifferent to suffering of others; hard-hearted; causing pain. **-ty**

**cruise** *v* sail about; fly or

drive at economical speed; *n* sea voyage

**cruis'er** warship; police car

**crumb** (krum) small bit of bread, cake, *etc*

**crum'ble** break into small bits

**crum'ple** wrinkle

**crunch** chew or grind noisily

**cru·sade'** *hist* **C.** Christian expedition to win back Holy Land; movement in favor of some cause. **-r**

**crush** press between two hard surfaces so as to squeeze out of shape or break (into small bits); crumple (dress); overpower

**crust** hard outer part of bread; hard outer covering or coating; scab on skin; outer portion of earth's surface

**crutch** stick with crosspiece to support lame person; sth that gives support; crotch

**crux** decisive point; difficult problem

**cry (cried)** produce sounds of fear, joy or sorrow, *usu* together with tears; call loudly; (of animals) make characteristic sound

**cryp'tic** secret; obscure

**crys'tal** clear transparent mineral resembling ice; brilliant cut glass; solid body with characteristic geometrical structure; glass covering face of watch

**crys'tal·ize** form into crystals; take on definite form

**cub** young of wild animals

**cu|be** solid figure with 6 equal square sides; product of a number multiplied twice by itself. **-bic**

**cub'ism** art style using geometrical forms

**cuck'oo** Eur. bird with distinctive call that lays its eggs in other birds' nests

**cu'cum·ber** (kyūkum-) (vine plant with) long fleshy green fruit used in salads

**cud** food returned from first stomach to mouth by cows, *etc*, to be chewed again

**cud'dle** hug tenderly; lie close (together); nestle

**cudg'el** *n* short club; *v* beat

**cue** (kyū) line in play giving signal for next speech or action; hint; rod used in billiards

**cuff** band of cloth attached to bottom of sleeve; turned-up fold at bottom of trousers; blow with fist or open hand; **off the c.** without preparation

**cui·sine'** (kwe-) (style of) cooking

**cu·li·nar·y** (kyū-) of kitchen or cooking

**cull** pick; select

**cul'mi·nate** reach highest point; end in

**cul'prit** accused person; one guilty of offense

**cult** system of worship; faddish interest

**cul'ti·va|te** till soil. **-tor;** improve; devote o. s. to

**cul'ture** (stage of) civilization; refinement through education; rearing of bacteria, etc

**cul'vert** drain crossing under road

**cu'mu·la·tive** (kyū-) increasing by successive additions

**cu·ne·i·form** (-nē-) wedge-shaped, as ancient type of writing

**cun'ning** a clever; sly; n slyness

**cup** small open container, usu with handle, to drink from; cooking measure; ornamental container awarded as prize; sth shaped like c.

**cup'board** (kuberd) closet with shelves for storing dishes, etc

**cur** worthless or nasty dog

**cur'a·tive** tending to cure

**cu·ra'tor** person in charge of museum, etc

**curb** restraint; part of bridle; raised edge of street

**curd** thickened soured part of milk

**cur'dle** thicken; coagulate

**cure** n medical treatment; remedy; v heal; preserve food, etc for storage

**cur'few** signal or hour at which people must be off streets; closing-hour

**cu'ri·ous** eager to know; strange; surprising. **curi·os'ity**

**curl** form (esp. hair) in spiral shape. **-er, -y**

**cur'rant** small seedless raisin; small edible acid berry of certain shrubs

**cur'ren·cy** circulation; money in use

**cur'rent** a circulating; in general use; now passing; n movement, esp. of air, water or electricity

**cur·ric'u·lum** plan of study at a school

**curse** expression of wish that evil may come upon someone; profane oath

**cur'so·ry** hasty; superficial; not thorough

**curt** short; rudely brief

**cur·tail'** cut short; reduce

**cur'tain** (kurten) (piece of) cloth hung (at window) to shut out light, conceal sth or separate stage from audience; rise or fall of theater c.

**curve** continuously bending line without angles

**cush'ion** bag of cloth, etc stuffed with soft material and used to sit, kneel or lie on; something used to soften shock or blow

**cus'tard** sweet dish made of eggs, milk, etc

**cus·to'di·an** keeper; guardian

**cus'to·dy** care; charge; arrest

**cus'tom** habit; usual practice; *pl* taxes on imports

**cus'tom·ar·y** habitual; usual

**cus'tom·er** buyer

**cut** *v* (**cut**) press sharp-edged instrument, as knife, into (so as to divide); wound; cross, as lines; shorten or reduce; perform, as caper; divide (pack of cards); refuse to recognize socially; have (tooth) come through gum; **c. across** or **through** take most direct path; **c. in** interrupt conversation, *etc*; **c. off** interrupt; bring to an end; disinherit; **c. out** stop; *n* wound, incision, *etc* due to cutting; act of cutting; piece cut off, *esp*. of meat; lowering (of wages, *etc*); manner in which clothes, *etc* are cut

**cut'back** return to earlier events, as in story; reduction (in production rate)

**cute** *US* pleasingly pretty; *UK* clever

**cu'ti·cle** skin around nails

**cut'ler·y** cutting tools, *esp*. for use at table

**cut'let** slice of meat, *usu* with bone

**cy·ber·net'ics** study of movement and control of information in machines, the human brain, *etc*

**cy'cle** repeating period (of events); complete series; bi-cycle

**cy'clone** violent twisting windstorm

**cyl'in·der** solid or hollow round body, longer than wide, and with flat ends; roll-er-shaped object; chamber in engine where steam, *etc* moves piston. **cylin'dri·cal**

**cym'bal** metal plate struck to produce sound

**cyn'ic** (sarcastic) person who doubts human goodness. **-cal, -cism**

**cy'press** (si-) cone-bearing tree with dark green leaves and hard wood

**cyst** liquid-filled sac formed in animal tissue

**czar** *hist* **C**. former emperor of Russia; s. o. with great power

# D

**d** fourth letter of English alphabet

**dab** *v* strike or pat lightly; put on (substance) with light strokes; *n* small wet lump or mass; slight tap

**dab'ble** splash; work at su-perficially

**dad, dad'dy** *infml* father

**daf'fo·dil** (bulb plant with) yellow spring flower

**dag'ger** weapon with short, two-edged, pointed blade

**dai'ly** done, happening or is-sued every day

**dain'ly** delicate; extremely clean or particular. **-tiness**

**dair'y** place where milk and cream are made into butter and cheese; shop or company that sells milk

**dai'sy** small flower with yellow center and white petals

**dai'sy wheel** (kind of typewriter or printer with) rotating printing wheel shaped like daisy, with letters at ends of "petals"

**dal'ly** amuse o.s.; loiter about; **d. with** toy with

**dam** barrier built to stop flow of water

**dam'age** injury, harm; pl money claimed or paid for loss or injury

**dam'ask** fabric with woven pattern

**damn** (dam) condemn; curse. **damna'tion**

**damp** a moist; v moisten; **d. down** depress; restrain; cause fire to burn more slowly

**damp'er** check in a stove, etc; thing that depresses

**dance** v move rhythmically (to music) in steps, turns, etc; leap about; bob up and down; n tune for dancing; social gathering for dancing; series of steps, turns, etc done to music

**dan'de·li·on** (-lī-) weed with

yellow flowers and edible leaves

**dan'druff** small scales of dead skin on scalp

**dan'dy** man over-concerned with dress, a fop

**dan'ger** (dānjer) possible injury, etc; source of harm or injury; risk. **-ous**

**dan'gle** hang loosely; offer sth as temptation

**dank** damp (and cold)

**dap'per** neat or smart in appearance

**dar'e** have the courage to do; take risk. **-ing:** challenge (person) to do

**dark** with little or no light; (of a color) near black; (of complexion) not fair; cheerless; sullen; hidden or unclear; secret; unenlightened; evil

**dark'room** room with special light, used to develop film

**dar'ling** person dearly loved or in great favor

**darn** repair torn cloth, etc by weaving close network of threads across hole with needle

**dart** n pointed object for throwing, esp. as weapon or in games; tuck sewn into garment to improve fit; v move quickly and suddenly

**dash** v run quickly; strike or throw violently, esp. so as to break to pieces; ruin, as plans; **d. off** or **down** write or sketch quickly; n small amount of sth; rush; horizontal line used in writing to mark break; the longer signal in Morse code

**dash'board** panel in car, *etc* holding instruments and dials

**das'tard·ly** cowardly; mean

**da'ta** (dā-, da-) facts; information; material for computer processing or storage

**date** *n* (statement of) time (day, month, year) when sth occurs; appointment for particular time; (palm tree with) oblong sweet fruit; *v* mark with date; bear date; belong to particular period; fix or determine date (of event, *etc*); meet s. o. on (regular) social basis; be or become old-fashioned

**daub** *v* smear; paint (unskillfully)

**daugh'ter** (dawter) one's female child

**daugh'ter-in-law** wife of one's son

**daunt** frighten; discourage

**daunt'less** fearless

**dawn** *n* first light, daybreak; beginning of anything; *v* become light; begin; (of idea, *etc*) **d. on** begin to be understood

**day** time between sunrise and sunset. **-light**; average time (twenty-four hours) required for earth to make one turn on its axis; particular

period of time; date of particular festival

**day'dream** (have) vision or fancy while awake

**daze** stun; confuse

**daz'zle** confuse by excessive light or display; impress with brilliance

**dead** (ded) no longer alive, in existence or use; out, as a fire; lacking vigor, movement, or liveliness; numb or unfeeling; dull; direct or straight; sudden; not transmitting, as electric wire; **d. end** closed at one end with no way out, as a street

**dead'en** (dedn) lessen liveliness, force, feeling, *etc*

**dead heat** race in which two or more finish together

**dead'line** time limit

**dead'lock** complete standoff due to equal strength of opponents

**deaf** (def) wholly or partly unable to hear; unwilling to listen. **-en**

**deaf-mute** s.o. unable to hear or speak

**deal** (dēl) *v* (**dealt**) (delt) distribute, *esp.* cards in game; deliver (blows); **d. in** trade or do business; **d. out** give out in shares, as food; **d. with** occupy o. s. with; handle; *n* business transaction; agreement; quantity or amount

**deal'er** person distributing

cards; trader, *esp. infml* one selling drugs illegally

**dean** church or college official

**dear** loved; high in one's regard; expensive

**dearth** (durth) great scarcity

**death** (deth) act of dying; end of life; state of being dead

**de·ba·cle** (dā-) sudden collapse or downfall

**de·base** reduce in quality

**de·bate** argue question in public; consider

**de·bauch** (-bawch) corrupt; seduce

**de·ben·ture** certificate of indebtedness; bond

**deb·it** (make) entry in account of sum owing

**de·bris** (dābrē) wreckage; ruins

**debt** (det) money, goods or service owed

**debt·or** (deter) one who owes

**de·bug** remove hidden listening devices; correct flaws in computer software

**de·bunk** *infml* remove false sentiments about

**de·but** (dābyū) first public appearance

**de·cade** ten years

**de·ca·dence** decline; decay. **-dent**

**de·camp** break or leave camp; go away suddenly or secretly

**de·cant·er** bottle for serving wine

**de·cap·i·tate** cut off head of

**de·cay** rot; lose quality; decline

**de·cease** death

**de·ceit** dishonesty; trick; misleading act or appearance. **-ful**

**de·ceive** mislead; cheat

**de·cel·er·ate** reduce speed

**De·cem·ber** twelfth and last month of year

**de·cent** respectable; not immodest or obscene; good enough. **-cy**

**de·cen·tral·ize** remove from center; do away with central control. **decentraliza'-tion**

**de·cep·tion** act or thing that deceives. **-tive**

**dec·i·bel** unit for measuring loudness of sound

**de·cide** settle (struggle, question, *etc*) by giving judgment, *usu* in favor of one side; settle doubt; make up one's mind on course of action. **-sion**

**dec·i·mal** proceeding by tens; of tenths or ten

**dec·i·mate** kill a large number of (originally, every tenth man)

**de·ci·pher** (disifer) make out meaning of; decode

**deck** *n* platform reaching from side to side of ship and covering space below; pack of playing cards; *v* dress (in fancy clothes)

**de·claim'** speak or recite formally. **decla·ma'tion**

**de·clare'** state publicly or formally; pronounce to be. **declara'tion**

**de·cline'** refuse; slope down; decrease; grow less or worse

**de·code'** translate from code

**dé·colle·té** (of a dress) low-necked

**de·com·pose'** separate into elements; rot. **decomposi·'tion**

**de·com·press|s'** reduce air pressure. **-sion**

**de·con·tam'i·nate** make safe by removing or neutralizing poison gas, *etc*

**dec'o·rate** furnish with ornaments; reward by medal

**de·co'rum** propriety of conduct

**de·coy'** that which lures into trap

**de·crease'** *v* grow or make less; *n* process of growing less; amount by which sth is lessened

**de·cree'** order by authority; court decision

**de·crep'it** feeble or broken down due to age or use

**ded'i·cate** set apart; devote; address (work of art, *etc*) to person

**de·duce'** draw as conclusion. **-ible**

**de·duct'** take away (sum or amount). **-ible**

**de·duc'tion** amount taken

away; conclusion drawn

**deed** act; achievement; document transferring land, *etc*

**deem** believe; judge

**deep** extending far down from top; reaching far in from front or outside; serious; fully absorbed in; strongly felt; (of sound) low and full; (of color, *etc*) rich; having or requiring profound understanding

**deep'en** make or become deep(er)

**deer** (*pl* **deer**) four-legged ruminant animal, male of which has antlers

**de·face'** disfigure; damage surface of. **-ment**

**de·fame'** attack good reputation; speak ill of. **defama'tion**

**de·fault'** fail to pay debt, appear in court or take part in competition

**de·feat'** overcome (in battle, contest, *etc*); thwart

**def'e·cate** discharge waste matter from bowels

**de'fect** *n* shortcoming; failing; flaw. **defec'tive**

**de·fec't** transfer loyalty to another group, country, *etc*. **-tion, -tor**

**de·fence'** see defense

**de·fend'** guard; ward off attack; speak in favor of; contest legal charge

**de·fend'ant** person sued or accused in court action

**de·fen|se'** act of defending; resistance against. **-sive**

**de·fer'** put off to a future time; yield to s.o. in judgment or opinion

**def'er·ence** yielding to opinions of another; respect

**de·fi'ance** bold resistance; open disobedience. **-ant**

**de·fi'cien|t** incomplete; defective; insufficient. **-cy**

**def'i·cit** amount lacking

**de·file'** make dirty. **-ment**

**de·fine'** declare exact meaning or nature of; fix boundaries of

**def'i·nite** clear; determined; with exact limits

**def·i·ni'tion** act of defining; exact statement of meaning (of word, *etc*); sharpness of image in television, *etc*

**de·fin'i·tive** final; determining; having most authority

**de·fla|te'** let air or gas out of; (cause to) lose confidence; decrease the amount or increase the value of money in circulation. **-tion**

**de·flect'** bend or turn aside. **-tion**

**de·fo'li·ate** remove leaves (chemically). **-ant**

**de·form'** put out of shape; make ugly. **deforma'tion**

**de·form'i·ty** malformation of body; (moral) flaw

**de·fraud'** cheat

**de·fray'** bear or pay (costs)

**de·frost'** remove frost from (refrigerator, *etc*); unfreeze

**deft** skillful

**de·funct'** dead; no longer existing

**de·fy'** resist openly; challenge to do; offer effective resistance to. **-fiance**

**de·gen'er·ate** lose former (high) qualities

**de·grade'** reduce in grade, quality, *etc*; lower in esteem

**de·gree'** stage; step; rank; division of measurement; academic title

**de·hy'drate** remove water from; lose water

**de·ice'** remove ice from (airplane, *etc*)

**de'i·fy** make a god of

**deign** (dān) condescend (to do)

**de'|is·m** belief in natural religion, but not in revelation. **-ist, deis'tic**

**de'i·ty** god or goddess

**de·jec|t'** make sad. **-tion**

**de·lay'** put off; hinder

**de·lec'ta·ble** delightful

**del'e·gate** *n* one elected to represent others; *v* send as representative; give authority to agent

**de·lete'** strike out (sth printed or written). **-tion**

**de·lib'e·rate** *v* (-āt) think over carefully; *a* (-it) well-considered; not hurried; intentional

**del'i·ca·cy** fineness; weakness of body; sensitiveness; choice kind of food

**del'i·cate** dainty; frail; sensitive; requiring tact

**del·i·ca·tes'sen** (shop selling) choice foods

**de·li'cious** (dilishes) extremely pleasing, *esp.* to taste or smell

**de·light'** (dilīt) (cause) great pleasure. **-ful**

**de·lim'it** fix limits of

**de·lin'e·ate** portray by drawing or description

**de·lin'|quen·cy** neglect of duty; guilt. **-quent**

**de·lir'i·|um** disorder of mind; great excitement. **-ous**

**de·liv'er** hand over (letters, ordered goods, *etc*) to (person for whom they are intended); set free or save (from); utter (speech, *etc*); direct (blow, attack, *etc*) at; relieve (woman in childbirth) of child. **-y**

**del'ta** triangular area of land deposited at mouth of large river

**de·lude'** deceive

**del'uge** great flood; downpour

**de·lu'|sion** act of deluding; false hope or belief. **-sive**

**de·luxe'** of very high quality

**delve** carry on intensive research

**dem'a·gogue** leader who appeals to base instincts of the people. **demagog'ic(al)**

**de·mand'** *v* ask for urgently, with authority or as right;

require; *n* (urgent) request; claim; desire (among possible buyers) to buy (specific goods)

**de·mand'ing** requiring effort

**de·mar·ca'tion** marking of boundaries

**de·mean'or,** *UK* **-our** behavior; outward appearance

**de·ment'ed** out of one's mind; insane; crazy

**de·mer'it** fault, misconduct; mark against person for misconduct

**de·mil'i·ta·rize,** *UK* **-rise** remove armed forces from

**de·mise'** (-mīz) death

**de·moc'ra·cy** system of government by the people, direct or representative, with formal equality of rights and privileges

**de·mog'ra·|phy** study of human population using statistics. **-pher**

**de·mol'ish** pull or throw down; destroy. **demoli'tion**

**de'mon** evil spirit; wicked person; person of great energy. **demo'niac**

**dem'on·strate** show (by experiment, *etc*); prove; take part in demonstration

**dem·on·stra'tion** act of proving or showing; public meeting to express opinion

**de·mor'al·ize** destroy discipline, courage, *etc*. **demoraliza'tion**

**de·mote'** reduce to lower grade

**de·mur'** object to. **-rer**

**de·mure'** sober, grave; affectedly modest

**den** home of wild animal; center of illegal activity; small private study room

**de·nier'** (denir) unit of thread weight of nylon, silk, *etc*

**den'im** heavy cotton cloth for jeans, *etc*

**de·nom·i·na'tion** name; religious sect; units in weights, money, *etc*

**de·nom'i·na·tor** part of fraction below the line

**de·note'** be sign of or name for; mean. **denota'tion**

**de·nounce'** accuse publicly; inform against; condemn

**dense** thick; close; compact; stupid. **-sity**

**dent** impression in surface, as from blow

**den'tal** of the teeth

**den'tin**, *UK* **-tine** hard substance forming mass of tooth

**den'tist** doctor who treats diseases of teeth and gums

**den'ture** set of (artificial) teeth

**de·nun·ci·a'tion** act of denouncing; condemnation

**de·ny'** declare untrue; refuse; disown. **-nial**

**de·o'dor|·ant** (substance) that destroys smells. **-ize**

**de·par|t'** go away; leave; die;

**d. from sth** deviate. **-ture**

**de·part'ment** division or branch of organized system, as in school, government, *etc*; **d. store** large store selling wide variety of goods

**de·pen|d'** be contingent on; rely on for support. **-dable, -dent, -dence**

**de·pic|t'** represent in drawing or words. **-tion**

**de·pil'a·to·ry** substance that removes hair

**de·plete'** reduce the amount of; make empty

**de·plor|e'** regret deeply; express disapproval. **-able**

**de·ploy'** spread out (troops)

**de·pop'u·late** greatly reduce population of (an area)

**de·port'** force (non-citizen) to leave country. **deporta'tion**; conduct o. s. **-ment**

**de·pos|e'** remove from high office; state under oath. **-al**

**de·pos'it** put or lay down; give in trust for safekeeping; give as security or in part payment

**de·pos'i·to·ry** storehouse

**de'pot** (dēpō) storage place; *US* railroad or bus station

**de·prave'** make bad; corrupt. **-ity, deprava'tion**

**de·pre'ci·ate** decline or reduce in value; belittle

**de·pre·ci·a'tion** decrease in value; allowance made for use (of machinery, *etc*)

**de·pres|s'** make sad; cause

**desperado**

(economy) to sink; push down, as lever, *etc.* **-sion**

**de·prive'** strip, take away; keep from enjoying. **depriva'tion**

**depth** being deep; measure downward or inward; deep part, as of sea; intensity, as of color, *etc.*; deepness of feeling, understanding, *etc.*

**dep'u·ty** person appointed to act for, or as assistant to, others. **-tize**

**de·rail'** (cause train to) leave the rails. **-ment**

**de·range|d'** mentally unbalanced; insane. **-ment**

**der'e·lict** *n* vagrant (alcoholic) person; *a* run-down; abandoned; lacking sense of duty

**de·ride'** laugh at scornfully; mock. **-sive, -sory, deri'sion**

**de·riv'a·tive** coming from a source; not original

**de·rive' from** get, come or originate from. **deriva'tion**

**der·ma·ti'tis** skin disease

**der·ma·to'lo·gy** study of skin, *esp.* its diseases

**de·rog'a·to·ry** tending to take away from or belittle

**der'rick** device for lifting heavy weights; framework over oil well

**de·scend'** go down; slope down; make sudden attack on; have origin from

**de·scen'dant** offspring

**de·scent'** downward slope; act of going down; line of origin

**de·|scribe'** set forth in words; draw or move in (circle, *etc*). **-scription**

**des'e·crate** deprive of sacred character

**de·seg're·gate** abolish separation according to race. **desegrega'tion**

**de·ser|t'** *v* give up; leave; run away from (military) duty. **-tion;** *n pl* (qualities deserving) reward or punishment

**des'ert** uninhabited barren region, *usu* sandy

**de·serve'** be entitled to reward or punishment

**de·sign'** (-zīn) plan; purpose; sketch for work of art, machine, *etc*

**des'ig·nate** indicate; describe; name; appoint

**de·sign'ing** crafty, scheming

**de·sir|e'** (-zir) want to have; long for; express wish. **-able, -ous**

**de·sist'** stop doing

**desk** piece of furniture with flat, sometimes sloping top for writing or reading at; place (in hotel, *etc*) where information, *etc* is given

**des'o·late** *a* (-it) left alone; uninhabited; wretched; *v* (-eit) lay waste; deprive of inhabitants; make wretched

**de·spair'** give up hope

**des·pe·ra'do** reckless criminal

**des'per·ate** hopeless; extremely dangerous; reckless from despair

**des'pi·ca·ble** contemptible

**de·spise'** look upon with contempt

**de·spite'** in spite of

**de·spon'den|t** dejected; without hope. **-cy**

**des'pot** tyrant; absolute ruler. **-ism**

**des·sert'** last course of dinner, *usu* sweet

**des·ti·na'tion** place for which person or thing is bound; ultimate goal

**des'tine** set apart for particular use or fate

**des'ti·ny** predetermined course of events; fate

**des'ti·tute** in utter want

**de·stroy'** ruin; make useless; kill, *esp.* sick animal

**de·struct'** US destroy (rocket, *etc*) deliberately

**de·struc'|tion** act of destroying; ruin. **-tive**

**des'ul·to·ry** disconnected; unmethodical; random

**de·tach'** unfasten and remove; separate from. **-able**, **-ment**

**de·tail'**, **de'tail** individual (small) part; particular item of plan, scheme, *etc*; small army force given special task; **in d.** item by item; giving particulars

**de·tach|ed'** standing apart; unemotional. **-ment**

**de·tain'** keep from going ahead; keep in custody. **deten'tion**

**de·tec't'** discover; find out **-tion**

**de·tec'tive** person, *esp.* policeman, whose job is to gather information in connection with crimes, *etc*

**de·tec'tor** device for detecting sth, as smoke, *etc*

**de·ter'** discourage or hinder by fear, doubt, *etc.* **-rent**

**de·ter'gent** (-jent) cleansing (agent)

**de·te'ri·o·rate** make or grow worse

**de·ter'mine** settle; define; be decisive; decide. **determina'tion**

**de·ter'mined** firmly decided

**de·ter'min·ism** theory that human action is directed not by free choice but by independent forces

**de·test'** hate

**det'o·na|te** (cause to) explode. **-tor**

**de'tour** (temporary) roundabout way

**de·tract'** take away from

**det'ri·ment** damage; harm. **detrimen'tal**

**deuce** (dyūs) two on cards or dice; score (40-40) in tennis, after which a player must win two consecutive points

**de·val'ue** reduce worth (of money). **devalua'tion**

**dev'as·tate** lay waste

**de·vel·op** bring or come to maturity; cause to grow or make progress; treat film to make picture visible; use (land) more fully; become apparent, as disease. **-ment**

**de·vi·ate** turn aside (from course, truth, *etc*). **-ant**

**de·vice'** invention; thing designed for a purpose; trick; emblem

**dev·il** *n* evil spirit, imagined as fighting against the forces of good; *v* prepare food with hot seasoning

**de·vi·ous** (dē-) winding; dishonest

**de·vise'** plan; invent; plot; give by will

**de·volve'** transfer; fall upon person as duty

**de·vote'** give up to or set apart for; dedicate

**de·vo·tion** great loyalty or affection; dedication; *pl* prayers

**de·vour'** eat greedily; swallow up

**de·vout'** pious; religious; heartfelt

**dew** moisture from air, which forms in drops during night on cool surfaces

**dex·ter·i·ty** cleverness; skill (in using one's hands). **dex't(e)rous**

**di·a·be·tes** disease in which body cannot make use of sugar

**di·a·bol·ic(al)** devilish; extremely wicked

**di·ag·no·sis** (*pl* **-ses**) identification of disease from symptoms

**di·ag·o·nal** (line) joinung opposite corners of square, *etc*; oblique (line)

**di'a·gram** sketch used to explain or illustrate problem, *etc*

**di'al** (dīel) face or plate marked with numbers or graduations, on which hands or pointers show time, pressure in engine, *etc*; plate on radio which shows stations; numbers on telephone for making connections

**di'·a·lect** form of speech peculiar to district, *etc*. **dialec'tal**

**di·a·lec'tic(s)** art of testing truth by discussion and logical reasoning

**di'a·logue** talk between persons; conversation in novel, play, *etc*

**di·al'y·sis** process for removing impurities from blood of s.o. with defective kidneys

**di·am'e·ter** line passing from side to side through center of a figure; measurement of width

**di'a·mond** extremely hard brilliant precious stone of (nearly) pure crystallized carbon; figure with four equal straight sides, two oblique and two acute angles; *US* baseball field

**di·a·per** absorbent cloth, *etc* wrapped around baby's buttocks to collect urine, *etc*; *Uk* nappy

**di·a·phragm** muscle between lungs and abdomen; membrane vibrated by sound; device for changing lens opening of camera; contraceptive device

**di·ar·rhe·a,** *UK* **-rhoe·a** (dīeree) excessive looseness of the bowels

**di·a·ry** (book with) daily record of events

**di·a·tribe** bitter criticism

**dice** *pl* of **die**

**di·chot·o·my** division into two (opposites)

**dic·ta·phone** speech recording machine used in offices

**dic·tate** *v* speak aloud (sth to be written down); give orders; *n* authoritative command

**dic·ta·tor** absolute ruler

**dic·tion** degree of distinctness in speaking; style of speaking or writing

**dic·tion·a·ry** (diksheneri) book containing words of a language in alphabetical order, which explains their meaning or gives their equivalent in another language

**did** see **do**

**di·dac·tic** meant to teach

**die** *n* (*pl* **dice**) a cube used in games; (*pl* **dies**) form for stamping, threading, *etc*

**die** *v* stop living or existing; come to an end; lose force or strength; **be dying for, to do,** *etc* have great desire

**die·sel** type of engine; heavy oil used as fuel in such engines

**di·et** (dī-) (prescribed) choice of food, *esp.* to improve health, lose weight, *etc*

**dif·fer** be unlike or distinct from; disagree. **-rent**

**dif·fer·ence** dissimilarity; point, feature, *etc* in which things are unlike; quantity by which one amount is greater or less than another; quarrel

**dif·fer·en·ti·ate** constitute difference; make or become unlike; make distinction

**dif·fi·cult** hard to do, understand, get along with, or satisfy; causing trouble. **-ty**

**dif·fi·dent** shy; lacking self-confidence. **-dence**

**dif·fuse'** *v* (-z) send forth; spread; *a* (-s) spread out; wordy

**dig** (**dug**) break up and turn over earth with spade, claws, *etc*; make hole in earth; search for; thrust (hand, heel *etc*) into; **d. out** or **up** uncover (by breaking up and removing earth)

**di·gest'** *v* absorb food in stomach and bowels. **-tion;** summarize; think over

**di·gest** *n* summary

**dig'it** any numeral from 0 to 9; finger or toe

**dig'i·tal** electrically encoded, as sound or video recording; measuring (time, temperature, *etc*) in numerals; of fingers or toes

**dig'i·tal com·pu'ter** (most common) type of computer based on binary system of two digits, 0 and 1

**dig'ni·fied** marked by stateliness

**dig'ni·fy** give rank or honor to

**dig'ni·ta·ry** person of high rank or office

**dig'ni·ty** true worth; high state or rank; nobility of manner

**di·gres|s'** turn from main subject. **-sion**

**dike, dyke** ditch, bank or wall against flooding

**di·lap'i·dat·ed** fallen into decay; in bad condition

**di·late'** make or become wider; speak at length (on). **dil(a)ta'tion**

**di·lem'ma** situation leaving only choice between two unwelcome possibilities

**dil·et·tante', UK -tan'te** lover of arts; one who pursues subject merely for amusement; *a* not thorough

**dil'i·gent** hardworking; industrious. **-gence**

**dill** aromatic herb used in pickling

**di·lute'** make thinner by adding water; reduce force of by adding something. **-tion**

**dim** not bright; faintly lighted; not clearly seen, heard, or understood

**dime** *US* coin worth 1/10 of a dollar or ten cents

**di·men'sion** measure of length, breadth, *etc* of object or figure; *pl* extent; size

**di·min'ish** make or become less. **diminu'tion**

**di·min'u·tive** tiny

**dim'ple** small natural hollow in cheek or chin

**din** loud, confused and continued noise

**din|e** eat dinner. **-er**

**din'er** railroad dining car; *US* small restaurant (built like dining car)

**din'ghy** (dinggi) small boat

**din'gy** (dinje) dark; dull; dirty

**din'ner** main meal of day, *usu* eaten in evening; formal (public) meal

**di'no·saur** (large) extinct reptile

**dip** put briefly into liquid; scoop (liquid) out of; lower briefly, as flag; sink below surface; slope downward. **-per**

**diph·the·ri'a** (dif-) infectious disease with severe throat inflammation

**diph'thong** (dif-) union of two vowels in one syllable

**di·plo·ma** official document; document conferring academic degree

**di·plo·ma·cy** (skill in) management of (international) relations; tact. **dip'lomat, diplomat'ic**

**dip·so·ma'ni·a** irresistible and excessive desire for alcohol. **-ac**

**dire** dreadful; urgent

**di·rect'** *v* guide or control; give order; point (sth) at; address (letter, words, *etc*) to; instruct actors in play, *etc*; tell (s.o.) which route to take; *a* straight; (of descent) in an unbroken line; without intervening agency; to the point

**di·rec'tion** act of directing; line along which anything moves or faces; *usu pl* instructions or orders

**di·rec'tor** member of managing board of company; person who directs play, *etc*

**di·rec·to·ry** (book containing alphabetical) list of names, *etc*

**dirge** funeral song

**dir'i·gi·ble** large gas-filled airship with motor and rudder

**dirt** any unclean matter, as mud, dust, *etc*; earth; anything foul or (morally) unclean. **-y**

**dis·a'ble** cripple; deprive of power. **-bled, disabil'ity**

**dis·ad·van'tage** unfavorable condition. **-taged, dis·advanta'geous**

**dis·a·gree'** be unlike; differ in opinion; quarrel; prove unpleasant. **-able**

**dis·ap·pear'** vanish from sight; cease to exist; be lost. **-ance**

**dis·ap·point'** fail to fulfill desire or hope. **-ment**

**dis·ap·prove'** have or express unfavorable opinion of; withhold approval

**dis·arm'** take away weapons; reduce armed strength of country. **-mament;** remove suspicion or unfriendliness

**dis·ar·range'** put into disorder

**dis·ar·ray'** confusion; disorder

**dis·as'ter** sudden or great misfortune. **-trous**

**dis·band'** break up, as club, organization, *etc*

**dis·bar'** to expel from practice as a lawyer

**dis·burse'** pay out (money). **-ment**

**disc** see disk

**dis·card'** cast aside; throw out; give up

**dis·cern'** see clearly with mind or senses; make out. **-ment, -ible, -ing**

**dis·charge'** dismiss; let go; fire (as gun); send out; pay (debt); carry out (duty); unload; lose stored electricity

**disguise**

**dis·ci·ple** follower

**dis·ci·pline** mental and moral training; order maintained in group; branch of instruction; punishment

**dis·claim'** deny connection with; give up claim to

**dis·close'** uncover, reveal. **-sure**

**dis·col'or**, *UK* **-our** change or spoil color of

**dis·com'fort** uneasiness; state of being uncomfortable

**dis·con·cert'** upset; throw into confusion

**dis·con·nect'** break or interrupt connection between

**dis·con'so·late** unhappy

**dis·con·tin'ue** put an end to; give up doing. **-ance**

**dis'cord** disagreement; disharmony; harsh noise. **discord'ant**

**dis·co·theque'** or **dis'co** club where people dance to records

**dis'count** *n* deduction from amount due; *v* sell at reduced price; disregard; allow for exaggeration

**dis·cour'age** deprive of confidence; try to dissuade. **-ment**

**dis'course** serious talk; formal speech or essay

**dis·cour'te·ous** rude; impolite. **-sy**

**dis·cov'e|r** learn of or find out (*esp.* sth unknown before). **-ry**

**dis·cred'it** refuse to believe; show to be undeserving. **-able**

**dis·creet'** wise; careful; unobtrusive

**dis·crep||an·cy** difference; inconsistency. **-ant**

**dis·cre'tion** freedom to decide at will; prudence. **-ary**

**dis·crim'i·|nate** make or observe difference between. **-nating**; make unfair distinction according to race, sex, *etc.* **-natory, discrimi·na'tion**

**dis·cur'sive** rambling

**dis'cus** heavy disk used in athletics

**dis·cus|s'** examine by argument; talk about. **-sion**

**dis·dain'** contempt; scorn. **-ful**

**dis·ease'** (dizēz) unhealthy condition; illness

**dis·en·chant'ed** freed of one's illusions

**dis·en·gage'** release o. s. from; (cause to) separate, as gears. **-ment**

**dis·en·tan'gle** free from complications; untwist. **-ment**

**dis·fa'vor**, *UK* **-vour** dislike; disapproval

**dis·fig'ure** mar beauty or appearance of

**dis·grace'** shame; dishonor; loss of favor. **-ful**

**dis·grun'tled** discontented

**dis·guise'** change appearance in order to mislead; hide or conceal sth

**dis·gust**¹ (cause) feeling of strong dislike

**dish** shallow glass, earthenware, *etc* container for holding food; food held or served in this, *esp.* of particular kind

**dis·har·mo·ny** disagreement; discord

**dis·heart·en** rob of courage

**di·shev·eled** with disordered hair; untidy

**dis·hon·est** (disonist) not honest; cheating

**dis·hon·o**⎮**r**, UK **-ou**⎮**r** disgrace. **-rable**

**dish'wash·er** person or *esp.* machine that washes dishes

**dis·in·fect**⎮**'** cleanse of germs. **-tant**

**dis·in·her·it** (-her-) cut off from inheritance

**dis·in·te·grate** reduce to particles; separate into parts

**dis·in·ter·est·ed** free from self-interest; impartial

**dis·joint·ed** having joints separated; incoherent

**disk**, UK **disc** a flat circular plate; layer of cartilage between spinal vertebrae; long-playing record; digital sound recording; **d. jockey** entertainer who plays records in a discotheque or on radio or television

**dis·lo·cate** put out of joint

**dis·loy·al** unfaithful. **-ty**

**dis·mal** depressing; gloomy

**dis·man·tle** strip of equipment, *etc*; take apart

**dis·may**¹ (fill with) fear and shock

**dis·mem·ber** tear or cut limb from limb

**dis·miss**¹ send away; remove from job, *etc.* **-al**

**dis·mount**¹ alight from cycle, horse, *etc*; remove from setting

**dis·o·⎮bey**¹ refuse to carry out order. **-bedience**

**dis·or·der** lack of order; illness; public riot

**dis·or·gan·ized** disarranged; lacking organization

**dis·own**¹ refuse to acknowledge as one's own

**dis·par·age** belittle; speak badly of

**dis·par·i·ty** high degree of difference

**dis·pas·sion·ate** free from emotion; calm; impartial

**dis·patch**¹ send off; kill; do something promptly

**dis·pel**¹ drive away; scatter

**dis·pen·sa·ry** place for handing out medicines, *esp.* in hospital, school, *etc*

**dis·pen·sa·tion** release from penalty, or duty; dealing out

**dis·pense**¹ deal out; make up (medicine); release from duty; **d. with** do without

**dis·pens·er** device supplying convenient amounts of soap, *etc*; vending machine

**dis·perse'** drive or go in different directions; spread evenly throughout, as color. **-sion**

**dis·place'** shift from its place; take place of; remove from office. **-ment**

**dis·play'** spread out in view; show

**dis·please'** offend; annoy; make angry. **-sure**

**dis·po·sa·ble** intended to be thrown away after use; (of money) available to be spent

**dis·pose'** arrange; settle; make inclined; **d. of** sell; get rid of; **-al**

**dis·po·si·tion** temperament; arrangement

**dis·pos·sess'** take away one's property

**dis·prove'** show to be false

**dis·pute'** argue; deny correctness of; quarrel; discuss. **disputa'tion**

**dis·qual'i·fy** make unfit (for purpose); deprive of right. **disqualifica'tion**

**dis·re·gard'** pay no attention to

**dis·rep'u·ta·ble** having a bad reputation. **disrepute'**

**dis·robe'** undress

**dis·rupt'** (cause) to break down; throw into disorder. **-tion**

**dis·sat'is·fy** make discontented. **dissatisfac'tion**

**dis·sect'** cut in pieces (to study structure, etc); criticize in detail

**dis·sem'ble** disguise; pretend (not to know)

**dis·sem'i·nate** distribute (news, etc) widely

**dis·sen'sion** (angry) disagreement

**dis·sent'** disagree. **-er**

**dis·ser·ta·tion** long treatment of subject, usu written to gain doctorate

**dis·si·dent** (one) disagreeing

**dis·sim'i·lar** unlike. **dissimilar'ity**

**dis·si·pate** scatter; waste

**dis·si·pat·ed** wasteful in pursuit of pleasure

**dis·so'ci·ate** separate (o. s.) from

**dis·so·lute** loose in morals

**dis·so·lu'tion** dissolving; decay

**dis·solve'** melt; waste away; put an end to (assembly)

**dis·so·nant** harsh in sound; out of harmony. **-nance**

**dis·sua'de** (-swād) persuade not to do. **-sion**

**dis'taff** spinning staff; **d. side** female side of family

**dis'tant** far away; separate in time, space, etc; reserved in manner. **-tance**

**dis·taste'** dislike. **-ful**

**dis·tend'** (cause to) swell, esp. from inside pressure. **-sion**

**dis·till'**, UK **-til** extract essence. **distilla'tion**

**dis·tinct'** separate; clear; different

**dis·tinc'|tion** difference; distinguishing quality; mark of honor. **-tive**

**dis·tin'guish** note or make difference between; be mark of; make prominent

**dis·tort'** twist out of shape; present falsely. **-tion**

**dis·trac'|t'** draw one's attention away from. **-tion**

**dis·tract'ed** confused; bewildered

**dis·traught'** deeply upset; crazed

**dis·tress'** suffering; want of money; situation of danger

**dis·trib'ute** deal out; divide into groups; supply (shops) with goods. **distribu'tion**

**dis·trib'u·tor** person or company supplying goods; device for spreading current to spark plugs of engine

**dis'trict** area or region, esp. one marked off as political or administrative unit; **d. attorney** US public prosecutor

**dis·turb'** interrupt quiet or peace of; upset; trouble. **-ance**

**dis·turbed** mentally unstable

**dis·use'** lack of use

**ditch** long narrow passage dug in earth, esp. as channel for water

**dit'to** the same (in accounts, etc)

**di·van'** (di-) sofa

**dive** jump into water, esp.

head first; go below surface of water. **-ing;** move suddenly downward; (of airplane) plunge steeply downward

**di·verge'** branch off from common point; differ. **-gence**

**di·verse'** varied; unlike. **-sify**

**di·ver'si·ty** difference; variety

**di·vert'** turn aside; amuse; distract. **-sion**

**di·vest'** strip of clothes, etc; deprive of (rights, etc)

**di·vide'** separate into parts; deal out in parts; share; cause to disagree; determine how many times a number is contained in another

**div'i·dend** share in profits; number to be divided; bonus

**div·i·na'tion** prophecy

**di·vine'** a godlike; sacred; n clergyman; v foresee

**di·vin'i·ty** condition of being divine; god; theology

**di·vis'i·ble** capable of being divided

**di·vis'ion** act of dividing; state of being divided; dividing line; administrative, political, etc section; large army unit

**di·vi'sor** number by which another is divided

**di·vorce'** dissolve marriage by legal judgment; separate entirely

**dominant**

**di·vulge'** make known; reveal

**diz'|zy** having the feeling of losing one's balance; (making) giddy. **-ziness**

**do** (**did, done**) perform: *d. one's duty*; carry out: *d. work*; complete; deal with in the manner required: *d. the dishes*; bring about: *d. good*; cover distance: *d. fifty miles*; be enough: *this will d. for now*; act: *d. as I d.*; get along: *how is he doing?*; serve purpose: *my suit will d. for another year*; **d. away with** put an end to; **d. up** wrap and tie up

**doc'ile** quiet and easily managed. **docil'ity**

**dock** *n* place in harbor where ship may anchor; enclosure in law court for prisoner; *v* cut off end (of tail); cut wages, *etc*; (of ship) bring or come into harbor

**dock'et** list of proceedings in legal action; agenda

**doc'tor** person licensed to practise medicine; person holding doctorate, the highest university degree. **-ate**

**doc'trine** (religious, *etc*) principles which are taught

**doc·u·ment** written or printed paper, *esp.* legal or official, which gives information or evidence. **documenta'tion**

**doc·u·men·ta·ry** investiga-

tive film based on fact

**dodge** move aside or down suddenly, as to avoid blow, *etc*; avoid giving clear or honest answer

**doe** female of certain animals, as deer, hare, *etc*

**dog** domestic four-footed animal related to wolf and jackal

**dog'ged** stubborn; unyielding

**dog'ger·el** trivial, *usu* comic, verse

**dog'ma** principle laid down by authority. **dogmat'ic**

**doi'ly** decorative mat

**dol'drums** inactivity; depression; calm area of ocean

**dole** *n* UK government grant to the unemployed; *v* **d. out** deal out sparingly

**doll** toy shaped like person

**dol'ly** wheeled device for moving heavy objects; wheeled camera platform

**dol'lar** unit of money in US and other countries

**dol'phin** (-fin) sea mammal similar to porpoise and whale

**do·main'** area of activity, *etc*; wine district or estate

**dome** high rounded roof; sth of this shape

**do·mes'tic** *a* of the home; (of animal) tame; *n* household servant

**dom'i·cile** dwelling place

**dom·i·nant** most important;

commanding; predominating. **-nance**, **-nate**

**dom·i·neer'** be overbearing. **-ing**

**do·min'ion** sovereignty; district governed

**don** *UK* university teacher

**do'nate** make gift of (money, *etc*). **dona'tion**, **do'nor**

**done** see **do**

**don'key** ass; stupid person

**doo'dle** draw or scribble aimlessly

**doom** (unhappy) fate; death

**dooms'day** judgment day

**door** (dōr) barrier of wood or metal, hinged or sliding, for shutting off room, house, cupboard, *etc*

**dope** *infml* any narcotic drug; *infml* stupid person

**dor'mant** sleeping; inactive

**dor'mi·to·ry** building or room in which many people sleep

**dor'sal** relating to the back

**dose** amount of medicine, *etc* to be taken at one time

**dot** small round spot or mark

**dote** be feeble-minded; **d. on** be extremely fond of

**dou'ble** *a* twice as great, strong, *etc*; forming a pair; twofold; of extra size, *etc*; of more than one meaning; *n* exact counterpart; substitute actor, singer, *etc*; *v* make twice as great; bend or fold over; clench (fist); **d. back** make sharp turn in running, *etc*

**dou·ble-deal'ing** deceit. **-er**

**doubt** (dout) be uncertain or undecided about; hesitate to believe. **-ful**, **-less**

**douche** (dūsh) (device for spraying) jet of cleansing liquid into or onto body

**dough** (dō) flour mixed with milk, fat, *etc* for making bread or cake

**dough'nut** (dōnut) sweet dough fried in deep fat

**douse** (dous) plunge into water; put out light, fire *etc*

**dove** (duv) pigeon

**dove'tail** *n* joint used in carpentry; *v* join or fit together neatly

**dow'a·ger** widow with title or property

**dow'dy** shabbily dressed

**dow'el** headless fastening pin

**down** *n* open, grassy upland; soft short feathers. **-y**

**down** *adv* from higher to lower (place, quality, rate); to the ground; from greater to lesser bulk; from earlier to later time; **pay d.** pay in cash and at once; **take** or **write d.** put on paper; *prep* downwards; at lower part of; *a* **d. and out** completely knocked out; without money or hope

**down'cast** directed downward, as eyes; depressed

**down'pour** heavy rainstorm

**down'right** quite; thorough; direct; blunt

**dread**

**down·town'** business center of city

**down·trod'den** oppressed

**down'ward(s)** toward lower point

**dow'ry** property bride brings into marriage

**doze** sleep lightly; be half asleep

**doz'en** group of twelve

**drab** dull; uninteresting

**draft** drawing or outline; preparatory version of law, book, *etc*; current of air, *esp.* in room or chimney; written order for payment of money by bank

**drafts'man** one who makes drawings or designs

**drag** pull with difficulty or heavily, *esp.* along ground; go (too) slowly; search (bottom of river) with net; **d. on** or **out** lengthen (proceedings) unnecessarily

**drag'on** fabulous winged (fire-breathing) monster

**drain** draw liquid off (through channel). **-age**; drink vessel empty; exhaust (funds or strength) gradually

**dram** small druggists' weight; small quantity

**dra·ma** play for stage, *etc*; plays as literary form. **-tist**; unusual series of events. **-tize** (*UK* **-tise**), **dramat'ic**

**drank** see **drink**

**drape** cover with cloth or arrange cloth in graceful folds

**dra'per·y** cloth fabrics; hangings

**dras'tic** acting strongly; violent; severe

**draught** (draft) device for regulating flow of air in stove; drawing of liquid from barrel, *etc*; drinking, or amount drunk at one time; depth ship sinks in water; see also **draft**

**draughts** see **checkers**

**draw** (**drew, drawn**) pull (after one, up, down, along, *etc*); bring out (liquid) from container; take in, as by breathing; attract; take or get from source; make picture of with pencil, *etc*; stretch out, as wire; deduce; move (towards, near, away, *etc*); (of game) end undecided. **d. out** make longer; get (person) to talk; **d. up** write out (document)

**draw'back** disadvantage

**draw'bridge** bridge which can be drawn up to open channel for ships or (*hist*) protect against attack

**draw'er** (drawr) compartment in desk, *etc* that can be drawn out; *pl* two-legged undergarment

**draw'ing** sketch in pen or pencil, *usu* without color

**drawl** to speak in slow drawn-out manner

**drawn** see **draw**

**dread** fear greatly; shrink from. **-ful**

**dream (dreamed** or **dreamt)** series of events pictured in mind (while asleep). **-less, -y**

**dream'er** one who dreams; impractical person

**drear'y** gloomy; cheerless

**dredge** n machine for scooping up earth, etc; v use d.; sprinkle with flour, etc

**dregs** pl sediment; worthless leftovers

**drench** wet thoroughly

**dress** v clothe; decorate, as store window; prepare (food, materials, etc) by special process; comb (hair); treat and bandage (wounds). **-ing;** n clothing, esp. outer garment worn by women

**dress'er** US bureau for toilet articles, etc; UK sideboard for dishes

**drew** see **draw**

**drib'ble** (let) flow in drops

**drift** n driving movement or force; current of water; tendency; mass of snow, etc driven together by wind; v be carried along by current; move along aimlessly. **-er**

**drill** pointed tool for boring holes; instruction and exercise, esp. in marching; strong twilled cotton cloth

**drink (drank, drunk)** swallow liquid; take alcoholic liquors, esp. as habit or to excess

**drip** fall or give in drops

**drip'-dry** that needs no ironing if hung when wet

**drip'ping** fat melted from roasting meat

**drive** v **(drove, driv'en)** start and direct movement of vehicle or animal; transport or travel in vehicle (which one guides o.s.). **-er;** force to move (in some direction); force to do; overwork; carry through (bargain, etc); **d. at** mean or aim at; n act of driving or being driven; natural instinct, as sex d.; organized effort, esp. to collect money for special purpose; personal initiative; device transmitting power to wheels of vehicle, etc; (private) road

**drive'-in** (bank, restaurant, etc) that can be used by car

**driz'zle** (a fine, misty) rain

**drone** n male bee; idler; unpiloted craft steered electronically; deep low sound; bass-pipe of bagpipes; v make deep humming sound; speak monotonously

**drool** slobber

**droop** hang or bend down; lose strength or courage

**drop** v (of liquid) fall in small round portions; (let) fall downward; (of road, cliff, etc) slope downward; pass without effort into (sleep, habit, etc); become lower, as prices, voice, etc; omit; stop having to do with; (of ani-

mals) give birth to; **d. back,
behind,** *etc* fail to keep up
with (main body); **d. in (on)**
visit casually; **d. out** withdraw

**drop'sy** disease in which fluid
collects in body

**drought** (drout) (period of)
great dryness

**drove** herd of cattle; crowd of
humans

**drove** see **drive**

**drown** kill or die by putting
or being completely under
water so as to make breathing impossible; make sound
unheard (by means of louder
sound)

**drows|e** be half-asleep. **-sy**

**drudge** work hard at uninteresting work; slave. **-ry**

**drug** any substance used as
medicine; any narcotic. **-gist**

**drum** *n* musical instrument
consisting of hollow cylinder
with ends covered by tightly
drawn skins which are beat-
en; any similar object; *v*
beat, *esp.* with rapid series of
strokes. **-mer**

**drunk** see **drink**

**drunk**('**en**) under the influence of alcoholic liquor

**dry** not wet; free of water;
without rain; thirsty; ironic;
uninteresting; (of goods)
solid; (of wines) lacking
sweetness. **-ness**

**dry'-clean** clean fabrics with
chemicals instead of water

**dry'er** device for removing
moisture from clothes, hair,
*etc*

**du'al** twofold, of two. **du-
al'ity**

**dub** name; add sound (effects) to film; furnish film
with dialogue in language
other than original. **-bed,
-bing**

**du'bi·ous** doubtful; of ques-
tionable value

**duck** *n* swimming bird whose
toes are connected by skin;
canvaslike cloth; *v* lower
(head) suddenly, as if to
avoid blow; thrust (s. o.)
suddenly into water

**duct** tube, canal

**duc'tile** easily drawn out or
molded; pliable

**dud** shell that fails to explode;
person or thing that is a failure

**dudg'eon** (dujen) anger

**due** owed, as a debt; payable;
suitable; proper; expected to
arrive (at a given time). **d. to**
owing to, because of

**du'el** fight with weapons between two persons; any contest

**du·et'** music for two performers

**duf'fel bag** long round canvas bag closed by draw-
string, used to carry
personal belongings

**dug** see **dig**

**dull** slow in understanding;

unfeeling; not sharp, bright, or intense; causing boredom

**du'ly** properly; in proper time; sufficiently

**dumb** (dum) lacking the power of speech; made, done, *etc* without speech; *infml* stupid

**dumb-found'** strike dumb with amazement. **-ed**

**dumb'wait-er** small elevator in wall for food, *etc*

**dum'my** imitation of sth; model of human figure used to tailor or display clothes; ventriloquist's model; *infml* stupid

**dump** *v* throw down in a heap; throw away; sell below market price; *n* place for garbage, *etc*; store of ammunition, *etc*; *infml* untidy place; *pl* depression

**dump'ling** round mass of steamed dough, served with meat, fruit, *etc*

**dump'y** short and fat

**dun** *a* dull grayish-brown; *v* press for payment of debt

**dunce** stupid person

**dune** hill of sand formed by wind

**dung** excrement, *esp.* of animals; manure

**dun-ga-rees'** heavy denim jeans, *usu* worn for work; overalls

**dun'geon** (dunjen) underground prison

**dunk** dip (food) into coffee, milk, *etc*

**du-o-dec'i-mal** of or progressing by twelves

**dupe** deceive(d person)

**du'pli-cate** (an exact) copy

**du'pli-ca-tor** machine for making copies

**du-plic'i-ty** deceitfulness

**du'ra-ble** lasting; not easily worn out. **durabil'ity**

**du-ra'tion** length of time (during which sth continues)

**du'ress** force; imprisonment; pressure based on threat of force

**dur'ing** (dyūr-, dūr-) throughout or at some point in a happening or course of

**dusk** partial darkness; darker stage of twilight. **-y**

**dust** *n* earth or other matter in fine dry bits; *v* sprinkle, as with powder or dust; rid of dust. **-y**

**du'te-ous** fulfilling duty; obedient. **-ness**

**du'ti-a-ble** subject to import taxes

**du'ty** what one is morally or legally bound to do; actions required by one's job or position; tax imposed on goods taken into or out of country, on the inheritance of property, *etc*

**dwarf** *n* person, plant, *etc* much smaller than usual size; small manlike being in fairy tales; *v* make seem small; prevent growth of

**dwell** (**dwelt**) live in; concentrate, speak or write at length on

**dwell'ing** house; residence

**dwin'dle** become smaller; fall in quality

**dye** (treat cloth, *etc* with) coloring matter. **-ing**

**dy'ing** see **die**

**dyke** see **dike**

**dy·nam'ic** of driving force; not at rest; active

**dy·na·mite** powerful explosive

**dy'na·mo** machine for changing mechanical into electrical energy

**dy'nas·ty** line of rulers from the same family

**dys'en·ter·y** painful disease of bowels with passing of blood

**dys·lex'i·a** brain defect causing reading problems because of inability to recognize shapes of letters

# E

**e** fifth letter of English alphabet

**each** every one of two or more, considered one by one

**ea'ger** (ēger) marked by keen desire or interest. **-ness**

**ea'gle** large bird of prey

**ea'gle-eyed** having sharp sight; watching attentively

**ear** organ of hearing; ability to hear differences in (musical) sounds well; part of cereal plant containing grains

**ear'drum** taut membrane in inner ear which is vibrated by sounds

**ear'lobe** soft pendant of flesh at bottom of outer ear

**ear'ly** (ur-) in first part of some period of time; before the usual or expected time

**ear'muffs** ear coverings connected by a band over the head, worn to protect against cold or loud noise

**ear'mark** *n* identifying mark; *v* set aside for special purpose

**earn** (urn) gain by work or merit; be worthy of; get as one's due. **-ings**

**ear'nest** *a* sincere; serious; *n* pledge

**ear'ring** ornament worn in earlobe

**earth** (urth) the planet on which we live; of the earth as opposed to sky; soil; safety connection to ground in electrical circuits

**earth'en·ware** pots, *etc* made of baked clay

**earth'quake** sudden movement of part of earth's surface

**eas|e** (ēz) *n* freedom from labor, suffering, or worry; freedom from stiffness or formality; ability to do sth without great effort; *v* free

**easel** from pain, pressure, worry, *etc*; make less difficult. **-ly**

**ea'sel** wooden frame to support painting, *etc*

**east** (near, towards) point (90° to right of north) where sun rises. **-ern, -ward(s)**

**eat** (ate, eat'en) take food into mouth, chew and swallow it; wear away

**eaves** *pl* overhanging edge of roof

**eaves'drop** listen secretly

**ebb** to flow back; decrease

**eb'on·y** (made or having color of) hard black wood

**e·bul'lient** boiling up; overflowing (of feelings)

**ec·cen'tric** not having the same center; not having axis at center; irregular; odd. **ec·centric'ity**

**ec·cle·si·as'ti·cal** of the church

**ech'e·lon** level of command within an organization

**ech'o** (ek̄o) sound sent back from surface by reflected sound waves; close imitation of another's ideas, words, *etc*

**ec·lec'ti|c** choosing freely from various sources. **-cism**

**e·clipse'** *n* darkening due to heavenly body moving in front of light source; *v* cast shadow on; outshine

**e·col'o·gy** (scientific study of) relationship and interaction of plants, animals and people with their environment. **-gist, ecolo'gical**

**e·co·nom'i·cal** saving; not wasteful

**e·co·nom'ics** science of production and distribution of wealth. **econ'omist**

**e·con'o·mize** reduce costs; avoid waste

**e·con'o·my** administration of resources of community; thrifty management

**ec'sta·sy** intense state of feeling; extreme delight. **ec·stat'ic**

**ec·ze'ma** itching inflammation of skin

**edge** (ej) *n* border; brink; line where two solid surfaces meet; thin sharp side of cutting instrument; **on e.** nervous; *v* move gradually, *esp.* sideways; provide or form border

**ed'i·ble** fit to be eaten

**e'dict** (ē-) order issued by authority

**ed'i·fice** (large) building

**ed'i|t** prepare for publication, broadcast, *etc*. **-tor**

**e·di'tion** (form of) literary publication; set of copies printed at one time

**ed·i·to'ri·al** article giving opinion held by newspaper

**ed'u·cate** bring up (young persons); train; instruct

**eel** long snakelike fish

**ee'rie** (frighteningly) strange; weird

**ef·fect'** *n* result; state of being operative; mental impression produced; *pl* personal property; *pl* lighting, sounds in film, *etc*; *v* bring about; result in

**ef·fec'tive** *a* producing an (intended) result; actually in effect; striking. **-ness**

**ef·fec'tu·al** answering its purpose; effective

**ef·fec'tu·ate** bring about

**ef·fem'i·nate** unmanly; womanishly soft

**ef·fer·ves'|cent** giving off bubbles; lively. **-cence**

**ef·fete'** weak; decadent; effeminate

**ef'fi·ca·cy** power to accomplish results. **effica'cious**

**ef·fi'cien|t** producing effect; capable. **-cy**

**ef'fi·gy** (crude) image of (hated) person

**ef'fort** exertion of power; attempt; achievement

**ef·fron'te·ry** rude impudence

**ef·fu'|sive** gushing. **-sion**

**e·gal·i·tar'i·an** asserting equality of all men

**egg** *n* hard-shelled oval reproductive body produced by reptiles or birds, *esp.* hens; contents of (hen's) egg as food; ovum; *v infml* **e. on** urge person (to do)

**egg'nog** drink made of eggs, sugar, milk (and spirits)

**egg'plant,** *UK* **au'ber·gine** (plant with) large purple fruit, used as vegetable

**e'go** (ē-) conscious thinking self; self-esteem

**e·go·cen'tric** self-centered

**e'go·ism** excessive selfishness

**e'go·tism** excessive talking about o. s.; self-conceit

**eight** (āt) a number (8), equal to seven plus one

**eigh·|teen'** a number (18), equal to eight plus ten. **-teenth**

**eighth** (ātth) next after seventh; being one of eight equal parts

**eight'y** (āti) a number (80), equal to eight times ten

**ei'ther** (*US* ēther, *UK* īdher) one or the other of two; each of two; used with *or* to state alternative choices: *either this or that*; used after negative sentences to mean the one and the other: *I will not go and he will not e.*

**e·jac'u·late** eject semen during orgasm; utter suddenly. **ejacula'tion**

**e·ject'** throw or push out; remove by force from office, property, *etc.* **-tion**

**eke out** supply what is lacking; manage to earn just enough to live on

**e·lab'o·rate** *a* (-it) carefully worked out; complicated; *v* (-eit) work out in (great) detail

**e·lapse'** (of time) pass

**e·las'tic** (material, as rubber)

recovering shape after stretching, *etc*; flexible; springy. **elastic'ity**

**e·la|t'ed** filled with joy or pride. **-tion**

**el'bow** *n* bend or joint between upper arm and forearm; any similar bend in road, river, pipe, *etc*; *v* push with elbow; make one's way by pushing

**eld'er** *a* older; *n* person who is older than o. s.; official in certain religious groups

**el'der**, *US* also **el'der·ber·ry** type of shrub with small white flowers and black berries

**e·lec|t'** choose (by vote). **-tion**

**e·lec'to·rate** body of persons entitled to vote

**e·lec'tri|c** of, using, charged with or produced by electricity; thrilling. **-cal**

**e·lec·tri'cian** person who installs or repairs electrical equipment

**e·lec·tric'i·ty** (ēlektrisiti) force, thought to be due to movement of electrons, capable of causing many effects, such as attraction and repulsion, lighting and heating, chemical changes, *etc*; electric current

**e·lec'tri·fy** charge or equip with electricity; excite

**e·lec'tro·cute** kill by electricity. **electrocu'tion**

**e·lec'trode** either pole of electric battery

**e·lec·trol'y·sis** separation of a liquid into its chemical parts by passing electric current through it; destruction of hair roots with electric current

**e·lec·tro·mag'net** iron bar which is made magnetic by electric current moving through coil around it

**e·lec'tron** extremely small particle charged with negative electricity. **electron'ic**

**e·lec·tron mi'cro·scope** instrument using focused beam of electrons to make minute objects visible

**el'e·gant** graceful; tasteful; refined

**el'e·gy** poem or song of lament

**el'e·ment** basic part; substance which cannot be changed chemically into simpler substance; environment to which an organism is adapted; heating coil in electric devices; *pl* forces of nature; *pl* basic principles of art or science. **elemen'tal, elemen'tary**

**el'e·phant** (elifent) large four-footed mammal with long grasping trunk and ivory tusks

**el'e·vate** lift up; raise, *esp.* to higher station

**embezzle**

**el·e·va·tor** (elivātēr) device for carrying persons and things vertically from one floor of a building to another; grain storehouse equipped with this; conveyor belt with buckets, *etc* for lifting materials

**e·lev·en** a number (11), equal to ten plus one

**elf** (*pl* **elves**) small (mischievous) fairy

**e·lic·it** draw forth or out

**el·i·gi·ble** fit to be chosen; qualified. **eligibil'ity**

**e·lim·i·nate** get rid of; remove

**e·lite'** (ālēt') choice or best of a group

**elk** large type of deer

**el·lipse'** oval (curve)

**elm** (hardwood of) large shade tree

**el·o·cu·tion** art of speaking in public

**e·lon·gate** lengthen. **elonga'·tion**

**e·lope'** run away to marry secretly

**el·o·quent** (of speech) fluent and effective. **-quence**

**else** other than the one mentioned: *somebody e.*; in addition: *what e. do you want?*; otherwise: *hurry, (or) e. you will be late*

**else'where** in, from or to another place

**e·lu·ci·date** explain; make clear

**e·lude'** escape; avoid obeying (law); be hard to remember. **-sive**

**e·ma·ci·a·ted** thin or feeble (from illness or hunger)

**em·a·nate** flow forth; come from

**e·man·ci·pate** free from legal, *etc* restraint

**e·mas·cu·late** weaken; castrate

**em·balm'** (-bahm) treat (dead body) so as to preserve from decay

**em·bank·ment** structure of earth, *etc* to hold back water or support roadway

**em·bar·go** (*pl* **-goes**) legal order forbidding trade

**em·bark'** put or go on ship. **embarka'tion; e. (up)on** start (sth new)

**em·bar·rass** make s.o. uneasy or ashamed; bring into financial difficulties.

**em·bas·sy** (building housing) ambassador and his staff; diplomatic mission (of these people)

**em·bed'** set solidly in surrounding matter

**em·bel·lish** make beautiful by ornaments; make (story) interesting by fanciful additions. **-ment**

**em·ber** piece of glowing coal, *etc* from a fire; *pl* smoldering ashes

**em·bez·zle** steal (money entrusted to one). **-ment**

**em·bit·ter** make bitter

**em·bla·zon** put heraldic signs on shield; deck in bright colors, *etc*

**em·blem** symbol representing idea, *etc*

**em·bod·y** give body to ideas, *etc*; express in concrete form; include in system

**em·bold·en** make bold

**em·bo·lism** blocking of blood vessel by clot of blood, *etc*

**em·boss** carve raised figures on surface

**em·brace'** hug; accept eagerly; include

**em·broi·der** ornament with needlework; exaggerate (story). **-y**

**em·broil'** bring into confusion or conflict

**em·bry·o** unborn offspring of living thing; early stage. **embryon'ic**

**e·mend'** remove errors from

**em'er·ald** green precious stone; clear deep green

**e·merge'** come out of (into view, knowledge). **-gence**

**e·mer'gen·cy** unforeseen situation demanding prompt action; urgent need

**e·mer'i·tus** retired because of age, *etc*., but retaining rank

**em'i·grate** leave country to settle elsewhere. **-nt**

**em'i·nent** high; standing above others; standing out clearly. **-ce**

**em'is·sar·y** person sent to deliver (secret) message

**e·mit'** send forth; give off; issue, as an order. **-ssion**

**e·mo'tion** strong feeling, as love. **-al**

**em'per·or** supreme ruler of an empire

**em'pha·sis** (*pl* **-ases**) stress; special importance. **emphat'ic**

**em'pire** group of nations ruled over by one ruler or government; supreme rule

**em·pir'i·cal** founded on experiment or observation only. **-ism**

**em·ploy'** use; use services of; put to work. **-ee, -ment**

**em·po'ri·um** (*pl* **-iums, -ia**) market place; large store with variety of goods

**emp'ty** *a* containing nothing; unoccupied, as a house; lacking some quality or thing; without meaning or effect; foolish; *v* make or become empty; discharge contents of

**e'mu** (ēmyū) large non-flying Australian bird

**em'u·late** try to equal; imitate

**e·mul'sion** creamy fluid with oily, *etc* particles which do not blend completely, as oil and water. **-fy**

**en·a·ble** give power, authority or means to do; make possible

**en·act'** make into law.
**-ment**; play part, as on stage

**e·nam'el** hard glossy coating
for metal, *etc*; hard smooth
covering of teeth

**en·am'ored,** *UK* **-oured**
filled with love; charmed

**en·camp'** settle in camp;
lodge in tents. **-ment**

**en·case'** cover (as) in a case.
**-ment**

**en·ceph·a·li'tis** inflammation of the brain

**en·chain'** bind (in chains)

**en·chant'** put under spell; delight. **-ment**

**en·cir'cle** form circle around;
surround. **-ment**

**en·close'** fence in; add to
contents of envelope. **-sure**

**en·com'pass** include; surround

**en'core** (ahngkōr') again!
(demand for repetition)

**en·coun'ter** meet(ing)

**en·cour'age** make brave;
support. **-ment**

**en·croach'** intrude on others'
rights, *etc*. **-ment**

**en·cum'ber** burden, *esp.*
with debts. **-brance**

**en·cy·clo·pe'di·a, -pae'di·a**
alphabetical work containing information on all
branches of knowledge or
one specific branch

**end** point at which sth ceases;
limit; last part; remnant;
purpose; result; death

**en·dan'ger** bring into danger

**en·dear'** make dear

**en·deav'or,** *UK* **-our** try

**en·dem'ic** regularly found in
an area or among certain
people, as a disease

**en'dive** curly-leaved salad
plant

**end'less** having no end

**en'do·crine gland** ductless
gland secreting hormone directly into blood

**en·dorse'** approve of or support; write (name, *etc*) on
back of check, *etc*. **-ment**

**en·dow'** furnish with funds,
privilege or ability. **-ment**

**en·dure'** bear pain, *etc*; continue to exist. **-ance**

**end'ways, end'wise** having
the end to the front; with
ends touching

**en'e·ma** (device for) injecting
(medicine, *etc*) into rectum

**en'e·my** one who hates and
opposes another; (armed
forces of) hostile nation; sth
harmful

**en·er·get'ic** very active;
forceful. **-ally**

**en'er·gy** force; strength; active operation; capacity for
doing work

**en'er·vate** weaken

**en·force'** give force to; compel (obedience)

**en·fran'chise** grant right to
vote; free (slave)

**en·gage'** bind by agreement,
*esp.* to marry; hire; fight
with; (cause to) interlock, as

gears; hold (attention). **-ment**

**en·gag·ing** attractive

**en·gen·der** (-jen-) give rise to; produce

**en·gine** (enjin) machine for changing energy into power or movement; railroad locomotive

**en·gi·neer** one skilled in designing, building or operating engines or works for public use, such as bridges, roads, *etc.* **-ing**

**en·grave** carve (figures, *etc*) on (hard surface); print from such a surface

**en·gross** occupy wholly

**en·gulf** swallow up

**en·hance** raise in degree, price, *etc.* **-ment**

**e·nig·ma** riddle. **enigmat'ic**

**en·joy** take pleasure in; have benefit of. **-ment**

**en·large** increase in size, quantity, *etc.* **-ment; e. on** speak or write at length

**en·light·en** teach; inform

**en·list** engage for military service; get aid or support of. **-ment**

**en·liv·en** make active, gay or cheerful

**en·mi·ty** hatred; hostility

**e·nor·mi·ty** great wickedness or crime

**e·nor·mous** (inuf) to the degree or in the amount required to satisfy want, fulfill purpose, *etc*

**en·rage** fill with rage

**en·rap·ture** fill with delight

**en·rich** make rich; improve quality

**en·roll**, *UK* **-rol** enter one's name in (army, school, *etc*) list; become or be made a member of. **-ment**

**en·sem·ble** (ahnsahmbl) matching or harmonious set; group (of musicians, actors, *etc*)

**en·sign** (-sīn) flag; badge of office; (-sin) *US* lowest-ranking naval officer

**en·slave** make into a slave. **-ment**

**en·sue** happen afterwards; result from

**en·sure** make sure; insure

**en·tail** make necessary as consequence; *law* settle property on fixed line of heirs

**en·tan·gle** make tangled; snare in obstacles. **-ment**

**en·ter** go or come into; pierce; put into; join or be admitted into, as school; record in list, register, *etc*; **e. into** take part in, assume obligation, be part of; **e. (up)on** begin

**en·ter·pris|e** undertaking; readiness to undertake (bold) projects. **-ing**

**en·ter·tain** treat as guest; amuse; consider. **-ment**

**en·thrall**, *UK* **-thral** make slave of; hold spellbound

**en·throne'** formally place on throne. **-ment**

**en·thuse'** make or become enthusiastic

**en·thu'si·asm** strong excitement in favor of a thing. **enthusias'tic**

**en·tice'** tempt; attract. **-ing**

**en·tire'** whole; complete; not broken. **-ty**

**en·ti'tle** give right or title to

**en'ti·ty** sth that has real, independent existence

**en·to·mol'o·gy** scientific study of insects. **-.gist**

**en'trails** pl bowels; inner parts

**en'trance** n door, gate, etc; act of entering; right of admission

**en·trance'** v put into trance; fill with emotion, esp. joy

**en'trap'** catch in a trap

**en·treat'** beg earnestly. **-ty**

**en·tree'** (ahntrā) right to enter; US main course of meal

**en·|trench'** establish in strong position. **-trenched**

**en·tre·pre·neur'** (ahn-) one who manages and bears business risks against possible profit

**en·trust'** give in trust to: give responsibility to

**en'try** act or place of entering; act of recording sth in list, etc; recorded item; s.o. or sth entered in contest, etc

**en·twine'** wind together or around

**e·nu'mer·ate** count; name one by one

**e·nun'ci·ate** state formally or definitely;    pronounce (words) clearly

**en·vel'op** cover completely

**en've·lope** covering, esp. for letter, etc

**en'vi·a·ble** arousing envy'

**en'vi·ous** marked by envy

**en·vi'ron·ment** (physical and social conditions, etc forming) surroundings

**en·vi·ron·men'tal·ist** one concerned with protecting natural environment

**en·vi'rons** pl area surrounding town, etc

**en·vis'age** imagine as possibility

**en'voy** (diplomatic) representative; messenger

**en'vy** (feel) discontent at another's success, etc and desire to have it

**en'zyme** substance produced by and causing changes in plants and animals

**e'on**, UK **ae'on** immeasurably long period of time

**ep'au·let**,    UK    **-lette** ornamental shoulder piece on uniform

**e·phem'er·al** short-lived

**ep'ic** long poem, film, etc about deeds of hero(es)

**ep'i·cen·ter** point of earth's surface above focus of earthquake

**ep'i·cure** lover of choice and dainty food

**ep·i·cu·re'an** (peron) devoted to pleasure. **-ism**

**ep·i·dem'ic** (disease) affecting many in district at one time

**ep·i·der'mis** outer layer of skin

**ep'i·gram** short witty poem or saying

**ep'i·lep·sy** nervous disease marked by fits. **epilep'tic**

**ep'i·log,** *UK* **-logue** (-log) speech or passage rounding out novel, play, *etc*

**e·pis'co·pal** of or governed by bishops

**ep'i·sode** period in life or part of story apart from whole; one part of serial story. **episod'ic**

**e·pis'tle** (ipisl) letter

**ep'i·taph** words in memory of dead

**ep'i·thet** word expressing characteristic quality

**e·pit'o·me** (-mē) typical example; ideal representation. **-mize**

**ep'och** period of history; *esp.* as marked by special events. **-al, e·making**

**eq'ua·ble** even; balanced

**e'qual** (ēkwel) *a* the same in number, quantitiy, size, rank, *etc*; having ability, *etc* needed to deal with sth or s.o.; evenly matched; *n* person e. to another; *v* be the same as; attain same level. **-ize, equal'ity**

**e·qua'tion** state of being equal; expression showing equality

**e·qua'tor** imaginary circle around earth halfway between poles

**e·ques'tri·an** of horse-riding

**e·qui·dis'tant** separated by equal distances

**e·qui·lat'er·al** having all sides equal in length

**e·qui·lib'ri·um** state of balance

**e'quine** of or like horses

**e'qui·nox** time at which day and night are equal in length

**e·quip'** furnish with necessary things. **-ment**

**eq'ui·ta·ble** fair; just

**eq'ui·ty** fairness; use of principles of justice to correct too narrow law; value of company's shares

**e·quiv'a·lent** (sth) equal in value, meaning, *etc*. **-lence**

**e·quiv'o·cal** of double meaning; uncertain; doubtful

**e·quiv'o·cate** use words of doubtful meaning; lie

**e'ra** historical period

**e·rad'i·cate** tear out by roots; destroy completely

**e·ra|se'** rub out, *esp.* writing. **-sure**

**e·rect'** *a* upright; (of penis) rigid from sexual excitement; *v* raise; build; assemble (machine). **-tion**

**ether**

**erg** (urg) unit of energy or work

**er'mine** (urmin) (valuable white winter fur of) animal of weasel family

**e·ro|de'** destroy slowly; wear away by action of wind, *etc*. **-sion**

**e·rot'ic** (of sexual) love

**err** make mistake; sin

**er'rand** short trip undertaken for specific purpose; purpose of trip

**er'rant** wandering in search of adventure; erring

**er·rat'ic** having no fixed course; wandering; irregular in behavior, *etc*

**er·ro'ne·ous** mistaken; incorrect

**er'ror** mistake; wrong or mistaken opinion; sin

**er'u·dite** learned. **erudi'tion**

**e·rupt'** break out or through. **-tion, -tive**

**es'ca·late** increase (by stages); make higher

**es'ca·la·tor** moving stairway

**es'ca·pade** mischievous adventure

**es·cape'** get away from; find way out; avoid; fail to be noticed

**es·chew'** shun

**es·cort'** guard (for protection or honor); accompany

**e·soph'a·gus** food canal from mouth to stomach

**es·o·ter'ic** meant for or understood by only a chosen few

**es·pe'cial·ly** (espesheli) in particular; to a very great degree; chiefly

**es·pi·o·nage** practice of spying or using spies

**es·pouse'** support (cause, *etc*); marry. **-al**

**es·pres'so** (cup of) strong coffee made with steam pressure

**es'say** short literary work on any subject; attempt

**es'sence** true nature; most important quality; distilled extract; perfume

**es·sen'tial** absolutely necessary; of a thing's essence

**es·tab'lish** set up (firm, *etc*); settle; make (belief, *etc*) accepted; prove

**es·tab'lish·ment** system set up by law, *etc*; house of business

**es·tate'** (landed) property

**es·teem'** think highly of; regard as

**es·thet'ics** see aesthetics

**es'ti·mate** judge (approximate size, value, cost, *etc*)

**es·trange'** turn away in feeling; alienate. **-ment**

**es'tu·ar·y** mouth of river subject to tides

**etch** engrave (picture, *etc*) on metal plate with acid. **-ing**

**e·ter'nal** everlasting. **eter'nity**

**e'ther** (ē-) inflammable colorless liquid used as solvent and anesthetic; upper regions of space

**e·the're·al** heavenly; airy; extremely delicate

**eth'ics** (science of) morals; principles; rules of conduct. **-al**

**eth'nic** of the races of man; *US* originating from particular (national, *etc*) group. **ethnol'ogy**

**eth·no·cen'tric** believing one's own race, nation, *etc* to be better than others

**et'i·quette** (-ket) conventional rules of behavior

**et·y·mol'o·gy** study of history and forms of words

**eu·ca·lyp'tus** (yūkalipt*es*) evergreen tree yielding strong-smelling oil used in medicines

**eu'lo·gy** (speech, *etc*) of high praise. **-gize** (*Uk* **-gise**)

**eu'nuch** (yūn*e*k) a castrated man

**eu'phe·mism** (substitution of) mild expression for blunt one. **euphemis'tic**

**eu'pho·ny** pleasing sound. **euphon'ic, euphon'ious**

**eu·pho'ri·a** sense of elation or well-being

**eu·rhyth'mics** system of moving body to musical rhythms as exercise

**Eu·ro·pe'an** (native) of Europe

**eu·tha·na'si·a** (yūthenāzh*e*) killing the incurably ill

painlessly

**e·vac'u·ate** remove people from (dangerous place); empty (the bowels)

**e·vade'** escape (from); get around (doing). **-sion, -sive**

**e·val'u·ate** judge or find out value of

**e·van·gel'i·cal** of Christian gospel, *esp.* in certain forms of Protestantism

**e·van'ge·list** preacher; one of writers of the four Gospels

**e·vap'o·rate** turn into vapor; disappear; remove water from

**eve** (ēv) evening or day before holiday or important event

**e'ven** (ēvn) *a* level; smooth; on the same level; uniform in quality, *etc*; equal in number, *etc*; calm; (of numbers) that can be divided exactly by two; *adv* (used in comparison) still, yet: *e. more tired*; (used to suggest a stronger or more unlikely alternative): *e. if he comes. I will not talk to him, e. his enemies respect him*; **get e. with** take revenge on

**eve'ning** last part of day and beginning of night

**e·vent'** anything that happens, *esp.* it is important; scheduled (sports) activity; **in the e. of** if; **in any e.** in any case

**e·ven·tu·al** finally resulting or happening

**e·ven·tu·al·i·ty** possible happening

**ev'er** at all times: *he is e. the same*; continuously: *e. since that day*; at any time: *did you e. meet him?*

**ev'er·green** (tree) that does not shed leaves; always fresh

**ev'er·y** each; all (members of any group) taken separately

**ev'er·y·bod·y** every person

**ev'er·y·day** happening, used, or suitable for every day; not unusual

**ev'er·y·one** everybody

**ev'er·y·thing** every object, event, fact, *etc*

**ev'er·y·where** in or to every place

**e·vict'** legally force (tenant) to leave. **-tion**

**ev'i·dence** *n* sign of; proof of; information given before court; *v* serve to show

**ev'i·dent** clear; obvious

**e'vil** (ēvĭl) (that which is) harmful or wicked

**e·voke'** call up (feelings, memories, *etc*). **evoca'tion**

**ev·o·lu'tion** (process of) development (from earlier forms). **-ary**

**e·volve'** develop gradually

**ewe** (yū) female sheep

**ex·act'** *a* strictly correct; **-titude;** *v* demand; insist on; enforce payment

**ex·act'ing** severe; difficult

**ex·ag'ger·ate** (igzaj-) overstate; go beyond limits of truth

**ex·alt'** (igz-) raise in rank, spirits, *etc*; praise highly. **exalta'tion**

**ex·am'ine** (igz-) inspect carefully; test knowledge of; question. **examina'tion**

**ex·am'ple** sample taken to show nature of whole; s.o. or sth worthy of imitation; warning case; problem to be solved in order to explain rule

**ex·as'per·ate** annoy to high degree

**ex'ca·vate** hollow out; dig out; unearth

**ex·ceed'** go beyond; be better or greater than

**ex·ceed'ing·ly** to an unusual degree

**ex·cel'** be better than or superior to

**ex'cel·lent** extremely good. **-lence**

**ex·cept'** *prep* (also **ex·cept'ing**) leaving out; other than; *v* leave out

**ex·cep'tion** act of excepting; sth excepted; sth that does not follow the general rule. **-al; take e.** object to. **-able**

**ex'cerpt** passage from book, *etc*

**ex·cess'** fact of exceeding; amount by which one thing exceeds another; extreme (degree, amount). **-sive**

**ex·change'** v give or get in place of; n central telephone office; place for buying and selling stocks, etc. **-able**

**ex·change' rate** price charged for money from another country

**ex'cise** inland tax on goods

**ex·cise'** cut out or away, as tumor

**ex·cite'** rouse (feelings, etc); cause; stir up. **-ment**

**ex·claim'** cry out; say loudly. **exclama'tion**

**ex·clude'** shut out (from); bar from (consideration, etc); expel. **-sion**

**ex·clu'sive** shutting out; desiring to keep others out; limited to one purpose. **-ness**

**ex·com·mu'ni·cate** expel from church membership

**ex'cre·ment** waste matter discharged from bowels

**ex·cre|te'** discharge waste matter from body. **-tion**

**ex·cru'ci·at·ing** (ikskrū-shiāt-)severely painful

**ex·cur'sion** short (pleasure) trip, *esp.* of group

**ex·cuse'** v (-kyūz) free from blame, etc (for sth done, omitted, etc); forgive. **-able;** **e. o.s.** ask to be released (from duty); n (-kyūs) apology; anything which frees from blame, duty, etc

**ex'e·cute** carry out; perform;

kill legally as punishment. **execu'tion**

**ex·ec'u·|tive** a concerned with carrying out (decisions, etc); n person or office administrating (laws, etc). **-tor**

**ex·e·ge'sis** (pl -ses) explanation, esp. of Bible

**ex·em'pla·ry** (igz-) worth imitating; serving as warning

**ex·em'pli·fy** (igz-) show by example; be example of

**ex·empt'** (igz-) v free from; a not subject to. **-tion**

**ex'er·cise** training to improve health, memory, etc; task set for this purpose; carrying out (of duty, etc); use of (right, etc); pl program of speeches, etc, as ceremony

**ex·ert'** (igz-) bring (influence, etc) to bear; **e. o.s.** make strong efforts. **-tion**

**ex·hale'** breathe out (air, gas, etc). **exhala'tion**

**ex·haus|t'** (igzawst) v draw off entire contents; drain (strength, etc); tire out; treat or study thoroughly; n (pipe for) waste gas from motor. **-tion**

**ex·hib'it** (igzib-) v show; display, n thing shown; document, etc brought as proof in court. **exhibi'tion**

**ex·hi·bi'tion·ism** tendency towards display in order to attract attention

**ex·hil'a·rate** (igzil-) make cheerful. **exhilera'tion**

**ex·hort'** (igzort) urge strongly; warn earnestly. **exhorta'·tion**

**ex·hume'** dig up dead body

**ex'i·gen·cy** (eksijensi) urgent need; emergency. **-gent**

**ex'ile** v expel from country (as punishment); n (place where) a person so expelled (lives)

**ex·is|t'** have being; live; continue to live. **-tence, existen'tial**

**ex'it** way out; leaving (stage etc); death

**ex'o·dus** going forth (of large number of people)

**ex·on'er·ate** free s.o. from blame

**ex·or'bi·tant** (igz-) going beyond reasonable limits

**ex·ot'ic** foreign; unusual

**ex·pan|d'** increase (in size, etc); spread out; express in fuller form; develop. **-sion**

**ex·panse'** wide area

**ex·pan'sive** tending to expand; covering wide range; friendly and outgoing

**ex·pa'tri·ate** expel from or leave native country

**ex·pect'** look forward to with confidence or as likely to happen; consider (s.o.) bound to do; be pregnant

**ex·pe'di|ent** a suitable under the circumstances; of advantage; n means to an end. **-cy**

**ex'pe·dite** speed up doing of; do (task) quickly

**ex·pe·di'·tion** (people, etc sent on) journey for some purpose; speed; promptness. **-tious**

**ex·pel'** drive or force out; shut out from school, etc

**ex·pen|d'** use up; spend **-dable, -diture**

**ex·pen|se'** cost; outlay of money. **-sive**

**ex·pe'ri·ence** knowledge resulting from personal observation; event that happens to a person

**ex·per'i·ment** test; trial. **experimen'tal**

**ex'pert** (person who is) specially skilled or knowledgeable,. **expertise'**

**ex'pi·ate** make good by paying penalty

**ex·pir|e'** breathe out (as if) from lungs; come to an end, as subscription, etc; die. **-y, expira'tion**

**ex·plain'** make clear or known in detail; account for. **explana'tion, explan'atory**

**ex'ple·tive** oath

**ex·plic'it** (-plis-) clearly expressed; definite; outspoken

**ex·plo'de'** (cause to) burst or fly into pieces with loud noise; express violent emotion; prove false. **-sion**

**ex·ploit'** v use for profit; make use of selfishly. **exploita'tion**

**ex'ploit** n (heroic) deed

**ex·plore'** travel through

country for purpose of discovery; examine closely. **explora'tion**

**ex·plo'sive** that can explode (as bombs, *etc*); (of question, *etc*) controversial

**ex·po'nent** one who explains; representative

**ex·port'** sell goods to other countries

**ex·pose'** leave unprotected; lay open to danger; present to view; make known; unmask (criminal); subject film to action of light. **-sure**

**ex·po·si'tion** act of explaining or exposing; explanatory discussion; show, as of manufactured goods

**ex·pos'tu·late** reason earnestly with person; protest (mildly)

**ex·pound'** set forth in detail; explain

**ex·press'** *v* put into words; show feelings. **-sion** squeeze out (juice, *etc*); *n* fast train or delivery; *a* speedy; clearly stated; special

**ex·pres'sive** serving to express; full of expression

**ex·pro'pri·ate** take away property (for public use)

**ex·pul'sion** act of expelling

**ex·punge'** remove; erase

**ex·pur'gate** cleanse; remove objectionable matter, *esp*. from book

**ex'qui·site** highly delicate or beautiful; keen (feeling, *etc*)

**ex'tant** (still) existing

**ex·tem·po·ra'ne·ous, ex·tem'po·re** done or spoken without preparation; offhand. **extem'porize** (*UK* **-ise**)

**ex·tend'** reach to; lengthen; make larger; stretch out (at full length); offer (hand, gift). **-sion**

**ex·ten'sive** large; far-reaching

**ex·tent'** area; degree

**ex·ten'u·ate** serve to make crime, *etc* less serious

**ex·te'ri·or** outer (surface); outside (area)

**ex·ter'mi·nate** destroy entirely

**ex·ter'nal** outside; to be applied to the outside; foreign

**ex·tinct'** that has died out; no longer burning, *etc*; (of volcano) no longer active. **-tion**

**ex·tin'guish** (-gwish) put out (fire, life, *etc*); wipe out debt; destroy

**ex·tol'** praise highly

**ex·tort'** obtain by threat, force, *etc*. **-tion**

**ex'tra** *a* beyond what is due, usual or necessary; *n* sth additional; actor who plays small parts; special edition of newspaper

**ex·tract'** draw out; copy passage; obtain by pressure, *etc*. **-tion**

**ex'tra·dite** return possible

criminal to his country for trial. **extradi'tion**

**ex·tra'ne·ous** coming from without; not belonging or proper to

**ex·traor'di·nar·y** (ikstror-) not usual; remarkable, **extraordinar'ily**

**ex·tra·sen'so·ry** beyond the ordinary senses

**ex·tra·ter·res'tri·al** outside the earth or its atmosphere

**ex'tra·ter·ri·to'ri·al** not subject to laws of place where one lives

**ex·trav'a·|gant** wasteful; going beyond reason. **-gance**

**ex·treme'** utmost; farthest from center; severe; beyond ordinary

**ex·trem'|is·m** advocating of radical (political) views. **-ist**

**ex·trem'i·ty** (-trem-) end; extreme need, degree or measure; *usu pl* limb of body, *esp.* hands or feet

**ex'tri·cate** disentangle; free

**ex'tro·vert** person interested mainly in things outside himself. **-ed**

**ex·u'ber·|ant** overflowing (in spirits, health); rich in growth. **-ance**

**ex·ude'** ooze out

**ex·ult'** (igz-) rejoice greatly; triumph

**eye** (ī) *n* organ of sight; ability to see; hole in needle for thread; part of fastener holding hook; leaf bud of potato; calm center of hurricane; *v* watch closely

**eye'ball** the whole of the eye

**eye'brow** hair growing on ridge over the eye

**eye'glass·es** pair of lenses to correct defective sight

**eye'lash** hair growing around edges of eyelid

**eye'let** hole for lace or cord

**eye'lid** movable fold of skin to cover the eye

**eye'lin·er** makeup applied to edge of eyelid

**eye shad'ow** makeup for eyelid

**eye'sore** sth ugly to see

**eye'tooth** canine teeth, *esp.* of upper jaw

**eye'wit·ness** person who sees sth happen, *esp.* a crime

# F

**f** sixth letter of English alphabet

**fa'ble** legend; moral story, *usu* with animals as characters

**fab'ric** woven material; structure

**fab'ri·cate** invent (lie); manufacture. **fabrica'tion**

**fab'u·lous** unbelievable; told about in fables

**fa·cade'** (fesahd) front of building; false outward appearance

**face** *n* front part of head; look; outward appearance; surface or outer part of anything; front; right side, as of cloth; dial of clock, *etc*; **f. to f.** opposite; confronting; *v* have face or front towards; come or stand before; deal with; put layer on surface of; line with different material, as cloth

**face'less** without identity

**face'-lift** surgery to remove wrinkles on face and improve appearance

**fac'et** one of small surfaces of cut gem; aspect

**fa·ce'tious** marked by (unsuitable) humor. **-ness**

**fac'ile** (fasil) easily done; fluent; superficial

**fa·cil'i·tate** make easy

**fa·cil'i·ty** state of being easy; skill; *usu pl* means, equipment, *etc* for making sth possible or easier

**fac·sim'i·le** (faksimile) exact copy

**fact** sth that is done; sth known or accepted as true; sth existing in reality; piece of information. **-tual**

**fac'tion** small (self-interested) group within party, *etc*; (spirit of) discord. **-tious**

**fac'tor** element contributing to result; agent

**fac'to·ry** building(s) where goods are manufactured

**fac'ul·ty** mental or physical power; ability (in special field); (*US* teaching staff of) department of university

**fad** intense, but passing interest, *etc*. **-dish**

**fade** grow weak; lose freshness or brilliance; grow gradually less clear, as picture on screen, radio wave, *etc*

**fae'ces** see **feces**

**Fah'ren·heit** (farenhīt) (of the) temperature scale on which water freezes at 32° and boils at 212°

**fail** miss or fail to succeed in some action, duty, *etc*; desert or disappoint s.o.; become bankrupt; decline or grow weaker; break down, as motor

**fail'ing** defect; fault

**fail'ure** unsuccessful person, attempt, *etc*; breaking down; lack of success; fact of not doing or performing; bankruptcy

**faint** *a* weak; (of color, sounds) not bright, clear, or loud; *v* lose consciousness; *n* act or state of fainting

**fair** *a* just; keeping to the rules; pleasing to the eye; light in color; blond; of average quality or amount; favorable, as weather; *n* exhibition of goods, farm products, *etc*

**fair'y** imaginary tiny being with magical powers

135 **fanfare**

**faith** complete confidence; (system of religious, *etc*) belief; loyalty. **-ful**

**fake** (make) sth that is not true or genuine

**fal'con** bird of prey (trained to hunt)

**fall** *v* (**fell, fall'en**) drop or hang freely; leave standing position suddenly, *usu* by accident; become lower; droop; lose virtue, station, *etc*; drop down wounded or dead (in battle); drop in quality, *etc*; happen; pass into a certain condition; *n* act or state of dropping; *US* autumn; descent of water; that which falls, as amount of rain, *etc*; the distance anything falls; loss of power; *etc*; ruin

**fal'la·cy** mistaken idea; idea based on false reasoning. **falla'cious**

**fal'li·ble** liable to error. **fallibil'ity**

**fal·lo·pi·an tube'** one of two ducts transporting eggs to the womb in females

**fall'out** dropping to earth of solid (radioactive) particles; aftereffect(s)

**false** wrong; not true. **-hood**; disloyal; artificial, as teeth

**fal'si·fy** forge document; make false. **falsifica'tion**

**fal'ter** stumble; stammer; lose courage

**fa|me** (favorable) public rep-utation. **-mous**

**fa·mil'i·ar** well-known; closely acquainted (with); (too) informal. **-ize** (*UK* **-ise**)

**fam'i·ly** parents and their children; one's wife or husband and children; any group having common ancestors; any group of related things, as plants, languages, *etc*

**fam'ine** severe lack of food in a district; great shortage

**fam'ish** (cause to) suffer from extreme hunger

**fan** *n* device for setting air into motion to cool room, *etc*; enthusiastic follower of pastime or admirer of celebrity; *v* cause (cool) air to blow on; stir up, as feelings; spread out from center

**fa·nat'ic** person filled with extreme (mistaken) enthusiasm. **-ical, -icism**

**fan belt** continuous band driving fan to cool motor

**fan'ci·er** person with special interest, as breeding plants, *etc*

**fan||cy** *n* imagination, *esp.* ability to imagine quaint or odd things; mental image or idea, *esp.* one without much foundation; whim; liking; *a* ornamental; extravagant; *v* picture to o.s.; believe without being sure; like. **-ciful**

**fan'fare** burst of trumpets; showy display

**fang** long sharp tooth of dog, snake, *etc*

**fan·ta·sy** (product of) imagination. **fantas'tic**

**far** *adv* at or to a great distance in space, time, degree, *etc*; by much; at or to a definite point or degree; up to now; **as** or **so f. as** to the extent that; *a* remote; distant; extreme

**far|ce** broadly humorous dramatic work; ridiculous affair; mockery. **-cical**

**fare** *n* passage money; paying passenger; food, *etc* offered; *v* get on (well, *etc*)

**fare·well'** good-bye; leave-taking

**far'fetched'** improbable

**far-flung'** widespread; remote

**farm** land *etc* used for growing crops, raising cattle, *etc*. **-er, -ing**

**far'sight·ed** marked by foresight or wisdom; seeing distant objects better than near ones

**far'ther** *adv* at or to a greater distance, extent, *etc*; *a* more distant or advanced

**far'thest** *adv* at or to greatest distance; *a* most distant

**fas'ci·nate** charm; hold spellbound

**fas'|cism** (fashizm)political system which exalts nation and race, allows no opposition and maintains control over all aspects of citizens' lives. **-cist**

**fash'ion** *n* custom or style in dress, manners, *etc* common at any (given) time; manner or way of doing sth; kind or sort; *v* form or shape. **-able**

**fast** *a* moving or able to move quickly; rapid; (of clock) showing time ahead of correct time; given to pursuit of pleasure, *etc*; firmly fixed or attached; unable to escape or be untied; lasting, as dye; deep or sound, as sleep; *v* eat little or no food, *esp* as religious custom; *n* act or period of fasting

**fas'ten** (fasen) attach or fix firmly, as buttons, door, *etc*. **-er, -ing**; fix (eyes, blame, *etc*) on

**fas·tid'i·ous** hard to please; having demanding tastes; easily disgusted. **-ness**

**fat** *a* having a great deal of fat; plump; well-fed; (of food) oily or greasy; thick; profitable; rich, as soil; *n* a substance, important source of energy as food, that does not dissolve in water; body tissue containing much greasy matter

**fa'tal** ending in death; deadly

**fa·tal·is·m** belief that all events are decided in advance by powers beyond control

**fa·tal'i·ty** death by accident, *etc*; deadliness

**fate** force beyond man's control supposed to determine events; destiny; fortune or final outcome

**fa'ther** male parent. **-hood;** founder or originator; F. title of respect for priest

**fa'ther-in-law** father of one's husband or wife

**fath'om** *n* unit of six feet used to measure depth of water; *v* get to bottom of; understand. **-able, -less**

**fa·tigue'** (-tēg) great weariness after hard work; weakening of a (metal) material due to stress

**fau'cet** tap for drawing water, *etc*

**fault** failing or flaw in character, structure, *etc*; failure to do what is right; responsibility for having done sth wrongly; break in earth's crust; **at f.** in the wrong; **to a f.** excessively; **find f.** criticize too much

**fau'na** animal life of region, period, *etc*

**fa'vor,** *UK* **-vour** *n* kind act or treatment; kindly regard or approval; (unjustified) privilege; **in f. of** approving; to one's advantage; *v* treat with special care, kindness, *etc* ; increase chances of success of; give aid or support to; look like. **-able**

**fa'vor·ite,** *UK* **-vour-** (person or thing) preferred above others; (competitor) considered most likely to win

**fawn** *n* young deer; *v* (of animals) show affection; (of humans) show excessive affection, respect, *etc*

**fax** *v* send material (letters, *etc*) in electronic form via telephone cables; *n* machine for this purpose; material sent

**fear** (have) painful feeling caused by being in danger, unsafe position, *etc*; (experience) dread of evil or unpleasant happening. **-ful, -less**

**fea'si·ble** capable of being done. **feasibil'ity**

**feast** (eat) rich meal; religious holiday

**feat** (remarkable) deed; action showing skill

**feath'er** one of light horny growths, consisting of shaft and threadlike filaments, which form outer coat of birds. **-y**

**fea'ture** *n* any part of face; characteristic part of thing; special article, *etc* in newspaper; full-length film; *v* display (as special attraction); play an important role

**Feb'ru·ar·y** second month of year

**fe'|ces,** *UK* **fae-** (fēsēz) waste matter expelled through anus. **-cal** (kel)

**fe'cund** (fē-) fruitful; fertile. **fecund'ity**

**fed'e·ral** of states united but keeping internal sovereignty; of the central government in a union of states. **-ism**

**fed·e·ra'tion** union of states, organizations, *etc*

**fee** amount charged for professional services; entrance money; money paid for schooling

**fee'ble** weak; not loud or strong.

**feed** (fed) give food to; supply (what is needed for growth, operation. or continued existene of sth); (*esp.* of animals) eat

**feel** (felt) touch; investigate or become aware of by touch; grope for; seem *esp.* to the touch; have emotion or (vague) impression; be conscious of; think or believe. **-ing**

**feel'er** movable organ of touch on heads of insects, *etc*; hint, *etc* put forward in order to find out views of other people

**feet** *pl* of **foot**

**feign** (fān) pretend

**feint** (fānt) trick; fake attack

**fe·lic'i·ty** happiness; skill in expression. **-tous**

**fe'line** (fē-) (of, like) animal of cat family

**fell** *v* cut down (tree); strike down by blow; see also **fall**; *a* cruel; deadly

**fel'low** *n* male person; member of group of scholars forming governing body of university; student supported by special fund; *a* joined by common interest, *etc*; equal in rank. **-ship**

**fel'o·ny** serious crime, as murder, *etc*. **felo'nious**

**felt** *n* heavy cloth made by rolling and pressing fibers together; *v* see **feel**

**fe'male** (member) of the sex that conceives and brings forth young; typical of, or done by, women or girls

**fem'i·nine** of woman; womanly. **feminin'ity**

**fem'i·nis·m** (movement in) support of women's rights

**fence** *n* enclosing railing; receiver of stolen goods; *v* surround with fence; deal in stolen goods; practise art of sword-play; **f. with** avoid direct reply by shifting argument

**fend: f. off** keep away (blows, *etc*); **f. for o.s.** get along on one's own

**fend'er** protective device on cars to keep off mud, lessen shock; *etc*; screen or frame placed before fireplace

**fer'ment** (cause to) undergo fermentation; be in or cause state of (political) unrest

**fer·men·ta'tion** chemical

change, with bubbling, caused by yeast, *etc*; excitement

**fern** flowerless seedless plant reproducing by means of spores

**fe·ro'ci|ous** fierce; wild; cruel. **-ty**

**fer'ret** *n* kind of weasel kept for hunting rats or rabbits; *v* search about for; hunt with ferrets; **f. out** discover by searching, *etc*

**fer'ric, fer'rous** of or containing iron

**fer'ry** place where persons are carried across river, *etc* in a boat; boat used for this

**fer'tile** fruitful; capable of having offspring; inventive. **-ize** (*UK* **-ise**), **fertil'ity**

**fer'til·iz·er** substance used to make soil more fertile

**fer'vent, fer'vid** burning with feeling. **-cy**

**fer'vor**, *UK* **-vour** zeal

**fes'ter** (of wound, *etc*) become infected and form pus; rot

**fes'ti·val** feast; season of special entertainment, as of music, *etc*

**fes'tive** gay; of or like a feast. **festiv'ity**

**fetch'ing** attractive

**fet'id** stinking

**fe'tish** image, *etc* supposed to have magic powers; object of blind devotion; object of abnormal sexual desire

**fet'ter** foot shackle; sth that hampers movement

**fe|tus**, *UK* **foe-** unborn or unhatched offspring. **-tal**

**feud** (fyūd) quarrel, *esp.* between families, groups, *etc*

**feu'dal·ism** *hist* medieval European system of receiving land from king or lord in return for homage, *etc*

**fe'ver** diseased condition marked by high body heat, thirst, fast pulse, *etc*. **-ish**

**few** (fyū) not many

**fi·an·cé'** *m*, **fi·an·cée'** *f* (-sā) one engaged to be married

**fi·as'co** total failure

**fib** (tell) trivial lie

**fi|ber**, *UK* **-bre** slender threadlike tissue. **-brous;** essential nature; strength

**fi'ber·board** stiff pressed sheets of wood fiber

**fi'ber·glass** spun glass used in insulating, *etc*

**fick'le** changeable, *esp.* in disposition

**fic'tion** something imagined or invented, as a story. **ficti'tious**

**fid'dle** *infml n* violin; *v* play violin; move fingers restlessly; **f. about, around, away** waste (time) on unimportant things; **f. with** occupy o.s. with sth; tamper with

**fi·del'i·ty** faithfulness; loyalty, exactness, as in a copy

**fidg'et** *infml* move about restlessly or uneasily. **-y**

**field** (fēld) any large open space or surface; land cleared for farming; land exploited for oil, minerals, *etc*; area where games are played or battle is fought; competitors in race, *etc*; range or sphere of activity, state, *etc*; area marked by certain effect, as magnetism

**field glasses** device uniting two small telescopes for outdoor use

**fiend** devil; wicked person; *infml* person excessively given to one sport, drug, *etc*. **-ish**

**fierce** (fērs) wild; cruel; raging; overpowering

**fi·er·y** like fire; burning; hot(-tempered); emotional

**fife** *mus* small shrill-toned wind instrument

**fif'|teen'** a number (15). equal to fourteen plus one. **-teenth**

**fifth** *a* next after fourth; *n* one of five equal parts

**fif'|ty** a number (50). equal to five times ten. **-tieth**

**fig** (broad-leaved tree with) soft pear-shaped fruit eaten raw or dried

**fight** (fīt) *v* (**fought**) struggle (against); *n* battle; boxing match; quarrel

**fig'ment** sth imagined

**fig'ur·a·tive** having a symbolic meaning; showing by resemblance. **-ly**

**fig'ure** *n* written sign that represents a number; shape, body, or form; likeness, *usu* of human form, as statue; drawing for illustration; series of dance steps; type or symbol; pattern or design, as in cloth; person, *esp*. in history or book; *v* reckon; *US infml* think; take (important) part in; play a role

**fig'ure·head** person who has office but no duties; small statue at front of ship

**fig·u·rine'** small carved or molded statue

**fil'a·ment** thin thread; wire in electric light bulb

**file** metal tool with cutting ridges for smoothing wood, metal, *etc*; folder, *etc* for keeping papers, records, *etc* in order; papers (on one subject) kept in this way; computer data stored under one label; row of persons or things one behind the other

**fi·let'** (fila), *UK* **fil'let** (filet) cut of meat or fish without bone

**fil'i·al** (filiel) of or fitting for son or daughter

**fil'i·bus·ter** delaying of action in parliament by long speech

**fill** make or become full; occupy the whole space of; satisfy a need or request; accept or hold (task, office); appoint s.o. to (vacant job); stop hole (in tooth, *etc*)

**fil'let** see **filet**

**fill'ing** material inserted into hole (in tooth, etc); food mixture inside pie, etc

**fil'ly** young female horse

**film** thin layer or coating; thin flexible strip, coated with chemicals, used to take pictures; motion picture

**fil'ter** (pass through) device for straining liquids, etc **filtra'tion**

**filth** disgusting dirt; moral corruption; obscene language, etc. **-y**

**fin** winglike steering organ on body of fish; any similar part on rocket, etc

**fi'nal** last; putting an end to; unchangeable. **final'ity**

**fi·nan|ce'**, **fi'nance** n pl funds, esp of government; sing management of money affairs; v provide or acquire money for. **-cial**

**finch** small songbird

**find** (**found**) discover; come upon by chance or by looking for; meet with; be of opinion; obtain; reach verdict

**fine** a of high quality; free of impurities or defects; not coarse or thick; of pleasing effect; showy or elegant; (of weather) good; (of feelings, taste, etc) refined or sensitive; n and v collect (sum of money) as penalty for offense

**fin'er·y** showy dress; ornament

**fi·nesse'** delicate skill; cunning

**fin'ger** n (part of glove covering) one of the five extremities of hand; anything resembling this; v touch with, or turn around in, fingers

**fin'ger-nail** hard horny growth on upper surface of tip of each finger

**fin'ger-print** (unique identifying mark made by) pattern of lines on bottom end of each finger; identifying characteristic or pattern

**fin'ick·y** fussy; too dainty

**fin'ish** come or bring to an end; defeat; treat surface by polishing, etc

**fi'nite** (finīt) having certain definite limits; not endless

**fiord** see **fjord**

**fir** evergreen tree of pine family, bearing erect cones

**fire** n light, heat and flame produced by burning; burning fuel etc; enthusiasm, sparkle, or brilliancy; shooting of guns; v shoot off, as gun; discharge from job; hurl; cause to burn; inspire; provide fuel for fire; bake, as pottery

**fire'arm** gun, pistol, etc

**fire'crack·er** paper tube with explosive powder, set off to make noise

**fire en·gine** vehicle transporting men and equipment to put out fires

**fire es·cape** way out of burning building, *esp.* outside metal stairway

**fire ex·tin·guish·er** (small) portable tank containing chemicals to put out fire

**fire'fly** winged beetle whose tail glows in the dark

**fire'man** person employed to put out fires; person who tends furnace, *etc*

**fire'place** recess in wall to hold an open fire

**fire'proof** that does not easily catch fire or burn

**fire'trap** building hard to get out of in case of fire

**fire'work** *usu pl* firecrackers or rockets which give off light, noise, *etc* when set off; spectacular display

**firm** *a* fixed to particular place; solid, not easily upset or weakened; showing decision and strength; (of prices) steady; *n* commercial company

**fir'ma·ment** the sky

**first** ahead of all others in order, time or rank; next after specified time, place, *etc*; of highest grade; *mus* carrying the melody

**first aid** treatment given at once to victim of accident, *etc* before medical aid is available

**first-class'** of the best or highest quality

**first'hand'** directly from the original source

**fis'cal** of the public treasury; financial

**fish** *n* cold-blooded vertebrate animal, living only in water and breathing only water, *usu* having scale-covered body and fins; *v* (try to) catch fish. **-erman, -ing**; search for sth hidden or buried; seek indirectly

**fish'y** of fish; suspicious

**fis'sion** (fish*en*) a splitting into parts, as atoms, *etc*

**fis'sure** (fish*er*) narrow crack due to splitting

**fist** hand with fingers curled tightly against palm

**fit** *a* suitable for some purpose, activity, *etc*; able to do sth; proper; in good health; *v* be suitable, proper, *etc*; be of right size or shape; make competent or ready (by teaching, giving needed equipment, *etc*); *n* manner in which sth fits; sudden violent attack, as of disease or cramps; sudden outburst, as of anger

**fit'ful** intermittent; irregular

**five** a number (5). equal to four plus one

**fix** make fast or stable; settle (definitely); adjust; arrange; make permanent; repair; direct (eyes, attention) at; (cause to) become solid or set

**fix·a'tion** unhealthy attachment; obsession; emotional tie formed in childhood which hinders further development

**fix'ture** sth or s.o. firmly established; *pl* sth firmly built in, as bath, *etc*

**fiz'zle** make hissing or bubbling sound; fail after a good start

**fjord** (fyord) narrow inlet of sea between high rocks

**flab'ber·gast** astound

**flab'|by** lacking firmness; soft; weak. **-biness**

**flag** *n* cloth with design(s) on it, *usu* fastened to pole, used as symbol of group, country, *etc* or to convey message; flat stone used for paving; (wild) iris; *v* mark (with flags, *etc*); droop or tire

**fla·gel·late** whip, *esp* for religious or sexual reasons. **-lant, flagella'tion**

**fla'gran|t** scandalous. **-cy**

**flag'ship** chief ship in a fleet; most important product of a (large) company

**flag'stone** flat paving stone

**flail** thresh; beat

**flair** natural ability or talent; stylish manner

**flak|e** light thin body or layer of anything, as of snow. **-y**

**flam·boy'ant** showy; richly colored

**flame** (body of) visible burning gas; state of blazing

**fla·min'go** long-legged, long-necked water bird with pink and red plumage

**flam'ma·ble** inflammable

**flange** a projecting flat rim used in machinery

**flank** side of body between ribs and hips; right or left side of building, body of troops, *etc*

**flan'nel** soft, loosely-woven woolen cloth

**flap** *n* movable part attached at one side (to cover opening, as of pocket); *v* hang loosely; move to and fro with beating motion, as wings

**flare** *v* blaze with unsteady light; spread or open outward gradually, as skirt; **f. up** become suddenly angry; *n* (sudden) blaze of light; blazing light used as signal

**flash** break forth in sudden flame; gleam; appear for a moment; send by telegraph, radio, *etc* as news; move swiftly; come to mind suddenly

**flash'back** return to past event, *esp* in film

**flash'bulb** lamp used to provide very bright, momentary light in photography

**flash'light** small battery-run electric light

**flash'y** showy, cheap

**flask** flat bottle for liquor, *etc*

**flat** *a* level; smooth; lying spread out; broad but not very deep; downright; *mus* below correct pitch; dull or depressed; having the air let out; tasteless; *n* level ground; *UK* apartment; tire without air. **-ten**

**flat'ter** praise (overmuch). **-y**

**flaunt** show off

**fla'vor,.** *UK* **-vour** (of food, drink) typical taste; special characteristic quality

**fla'vor·ing,** *UK* **-vour-** used to give food special taste

**flaw** *n* imperfection; defect; *v* make imperfect

**flax** plant yielding oil and fiber, for linen

**flay** strip of skin

**flea** tiny jumping insect which feeds on blood

**fleck** spot; speck; patch of color

**fledg'ling** bird which has just learned to fly; inexperienced person

**flee (fled)** run away, as from danger

**fleece** *n* sheep's wool. **-y**; *v* cut wool from sheep; *infml* cheat or rob s.o. by trick

**fleet** *n* group of ships, *etc* under one command or management; *a* swift

**fleet'ing** brief; passing quickly

**flesh** soft parts of (animal) body between skin and bones; pulp of fruit or vegetable; human body, as distinct from soul

**flew** see **fly**

**flex'i·ble** capable of being bent without breaking; easily managed; adaptable. **flexibil'ity**

**flick** light snapping stroke

**flick'er** flutter; give light unsteadily

**fli'er, fly'er** pilot of airplane; fast train or bus; reckless chance; advertising leaflet for mass distribution

**flight** act or manner of flying; distance flown at one time; stairs from one floor to the next; flying group of birds or insects; act of running away, *esp.* from danger

**flight'ly** subject to sudden moods; irresponsible. **-i-ness**

**flim'sy** easily destroyed; not strong; thin. **-iness**

**flinch** draw back (from fear, *etc*)

**fling (flung)** *v* throw, *esp.* suddenly or forcibly; toss, as dice; *n* time of indulgence; athletic dance

**flint** (piece of) hard stone which strikes fire with steel. **-y**

**flip** throw or turn over (with the fingertips)

**flip'pant** lacking in earnestness; disrespectful. **-cy**

**flip'per** broad flat limb of seals, *etc*, used for swim-

**fluctuate**

ming; broad rubber shoe, used for skin-diving

**flirt** arouse (sexual) interest without serious intent; play with (idea, danger, *etc*)

**float** *v* rest or move on surface of liquid; hang, as dust in air; (of stock) put on market; allow price of money to vary freely; *n* sth that floats, as a raft, cork on fishing line, *etc*; (vehicle carrying) display in parade; soft drink with ice cream in it

**flock** *n* group of animals, *esp* birds, sheep or goats; crowd of people; small bits of wool, *etc* for filling cushions, *etc*; *v* move together in large numbers

**floe** sheet of floating ice

**flog** whip

**flood** tide; great flow of rising water that overruns the land; any great stream or flow, as of words, light, *etc*

**flood'gate** device to control flow from body of water

**flood'light** (lamp producing) broad beam of bright light, used to light sports arenas, *etc*

**floor** *n* bottom surface of room; any ground surface; story of building; main part of meeting-room; **the f.** the right to speak before a meeting; *v* install f.; knock down; *infml* defeat

**flop** flap about; throw oneself heavily or carelessly (into chair, *etc*); fail

**flop'py disk'** piece of magnetic plastic for storing computer data

**flo'ra** plant life of region, period, *etc*

**flo'ral** of or like flowers

**flor'id** too flowery in style; flushed with red. **-ly**

**flo'rist** person who sells flowers

**flot'sam** floating wreckage

**floun'der** *v* struggle (along), as in mud; make mistakes; *n* flat saltwater food fish

**flour** powder made by fine grinding of wheat or other grain

**flour'ish** (flur-) *v* grow healthily; be successful; wave about, as a sword; *n* ornament in handwriting; *mus* fanfare

**flout** mock; insult

**flow** move along as a liquid or stream does; (of tide) rise; move easily and smoothly, as talk, poetry, *etc*; hang or fall loosely, as dress

**flow'chart** diagram showing movement, *etc* within a complex system

**flow'er** (colorful) part of plant producing seed or fruit; state of blooming; best part

**flown** see **fly**

**flu** *infml* influenza

**fluc'tu·ate** rise and fall; change irregularly

**flue** channel (in chimney) for heat or smoke

**flu'ent** speaking or writing quickly and easily; flowing. **-cy**

**fluff** n light feathery bits or mass, as of wool; v shake into feathery mass. **-y**

**flu'id** (substance) capable of flowing freely; not fixed. **fluid'ity**

**fluke** infml lucky chance

**flung** see **fling**

**flunk** US infml (cause to) fail in an examination

**flun'ky**, UK **-key** (uniformed) servant; fawning person

**flu·o·res'cence** light given off by certain substances when exposed to ultraviolet or X-rays. **-cent**

**flu'o·ri·date** add fluoride to (water supply)

**flu'o·ride** chemical compound which helps to prevent tooth decay

**flur'ry** sudden disturbance or excitement; sudden wind or light snowfall

**flush** v make clean by running water through, as toilet; (of face) turn hot and red with rush of blood due to excitement, illness, etc; a even with a surface; infml well-supplied (with money); n set of cards of same suit

**flus'ter** make nervous or confused

**flute** musical pipe; groove

**flut'ter** flap wings; move in air, as flag; move quickly or jerkily

**flux** a (state of) flowing; series of changes; unhealthy discharge from bowels, etc

**fly** v (**flew, flown**) move through the air on wings; be carried in, or guide flight, of, airplane; float in air; pass (quickly) through air; move swiftly; n small two-winged insect, esp. housefly; flap covering zipper, etc of trousers; flap forming door of tent

**fly'leaf** blank leaf at front or back of book

**fly'wheel** heavy wheel for equalizing speed of machinery

**foal** young horse

**foam** mass of tiny bubbles formed on liquid, skin etc; chemical froth used to put out fires; froth of saliva; lightweight buble-filled material of rubber or plastic

**fo'cus** (pl **fo'cus·es** or **fo'ci** [fōkesiz, fōsī]) point at which rays meet; center of interest, activity, etc. **-cal**

**fod'der** dried hay, etc fed to cattle

**foe** enemy

**foe'tus** see **fetus**

**fog** (cover over with) thick mist; (produce) confused or unclear state. **-gy**

**fo'gy** old-fashioned person

**footnote**

**foi'ble** weak point in character

**foil** *n* paper-thin sheet metal; sth which provides contrast to another; light sword for fencing; *v* outwit; defeat

**foist** impose sth unwanted on another; pass off fake as sth genuine

**fold** *v* bend (paper, cloth, *etc*) over upon itself; bend back or down; bend parts of thing together so as to form compact mass; (of limbs) press together; enclose, wrap; *n* part that is folded, as of cloth; enclosure, *esp.* for sheep

**fold'er** folded cardboard cover for papers

**fo'liage** leaves of tree, *etc*

**fo'li·o** (size of) book page; leaf of paper

**folk** people of a nation or race; *pl* people in general; *pl* members of one's family

**fol'low** go or come after (in natural order, time, *etc*); pursue moving thing or person; go along (path, *etc*); accept leadership or be admirer of; result from; act according to (advice, law, *etc*); observe; understand. **-er**

**fol'ly** foolishness; want of good sense; unprofitable undertaking

**fo·ment'** stir up, as discontent

**fond** loving; tender; (foolishly) doting

**fon'dle** touch or stroke lovingly

**fon·due'** dish of melted, flavored cheese; bits of meat or fruit dipped into hot oil, melted chocolate, *etc*

**food** what is eaten, *esp.* if solid; any kind of (solid) nourishment

**fool** *n* one who lacks sense; *hist* jester; **make f. of** trick or make appear ridiculous. **-ish** *v* deceive; joke; **f. around** potter aimlessly; **f. away** waste (time or money)

**fool'har·dy** foolishly bold

**fools'cap** paper measuring 13 x 16 inches

**fool'proof** so simple, *etc* as to exclude error or failure

**foot** *n* (*pl* **feet**) part of leg below ankle, on which person or animal stands; anything similar to this in position or use; lower or lowest end or part; measure of length, equal to 12 inches; unit of verse with *usu* one stressed syllable; *v infml* pay, as bill

**foot'ball** air-filled ball; game played with it

**foot'hold** firm place for feet to stand on; base for advancing further

**foot'ing** firm placing of the feet; relative position or base

**foot'lights** *pl* row of lights at front of stage floor

**foot'note** note at bottom of

page containing additional information

**fop** man vain about his appearance. **-pish**

**for** prep toward an aim or goal: *leave f. home*; in order to gain: *work f. money*; in return or instead of: *an eye f. an eye*; as being: *take s.o. f. honest*; because of: *chosen f. her beauty*; in spite of: *admirable, f. all his faults*; amounting to: *a check f. five dollars*; during: *f. many years*; representing: *he stands f. his country*; on behalf of: *he did it f. her*; *conj* because: *I know it is sweet, for I have tasted it*

**for'age** n food for animals; v hunt for food; search for

**for'ay** raid; excursion

**for'bear'** (**for-bore'**, **for-borne'**) v do without; refrain from doing; be patient. **-ance**

**for'bear** n see **forebear**

**for-bid'** (**-bade** or **-bad**, **-bid'den**) command not to do; not permit; prevent

**for-bid'ding** causing fear

**force** n strength, energy, or active power; (of argument, words, *etc*) power to convince; vividness; (of law, *etc*) binding effect; organized body of soldiers, policemen, *etc*; power or violence exerted on a person or thing; v do violence to; compel; get, win

or overcome by violence; strain; hasten, as growth, by artificial means

**for'ceps** (surgical) pincers

**for'ci-ble** of or done by force

**ford** shallow river crossing

**fore** n front; a, adv in or towards the front

**fore'arm** part of arm between elbow and hand

**fore'bear** usu pl forefather

**fore'bode** create feeling of coming misfortune

**fore-bod'ing** omen; feeling of approaching evil

**fore-cast'** tell beforehand, as the weather

**fore-clo'se'** reclaim property for failure to pay mortgage. **-sure**

**fore'fin-ger** finger next to thumb

**fore-go'** (**-went, -gone**) precede

**fore'go-ing** (the one) preceding

**fore-gone'** previous; **f. conclusion** certain or foreseeable result

**fore'ground** part of landscape, scene, *etc* that is nearest to viewer

**fore'head** (forid) part of face above eyes

**for'eign** of, to, about or in a country other than one's own. **-er**; not related to what is being said or done; not belonging

**fore'man** chief man in a group, as of workers

**fore'most** first in place, order or importance

**fore·or·dain'** decide or fix beforehand

**fore'run·ner** person or thing that comes before another and prepares the way for, or indicates, his or its coming

**for·see'** see or know beforehand

**fore·shad'ow** be sign of event to follow

**fore·short'en** draw detail in picture shorter to give natural effect

**fore'sight** power to know of sth beforehand; care or provision for the future

**fore'skin** fold of skin at end of penis

**for'est** large area covered with trees. **-er, -ry**

**fore·stall'** prevent sth by acting beforehand

**fore'taste** advance sample, as sign or warning

**fore·tell'** tell of event to happen

**fore'thought** thinking beforehand; care for the future

**for·ev'er(·more)** for time without limit; always

**fore·went'** see **forego**

**fore'wom·an** female foreman

**fore'word** short introduction to book, *etc*

**for'feit** (-fit) thing lost owing to crime or fault; penalty;

price. **-ture**

**for·gave'** see **forgive**

**forge** *n* place where metal is worked; *v* shape by heating and hammering; imitate (signature, *etc*) for dishonest purpose. **-er, -ery; f. ahead** make way (under difficulties)

**for·get'** (-got', -got'ten) lose memory of; neglect to do by failing to remember. **f. o.s.** lose one's temper; behave in unsuitable way

**for·get'-me-not** (herb with) small, *usu* bright blue flower

**for·give'** (for·gave', forgiv'en) stop feeling angry with s.o. for wrongs done; pardon

**for·go'** (-went, -gone) give up; refrain from

**for·got', for·got'ten** see **forget**

**fork** tool with two or more prongs, used for picking up, holding or tossing things; one of two or more parts into which road, river, tree, *etc* divides; place where this division starts

**for·lorn'** deserted; in pitiful condition

**for|m** *n* shape as distinguished from content; mold used to give shape; general plan or design (of a work of art); condition, *esp.* of athlete; printed document with blank spaces where information is to be written; v give (certain) shape to; make up or be part of a whole; develop, as a habit; arrange in a certain order; take shape. **-mative, forma'tion**

**for'mal** of the outward form; following a set ceremonial; having the form without the spirit; stiffly correct. **formalis'tic, formal'ity**

**for'mat** size, shape, *etc* of sth, *esp.* a book; plan of organization

**for'mer** earlier in time. **-ly**; the first of two things, *etc*

**for'mi·da·ble** arousing fear; hard to overcome

**for'mu·la** (*pl* **-las, -lae** [-lē]) set form of words for ritual, *etc*; fixed rule; rule, fact *etc* written in symbols; list of (chemical) ingredients; *US* milk substitute for babies

**for'mu·late** express in a formula; state clearly

**for·sake'** (**-sook, -sak'en**) give up; leave entirely

**for·swear'** (**-swore, -sworn**) promise to give up

**forth** onward; out into view

**forth·com·ing** about to appear or happen

**forth'right** straightforward; outspoken

**forth·with'** at once

**for·ti·fi·ca'tion** sth that strengthens, *esp.* structures for military defense

**for'ti·fy** strengthen (phys-

**for'ti·tude** bravery in meeting pain or danger

**fort'night** period of two weeks

**For'tran** computer language, used *esp.* for scientific calculations

**for'tress** fortified place

**for·tu'i·tous** happening by chance

**for'tu|ne** chance; (good or bad) luck; fate; wealth. **-nate**

**for'|ty** a number (40), equal to four times ten. **-tieth**

**fo'rum** (place of) public discussion

**for'ward** a near, toward or belonging to the front part; ahead of the ordinary; (of persons) impertinent; *adv* (also **for'wards**) to(wards) the front; v send ahead or on, as mail; help get ahead

**for·went'** see **forgo**

**fos'sil** hardened remains in earth's crust of ancient plants or animals; out-of-date person or thing. **-ize** (*UK* **-ise**)

**fos'ter** a giving nourishment and care, though not related; v care for; nourish; encourage

**fought** see **fight**

**foul** disgusting to the senses, *esp.* to sense of smell; very dirty; (of weather) wet and stormy; morally offensive or unclean; against the rules of a game; entangled, as rope

**foun·d** lay base of; begin building; set up (hospital, *etc*) and provide with funds.

**founda'tion;** melt and mold (metals). **-dry**

**founded** see **find**

**found'ling** baby found after unknown parents have deserted it

**foun'tain** water spring; jet of water; source

**four** a number (4), equal to three plus one; **on all fours** on hands and knees

**four·teen'** a number (14), equal to thirteen plus one. **-teenth**

**fourth** *a* next after third; *n* one of four equal parts

**fowl** any bird; farm bird, *esp.* hen, kept for eggs and meat

**fox** bushy-tailed animal of dog family, *usu* red in color and known for its cunning

**fox'trot** (music for) ballroom dance in $^4/_4$ time

**fra'cas** (frak-) noisy quarrel

**frac'tion** (small) part of whole

**frac'ture** *n* breaking, *esp.* of bone; *v* (cause to) break

**frag'ile** (fraj-) easily broken; delicate. **fragil'ity**

**frag'men|t** part broken off; incomplete part. **-tary**

**fra'|grant** (frā-) sweet or pleasant of smell. **-grance**

**frail** weak; easily broken. **-ty**

**frame** *n* border of wood, *etc* for picture; structure of parts fitted together, as skeleton of house, *etc*; any structure of fitted parts; build of body; state (of mind); *v* shape, *esp.* by fitting parts together; compose, as law, poem, *etc*; shape (words with lips); imagine, as idea; put border around picture; *infml* bring false charge against or invent evidence to make innocent person seem guilty

**fran'chise** right to vote; sales license

**frank** open or straightforward in speech; undisguised

**frank'furt·er** seasoned reddish sausage of beef, pork, *etc*, in US also called hot dog or wiener

**fran'tic** wildly excited (with fear, *etc*)

**fra·ter'nal** brotherly

**fra·ter'ni·ty** group with common interests; *US* club of male college students

**frat'er·nize** make friends with; associate with (enemy). **fraterniza'tion**

**frat'ri·cide** murder(er) of one's own brother

**fraud** deceit for criminal purpose; impostor. **-ulent**

**fraught** (frawt) laden with; full of; accompanied by

**fray** *n* fight; battle; *v* wear through by rubbing; become ragged at edge

**freak** sudden unexplainable change of mind; any abnormal specimen, as animal with two heads

**freck'le** small brownish spot on skin, *esp.* on face or arms

**free** (fre'er, fre'est) (frē, frēer, frēist) not confined; having full social rights; not subject to domination by, or will of, others; not subject to limitations or rules; clear of obstacles; (of chemicals) not combined with others; open to all, as game; loose; not paying attention to rules of social behavior; without charge; generous; (of translations) not literal; frank

**free'dom** state of being free or acting freely

**free'lance** (person) working in some professional field but with no fixed employer

**freeze** (froze, fro'zen) become hard or solid due to cold; reach temperature at which water becomes ice; store (food) at temperatures below this level; die of frost or cold; stop upward or downward movement of prices, rents, *etc*, *usu* by government order; be chilled by cold, fear, *etc*

**freeze'-dry** preserve (food) by freezing and removing ice crystals in a vacuum

**freez'er** room or compartment for freezing or keeping food frozen

**freight** (frāt) transport of goods; price paid for this; goods transported

**fren'|zy** wild excitement; (fit of) madness. **-zied**

**fre'quen|t** *a* happening often or in close succession. **-cy**

**fre'quent** *v* visit often

**fres'co** (method of) painting made on wet plaster of wall, *etc*

**fresh** newly made, arrived, met with, *etc*; another; (of water) not salty; (of food) in natural unpreserved state; not faded, stale or worn; (of air) cool or pure; looking or being healthy; (of wind) of medium strength; forward; impolite

**fresh'man** first-year (college) student

**fret** worry; chafe at sth; wear away. **-ful**

**fric·as·see'** dish of cut-up meat with sauce

**fric'tion** rubbing of one surface against another

**Fri'day** fifth day of week, between Thursday and Saturday

**friend** (frend) person who shares mutual regard and affection with another; supporter; one who is not an enemy. **-ship**

**fright** (frīt) sudden strong fear; one who looks grotesque or shocking. **-en, -ful**

**frig'id** (frijid) cold; without feeling; stiff. **frigid'ity**

**frill** decorative band of material; *etc*; *usu pl infml* sth not essential

**fringe** (frinj) ornamental border of hanging threads; outskirts; edge; **f. benefit** privilege granted by employer in addition to wages

**frisk** dance or leap around

**frit'ter** *n* fruit, *etc* dipped in batter and fried in oil; *v* **f. away** waste (time, money, *etc*)

**friv'o·lous** not serious; not worthy of notice; silly. **frivol'ity**

**friz'zly, friz'zy** curly, *esp.* hair

**fro: to and f.** back and forth

**frog** tailless web-footed jumping animal living both on land and in water: hoarseness in throat

**frol'ic** frisk about merrily. **-some**

**from** *prep* expressing: starting point: *f. this day on*; removal or seperation: *he took the papers from her*; source: *a man f. New York*; cause: *sick f. over-eating*; distinction: *tell one f. the other*

**front** (frunt) foremost part of anything; place or position directly before anything; (foremost) line of battle; union of various groups for a particular purpose; area of activity; boundary between masses of warm and cold air; person or object used to conceal the actual agent

**front'age** front (extent) of building or land

**fron'tier** (frontir) boundary between countries; border of inhabited or explored area; border of knowledge

**frost** *n* white powder of ice crystals which forms on cold surfaces; process or temperature of freezing; weather with temperature below freezing; *v* cover with ice crystals; make glass opaque by coating; cover cake, *etc* with frosting

**frost'bite** dangerous condition in which part of body is frozen by exposure to cold

**frost'ing** mixture of sugar, egg whites, *etc* for covering cake, *etc* **-y**

**froth** mass of small bubbles; foam. **-y**

**frown** wrinkle brow. *esp.* in displeasure or thought

**froze, fro'zen** see **freeze**

**fru'gal** economical; sparing in use; costing little. **frugal'ity**

**fruit** seed-bearing part of plant, often used as food, as cherry, apple, *etc*; offspring; product or result. **-ful**

**fru·i'tion** fulfillment (of hopes, plans, *etc*); state of bearing fruit

**frus'trate** defeat (attempts); disappoint; thwart (person)

**fry** v (**fried**) cook in fat; young of fish or other small animals

**fudge** soft candy containing sugar, chocolate, *etc*

**fu'el** material for burning as source of heat or power

**fu'gi·tive** (fyūji-) n person who flees from police, *etc*; a fleeting; quickly passing; having fled or run away

**ful'crum** support on which a lever turns

**ful·fill'**, UK **-fil** carry out, as promise; satisfy; bring to an end. **-ment**

**full** a containing as much as can be held; complete; coming to a given or usual limit: *f. moon*; (of clothes) having many folds; containing many or much: *house f. of people*; plump; rich; adv exactly: *hit him f. in the face*; quite: *know f. well*

**full'-blood·ed** of pure ancestry; vigorous

**full-blown'** in full bloom; fully mature

**ful'mi·nate** explode (with loud noise); express angry opposition

**fum'ble** handle clumsily; grope about

**fume** n (offensive) smoke or vapor; v give off fumes; be angry

**fu'mi·gate** (fyū-) expose to

fumes so as to kill insects, germs, *etc*

**fun** (activity giving rise to) pleasure and merriment; **for** or **in f.** meant as a joke; **make f. of** expose to unkind laughter

**func'tion** activity proper to person, thing, *etc*; duty or office; formal public ceremony. **-al**

**func'tion·ar·y** an official

**fund** supply; sum of money, *etc*, *esp*. for specific purpose; *pl* money available

**fun·da·men'tal** of the basis or foundation; primary; essential

**fu'ner·al** ceremony at which dead person is buried, cremated, *etc*

**fun'gus** (pl **-gi** or **-guses**) mushroom or similar plant, including molds

**fun'nel** cone-shaped tube for pouring liquid, *etc* into smaller opening; smokestack; air shaft

**fun'ny** giving rise to laughter; amusing; strange or odd

**fur** hairy coat of certain animals, as bear, beaver, *etc*; skin with this hair used for outer garments or trimming; any coating resembling this. **-ry**

**fur'bish** polish up; make sth look new

**fu'ri·ous** full of rage; violent; with great energy, speed, *etc*

**furl** roll up (sail, flag, *etc*)

**fur'lough** (-lō) leave of absence, *esp.* that of soldier

**fur'nace** structure in which heat is produced for houses, *etc*

**fur'nish** supply; fit (house *etc* with furniture)

**fur'ni·ture** movable objects, such as beds, chairs, tables, *etc* used in dwellings, offices, *etc*

**fu'rore** fashionable craze; uproar

**fur'row** narrow rut (made by plow); facial wrinkle, *esp.* of forehead

**fur'ther** *adv* to or at a greater distance in time, space, or development; in addition; to greater extent; *a* farther; additional; *v* promote (cause, *etc*)

**fur'ther·more** in addition

**fur'thest** most distant

**fur'tive** done secretly; sly

**fu'ry** wild anger or rage; violence; goddess of revenge; angry woman

**fuse** *v* melt together; blend by melting. **-ible, fusibil'ity;** *n* safety device in electric circuit; device for exploding bomb, *etc*

**fu'se·lage** body of airplane

**fu·si·lade'** continuous discharge of shots; outburst, *esp.* of criticism

**fu'sion** (fyūzhen) joining together (as if) by melting

**fuss** unnecessary or exaggerated excitement or activity

**fu'tile** useless; not successful. **futil'ity**

**fu'ture** (fyūcher) (what will be or happen in) time to come

**fuzz** (mass of) loose, fluffy matter

# G

**g** seventh letter of English alphabet

**gab'ar·dine** strong woven cloth, used *esp.* for coats

**ga'ble** triangular part of wall at end of roof

**gadg'et** small mechanical device

**gag** sth placed in or over mouth to prevent person from speaking; joke or comic effect (used by comedian)

**gage** see **gauge**

**gai'e·ty** state of being cheerful or merry; merrymaking

**gain** get, *esp.* sth useful, desired, *etc*; make, as profit; get an increase or addition, as weight; arrive at, as goal; make progress; (of clock) run too fast; **g. on** get nearer (to s.o. or sth chased)

**gain·say'** deny; speak against

**gait** way of walking; pace

**ga'la** festive occasion

**gal'ax·y** one of the large

groups of stars which make up the universe; brilliant gathering. **galac'tic**

**gale** strong wind; sudden burst, *esp.* of laughter

**gall** *n* secretion of liver; anything very bitter; bitterness; *v* make sore by rubbing; make angry

**gal'lant** brave; polite to women. **-ry**

**gall'blad·der** sac containing gall from liver

**gal'ler·y** room or group of rooms used for showing works of art; balcony inside theater, *etc*; covered walk, open at one or both sides; long narrow passage

**gal'ley** kitchen of ship or airplane; old type of ship using sails and oars

**gal'li·vant** *infml* roam about

**gal'lon** liquid measure, equal to four quarts

**gal'lop** (a ride or run at) fastest pace of horse, *etc*

**gal'lows** *hist* wooden frame for hanging criminals

**gall'stone** unnatural stone formed in gallbladder

**ga·lore'** in plenty

**ga·losh'** *usu pl* waterproof (rubber) overshoe

**gal'va·nize** rouse as if by electricity; coat with metal (by electricity)

**gam'bit** chess opening in which piece is given up to

gain advantage; opening remark; trick

**gam'ble** play dice, cards, *etc* for stakes; take risk on sth whose outcome is uncertain. **-bler**

**gam'bol** frisk about

**game** *n* contest under agreed rules; pastime or amusement; wild animals hunted for sport or food; *a* having courage; lame

**gam·ma glob'u·lin** blood plasma rich in antibodies, used against certain diseases

**gam'ma ray** *usu pl* type of X-ray given off by radioactive substance

**gam'ut** whole scale or range

**gan'der** male goose

**gang** group of criminals; group of persons working or playing together; set of similar instruments connected to act together, as saws

**gan'gling** tall and clumsy

**gang'plank** movable bridge to enter or leave ship

**gan·grene'** dying of body tissue due to lack of circulation

**gang'ster** member of criminal gang

**gang'way** passage between seats, *etc*

**gaol** (jāl) *UK* jail. **-er**

**gap** opening due to break, missing part, *etc*

**gape** open (mouth) wide; stare at

**ga·rage'** (-rahzh') building

where automobiles are kept or repaired

**garb** (distinctive) clothing

**gar·bage** kitchen waste, refuse; trashy literature; worthless ideas, *etc*

**gar·ble** distort or corrupt (text, *etc*)

**gar·den** piece of ground used for growing flowers, vegetables or fruits. **-er**

**gar·de·ni·a** (tropical shrub with) fragrant white or yellow flower

**gar·gle** rinse throat with liquid kept in motion by blowing air from lungs

**gar·ish** gaudy; glaring

**gar·land** wreath of flowers

**gar·lic** (plant with) strong-scented bulb, used in cooking

**gar·ment** article of clothing

**gar·ner** gather; collect

**gar·net** dark red gem; (of) this color

**gar·nish** decorate, *esp* food

**gar·ret** room in building just under the roof

**gar·ru·lous** given to talk; wordy. **garru·lity**

**gar·ter** elastic band to hold up stocking

**gas** substance whose molecules move freely and can expand indefinitely; any of various kinds of this, used for heating, as light source, *etc*. **-eous**

**gash** deep long cut

**gas·ket** packing to prevent escape of liquid, *etc* in pipes or joints

**gas·o·line** *US* liquid distilled from petroleum, used as engine fuel, as solvent, *etc*

**gasp** catch breath suddenly; struggle for breath; speak convulsively, as if unable to breathe

**gas·tric** of the stomach

**gas·tron·o·my** art of good cooking

**gate** movable entrance barrier across opening in fence, wall, *etc*; means of entrance or exit, *esp.* at an airport; total admission fees or spectators at (sports) event; device for regulating flow of water, steam, *etc*, in canal, pipe, *etc*

**gath·er** collect; bring or come together; pick (crops, *etc*); develop gradually, as speed; understand or guess; take (person) into one's arms; collect one's wits, *etc*; draw into folds, as material, brow, *etc*

**gaud·y** (vulgarly) showy

**gauge** (gāj) (standard) measure; measuring instrument; thickness of wire, *etc*; width of barrel of gun; distance between rails of railroad

**gaunt** unusually thin; worn-looking. **-ness**

**gauze** thin transparent fabric

**gave** see **give**

**gav'el** chairman's, judge's or auctioneer's hammer

**gawk'y** bashful; awkward

**gay** glad, light-hearted, happy; (of colors, *etc*) bright; *infml* homosexual. **-ness, gai'ety**

**gaze** look steadily

**ga·zelle'** small graceful antelope with soft beautiful eyes

**ga·zette'** (official) journal

**gear** device for transmitting motion; part of machinery with special function, as for steering, landing, *etc*; equipment; *infml* clothes

**gear'shift** lever for changing gears of engine

**geese** *pl* of **goose**

**Gei'ger coun'ter** device for detecting and measuring radioactivity

**gel·a·tin,** *UK* **-tine** clear substance forming basis of jellies, glues, *etc*

**geld'ing** castrated animal, *esp.* horse

**gem** precious cut stone

**gen'der** set of classes in which nouns are grouped; sex

**gene** (jēn) cell unit by which hereditary characteristics are passed on to offspring

**ge·ne·al'o·gy** (investigation of) line of family descent. **genealog'ical**

**gen'e·ra** *pl* of **genus**

**gen'er·al** *a* of or affecting all members of a class, *etc*; done by, or common to, many or the most part; not specific or detailed; *n* high-ranking officer in army or air force; **in g.** usually; as a rule

**gen·er·al·ize,** *UK* **-ise** make general; draw general conclusion from facts; make general statements; speak vaguely. **-ity. generaliza'-tion**

**gen'er·ate** bring into existence; produce. **-tive**

**gen·er·a'tion** period of about 30 years; all persons or family members born at about the same time; production; act of generating

**gen'er·a·tor** machine which turns mechanical into electrical energy; machine which produces gas, steam, *etc*

**ge·ner'ic** of a whole group or class; not protected by trademark

**gen'er·ous** free in giving; not mean or small; plentiful. **generos'ity**

**gen'e·sis** origin; production; creation

**ge·net'ic code'** individual pattern of genes guiding development of any living thing

**ge·net'ics** scientific study of heredity

**gen'ial** (jēnyel) cheerful; friendly. **genial'ity**

**gen'i·tal** *a* of generation or the organs of generation; *n pl* the external sex organs

**gen'ius** (jēnyes) (person with) unusually high intellectual or artistic power; spirit of place, person *etc*; distinctive character, as of nation, period, *etc*

**gen'o·cide** (je-) planned destruction of a people

**gen·teel'** (jentēl) (affectedly) polite or well-bred

**gen'tile** (jentīl) (person, *esp.* a Christian, who is) not Jewish

**gen·til'i·ty** (affected) politeness or refinement

**gen'tle** kind or friendly; soft and soothing; not rough or violent; tame, as horse

**gen'tle·man** man of good family; man characterized by fine feelings, good education, consideration for others, *etc*

**gen·tri·fi·ca'tion** redevelopment of rundown city areas, *usu* at the expense of poor people

**gen'u·ine** real; sincere. **-ness**

**ge'nus** (*pl* **gen'er·a**) class or group

**ge·og'ra·phy** science of the earth's surface, climate, political divisions, *etc*; physical arrangement (of particular area, *etc*). **geograph'ical**

**ge·ol'o·gy** science of the earth's crust and its changes. **geolog'ical**

**ge·om'e·try** science of the properties and relations of lines, surfaces and solids.

**geomet'rical**

**ge·o·po·li'tics** politics as influenced by geographical factors

**ge·ra'ni·um** (jirā-) (garden plant with clusters of) red, pink or white flowers

**ger·i·at'rics** medical branch dealing with diseases and problems of old age

**germ** tiny organism causing disease; living substance that can develop into (part of) new organism

**ger'mi·cide** substance that kills germs

**ger'mi·nal** creative; in the earliest stage of development

**ger'mi·nate** begin to grow; sprout; produce

**ger·on·tol'o·gy** scientific study of aging

**ges·ta'tion** act or period of carrying offspring in womb till birth

**ges·tic'u·late** express ideas, *etc* by or with motions, *esp.* of hands and arms

**ges'ture** movement of body, *esp.* hands, to express idea, *etc*

**get** (**got**, **got** or *US* **got'ten**) obtain by effort, asking, *etc*; receive; reach, as destination; (of disease) catch; (cause to) be in specified condition: *g. one's feet wet*; (cause to) move or be taken away: *g. these books out of* *here*; make ready: *g. supper*; persuade: *g. her to come along*; become: *he gets tired early*; **g. along** manage; move ahead; have (specified) success; be on friendly terms; **g. off** come down from; **g. through** finish, as work

**gey'ser** (gizer) natural spring emitting jets of hot water and steam from time to time

**ghast'ly** horrible; shocking; deathly pale

**ghet'to** part of city inhabited by minority group(s) because of legal, social or economic pressure

**ghost** (spirit of) dead person which supposedly appears to the living; faint shadow; false second image on film, *etc*; **g.** (**writer**) person who writes books, *etc* for s. o. else

**gi'ant** (jī-) legendary being similar to man but of enormous size; very large person, animal, *etc*; person of unusual talent

**gib'ber·ish** (jib-, gib-) senseless talk; chatter

**gib'bon** (gib-) smallest of manlike apes

**gibe** (jib) mock; jeer

**gid'dy** (g-) (causing to be) dizzy; light-headed. **-diness**

**gift** sth given as present; natural talent. **-ed**

**gi·gan'tic** (jī-) like a giant; huge

**gig'gle** (g-) laugh in silly way

**gild** (gild'ed or gilt) (g-) cover with thin layer of gold; make brighter or more pleasing; see also **guild**

**gill** (g-) breathing organ of fish

**gilt** *n* thin layer of gold; *a* covered with gilt; golden in color

**gim'mick** (g-) *infml* sth to attract attention

**gin** (j-) alcoholic liquor; machine for removing seeds from cotton; trap for animals

**gin'ger** (jinjer) (tropical plant with) hot spicy root, used in cooking, *etc*; (of) orange-brown color

**ging'ham** (g-) cotton fabric

**gin·gi·vi'tis** (jinje-) painful swelling of the gums

**gip'sy** (j-) see **gypsy**

**gi·raffe'** (j-) cud-chewing African animal with very long neck, tallest of four-footed animals

**gird** (gird'ed or girt) fasten to or around, as sword; prepare o. s. (mentally) for action

**gird'er** main horizontal supporting beam

**gir'dle** light corset reaching from top of legs to waist

**girl** female child; female servant; sweetheart

**girth** measurement around anything

**gist** (j-) main points or substance of a matter

**give** (gave, giv'en) hand over or let another have sth in one's possession, *esp.* without return; deliver or put at another's disposal; utter, as shout, answer, *etc*; grant, as favor; pledge (one's word); supply: *a lamp gives light*; offer: *he gave her his hand*; yield to force: *the floor gave beneath his weight*; cause to or let have: *gave me a headache, gives him the right*; **g. in** admit defeat; **g. up** abandon; stop (doing); pronounce hopeless or insoluble; stop trying to fight against

**giz'zard** stomach of a bird for grinding food

**gla'cier** (glä'sher) slow-moving mass of ice

**glad** happy; causing joy

**glad'i·a·tor** fighter (*esp.* at ancient Roman shows)

**glad·i·o'||lus**, also **-la** (*pl* **-li**) plant with sword-shaped leaves and spikes of brilliantly colored flowers

**glam'or**, UK **-our** fascinating (deceptive) charm. **-ous**

**glance** look briefly; flash; **g. off** bounce off sth instead of hitting it squarely

**gland** organ of secretion in body. **-ular**

**glare** shine with strong dazzling light; look at fiercely; be conspicuous

**glass** hard brittle, *usu* transparent substance, made by melting sand together with other chemicals and used for windows, dishes, *etc*. **-y**; *pl* eyeglasses

**glass'house** greenhouse

**glau·co·ma** eye disease marked by increased pressure in eye, which can lead to blindness

**gla|ze** fit (window frame) with glass. **-zier;** coat with thin surface or layer resembling glass; (of eye) become glassy

**gleam** faint glow of light

**glean** gather slowly and in small bits (what is left by others). **-ings** *n pl*

**glee** joy; unaccompanied song for three or more voices

**glen** narrow valley

**glib** fluent and easy (but insincere) in talking or writing; slick. **-ness**

**glide** move with smooth quiet continuous motion; (of airplane) float through air without engine power

**glid'er** plane with no engine which floats on air currents after being pulled into the air

**glim'mer** shine faintly or unsteadily

**glimpse** brief view

**glint** flash; glitter

**glis'ten** (glisn) shine with damp luster

# glitter

**glit'ter** shine brilliantly; sparkle

**gloat** look or dwell on sth with (evil) satisfaction

**glob|e** sphere, *esp.* the earth. **-al, -ular**

**globe'trot·ter** person who travels widely. **-ting**

**glob'ule** tiny round drop of (oily) liquid

**gloom** darkness; depressed mood or atmosphere. **-y**

**glo'|ry** *n* high praise; honor; praise in thanksgiving; shining majesty or beauty; heavenly light. **-rious, -rify, glorifica'tion**; *v* **g. in** rejoice proudly; be boastful

**gloss** (superficial) polish or glow; note in margin, *etc* explaining text; (misleading) interpretation

**glos'sa·ry** list explaining special (technical) terms

**glove** leather, wool, *etc* covering for hand, *usu* with separate sheath for each finger

**glow** give off light and heat without flame; have warm color (because of physical exercise or emotion)

**glow'worm** beetle which gives off a greenish light

**glue** sticky substance made by boiling animal bones, skin, *etc*, used to paste things together

**glum** sad; sullen. **-ness**

**glut** overfill (with food); provide with too much

**glut'ton** one who eats to excess. **-ous**

**gnarled** (nahrld) knotty; weather-beaten in appearance

**gnash** (nash) strike or grind (teeth) together

**gnat** any of group of small, *usu* stinging flies

**gnaw** wear away by constant biting; bite on persistently

**gnome** dwarf; goblin

**gnu** (nū) kind of African antelope resembling ox

**go** (**went, gone**) (start to) move along on foot or in vehicle; leave; travel or advance; extend (in given direction), as road; (of time) pass; (of machines, *etc*) work or run; move in specified manner; be known (by certain name); pass into or continue in (given) condition, *etc*; be awarded, addressed, *etc*, to particular person or purpose: *my money goes to him*; be sold (for given price, *etc*); result or tend (to show, *etc*); belong in given place); (of colors, *etc*) harmonize; die; be ended or worn out; (start to) take certain action; **g. around** move about; be enough for all; **g. at** attack; **g. into** be contained: *3 goes into 9*; investigate; **g. out** leave house, *etc*; (of light, *etc*) stop burning; cease; **g. under** be defeated or ruined;

**good**

sink below surface of water; drown

**goad** n pointed stick for driving cattle; v urge or drive ahead (by annoyance)

**goal** (gōl) point at which race ends; point to which ball, etc is to be driven; aim or purpose; place to be reached, as by journey

**goat** horned cud-chewing animal related to sheep

**goat·ee** pointed beard

**gob'ble** eat hurriedly in large pieces; make sound like turkey

**gob'lin** small (ugly) fairy that is mischievous or evil

**go'-be·tween** person who acts as intermediary between two persons, groups, etc

**god** being of superhuman qualities and powers, thought to rule (part of) the world; idol. **-dess** God creator and ruler of universe in certain religions

**god'child** baby for whom person acts as sponsor at Christian baptism. **-son, -daughter, -father, -mother, -parent**

**god'send** (urgently hoped for) thing or event which comes suddenly, like gift from God

**gog'gle** v roll eyes; stare; n pl close-fitting glasses to protect eyes from dust, water, etc

**goi'ter,** UK **-tre** unhealthy enlargement of thyroid gland

**gold** highly valuable soft yellow metal; coins, jewelry, etc made of this; wealth. **-en**

**gold'fish** small usu orange fish kept in aqauriums and ponds

**golf** game played on special course using clubs to drive small ball into series of holes

**gon'do·la** long narrow boat used on canals of Venice; passenger car attached to balloon, etc

**gone** see **go**

**gong** metal disk which gives off resounding tone when struck

**gon·or·rhe'a,** UK **-rhoe'a** (gonerēe) contagious sexual disease

**good** (bet'ter, best) a having right, satisfactory or pleasing qualities; of high moral quality; kind; having desirable, beneficial, etc effects; right and proper; (of children) well-behaved; suited for given task or purpose; considerable: a g. deal; full: a g. five miles away; valid: a g. will; **as g. as** almost: I am as g. as ready; **make g.** make up for (damage, etc); fulfil (promise); accomplish what one has set out to do; n what is advantageous, beneficial, etc: for his own g.; pl objects bought and sold in trade

**good-bye'** phrase said when taking leave

**goose** (pl **geese**) large long-necked, web-footed bird

**goose'flesh** condition caused by cold or fear in which skin rises in small bumps

**go'pher** (gō-) American rodent which lives in burrows

**gor|e** n clotted blood; v pierce with horns or tusks. **-y**

**gorge** n narrow steepwalled valley; contents of stomach; v feed greedily; stuff with food

**gor'geous** splendid; very beautiful

**go-ril'la** largest kind of ape

**gos'pel** sth accepted as absolute truth

**gos'sa·mer** film of cobwebs floating in calm air; thin delicate material

**gos'sip** idle talk(er) about other people's affairs; rumor

**got, got'ten** see **get**

**gouge** (gouj) n chisel; v scoop or force out; sl cheat grossly

**gou'lash** highly-seasoned stew

**gourd** (gōrd, goord) (vine with) melon-like fruit; its dried rind used as vessel, etc

**gour'mand** (goor-) one overfond of good eating

**gour'met** (goormā) expert in good food and drink

**gout** (gout) painful disease affecting joints

**gov'ern** rule with authority; carry on affairs of state, company, etc; influence; hold in check

**gov'ern·ment** political rule; governing body. **govern'men'tal**

**gov'er·nor** head of state (US), province, etc; member of group directing school, hospital, etc; automatic regulator of speed, fuel, etc

**gown** woman's dress, esp. for formal wear; loose garment worn by priest, surgeon, etc

**grab** take hold of suddenly with hands; snatch greedily; take (land, etc) unlawfully or by unscrupulous means

**grace** charm or elegance in movement, manner, etc **-ful**; state of being favored by influence of God; extra time granted to pay debt, etc; short prayer of thanks before or after meal; decency of conduct; **G.** form of address for archbishop, duke, etc

**gra'cious** kind (esp. to inferiors); merciful. **-ness**

**gra·da'tion** series of changes by degrees; stage of change; pl arrangement in such degrees

**grade** degree in system of rank, quality, etc; step or stage in development, etc; US division of school based on age or progress of pupils;

*US* mark given for student's work; (degree of) slope of road, *etc*

**grad'u·al** taking place by (small) degrees; moving slowly; not sudden

**grad'u·ate** mark in degrees; change gradually; take or give academic degree. **gradua'tion**

**graf·fi'ti** drawings or writing on a wall

**graft** insert cutting from one plant into another; transplant living skin

**grain** seed(s) of any cereal plant; cereal plants; any small hard bit, as of sand, salt, *etc*; smallest unit of weight; direction of fibers in wood; grainlike texture of stone, *etc*

**gram,** *UK* **gramme** weight unit in metric system

**gram'mar** (study of) interrelation of parts of a language; textbook treating this. **grammar'ian, grammat'ical**

**gran'a·ry** storehouse for grain

**grand** impressive or stately in appearance, manner, *etc*; (of ideas, *etc*) having high or noble aims; of highest importance or greatest rank

**grand'|child** child of one's son or daughter. **-daughter, -son**

**gran'deur** (-jer) splendor; majesty

**gran·dil'o·quence** pompous or lofty speech

**gran'di·ose** giving an impression of greatness; pompous

**grand'|par·ent** mother or father of either of one's parents. **-father, -mother**

**grand'stand** main stand for onlookers at race, *etc*

**gran'ite** very hard granular kind of rock

**grant** *v* agree to fulfil request; give, *esp.* by formal act; admit as true for sake of discussion; *n* money given for some purpose

**gran'u·la|te** form into grains; roughen surface of. **-r**

**grape** edible berry, growing in bunches on vines, from which wine is made

**grape'fruit** large yellow citrus fruit

**grape'vine** informal way of spreading news or gossip; vine bearing grapes

**graph** (graf) diagram representing a system of connections or interrelations

**graph'ic** of drawing, writing, diagrams, *etc*; lifelike in description

**graph'ics** (computer) production of charts, diagrams, *etc*

**graph'ite** soft black carbon used in pencils, as lubricant, *etc*

**gra·phol'o·gy** study of hand-writing

**grap'ple** take hold of; grip; struggle with; try to deal with

**grasp** take hold of tightly or eagerly with fingers; understand; **g. at** try to get hold of; reach for

**grass|s** plant with narrow spearlike blades, used fresh or dried as food for cattle, *etc*; pasture land; lawn. **-sy**

**gross'hop·per** plant-eating jumping insect

**grass roots'** society at the local level of opinion; voters

**grat|e** *n* frame of metal bars in oven, *etc* or used as partition or cover. **-ing;** *v* make small by rubbing on rough surface; rub with harsh noise; irritate

**grate'ful** feeling or showing thankfulness

**grat'i·fy** please (by satisfying desires). **gratifica'tion**

**gra'tis** free of cost

**grat'i·tude** thankfulness

**gra·tu'i·tous** done without good reason; uncalled for; got or given free of cost

**gra·tu'i·ty** gift of money; tip

**grave** *n* hole dug in ground in which dead person is buried; death; *a* important; serious; dignified; earnest. **-ly**

**grav'el** small pebbles and coarse sand. **-ly**

**grave'stone** stone placed at grave bearing name, *etc* of dead person(s)

**grave'yard** cemetery

**grav'i·tate** move by force of gravity towards sth. **gravita'tion**

**grav'i·ty** force attracting bodies to center of earth; importance; dignity of manner

**gra'vy** (sauce made from) juice that drips from roasting meat

**gray,** *UK* **grey** *n* (of the) color made by mixing black and white, as ashes, *etc*; *a* gloomy or dull; gray-haired; uncertain or unexplored

**graze** (cause to) feed on growing grass; touch or scrape in passing

**grease** animal fat, *esp.* when soft or melted; any thick oily matter, as that used to lubricate machinery

**great** (grāt) large in size, number, importance, *etc*; more than the ordinary; famous; of excellent qualities

**great-grand'|child** grandchild of one's son or daughter. **-daughter, -son**

**great-grand'|par·ent** parent of one's grandfather or grandmother. **-father, -mother**

**greed** unusually large appetite; grasping desire for wealth, *etc*. **-y**

**green** *n* (of the) color made by mixing yellow and blue, as grass, *etc*; *pl* (dish of) green vegetables; *a* covered with growth, as grass or leaves. **-ery**; not ripe; not seasoned or dried; inexperienced; of or for ecological approach to political problems

**green'horn** *infml* gullible or inexperienced person

**green'house** heated building with glass roof and walls where tender plants are grown; **g. effect** gradual warming of earth's atmosphere caused by burning coal, oil, *etc*

**greet** say words of welcome to; receive person, action, *etc* with specified words or in specified manner; meet (eye, ear, *etc*)

**gre·gar'i·ous** living in communities; fond of company. **-ness**

**grem'lin** mischievous spirit supposed to cause equipment to fail

**gre·nade'** small explosive shell thrown by hand, *etc*

**grew** see **grow**

**grey** see **gray**

**grid** grating; system of numbered squares, used in maps to locate positions

**grid'dle** round iron plate for baking pancakes

**grid'i·ron** metal frame for broiling; *US* football field

**grief** deep sorrow; trouble

**griev'ance** ground for complaint

**grieve** (cause to) feel deep sorrow

**grill** cook over or under direct heat, broil; *infml* question severely

**grille** decorative grating

**grim** without mercy; harsh and stern in appearance; unpleasant

**gri·mace'** facial contortion expressing annoyance, *etc*

**grim|e** dirt; soot. **-y**

**grin** draw back lips so as to show teeth, *esp.* in amusement

**grind (ground)** make powder of by crushing or rubbing; wear down, polish or sharpen by rubbing; make (handmill, *etc*) work by turning handle; rub harshly together, as teeth

**grip** *v* hold tightly; *n* firm grasp or hold; manner of, or device for, holding

**gripe** cause or feel sharp pain in bowels; *infml* complain

**gris'ly** causing horror or dread

**gris'|tle** (grisl) animal cartilage. **-tly**

**grit** *n* small particles of stone or sand; *infml* unyielding courage; *v* grate or grind, as teeth. **-ty**

**griz'|zled** gray(-haired). **-zly**

**groan** (make) deep sound of pain, sorrow, *etc*

**gro'cer** dealer in food. **-y**

**gro'ce·ries** pl goods sold by grocer

**grog'gy** weak and unsteady, as from medicine, etc

**groin** hollow where thigh joins belly

**groom** n servant having care of horses; man about to be or newly married; v tend horses; make (o. s.) neat and tidy

**groove** channel or furrow; fixed routine

**grope** feel about, as in dark; seek by feeling

**gross** n twelve dozen; a total; without any deductions; glaring; too fat; coarse; indecent

**gro·tesque'** (-tesk) comically ugly; fantastically distorted; absurd

**ground** v see **grind**

**ground** n (surface of) the earth; land; soil; (often pl) area of particular kind or use; bottom, as of sea; pl dregs, as of coffee; (often pl) reasons, as for action; v touch or strike bottom, as ship; prevent from flying; (electric circuit) connect with ground

**ground'work** basis for sth; foundation

**group** number of persons or things standing near to each other, or having some common feature

**grove** small wood

**grow** (**grew, grown**) develop, as living plant or animal; increase in size, strength, number, etc; produce by cultivation, as beard, flowers, etc. **growth**

**growl** (make) deep threatening sound, as that of angry dog

**grown'-up** adult (person)

**grub** n insect larva; v dig with hands or paws

**grub'by** dirty

**grudge** v be unwilling to give or let have; n feeling of ill-will

**gru·el·ing,** UK **-el·ling** exhausting; severe

**grue'some** horrible; causing fear or disgust

**gruff** (of voice) low and rough; (of manner) harsh and unfriendly

**grum'ble** make deep rumbling sound; complain (ill-naturedly)

**grunt** (make) deep sound in throat like that of pig

**gua'no** (gwa-) dung of seabirds used as fertilizer

**guar·an·tee'** (gar-) n person giving or receiving security; manufacturer's promise to repair or replace sth for stated period of time; v be or give a guarantee; answer for fulfillment or genuineness; secure against risk or loss. **guar'antor**

**guard** (gahrd) *n* person(s) watching over place or person; device to protect against dirt, injury, *etc*; state of watchful attention; *UK* railway conductor; *v* keep safe by watching over; watch over (door, house to prevent unauthorized entry, or prisoner to prevent escape); **g. against** take precautions to prevent

**guard'i·an** keeper; protector; one given custody of person or property of another. **-ship**

**gu·ber·na·to'ri·al** *US* of a governor

**guer·ril'la** (ger-) person carrying on irregular warfare

**guess** (ges) form opinion without having definite facts; estimate; think possible or probable

**guest** (gest) person received at another's house and given food, lodging, *etc*; person staying at hotel; **g. worker** person who works in foreign country for a period of time

**guid|e** (gīd) *n* one who shows way; book of rules, instruction, or (geographical) information; device on machine directing motion of hand, material, *etc*; *v* show way, *esp.* to tourists; direct course of. **-ance**

**guid'ed mis·sile** aerial weapon, as rocket, directed electronically, *etc*

**guild** professional association of persons with common goal for mutual aid

**guile** (gīl) cunning; treachery. **-ful, -less**

**guil'lo·tine** (gil-) machine for beheading criminals

**guilt** (gilt) fact or condition of having committed crime or moral offense. **-less, -y**

**guin'ea pig** small short-tailed rodent, often kept as pet or used in scientific tests; person used in (medical) experiment

**guise** (gīz) (assumed) outer appearance

**gui·tar'** *mus* instrument with six or twelve strings plucked by hand

**gulch** *US* narrow ravine

**gulf** area of sea partly surrounded by land; deep chasm; unbridgeable gap

**gul'li·ble** easily fooled. **gullibil'ity**

**gul'ly** little valley cut by water; ditch; gutter

**gulp** swallow food or drink quickly; catch one's breath as if in swallowing

**gum** sticky mass given off by some plants, used in making glue, or mixed with sugar to make chewing gum. **-my;** *usu pl* flesh around teeth

**gun** device, consisting of metal tube, firing mechanism, *etc*, for shooting bullets, shells, *etc*; similar device for spraying paint, *etc*

**gun'pow·der** explosive mixture of saltpeter, *etc*, used for firing guns

**gur'gle** (make) bubbling sound, as of water flowing from bottle

**gush** flow suddenly in strong stream; talk with (affected) emotion. **-ing, -y**

**gust** sudden strong rush of wind, *etc*. **-y**

**gus'to** hearty enjoyment in eating, *etc*

**gut** *n* bowels, *esp*. of animals; tensile thread or string used in surgery, musical instruments, *etc*; *v* take guts out of; destroy or rob interior of

**gut'ter** *n* channel at side of roof or street for water; low-

est social class; *v* (of candle) flicker

**gut'tur·al** of the throat; harsh and throaty

**guz'zle** drink frequently and greedily

**gym(·na'si·um)** place for gymnastics

**gym·nas'tics** physical exercises

**gy·ne·col'o·gy**, UK **gy·nae-** (gīne-, jīne-) medical branch dealing with women and their diseases

**gyp'sy** one of a wandering race of Indian origin

**gy'rate** move in circles or spirals; whirl

**gy'ro·scope** heavy wheel which spins inside frame, used to keep planes and ships steady

# H

**h** eighth letter of English alphabet

**hab·er·dash·er** dealer in small articles of (men's) dress. **-y**

**hab'it** practice of doing particular thing repeatedly or regularly; characteristic dress, *esp*. of nuns, *etc*

**hab'it·a·ble** capable of being lived in

**hab'it·at** natural home of plant or animal

**hab·i·ta'tion** (act of living in) place of dwelling

**ha·bit'u·al** customary; given

to a habit

**ha·bit'u·ate** accustom to

**hack** *v* cut; chop; cough drily; *n* hired horse; old worn-out horse; hired (literary, *etc*) drudge; second-rate writer; *US infml* taxi

**hack'neyed** trite; stale

**had** see **have**

**had'dock** common food fish of N. Atlantic

**Ha'des** (hādēz) *Gr. myth.* abode of the dead; hell

**hag** ugly (evil) old woman; witch

**hag'gard** wild-looking, as from suffering, want, *etc*

**hag'gle** bargain stubbornly over small amount; dispute

**hail** *n* frozen raindrops; shower of questions, *etc*; *v* pour down on (as hail); greet; call out to

**hair** fine threads growing from skin of animals and (*esp.* on head) humans; **split hairs** make too fine differences

**hair'dres·ser** person who cuts and arranges hair

**hair'-rais·ing** causing terror, excitement or surprise

**hale** healthy

**half** (*pl* **haives**) (haf, havz) one of two equal parts into which thing is or can be divided

**half'-breed** offspring of parents of different races

**half-broth·er**, **half-sis·ter** brother or sister with only one parent in common

**half'heart·ed** lacking interest or enthusiasm

**half'-mast'** position of flag halfway up mast, as sign of mourning

**half·way'** at the midpoint between two things; partial

**half'-wit'ted** feeble-minded; foolish

**hal'i·but** large flat saltwater food fish

**hal·i·to'sis** bad-smelling breath

**hall** (hawl) large room for formal events; entrance room of house; *US* corridor; large (public) building for administration, students' residence, *etc*

**hal·le·lu'ja** (-ye) (shout, *etc* of) praise or thanksgiving

**hall'mark** official mark showing purity of gold, *etc*; typical (high) quality, *etc*

**hal'low** make or honor as holy

**hal·lu·ci·na'tion** seeing or hearing sth that does not actually exist

**hal·lu·ci·no·gen'ic** (of drugs, *etc*) producing hallucinations

**ha'lo** circle of light around sun or moon; ring of light shown surrounding head of saint

**hal'ter** rope for leading cattle; brief woman's (sports) top tied around neck and across back

**halve** (hav) divide into halves; reduce to half

**halves** see **half**

**ham** (meat from) thighs of buttocks of hog, *esp.* when salted and smoked; bad but showy actor. **-my**; amateur radio operator

**ham'burg·er** flat cake of fried or broiled ground beef

**ham'let** small village

**ham'mer** tool with (*usu*) metal head attached to wooden handle, used to drive in nails, beat iron, etc; device for striking another object, as in piano, gun, etc; **come under the h.** be sold at auction

**ham'mock** hanging bed of canvas, etc

**ham'per** n large basket; v hinder movement

**ham'ster** small rodent kept as pet

**ham'string** n tendon at back of knee; v cripple (by cutting this); hinder

**hand** n part of human arm below wrist, ending in five fingers; worker in farm, factory, etc; active cooperation: *he had a h. in this*; source: *news at first h.*; (left or right) side; skill or style: *work showing the h. of an expert*; style of handwriting; control or responsibility: *the decision is in their hands*; pointer on clock or dial; (in card games) cards dealt to player in one round; pledge of marriage; measure (= 0.1 m) of horse's height; cluster of many bunches of bananas; round of applause; **at h.** near by; **from h. to h.** from one person to another; **from h. to mouth** without care for the future; **in h.** under control; **on h.** in stock or readily available; **out of h.** out of control; **win hands down**

win easily; v pass sth with the hand; help person (into car, etc) with the hand

**hand'bag** small bag, esp. one used by women for small personal items

**hand'bill** small leaflet

**hand'book** reference book with basic information on specific subject; manual

**hand'cuffs** pair of metal wristbands, connected by chain, for securing prisoner

**hand'ful** enough to fill the hand; small quantity; difficult person or task

**hand'i·cap** physical or mental disability; disadvantage. **-capped**

**hand'i·craft** manual skill or trade

**hand'ker·chief** square piece of cloth or soft paper, used for wiping nose, etc

**han·dle** n (specially-shaped) part or device by which thing is grasped, opened, guided, etc; v touch or move about with hand(s); manage thing or person; treat (in given manner); deal in (goods, etc)

**han·dle·bar(s)** curved or straight metal rod, esp. one for steering bicycle

**hand'out** food, clothes, etc given to poor; printed information to be distributed at lecture, etc

**hand'some** (hansəm) of fine appearance; (of behavior,

*etc*) generous; (of amount) considerable

**hand'y** within easy reach; easy to handle; skilful with one's hands

**han'dy·man** man who does odd jobs

**hang** (hung) fasten thing at its top point or upper part, so that it can swing freely; place picture, wallpaper, *etc* on wall; (of dust, *etc*) float in air; (let) droop, as head; keep (jury) from reaching verdict (by refusing to agree); (*usu* hanged) execute by putting rope about neck and suspending from gallows; **h. about** or **around** loiter; **h. back** be unwilling to move ahead or act; **h. on** keep stubborn hold of; **h. together** (of story, *etc*) be consistent; (continue to) be united; **h. up** delay; (of telephone) put receiver on hook

**hang'ar** shed for housing, repairing, *etc* airplanes

**hang'er** wooden, *etc* bar on which clothes are hung; loop, *etc* by which sth is hung up

**hang'ing** execution on gallows; (*usu pl*) curtains for wall or window

**hang'man** man whose job is to hang criminals

**hang'nail** loose skin at base or side of fingernail

**hang'o·ver** sth left over from the past; unpleasant physical condition, *esp.* after too much alcohol

**han'ker** long for

**hap·haz'ard** dependent on chance; lacking plan and order

**hap'less** unlucky

**hap'pen** take place, *esp.* by chance or unexpectedly; **h. on** meet or find by chance

**hap'|py** feeling pleased, content or glad; (of event, *etc*) bringing good fortune; apt, as remark. **-piness**

**hap·py·go·luck'y** carefree; taking things as they come

**ha·rangue'** (-rang) (attack in) loud or long impassioned speech

**har·ass'** annoy by repeated attacks; worry

**har'bor**, UK **-bour** *n* sheltered place on coast for ships; *v* give shelter to; hide, as criminals; (of suspicion, *etc*) have in mind

**hard** solid and firm; not yielding to touch; (of task, *etc*) difficult; (of work, *etc*) done with, or requiring, great strength or effort; (of rain, snow, *etc*) violent or heavy; harsh or unfriendly, as person, feeling, *etc*; difficult to bear, as fate; (of money) in coins; *US* (of drinks) containing much alcohol; (of water) containing minerals which hinder cleaning effect of soap. **-ness**; **h. of hearing** partly deaf; **h. by** near by; **be h. on** be severe with

**hard'back** (book) having a stiff cover

**hard'-bit'ten** tough and stubborn

**hard' cop·y** readable computer data, *esp.* in printed form

**hard disk'** piece of coated metal for storing large amounts of computer information

**hard'en** (cause to) become hard; make hardy

**hard'head·ed** not easily moved or fooled; stubborn

**hard'heart·ed** unfeeling

**hard'ly** almost not at all; unlikely; with difficulty

**hard'ship** circumstance that is hard to bear

**hard'ware** metal goods, as tools, nails, *etc*; machinery (housing, keyboard, monitor) making up a computer; physical equipment as part of a system

**hard'wood** (tree with) strong dense wood, as oak, used for furniture, floors, *etc*

**har|dy** able to stand cold, bad weather, *etc*; robust. **-diness**

**hare** long-eared mammal like a rabbit, with long hind legs adapted to great speed

**hare'brained** rash; wild

**hare'lip** divided upper lip

**har'em** women's tract in Moslem house, its inhabitants

**hark** listen; **h. back** come back to earlier point

**har'lot** a prostitute

**harm** (cause) damage or injury. **-ful, -less**

**har·mon'i·ca** *mus* instrument played by holding to mouth and blowing or sucking air through it

**har'mo·ny** agreement; pleasing arrangement of parts; combination of simultaneous notes. **-nize** (*UK* **-nise**), **harmo'nious**

**har'ness** *n* gear for horse, *etc*; *v* put in a harness; make use of (natural forces such as water)

**harp** large musical instrument of triangular shape with strings plucked by fingers. **-ist**

**har·poon'** fishing spear attached to rope

**har'row** farm machine with metal teeth for breaking up soil

**har'row·ing** causing anxiety and great mental distress

**harsh** rough to touch, hearing, *etc*; (of behavior) unfeeling and severe. **-ness**

**har'vest** (time of) gathering in ripe crops; any supply of ripened and gathered products, as fruit

**has** see **have**

**hash** dish of meat and potatoes, cut small and fried; muddle

**hash'ish** narcotic drug got from hemp

**hasp** fastening device for door

**has'sock** footstool

**hast|e** speedy action; (rash) speed. **-y**

**hat** covering, often with brim, for the head

**hatch** v bring forth or emerge from egg; form (plot); n (cover for) opening in deck, wall, etc

**hatch'et** small ax

**ha|te** dislike strongly. **-tred**

**haugh'|ty** (hawti) arrogant; proud. **-tiness**

**haul** draw or pull with force; transport, esp. by truck

**haunch** hip; hind quarter or thigh of animal

**haunt** visit place or person often, as ghosts do

**have** (**had; has**) own or possess; hold, esp. in the mind; bear (children); experience, as an accident; show; as pity; get: *you can h. it if you wish*; cause to be done: *h. a letter written*; **h. to** be forced to: *I. h. to go*

**ha'ven** harbor; shelter

**hav'oc** destruction; disorder

**hawk** n bird of prey known for keen eyes; v carry goods about for sale. **-er;** clear throat noisily

**hay** grass, clover, *etc* cut and dried and used as food for cattle

**hay fe'ver** allergy affecting nose and throat, caused by breathing in pollen

**hay'wire** *infml* out of order

**haz'ard** risk; chance; danger. **-ous**

**haze** thin mist; mental confusion

**ha'zel** (wood of) small nut-bearing tree; (of) light brown color

**ha'zy** misty; vague

**H'-bomb** hydrogen bomb

**he** (**him, his**) male person or animal already mentioned

**head** (hed) n part of body above neck, containing brain and organs of taste, smell and hearing; this part referred to as seat of intellect, understanding, *etc*; an individual, *esp.* of cattle; front or upper end, as of waiting line, bed, *etc*; cutting or striking part of tool, flat end of nail, *etc*; person in leading position; part of boil, *etc* which breaks open; source, as of river; pressure, as of steam; foam at top of beer; v lead or be at top of; point in a certain direction; **h. off** stop or turn aside, as a pursuer

**head'ache** pain in head; *infml* troublesome problem or person

**head'ing** (hed-) title, *esp.* one printed at top of page, *etc*

**head'light** lamp with reflector at front of car, *etc*

**head'line** line of (thick) print at top of newspaper article, summarizing its contents

**head'long** with head first; rashly; hastily

**head'mas·ter, -mis·tress** *esp. UK* principal teacher or administrator of school

**head-on¹** (of collision, *etc*) with head or front foremost

**head'phones** device fitting against the ears and held by band across head, used for listening to radio, *etc*

**head'quar·ters** *pl* or *sing* center of operations

**head'room** space overhead in tunnels, vehicles, *etc*

**head'stone** gravestone

**head'strong** bent on having one's own way

**head'way** progress

**head'wind** wind blowing directly from the front

**head'y** intoxicating

**heal** bring (sick person) back to health; (of wound) become whole again

**health** (helth) freedom from illness; general condition of body: *he is in good/bad h.* **-y;** toast in honor of

**heap** number of things lying on one another

**hear** (**heard**) (hēr, hurd) take in sounds by the ear; listen to; (of court, *etc*) give witness, *etc* order or opportunity to speak; be informed; **h. from** get letter, *etc*

**hear'ing aid** electronic device worn in or behind the ear to make sounds louder

**hear'say** gossip; rumor

**hearse** vehicle for transporting coffins of the dead

**heart** (hahrt) muscular organ which contracts and expands to pump blood through body; this organ viewed as center of life, feelings, *etc*; sth shaped like heart; pity; courage; vital or central part of anything; **by h.** from memory

**heart'ache** sadness

**heart'burn** sharp burning feeling in chest due to acid coming from stomach

**heart'en** give courage to

**hearth** (hahrth) floor of fireplace

**heart'y** sincere; friendly; vigorous; (of meal) large

**heat** form of energy causing temperature of any substance to rise; state of being hot or of having high temperature; strength of feeling, as in anger; (in female animals) condition of sexual excitement; (preliminary) race

**hea'then** uncivilized (person)

**heave** raise or lift with effort; rise and fall with swelling motion; breathe with effort

**hem**

**heav·en** (hev-) place where dead souls are supposed to go; place of great happiness; *usu pl* the sky. **-ly**

**heav·y** (hev-) hard to lift or carry because of great weight; hard to bear, as fate; (of sleep) deep; (of sky) overcast; strong, as storm; (of sounds) loud and deep; (of food) not easy to digest; of unusual thickness, as clothes; more than is usual: *h. traffic*

**heav·y-du·ty** built for a lot of (rough) use

**heav·y-set** of stocky (stout) build

**heck·le** bother

**hec·tic** feverishly excited

**hec·to·gram** 100 grams

**hec·to·li·ter**, *UK* **-tre** 100 liters

**hec·to·me·ter**, *UK* **-tre** 1oo meters

**hedge** *n* thick growth of shrubs planted in straight line, often serving as fence; *v* enclose by hedge; avoid committing o.s.

**he·do·nis·m** doctrine that pleasure is the highest good. **-nist**

**heed** take notice of; pay attention to. **-ful, -less**

**heel** *n* back part of foot, stocking or shoe; raised part of shoe; *v* **h. over** (of ships) lean over to one side

**heft·y** heavy; big and strong

**he·ge·mo·ny** dominance (of one nation over others)

**heif·er** (hef-) young cow

**height** (hīt) distance from base or ground to top of house, hill, *etc*; highest point or degree

**height·en** raise high(er); make more intense

**hei·nous** (hā-) shockingly evil

**heir** (ār) person receiving property of s.o. who has died

**heir·loom** family possession handed down through generations

**held** see **hold**

**hel·i·cop·ter** aircraft with horizontally-revolving blades that can take off and land vertically

**hel·i·port** airport for helicopters

**he·li·um** (hē-) colorless gaseous element, nonburning and of very light weight

**hell** place of damned souls; place or state of misery or suffering

**helm** wheel, *etc* for steering ship. **-sman**

**hel·met** protective head covering for soldiers, firemen, motorcyclists, *etc*

**help** give aid or relief to. **-ful**; serve; prevent or avoid: *I can't h. laughing*; **-** in assistance; household servant(s)

**help·ing** portion of food

**hem** *n* border made by folding back and sewing down cloth; v make such a border; **h. in** surround

**hem'i·sphere** (-sfēr) half of sphere; half of the earth; each half of brain

**hem'lock** poisonous herb; tree of pine family

**he·mo·glo'bin** red coloring matter of blood

**he·mo·phil'i·a** (hereditary) tendency to bleed excessively due to inability of blood to coagulate. **-ac**

**hem'or·rhage** (hemerij) copious flow of blood, as from broken blood vessel

**hem'or·rhoid** swelling of veins in lower rectum

**hemp** plant from which rope, etc is made

**hen** female of domestic fowl and other birds

**hence** forward in time: a week h.; therefore

**hence·forth'** from this time on

**hench'man** trusted follower; (unscrupulous) supporter

**hen'na** (red dye of) tropical shrub

**hep·a·ti'tis** liver disease causing weakness and yellowing of skin

**hep'ta·gon** figure with seven sides

**her** word indicating possession by female: h. dress; as object, female person or animal already mentioned: I like h. very much

**her'ald** n (state or royal) messenger; v announce coming of. **herald'ic**

**herb** group of seed plants with soft stem and with leaves used as flavoring, in medicine, etc

**herd** group of animals, esp. cattle, grazing or moving together; people seen as mindless group

**here** in, at or to this place; in this life

**here·af'ter** in the future

**he·red'i·tar·y** passing (naturally or by law) from parents to offspring

**he·red'i·ty** (theory of) transmission of characteristics from parents to offspring

**her'e·sy** opinion in conflict with accepted (religious) doctrine. **-tic**

**her'it·age** what is or may be inherited

**her·maph'ro·dite** animal or flower having both male and female sex organs

**her·met'ic** made airtight by sealing. **-ical**

**her'mit** person living in solitude. **-age**

**her'ni·a** protrusion of part of organ through break in surrounding tissue, as bowel through navel, etc

**he'ro** (pl **-roes**) person honored for his outstanding deeds and high qualities, esp.

bravery; chief male character in play, *etc.* **hero'ic, her'oine**

**her·o·in** powerful addictive drug made from morphine

**her'on** long-legged, long-necked wading bird living in swamps, *etc*

**her'pes** contagious disease causing painful blisters, *esp.* on face or genitals

**her'ring** North Atlantic food fish

**her·self'** emphasizing or reflexive form of she: *she h. says so, she washed h.*

**hes'i·tate** hold back in doubt or indecision; be unwilling. **-tant**

**het'e·ro·dox** not agreeing with accepted apinions. **-y**

**het·e·ro·ge'ne·ous** composed of different elements

**het·e·ro·sex'u·al** (person) attracted sexually to opposite sex

**hew** (hyū) (**hewed, hewed** or **hewn**) cut or chop (into shape); cut down

**hex'a·gon** figure with six sides

**hey'day** period of highest activity or success

**hi'ber·nate** spend winter in sleeping state, as certain animals

**hic'cup, hic'cough** (hikup) sharp gulping sound caused by sudden cramping of breathing muscles

**hick'o·ry** (hardwood of) N. Amer. nut-bearing tree

**hide** *v* (**hid, hid'den**) put sth where it cannot be seen or found; keep secret; block view of; turn (face) away in shame; *etc*; *n* skin of an animal

**hide'bound** narrow-minded

**hid'e·ous** horribly ugly; morally shocking. **-ness**

**hi'er·arch·y** (rigid) system of graded classes; body of persons in command

**hi'er·o·glyph** (hīreglif) drawing of object standing for word, *etc* as in ancient Egyptian writing; secret symbol. **hi·e·ro·glyph'ic**

**hi'fi'** (hīfī) high fidelity sound; electronic equipment to produce such sound

**high** (hī) *a* being some distance above any given point; being (given) distance above ground: *ten feet h.*; (of sound) shrill or sharp; noble in quality, character, *etc*; of great importance; (of wind) strong; of greater than usual degree, content, *etc*: *h. prices*; *adv* far upward; in, at or to high level

**high'brow** intellectual

**high'-chair** chair with long legs for child

**high fi·del'i·ty** quality of recorded sound very near the original

**high'hand'ed** overbearing. **-ness**

**high'light** v make prominent; n bright part of painting; important or striking part

**high'-rise** (building) having many floors

**high school** US school above elementary level

**high sea** usu pl open sea not close to any shore

**high'-strung** very nervous or sensitive

**high'way** main (overland) road

**hi'jack** seize illegal control of (plane, etc); stop moving truck, etc to steal freight. **-er, -ing**

**hi·lar·i·ous** full of or causing (loud) mirth. **-ty**

**hill** piece of land, usu rounded, which is higher than its surroundings; small heap of earth. **-y**

**hilt** handle of sword, etc

**him** as object, male person already mentioned: I know h.

**him·self** emphasizing or reflexive form of **he**: he said it h., he hurt h.

**hind** n female (red) deer; a situated at the back

**hin'der** keep back; prevent from doing. **-drance**

**hind'most** farthest to the rear

**hind'sight** understanding sth after it has happened

**hinge** (hinj) jointed piece of metal on which door, lid, etc swings

**hint** indirect suggestion

**hip** fleshy part of body just below waist on either side; red fruit of rose

**hi·po·pot'a·mus** large fat Afr. animal with thick hairless skin and short legs, living chiefly in rivers, etc

**hire** employ (worker, etc) or rent (car, etc) for pay

**his** word indicating possession by male: h. body

**hiss** (make) sharp sound of letter s, esp. as sign of disapproval, etc

**his·tol'o·gy** scientific study of organic tissues

**his·to'ri·an** person who studies and/or writes about history

**his·to·ry** record of past (public) events; study of course of human affairs. **histor'ical**

**his·tor'ic** well-known or important in history

**his·tri·on'ic** of actors or acting; affected

**his·tri·on'ics** acting; artificial behavior for effect

**hit** v (hit) (cause to) touch with force, as by blow or missile; deliver, as a blow; affect severely; n blow; stroke (of luck); sth successful, as play, song, etc

**hitch** v move (thing) with a jerk; tie (with knot); n jerk; obstacle or difficulty; knot

**hitch'hik|e** travel by free rides in other people's cars. **-er**

**hith·er·to'** (-tū) up to this time

**hive** container for housing bees; *pl* itching skin rash

**hoard** store for future use, *esp.* more than usual

**hoarse** harsh and grating, as voice, cry of bird, *etc*

**hoar'y** white, *esp.* with age

**hoax** (hōks) (humorous) deception; practical joke

**hob'ble** limp; tie (legs of animal) to prevent free motion

**hob'by** activity pursued in one's free time for relaxation

**ho'bo** US homeless wandering person; tramp

**hock'ey** game played on field or ice rink with ball or small hard rubber disk and curved sticks

**ho·cus-po'cus** formula used by magicians; any trick designed to cover up fact of deceit

**hod** container on pole for carrying bricks, *etc*

**hodge'podge,** *UK* **hotch'-potch** mixture of many things; jumble

**hoe** garden tool for weeding and loosening soil

**hog** pig, *esp.* if fully-grown

**hoist** raise or lift by mechanical device

**hold** (**held**) grasp; support; contain; keep in given condition: *h. the soil moist*; continue: *the rain held for days*; remain firm: *the dam held against the water*; cause to happen: *h. a meeting*; have (opinion, *etc*); be true: *this saying holds for all cases*; **h. forth** speak at great length (on topic); **h. over** postpone; keep; **h. up** delay; stop in order to rob; use as example

**hold'ing** land or stocks owned

**hole** opening; hollow place

**hol'i·day** day of rest or celebration; period of relaxation when no work is done; vacation

**hol'low** *a* not solid or filled out; empty; worthless or false; *n* shallow dent in surface, as of land

**hol'ly** evergreen shrub with glossy spiny leaves and red berries

**hol'o·caust** great destruction of life, *esp.* by fire

**hol'o·gram** three-dimensional laser photograph

**hol'ster** leather case for pistol worn at hip, *etc*

**ho'ly** sacred; spiritually pure; awesome

**hom'age** (homij) respect paid to person or value

**home** place where one lives; city or country of birth; asylum for orphans, old people, *etc*

**home'ly** plain; modest; not good-looking. **-liness**

**home'sick** longing for one's home

**home'spun** spun at home; plain

**home'work** studies, *etc* to be done at home

**hom'i·cide** *law* the murder or the murderer of another human being. **homicid'al**

**ho·mo·ge'ne·ous** (consisting of parts) of the same kind

**ho·mo·sex'u·al** (person) attracted sexually to same sex. **homosexual'ity**

**hone** sharpen (knives, *etc*)

**hon'es|t** (onist) truthful; not deceiving. **-ty**

**hon'ey** (huni) sweet sticky fluid made by bees from flower nectar and used as food

**hon'ey·comb** (-kōm) mass of wax cells built by bees

**hon'ey·dew mel·on** pale smooth melon with sweet greenish flesh

**hon'ey·moon** vacation taken by newlyweds; early period of harmony (following marriage, election, *etc*)

**honk** (make) cry of goose or similar sound, as that of automobile horn

**hon'or**, *UK* **-our** respect paid to worth or achievement; high moral conduct; good reputation; *pl* high grades for excellence in studies. **-able, -ary**

**hood** covering for head and neck or for part of machine, automobile, *etc*

**hood'wink** deceive; trick

**hoof** (*pl* **hoofs, hooves**) hard protective covering on feet of horses, cattle, *etc*

**hook** curved piece of metal, *etc* for catching, holding or pulling; cradle holding telephone receiver; short thrusting blow; **by h. or by crook** using all possible means (to do sth)

**hoo'li·gan** troublemaker; thug. **-ism**

**hoop** round band of wood or metal to hold together the wooden slats of a barrel, *etc*

**hoo·ray'** *see* **hurrah**

**hoot** (give) loud shout, *usu* of scorn; cry of the owl

**hop** *v* move by quick short jumps, as birds, *etc*; jump (on one foot); *n* short jump; distance between plane stops; twining vine whose seed cones are used in making beer, *etc*

**hope** expectation that sth will happen as desired; thing desired; *s.o.* or sth promising success. **-ful, -less**

**horde** moving throng of people or animals

**ho·ri'zon** line at which earth and sky appear to meet; level of one's development

**hor·i·zon'tal** parallel to place of horizon or to a base line; level; flat

**hor'mone** substance secreted into blood to regulate growth, function of body organs, *etc*

**horn** hard (long, curved) growth, one of a pair, on heads of many hoofed animals; tough material of which this growth, hoofs, nails, *etc* consist; *mus* (spiral) wind instrument made of metal; device for making warning sound, as on automobile

**hor·net** very large wasp

**hor·o·scope** art of foretelling future by observing position of stars and planets

**hor·ri·ble** exciting horror; hideous; very unpleasant

**hor·rid** shocking

**hor·|ror** (sth causing) great fear; extreme dislike. **-rify**

**horse** large hoofed four-footed domestic animal with mane and tail, used for riding on or pulling wagons, *etc*

**horse·pow·er** unit for measuring power of an engine

**horse·rad·ish** white-flowered herb whose root is used to make a pungent sauce

**hor·ti·cul·ture** art of gardening

**hose** (*pl* hose) stockings; (*pl* hos·es) flexible tube for transporting liquids

**hos·pi·ta·ble** kind and generous to guests or strangers. **hospital·ity**

**hos·pi·tal** building where sick or injured are given medical care, rest, *etc*

**hos·pi·tal·ize** put s.o. in hospital for treatment

**host** one who entertains guest; plant or animal on which parasite lives; large number

**hos·tage** (hostij) person given or held as security

**hos·tel** lodging place for young travelers or students

**hos·tile** unfriendly; of an enemy. **hostil·ity**

**hot** very much above ususal temperature; marked by strong emotions, as excitement, anger, *etc*; pressing closely, as in pursuit; stinging, as mustard

**hotch·potch** see **hodge-podge**

**hot dog** frankfurter in long bread roll

**ho·tel** house providing rooms, and sometimes meals, for travelers

**hot·house** greenhouse

**hot·plate** metal plate, *usu* part of portable cooker, used to prepare or keep food hot

**hound** *n* (hunting) dog; *v* chase; harass

**hour** period of 60 minutes, 24th part of day; any particular time; a classroom period

**hour·glass** glass device in which fixed quantity of sand runs from upper chamber through narrow hole into lower. chamber in one hour

**house** building for living in; any building in which sth specific is kept; a family, *etc* a royal one; body of law-makers; place of business or entertainment; audience (section) of theater

**house'hold** people, *esp.* family, living under one roof

**house'wife** married women in charge of household

**house'work** cleaning, cooking, *etc*

**hous'ing** (provision of) buildings to live in; protective case, *esp.* for machinery

**hov'el** open shed; small poor dwelling

**hov'er** hang fluttering in the air; wait nearby; be in undecided state

**how** in what way or condition; to what extent or degree

**how·ev'er** in any manner or degree that can be thought of; nevertheless

**howl** (make) long sad cry, as wolf or dog

**hub** central part of wheel; central point

**hub'bub** loud confused noise; uproar

**huck'le·ber·ry** (N. Amer. shrub with) edible blue-black berry

**huck'ster** street salesman

**hud'dle** heap or crowd together; crouch; nestle closely together

**hue** (shade of) color; **h. and cry** outcry (of pursuit or protest)

**huff** *n* fit of anger; *v* emit (breath) in puffs; bluster. **-y**

**hug** hold tightly in arms (as sign of love); stay close to; follow closely; cling to

**huge** (hyūj) very great; extremely large. **-ly, -ness**

**hu'la** Hawaiian dance

**hulk** body of old wrecked ship; mass; big person

**hull** outer covering of fruit or seed; frame of ship

**hum** make low, steady murmuring sound, as bee; sing with closed lips

**hu'man** (of, like, or belonging to) man, woman or child. **-ize** (*UK* **-ise**)

**hu·mane'** (-mān) kind and pitying towards suffering

**hu'man·ism** system of thought concerned with man's interests; Renaissance revival of ancient Greek and Roman thought

**hu'man·ist** student of human affairs; student of Roman and Greek literature. **hu-manis'tic**

**hu·man·i·tar'i·an** (person) having regard for the welfare of mankind. **-ism**

**hu·man'i·ty** mankind; human nature; kindness; *pl* learning concerned with human culture

**hum'ble** very modest; of low station in life

**hum'bug** sham; impostor; nonsense

**hum'drum** commonplace; dull

**hu'mid** moist or damp. **hu·mid'ity**

**hu·mil'i·ate** cause to feel ashamed; cause loss of dignity to

**hu·mil'i·ty** humbleness; modesty

**hum'ming-bird** tiny brilliantly-colored Amer. bird whose wings hum when moving

**hu'mor**, *UK -mour* quality of being funny; ability to be aware of funny things; mood; *v* give in to whims of (s.o.)

**hu'mor·ous** amusing; comical; having (sense of) humor

**hump** rounded bulge, as that on back of camel; small rounded rise in ground

**hu'mus** organic fertilizing matter in soil

**hunch** *n* idea based on intuition; *v* bend so as to form a hump

**hunch'back** (person with) humped or crooked back

**hun'|dred** a number (100), ten times ten. **-dredth**

**hung** see **hang**

**hun'|ger** (exhausted condition due to) need of food; strong desire for food, *etc.* **-gry**

**hunk** large piece

**hunt** chase and kill wild animals for food or sport; search for

**hur'|dle** barrier to be jumped over in race; obstacle

**hurl** throw with great force

**hur·rah'**, **hur·ray'**, **hoo·ray'** shout of joy or applause

**hur'ri·cane** violent storm

**hur'|ry** move or act with (excessive) haste; drive (s.o.) to move fast. **-ried**

**hurt** (hurt) cause sickness of body or mind; interrupt healthy or natural bodily functions, *etc.* by wounding or disease; cause or have bodily pain; cause damage to; wound feelings

**hur'tle** (cause to) move or rush swiftly

**hus'band** *n* a married man; *v* manage carefully and economically

**hus'band·ry** farming

**hush** order to be, or become, silent or quiet

**husk** dry outer covering of certain fruits or seeds

**hus'|ky** big and strong; somewhat hoarse. **-kiness**

**hus'tle** push (one's way) roughly; shove person hurriedly; hurry

**hut** small simple roughly--built house

**hutch** small pen for rabbits; *etc*

**hy'a·cinth** (bulb plant with) fragrant cluster of blue, pink or white flowers

**hy′brid** (hībrid) (offspring) of animals or plants of different kinds; (thing) composed of mixed elements

**hy′drant** pipe in street for drawing water

**hy·draul′ic** operated by or employing water or other liquid

**hy·dro·e·lec′tric** of or producing electricity by water-power

**hy′dro·foil** boat equipped with device to lift it out of water at high speeds

**hy′dro·gen** gaseous chemical element, the lightest substance known

**hy′dro·gen bomb** bomb based on release of nuclear energy from hydrogen

**hy·dro·pho′bi·a** morbid fear of water; rabies

**hy′dro·plane** plane which can land on water; light motorboat

**hy·dro·ther′a·py** use of water to treat diseases

**hy·e′na** (hiēne) four-footed doglike animal of Africa and Asia, feeding mainly on animals killed by others

**hy′giene** science and principles of health through cleanliness. **hygien′ic**

**hy·grom′e·ter** instrument for measuring moisture in the air

**hymn** (him) song in praise of God, nation, etc

**hym′nal** book of hymns

**hy·per′bo·la** curve whose two ends are never parallel

**hy·per′bol·e** (-bēlē) exaggeration for effect

**hy·per·crit′i·cal** too critical

**hy·per·son′ic** of speeds more than 5 times the speed of sound in air

**hy·per·ten′sion** abnormally high blood pressure

**hy·per′tro·phy** unusual enlargement of organ of body

**hy′phen** short line used to join words or indicate break at end of line. **-ate**

**hyp·no′|sis** (artificially produced) state resembling sleep in which person acts on outside suggestion. **-tic, hyp′notism**

**hy·po·chon′dri·|a** (-kon-) excessive fear about one's health. **-ac**

**hy·poc′ri·sy** pretense of goodness, virtue, etc. **hyp′ocrite**

**hy·po·der′mic** hollow needle for inserting drugs beneath the skin

**hy·pot′e·nuse** side opposite right angle of triangle

**hy·poth′e·sis** (pl **-ses**) idea proposed as explanation or basis for reasoning. **hypoth′et·ical**

**hys·te′ri·a** disturbance of nervous system marked by excessive excitement; etc; violent emotional outbreak

**hys·ter′i·|cs** fit of hysteria. **-cal**

**I**

**i** ninth letter of English alphabet

**I** (me, my) pronoun used when speaker, writer, *etc* refers to himself as subject of sentence; roman numeral 1

**ic|e** *n* solid form of water and other liquids when frozen. **-y**; *US* frozen dessert; *UK* ice cream; *v* cool with ice; cover (cake) with icing

**ice'berg** large mass of ice floating in sea

**ice'box** box where food is kept cool by ice

**ice cream** dessert made by freezing mixture of cream and sugar; *etc*

**i'ci·cle** (isikl) hanging tapering mass of ice formed by freezing of dripping water

**ic'ing** (is-) coating for cake, made of sugar, *etc*

**i·con'o·clast** person who attacks established (religious) beliefs. **iconoclas'tic**

**i·de'a** a concept formed in the mind by thinking, in reaction to events in the outside world or as a result of feelings; notion; pattern of anything held in the mind, as distinguished from any individual sample of this thing in reality; plan; opinion; vague belief

**i·de'al** (sth) in accordance with one's highest conceptions; (sth) existing only as an idea; (sth) perfect

**i·de'al·ism** pursuit of high ideals; showing things in an ideal form; system of thought in which everything is held to consist of ideas

**i·den'ti·cal** being the same in every detail; the same; (of twins) born from one egg and looking alike

**i·den'ti·fy** prove identity of; discover; associate or share with; declare identical with. **identifica'tion**

**i·den'ti·ty** state of being specific person or thing; state of being o.s.; exact sameness

**i·de·ol'o·gy** ideas underlying political, *etc* theory

**id'i·om** an expression peculiar to a language; characteristic language. **idiomat'ic**

**id·i·o·syn'cra·sy** view, attitude, *etc* peculiar to a person

**id'i·ot** person incapable of mental development from birth; complete fool. **-cy**

**i'dle** *a* doing nothing; unemployed; not in operation; (of talk, promises, *etc*) worthless or unimportant; groundless, as fear; *v* be idle; (of engine) run at low speed with gears disconnected. **-ness**

**i'dol** image of god used as object of worship; person blindly adored. **-ize** (*UK* **-ise**)

**i'dyll** (īdl) (description of) charming (country) scene. **idyl'lic**

**if** in the case that: *i. he comes, I will speak to him;* on condition that: *i. you try hard, you will succeed;* supposing that: *i. I knew his address, I would write to him;* whether: *see i. he is there;* **as i.** as it would be if

**ig'loo** Eskimo hut of snow

**ig·nite'** set on or take fire

**ig·ni'tion** igniting; electrical device for starting engine

**ig·no'ble** of low character or birth

**ig·no·min'i·ous** shameful; disgraceful

**ig·no·ra'mus** ignorant person

**ig'no·rant** lacking knowledge; unaware. **--rance**

**ig·nore'** refuse to take notice of

**i·gua'na** large tropical lizard

**i·ke·ba'na** Japanese art of arranging flowers

**ill** *a* not in good health; sick. **-ness;** (of manners, *etc*) rough and unfriendly; (of feelings) hostile; (of luck, *etc*) unfavorable; *n* evil; **i. at ease** uncomfortable or nervous

**ill-ad·vised'** unwise

**il·le'gal** unlawful. **illega'lity**

**il·leg'i·ble** impossible to read. **illegibil'ity**

**il·le·git'i·ma**te not authorized by law; not born of married parents. **-cy**

**ill'fat·ed** bringing, or destined to, misfortune

**ill'-fa'vored** ugly; displeasing

**ill'-got'ten** gained by evil means

**il·lib'er·al** narrow-minded; stingy; without culture

**il·lic'it** unlawful; forbidden

**il·lit'er·a**te unable to read or write; lacking education. **-cy**

**il·log'i·cal** against or lacking logic or reason

**il·lu'mi·nate** light up; throw light on; make clear; decorate with lights; *esp. hist* decorate (manuscript) with gold, *etc*

**il·lu'|sion** sth that deceives by its appearance; false impression. **-sory**

**il'lus·tra|te** make clear (by examples); furnish book, *etc* with pictures, drawings, *etc*. **-or, illus'trative**

**il·lus·tra'tion** picture, *etc* in book; example; act of illustrating

**il·lus'tri·ous** famous

**im'age** imitation of outer form of object, such as picture; reflection, as in mirror; mental picture; public perception of; simile or metaphor; (exact) likeness. **-ry**

**im·ag'i·ne** form mental picture of; suppose; guess. **-nary**, **-native**, **imagina'tion**

**i·mam'** leader of prayer in mosque; Moslem leader

**im·bal'ance** lack of balance; difference in number or quality

**im'be·cile** person of very weak mental powers; just above idiot. **imbecil'ity**

**im·bibe'** drink (in)

**im·bue'** inspire (with ideas, *etc*); soak or dye thoroughly

**im'i·ta|te** follow example of; copy; be like. **-tive**, **-tor**, **imita'tion**

**im·mac'u·late** pure; spotless; faultless. **-ly**

**im'ma·|nent** existing or remaining within; indwelling. **-nence**

**im·ma·te'ri·al** unimportant; not consisting of matter

**im·ma·tur|e'** not fully developed. **-ity**

**im·meas'ur·a·ble** not measurable; limitless

**im·me'di·ate** done at once or without delay; not separated by any object or by space or time: *his i. neighbor, the i. future*; direct. **-ly**

**im·men|se'** huge. **-sity**

**im·mer|se'** dip (completely) into liquid; baptize thus; involve deeply. **-sion**

**im'mi·|grate** come to live permanently in new country. **-grant**

**im'mi·|nent** soon to happen. **-nence**

**im·mo'bi|le** fixed; motionless. **-lize** (*UK* **-lise**), **immobil'ity**

**im·mod'er·ate** beyond reasonable limits. **-ness**

**im·mod'est** indecent; bold

**im·mor'al** against moral rules. **immoral'ity**

**im·mor'tal** that never dies; famous for all time. **-ize** (*UK* **-ise**), **immortal'ity**

**im·mov'a·ble** (-mūv-) that cannot be moved; firm; unyielding. **immovabil'ity**

**im·mun|e'** free from disease, tax, *etc* by nature or law. **-nity**, **immunize** (*UK* **-ise**)

**im·mu'ta·ble** unchangeable

**imp** little devil; mischievous child

**im'pact** striking of one body against another; influence

**im·pair'** make worse; weaken; damage

**im·pale'** pierce, as with sharp stake

**im·pal'pa·ble** not able to be felt by touch; hard to grasp

**im'part'** give; make known

**im·par'tial** just; not prejudiced. **impartial'ity**

**im·pass'a·ble** that cannot be passed along or over

**im'passe** deadlock

**im·pas'sioned** filled with strong feelings

**im·pas'sive** without emotion

## impatient

**im·pa·**|**tient** (-pashent) not
bearing pain, bad luck, *etc*
with calmness; restlessly desiring; not willing to bear interruption, contradiction,
*etc* calmly. **-tience**

**im·peach'** accuse (public
official) of misconduct in
office; cast doubt on. **-ment**

**im·pec·ca·ble** faultless;
blameless. **impeccabil'ity**

**im·pede'** hinder. **-iment**

**im·pel'** drive (person to do)

**im·pend'ing** near at hand;
about to happen

**im·pen'e·tra·ble** that cannot
be entered into or passed
through; that cannot be
(easily) understood. **impen-
etrabil'ity**

**im·per'a·tive** urgent; not to
be avoided; commanding

**im·per·cep'ti·ble** very slight;
not noticeable

**im·per'fect** faulty; not fully
formed or done.
**imperfec'tion**

**im·pe'ri·al** of an empire or
emperor; very grand; of UK
system of weights and measures

**im·pe'ri·al·ism** imperial government; policy of rulling
other countries directly by
colonization or indirectly by
economic or political control. **imperialist'ic**

**im·per'il** bring into danger

**im·per'son·al** showing no
personal feeling; not refer-

ring to any person

**im·per'son·ate** pretend to be
s.o. by imitation

**im·per'ti·nent** offensively
impolite. **-nence**

**im·per·turb'a·ble** that cannot be excited; calm

**im·per'vi·ous** that does not
permit passage through; not
easily affected. **-ness**

**im·pet'u·ous** impulsive; acting rashly. **-ness**

**im'pe·tus** moving force; incentive; impulse

**im·pi'e·ty** lack of respect (*esp.*
for God). **im'pious**

**imp'ish** mischievous

**im·pla·ca·ble** that cannot be
soothed or appeased.
**implacabil'ity**

**im·plant'** plant (into); insert
(graft, *etc*) in living tissue

**im'ple·ment** *n* tool; utensil; *v*
put into effect. **implemen-
ta'tion**

**im'pli·cate** involve (in crime,
*etc*)

**im·pli·ca'tion** sth implied;
possible effect; act of involving

**im·plic'it** taken for granted
though not stated; (of confidence, *etc*) unquestioning

**im·plode'** burst inward.
**-sion**

**im·plore'** beg earnestly and
urgently

**im·ply'** suggest or express indirectly; involve as necessary
or natural

**im·po·lite** rude; not polite

**im·pon·der·a·ble** not able to be weighed or measured exactly. **imponderabil'ity**

**im·port'** v bring in (goods), from foreign country; n meaning; importance; sth brought in from abroad

**im·por**|**tant** meaning or mattering a great deal; having far-reaching results; of great influence or standing; **self-i.** tending to exaggerate one's standing or significance. **-tance**

**im·por·tune'** beg repeatedly

**im·pose'** lay (tax, etc) on; thrust (o.s.) on or take advantage of others. **im·posi'tion**

**im·pos'ing** impressive, esp. in size or appearance

**im·pos·si·ble** that cannot happen, exist, or be done; (of person, behavior, etc) hard to accept or deal with. **impossibil'ity**

**im·pos'**|**tor** person who passes himself off as s.o. else; swindler. **-ture**

**im·po**|**tent** powerless; helpless; (of males) unable to have sex. **-tence**

**im·pound'** shut up, as stray animals; (law) seize and hold goods

**im·pov·er·ish** make poor

**im·prac·ti·ca·ble** not suited for actual practice or use. **impracticabil'ity**

**im·prac'ti·cal** unskilled in everyday affairs; unrealistic; idealistic. **impractical'ity**

**im·preg'na·ble** resisting all attack. **impregnabil'ity**

**im·preg'nate** make pregnant; soak thoroughly; spread throughout

**im·press'** press (mark) onto sth; influence deeply; fix firmly on the mind. **-sive**

**im·pres'sion** impressing; effect on mind; (vague) memory or belief; print taken from type; copies forming one issue of book, etc

**im'print** print or press (mark) on sth

**im·pris'on** put into prison. **-ment**

**im·prob'a·ble** not likely to happen or be true. **improbabil'ity**

**im·promp'tu** done without previous preparation

**im·prop'er** incorrect; unseemly; indecent

**im·prove'** make or become better. **-ment**

**im·prov'i·dent** careless; failing to provide for future needs. **-dence**

**im'pro·vise** compose or make without preparation. **improvisa'tion**

**im·pu'dent** very rude; disrespectful. **-dence**

**im·pugn'** (-pyūn) attack by words; cast doubt on

**im'pulse** sudden feeling

leading to action (without thinking); driving force.

**im·pul'sive**

**im·pu'ni·ty** freedom from punishment or harm

**im·pu|re'** unclean; mixed with foreign matter. **-rity**

**im·pute'** attribute (fault, *etc*) to. **imputa'tion**

**in** *prep* used to express position within given time, space, event, *etc*: *i. the seventeenth century*; *i. half an hour*, *i. New York, he acts i.the movies*; to indicate given circumstances: *i. a hurry, i. service, dressed i. blue*; to express share or part: *share i. a company, pleasure i.reading*; to indicate purpose: *i. honor of, i. reply to*; to show proportion: *one i. ten*; *break i. pieces, put i. motion*; **in so far** see **insofar**

**in·a·bil'i·ty** lack of means or power (to do)

**in·ac·ces'si·ble** that cannot be reached. **inaccessibil'ity**

**in·ac'cu·ra|te** not exact; in error. **-cy**

**in·ac'tive** not active; sluggish

**in·ad'e·qua|te** not enough (for the purpose). **-cy**

**in·ad·mis'si·ble** that cannot be allowed or admitted

**in·ad·ver'|tent** unintentional; accidental. **-tence**

**in·al'ien·a·ble** unable to be taken away or transferred

**in·an|e'** empty; senseless; silly **-ity**

**in·an'i·mate** not alive

**in·ap·pro'pri·ate** not fitting or suitable

**in·apt'** unsuitable; unskillful

**in·ar·tic'u·late** (of speech) indistinct; unable to express o.s. clearly

**in·as·much'** as since; to the degree that

**in·au'di·ble** not able to be heard

**in·au'gu·|rate** place s.o. in office; start undertaking, *etc* with ceremony. **-ral**

**in'born** being part of one's nature from birth

**in'bred** belonging to by nature or training

**in'breed·ing** mating of closely-related animals

**in·cal'cu·la·ble** not able to be reckoned or estimated (beforehand); uncertain

**in·can·des'|cent** glowing with heat; shining brightly. **-cence**

**in·can·ta'tion** (speaking of) magical words; spell

**in·ca'pa·ble** not able to do; lacking ordinary skill; not qualified

**in·ca·pac'i·|tate** make unfit or unable. **-ty**

**in·car'cer·ate** imprison

**in·car'nate** embodied in (human) form

**in·cen'di·ar·y** causing fires; tending to stir up strife

**in'cense** *n* substance smelling sweetly when burned

**in·cense'** *v* make very angry

**in·cen'tive** sth which rouses or promotes action

**in·cep'tion** beginning

**in·ces'sant** that does not stop; repeated; continuing

**in'cest** sexual intercourse between close relatives. **inces'-tuous**

**inch** *n* unit of length (= 2.54 centimeters), one twelfth of a foot; small amount or degree; *v* move by small degrees

**in'ci·dence** occurrence; rate at which sth happens

**in'ci·dent** event (happening alone or in connection with something else)

**in·ci·den'tal** happening by chance; of minor importance

**in·ci·den'tal·ly** by the way

**in·cin'er·a|te** burn to ashes. **-tor**

**in·cip'i·ent** beginning (to be); in an early stage

**in·ci|se'** make a cut in. **-sion**

**in·ci'sor** front cutting tooth

**in·cite'** stir up. **-ment**

**in·clem'ent** (of weather) cold or stormy

**in·cline'** *v* lean (forward or downward); have mental or bodily tendency towards; *n* slope. **inclina'tion**

**in·clu|de'** contain; take in (a part of larger whole). **-sion,** -sive

**in·cog'ni·to** having one's identity concealed (*esp.* to avoid attention)

**in·co·her'|ent** not logically connected. **-ence**

**in'come** money received regularly from business, *etc*

**in·com·men'su·rate** out of proportion; inadequate

**in·com'pa·ra·ble** matchless; not to be compared

**in·com·pat'i·ble** opposed in character; that cannot exist together in harmony. **incompatibil'ity**

**in·com'pe|tent** not qualified or able (to do). **-tence**

**in·com·plete'** lacking part; not complete

**in·com·pre·hen'|si·ble** not understandable. **-sion**

**in·con·ceiv'a·ble** that cannot be imagined

**in·con·clu'sive** producing no conclusion or result

**in·con'gru·ous** out of place. **incongru'ity**

**in·con·sid'er·a·ble** of small size, value or importance

**in·con·sid'er·ate** thoughtless; lacking in regard for others

**in·con·sist'ent** contradictory; lacking agreement; erratic, changeable

**in·con·sol'a·ble** incapable of being comforted

**in·con·spic'u·ous** hardly noticeable

**in·con'stan|t** fickle; subject to change. **-cy**

**in·con·test'a·ble** beyond doubt; indisputable

**in·con'ti·nent** unable to control one's bladder or bowels. **-nence**

**in·con·ve'nient** causing trouble or annoyance. **-nience**

**in·cor'po·rate** form into a corporation; include as part; combine into one

**in·cor·po're·al** not consisting of matter

**in·cor·rect'** not true; (of manners, *etc*) not proper

**in·cor'ri·gi·ble** (-rijibl) bad beyond reform. **incorrigi·bil'ity**

**in·cor·rup'ti·ble** that cannot be (morally) corrupted or decay

**in·crease'** make or become greater

**in·cred'i·ble** unbelievable; extraordinary. **incredibil'ity**

**in·cred'u·lous** skeptical; doubting. **incredul'ity**

**in'cre·ment** sth added; profit

**in·crim'i·nate** accuse of crime; involve in accusation

**in'cu·bate** hatch eggs by keeping them warm; cause (infection) to develop. **in·cuba'tion**

**in'cu·ba·tor** apparatus in which babies born too early

are kept alive; device for hatching eggs or developing bacteria

**in·cul'cate** impress ideas, *etc* upon mind

**in·cum'bent** *a* resting on, as duty; *n* holder of an office

**in·cur'** bring upon o.s.

**in·cur'a·ble** that cannot be cured

**in·debt'ed** owing money, gratitude, *etc*. **-ness**

**in·de'cent** against good taste; obscene. **-cy**

**in·de·ci'|sion** inability to decide; hesitation. **-sive**

**in·deed'** in truth; really (used to express emphasis, surprise, irony, *etc*)

**in·de·fat'i·ga·ble** untiring

**in·de·fen'si·ble** that cannot be defended or excused

**in·de·fin'a·ble** hard to define or describe exactly

**in·def'i·nite** not definite; not clear; vague

**in·del'i·ble** that cannot be rubbed out

**in·del'i·ca|te** coarse; tactless. **-cy**

**in·dem'ni·fy** secure against or compensate for loss. **indem·nifica'tion**

**in·dem'ni·ty** security against or compensation for damage or loss

**in·dent'** make (toothlike) notches in; set back from margin (to mark paragraph). **indenta'tion**

**in·de·pen|dent** free from rule or influence; not depending on others; unwilling to accept aid of others. **-dence**

**in·de·struc'ti·ble** that cannot be destroyed. **indestructibi'lity**

**in·de·ter'mi·na|te** not fixed in extent, *etc*; vague. **-cy**

**in'dex** (*pl* **-dexes, -dices**) alphabetical guide to information, as in book; sth serving as a pointer or sign; system allowing comparison of prices, *etc*; list of restricted (reading) material; **i. finger** forefinger

**In'di·an** of the original inhabitants of the Americas; (of a native) of India

**in'di·cate** point out; be sign of. **indic'ative**

**in·dict'** (-dīt) *law* accuse (by legal process). **-ment**

**in·dif'fer·|ent** without interest; neutral; not very good. **-ence**

**in·dig'e·nous** native; natural to

**in'di·gent** poor; needy. **-gence**

**in·di·ges'ti·ble** that cannot be (easily) digested. **-tion, indigestibil'ity**

**in·dig·na'tion** anger at something considered unjust. **indig'nant**

**in'di·go** deep blue (dye)

**in·di·rect'** not direct

**in·dis·creet'** unwise; not cautious. **indiscre'tion**

**in·dis·crim'i·nate** making no (moral) distinctions. **-ly**

**in·dis·pen'sa·ble** necessary; that cannot be done without. **indispensabil'ity**

**in·dis·posed'** not in good health; unwilling. **indisposi'tion**

**in·dis'pu·ta·ble** that cannot be doubted or denied

**in·dis·sol'u·ble** that cannot be dissolved; lasting

**in·dis'tinct'** not clear

**in·dis·tin'guish·a·ble** that cannot be clearly marked off or seen

**in·di·vid'u·al** *a* single; special; having distinct character; *n* single human being. **individual'ity**

**in·di·vid'u·al·is·m** belief that rights of the individual are the most important in a society

**in·di·vis'i·ble** that cannot be divided. **indivisibil'ity**

**in·doc'tri·nate** teach unquestioning acceptance of certain ideas

**in'do·|lent** lazy. **-lence**

**in·dom'i·ta·ble** that cannot be subdued

**in'doors** in or into a building

**in·du'bi·ta·ble** beyond doubt; unquestionable. **-bly**

**in·duce'** bring person to do; cause. **-ment**

**in·duct'** introduce or bring into; admit as member

**in·dul|ge'** grant (wish, *etc*); yield to (feeling). **-gence**

**in·dus'tri·ous** hard-working

**in'dus·try** (branch of) manufacture and those engaged in it; the entire manufacturing section of an economy; steady hardworking activity

**in·ed'i·ble** not fit to eat

**in·ef'fa·ble** that cannot be expressed in words

**in·ef·fec'tive, in·ef·fec'tu·al** not having the desired effect; not capable. **-ness**

**in·ef·fi'cient** not fully capable (of doing something well or economically). **-cy**

**in·el'i·gi·ble** not qualified; not fit to be chosen

**in·ept'** clumsy; out of place

**in·eq'ui·ta·ble** not just

**in·ert'** not having the power to move; chemically inactive. **-ness**

**in·er'tia** force holding matter in given state unless acted upon by outside force; inertness

**in·es·ca'pa·ble** impossible to avoid

**in·es'ti·ma·ble** too great, *etc* to be estimated

**in·ev'i·ta·ble** that cannot be avoided; sure to happen. **inevitabil'ity**

**in·ex·cus'a·ble** that cannot be excused

**in·ex·haust'i·ble** that cannot be used up or tired out

**in·ex'o·ra·ble** unyielding; without pity

**in·ex·pe'di·ent** not practical or convenient

**in·ex·pen'sive** costing little

**in·ex·pli'ca·ble** that cannot be explained

**in·ex·press'i·ble** that cannot be said in words

**in·fal'li·ble** that cannot be in error; unfailing

**in'fa·mous** of very bad reputation; wicked. **-my**

**in'fant** baby; *law* person under eighteen. **-cy**

**in·fan'ti·cide** murder(er) of infant

**in'fan·tile** of or like a baby

**in'fan·try** foot soldiers

**in·fat'u·a·ted** inspired with a (brief) foolish passion. **infatua'tion**

**in·fect'** fill (air) or affect (person) with disease germs, *etc*. **-tion, -tious**

**in·fer'** gather or draw conclusion (from facts) by reasoning. **in'ference**

**in·fe'ri·or** lower; poor (in quality, rank, *etc*). **inferior'ity**

**in·fer'nal** of hell

**in·fer'no** (place or state like) hell; large uncontrollable fire

**in·fest'** overrun in troublesome manner, as mice, *etc*

**in'fi·del** nonbeliever (in a particular religion)

**in·fi·del'i·ty** unfaithfulness, *esp.* in marriage; breach of trust

**in·fight·ing** (bitter) competition within group

**in·fil·trate** pass into or through; enter group, area, *etc* secretly and gradually, *usu* with hostile intent

**in·fi·nite** without end or limits; very great. **infin'itude**

**in·fin·i·tes'i·mal** extremely small

**in·fin'i·ty** state of being infinite; infinite space, time, size, *etc*

**in·firm'** weak in body or mind, *esp.* from age; not stable. **-mity**

**in·fir'ma·ry** hospital; rooms for treating the sick in schools, *etc*

**in·flame'** raise (body tissues) to feverish heat. **inflamma'tion;** raise passions or feelings

**in·flam'ma·ble** easily set on fire; easily excited

**in·flam'ma·to·ry** tending to arouse passions

**in·flate'** swell or puff out with gas or air; increase (amount of currency); raise (price) artificially. **-tion**

**in·flec|t'** bend; regulate (tone of voice). **-tion**

**in·flex'i·ble** unbendable; unyielding; not permitting change. **inflexibil'ity**

**in·flic|t'** impose (sth damaging or unwanted) on. **-tion**

**in·flow, in·flux** flowing in

**in·flu·ence** (make use of) power to affect acts, thoughts, *etc* of another by means of argument, moral or emotional pressure, *etc*; (exert) invisible action by one thing on person or other thing: *the weather has an influence on our well-being.* **influen'tial**

**in·flu·en'za** contagious disease causing great weakness, high fever, and *usu* disorder of throat and nose

**in·for|m'** tell; give information, *etc* to: **i. on|against** accuse. **-mant, informa'tion**

**in·for'mal** without formality; casual

**in·frac'tion** (example of) breaking of rules, *etc*

**in'fra·struc·ture** (system of) permanent installations necessary to run country, company, *etc*

**in·fre'quen|t** not happening often. **-cy**

**in·fringe'** break (rules, *etc*); overstep boundary. **-ment**

**in·fu'ri·ate** make very angry

**in·gen'ious** clever at inventing; cleverly invented. **ingenu'ity**

**in·gen'u·ous** frank; naive. **-ness**

**in·ges|t'** take in (food, *etc*). **-tion**

**in·glor'i·ous** shameful

**in'got** block of cast metal

**in·grained'** firmly fixed; deep-rooted

**in·grate** ungrateful person

**in·gra'ti·ate** bring oneself into favor with others

**in·grat'i·tude** lack of gratefulness

**in·gre'di·ent** element or component part of mixture

**in'grown** having grown into the flesh, as toenail

**in·hab'it** live in. **-tant**

**in·hale'** breathe in. **inhala'tion**

**in·her'ent** (of qualities, *etc*) existing in as permanent and natural element

**in·her'it** receive (property, *etc*) from former owner or (genetic qualities) from parents. **-tance**

**in·hib'it** restrain (impulses, *etc*); forbid. **inhibi'tion**

**in·hos'pi·ta·ble** not hospitable; (of region) not giving shelter, *etc*

**in·hu'man** unfeeling; brutal. **inhuman'ity**

**in·im'i·cal** hostile; harmful

**in·im'i·ta·ble** that cannot be imitated

**in·iq'ui·ty** extreme injustice; wickedness. **-tous**

**in·i'tial** *a* of or happening at the beginning; *n* first letter of (person's) name; large letter

**in·i'ti·ate** begin; instruct in principles of sth; introduce into secret society, *etc*

**in·i'ti·a·tive** (readiness and ability to take) first step or lead

**in·ject'** force (fluid) into; introduce. **-tion**

**in·junc'tion** *law* order to do or not do sth

**in'jure** hurt; do wrong to. **-ry, inju'rious**

**in·jus'tice** lack of fairness; unjust act

**ink** colored liquid used for writing, drawing or printing

**ink'ling** hint; slight knowledge or suspicion

**in'laid** having a pattern of wood, stones, *etc*, set in surface, as of table

**in'land** of, to or in the interior of a country

**in'-laws** *infml* relatives by marriage, *esp.* parents of spouse

**in'let** small narrow bay; way in

**in'mate** person confined in prison, hospital, *etc*

**in'most, in'ner·most** most inward

**inn** public house offering rooms and food to travelers; tavern

**in·nate'** inborn; natural

**in'ner** located near center; interior; internal

**in·no'cent** free from moral wrong; not guilty; harmless. **-cence**

**in·noc'u·ous** harmless

**in'no·vate** bring in sth new

**in·nu·en'do** (insulting) hint

**in·nu'mer·a·ble** countless

**in·oc'u·late** implant disease,

*etc* as protective measure. **inocula'tion**

**in·of·fen'sive** causing no offense or harm. **-ness**

**in·op'er·a·ble** that cannot be cured by surgery; not practical

**in·op·por·tune'** unsuitable, *esp.* with regard to time

**in·or'di·nate** excessive

**in·or·gan'ic** not organized like a living body; of dead matter, as stone, *etc*

**in'put** sth that is put in for use, *esp.* energy, information for a computer, *etc*

**in'quest** legal inquiry into cause of person's death

**in·quire'** ask; seek information, search into. **-ry**

**in·qui·si'tion** (official) inquiry; ruthless questioning; *hist* **I.** Roman Catholic tribunal to punish false beliefs. **inquis'itor**

**in·quis'i·tive** (unduly) curious. **-ness**

**in'road** invasion; activity (for) producing change

**in·sane'** mentally ill; mad; foolish. **-ity**

**in·sa'ti·a·ble** that cannot be satisfied

**in·scribe'** write in or on; engrave; enter, as on official list. **inscrip'tion**

**in·scru'ta·ble** not easily understood; mysterious. **inscrutabil'ity**

**in'sect** any of the class of small animals having no backbone, a body divided into three parts, six legs and *usu* two (pairs) of wings

**in·sec'ti·cide** substance for killing insects

**in'se·cure** unsafe; not firm, unsure (of o.s.). **insecu'rity**

**in·sem'i·nate** place semen in (female)

**in·sen'si·ble** unconscious; lacking feeling

**in·sen'si·tive** not sensitive. **insensitiv'ity**

**in·sep'a·ra·ble** that cannot be separated

**in·sert'** put in(to). **-tion**

**in·side'** *n* part near the center; inner side; *a* of, on or in the inside; *adv* at or to the inner side; *prep* within; in less time than

**in·sid'i·ous** deceitful; treacherous; proceeding secretly. **-ness**

**in'sight** (intuitive) understanding of situation, inner truth, nature of a thing, *etc*

**in·sig'ni·a** *pl* badges of office, *etc*

**in·sig·nif'i·|cant** unimportant; meaningless. **-cance**

**in·sin·cere'** not honest or frank. **-ity**

**in·sin'u·ate** hint slyly; bring (o.s.) into favor, *etc* by sly or indirect methods

**in·sip'id** lacking flavor; dull. **-ness, insipid'ity**

**in·sist'** lay stress on; demand. **-tence**

**in·so·far'** as to the extent that

**in'so·lent** disrespectful; insulting. **-lence**

**in·sol'u·ble** that cannot be (dis)solved

**in·sol'vent** unable to pay debts. **-cy**

**in·som'ni·a** sleeplessness

**in·spect'** look closely at; examine officially. **-tion**

**in·spec'tor** higher police officer; person whose job it is to inspect

**in·spire'** influence; bring about; rouse feeling, etc in (by divine influence). **inspi·ra'tion**

**in·sta·bil'i·ty** lack of permanence or steadiness

**in·stall'** place in office, etc (with ceremony); place in position for use, as machine, etc. **installa'tion**

**in·stall'ment**, UK **-stal-** one of successive part payments or parts supplied

**in'stance** example; particular case

**in'stant** n (exact) moment; a (of time) present; urgent; immediate. **-cy**

**in·stan·ta'ne·ous** done or happening in an instant

**in·stead'** (-sted) in place of (s.o. or sth)

**in'step** upper surface of foot between toes and ankle; part of shoe, etc fitting this

**in'sti·gate** bring about action; urge s.o. to action

**in·still'**, UK **-stil** put in slowly, as ideas in the mind

**in'stinct** inborn impulse or skill. **instinc'tive**

**in'sti·tute** n (building housing) organization for scientific, etc purpose; v set up; start; found

**in·sti·tu'tion** act of instituting; established custom or law; (charitable) institute; mental hospital. **-al**

**in·struct'** direct; teach; inform. **-tion, -tive, -tor**

**in'stru·ment** tool; device for producing musical sounds; measuring device. **instru·men'tal**

**in·stru·men·ta'tion** mus arrangement for instruments; complex system of instruments, as in airplane

**in·sub·or'di·nate** refusing to obey

**in·sub·stan'tial** slight; not real

**in·suf'fer·a·ble** unbearable

**in·suf·fi'cient** not enough. **-cy**

**in'su·lar** narrow-minded; of or like an island

**in'su·late** surround (wire, etc) with non-conducting material. **-tor, insula'tion;** cut off from surroundings

**in'su·lin** medicine for diabetes, obtained from pancreas of animals

**in·sult'** offensive speech or action

**in·sup·port'a·ble** unbearable

**in·sure'** make certain; protect against loss, damage, *etc.* **-ance**

**in·sur'gent** rebel(lious)

**in·sur·mount'a·ble** that cannot be overcome

**in·sur·rec'tion** (armed) rising against authority

**in·tact'** whole; undamaged

**in'take** act or place of taking in; amount taken in

**in·tan'gi·ble** (-tanj-) that cannot be touched or grasped by the mind

**in'te·ger** (-tej-) whole number

**in'te·gral** of or necessary to a whole

**in'te·grate** bring into a whole; bring about (racial, *etc.*) equality. **integra'tion**

**in·te·grat·ed cir'cuit** tiny silicon chip containing complex electrical circuit, used in computer systems, *etc*

**in·teg'ri·ty** strength of character; honesty; wholeness

**in'tel·lect** power of knowing, reasoning and understanding. **intellec'tual**

**in·tel'li·gence** ability to understand.  **-gent;** (people who gather) *esp.* secret information

**in·tel'li·gi·ble** (-ji-) that can be understood.  **intelligi'bil'ity**

**in·tem'per·ate** immoderate, *esp.* in drinking alcohol. **-ance**

**in·tend'** have in mind (to do); be meant for a particular purpose

**in·tense'** existing in a high degree, as heat, *etc*; (of feelings) very strong.  **-sify, -sity, -sive**

**in·tent'** *n* aim or purpose; *a* firmly decided on (doing) sth; eager; fixed, as gaze.  **-ly**

**in·ten'tion** purpose

**in·ten'tion·al** done on purpose

**in·ter'** bury.  **-ment**

**in·ter·act'** act upon each other.  **-tion**

**in·ter·breed'** (cause to) produce young from parents of different breeds, *etc*

**in·ter·cede'** plead (with one person for another); mediate.  **-cession**

**in·ter·cept'** stop or check (natural course of); catch on the way from one place to another.  **-tion, -tor**

**in·ter·change'** *v* exchange things with each other. **-able;** *n* exchange; small roads linking major highways at different levels

**in'ter·com** system of two-way communication via microphone and loudspeaker

**in·ter·con·ti·nen'tal** (carried on) between continents

**in·ter·course** dealings, talk *etc* between persons; sexual relations

**in·ter·de·pen'dent** dependent on each other. **-dence**

**in·ter·dict'** forbid; restrain. **-tion**

**in·ter·dis·ci·plin·ary** of or among different branches of learning

**in·ter·est** readiness to be concerned with s.o. or sth; power to give rise to such feeling; share in property, *etc*; business, cause, *etc* involving or promising advantage, profits, *etc* to one or more persons; (rate of) payment made in return for use of money borrowed; **in the i. of** on behalf of

**in·ter·face** point of interaction between two systems

**in·ter·fer|e'** (of interests, actions, *etc*) clash; hinder; meddle. **-ence**

**in·ter·im** in the meantime; *a* temporary; of the time between two events

**in·te·ri·or** lying within; internal

**in·ter·ject'** throw in (remark) suddenly

**in·ter·lace'** weave together

**in·ter·lin·e·ar** between the lines

**in·ter·link'** join together

**in·ter·lock'** connect so that movement in one part affects other parts

**in·ter·lop·er** intruder

**in·ter·lude** time, event, *etc* that lies between; entertainment between acts

**in·ter·me'di·ar·y** (person) acting between parties

**in·ter·me'di·ate** being or happening between two things

**in·ter·mi·na·ble** (seeming) without end

**in·ter·min·gle** mix (together); mingle with

**in·ter·mis·sion** pause

**in·ter·mit'tent** alternately stopping and beginning again

**in·tern'** *n* assistant doctor residing in hospital

**in·tern'** *v* imprison or limit freedom of movement. **-ment**

**in·ter·nal** of or lying in the inside; of the mind or soul; of the inner affairs (of a country)

**in·ter·na·tion·al** existing or carried on between different nations

**in·ter·na·tion·al·ize**, UK **-ise** bring under international control

**in·ter·play** influence, *etc* of two or more things on each other

**in·ter·po·late** insert (words) into text or conversation; introduce additional material

**in·ter·pret** explain; understand in a particular way;

**introspective**

describe or perform (work of art); translate what is said in foreign language. **-er, inter·pre'ta·tion**

**in·ter·re·late'** be mutually connected. **-tion(ship)**

**in·ter'ro·gate** question formally. **in·ter·ro·ga'tion**

**in·ter·rupt'** (cause) to break off action, speech, *etc.* **-tion**

**in·ter·sect'** cut across each other, as streets. **-tion**

**in·ter·sperse'** scatter among other things

**in·ter·state'** existing or carried on between states, *esp.* those of the *US*

**in'ter·val** space or time between points or events; pause

**in·ter·vene'** happen in the meantime; come between persons, *etc*; interfere in action. **-tion**

**in'ter·view** (ask questions at) meeting to obtain information, news story, *etc*

**in·tes'tine** *usu pl* bowels

**in'ti·mate** *a* (-mit) close in friendship, *etc*; familiar with; closely personal; *n* close friend. **-cy**

**in'ti·mate** *v* (-māt) make known indirectly; hint

**in·tim'i·date** make afraid; influence by threats

**in'to** to the inside of: *i. the house*; to a specified condition: *he fell i. disgrace*; against: *the car ran i. the wall*; indicating insertion, *etc: put i. a will*; in the direction of: *look i. the camera*

**in·tol'er·a·ble** unbearable

**in·tol'er|ant** not allowing contrary opinions, *esp.* in matters of race, religion, *etc.* **-ance**

**in·to·na'tion** (pattern of) rise and fall of the voice in speech

**in·tone'** chant

**in·tox'i·cate** make drunk; excite beyond self-control

**in·trac'ta·ble** difficult to deal with

**in·tra·mu'ral** of or within a place, college, *etc*

**in·tran'si·gent** unable to compromise

**in·tra·ve'nous** into or within vein(s)

**in·tra·u'ter·ine de·vice'** (also *IUD*) plastic, *etc* object placed in womb as contraceptive

**in·trep'id** fearless

**in'tri·ca|te** (confusingly) entangled or involved. **-cy**

**in·trigue'** arouse interest or curiosity; form (secret) plot

**in·trin'sic** belonging naturally to a thing

**in·tro·duce'** make one person known to another; bring or place in; bring into use; make opening remarks. **-tion, -tory**

**in·tro·spec|'tive** tending to examine one's own thoughts or feelings. **-tion**

**in·tro·vert** person concerned chiefly with his own thoughts and feelings. **-ed, introver'sion**

**in·trude** thrust or force (o.s.) upon; come uninvited. **-sion**

**in·tu·i'tion** immediate grasping by the mind without reasoning. **intu'itive**

**in·un·date** flood

**in·ure'** accustom (to hardships)

**in·vade'** enter country, etc to attack; encroach upon. **-sion, -sive**

**in·va·lid** (person) weakened by illness or disability

**in·val'|d** having no (legal) force. **-date, invalid'ity**

**in·val'u·a·ble** (useful) beyond measure

**in·va'ri·a·ble** unchangeable; always the same

**in·vec'tive** violent attack in words

**in·veigh'** (-vā) attack violently in words

**in·vei'gle** bring person to do by flattery, etc

**in·vent'** create new device, etc; think up (false) story. **-tion, -tor**

**in·ven·to·ry** detailed list of goods in stock

**in·vert'|t** turn upside down or backwards; reverse order, etc. **-sion**

**in·ver'te·brate** (animal) having no backbone

**in·vest'** put in (money) to use by purchase, etc so as to bring returns; clothe (with signs of office, qualities, etc). **-ment**

**in·ves'ti·gate** examine; search into. **-tor, investiga'tion**

**in·vig'o·rate** give life and energy to

**in·vin'ci·ble** that cannot be defeated. **invincibil'ity**

**in·vis'i·ble** that cannot be seen. **invisibil'ity**

**in·vite'** ask to come (as guest) or to accept (an offer); ask to give voluntarily, as suggestions, donations, etc. **invita'tion**

**in·vit'ing** attractive

**in·voice** bill sent with goods shipped

**in·voke'** call upon (in prayer, etc); appeal to authority; ask earnestly for. **invoca'tion**

**in·vol'un·tar·y** not done by one's own will; unintentional

**in·volve'** entangle (person in affair, etc); make necessary as consequence; include. **-ment**

**in·vul'ner·a·ble** that cannot be hurt. **invulnerabil'ity**

**in'ward** a towards or at inside or center; mental or spiritual; **inward(s)** adv towards the inside

**i'o·dine** (īedïn) strong-smelling nonmetallic element used as disinfectant, etc

**i'on** type of electrically charged particle

**i·on·o·sphere** atmosphere high above earth containing ions by which radio waves can be sent around the globe

**i·o·ta** very small quantity; jot

**IOU** (īōyū) ( = "I owe you") paper containing sum owed and signature as proof of debt

**i'rate** (īrāt) angry

**ire** anger

**ir·i·des'|cent** having colors of rainbow which shift with light. **-cence**

**i'ris** (īris) colored ring in center of eye; (plant with spearlike leaves and) showy blue or yellow flower

**irk** annoy. **-some**

**i'ron** n soft silver-gray metallic element, which is magnetic, rusts easily and is used to make steel; hand-held electric device for pressing clothes; golf club with metal head; pl bands used to fasten prisoner's wrists or ankles; v to press, as clothes

**i'ron·ing-board** long narrow (folding) table to hold clothes for ironing

**i'ro·ny** expression of one's meaning by words seeming to say the opposite (for purposes of ridicule); sequence of events having outcome contrary to what was expected. **iron'ical**

**ir·ra'tion·al** lacking reason; not logical

**ir·re·con·cil'a·ble** that cannot be made to agree

**ir·re·fu'ta·ble** that cannot be proven false

**ir·reg'u·lar** not regular; contrary to rule; uneven. **irreg·ular'ity**

**ir·rel'e·|vant** not to the point. **-vance**

**ir·re·lig'ious** not religious; hostile to religion

**ir·rep'a·ra·ble** beyond repair

**ir·re·place'a·ble** that cannot be replaced

**ir·re·pres'si·ble** beyond restraint; lively

**ir·re·proach'a·ble** blameless

**ir·re·sist'i·ble** too strong, charming, *etc* to be resisted

**ir·res'o·lute** undecided; hesitating. **irreso·lu'tion**

**ir·re·spec'tive of** without regard to

**ir·re·spon'si·ble** not capable of being responsible; without due sense of responsibility

**ir·rev'e·rent** disrespectful

**ir·re·vers'i·ble** that cannot be reversed

**ir·rev'o·ca·ble** that can no longer be changed

**ir'ri·gate** supply (land) with water

**ir'ri·ta·ble** quickly made angry; highly sensitive to touch, *etc.* **irritabil'ity**

**ir'ri·|tate** make angry; annoy; make (skin, *etc*) sore or inflamed. **-tant**

**is** see **be**

**is·land** (īlend) body of land surrounded by water; isolated group or area. **isle, is·let** (īl, īlit)

**i·so·late** place apart or alone; cut off from surroundings. **isola·tion**

**i·so·la·tion·is·m** policy of staying aloof from other countries, etc. **-ist**

**i·so·tope** one of two or more forms of element with different atomic weights but same chemical properties

**is·sue** (ishū) act of sending or going out; point in question; outcome; offspring; number of newspaper copies, etc published at one time

**isth·mus** (ismes) narrow strip of land connecting two continents, etc

**it** (its) thing, event, etc already mentioned; word used as subject of impersonal verb: *i. is hot*; word standing for (logical) subject mentioned later: *i. is hard to understand him, i. was I who did it*

**i·tal·ics** pl (type of print with) sloping letters. **-cize** (UK **-cise**)

**itch** uneasy tickling feeling of the skin; skin disorder causing this; strong restless desire

**i·tem** article on a list; news story. **-ize** (UK **-ise**)

**i·tin·er·ant** (person) traveling from place to place

**i·tin·er·a·ry** plan of travel; guidebook for travel

**its** of or belonging to it

**it·self** emphasizing or reflexive form of it: *this is a contradiction in i., the horse hurt i.*

**IUD** see **intrauterine device**

**i·vo·ry** (color of) hard substance forming tusk of elephant, etc; sth made from this

**i·vo·ry tow·er** retreat for avoiding problems, etc of everyday life

**i·vy** climbing evergreen plant

# J

**j** tenth letter of the English alphabet

**jab** stab; poke roughly

**jack** device for lifting heavy weights; playing card bearing picture of soldier or servant

**jack·al** small wild animal of dog family

**jack·ass** male ass; stupid person

**jack·et** short coat with long sleeves; potato skin; wrapper, as of book

**jack·knife** large folding pocket knife; dive made by bending to touch ankles and then straightening body

**jade** (green color of) precious stone used in jewelry, *etc*

**jag'ged** (jagid) having ragged or notched edges

**jag'uar** large, leopard-like spotted cat of tropical Amer.

**jail** (*UK* gaol) prison, *esp.* building where persons are kept for minor crimes or while awaiting trial

**jam** *v* squeeze or press into narrow space; push or apply suddenly, as brake; interfere with radio transmission; wedge or fix (machine, *etc*) so that it cannot work; *n* mass of cars, *etc* packed close together; fruit boiled with sugar until thick, as spread for bread

**jamb** side post of door, window, *etc*

**jan'gle** (cause to) make harsh metallic sound; irritate

**jan'i·tor** doorkeeper; *US* man who takes care of building

**Jan'u·ar·y** first month of year

**jar** *n* deep wide-mouthed glass or earthenware container; *v* make harsh or unpleasant sound; have harsh effect; clash

**jar'gon** talk that cannot be understood; language of particular profession or group

**jaun'dice** liver disease causing skin, *etc* to turn yellow

**jaunt** (short) pleasure trip

**jaun'ty** cheerful; sprightly

**jave'lin** light spear

**jaw** bone(s) containing teeth; *pl* mouth; *pl* parts of machine, *etc* for grasping sth

**jay** brightly-.colored bird of crow family

**jay'walk** cross street at wrong place or against traffic light

**jazz** music of black Amer. origin marked by improvisation and strong syncopated rhythm

**jeal'ous** (jeles) suspicious of rivals for someone's love or interest; feeling spiteful envy towards anyone more successful; possessive. **-y**

**jeans** *pl* trousers of denim

**jeep** small all-purpose car with four-wheel drive

**jeer** mock; sneer

**jel'ly** solid but elastic substance made by boiling fruit juices, certain animal substances, *etc*

**jel'ly·fish** jelly-like sea animal often having long feelers with stings

**jeop'ar·dy** (jep-) danger. **-dize** (*UK* **-dise**)

**jerk** give short pull or twist (to); throw with short quick movement; move abruptly or with jolts. **-iness, -y**

**jer'ry-built** of cheap, bad construction

**jer'sey** (jurzi) knitted fabric of cotton, silk, *etc*; sweater made of this

**jest** joke

**jest'er** one who makes jokes (*esp. hist* royal fool)

**jet** airplane with jet engine; spurt of liquid, gas, *etc* from small opening; such an opening; black mineral; **j. engine** one driven by exhaust gases

**jet'lag** tired or confused feeling caused by crossing several time zones in jet

**jet'sam** goods cast overboard to lighten ship

**jet'set** international group of wealthy, fashionable people

**jet'ti·son** throw (goods) overboard; abandon

**jew'el** (jūel) (ornament of) precious (cut) stone

**jig** (music for) lively dance

**jig'gle** make quick, jerking movements

**jilt** cast off (lover) or refuse to marry as promised

**jin'gle** (make) metallic noise of bells, coins striking together, *etc*; short simple song used in advertising

**jiu·jit'su** see **jujitsu**

**job** regular paid position; piece of work; task

**jock'ey** *n* one who rides a horse in races, *v* manage cleverly

**joc'u·lar** joking; humorous. **jocular'ity**

**jog** move along at slow speed; run for exercise; push slightly; call to mind: *j. one's memory*

**join** fasten together; become member, as of club; combine (efforts, *etc*); gather together in one body

**join'er** maker of furniture, *etc*. **-y**; s.o. who joins many clubs, *etc*

**joint** flexible connection between two bones; cut of meat; place where two parts, *etc* meet, as in a joke; *a* united; shared by two or more persons

**joist** wooden crosspiece for ceiling or floor

**joke** sth said or done to cause laughter

**jol'ly** pleasant; merry

**jolt** shake roughly or suddenly, as in riding

**jos'tle** push or shove against

**jot** *n* small amount; *v* write down briefly

**joule** unit for measuring work or energy

**jour'nal** newspaper or serious magazine; book for listing daily events, *etc*

**jour·nal·is·m** business of writing for newspapers, *etc*. **-ist**

**jour'ney** (jurni) travel from one place to another

**jo'vi·al** merry; in good humor. **jovial'ity**

**jowl** cheek; jawbone; fold of flesh hanging from jaw

**joy** feeling of great happiness; cause of this. **-ful, -ous**

**joy'stick** upright handle to

209

**just**

control movement of airplane, computer game, *etc*

**ju·bi·lant** feeling or showing great joy. **jubila'tion**

**ju·bi·lee** (celebration of special) anniversary, *esp.* 50th

**judge** *n* public official with power to decide questions brought before court; person deciding winner in contest, *etc*; competent critic; *v* decide question brought before court; establish winner, *etc*; estimate worth or quality of. **-ment, judgment**

**ju·di·cial** (-dishel) of or pertaining to a court of law, judge or judgment

**ju·di·ci·ar·y** (-dishes) (the system of) courts and judges of a country

**ju·di·cious** (-dishes) sound in judgment; wise. **-ness**

**jug** pitcher; *US* deep large container with narrow mouth

**jug|gle** keep several objects in motion at the same time; manipulate. **-gler**

**jug'u·lar** (vein) of the neck

**juice** (jūs) liquid part of plants or animal bodies

**ju·jit'su** Japanese art of self-defense using opponent's strength and weight against him

**Ju·ly'** seventh month of year

**jum'ble** mix (individual things) in confused mass

**jum'bo** larger than others of its kind

**jump** spring into the air; rise suddenly, as temperature

**jump'er** long loose blouse; sleeveless dress; *UK* sweater

**jump'suit** one-piece garment combining trousers and top

**jump'y** nervous

**junc'tion** place or point of meeting, as of railway lines, *etc*

**junc'ture** critical moment (at which events concur)

**June** sixth month of year

**jun'gle** (tropical) land overgrown with tangled underbrush and trees; jumble; place of ruthless struggle

**jun'ior** (-yer) younger; of lower standing

**junk** *n* kind of Chinese ship; any waste or worthless material; *v* give up (using) as worthless

**ju·ris·dic'tion** (extent or area of) authority, *esp.* to decide questions of law

**ju·ris·pru'dence** science or study of law

**ju'rist** one trained in law

**ju'ror** one serving on a jury

**ju'ry** body of (12) persons sworn to decide legal question; judges of contest

**just** *a* fair; (of punishment) deserved; right according to law; *adv* exactly; now or a short while ago: *my friend has j. come*; by a very small space or time: *j. a little too*

*late*; simply or only: *j. excited*

**jus'tice** (administering of)
what is deserved or right,
*esp.* according to law; a
judge ·

**jus'ti·fy** show to be just, right
or reasonable; make printed
lines even in length. **jus-**

**ti'fica'tion**

**jut** stick out

**jute** plant fiber used in making rope or burlap

**ju've·nile** *a* young; of or for
youth; childish; *n* (actor
playing) young person

**jux·ta·pose'** place side by
side. **juxtaposi'tion**

# K

**k** eleventh letter of English alphabet

**ka·lei'do·scope** tube
through which constantly
changing color patterns can
be seen; changing pattern or
scene

**kan·ga·roo'** plant-eating
Australian animal, with
strong hind legs for leaping
and a pouch in which young
are carried

**ka'pok** fleecy material, used
to stuff cushions, *etc*

**ka·ra'te** Japanese style of
fighting using hands and feet
as weapons

**keel** bottom timber of ship

**keen** sharp; eager; quick in
understanding. **-ness**

**keep (kept)** retain possession
of; save; (cause to) continue
in action or state: *k. the fire
burning, k. walking*; guard or
protect, as prisoner, *etc*; prevent from doing: *k. him from
leaving*; have customarily in
stock or for use; manage, as

shop, household, *etc*; withhold from use or knowledge:
*k. it a secret*; record events,
business transactions, *etc*,
regularly: *k. books*; provide
living for person, *etc*; go on
having: *k. one's looks*; remain fresh (of food, *etc*);
observe, as law, festival, *etc*;
fulfill, as promise; **k. off**
ward off; stay away; **k. on** go
on doing

**keep'sake** thing kept in
memory of giver

**keg** small barrel

**ken** range of sight or knowledge

**ken'nel** house for keeping
dogs in

**ker'chief** cloth used to cover
head

**ker'nel** (edible) part inside
nutshell, *etc*; seed within
husk

**ketch'up** spiced tomato sauce

**ket'tle** (metal) pot *usu* covered and with spout, for
boiling water, *etc*

**kink**

**key** (metal) object for winding clock, starting car, opening or locking door, *etc*; sth giving explanation or aid(s) to understanding; lever on piano, typewriter, *etc* pressed with finger to work the mechanism; *mus* system of related notes with particular note as base

**kha'ki** dull brownish yellow (cloth)

**kick** strike something with foot; strike out with foot

**kid** *n* (leather made from hide of) young goat; youngster; *v* tease; fool

**kid'nap** carry (person) away by unlawful force, *esp*. to gain ransom

**kid'ney** one of pair of beanshaped organs in vertebrates, located near spine and giving off urine

**kid'ney ma·chine** apparatus to cleanse blood of patient with defective kidney(s)

**kill** cause death of; destroy; neutralize effect of disease, *etc*; cause to stop; (of time) cause to pass; defeat or veto, as law

**kiln** oven for burning or baking pottery, *etc*

**ki'lo·byte** 1000 or 1024 bytes of computer information

**kil'o·gram** unit of weight equalling 1,000 grams

**kil'o·me·ter** unit of length equalling 1,000 meters

**kilt** pleated skirt, *usu* tartan, worn by Scotsman

**-folk** (*UK* **-sfolk**); *a* related people

**kind** *a* of a friendly or gentle nature. **-liness, -ness, kind'-heart'ed;** *n* class, *esp*. of animals, plants, *etc*. having the same characteristics; nature of a thing or individual as determining likeness to, or difference from, others: *they are of the same k.*; particular quality or sort; *this is the k. of house I like*; giving a more or less exact description: *it is a k. of desk*; **in k.** of the same nature as thing received

**kin'der·gar·ten** school or class for children aged 4-6

**kin'dle** set on or catch fire; (cause to) become excited

**kin'dling** material for starting a fire

**kin'dred** *n* one's relatives; *a* related; similar

**ki·net'ic** of or relating to (forces of) motion

**king** male (hereditary) ruler of a country; most powerful or outstanding person, animal, *etc* of its kind; playing card bearing picture of k.; main piece in chess

**king'dom** state governed by king or queen; province, *esp*. of nature: *animal, vegetable and mineral kingdoms*

**kink** sharp twist or bend (in rope, *etc*). **-y**

**ki'osk** small stand for selling newspapers, *etc*

**kip'per** salted smoked fish, *esp.* herring

**kiss** *v* touch with lips as sign of love, greeting, *etc*; touch lightly, as wind; *n* act of kissing; slight touch; *US* small piece of candy, *usu* wrapped in paper, *etc*

**kit** set of tools, utensils, *etc* carried in bag; set of parts to be assembled

**kitch'en** room where food is prepared and cooked

**kitch·en·ette'** small kitchen (as part of larger room)

**kite** light (wooden) frame covered with thin paper, to be flown in wind at end of long string; bird of prey

**kitsch** worthless artistic or literary material

**kit'ten** young cat

**kit'ty** pet name for cat; pool (in card game) into which money is put

**Kleen'ex** *TM* paper handkerchief

**klep·to·ma·ni·a** neurotic urge to steal regardless of personal need. **-ac**

**knack** (nak) special skill in doing sth

**knead** (nēd) work dough, clay, *etc* with fingers so as to mix; massage

**knee** (nē) (part of garment covering) joint between thigh and lower part of leg

**knee'cap** bone at front of knee

**kneel** (nēl) (**knelt** or **kneeled**) fall or rest on knee(s), as when praying

**knew** see **know**

**knick'knack** (niknak) small cheap ornament

**knife** (nīf) *n* (*pl* **knives** [nīvz]) pointed cutting instrument with sharp-edged (steel) blade fitted into handle; *v* stab with knife

**knight** (īt) *hist* man of noble birth, raised to honorable military rank; similar rank granted by king, *etc*, for services. **-hood;** chess piece

**knit** (nit) (**knit** or **knit'ted**) make garment of interlocking loops of yarn using knitting needles or machine. **-ter, -ting;** join (parts) closely and compactly; draw into folds, as brow

**knit'wear** knitted clothing

**knob** (nob) projecting part, *usu* rounded, forming handle on door, drawer, *etc*; round lump on surface or at end of thing, as at head of walking stick; rounded (isolated) hill

**knock** (nok) strike sth, as door, with knuckles, fist or hard object, so as to call for attention; hit (person) in this manner; make pounding noise; **k. about** hit (person) repeatedly; wander aimlessly; **k. against** collide with; **k. down** strike (person) down; (in auctions) announce sale by blow with hammer; **k. off** stop doing, *esp.* work; **k. out** (in boxing) make opponent unconscious

**knock'er** (nok-) (metal) knob, *etc*, hinged to door, for knocking

**knock'-kneed** (noknēd) having legs that curve inward at knee

**knot** (not) fastening in rope, *etc*, formed by tying ends together; hard lump in tissue of plant or animal, or in wood (*esp.* where branches meet); measure of speed of ship or plane (= one nautical mile per hour)

**knot'ty** full of knots; difficult, as problem

**know** (nō) (**knew** [nyū, nū], **known**) understand or be aware of by realizing nature of a thing or idea, or by experience, learning, *etc*; have fixed in mind by learning; be familiar with person, place, *etc*; be able (to do) through experience, *etc*; be able to tell one from another.

**knowl'edge**

**knowl'edge·a·ble** well-informed

**knuck'le** (nukl) *n* joint of finger; joint of meat from lower part of fore or hind legs of pig, *etc*; *v* **k. down** work hard; **k. under** give in (to pressure)

**ko·a'la** (bear) small Australian animal which lives in trees and has thick gray fur

**kohl·ra'bi** (plant with) turnip-like vegetable

**Ko·ran'** sacred writings of the Moslems

**ko'sher** (of food, *etc*) fulfilling requirements of Jewish law; *infml* right; proper

**kow·tow'** (kōtou) show obedience, *etc* (by touching ground with forehead)

# L

**l** twelfth letter of English alphabet

**la'bel** strip of paper, attached to sth to identify it, show ownership, *etc*; descriptive phrase

**la'bor**, *UK* **-bour** work, *esp.* for economic production; body of those doing such work; task; act of giving birth

**lab·o·ra·to·ry** room used for scientific work, tests, *etc*

**la'bored**, *UK* **-boured** done with much care or effort; not easy or natural

**la·bo'ri·ous** requiring or showing signs of hard work; hard-working

**la·bor u·ni·on** see **trade un·ion**

**lab'y·rinth** network of many passages and blind alleys through which it is hard to find a way; complicated situation. **labyrin'thine**

**lac|e** openwork fabric in ornamental pattern, made of threads. **-y**; string threaded through holes, for drawing together edges of shoes, etc

**lac'er·ate** tear roughly; hurt

**lack** be without; not have sth needed or wanted

**lack·a·dai'si·cal** lacking enthusiasm; lazy

**lack'ey** liveried servant; slavish person

**lack'lus·ter,** UK **-tre** dull; unexciting

**la·con'ic** using few words; terse

**lac'quer** (laker) varnish; spray to keep hair in place

**lad** boy; (young) fellow

**lad'der** structure of two parallel bars or ropes connected by crosspieces (rungs) and used for climbing up or down; UK run in stocking

**la'den** loaded

**la'dle** long-handled spoon with deep bowl for dipping soup, etc

**la'dy** polite term for any woman; woman of good family. **-like**; also **L.** (UK) title for woman of high noble rank. **-ship**

**lag** go too slow; fall behind. **-gard**

**la'ger** (lah-) (glass of) light beer

**la·goon'** lake of saltwater (partially) separated from sea by banks of sand, etc

**laid** see **lay**

**lain** see **lie**

**lair** resting place of wild animal

**la'i·ty** lay people; people outside of a particular profession

**lake** large body of water surrounded by land

**lamb** (lam) (meat of) young sheep; gentle or weak person

**lame** crippled, esp. in foot or leg; unable to walk (properly); (of excuse, etc) weak

**la·ment'** express or feel grief; mourn for; regret. **la'men·table, lamenta'tion**

**lam'i·nate** beat or roll into thin plates; make by putting layer on layer

**lamp** (movable) device for giving light or heat

**lance** long spear

**lan'cet** small pointed two-edged knife, used in surgery

**land** n solid part of earth's surface; soil, esp. with regard to its use or type; a country; ground owned publicly or privately; v bring to shore, esp. from ship; (cause to) come to certain place or condition; *l. a plane*, *l. him in trouble*

**land'fall** first sight of land from ocean or air

**land'ing** act of arriving on land; place where ships dock; even surface at top (of or between) flight(s) of stairs

**land'locked** (almost) entirely surrounded by land

**land'lord,** ∫ **land'la-dy** person who owns and leases buildings, *etc*, or who runs boarding house, *etc*

**land'mark** easily-seen object on land that serves as a guide; important event (in history)

**land'scape** (picture representing) country scene

**land'slide** sliding down of mass of land; overwhelming election victory

**lane** narrow way between fences, houses, *etc*; fixed course travelled by ship, *etc*; division of highway for one line of traffic; division of track, *etc* for race

**lan'guage** communication among human beings using words; system of such words as used by people of one nation, professional group, *etc*; (particular) manner of speech or writing

**lan'guid** (-gwid) slow; weak; lacking in energy or spirit

**lan'guish** become or be weak; suffer (under unfavorable conditions); long for

**lan'guor** (langger) lack of energy; tender mood. **-ous**

**lank** (of hair) straight and limp

**lank'y** tall and thin

**lan'o-lin** fatty substance from sheep's wool, used in face cream, *etc*

**lan'tern** (lamp with) case of glass, parchment, *etc*, to protect light from wind; chamber at top of lighthouse

**lap** *n* hollow of body between waist and knees formed when sitting; amount of rope, cloth, *etc*, required to go round reel, *etc* once; single round of race course; (sound of) washing of water against shore; *v* fold over or around, or wrap around (sth); take or lick up water, *etc*, with tongue

**la-pel'** part of coat front attached to collar and folded back

**lapse** slip (of memory, *etc*); falling (into wrong or to lower state); passage of time; ending of privilege due to disuse, *etc*

**lar'ce-ny** *law* theft. **-nous**

**larch** (wood of) kind of pine-tree which sheds its needles each year

**lard** *n* rendered fat of pigs; *v* enrich lean meat with bacon, *etc* before cooking; decorate (talk) with foreign words, *etc*

**lard'er** pantry

**large** of more than usual size, amount; *etc*; of broad scope or range; **at l.** free, unconstrained; as a whole

**lark** amusing trick or adventure; any of various songbirds, *esp.* skylark

**lar'va** wormlike young of insect from time of leaving egg to pupa stage

**lar·yn·gi'tis** inflamed swelling of the larynx

**lar'ynx** hollow in throat containing vocal cords

**la'ser** (device for producing) intense narrow beam of light, used for cutting metal, *etc* or in surgery

**lash** *n* (blow with) flexible end of whip, *etc*; quick switching movement, as of animal's tail; sharp stroke; sharp criticism; violent beating, as of rain; eyelash; *v* bind (to sth) with rope; beat (as if) with a whip

**lass** girl; sweetheart

**las'so** rope with running noose, used to catch cattle

**last** *a* coming after all others; being immediately before the present; being the only one('s) left; least likely; *v* continue living or being as before; take, or be enough for, specified time; *n* end; model of foot on which shoe is shaped

**last'ing** permanent; enduring

**latch** door-fastening device

**late** coming, or continued until, after the usual or proper time; (of time) immediately before present; happening in or belonging to advanced stage of development, history, *etc*; no longer alive

**late'ly** recently

**la'tent** (lā-) hidden; existing but not developed. **-cy**

**lat'er·al** of, at or toward the side

**la'tex** (lā-) milky fluid of certain plants, *esp.* the rubber tree; synthetic substance like this used in paints, *etc*

**lathe** (lā-) machine for shaping wood, metal, *etc*

**lath'er** froth of soap and water; frothy sweat of horse

**lat'i·tude** distance (of point on its meridian) N. or S. of equator; freedom from narrow restrictions

**la·trine'** (outdoor) toilet, *esp.* in camp, *etc*

**lat'ter** being second mentioned of two; later; of or near end of a period

**lat'tice** structure of crossed wooden or metal strips

**laud'a·ble** worthy of praise

**laud'a·to·ry** praising

**laugh** (-af) give off the inarticulate sounds which express joy, amusement, contempt, *etc*. **-ter; l. at** make fun of

**launch** *v* set (ship) afloat;

send (rocket) into space; start sth, as campaign; send or go forth; throw; *n* act of launching; heavy open motorboat

**laun·der** wash and iron (clothes, *etc*)

**laun·dro·mat** self-service laundry; also *UK* **launder·ette**

**laun·dry** room or business where clothes are washed, (and ironed); dirty clothes, *etc*

**lau·rel** evergreen shrub; leaves of this as symbol of victory or honors won

**la·va** melted rock flowing from volcano; such rock when hardened

**lav·a·to·ry** room for washing; *UK* toilet

**lav·en·der** (small shrub with) pale-blue sweet-smelling flower; (of) this color

**lav·ish** giving or using generously; (too) abundant

**law** system of rules recognized by and governing conduct of nation, *etc*; rule issued by legislative body and enforceable by the courts. **-ful**; division of knowledge concerned with these rules, or body of persons dealing with them; (statement of) rule which unchangingly applies in physics, *etc*

**lawn** plot of well-tended,

grass-covered land

**lawn·mow·er** machine for cutting grass

**law·suit** private claim before a court

**law·yer** person licensed to give legal advice and represent client in court

**lax** loose; not strict; careless. **-ity, -ness**

**lax·a·tive** (medicine) causing bowels to empty

**lay** *v* (**laid**) see also **lie**; put in certain position or place, *esp*. one of rest, or cause to be in certain state, *etc*; put sth in proper position; (cause to) calm down; bury; (of birds) produce (eggs); make bet: *lay him five to one*; bring to person's, *etc* attention; bring forward as charge; attribute (fault, *etc*) to person; place on, as burden; prepare or make ready, as plan, table for meal; *etc*; **l. bare** reveal; **l. by** put aside for later use; **l. hold of** grasp; **l. off** dismiss (worker), *esp*. for short time; **laid up** confined to bed through illness; *a* not of the clergy; not professional. **-man, -person, -woman**

**lay·er** a thickness of material; sth put or spread on a surface, as paint

**lay·out** arrangement or plan, as of newspaper

**lay·o·ver** stopover

**la'|zy** unwilling to do work or strain o.s.; slow-moving, as river. **-ziness**

**lead** (lēd) v (**led**) show the way by going ahead; cause horse, *etc* to follow one by holding bridle; guide in certain action, course, *etc*; (of road, *etc*) serve to bring (person) to given place; go or be at head of troops, team, enterprise; direct, as discussion, orchestra, *etc*; pass (life) in specified manner; play first in game of cards; *n* first or most important position, part in play, *etc*; extent of being ahead; thing or fact that serves as guide; clue

**lead** (led) heavy, soft, bluish-gray metal; lump of this suspended from line and used to measure depth of water; small bullets; (stick of) graphite used in pencils

**lead'en** (ledn) (as if) made of lead; heavy; dull (gray)

**lead'er** one or that which leads. **-ship**; *esp. UK* paper editorial

**lead'ing** most important; main

**leaf** (*pl* **leaves**) part of plant, *usu* green, which grows from stem; foliage of tree; sheet of paper folded once, as two pages in book; hinged flat part, as of door, table, *etc*

**leaf'let** division of leaf; young leaf; small (folded) sheet of paper printed with information, *etc*

**league** agreement between groups, states, *etc* for mutual aid; group of competing sports clubs; old unit of distance (about 3 miles)

**leak** (of liquids, gases, *etc*) flow into or run out of vessel through crack or hole; (of secrets, *etc*) become known by accident, *etc*. **-age, -y**

**lean** v (**leaned** or **leant**) bend from upright position or in particular direction; (cause to) rest against or on sth; tend toward certain ideas, attitudes, *etc*; rely on; *a* (of persons or animals) not having much flesh; (of meat) not fat; meager

**leap** (**leaped** or **leapt**) jump from one point to another; jump over sth; jump to (conclusion *etc*)

**leap year** year with extra day (29 February) occurring every fourth year

**learn** (**learned** or **learnt**) get knowledge or skill by study, experience, *etc*. **-er, -ed, -ing**; become aware of; memorize; find out

**lease** v rent (land, *etc*) by contract; *n* rental contract

**leash** line for leading dog

**least** less in size, weight, amount, *etc* than all others; **at l.** in any case; not less

**legislation**

than; **in the l.** at all: *not in the least likely to happen*

**leath'er** (ledher) skin of certain animals prepared by tanning for use in shoemaking, *etc*

**leave** *v* (**left**) go away from place, person, *etc*; allow to stay in specified condition, or (person) to do without interference; let work, *etc*, remain for future action; let remain behind; hand down through a will; give in charge: *l. the child to his care*; **l. off** stop (doing); **l. out** fail to include; *n* permission to do sth; period for which permission to be absent is given; farewell

**leav'en** (leven) substance, *esp.* yeast, for raising dough; influence which works a (gradual) change. **-ing**

**lec'ture** (give) talk before class, *etc* on given subject. **-er;** (issue) reproof or warning

**led** see **lead**

**ledge** narrow shelf projecting from wall, cliff, *etc*

**ledg'er** book of accounts recording money spent and earned

**lee** side sheltered from wind

**leech** bloodsucking worm

**leek** vegetable with long white stalk and mild onion flavor

**leer** (look with a) side glance,

*esp.* a sly or indecently suggestive one

**left** *v* see **leave;** *a* of or belonging to side of person or thing which points to the west when facing north; near, on or by this side; of or belonging to the political left, as Socialist, *etc*. **-ist, -wing**

**left'o·ver** not used; remaining

**leg** one of limbs (in humans from hip to ankle) by which human or animal body is supported and moved; part of clothing covering this; leg of animal as food; support of chair, *etc*; one part of a course, race, trip, *etc*; **pull (someone's) leg** make fun of

**leg'a·cy** gift by will; anything handed down by ancestor

**le'gal** of or required by law; lawful. **-ize** (UK **-ise**), **legal'ity**

**le·ga'tion** (residence of) diplomatic minister and staff

**leg'end** traditional story popularly regarded as true; famous person or thing. **-ary;** motto on coin, *etc*

**leg'gings** *pl* outer covering for leg up to knee

**leg'i·ble** (of handwriting, *etc*) readable. **legibil'ity**

**le'gion** vast number; *hist* division in Roman army

**leg·is·la'tion** (lej-) (making

of) laws; body of laws. **leg'islative**

**leg·is·la·ture** legislative body of a state. **-tor**

**le·git'i·mate** lawful; proper or regular; reasonable; born of married parents. **-cy**

**leg'room** space for legs when seated (in vehicle, etc)

**leg'ume** (fruit or seed of) pod-bearing plant, as bean, pea, etc

**lei'sure** time at one's disposal, free from work or duty. **-ly**

**lem'on** (subtropical tree bearing) yellow citrus fruit; (of) pale yellow color

**lem'on·ade** drink of sweetened lemon juice and water

**lend (lent)** allow (person) use of money, etc, for certain time, usu at interest, with an understanding that it or sth equal in value or kind will be returned. **-er**; give (temporary) effect or service to: l. dignity to his looks, l. one's aid; **l. oneself** or **itself** to be useful or appropriate to

**length** extent of thing when measured or considered from end to end or (of time, book, etc) from beginning to end; (long) stretch; piece having given measurement; vertical measure of clothing; degree to which sth is carried: go to any/great, etc lengths; **at l.** in detail

**le·ni·en|t** mild; tolerant. **-cy**

**lens** glass for concentrating or spreading light rays, used in eyeglasses, cameras, etc; transparent body in eye which focuses light rays on retina

**leop'ard** (leperd) large wild animal of cat family found in Africa and Asia

**le·o·tard** close-fitting, one-piece garment worn by dancers, etc

**lep'ro·sy** infectious disease of skin and nerves causing loss of fingers, etc. **-er, -rous**

**les·bi·an** (of or relating to) woman attracted sexually to other women

**le'sion** wound; abnormal change in organ, esp. due to injury or disease

**less** a smaller in size, amount, importance, etc; prep minus

**less'en** make or become less

**les'son** (instruction in) thing to be learned; time or task assigned for particular study; experience serving as warning, etc

**lest** in order that ... not; for fear that

**let (let)** allow (person, animal or thing) to come, go, have, escape, etc; l. him in, l. the dog run, l. the steam out; offer for rent or hire: l. rooms

**le'thal** (lē-) of or causing death

**leth'ar·gy** (unnatural) drowsiness, state of dullness and lack of interest. **lethar'gic**

**let'ter** written or printed message to other person(s); (printing-type bearing) one of the signs representing speech sounds making up the alphabet; actual wording of law, *etc*; *pl* literature. **-ed, -ing**

**let'ter·head** name and address (of business) printed at top of sheet of paper

**let'ter·press** printing from raised type

**let'tuce** salad plant with large crisp leaves

**lev'ee** embankment against river floods

**lev'el** horizontal; flat; smooth; steady

**le'ver** bar transmitting mechanical force, as in lifting, cutting, *etc*. **-age;** handle for operating machine, *etc*

**le'vis** (lēvīs) also **L.** (TM) *pl* close-fitting jeans with copper rivets

**lev'i·tate** (cause to) rise or float in air

**lev'i·ty** lack of (suitable) seriousness

**lev'y** raising and collecting, as taxes, troops, *etc*; amount or number so raised

**lewd** (lūd) lustful; indecent. **-ness**

**lex·i·cog'ra·phy** making of dictionaries. **-pher**

**lex'i·con** dictionary

**li'a·ble** (legally) responsible for; susceptible to; subject or open to sth that may happen. **liabil'ity**

**li·ai·son'** (lēazon) connection, *esp.* between military units; (unlawful) sexual affair

**li'ar** one who tells lies

**li'bel** (published) statement damaging to person's reputation. **-ous** (*UK* **-lous**)

**lib'er·al** generous; openminded; in favor of progressive reforms; not strict. **liberal'ity**

**lib'er·ate** set free

**lib'er·ty** freedom from control, imprisonment, *etc*; power of acting according to one's own choice; (improper) freedom in behavior

**li·bi'do** (-bē-) psychic energy, *esp.* the sexual urge

**li'bra·ry** room or building where books are kept for reading, study, *etc*; collection of books, records, *etc*. **librar'ian**

**li·bret'to** text of opera

**lice** *pl* of louse

**li'cense** permission, *esp.* from government, to marry, do business, *etc*; (excessive) freedom

**li·cen'tious** immoral; lewd

**lick** pass tongue over to taste, moisten, *etc*; (of waves or flames) play lightly over surface

# lid

**lid** hinged or movable cover for pot, box, *etc*; eyelid

**lie** (**lay, lain; ly'ing**) be in a horizontal position, as on bed; be in specified condition: *l. idle*, or in specified place: *the book lay on the table*; be situated; rest (upon): *responsibility lies with the government*

**lie** (**lied; ly'ing**) *v* tell lie(s); have misleading appearance; *n* statement which speaker knows to be untruthful; false belief, impression, *etc.* ; **give the l. to** show to be wrong

**li'en** (lēn) *law* right to hold another's property till debt on it is paid

**lieu** (lū): **in l. of** instead of

**life** (*pl* **lives**) state of constant change and functioning, arising from internal organic structure, which distinguishes plants and animals from organic substances; period during which this state exists; a being while in this state; a group of such beings collectively: *animal l.*; manner of existence; quality of being lively or alive. **-less**

**life belt** see **life preserver**

**life'boat** boat carried on ship for rescuing people

**life pre·serv·er** belt or other device for keeping persons afloat in water

**lift** *v* move or raise upward; raise in rank; improve one's spirits, *etc*; remove, as restrictions, *etc*; (of voice) make louder; steal; *n* act of raising; ride in car, given to walking person; device for raising; *UK* elevator

**lift'-off** vertical start of rocket or spacecraft

**lig'a·ment** strong band of tissue connecting bones or supporting organs in body

**light** *a* bright; of small or less than usual or proper weight; small in degree, force, importance, *etc*; (of food) not heavy; graceful or quick in movement; dizzy. **-ness;** *n* form of energy, as that given off by sun, lamp, *etc*, which makes things visible to the eyes; source of such energy; amount or degree of brightness; daylight or dawn; aspect in which thing is seen or takes on certain appearance: *in the l. of these facts*; means of making sth burn; traffic signal; **see the l.** come into being; understand idea, *etc*; *v* (**light'ed** or **lit**) make lamp, *etc* burn; make or become bright; settle on; get off horse; come (upon) by chance or choice

**light'en** make or become bright(er); reduce weight or load; relieve

**light'ning** sudden flash of light between clouds, caused

by discharge of electricity in air

**lig'nite** kind of brown coal with woody texture

**like** *a* resembling or being similar to (person or thing referred to). **-ness;** characteristic; *prep* similar to; in the manner of; typical of; such as; giving promise of happening: *it looks l. rain;* **feel l.** feel in mood for; *v* feel friendly towards; find pleasing; wish (to do or have)

**like'ly** probable; looking as if it might well happen, be true, *etc;* looking suitable, promising, *etc.* **-lihood**

**lik'en** (lī-) compare (persons or things) to

**like'wise** also, similarly

**li'lac** shrub with clusters of sweet-smelling pale violet or white blossoms; (of) pale violet color

**lil'y** (bulbous plant with) large, trumpetlike (white) flower

**limb** (lim) leg or arm of person or animal; wing of bird; large branch of tree. **-less**

**lim'ber** bending easily; supple

**lim'bo** place of souls barred from heaven, as unbaptized infants, *etc;* state of neglect or uncertainty

**lime** white earthy substance used in making cement, *etc;*

mixture of calcium used to improve crop-bearing soil; (tree bearing) green citrus fruit like lemon; (of) pale green color; linden

**lim'e·rick** (humorous) poem with five lines

**lim'it** boundary line; farthest point (of extent, *etc*); bound, amount, *etc* that may not be passed. **limita'tion**

**lim·ou·sine'** luxurious motor car, often driven by hired driver

**limp** *v* walk lamely; *a* not stiff; without firmness

**lim'pid** (of water, literary style, *etc*) clear

**lin'den** (wood of) tree with heart-shaped leaves and fragrant yellow blossoms

**line** (straight) long narrow mark made on surface with pen, tool, *etc*; sth like this, as furrow, wrinkle on face, boundary mark; objects or persons arranged in row, as trees, printed letters, body of troops; course of action or thought, or of direction; unbroken series of persons, *esp.* with regard to descent; particular kind or branch of activity, business, *etc*; system of transportation, as buses of a town; rope, cord, *etc*; *pl* words of actor's part; shape; manner of construction, *etc*; *v* cover inner side with sth, *esp.* with different

**lin·e·age** (liniij) line of descent from a particular ancestor. **-al**

**lin·e·ar** of measurement in one dimension; of, in or like a line

**lin·en** (linen) fabric made of flax; sheets, tablecloths, *etc*

**lin·er** (lī-) ship or plane used for regular passenger transport; eyeliner

**lin·ger** put off leaving; dwell on subject; continue to exist feebly though dying

**lin·ge·rie** (lahnzherē) women's underwear

**lin·guis'tics** science of languages. **linguist**

**lin·i·ment** liquid rubbed on body to relieve pains, *etc*

**link** *n* one ring of a chain; sth connecting one thing with another. **-age**; *v* (cause to) be connected

**links** golf course

**li·no·le·um** shiny material for covering floors made by coating canvas with special mixture

**lint** soft linen material for dressing wounds; fuzz of thread, short fibers, *etc*

**li·on** large powerful wild animal of cat family with tawny hide and (in the male) mane, found *esp.* in Africa; important person. **-ess**

**lip** one of the two fleshy red folds at opening of mouth; sth shaped like this, as spout of pitcher

**lip'stick** (stick of) rouge for coloring lips

**liq·ue·fy** make or become liquid. **liquefac'tion**

**liq'uid** (likwid) (substance that is) neither solid nor gaseous, as water, wine, *etc*; clear or smooth like water; (of assets) that can easily be changed into cash

**liq'ui·date** pay debt; change assets into cash; end affairs of a firm; do away with

**liq'uor** (liker) alcoholic drink, as whisky, *etc*

**lisp** pronounce *s* and *z* like the sounds of *th*

**list** group of items set down on paper one below the other; strip of material; a leaning to one side, as of ship

**lis'ten** (lisn) hear (person speaking, sound, *etc*) by giving attention with ear; accept advice. **-er**

**list'less** lacking energy, interest, *etc*

**lit** see **light**

**lit'a·ny** (li-) prayer with responses from congregation

**li'ter**, *UK* **-tre** liquid measure in metric system, about 1 quart

**lit'er·al** following the exact words or letters of original; of words in their usual and original meaning; true to fact. **-ly**

**lit'er·a·ry** (of the art or study) of literature

**lit'er·ate** able to read and write; educated. **-acy**

**lit'er·a·ture** literary production (of a country, period, *etc*); writings dealing with a particular subject

**lithe** bending or moving easily. **-ness**

**lith'o·graph** picture, *etc* made from engraved stone or metal. **litho'graphy**

**lit'i·gate** *law* carry on lawsuit. **litiga'tion**

**lit'ter** stretcher for carrying wounded; young of animals brought forth at one birth; objects, *esp.* paper, strewn about

**lit'tle** (**less** or **less'er**, **least**; or **lit'tler**, **lit'tlest**) not big in size, amount, importance, *etc*; (of time or distance) short; (of sounds) weak; mean or narrow in outlook

**lit'ur·gy** form of public worship. **litur'gical**

**live** (lĭv) *v* have or be capable of functions of life; go on in existence; dwell at given place; pass life in specified manner; maintain life or feed (upon): *l. on one's income*, *l. on potatoes*. **live'lihood** (lĭv-); **l. down** make fault, *etc*, be forgotten by manner of one's living; **l. in** dwell at place where one works

**live** (līv) *a* of or having life; (of coals, *etc*) glowing; (of shells) unexploded; (of wire) charged with electricity; (of broadcast) sent directly, not recorded

**live'ly** (līv-) full of life and energy; active; gay; (of color) bright

**liv'en up** (līv-) (cause to) become lively

**liv'er** (lĭv-) large reddish-brown organ which produces bile and purifies blood; this organ from animals as food

**live'stock** (līv-) animals kept on farm for use or profit

**liv'id** (lĭv-) discolored, as by bruise; *infml* very angry

**liv'ing room** (lĭv-) main room in house, *etc*, used for social activity

**liz'ard** (lĭzerd) insect-eating reptile with long body and tail and scaly skin

**lla'ma** (lame) humpless S. Amer. animal related to camel, used for carrying and as source of wool

**load** (quantity of) that which is to be carried or transported at one time; that which is borne or supported; something that weighs heavily on one, as sorrows; charge of gun, *etc*; amount of power supplied by generator, *etc*

**loaf** *n* (*pl* **loaves**) bread, *etc*, baked in certain form, *usu* longer than wide, v *infml* idle away time. **-er**

**loam** kind of rich soil

**loan** sth lent, *esp.* money; act of lending

**loan'word** word taken over from another language

**loath, loth** reluctant

**loath|e** feel hate or disgust for. **-ing, -some**

**lob'by** n entrance hall; pressure group formed to influence legislation, *etc*; v influence members of legislature (to vote for bill, *etc*)

**lobe** rounded projecting part, as that of the lower ear, or several such parts divided by clefts, as in brain

**lob'ster** hard-shelled sea animal with claws, stalk-eyes and white meat used as food

**lo'cal** of or at a particular place; restricted to one area. **-ly**

**lo'cale'** scene of events

**lo'cal'i'ty** place; district

**lo'cate** discover or state place of; settle in a place

**lo'ca'tion** place occupied; act of locating; place outside of film studio where scenes are photographed

**lock** n device for fastening door, lid, *etc*, by means of bolt(s) moved by key, dial, *etc*; device to keep wheel from turning; portion of canal, *etc*, with gates at each end, for moving boats from one level to another; portion of hair, *etc*; *pl* hair of head; v fasten by means of l.; shut (prisoner, *etc*) up in safe place; join firmly by engaging or linking parts; become fixed or blocked, as wheels

**lock'er** closet, *etc*, reserved for one person in public place

**lock'out** closing of business as measure of force against employees

**lock'smith** person who makes or repairs locks

**lo-co-mo'tion** (power of) movement

**lo-co-mo'tive** engine for pulling trains

**lo'cust** winged insect which migrates in large swarms and feeds on crops, *etc*, destroying whole areas; N. Amer. tree

**lo-cu'tion** phrase; style of speech

**lode** vein of metal ore in the earth

**lode'stone** (piece of) magnetic iron ore; sth which attracts

**lodg|e** n cottage serving as summer house, gatekeeper's dwelling, *etc*; (meeting-place of) members of branch of Freemasons, *etc*; v have or furnish with (temporary) living-quarters at house, *etc*, *usu* for payment. **-er, -ing**; bring to or be held in certain place or position; deposit, as for safe-keeping; (of complaint, *etc*) bring before court; give power to detain

**loft** upper floor under roof; room over stable for hay, *etc*

**loft'|y** of impressive height; haughty; elevated (in character, *etc*). **-iness**

**log** (large) unhewn piece of wood; device for measuring speed of ship; also **log book** detailed official record of sea or air voyage

**log'ger·head** fool; **at loggerheads** disagreeing strongly

**log'ic** science of reasoning and proof; chain of reasoning; sound sense. **-al**

**lo·gis'ti|cs** planning, *etc* required in any large operation, *esp.* in moving and supplying troops. **-cal**

**lo'go** symbol or sign of (business) organization; **LO'GO** computer language of ten used in schools

**loin** (*usu pl*) part of body on either side of spine between ribs and hipbone; cut of meat from this part of animal's back

**loi'ter** stay (aimlessly) at a place; linger on the way

**loll** hang loosely, as tongue; stand or sit around lazily

**lol'li·pop** hard candy on a stick

**lon|e** being without company; being far away from human habitations; standing

apart. **-er,** lonely

**long** *a* having a great or specified extent in space or time: *a l. journey, twelve feet l.*; of more than normal extent in space, amount, *etc*; *a l. dozen*; far-reaching: *l. sight, l. memory*; **in the l. run** in the final result; *v* wish strongly for

**lon·gev'i·ty** (lonjev-) length of life; long life

**long'hand** normal handwriting

**lon'gi·tude** (lonji-) distance E. or W. from a meridian, such as that of Greenwich, to any given meridian

**long'shore·man** man employed in loading ships, *etc*

**long'wind·ed** (of talking or writing) at great length

**look** turn eyes in certain direction or fix them upon sth in order to watch, examine, seek *etc*; have specified expression or appearance; (of conditions prospects, *etc*) seem to be; (of house, *etc*) face in given direction; **l. after** follow with eyes; take care of; **l. in** make short visit; **l. on** watch (activity) without taking part. **-er-on; l. out** be watchful; take care; **l. to** give attention to (task, *etc*); direct hope, *etc*, to; **l. up** search for; **l. up to** respect

**loom** *n* machine for weaving;

*v* come into view indistinctly or in large (and threatening) shape

**loop** piece of string, *etc*, folded back upon itself so as to form a circle or oval; anything shaped like this

**loop'hole** means of getting around rule, *etc*

**loose** free to move or be moved; not bound together or packaged; unrestrained in speech, behavior, *etc*; (of fabrics) not closely woven; (of thoughts, *etc*) not exact. **-en; at l. ends** in a disorderly or unsettled state

**loot** *n* goods taken illegally from enemy in war; stolen goods; *v* steal

**lop** cut off (branches of tree)

**lop'sid'ed** having one side lower, heavier, *etc* than the other; unbalanced

**lo·qua'ci·ous** tending to talk (too) much. **-ty**

**lord** *n* one who has power over others; also **L.** (*UK*) (title of) nobleman. **-ship; L.** God or Christ

**lore** body of knowledge and traditions on a subject

**lor'ry** *UK* truck

**lose** (**lost**) cease to have through chance, death, *etc*: *l. a purse, l. one's life*; fail to keep: *l. one's hold; l. the way*; stop having: *l. fear*; fail to win (battle, *etc*) or get (profits, *etc*); have less of: *l. one's*

hair; be occupied exclusively with: *be lost in a book*; leave or be left behind in race, *etc*; fail to put to use: *time lost in waiting*

**loss** sth lost; act of losing; **at a l.** be bewildered (for lack of words, *etc*)

**lot** great number; (set of) article(s) offered at sale; distinct piece of land; method of deciding choice by drawing numbered slips; one of such slips, *etc*; one's share; place where motion picture is filmed

**lo'tion** liquid used for healing wounds, clearing skin, *etc*

**lot'ter·y** sale of numbered tickets, some of which entitle to prize

**loud** (of sound) strongly affecting the sense of hearing; (of place, *etc*) be filled with noise; (of colors) overly showy; (of behavior *etc*) vulgar

**loud'speak·er** electronic device to make sounds louder

**lounge** *v* go or sit lazily; pass time in this manner; *n* area for sitting in hotel, *etc*, often where drinks are served

**louse** (*pl* **lice**) small parasitic insect feeding on blood or plant juices

**love** strong feeling of affection; object of this feeling; sexual desire and its fulfillment. **-er**

**love'lorn** longing for or deserted by one's lover

**love'ly** of charming or touching beauty

**low** *a* being or happening near to ground or below normal level; not reaching far upwards; (of dress) having deeply-cut neckline; (of region) lying near to sea; not having usual depth, as river; lacking (or giving little) strength; small in amount, degree, *etc* within given scope; far down in rank, estimation, *etc*; lacking in moral principle or superior quality; (of mood) depressed; (of sounds) not loud; (of organisms) of simple structure. **-er;** *v* utter cry of cow. **-ing**

**low'er** (louer) look dark and threatening, as sky; frown. **-ing**

**loy'al** faithful (to duty, government, *etc*). **-ty**

**LP** long-playing (record or album)

**LSD** illegal mind-expanding drug, often causing hallucinations

**lu'bri·|cate** make slippery or smooth by putting on liquid or grease. **-cant**

**lu'cid** clear (*esp.* of reasoning). **lucid'ity**

**luck** good or bad fortune; success due to chance. **-y**

**lu'cra·tive** (lū-) profitable

**lu'di·crous** absurd; laugh-able. **-ness**

**lug** pull or carry with great effort

**lug'gage** *esp. UK* baggage; suitcases, *etc* carried when traveling

**lu·gu'bri·ous** mournful

**luke'warm** tepid; indifferent

**lull** *v* put to sleep by soothing means; quiet; *n* short break (in storm)

**lul'la·by** song to put child to sleep

**lum·ba'go** rheumatic pain in lower back

**lum'ber** *n* sawed timber; disused furniture, *etc*; *v* move clumsily

**lu'mi·nous** giving or reflecting light. **luminos'ity**

**lump** *n* solid shapeless mass; swelling, as one caused by bruise; square of sugar; *v* **l. together** consider as unit

**lu'na·cy** insanity

**lu'nar** of the moon

**lu'na·tic** insane (person)

**lunch** (light) meal taken around noon

**lung** either of the two organs of breathing located in chest of humans and most vertebrates

**lunge** (make) sudden forward thrust or movement

**lurch** *n* sudden leaning or rolling; *v* stagger

**lure** sth used to attract; bait

**lu'rid** lighted by ghastly, unnatural light; shocking

**lurk** 230

**lurk** wait (unnoticed) in hiding

**lus'cious** (richly or excessively) sweet in taste, smell, *etc*. **-ness**

**lush** thriving; abundant; juicy

**lust** (strong) sexual desire; passionate enjoyment or desire

**lus'ter**, *UK* **-tre** sheen, as of polished surface; glow; glory. **lus'trous**

**lust'y** healthy and lively

**lux·u'ri·ant** growing or producing richly; richly ornamented

**lux'u·ry** (use of) costly food, dress, *etc*; sth desirable but not necessary. **luxu'rious**

**ly'ing** see **lie**

**lynch** put to death without authority or proper process of law

**lyr'ic** *a* (of poems) songlike; expressing writer's feelings. **-cal**; *n* such a poem; *pl* words of a song. **-cist**

# M

**m** thirteenth letter of English alphabet

**ma·ca'bre** gruesome; having death as subject

**mac·a·ro'ni** pasta shaped in long tubes

**mach·i·na'tion** (mak-) (*usu pl*) plot; intrigue

**ma·chine'** apparatus designed to do certain work by use of mechanical or electrical power, consisting of several parts with separate functions; wheeled vehicle or aircraft; computer; body of persons controlling political party, *etc*. **-ry, machin'ist**

**ma·chine gun** automatic gun giving rapid and continuous fire

**ma'cho** (man who is) ostentatiously manlike

**mack'e·rel** sea fish used as food

**mac·ra·mé'** (work made by) knotting string into patterns

**mac·ro·bi·o'tic** of or following diet of whole grains, *etc*

**mac'ro·cosm** the universe; any great whole

**mad** mentally ill; very foolish; wildly eager or excited (about, after, *etc*); (of dogs, *etc*) having rabies; very angry. **-den, -ness**

**mad'am** polite term used to address woman; woman in charge of brothel

**made** see **make**

**ma·don'na** (picture, statue of) the Virgin Mary

**mael'strom** great whirlpool

**maes'tro** (mīstrō) great composer or musician, *esp.* a conductor

**make**

**ma'fi·a** international criminal organization

**mag'a·zine** periodical publication; cartridge chamber in gun, camera, *etc*; storage house for weapons, *etc*

**mag'got** larva of fly

**mag'ic** pretended art of producing effects by supernatural power. **magi'cian**

**mag'is·trate** (maj-) judge dealing with minor offences

**mag·nan'i·mous** generous and noble in feeling, *etc*. **magnanim'ity**

**mag'nate** person of great wealth and power

**mag·ne'si·um** silver-white metallic element

**mag'net** metal substance attracting iron; sth that attracts. **magnet'ic**

**mag'net·ize**, UK **-ise** make magnetic, as by electricity; attract strongly

**mag·nif'i·cent** splendid (in appearance). **-cence**

**mag'ni·fy** make sth appear larger; exaggerate. **-fier, magnifica'tion**

**mag'ni·tude** size; greatness; importance

**mag·no'li·a** (tree with) large fragrant flower

**mag'pie** noisy bird with long tail and black and white feathers

**ma·hog'a·ny** (tropical tree yielding) hard reddish-brown wood; (of) reddish-brown color

**maid** woman servant

**maid'en** (mā-) unmarried (girl); happening, appearing, *etc*, for the first time: *m. voyage*

**mail** postal system; letters, *etc* sent by post; *hist* armor of rings or chainwork

**maim** cripple

**main** *a* most important; chief in rank, size, *etc*; (of physical force, *etc*) exerted fully; *n* principal pipe or wire, as for water, electricity, *etc*; also **main'land** land as distinguished from islands, *etc*

**main'frame** very powerful stationary computer

**main'stream** (of or concerning) prevailing climate of opinion

**main·tain'** keep up; support (by giving food, *etc*); keep in repair. **main'tenance;** state as true

**maize** UK corn

**maj'es·ty** stately dignity; splendor. **majes'tic**

**ma'jor** *a* greater in importance, number, *etc*; notable; serious; *n* military rank; *US* main course of studies; *law* person of full legal age

**ma·jor'i·ty** greater number or part; amount by which number of votes, *etc* is greater; *law* full legal age

**make** *v* (**made**) produce sth by constructing from material, joining parts, *etc*: *m. a chair*; cause to be (in certain condition, form, *etc*); bring about: *m. trouble*; prepare for use, *etc*: *m. dinner, a bed*; bring (person, *etc*) to do sth: come to have or be by work, development, *etc*: *m. profits, he will m. a good scholar*; lay down, as rules; form in mind, as decision; judge as to nature, meaning, *etc*: *what do you m. of this?* serve for given purpose: *this makes good reading*; amount to; reach by travelling: *m. one's destination*; deliver, as speech; cause to appear as; **m. away with** get rid of; kill; **m. believe** pretend; **m. out** write out (check, *etc*); understand (to be); pretend; get along; **m. over** give (property) into another's possession, *etc*; change; **m. up** put together (parts); invent (story, *etc*); compensate; settle (quarrel, accounts, *etc*); apply cosmetics; **m. up to** pay special attention to (person); *n* manner or form in which thing is constructed; origin of product

**make'shift** (being) temporary device or substitute

**mal'ad·just·ed** badly adjusted

**mal·a·droit** (-droit) awkward; unskillful. **-ness**

**mal·aise'** feeling of illness, worry, *etc*

**ma·lar'i·a** disease causing repeated attacks of fever

**mal'con·tent** discontented (person)

**male** (person, animal or plant) belonging to the sex that does not bear offspring or fruit; (of machine parts, *etc*) made to fit into a hollow part

**mal'e·fac·tor** criminal; evildoer

**ma·lev'o·lent** wishing evil to others. **-lence**

**mal·for·ma'tion** sth, *esp.* part of body, badly or wrongly shaped

**mal·func'tion** fail(ure) to perform in normal way

**mal'ice** desire to make others suffer. **malic'ious**

**ma·lign'** (-līn) *v* slander; speak badly of; *a* evil in effect. **-nity** (-lig-)

**ma·lig'nan|t** (-lig-) bearing strong ill will; (of disease) very dangerous; (of tumor) infected with cancer. **-cy**

**ma·lin'ger** pretend sickness to escape work, *etc*. **-er**

**mal'le·a·ble** that can be shaped or formed by hammering; easily managed. **malleabil'ity**

**mal'let** wooden hammer

**mal·nu·tri'tion** (poor health from) lack of proper food

**mal·prac'tice** wrong professional conduct, *esp.* by doctor towards patient

**malt** grain, *usu* barley, prepared for making beer, *etc*

**mal·treat'** treat badly. **-ment**

**mam'mal** animal that feeds on milk from mother's body when young

**mam'moth** *a* huge; *n* extinct hairy elephant

**man** *n* (*pl* **men**) the human being or race as highest form of animal development; a person; (grown-up) male; husband; male servant; *pl* workmen, soldiers, *etc*; *v* furnish ship, *etc*, with men

**man'a·cle** *usu pl* handcuff

**man'age** take care of or control, as business, property, *etc*; succeed in doing sth, achieving one's aim, *etc*; influence (person) by flattery, *etc*; handle, as tool; get along on small amount of money, *etc*. **-able, -ment, -r**

**man'date** command; political instructions given to representative by voters; commission given to a state to govern foreign territory. **-to·ry**

**mane** long hair on neck of horse, lion *etc*

**ma·neu'ver**, *UK* **-noeuvre** skillful plan or move; *pl* large-scale military exercise

**mange** skin disease of hairy animals

**man'ger** eating trough for cattle, *etc*

**man'gle** *v* cut or hurt so as to disfigure; press clothes with m.; *n* machine with heated rollers for pressing washed clothes

**man·han·dle** handle roughly

**man'hole** entry to a sewer

**ma·ni·a** (mā-) mental disorder marked by violent excitement; great enthusiasm. **-ac, man'ic** (ma-)

**man'i·cure** care of hands, *esp.* cutting fingernails, *etc*

**man'i·fest** *a* clear (to the eye or mind); *n* list of ship's cargo; *v* show plainly. **manifesta'tion**

**man·i·fes'to** public declaration, as of political group

**man'i·fold** *a* many; various; *n* pipe with several outlets, as in car exhaust

**ma·nip'u·late** handle (with skill); manage (to one's own advantage). **-tor**

**man'kind'** human race

**man'ner** (customary) way sth is done or happens; person's way of behaving; sort; *pl* (polite) social behavior

**man'ner·ism** special style or manner carried to excess

**ma·nœ'vre** see **maneuver**

**man'sion** (-shen) large stately house

**man'slaugh·ter** (-slaw-) *law* crime of killing person without meaning to do so

**man'tel, man'tel·piece** shelf or ledge above and around fireplace

**man·u·al** *a* of or done with the hand; *n* (small) book of instructions; *mus* keyboard of organ

**man·u·fac'ture** make articles by hand or machine (on large scale); invent, as story. **-er**

**ma·nure'** dung used to enrich soil

**man·u·script** book *etc* written by hand; author's copy for printer

**man'y (more, most)** (forming) a large number; (forming or being) part of a certain number: *as m. as ten persons, m. a tear*

**map** *n* drawing, *etc*, showing geographical, political, *etc* features of (part of) earth's surface, heaven or heavenly body; *v* make a map of; **m out** plan in detail

**ma'ple** (hardwood of) tree grown for wood and for sap, used to make m. syrup and m. sugar

**mar** damage seriously; spoil appearance of

**mar'a·thon** footrace of about 26 miles; test of endurance

**mar'ble** hard, smooth limestone much used in architecture and sculpture; small ball (of glass), used in child's game

**march** *v* (cause to) walk in regular (slow) step, as soldiers; *n* act of or distance covered by marching; forward movement, as of time; piece of music meant to accompany marching; **M.** third month of the year

**mare** female horse

**mar'ga·rine** (-je-) food like butter, made from vegetable or animal fats

**mar'gin** edge or border; reserve of time, money, *etc.* **-al**

**mar·i·hua'na, mar·i·jua'na** (-hwa-) dried leaves of hemp, smoked for drugging effect

**mar'i·nate** steep (meat, *etc*) in pickling sauce

**ma·rine'** of the sea or ships.

**mar'iner, mar'itime**

**mar·i·o·nette'** doll moved by strings or hand

**mar'i·tal** of marriage

**mar'jo·ram** sweet-smelling herb, used in cooking

**mark** *n* line, scratch, symbol, *etc*, on anything, whether produced by growth, accident, or made for identification, *etc*; sign used in writing, as for punctuation; symbol serving to show quality of work, *etc*, as of pupils; object aimed at in shooting, *etc.* **marksman;** goal; sign of affection, *etc*; standard or distinguishing feature; *v* make mark; single out; assign value to; be sign of; take down, as score; pay attention to; **m. down** reduce price; give lower score; **m. off** separate by lines; **m. time** move feet as in marching, but without moving forward; **m. up** raise price; give higher score

**mar'ket** place where people meet to sell or buy food, *etc*; trade in, or demand for, particular kind of goods: *the cotton m.*

**mar'ma·lade** jam made of oranges, lemons, *etc*

**ma·roon'** *v* leave (person) stranded on deserted island, *etc*; *n* brownish-red color

**mar·quee'** (-kē) canopy over entrance to theater, *etc*

**mar'riage** (-ij) union of man and woman legalized by church or civil ceremony; any close union

**mar'row** soft fatty tissue at center of bones; essential part

**mar'ry** unite or take in marriage

**marsh** low wet land

**mar'shal** *n* officer of highest military rank; *US* court or police officer; *v* arrange in proper order; lead s.o. ceremoniously

**mart** market; shop or store

**mar'tial** warlike; of warfare; **m. law** military government

**mar'tyr** one who suffers death or torture rather than give up his religion, or principles. **-dom**

**mar'vel** wonderful thing; extraordinary example. **-ous** (*Uk* **-lous**)

**mas·ca'ra** substance for coloring eyelashes

**mas'cot** person or thing supposed to bring good luck

**mas'cu·line** manly; of the male sex. **masculin'ity**

**mash** *v* crush to soft pulp, as cooked potatoes; *n* soft pulpy mass; crushed malt mixed with hot water, used in making beer, *etc*

**mask** covering for the face, worn as disguise, for protection, *etc*; wax or plaster likeness of face, *esp.* one molded after death

**mas'och·ism** (mazok-) gaining of (sexual) pleasure from suffering pain, *etc*. **masochis'tic**

**ma'son** person who builds with stone, *etc*; M. man belonging to secret society

**mas·quer·ade'** (-ker-) false outward show; ball where masks are worn

**mass** shapeless body of matter; large number; main body or part; **the masses** the body of ordinary people; **m. production** making large numbers of a product using machines

**mas'sa·cre** (-ker) cruel or wanton killing, *esp.* of a large number of (helpless) people

**mas·sage'** (treat by) rubbing or kneading of the body. **masseur', masseuse'**

**mas'sive** large and heavy; solid

**mast** beam rising from deck of ship and supporting sails; metal pole to support antenna, *etc*; chestnuts, acorns, *etc*, as food for pigs

**mas·tec'to·my** surgical removal of breast

**mas'ter** *n* one who has authority over others or the power of controlling people or things; ship's commander; person of outstanding skill or knowledge in his field; sth, as tape, from which copies are made; (holding) advanced college degree; *UK* male teacher; *a* chief; skilled; *v* gain thorough knowledge or skill; overcome

**mas'ter·ful** in control; commanding

**mas'ter key** key opening many types of locks

**mas'ter·piece** superb (artistic) work

**mas'ter·y** control; masterly skill; victory

**mas'ti·cate** chew

**mas'tur·bate** practice sexual self-gratification

**mat** *n* fabric of straw, plaited rushes, *etc*, used as floor covering, *etc*, **-ting;** *a* (of surfaces, colors, *etc*) dull

**match** short thin stick of wood tipped with substance which burns when rubbed on rough surface; person or thing exactly like another, or having similar or equal qualities; contest of skill; marriage

**mate** *n* companion; one of a pair; ship's officer; *v* join in marriage; pair (for breeding)

**ma·te'ri·al** *a* of matter; physical; important; *n* matter from which things are made; elements of a piece of work; cloth

**ma·te'ri·al·ism** theory that nothing exists but matter and its movements; stressing of material well-being. **materialis'tic**

**ma·te'ri·al·ize** (make) appear in bodily form; become actual fact

**ma·ter'nal** of a mother; motherly; related on mother's side

**ma·ter'ni·ty** (of) motherhood

**math·e·mat'ic**s science of space and number. **-cal, mathemati'cian**

**mat'i·nee** afternoon theatrical, *etc* performance

**mat'tri·arch** (mātriahrk) woman who rules family, group or state. **-chy**

**ma'tri·cide** murder(er) of one's own mother

**ma·tric'u·late** enroll in college, *etc*

**mean**

**mat·ri·mo·ny** (state of) marriage. **matrimo'nial**

**ma'trix** (*pl* **ma'tri·ces** or **ma'trix·es**) an enveloping place or element in which sth develops; mold in which type, *etc* is cast

**ma'tron** married woman; woman supervisor in hospital, *etc*

**mat'ted** tangled

**mat'ter** *n* substance of which physical things are composed; sth of importance or consequence: *a m. of life and death*; sth offering ground for action, feeling, *etc*: *a m. of complaint*; time or distance reckoned approximately: *a m. of time*; things written or printed; material of book, *etc*, as distinguished from form; substance given off by living body, *esp.* pus; *v* be of (relative) importance

**mat·ter-of-fact'** relying on fact rather than imagination; practical

**mat'tress** rectangular sack (with springs) filled with wool, foam rubber, *etc*, used to sleep on

**ma·tu're** ripe; completely developed; (of debts, *etc*) due. **-rity**

**maud'lin** overly sentimental, *esp.* when drunk

**maul** damage, as with claws; beat and bruise; handle roughly

**mau·so·le'um** large tomb, *esp.* building containing niches, *etc* for burial above ground

**mav'e·rick** independent-minded person; *US* unbranded (*esp.* motherless) calf

**max'im** general truth or rule of conduct briefly expressed

**max'i·mum** (being the) greatest posible size or amount

**may (might)** verb expressing possibility: *it m. be true*; permission: *you m. come in*; wish, fear, *etc*: *hope that he m. succeed*; purpose: *take such steps as m. prevent difficulties*; *n* M. fifth month of the year

**may'be** perhaps

**may'hem** great damage or confusion

**may'or** chief official of a city

**maze** confusing network of paths, *etc*

**me** as object, used for person speaking, writing, *etc*

**mead'ow** field of grass land, *esp.* for growing hay or grazing cattle

**mea'ger**, *UK* **-gre** thin; lacking richness; scanty

**meal** food taken at one, mostly fixed, time; coarsely ground grain

**mean** *v* (**meant**) have in mind; (of persons, things, actions *etc*) be intended fo͏—

given purpose; (of words, *etc*) have (given) sense or importance; *n* average; midpoint; *pl* that which helps bring about intended result; financial resources; *a* low in quality, importance, *etc*; base; stingy; equally far from two extremes

**me·an·der** *v* wind and turn; wander aimlessly

**mean'ing** significance; importance. **-ful, -less**

**mea'sles** *pl* contagious disease marked by fever and red rash

**meas'ure** (mezher) *n* step taken to secure aim, as law, *etc*; (due or given) extent, quantity, degree, *etc*, of sth; instrument or system used for determining this; unit of length, capacity, *etc*; rhythm of piece of music, poem, *etc*; *v* determine (person's, thing's) size, quality, *etc*, by fixed standard; mark off (given length); test one's strength, *etc*, by competing with another

**meat** flesh of animals used for food, excluding fish; edible part of nut, *etc*

**me·chan'ic** skilled worker repairing or using machines

**me·chan'i·cal** of, like or done by machine; automatic. **mech'a|nize** (*UK* **-nise**)

**me·chan'ics** science of the action of forces on bodies;

science of machinery; technical and practical details, as of playwriting

**mech'a·nism** structure (of working parts) of a machine

**med'al** metal disk inscribed in memory of event or given as award

**med'dle** (-dl) busy oneself with affairs of others; interfere. **-some**

**me·di·a** means of public communication: newspapers, radio, television

**me·di·ae'val** see **medieval**

**me'di·al** in the middle; average

**me'di·an** (line) lying in or passing through the middle

**me'di·ate** act as agent between parties to settle quarrel, *etc*; produce agreement in this way. **-tor**

**med'i·cal** of medicine

**med·i·ca'tion** healing substance; drug

**med'i·cine** science of preventing, treating and curing diseases, *esp.* as opposed to surgery, *etc*; any substance used in treating diseases

**me·di·e'val** *hist* of the Middle Ages; *infml* old(-fashioned)

**me·di·o'cre** of middle quality; neither very good nor very bad. **medioc'rity**

**med'i·tate** consider mentally; dwell in thought (on subject). **-tive, medita'tion**

**me'di·um** (*pl* **-diums, -dia**) method of communication (see also **media**); substance through which a force acts or by means of which a result is achieved; middle condition or degree; person claiming ability to communicate with spirits

**med'ley** mixture of many things

**meek** gentle; submissive

**meet** (**met**) come upon or together, *esp.* with person; be introduced to or go to place of arrival: *m. a train*; experience, as conditions, attitude, *etc*; fulfill (demands, obligations, *etc*); compete against; (of roads, *etc*) join or cross

**meg·a·lo·ma'ni·a** mental disorder brought by delusions of great power, *etc*. **-ac**

**meg'a·phone** trumpetlike speaking device to make voice sound louder

**mel'an·chol·y** (tendency to) sadness and depression

**mel'low** (of fruit) ripe and tender; (of wine) well-aged; (of character) made gentle by age; full and pure; without harshness. **-ness**

**me·lo'di·ous** of melody; sweet-sounding. **-ness**

**mel'o·dra·ma** sensational drama appealing strongly to emotions. **melodramat'ic**

**mel'o·dy** succession of (musical) sounds so arranged as to

please the ear; main part of musical composition

**mel'on** (large) fruit with hard rind and sweet edible flesh

**melt** become liquid by application of heat; become soft; (cause to) lose clear outline; dwindle away

**mem'ber** person belonging to a society, organization, *etc*, or elected to a legislative body. **-ship**; limb or organ, *esp.* penis, of animal body; part of a whole

**mem'brane** thin sheet of (animal) tissue, *etc*

**me·men'to** sth serving to remind or warn; sth kept as souvenir

**mem'o** see **memorandum**

**mem'oir** (memwahr) usu pl story of one's experiences and recollections

**mem'o·ra·ble** worth remembering; remarkable

**mem·o·ran'dum** (*pl* **-dums** or **-da**) note (to help the memory); informal letter on special subject

**me·mo'ri·al** statue, *etc* serving to keep alive memory of person, *etc*

**mem'o·rize** learn by heart

**mem'o·ry** faculty of keeping in mind or recalling impressions, facts, *etc*; time or events which can be called to mind: *within living m., his first memories*; part of computer in which data is stored

**men** pl of **man**

**men'ace** threat(en)

**me·nag'er·ie** collection of wild animals in cages

**mend** repair; correct (bad habits, etc); improve in health

**men·da'ci|ous** lying; false. **-ty**

**me'ni·al** low; degrading

**men'o·pause** time in middle age when woman's periods stop; change of life

**men'stru·|ate** discharge blood during monthly period. **-al, menstrua'tion**

**men'tal** of, in or done by the mind

**men·tal'i·ty** mental power; attitude

**men'thol** mintlike substance

**men'tion** speak of briefly or incidentally; specify or name

**men'u** list of dishes served at restaurant; list of choices in a computer program

**mer'can·tile** commercial; of trade

**mer'ce·na·ry** a interested only in money; n hired soldier in foreign service

**mer'chan·dise** goods for sale

**mer'chant** one who trades in goods for profit; storekeeper; UK wholesale dealer

**mer'cy** feeling or act of pity or forgiveness towards enemy, criminal, or person in one's power. **-ciful, -ciless**

**mere** being nothing more than stated: a m. child

**merge** (cause to) combine or unite (gradually) into one thing

**merg'er** (-jer) act of merging; uniting of two or more companies

**me·rid'i·an** any circle around earth passing through the poles, used on maps to show position; point of highest development, etc; sun's highest point at noon

**me·ri'no** (soft fine wool from) type of sheep

**mer'it** quality of deserving reward, praise, etc; excellence; substance of a matter

**mer·i·to'ri·ous** deserving reward or praise

**mer'maid** imaginary being with upper body of woman and tail of fish

**mer'ry** cheerful and gay. **-riment**

**mesh** n open space in net; network; v fit together; engage, as gear teeth

**mes'mer·ize,** UK **-ise** fascinate; hold one's complete attention

**mess** dirty or untidy condition or mass of things; military dining-room; meal taken there; (portion of) soft or liquid (unappetizing) food; **make a m. of** spoil; bungle

**mes'sage** (-ij) information, instructions, etc, sent from one person to another

**mes·sen·ger** (-inj-) person who carries a message or runs errands

**met** see **meet**

**me·tab·o·lism** process in organism by which food is converted into energy

**met·al** (solid) mineral substance, as silver, iron, *etc*. **metal'lic**

**met·a·mor·pho·sis** complete change of form, *etc*

**met·a·phor** (use of) descriptive term which is not literally true but which suggests resemblance. **metaphor'ical**

**met·a·phys·i·cs** part of philosophy dealing with nonphysical fundamental causes of universe. **-cal**

**mete out** deal out in portions

**me·te·or** small body travelling through space which glows when it enters earth's atmosphere. **meteor'ic**

**me·te·or·ol·o·gy** science of atmosphere, *esp.* as relating to weather. **-gist**

**me·ter** device measuring amount of sth, as gas, or time elapsed

**me·ter,** *UK* **-tre** unit of length in metric system; any of the forms of poetic rhythm

**meth·od** way of doing sth according to plan; orderly arrangement. **method'ical**

**me·tic·u·lous** extremely careful about the smallest details

**met·ric** of the decimal measuring system

**me·trop·o·lis** chief city of a country, *etc*. **metropol'itan**

**met·tle** (characteristic) spirit; courage. **-some**

**mew** (make) sound of cat

**mez·za·nine** (mezenēn) low story, *esp.* between ground and second floor; *UK* (first rows of seats in) lowest balcony of theater

**mice** *pl* of mouse

**mi·crobe** tiny living being, *esp.* one causing disease

**mi·cro·bi·ol·o·gy** scientific study of tiny organisms, as bacteria

**mi·cro·cosm** man, community, *etc* viewed as (tiny) replica of larger whole

**mi·cro·fiche** sheet of film containing tiny photos of documents, *etc*

**mi·cro·film** (roll of) film used to make tiny copies of books, *etc* for easy storage

**mi·cro·phone** instrument for converting sound waves into electrical energy

**mi·cro·read·er** device for reading microfilm, *etc*

**mi·cro·wave** very short electromagnetic wave, used in radar, *etc* and *esp.* in cooking; an oven using this technique

**mid·day** noon

**mid·dle** being at equal distance from two (given) points or extremes in space, time, degree, *etc*; M. Ages period of history between ancient and modern times (500–1500 A.D.)

**mid·dle-aged'** between youth and old age

**mid'dle·man** dealer between producer of goods and shopkeeper or user

**midg'et** very small person or thing

**mid'night** twelve o'clock at night

**mid'riff** part of body between chest and belly

**midst** middle; state of being entirely surrounded

**mid'wife** person, *usu* woman, who assists woman in giving birth to children

**mien** (mēn) air or look of person as showing mood, *etc*

**might** *v* see **may**

**might** *n* (great) strength or power. **-y**

**mi'graine** (disorder marked by) severe repeated headache

**mi'grant** (person) moving from one place to another

**mi'gra|te** move from one place, *esp.* country, to another; (of birds, *etc*) come and go with the seasons. **-to·ry, migra'tion**

**mild** (-ī-) gentle; not harsh or rough; slight; (of weather) calm and warm; (of food, *etc*) not sharp or strong-tasting

**mil'dew** (-dū) tiny harmful fungus attacking plants, linen, *etc*

**mile** (-ī-) unit for measuring distance, equal to 5,280 feet

**mile'age** number of miles between places; total miles traveled; travel allowance or charge per mile

**mi'lieu** (social) environment

**mil'i·tant** (person) aggressively active or tending to force

**mil'i·ta·ris·m** undue stress on the military in a state. **-rist**

**mil'i·tar·y** *a* of or like soldiers; of war; *n* troops; the army

**mi·li'tia** (-lishe) emergency military force made up of citizens

**milk** white fluid given off by female mammals for nourishment of young, *esp.* that of cows as food; any liquid resembling this

**milk'y** of or like milk; (of liquids) cloudy; **M. Way** band of light from countless stars stretching across the night sky

**mill** *n* (building fitted with) machinery for manufacture of steel, cotton, *etc* or for grinding grain into flour; machine for grinding coffee, *etc*; *v* grind or work in or with mill; move around confusedly, as cattle

**mil·len'ni·um** period of 1000

years; future time of justice and happiness on earth (under Christ's reign)

**mil·li·gram** one thousandth of a gram

**mil·li·me·ter** one thousandth of a meter

**mil·lion** one thousand times one thousand

**mil·lion·aire'**, *f* **-ess** very rich person who has a million dollars, pounds, *etc*

**mim'ic** (one that can) copy in action, speech, *etc*. **-cry**

**min·a·ret'** slender tower on mosque

**mince** chop fine; use mild or polite words in criticism; speak or walk with affected delicacy

**mind** *n* that which thinks and feels, and is capable of memory, judgment, *etc*, as opposed to body; (person having) intellectual power; way or direction of thinking, feeling, *etc*; *v* pay attention to and obey (instructions, *etc*); occupy o.s. with (task) or take care of; be careful about; feel concern about or object to

**mine** *pron* word indicating possession by speaker, writer, *etc*: *this house is m.*

**mine** *n* excavation dug in earth to get at deposit of coal, minerals, *etc*; rich store of information, *etc*; container filled with explosives placed in the ground or sea, to blow up enemy tanks, ships, *etc*

**min·er·al** (of) any substance neither animal nor vegetable. **mineral'ogy**

**min·gle** mix among; blend

**min'i** *infml* sth small of its kind, *esp.* very short skirt, *etc*

**min·i·a·ture** *n* very small portrait or copy; *a* on a very small scale

**min·i·mal** very small; the smallest possible

**min·i·mize** reduce to smallest possible amount or degree; belittle

**min·i·mum** (being) the smallest amount possible

**min·is·ter** *n* person at head of government department or sent as diplomatic agent; clergyman; *v* give aid or service. **-try**

**mink** (valuable fur of) small weasel-like animal

**mi'nor** lesser; under age

**mi·nor·i·ty** smaller number or part, *esp.* of votes; part of population differing from the rest in race, *etc*; being under age

**mint** place where money is coined; aromatic herb used in cooking, *etc*

**mi'nus** (-ī-) less by deduction of: *eight m. four is equal to four*; lacking; (of qualities, *etc*) negative

**min'ute** *n* (mi-) sixtieth part of hour or of a degree; brief time; *pl* official written notes of proceedings at meeting

**mi·nute'** *a* (mīnūt') very small; very accurate

**mir'a·cle** marvelous event (that cannot be explained by any law of nature). **mirac'ulous**

**mi·rage'** (-rahzh') optical illusion seen on sea or desert

**mire** swampy ground; mud

**mir'ror** polished (glass) surface which reflects images

**mirth** merriment. **-ful**

**mis·ad·ven'ture** mishap

**mis·al·li'ance** unsuitable union, *esp.* marriage

**mis'an·thrope** one who hates mankind. **misanthrop'ic, misan'thropy**

**mis·ap·pre·hen|d'** misunderstand. **-sion**

**mis·ap·pro'pri·ate** put (another's money) to wrong use

**mis·cal'cu·late** reckon wrongly

**mis·car|ry** (of plans, *etc*) be unsuccessful; give birth too early. **-riage**

**mis·cel·la'ne·ous** varied; of mixed character or various kinds

**mis'cel·la·ny** mixture, *esp.* of writings on various subjects

**mis'chief** harm or trouble (caused by person); pranks. **mis'chievous**

**mis·con·ceive'** understand

wrongly. **-ception**

**mis·con'duct** improper behavior

**mis·con·|strue'** mistake meaning of. **-struction**

**mis·deed'** wrong deed; crime

**mis·de·mean'or** *UK* **-our** minor crime

**mi'ser** person who lives poorly so as to hoard money. **-ly**

**mis'er·|y** wretchedness due to poverty or suffering. **-able**

**mis·fire'** fail to go off or ignite (at the right time); fail to have the desired effect

**mis'fit** poor fit; person not suited to his environment

**mis·for'tune** (instance of) bad luck

**mis·giv'ing** (feeling of) feat distrust or doubt, *esp.* about some future event

**mis·guid'ed** acting according to wrong ideas

**mis·han'dle** handle roughly; treat badly

**mis·hap'** unlucky accident

**mis·in·form'** give (s.o.) wrong information

**mis·in·ter'pret** understand wrongly

**mis·judge'** judge wrongly

**mis·lay'** (-laid') put thing by accident where it cannot be found; lose

**mis·no'mer** wrong name

**mis·place'** put in wrong place; mislay

**mis·print** mistake in printing

**mis·pro·nounce'** pronounce wrongly. **mispronuncia'tion**

**mis·rep·re·sent'** give wrong account of

**miss** (of person, shot, *etc*) fail to hit, meet, get, get, perform duty, understand, be present, *etc*; escape (sth); feel loss or absence of, *esp.* with regret

**miss** *n* (*pl* **miss'es**) (form of address for) unmarried woman or girl: *Miss Smith*

**mis'sile** (misil) object suitable for throwing (as a weapon); see also **guided missile**

**mis'sion** messenger's errand; special embassy; body of ministers sent by church to convert nonbelievers. **mis'sionary**

**mis·spell'** spell wrongly

**mist** cloudlike mass of tiny drops of water near or above ground; something which dims the view

**mis·take'** (-took, -taken) fail to understand or recognize sth properly

**mis'ter** form of address for man: *Mr. Miller*

**mis'tress** woman who has authority over others, as in household, or power of controlling sth; woman sexually allied to man without being married; *UK* female teacher

**mis·tri'al** trial that has no le-

gal effect because of error

**mis·un·der·stand'** (-stood) fail to understand; understand wrongly

**mis·use'** wrong use. **-age**

**mite** kind of tiny insect; small child; tiny amount

**mit'i·gate** make or become less severe (as pain, *etc*); soothe

**mit'ten** glove enclosing the four fingers together and thumb separately

**mix** combine substances, persons, *etc*, so that they form one mass, group, etc. **-ture;** be sociable: *he mixes easily with people;* **m. up** confuse, as facts, *etc*

**mix'er** (electric) device for mixing substances, as cake, cement, *etc*

**moan** (utter) low, drawn-out sound of pain or grief

**moat** deep (water-filled) ditch around castle or around zoo animals to prevent their escape

**mob** disorderly (violent) mass of people

**mo'bile** easily moved or changing. **mobil'ity**

**mo'bi·lize** collect and make ready for use, *esp.* troops. **mobiliza'tion**

**mock** make fun of, *esp.* contemptuously; treat with scorn. **-ery**

**mock'-up** full-scale model built for testing or display

**mode** manner of doing or being; fashion

**mod'el** small-scale copy of thing or representation of house, road, *etc*, to be built; example or pattern proposed for imitation; person who serves as subject for artist, *etc*, or wears dresses, *etc*, for display to customers; particular product design or type

**mod'er·ate** not excessive or extreme; ordinary

**mod'er·a·tor** chairman of (church, *etc*) meeting or discussion

**mod'ern** (typical) of the present or recent time. **-ize** (*UK* **-ise**), **modernis'tic**

**mod'est** not boastful; shy; not excessive; decent. **-ty**

**mod'i·fy** change somewhat; make less in degree, *etc*. **modifica'tion**

**mod'u·late** vary in tone; regulate, as radio waves

**mod'ule** independent structural unit which can be combined with others

**mo'hair** (fine silky wool from) hair of Angora goat

**moist** slightly wet; damp. **-ture**

**moist'en** (-sen) make damp

**mo'lar** large grinding-tooth

**mo·las'ses** thick, light to dark brown syrup separated from raw sugar

**mold**, *UK* **mould** wooly fungus growth (on bread, *etc*); earth rich in organic matter; frame or form in which sth is shaped

**mole** dark permanent spot on skin; breakwater structure laid in sea; small, insect-eating mammal living mostly underground in burrows

**mol'e·cule** smallest particle of substance retaining all the qualities of the substance. **molec'ular**

**mo·lest'** annoy (sexually); harm. **molesta'tion**

**mol'ten** melted by great heat, as rock or metal

**mo'men|t** very short period of time. **-tary**; point in time; importance

**mo·men'tous** very important

**mo·men'tum** quantity of motion; moving force

**mon'ar|ch** hereditary ruler, as king, queen *etc*. **-chy**, **monar'chial**

**mon'as·ter·y** group of buildings in which monks live

**mo·nas'tic** of monks and nuns or monasteries; cut off from wordly affairs

**Mon'day** first day of the week, between Sunday and Tuesday

**mon'e·tar·y** of money

**mon'ey** coins of precious metal, banknotes, *etc*, issued by government and used to pay debts, buy goods, *etc*

**mope**

**mon'grel** (animal, *esp.* dog) of mixed breed

**mon'i·tor** device to control the functioning of sth or to detect sth; computer screen; pupil with duty of keeping class in order; one who listens to and reports on foreign broadcasts

**monk** (mungk) member of religious order living withdrawn from world

**mon'key** highly-developed mammal of a group similar to man

**mo·nog'a·my** marriage with but one person at a time. **-mous**

**mon'o·graph** book *etc* on one particular subject

**mon'o·logue** (-log) long speech, sketch, *etc* spoken by one actor

**mo·nop'o·ly** exclusive control over sth, as a product, service, *etc*. **-lize** (*UK* **-lise**), **monopolis'tic**

**mon'o·syl·la·ble** word of one syllable. **monosyllab'ic**

**mon'o·the·ism** belief that there is only one God

**mo·not'o·nous** uttered in one unchanging tone; tiringly uniform. **-ny**

**mon·soon'** (rainy season brought by) periodic wind in S. Asia

**mon'ster** horrible-looking animal or plant (in fable); extremely wicked person; thing of huge size. **-strous**

**mon·stros'i·ty** (large) ugly thing

**month** any of the twelve (approximately 30-day) periods into which year is divided

**mon'u·ment** statue or structure in memory of person or event

**mon·u·men'tal** like a monument; massive

**moo** (make) lowing sound of cow

**mood** state of mind or feeling, *esp.* at a particular time; fit of gloominess, *etc*. **-y**

**moon** *n* the heavenly body which moves around the earth in monthly rhythm and shines at night by reflecting sunlight; any similar body moving around a planet; *v* wander around or spend time idly or listlessly

**moon'light** *n* light of the moon; *v* *infml* have two jobs (without paying proper income tax)

**moor** *n* stretch of boggy wasteland; *v* tie ship in place (in harbor)

**moose** N. Amer. elk

**moot** open to discussion or debate

**mop** *n* coarse yarn or cloth fastened to end of stick, for cleaning floors, *etc*; thick mass, as of hair; *v* wipe (clean)

**mope** be in low spirits

**mor'al** *a* concerned with distinction between right and wrong; virtuous; lesson contained in story; *pl* principles of proper conduct. **-ize** (*UK* **-ise**), **moral'ity**

**mo-rale'** mental state, *esp.* level of confidence

**mo-rass'** wet, soft ground

**mor-a-tor'i-um** official period of delay or stopping of activity

**mor'bid** unhealthy, *esp.* mentally; diseased

**more** (in or to) greater amount, degree, number, *etc*; further

**more-o'ver** in addition (to what has been said)

**morgue** *US* official place where bodies of persons found dead are kept for identification or until released for burial; *UK* mortuary

**morn'ing** first part (from midnight to noon) of the day

**mo'ron** adult whose mental development is about that of a child of 12

**mo-rose'** ill-humored and unfriendly. **-ness**

**mor'phine** habit-forming drug from opium, used to dull pain

**mor'sel** mouthful; small piece

**mor'tal** *a* subject to or causing death; deadly; human; very great: *m. fear*; *n* human being

**mor-tal'i-ty** being mortal; number or rate of deaths

**mor'tar** cement for joining bricks, *etc* together; sturdy bowl for pounding food, *etc*; short cannon

**mort'gage** (morgij) transfer property as security for debt; pledge

**mor'ti-fy** bring (desires) under control by self-denial, shame; hurt (feelings). **mortifica'tion**

**mor'tu-ar-y** place where dead are kept before burial

**mo-sa'ic** (of or like) pattern, *etc* formed by bits of colored stone, glass, *etc*

**Mos'lem** see **Muslim**

**mosque** (mosk) Muslim house of worship

**mos-qui'to** gnat-like stinging insect which sucks blood from animals and man

**moss** low-stemmed plants without true flowers and seeds, growing in tufts on moist ground, stones, *etc*

**most** (in or to) the greatest amount, degree, number, *etc*

**most'ly** mainly; for the most part

**mote** small grain (of dust)

**mo-tel'** motor hotel with parking space near each room

**moth** four-winged, (mostly) nocturnal insect; larva of this insect deposited in wool, fur, *etc*

**moth'er** (mudher) *n* female parent. **-hood; m. superior** head of convent; *a of*, characteristic of, or obtained from (one's) mother: *m. love, m. tongue*

**moth'er-in-law** mother of one's wife or husband

**mo·tif'** (tēf) main idea, *etc* in artistic work; repeated pattern, *etc*

**mo'tion** *n* act of moving or changing place; formal proposal at meeting; bodily action or gesture; *v* direct by sign or gesture

**mo·tion pic'ture** *US* series of pictures on film, projected onto screen in rapid succession to simulate movement; *UK* cinema film

**mo'tive** that which prompts person to act, as fear, desire, *etc*

**mo'ti·vate** supply or be reason for action. **motiva'tion**

**mot'ley** of various colors or kinds

**mo'tor** (driven by) small powerful engine which converts energy into motion, as device for driving machinery. **-ize** (*UK* **-ise**)

**mo'tor·ist** person who drives car

**mot'tled** marked with spots of different colors

**mot'to** short sentence giving rule of conduct or guiding principle of institution,

country, *etc*

**mould** see mold

**mound** raised bank; small hill

**mount** get on (bicycle, *etc*); rise; climb; fix in place

**moun'tain** natural elevation rising from earth's surface, *usu* of considerable height. **-ous**

**mourn** feel or show sorrow or regret for. **-ful**

**mouse** (*pl* mice) small, long-tailed rodent living in fields and houses; hand--moved control box for directing computer programs; shy person

**mous·tache'** see mustache

**mouth** (-th) *n* (*pl* mouths [-dhz]) opening in head of man or animals through which food is taken in and sounds or speech are formed; opening leading into cave, *etc*; part of river, *etc* where its waters flow into larger body of water **mouth** (-dh) *v* move lips as if speaking; speak pompously

**mouth'ful** (-th-) quantity that fills the mouth

**mouth'piece** (-th-) part of pipe, telephone, *etc* placed in or near mouth; spokesman

**mov|e** (mūv) change (one's own or thing's) place, position or residence. **-able;** (cause) to be in forward, revolving, *etc*, action, as a machine; (cause) to take (given) action; arouse feelings, *esp.* of pity or tenderness. **-ing**

**move'ment** act or (special) manner of moving; series of actions of group of persons, directed toward certain aim; progress or trend of affairs, events, *etc*; moving parts of machinery, *esp.* watch or clock; *mus* division of symphony, *etc*; an emptying of the bowels

**mov'ie** (mūvi) *US* film

**mov'ies** *US* cinema

**mow** (mō) (**mowed, mowed** or **mown**) cut grain, grass, *etc*. **-er**

**much** (in or to) a great amount, measure or degree; nearly: *m. the same size*

**mu'|cus** (myū-) slimy substance secreted by certain membranes in body. **-cous**

**mud** wet soft earth, as that on bottom of river

**mud'dle** mix up or bungle (affairs, things, *etc*); (cause to) be confused, *esp.* owing to drink

**muf'fin** small round cake of bran, *etc*, *usu* served hot with butter

**muf'fle** wrap up to protect or deaden sound of

**muf'fler** scarf; device to deaden sound, as of car engine

**mug** (heavy) drinking cup, *usu* with handle; *v* attack person in order to rob him

**mug'gy** uncomfortably warm and humid

**mule** offspring of mare and donkey, noted for its stubbornness; slipper with no back

**mul'ti-col-ored**, *UK* **-oured** of many colors

**mul-ti-far'i-ous** many and varied. **-ness**

**mul-ti-lat'e-ral** among three or more parties

**mul'ti-ple** having many parts or varieties; many. **multi-plic'ity**

**mul'ti-ply** increase in number. **multiplica'tion**

**mul'ti-tude** great number; crowd. **multitu'dinous**

**mum'ble** speak unclearly; chew as with toothless gums

**mum-bo-jum'bo** meaningless (religious) activity; gibberish

**mum'|my** body treated so as not to decay. **-mify**

**mumps** *pl* infectious disease marked by swelling of glands below ear

**munch** chew noisily

**mun'dane** of this world; dull and ordinary

**mu-nic'i-pal** of self-government of a city

**mu-nic-i-pal'i-ty** town, *etc* having local self-government

**mu-nif'i|cent** very generous. **-cence**

**mu-ni'tions** military weapons, bombs, *etc*

251

**mu'ral** picture painted on wall

**mur'der** kill(ing) human being unlawfully and intentionally. **-er, -ess, -ous**

**murk'y** dark; gloomy; hazy

**mur'mur** (make) low continuous sound, as of wind in the trees, or of low unclear voices

**mus'|cle** (musl) band of fibrous tissue in animal body whose contraction produces movement. **-cular**

**muse** v think in reverie; n one of nine Greek goddesses of arts and sciences

**mu·se'um** building for keeping and displaying objects of art, science, etc

**mush** soft thick matter, esp. US boiled cornmeal

**mush'room** n (edible) flowerless plant with fleshy stalk and umbrella-shaped cap; v grow rapidly

**mu'sic** (myūzik) art of arranging sounds in definite pattern so that they have pleasing effect, express emotion, etc; written or printed score of such an arrangement. **musi'cian**

**mu'si·cal** a of, for producing music; n play or film with songs and usu also dances

**musk** animal secretion used in perfumes. **-y**

**Mus'lim** of, believing in or belonging to religion founded by Moham.

**mus'sel** edible se. animal with black s.

**must** v (must) be oblig. do; be certain to do, be happen; happen, do, be as it compelled by perverse destiny or desire: just as I didn't want to see him, he m. come in the room; (in negative sense) may: this m. not happen; n sth necessary or important; new wine

**mus·tache** UK **mous-** hair growing on man's upper lip

**mus'tard** yellow-flowered herb; its seeds: a paste made from these to season food

**mus'ter** assemble (troops for inspection, etc)

**must'|y** stale or moldy in smell or taste; out of date. **-iness**

**mu'ta·ble** fickle; changing. **mutabi'lity**

**mu'tant** (sth) produced by mutation

**mu·ta'tion** change in form, etc (esp. one resulting in variation from parent)

**mute** (one who is) silent or unable to speak

**mu'ti·late** cut off limb, etc of person or animal; ruin

**mu'ti|ny** (engage in) open (esp. military) revolt against authority. **-nous, mutineer'**

**mut'ter** speak unclearly in low tone; grumble

**mut'ton** flesh of sheep as food

**au·tu·al** (of actions, feelings, *etc*) done, felt by each of two or more towards the other(s); common to two or more

**muz·zle** projecting jaws and nose of animal; covering for mouth of animal to prevent it from biting or eating; open end of gun from which bullet is fired

**my** belonging to or done by speaker; writer, *etc*: *m. house*

**my·o·pi·a** near-sightedness; inability to see distant objects clearly. **-pic**

**myr·i·ad** (of a) very great number

**myr·tle** evergreen shrub with shiny leaves and fragrant white flowers

**my·self** emphasizing or re-flexive form of **I** or **me**: *I will go m., I hurt m.*

**mys·ter·y** secret or unexplainable matter; secret religious truth or ceremony. **myste·rious** fictional story about crime, *esp.* murder

**mys·tic, mys·ti·cal** of hidden meaning; creating feeling of awe and wonder

**mys·ti·fy** purposely confuse; wrap in mystery

**myth** legendary story about supernatural persons, *etc*; imaginary or invented person or thing; unfounded belief. **-ical**

**my·thol·o·gy** body of myths of particular country, *etc*; study of myths. **-gist, mythol·og·ical**

# N

**n** fourteenth letter of English alphabet

**na·dir** (nā-) lowest point

**nag** *v* annoy by constantly finding fault, complaining, *etc*; *n* (old) horse

**na·iad** (nāad) water nymph

**nail** slender piece of metal with point and flattened head, driven in wall, through wood, *etc*, as peg, for holding parts together, *etc*, horny covering at tip of finger or toe

**na·ive** (nahēv) (amusingly) simple in mind or manner. **naiveté**

**na·ked** (nākid) without clothing, (usual) covering, vegetation, *etc*; defenseless; undisguised; (of sight, *etc*) unaided by telescope, *etc*

**name** word(s) by which person, thing, class, place, *etc*, is called or referred to. **-less;** famous person; reputation of given kind: *he has a bad n.*; existence not in fact but only by designation: *hero in n. only*; **in the. n. of** appealing to: *in the n. of common sense*; on behalf of: *in the n. of my brother*

**name'ly** that is to say

**name'sake** person with same name as, *esp.* one named after, another

**nap** short sleep; wooly or hairy surface of cloth

**nape** back of neck

**nap'kin** square piece of linen, paper, *etc*, for wiping fingers and mouth after eating; *UK* diaper

**nar·co'sis** state of numbness or sleep due to drugs

**nar·cot'ic** habit-forming drug which causes sleep or makes insensible to pain

**nar·ra|te'** tell story; give report of event. **-tion, -tor, nar'rative**

**nar'row** of little width as compared to length; not wide; limited in scope or size; (of viewpoint) prejudiced; (of means, *etc*) barely sufficient; careful, as examination, *etc*

**na'sal** of the nose

**nas'cent** beginning to exist

**nas'ty** disgustingly dirty or disagreable to taste, *etc*; ill-natured; spiteful; obscene; harmful

**na'tal** of birth

**na'tion** people of (large) region sharing the same language, history, *etc, etc* when united under independent government. **-al, -alism, -alist, national'ity**

**na·tion·al·ize**, *UK* **-ise** make

land, railways, *etc* national property. **nationaliza'tion**

**na'tive** belonging by birth or nature; of (the place of) one's birth; belonging to a place, as plants, *etc*

**na·tiv'i·ty** birth, *esp.* of Christ

**nat'u·ral** (nacherel) inborn; happening in or typical of normal course of nature; existing in nature, not artificial, manufactured, *etc*; of the physical world; lifelike; unaffected; born of unmarried parents

**nat'u·ral·ize**, *UK* **-ise** give foreigner citizenship; introduce (plant, foreign word, *etc*) into new country. **naturaliza'tion**

**na'ture** (nācher) (the whole of) physical phenomena and forces of the material world; essential quality or inborn character of thing or person; sort; vital functions, needs, *etc*, of man or animals

**naugh'ty** (nawti) (*usu* of children) badly behaved or failing to obey; mildly indecent

**nau·se·a** (nawshie) sickness with urge to vomit; disgust. **-ate, -ous**

**nau'ti·cal** of sailors or ships; **n. mile** international measure of air or sea distance (1852 meters or about 6076.1 feet)

**na'val** of ships or the navy

**na'vel** depression in middle

of belly left by cutting of umbilical cord

**nav·i·ga·ble** (of river, *etc*) allowing ship to pass; (of ship, plane, *etc*) that can be steered

**nav·i·gate** steer course of (ship or plane); plot route. **-tor, naviga'tion**

**na·vy** (all of) nation's warships, their crews, equipment, *etc*; (of) dark blue color

**nay** a vote(r) against sth

**near** *a* to, at or within short distance in space or time; close; closely related; almost; the closer of two things; *prep* not far from; *v* approach

**near·ly** almost

**neat** elegant and simple in line or arrangement; skillful; tidy; (of liquor) not mixed with ice, *etc*

**neb·u·lous** vague or confused; cloudlike

**nec·es·sar·y** (nesˈeseri) that must be done; that canot be done without; certain to be or happen as inevitable result

**ne·ces·si·tate** make necessary

**ne·ces·si·ty** urgent need; sth absolutely required; strong power of circumstances

**neck** (part of dress, *etc*, covering) part of body that connects head and shoulders;

sth like this in shape or position, as slender part of bottle, narrow stretch of land, *etc*

**neck·lace** (-lis) string of precious stones, beads, *etc*, worn around neck

**neck·tie** band of silk, *etc* worn around shirt collar and knotted in front

**nec·tar** sweet fluid gathered from flowers and made into honey by bees

**nec·tar·ine** smooth-skinned peach

**need** be in want of; (urgently) require; be obliged (to do)

**nee·dle** thin pointed piece of steel with an eye at one end to put thread through, used in sewing; thin rod used in knitting, *etc*; sharp metal tube of hypodermic syringe; pointed piece of (magnetized) metal used as indicator on dial, for picking up vibrations of record, *etc*; leaf of pine, *etc*

**nee·dy** poor

**ne·far·i·ous** very wicked, *etc*. **-ness**

**ne·gate'** deny; make invalid. **-tion**

**neg·a·tive** *a* marked by denial or refusal; lacking positive qualities; (of electrical energy) carried by electrons; (of a number) less than zero; *n* refusal; exposed film showing reverse image

**neg·lect**¹ withhold (necessary) care or attention; leave undone carelessly or on purpose. **-ful**

**neg'li·gent** guilty of neglect; careless. **-gence**

**neg·li·gi·ble** that need not be regarded; unimportant

**ne·go'ti·ate** (shēāt) discuss matter in order to reach agreement. **-ator**; deal with successfully; change checks, etc into cash. **-able** (ebel)

**Ne'gro** (nē-) f **-gress** (pl **-oes**) (of) a black person

**neigh** (make) cry of a horse

**neigh'bor**, UK **-bour** (naber) person living next door or near another. **-hood**

**nei'ther** (US nēdher, UK -nī-) a, pron not the one or the other; adv also not; conj not either

**nem'e·sis** vengeful justice

**ne'on** (nēon) gaseous element used as light source in low-pressure tubes through which electricity is passed

**neph'ew** son of one's brother or sister

**nep'o·tis·m** giving preference to one's relatives, esp. in awarding offices, jobs, etc

**nerve** (bundles of) thread-like tissue carrying sensations to brain and impulses from brain to other parts of body; self-control; coolness in danger, etc; rib in leaf or insect wing; pl (degree of)

physical and psychical sensitivity. **-vous**

**nest** shelter made by bird for laying and hatching its eggs; any similar shelter

**nes'tle** snuggle close; settle down comfortably; lie sheltered

**net** n fabric of cords, strings, etc, crossing each other so as to leave open spaces in between; piece of this used for covering, protection, etc, or for catching fish, etc; a clear of charges and deductions, as profit; (of weight) not including packaging, etc

**neth'er·most** lowest

**net'tle** n plant with stinging hairs; v annoy

**net'work** fabric or structure of threads, wires, etc, crossing each other at certain intervals and joined together at crossing; similar system of channels, roads, etc; system of connected broadcasting stations or computers

**neu·rol'o·gy** study of nervous system and its diseases. **-gist, neurolog'ical**

**neu·ro'sis** (pl **-ses**) nervous disorder which interferes with bodily function. **-tic**

**neu'ter** neither male nor female

**neu'tral** taking neither side in conflict; lacking pronounced qualities, color, etc. **neutral'ity**

**neu'tral·ize,** UK **-ise** make ineffective or neutral

**nev'er** at no time; not ever

**nev·er·the·less'** all the same

**new** recently made, invented, become known, etc; not owned or used by someone before; different or changed from the former or accustomed state

**new'ly-wed** (person) recently married

**news** pl (with sing verb) fresh information; (broadcast of) report of recent events, etc

**news'pa·per** publication printed daily, weekly or monthly, containing news, editorial comments, reviews, etc

**news'print** paper used in printing newspapers

**news'reel** motion picture giving events of the day

**next** nearest (to); immediately following in order, time, place, etc

**nib'ble** bite gently; take small bites of

**nice** pleasing, friendly, etc; requiring or showing great care, skill, close attention, etc, fine, as distinction; well-mannered. **-ty**

**niche** (nich) hollow in wall (for vase, etc); suitable position, etc

**nick** n mark or broken place on edge or surface; similar mark serving as catch, indi-

cator, etc; v chip; make nick in

**nick'el** hard, silvery, rust-resistant metallic element; US and CAN five-cent piece

**nick'name** (humorous) name added to or replacing (person's) actual name

**nic'o·tine** poisonous substance found in tobacco

**niece** (nēs) daughter of one's brother or sister

**nig'gard** stingy person

**nig'gard·ly** (of person) stingy; (of sum) scanty; meager

**night** period between sunset and sunrise; evening occasion; (period of) darkness

**night'ly** (taking place) every night

**night'fall** end of day

**night'in·gale** brown bird noted for sweet song

**night'ly** (taking place) every night

**night'mare** frightening dream or experience

**ni'hil·ism** belief that all existence is meaningless; belief that existing religious, political, etc principles or systems are so bad that they should be destroyed. **nihilis'tic**

**nil** nothing

**nim'ble** quick and light in movement; quick to understand

**nim'bus** halo; rain cloud

**nine** a number (9), equal to eight plus one

**nine·|teen'** a number (19) equal to ten plus nine. **-teenth**

**nine·|ty** a number (90), ten times nine. **-tieth**

**ninth** (nīnth) next after eighth; being one of nine equal parts

**nip** pinch or squeeze sharply between two surfaces, *etc*; check growth or development (of)

**nip'ple** small projection on breast, connected in female to milk ducts; sth resembling this, as cap on nursing bottle

**ni'trate** chemical substance, used to improve soil

**ni'tro·gen** gaseous element making up four-fifths of earth's atmosphere and present in all living tissues

**ni·tro·glyc'er·in** highly explosive oil used in dynamite, *etc*

**no** (*pl* **noes**) *n* word used to express refusal to do or give, denial, or disagreement; vote(r) against sth; *a* not any: *n*. food; not in any degree: *they are n. better than the rest*

**no'ble** high in rank or birth. **-man, -woman,** *etc*; grand. **nobil'ity**

**no'bod·y** no person; person of no importance

**noc·tur'nal** of, occurring or active at night

**nod** bend head slightly, as in greeting, agreement, *etc*; (of flowers) hang down, *esp.* with swaying motion

**noise** sound, *esp.* of loud, confused or unwanted kind. **-less, noisy**

**noi'some** harmful; ill-smelling

**no'mad** member of wandering tribe. **nomad'ic**

**mo'men·cla·ture** system of names or naming, *esp.* in sciences, *etc*

**nom'i·nal** of names; existing in name only; not large, as sum of money

**nom'i·na|te** name or propose for office. **-tor, nomina'tion**

**nom'i·nee** person nominated

**non·cha·|lant** cool in feeling; unexcited. **-lance**

**non·com·mit'tal** refusing to declare o.s. in favor of particular course, view, *etc*

**non·con·duc'tor** substance which permits little or no sound, heat or electricity to pass through it

**non·con·form'ist** (person) rejecting accepted standards of religion, politics, *etc*

**non'de·script** not easily described; having no marked characteristics

**none** no one; not any (of): *n. of them were here*; no part: *n. of this is true*

**non·en'ti·ty** person of no importance

**none'such** person or thing having no equal

**non-plus'** render helpless as to what to say, do, *etc*

**non'sense** words, actions, *etc* which make little sense; foolishness

**non-stop'** uninterrupted(ly)

**noo'dle** strip of dough, dried and then boiled in water

**nook** (out-of-the-way) corner; recess

**noon** twelve o'clock in the day

**noose** loop with running knot which tightens as rope, *etc* is pulled

**nor** (used after neither) and not either: *neither he n. my brother;* continuing a negative: *they never overate, n. did they drink much*

**nor|m** that which is the rule or standard. **-mal**

**north** (towards or lying in) the region to the right of person facing the setting sun. **-ern**

**North Pole** northernmost point of earth

**nose** projecting part of face between mouth and eyes, allowing passage of air in breathing and serving as organ of smell; sth similar to this in shape or position, as spout of vessel, forward end of ship, *etc*

**nos·tal|gi·a** fond or wistful longing for sth past. **-gic**

**nos'tril** one of outer openings of nose

**not** word expressing denial, refusal, disagreement, negation or prohibition: *I did n. see him, he did n. want it, I do n. think so, we do n. have anything to eat; you must n. do that*

**no'ta·ble** worth noting; important. **notabil'ity**

**no'ta·ry** public officer who draws up and verifies documents. **notar'ial**

**notch** V-shaped mark on surface of edge; degree; *US* deep narrow pass

**note** characteristic or distinguishing sign, feature, style, *etc*; (written sign showing length and pitch of) a musical sound; *usu pl* short record of events, facts, *etc*, explanation, *etc*, on margin of page; short letter; paper acknowledging and promising payment of debt: *bank n.*; (outstanding) reputation; attention paid to (command, *etc*)

**noth'ing** (nuth-) no thing; not anything; unimportant person, event, *etc*; no amount or part

**noth'ing·ness** nonexistence; utter void; insignificance

**no'tice** (formal) information or announcement, *esp.* by party to agreement, *etc*, that it is to end within given time;

(sign giving) warning, instructions, *etc*; act of observing and fixing in mind; (polite) attention paid to person, words, *etc*; (newspaper) announcement or review of book, *etc*

**no'ti·fy** inform; give notice. **notifica'tion**

**no'tion** idea; opinion; *pl US* small wares, as thread, *etc*

**no·to·ri·ous** widely (but unfavorably) known. **notori'ety**

**not·with·stand'ing** in spite of

**nought** (nawt) nothing; zero

**nour'ish** feed; nurse (feelings, *etc*). **-ment**

**nov'el** *a* of new kind; new. **-ty;** *n* long published story of invented characters and events

**No·vem'ber** eleventh month of year

**nov'ice** (-is) beginner (*esp.* in religious order)

**now** *adv* at the present time; under the present circumstances; immediately; a moment ago: *he came just n.;* at time spoken of: *n. came the king; conj.* **n. (that)** seeing that; since

**now'a·days** at the present time; in these (modern) days

**no'where** (in, at or to) no place

**nox'ious** (nokshes) harmful. **-ness**

**noz'zle** spout fitted to end of hose, water pipe, *etc* to control flow of liquid, *etc*

**nu'cle·ar** relating to or being a nucleus; of, relating to or using atomic energy

**nu'cle·us** central part around which others are grouped; central core of atom, cell, *etc*

**nude** naked (person, *esp.* in painting, *etc*). **-dist, -dity**

**nudge** push slightly (*esp.* with elbow), so as to call attention, *etc*

**nug'get** lump of gold, *etc* as found in nature

**nui'sance** person, thing, *etc*, highly annoying to others

**null** having no value, effect or legal force. **-lify, -lity**

**numb** (num) lacking feeling, *esp.* from cold; lacking emotion

**num'ber** total of units, things, *etc*, or of persons united in company, group, *etc*; word(s) or symbol(s) used in counting, or given to sth to show its place in a series: *he lives at No 5;* single edition of magazine, *etc*, or part of program, *etc*; *pl* large amount or quality, *etc*

**nu'mer·al** sign expressing a number. **numer'ical**

**nu'mer·ous** many; having many units

**nun** woman living in convent under religious vows

**nup'tial** of marriage (ceremony)

**nurse** *n* person who (professionally) takes care of the sick or injured; woman employed to take care of small children; *etc*; encourage growth; suckle (baby)

**nurs·er·y** place where small children are cared for temporarily; place where plants *etc* are raised for transplanting or sale

**nur·ture** feed, train or bring up children

**nut** fruit with dry edible kernel and hard or leathery shell. **-ty;** (metal) block screwed onto a bolt to fasten it

**nut·meg** aromatic spice added to food

**nu·tri·tion** food; act of giving or receiving food. **-tious, nu·tritive**

**nuz·zle** burrow with nose, or press nose against or in, as animal does

**ny·lon** synthetic plastic material of great strength, used in industry, for stockings, *etc*

**nymph** minor goddess of sea, woods, *etc*

**num·pho·ma·ni·a** excessive sexual desire in a woman. **-ac**

# O

**O** fifteenth letter of English alphabet

**oaf** awkward or stupid person

**oak** (hardwood of) large tree which has jagged leaves and bears acorns

**oar** (wooden) pole with blade at one end, used for moving boat

**o·a·sis** (*pl* **-ses**) place in desert where water is found

**oat** *usu pl* (grain of) cereal grown as food for people and animals

**oath** solemn promise; statement sworn to be true; expression of anger, *etc* using taboo word(s)

**ob·du·ra·te** hardened in feeling; stubborn. **-cy**

**o·be·di·ent** willing to obey. **-ence**

**o·bei·sance** (-bā-) bow of respect or greeting

**o·be·se·** very fat. **-sity**

**o·bey·** carry out orders, instructions (of)

**o·bit·u·ar·y** notice of person's death in newspaper

**ob·ject** *n* thing (that can be seen or felt); person or thing at which feelings are directed; aim

**ob·ject·** *v* state opposition to; disapprove. **-tion**

**ob·jec·tion·a·ble** giving rise to objection; unpleasant

**ob·jec·tive** *a* of things, *etc* outside the mind; real; not prejudiced; not dealing with thoughts or feelings. **ob·jectiv'ity**; *n* goal aimed at

**ob'li·gate** put person under duty to do. **oblig'atory**

**ob·li·ga'tion** binding assistment; duty; debt of gratitude

**o·blige'** compel; do a favor for

**ob·lique'** slanting; indirect

**ob·lit'er·ate** destroy; blot out; leave no trace of

**ob·liv'i·on** state of having or being forgotten

**ob'long** (shape or object) longer than broad and with parallel sides

**ob·nox'ious** (-nokshᵉs) offensive; unpleasant

**ob·scen|e'** indecent. **-ity**

**ob·scur'ant·ism** hindering of the spread of knowledge

**ob·scure'** dark; dim; hidden; little known; unclear. **-rity**

**ob·serv'ance** keeping of a law or custom; ceremonial act

**ob·serv'ant** taking careful notice of things

**ob·ser'va·to·ry** building or place for scientific observation, *esp.* of the heavens

**ob·serve'** keep or follow custom, law, *etc*; watch; notice; make remark on. **observa'tion**

**ob·ses|s'** haunt; fill one's mind completely. **-sion, -sive**

**ob·so·les'|cent** going out of use. **-cence**

**ob'so·lete** out of use or date

**ob'sta·cle** thing that hinders movement, action, progress, *etc*

**ob·stet'ri|cs** science of assisting women in childbirth. **-cal, obstetri'cian**

**ob'sti·na|te** stubborn; not yielding. **-cy**

**ob·struct'** stand in way of; hinder; make difficult. **-tion, -tive**

**ob·tain'** get by effort; exist; be in general use

**ob·trude'** thrust forward (without being asked). **-sive**

**ob·tuse'** slow to understand. **-ness**; (of angle) between 90 and 180 degrees

**ob'vi·ate** make unnecessary; get rid of (difficulty)

**ob'vi·ous** clear to the eye or mind; plain. **-ness**

**oc·ca'sion** particular or special time, event, *etc*; time particularly suited for doing something; reason or (secondary) cause for action or result; **on o.** now and then

**oc·ca'sion·al** not regular; infrequent

**Oc'ci·dent** the western world, *esp.* Europe, N. and S. Amer. **occiden'tal**

**oc·cult'** secret; mysterious; of the supernatural or magical

**oc·cu·pa'tion** job; activity; act of occupying or being occupied

**oc'cu·|py** hold; fill (space,

*etc*); live in; keep busy; take possession of. **-pant, -pancy**

**oc·cur'** happen; come to mind; be found. **-rence**

**o'cean** (any of the geographical divisions of) large body of salt water covering most of the Earth's surface. **ocean'ic** huge space or quantity

**o'clock** of the clock, used in specifying the hour of the day: *it is 5 o'clock*

**oc'ta·gon** figure with eight sides and eight angles

**Oc·to'ber** tenth month of year

**oc'to·pus** deep-sea animal with soft body and eight sucker-bearing arms around mouth

**oc'u·lar** of the eye(s)

**oc'u·list** specialist in eye defects and diseases

**odd** different from the ordinary, usual or accepted. **-ity** occurring occasionally; not part of definite group, *etc*; (of number) not divisible by two; additional to a stated number: *he has some 30-odd tapes*; separated from pair or series: *an o. glove*

**odds** advantage favoring one of two opposed things, *etc*; chances in favor of or against result, *etc*; these chances expressed as ratio for betting; **at o.** (being) in disagreement

**ode** poem of lofty style

**o'di·ous** hateful; disgusting. **-ness**

**o'di·um** hatred; disgrace attached to sth hateful

**o'dor,** *UK* **-dour** smell; scent **of** *prep* used to indicate: distance, direction, separation, deprivation, *etc*: *within ten miles o., to the north o., take leave o., be robbed o.*; origin, source, cause, *etc*: *o. good family, the works o. Bacon, to die o. cold*; material, identity: *table o. wood, the city o. New York*; belonging, connection, *etc*: *the property o. my uncle, a friend o. mine*; objective relation: *love o. music*; reference: *talk o.peace*; quality, *etc*: *a woman o. great kindness*; day, month in dates: *10th o. May*; minute, hour in times: *ten minutes o. six*; inclusion in a whole, *etc*: *six o. us*

**off** *adv, adj* away from former position, connection, *etc*, or to distance, in certain direction, *etc*: *run o. to the woods, see one o. on a trip*; varying from the normal or regular; as deduction: *5% o. on wholesale purchases*; away in time or space: *Easter is five weeks o., the city is some 20 miles o.*; out of operation or interrupted: *the current is o., lay o. work*; so as to bring to end or finish completely: *kill*

o. mice; in state of cancellation, etc: the deal was o.; in state of fulfillment, success, etc: the deal came o.; in or into state of removal or reduction: he took his coat o., the paint wore o.; not at work: she has the week o.; of less than usual quality, activity, etc: the o. season (of chances) unlikely; **o. and on** now and then; **right o.** immediately; prep away from: he jumped o. the wall; near: an island o. the coast; no longer (up)on: he got o. the chair

**off·fend'** hurt feelings of; annoy; sin

**of·fen|se'**, UK **-fence** wrongdoing, crime; (cause for) hurt feelings; attack. **-sive**

**of'fer** put (thing, idea, etc) forward for acceptance or refusal; express or show readiness or intention (to do, give help, etc); present for sale or tend as price: o. a car for sale, o. ten dollars; (of things, opportunity, etc) present, provide; present (sacrifice, etc) as act of worship

**off'hand'** casual; without preparation

**of'fice** place for doing business, clerical or administrative work, etc: (duties, functions, etc, belonging to) responsible position, esp. in

government; place offering special service or type of business; government department; (prescribed form of) church service or ceremony

**of'fi·cer** person holding public, church, commercial, etc, office; person holding position of authority in army or similar body; policeman

**of·fi'cial** (of, from or about) person(s) holding public office or position of authority

**of·fi'ci·ate** act in priestly or other office, esp. on particular occasion

**of·fi'cious** offering unwanted services; meddlesome. **-ness**

**off'ing: in the o.** likely to happen in the near future

**off'set** balance; compensate for

**off'shoot** side branch or shoot; descendant

**off'shore** away or at a distance from shore

**off'spring** child or children of particular parents

**of'ten** many times: he came o.; in many cases: patients o. die of this disease

**o'gle** look at amorously

**o'gre** man-eating giant

**oil** petroleum; any of large number of thick, liquid fatty, substances from plants, animals, etc, used as source of heat or light, in cooking, for lubricating, in perfumes, *etc.* **-y;** (painting done in) oil color

**oil'skin** (garment of) cotton fabric made waterproof by treatment with oil

**oint'ment** greasy substance for healing skin, *etc*

**old** having existed or lived for a long time; having a specified age; characteristic of advanced age or worn, *etc*, through long use; belonging to period far back in history; former; long known: *o. customs*

**old-fash'ioned** out of date

**ol·fac'to·ry** of the sense of smell

**ol'i·garch·y** (-ki) government by a few. **oligar'chic(al)**

**ol'ive** (tree growing in warm regions and bearing) small oval fruit which yields oil and is dull yellowish-green when unripe; (of) this color

**o'men** event supposed to warn of things to come

**om'i·nous** warning of some future evil

**o·mit'** leave out; fail to do. **-mission**

**om'ni·bus** book containing reprints of several works, *esp.* by one author; bus

**om·nip'o·tent** having unlimited power. **-tence**

**om·ni·pres'ent** present everywhere. **-ence**

**om·ni'·scient** (-shent) knowing all things. **-science** (-shens)

**om·niv'o·rous** feeding on everything, both vegetable and animal

**on** used to express as *prep*: position above and supported by surface: *a hat lay o. the chair, sit o. a horse*; position, state, condition, *etc*: *hair o. his head, o. duty, o. fire*; closeness to, direction of movement, *etc*: *house bordering o. the river, o. the right*; support, *etc*: *carriage o. wheels, key o. a chain*; means: *we heard it o. the radio, travel o. horseback*; (of time) at the time of, during: *the train was o. the hour, o. Sunday morning*; object or reference of thought, action, *etc*: *speak o. a subject*; as *adv*: showing (continuous) action, process, *etc*: *he went o. for days*; showing movement forward, *etc*: *further o., as time went o.*; so as to make active, put in operation: *turn the water/light o.*; so as to cover, be situated, *etc*: *put one's clothes o., put the kettle o.*; attached or fast to: *hold o.*

**once** (wuns) *adv* a single time: *he came only o.*; ever, even a single time: *if o. he learns about this*; at some time in the past (also **o. upon a time**): *a o. well-known poet*;

*conj* when; as soon as: *o. he knows you better*; **o. and for all** finally and definitively; **o. again** one more time; as in the past; **all at o.** suddenly; **at o.** immediately; at the same time

**one** *n* the first and lowest number (1), designating a single item, person, *etc*, in contrast to two or more; a whole or single through union, agreement, *etc*: *they were as if o.* **-ness;** *a* some (day, *etc*, in the future): *o. day he will come*; same: *they all took o. direction*; of a particular kind, *etc*: *of o. sex/race*; of particular past date, *etc*: *o. morning last summer*; only: *she was the o. person I met*; a certain (otherwise unknown, *etc*, person): *o. Mr. Smith came to see me*; *pron* any person, *esp.* of the speaker's kind: *every o.*, *o. should think that*; person of specified kind: *the brown-haired o.*; thing of specified kind: *I don't have o.*

**on·er·ous** burdensome

**one·self** form of **one** used for emphasis or reflexively: *one cannot do that o.*, *to hurt o.*

**one-sid·ed** (-si-) lopsided; considering or preferring only one side; unfair; not equal: *a o. fight*

**on·ion** (plant with) strong-tasting many-layered bulb, much used in cooking, pickling, *etc*

**on·ly** *a* without others of the same class or kind: *o. one book was left, an o. son*; *adv* merely, no more than: *I o. heard him come, if you would o. agree*; *conj* but: *I would have been there, o. the train was late*

**on·set** attack; beginning

**on·slaught** (-slawt) furious attack

**on·to** to a place, position, *etc* on

**on·ward(s)** toward or at a point ahead in space or time

**ooze** *v* leak out slowly and gradually; *n* soft mud; that which oozes

**o·paque'** not letting light through; that cannot be seen through

**o·pen** *a* not shut, closed, covered, enclosed by gates, *etc*: that may be used, entered, competed for by all, or that is available, accessible, *etc*: *an o. meeting, an o. road*; (of time, positions, *etc*) not occupied; (of questions, *etc*) undecided; spread out, as a newspaper; having gaps or openings: *o. ranks, o. texture*; (of accounts) not yet balanced; existing, carried on, *etc*, so as to be exposed to general view or knowledge; frank in manners, *etc*; generous; willing to accept ideas, *etc*: *an o. mind*; *v* make or become open; remove covering, obstacles, *etc*, or move (door, *etc*) from shut position, so as to permit passage, expose to view, *etc*; make available for use: spread out: *o. a book/umbrella*; set up for (general) use: *o. a shop*; begin action, *etc*: *o. the contest*; come apart; *n* outdoors

**op'er·a** a drama in which the words are sung to orchestral accompaniment. **operat'ic**

**op'er·a|te** (cause to) perform work; produce effect; carry on business, *etc*; manage. **-ble, -tive**

**o'pi·ate** drug containing opium which eases pain or brings sleep

**o·pin'ion** judgment; belief; view

**o·pin'ion·at·ed** stubborn in holding to one's opinions

**o'pi·um** habit-forming drug used as narcotic, *etc*

**op·po'nent** one who opposes

**op·por·tune'** timely; well-timed; suitable

**op·por·tun'|is·m** policy of following course offering immediate gain, at cost of principles. **-ist**

**op·por·tu'ni·ty** chance; good occasion to do sth

**op·pose'** resist or act against;

set against or in contrast. **opposi'tion**

**op'po·site** facing; wholly different; being the other of a pair

**op·press|s'** weigh down or crush (by force, worries, *etc*); subject to continual cruelty. **-sion, -sive, -sor**

**opt** make a choice

**op'ti·cal** of sight or the eye; of or using optics

**op·ti'cian** maker or seller of eyeglasses

**op'tics** scientific study of light

**op'ti·|mis·m** belief that everything is as good as possible; natural tendency to be hopeful about everything. **-mist, optimis'tic**

**op'ti·mum** most favorable (condition, degree, *etc*)

**op'tion** (freedom of) choice; right to buy sth at fixed price at a certain time

**op'u·|lent** rich; plentiful. **-lence**

**o'pus** artistic work

**or** word used to introduce alternative(s): *apples o. peaches; apples o. peaches o. pears; apples, peaches o. pears*; to connect alternative terms: *a sound o. healthy mind*; to express correlation: *either ... o., o. ... o., whether .. o.*

**or'a·cle** person in ancient Greece who uttered prophecy or divine message; wise person or statement. **orac'ular**

**o'ral** of the mouth; spoken

**or'ange** (orinj) (citrus tree bearing) round juicy fruit with reddish-yellow rind; (of) this color

**o·ra'tion** formal speech. **or'ator**

**or'a·to·ry** art of public speaking. **orator'ical**

**or'bit** eye socket; path of one body circling another, as earth around sun; range of influence. **-al, -er**

**or'chard** (enclosed) area where fruit trees are grown

**or'ches·|tra** body of musicians playing various instruments and performing symphonies, operas, etc. **-trate, orches'tral**

**or'chid** (plant with) showy flower, often of brilliant color and extraordinary shape; (of) light purple color

**or·dain'** appoint to (churchly) office; command (to be done)

**or·deal'** painful or troublesome

**or'der** direction, instruction, etc, esp. one which must be obeyed; manner in which things, persons, etc, follow one after another in space, time, etc; state in which everything is in its right place; (satisfactory or efficient)

condition: *the motor is out of o.*; state of society or other bodies marked by absence of revolt, disturbance, etc and by observance of law and authority; established or customary manner of proceeding, esp. in debates etc; class or kind of things, persons, etc, distinguished from others by nature, character, status, etc; any of the grades of clerical office in the Christian churches; instruction to manufacture, deliver, etc, goods, pay money, etc: *an o. for ten stoves, money o.*; **in o. that, in o. to** so that

**or'der·ly** a arranged in, characterized by, or observant of order; n attendant in hospital or to an officer

**or'di·nar·y** normal; common; (somewhat lower than) average

**ore** metal-bearing rock

**or'gan** part of animal or plant having specific and vital function, as kidneys, etc; (official) organization with some specific purpose; means of communicating certain opinions, as a party newspaper; mus instrument with set(s) of pipes sounded by means of compressed air and played by means of keyboard(s)

**or·gan'ic** of bodily organs; of

living things; of a system of specialized parts; being a necessary part of such a system; (of food) grown without use of chemicals

**or'gan·ism** any form of animal or plant life; whole system of specialized parts

**or'gan·ize** form into organic or orderly whole; set up or arrange; US enroll (workers) in trade union. **organiza'tion**

**or'gasm** height of sexual excitement

**or'gy** wild (drunken) festivity; happening marked by wild unchained passion. **orgias'tic**

**o·ri·ent** n O. the East or eastern countries. **-tal;** v bring into clearly understood relations; determine position. **orienta'tion**

**or'i·fice** opening, esp. in body

**or'i·gin** beginning; starting-point; source. **orig'inate**

**o·rig'i·nal** first; earliest; new; not imitated; being that from which a copy, translation, etc is made. **original'ity**

**or'na·ment** that which adorns; addition serving to make appearance more beautiful. **ornamen'tal**

**or·nate'** richly ornamented

**or·ni·thol'o·gy** scientific study of birds. **-gist**

**or'phan** child whose parents

are both dead. **-age**

**or'tho·dox** having the correct or generally-accepted (religious) opinions. **-y**

**os'cil·late** swing between two points; vibrate

**os·mo'sis** slow passage or diffusion of fluid through a membrane

**os·ten'si·ble** put forward to appear as such; pretended

**os·ten·ta'tion** showing off; unnecessary display. **-tious**

**os·tra·cize,** UK **-cise** exclude by general consent from society. **-cism**

**os'trich** the largest of birds, flightless, swift-running and valued for its showy wing and tail plumes

**oth'er** different from the one(s) mentioned or thought of: *let's have some o. ideas on this subject;* different in nature, etc: *I wouldn't want any o. food than bread;* additional: *she and one o. friend;* being the remaining one(s) of two or more: *his o. eye;* **the o. day** one or two days ago; **every o. day** every second day

**oth'er·wise** in a different manner; in other circumstances; in other respects: *o. she was happy*

**ot'ter** (fur of) fish-eating water animal

**ouch** cry of sudden pain

**ought** (awt) am (is, are) or

was (were) bound in duty or because of moral obligation, on grounds of justice, probability, etc: I o. to help her, this o. to be done, they o. to have been here by ten

**ounce** unit of weight equal to 1/16 lb. avoirdupois; small amount

**our(s)** possessive form of we; of us: *our brother, ours is a great tradition*

**our·selves**¹ used as reflexive form of **we** or for emphasis: *we had o. to blame, we will do this o.*

**oust** (oust) drive out of place occupied

**out** away from or not in (former) place, position, state, etc: *he took the dog o., the workers were o. on strike, it's very humid o.*; so as to finish: *put the fire o.*; not burning: *the candle is o.*; in(to) the open, existence, etc: *a fire broke o., the secret was o.*; so as to extend: *troops fanned o.*; not at home, etc: *she was o. for the day*; not in usual state, shape, etc: *to be tired o., to spread o.*; loudly: *cry o.*; in(to) confusion, disharmony, etc: *fall o. about sth*; (with *of*) away from (former) place, state, etc: *he went o. of the room, o. of sight, o. of danger*; so as to (make) be without: *cheat him o. of his money, we are o. of cash*;

from a source, ground, etc: *made o. of linen, asked o. of ignorance*; from among: *one o. of many*; at (given) distance: *7 miles o. of town*; away from what is correct: *o. of line, o. of order*

**out·bid**¹ make higher offer than

**out·break** (sudden) onset of disease, emotion, war, etc

**out·burst** (sudden and violent) bursting forth, as of tears

**out·cast** (person) expelled from country, home, etc

**out·come** result

**out·cry** public protest

**out·dat·ed** obsolete

**out·do**¹ do better than

**out·er** on the outside; located (farther) away from center

**out·fit** set of articles needed for particular purpose

**out·go·ing** departing; friendly

**out·growth** natural result, product, etc; additional result; that which grows out, as an offshoot

**out·house** outbuilding, *esp. US* an outside toilet

**out·ing** pleasure trip

**out·land·ish** foreign; strange

**out·law** one declared outside the protection of law; criminal who has not been caught

**out·lay** money spent

**out·let** opening for letting sth out, as gas, electric, etc;

# outline

shop, *etc* serving as market for goods

**out·line** line showing shape or limits of object; rough sketch; short description of important parts of plan, etc

**out·look** view (of the future)

**out·ly·ing** far from the center

**out·num·ber** be larger in number than

**out·pa·tient** person being treated at hospital though living at home

**out·post** settlement at a frontier

**out·put** goods, *etc* produced in given period

**out·rage** shameful wrong; violation of other's rights or feelings. **outra'geous**

**out·right** direct; complete; open

**out·set** beginning

**out·side|'e** *n* surface, exterior or outer appearance, or outer appearance; space or position beyond boundary, *etc*; the utmost limit: *you will get ten dollars at the o.; a* on, to or of the outer side, or space without; not belonging to group, society, *etc*: *o. influences.* **-er**

**out·size** larger than the norm

**out·skirts** *pl* section at outer edge of city

**out·spo·ken** speaking openly or frankly

**out·stand·ing** standing out; deserving attention or praise; unpaid, as bills

**out·ward** to, at, or of the outside

**out·wit** get the better of by cleverness

**o·val** (sth) egg-shaped

**o·va·ry** female reproductive organ in which eggs are produced; part of plant producing seeds

**o·va·tion** enthusiastic public reception

**ov·en** brick, metal, *etc*, chamber for cooking food, baking clay, *etc*

**o·ver** *prep* above in position, authority, *etc*: *the sky o. our heads, he rules o. us;* to or on the other side of: *he jumped o. the wall, they live o. the hill;* on top of (so as to cover): *she put a cloth o. the birdcage;* beyond the rim or edge: *coffee ran o. the side of the cup;* in excess of or addition to (quantity, limit, *etc*): *o. the correct weight, costs o. ten dollars;* while doing sth: *they met o. chess;* in many parts of: *paint spilled o. the floor;* during: *o. the weekend;* in connection with: *in trouble o. this matter; adv* away from erect position: *topple o.;* covering (entire) surface: *paint the house all o.;* above and beyond edge, *etc*: *water boiled o.;* so as to show another side: *turn the page o.;* across space: *went o. to see him;* so as to change position, adherence, *etc*: *went o. to the enemy*; from beginning to end, or repeatedly: *count the money o.*, *do it all o. again*; from one (person, *etc*) to another: *he handed it o.*; ended: *after the war was o.*; remaining: *the money is left o.*

**o'ver·act'** act (theatrical part) in exaggerated manner

**o'ver·all** *a* including everything; *adv* as a whole; *n UK* protective work coat; *pl* one-piece top and trousers worn at work, *etc*, to protect clothing

**o'ver·bear'ing** arrogantly commanding

**o'ver·board** over side of ship (into the water)

**o'ver·cast** cloudy

**o'ver·coat** heavy winter coat worn over clothes

**o'ver·come' (-came, -come)** get the better of; affect strongly, as feelings

**o'ver·do' (-did, -done)** exaggerate; cook (food) too long

**o'ver·dose** too large a dose

**o'ver·draw' (-drew, -drawn)** issue check larger than bank balance

**o'ver·drive** engine device allowing higher gear ratio than that of normal top gear

**o'ver·due'** left unpaid or unattended too long; late

**o'ver·grown'** covered with growth

**o·ver·hang' (-hung)** jut out, as cliff

**o·ver·haul'** examine thoroughly and make repairs; overtake

**o·ver·head**, *UK* **-heads** general costs of a business

**o·ver·hear' (-heard)** hear secretly or by accident

**o·ver·land'** across the countryside by land routes

**o·ver·lap'** cover and extend beyond

**o·ver·look'** view from or be situated at higher position; inspect; miss seeing or noticing something

**o·ver·night'** during or for the night; suddenly

**o·ver·pass'** road crossing over another by a bridge

**o·ver·pow'er** defeat; master; be too strong, as heat

**o·ver·ride' (-rode, -ridden)** pursue course, *etc* in disregard of (advice, orders, *etc*)

**o·ver·rule'** set aside by higher authority; rule against (suggestion)

**o'ver·sea(s)** (situated) beyond the sea; foreign

**o·ver·|see' (-saw, -seen)** supervise. **-seer**

**o·ver·shad'ow** cast shadow over; make unimportant by comparison

**o'ver·shoe** rubber, *etc* shoe worn for protection in wet weather, *etc*

**o·ver·sight** (mistake due to) failure to notice

**o·ver·strung'** too sensitive or nervous

**o'vert** openly done; not secret. **-ly**

**o·ver·take'** (**-took**, **-taken**) catch up with

**o·ver·tax'** tax too heavily; make too great demands on

**o·ver·throw'** (**-threw**, **-thrown**) upset; bring to a fall

**o'ver·time** (pay collected for) time worked beyond the usual hours

**o'ver·ture** opening of discussions; formal offer; *mus* piece at beginning of opera, ballet, *etc*

**o·ver·turn'** overthrow

**o'ver·view** (short) survey or summary

**o·ver·whelm'** overcome by amount, strength, *etc*

**o·ver·wrought'** very excited

**ov'u·late** produce and discharge eggs from ovary

**o'vum** (*pl* **o'va**) female reproductive cell in animals

**owe** (ō) be under obligation to repay borrowed money, return something received or render service, honor, *etc* (to person)

**owl** (oul) soft-feathered, large-eyed bird of prey, hunting at night

**own** (ōn) *a* belonging or peculiar to o.s. or itself: *this house is my o.*, *love truth for its o. sake*; *v* have as property. **-er;** acknowledge or admit (as true, existent, *etc*): *a child nobody will o.*, *o. to having done it*

**ox** (*pl* **ox'en**) any cod-chewing, even-toed hoofed mammal; castrated adult male of domestic cattle

**ox'i·dize** (cause to) combine with oxygen; cover with rust or other oxide. **oxida'tion**

**ox'y·gen** gaseous element making up one-fifth of atmosphere and essential to all life on earth

**oys'ter** edible sea animal with hinged shell, some kinds of which produce pearls

**o'zone** form of oxygen, *esp.* noticeable in air after thunderstorm

# P

**p** sixteenth letter of English alphabet

**pace** *n* (length of) step in walking or running; manner or speed of moving; *v* move with slow, measured steps; measure (distance) by paces; set tempo of movement for

**pace'mak·er** one that sets pace; electronic device inserted in heart to control heartbeat

**pach'y·derm** any thick-skinned four-legged mammal, *esp.* elephant, rhinoceros, *etc*

**pac'i·fist** person opposed to war and refusing to bear arms. **-fism**

**pac'if·y** calm (anger, *etc*); bring to state of peace

**pack** *n* bundle of things wrapped up, *etc* for carrying, *esp.* on back; number or quantity of similar persons, animals or things; set of items, as cigarettes, wrapped for selling; set of playing cards; application of healing or cosmetic paste to body, *esp.* face; *v* put things together in box, *etc* for transport or storing. **-er**; fill (container, *etc*) closely; crowd (people, animals) together; select (jury) so as to make sure of desired verdict

**pack'age** bundle of things packed for transport, *etc*; parcel; set of related items treated as unit

**pack'et** small package; ship carrying mail and passengers

**pact** agreement (*esp.* between nations)

**pad** *n* cushion or mass of soft material for filling out hollows, *etc* or for sitting on. **-ding**; sheets of paper fastened together at one edge; cushion under foot of cer-

tain animals; floating leaf, as of water-lily; *v* walk with soft footsteps; stuff or fill out

**pad'dle** long-handled broad-bladed implement for moving small boat; anything shaped like this

**pad'lock** detachable lock

**pa'gan** heathen (person). **-ism**

**page** *n* one side of written or printed sheet in book, letter, *etc*; boy employed to run errands, *etc*, *esp.* in hotel; *hist* youth training for knighthood or attending person of high rank; *v* seek out person by calling out his name, *esp.*, through loudspeaker

**pag'eant** (pajent) great open-air public (historical, *etc*) show; any brilliant spectacle. **-ry**

**pa·go'da** temple in India, China, *etc*

**paid** see **pay**

**pail** *esp.* *US* bucket; (also **pail'ful**) amount contained in p.

**pain** suffering of body or mind, as that due to injury, grief, *etc*. **-ful**, **-less**; *pl* trouble taken

**pains'tak·ing** very careful (in work)

**paint** *n* solid coloring matter, mixed with oil, *etc* which will stick to surface; *v* make picture of in colors, as on canvas, *etc;* apply coloring matter to wall. *etc* **-er, -ing;** describe in words

**pair** set of two, *esp.* of things similar to each other or used or existing together: *a p. of shoes;* thing consisting of two corresponding pieces: *p. of scissors;* two persons or animals of opposite sex associated together, as in marriage

**pa·ja·mas** UK **py–** *pl* trousers and jacket worn as sleeping garment

**pal'ace** (palis) large stately house, *esp.* as residence of king, bishop, *etc*

**pal'at·a·ble** pleasant (to the taste)

**pal'ate** roof of mouth; (sense of) taste

**pa·la·ver** long discussion; idle talk

**pale** *a* of light color; (of skin) whitish; (of light) not bright. **-ness;** *n* pointed piece of wood for fence; **beyond the p.** outside limits of acceptable behavior

**pal'i·sade** fence of poles; *pl* line of cliffs

**pall** *v* become boring or uninteresting; *n* cloth spread on coffin; anything that covers, *esp.* with darkness

**pall'bear·er** person who carries coffin at funeral

**pal'let** (straw) mattress; portable (wooden) platform for moving or storing heavy goods

**pal'lid** (unhealthily) pale

**pal'lor** (unnatural) paleness

**palm** (pahm) *n* inner surface of hand between wrist and fingers; (sub)tropical tree with tall unbranched trunk and crown of large fan-shaped leaves; leaf of this tree (as sign of victory); *v infml* **p. off** get rid of by trickery

**pal'pa·ble** able to be touched or felt; readily seen or understood

**pal'pi·tate** throb; tremble (with fear, *etc*)

**pal'sy** condition marked by trembling of limbs. **pal'sied**

**pal'try** worthless; petty

**pam'phlet** small unbound book, *esp.* on subject of current interest

**pan** *n* round metal vessel for cooking, separating ore from gravel, weighing sth on a pair of scales, *etc; v* wash gravel, *etc* to separate ore; (cause camera to) follow action, *etc; infml* criticize severely

**pan·a·ce'a** remedy for all

**pan'cake** thin flat (breakfast) cake made of batter and fried on griddle

**pan'cre·as** large gland discharging digestive fluid and insulin into intestine

**pan·de·mo'ni·um** wild uproar; utter confusion

**pane** (framed) sheet of glass

**pan·e·gyr·ic** (-jir-) speech or writing in praise of person or thing

**pan'el** group of persons with special task, as jury. **-ist** (*UK* **-list**); enclosed part of surface, as in door; board holding controls, dials, *etc*; piece of different color, *etc* in dress

**pang** sudden sharp pain or feeling of worry, *etc*

**pan'ic** (feel or cause to feel) unreasoning terror affecting group of persons or animals

**pan·o·ra·ma** wide view of landscape; continuous passing scene

**pant** breathe hard and fast; gasp for breath; long to do something

**pan'the·ism** doctrine that God and nature are one

**pan'ther** (black) leopard; *US* puma or cougar

**pan'to·mime** play in which gestures are used instead of words

**pan'try** room where food or china, *etc* is kept

**pants** *pl US* trousers

**pa'pal** of the Pope

**pa'per** substance made from rags, wood, *etc*, in thin sheets, for writing on, wrapping, *etc*; piece of this bearing writing or printing, as document, *etc*; set of questions or answers in examination; article on particular subject; newspaper; *pl* documents showing person's or ship's identity; *v* decorate wall of room with wallpaper

**par** equality in value or standing; average or normal amount; face value

**par'a·ble** story teaching moral or religious lesson

**par'a·chute** umbrella-like safety device for jumping from airplane

**pa·rade'** public procession through streets; (place of) regular assembly of troops for inspection, *etc*; ostentatious show; *UK* promenade

**par'a·digm** (-dīm) example; pattern

**par'a·dise** heaven, as the final dwelling-place of the good; place or state of utter bliss

**par'a·dox** (seemingly) absurd or self-contradictory statement or situation. **para·dox'ical**

**par'a·gon** model of excellence

**par'a·graph** division in book, *etc* containing one or more sentences and starting on new line

**par'al·lel** having the same direction and remaining equally distant at all points; corresponding; similar

**par·al·lel'o·gram** four-sided figure whose opposite sides are equal in length and parallel

**pa·ral'y·sis** (partial) loss off feeling in body or ability to move muscles; inability to act, think, *etc*. **paralyt'ic**

**par'a·lyze**, *UK* **-lyse** affect with paralysis; make powerless

**par'a·mount** above all others in importance, *etc*; supreme

**par·a·noi'a** mental disease marked by false belief in one's importance or in others' hatred of one. **-ac**

**par·a·pher·na'li·a** personal belongings; equipment (for particular activity)

**par'a·phrase** statement of (meaning of) text in other words

**par·a·ple'|gi·a** paralysis of body from waist downward. **-gic**

**par'a·site** animal or plant living in or upon another and feeding on it

**par'boil** partly cook by boiling

**par'cel** goods, *etc* wrapped up together; piece of land

**parch** make or become hot and dry, as by sun

**parch'ment** skin, *esp.* of sheep, used to write on; sth written in this way

**par'don** polite allowance made in excusing fault, *etc*: *I beg your p.*; forgiving of offense; freeing from punishment

**pare** cut off outer skin or layer; make less or smaller little by little

**par'ent** a father or mother. **-age, -hood**

**pa·ren'the·sis** (*pl* **-ses**) words inserted in sentence but not grammatically part of it; round bracket. **pa·renthet'ic(al)**

**pa·ri'ah** (-ri-) social outcast

**par'ish** district having with church and clergyman

**par'i·ty** equality

**park** *n* large enclosed piece of land with trees, meadows, *etc* set apart for public use or belonging to country house; ground set apart for sports, leaving cars, amusement *etc*; *v* place and leave, as car, *etc*

**par'lance** way of speaking

**par'ley** discussion of terms, *esp.* between enemies

**par'lia·ment** (-le-), P. lawmaking body of Great Britain, consisting of House of Lords and House of Commons; similar lawmaking body elsewhere

**par'lor**, *UK* **-lour** sitting room; *US* business offering special service, as massage p., funeral p.

**pa·ro'chi·al** (-kiel) of a parish; narrow in interests **-ism**

**par'o·dy** humorous imitation (of style of writing, *etc*); poor imitation

**pa·role'** release of prisoner

before sentence is completed on promise of good behavior

**par'ox·ysm** sudden violent fit of feeling, coughing, etc

**par'ri·cide** murder(er) of one's own parent or close relative

**par'rot** any of various kinds of hook-billed tropical birds with multi-colored feathers, some of which can be taught to imitate words

**par'ry** ward off (blow, etc); evade, as question

**par·si·mo'ni·ous** careful in spending money; stingy. **par'simony**

**par'son** (parish) clergyman

**part** that which is less than, and together with others of similar or equal kind makes up a whole; division of story, etc, share; one of sides to a contest, agreement, etc; line made by dividing hair on head; often pl region; music assigned to particular voice or instrument in a composition; (lines of) dramatic role; (one's) share in some action, etc; v (cause to) become divided, separated or come apart; leave; die; **p. with** give up

**par·take'** (-took, -tak'en) take part in; have a share of, as food

**par'tial** forming only a part; prejudiced in favor of one side. **partial'ity**

**par·tic'i·pate** have share in; take part in. **-pant, partic·ipa'tion**

**par'ti·cle** very small piece

**par·tic'u·lar** a relating to one rather than to all; special; different from the others or the usual; hard to please; extremely exact about details; in p. especially; n individual fact or point. **particular'ity**

**par'ti·san** n supporter of party or cause; person engaged in underground fighting against occupying enemy; a (heavily) slanted in favor of

**par·ti'tion** division into parts; part; dividing wall

**part'ly** to some degree; not entirely

**part'ner** person who participates in some action with other person(s), esp. in business; husband or wife; one of couple

**par'ty** body of persons united in cause, contest against another side, etc, esp. organized political group holding certain views on public questions and offering candidates for election to office, etc; group of persons meeting for social enjoyment, travelling, etc; each of the two or more persons forming the two sides in lawsuit, agreement, etc

**pass** v (cause to or let) move

onward, along, over, *etc*, or (cause to) change place, condition, possession, *etc*: *p. along the street, money passed hands, let him p.*; be accepted as: *she could p. as a boy*; (of law, *etc*) be accepted; succeed in: *p. one's examinations*; take place: *I saw what was passing*: (of time) go by; hand down judgment in court; (in card games) refuse to join bidding, *etc*; put (string, *etc*) around something; spend (time) in given manner; **p. away** die; **p. on** die; move on; **p. over** not remark on some action, *etc*; *n* (written) permission to come and go, enter, *etc*; narrow opening through mountains; *infml* condition of affairs

**pas'sage** act or means of passing; part of text

**pas'sen·ger** (pasinjer) one who travels in a (public) vehicle but is not the driver

**pas'sion** strong feeling, *esp.* love; strong anger. **-ate**

**pas'sive** not acting but being acted upon; offering no opposition. **passiv'ity**

**pass'port** official document authorizing bearer to travel abroad and entitling him to protection

**past** *a* of, belonging to events, things, *etc*, which happened or existed formerly

or in time just before the present; *prep* beyond; *n* time before the present

**pas'ta** mixture of flour, eggs and water, dried in various shapes and then boiled in water

**paste** adhesive mixture of flour and water, *etc*; mixture of flour, shortening, *etc*, for baking pies, *etc*; any soft preparation, as tooth p.; brilliant glasslike substance for making artificial gems

**paste'board** sheets of paper pasted together into stiff board, used for book cover

**pas'tel** (of) soft pale color

**pas'teur·ize**, *UK* **-ise** treat (milk, *etc*) with heat to kill germs

**pas'time** sth entertaining that helps one to pass time pleasantly

**pas'try** (pā-) (pies, tarts, *etc* made of) dough of flour, shortening, *etc*

**pas'ture** ground on which cattle can feed

**pat** *v* strike lightly with flat surface, as with palm of hand; stroke gently with fingers or palm; *a* ready for (any) occasion: *he always had a p. answer*

**patch** *n* piece of material used to mend hole, tear *etc*, or to cover wound; small piece of land; large (irregular) spot on surface; *v* repair by putting patches on; **p. up** settle (quarrel, *etc*); mend hastily

**pate** (top of) head

**pa'tent** *a* open; evident; *n* official right (protecting invention)

**pa'ter·nal** of or like a father; fatherly; related through the father. **-ism**

**pa·ter'ni·ty** fatherhood

**path** narrow way, *esp.* one beaten by feet of men or animals; course along which something moves; line of action, conduct, *etc*

**pa·thet'ic** causing pity, sorrow or contempt

**pa·thol'o·gy** scientific study of disease. **-gist, pathol'ical**

**pa'thos** (pā-) quality in literature or life that arouses pity or sadness

**pa'tient** (pāsh*e*nt) *a* enduring pain, annoyance, *etc* calmly or with self-control; not giving up in spite of difficulties. **-tience;** *n* person under medical care

**pa'ti·o** (roofed) space, *usu* paved, attached to house and used for dining outdoors, *etc*

**pa'tri·arch** (pātriahrk) father and ruler of family or tribe; respected old man. **patriar'chal**

**pat'ri·cide** murder(er) of one's own father

**pa'tri·ot** one who loves and defends his country's interests. **patriot'ic**

**pa·trol'** (guard of police, *etc*) making round of area to watch it; troops sent out to gather information or protect area

**pa'tron,** *f* **-ess** (wealthy) person who protects or supports; regular customer. **-age**

**pa'tron·ize,** *UK* **-ise** act as patron; behave as if superior to another person

**pat'ter** beat or move with short tapping sounds, as rain on roof, or children running; talk, very fast or glibly

**pat'tern** anything made as guide for others to copy; excellent example; (decorative) design

**paunch** belly, *esp.* fat one in a man. **-iness, -y**

**pau'per** very poor person

**pause** temporary stop in action or speech; delay

**pave** cover (road, *etc*) with stones, concrete, *etc* so as to make level surface. **-ment;** prepare (way) for

**paw** foot of animal with nails or claws

**pawn** *v* deposit sth (of value) as security for money lent. **-broker;** *n* state of being pawned; least valuable piece in chess; unimportant person

**pay** (**paid**) give money, services, *etc* in discharge of debt, for work of services done, goods received, *etc*. **-able, -ment;** (of business *etc*) be profitable; suffer punishment for; give attention, compliment, *etc* to; make visit; **p. off** *or* **up** pay in full

**pea** (widely cultivated plant with) edible round green seed

**peace** freedom from, or stopping of, war; condition in which public order and security is undisturbed; mental calm. **-ful**

**peach** (tree bearing) large sweet juicy fruit with downy yellow or pinkish skin and rough stone; (of) yellowish pink color

**pea‖cock** bird (male peafowl) with sparkling blue and green feathers and large tail which can be spread out like fan, taken as symbol of vanity. **-hen**

**peak** *n* pointed top of hill, *etc*; highest point; foremost part of brim of cap; *v* reach highest point

**peal** (make) loud ringing sound, as of thunder, bells, *etc*

**pea‖nut** (plant bearing pod with) oily seed, used as food

**pear** (tree with) fleshy fruit of rounded shape narrowing towards stem

**pearl** (purl) (valuable gem of) hard smooth lustrous substance of varying color, formed within shell of oysters; finest example of its kind

**peas‖ant** (now *usu hist*) farmer or farm laborer; *infml* uncouth person

**peb‖ble** small stone rounded by action of water. **-bly**

**peck** *n* dry measure, equal to 8 quarts; *v* strike at or make dent in with quick short movements of beak, pointed instrument, *etc*; eat (food) bit by bit

**pe·cu·li·ar** (pikyūlyer) odd; unusual; special; belonging exclusively to; distinctive. **peculiar'ity**

**pe·cu·ni·ar·y** (consisting of) money

**ped'a·go·gy** science or practice of teaching. **pedagog'-ical**

**ped'al** (pedl) lever or leverlike part moved by foot to work machinery, play instrument, as organ, *etc*, or propel bicycle

**ped'ant** one who shows off his learning or insists on too strict attention to unimportant details. **-ry**

**ped‖dle** carry goods about for retail sale; deal out in small quantities. **-dler** (*UK* **-lar**)

**ped'es·tal** base of column,

statue, *etc*; foundation; position of esteem

**pe·des'tri·an** *a* lacking imagination; dull; of walking; *n* person on foot

**pe·di·at'rics** medical branch dealing with children and their diseases. **pediatric'ian**

**ped'i·gree** (table showing) line of descent

**peek** peep; peer

**peel** *v* strip or cut off skin or rind of fruit, bark of tree, *etc*; lose skin, bark, *etc*; *n* skin or rind of fruit, *etc*

**peep** look through narrow opening. **-hole;** look slyly or secretly, as from hiding place; come into view slowly or partially

**peer** *v* look with narrowed eyes at or into, as if hard to see; *n* an equal in age, class, *etc*; nobleman

**pee'vish**          bad-tempered; complaining

**peg** small, *usu* pointed piece of wood, *etc*, for fastening together boards, hanging things on, marking scores, *etc*

**pel'i·can** large water bird with pouch under beak for storing fish

**pel'let** little ball; bullet; pill

**pelt** *n* skin of fur-bearing animal; *n* hit repeatedly, as with stones

**pel'|vis** basin-like cavity formed by hip bones and spine. **-vic**

**pen** small enclosed place for keeping animals; instrument for writing with ink

**pe'nal** (pē-) of or liable to punishment

**pe'nal·ize,** *UK* **-ise** (pē-) put penalty on

**pen'al·ty** punishment (for breaking law, rules of game, agreement, *etc*)

**pen'ance** act showing sorrow for sin

**pence** *UK pl* of **penny**

**pen'cil** thin stick of black lead, colored chalk, *etc*, *usu* enclosed in wooden cylinder, for drawing, writing, *etc*; object of similar form used as cosmetic

**pend'ant** hanging ornament; thing that matches or balances

**pend'ing** *a* not yet decided, as lawsuit; *prep* until

**pen'du·|lum** body hung so as to swing freely, *esp*. in clock. **-lous**

**pen'e·trate** pass or see into or through; pierce. **penetra'tion**

**pen'guin** non-flying water bird of southern half of earth, with paddle-like wings for swimming

**pen·i·cil'lin** powerful antibiotic produced by certain forms of mold

**pen·in'su·|la** land nearly surrounded by water. **-lar**

**pe·nis** male organ used to urinate and to copulate

**pen·i·tent** feeling sorrow or regret for one's sins. **-tence**

**pen·i·ten·tia·ry** *esp. US* prison (for major offenses)

**pen·nant, pen·non** long narrow pointed flag for signalling, as emblem, *etc*

**pen·ny** (*pl* -**nies,** *UK* **pence**) hundredth part of British pound; in US and Canada, one cent; small amount of money. **-niless**

**pen·sion** regular payment made to retired person

**pen·sive** deep in thought. **-ness**

**pent in** or **up** confined

**pen·ta·gon** figure with 5 sides and 5 angles

**pent·house** house or apartment built on roof of tall building

**pen·u·ry** poverty

**peo·ple** human beings as distinct from animals; body of persons composing country, race or tribe, or of particular place, or united by common culture, cause, *etc*; persons in general; one's family; the body of citizens having right to vote

**pep·per** pungent black or white seasoning from dried berries of several plants; (plant with) thick-rinded many-seeded fleshy green, red or yellow fruit, used as vegetable or dried and ground into hot spice

**per** for each; by means of

**per·am·bu·la·tor** or **pram** *UK* baby carriage

**per·ceive** come to know through the senses, *esp.* sight; understand; notice

**per cent, per·cent** frequency or quantity in proportion to a total amount of 100 units: *he sold 75 p. c. of his land*

**per·cent·age** rate; proportion

**per·cep·tion** act or faculty of perceiving. **-tible, -tive**

**perch** place where bird rests; raised or secure position; freshwater fish, used as food

**per·co·late** (cause to) filter or ooze through small holes; make coffee by this method

**per·cus·sion** sharp striking of one object against another; striking of sound on ear; beating or striking of a musical instrument. **-ist**

**per·di·tion** ruin; entire loss, *esp.* of one's soul

**per·emp·to·ry** brooking no delay, *etc*; arrogant

**per·en·ni·al** lasting long or forever; persistent; (of plants) living for several years

**per·fect** *a* lacking no essential part, quality, *etc*, faultless; thoroughly skilled; exact: *p. circle.* **perfec'tion**

**per·fec**|**t**' *v* make perfect.
**-tionist**

**per·fi**|**dy** faithlessness; treachery. **perfid**|**ious**

**per·fo**|**rate** make hole(s) in

**per·form** do; carry out an action; play instrument, sing, act, *etc*, *esp*. in public.
**-ance, -er.**

**per·fume** sweet smell; sweet-smelling liquid, used *esp* by women as a scent

**per·func**|**to·ry** done merely for sake of getting through a duty; done with little interest

**per·haps** possibly but not certainly

**per·il** danger. **-ous**

**per·im**|**e·ter** outline of a closed figure; border or outer edge

**pe·ri**|**od** (pē-) *n* portion of time; particular historical time; menstruation; division of school day; complete sentence; mark (.) indicating end of sentence or abbreviated word; *a* (characteristic) of (past) period of time

**pe·ri·od**|**i·cal** *a* happening at regular stated times; *n* magazine published at regular times, as weekly, *etc*

**pe·riph**|**er·y** outer boundary

**per·ish** be destroyed; die

**per·ish·a·ble** (sth) liable to spoil quickly, as food

**per·ju**|**re o.s.** swear sth one knows to be false. **-ry**

**perk up** lift one's body or

head briskly; become cheerful

**per·ma·frost** permanently frozen soil beneath earth's surface in cold zones

**per·ma·nent** lasting; not changing. **-nence**

**per·me·a**|**te** pass through; seep into and spread throughout. **-ble**

**per·mis**|**sion** formal consent; leave (to do). **-ble**

**per·mit**' *v* allow

**per·mit** *n* written permission (by authority)

**per·ni·cious** very destructive; wicked. **-ness**

**per·pen·dic·u·lar** (line *etc* which is) exactly upright or at right angle to a base. **perpendicular**|**ity**

**per·pe·trate** carry out (crime, *etc*)

**per·pet·u·al** endless; everlasting. **-ate**

**per·plex**' confuse; make (problem) more difficult

**per·se·cute** cause to suffer (*esp.* because of religious or political beliefs); annoy by repeated attacks. **persecution**

**per·se·ver**|**e**' continue in some course of action in spite of difficulties, *etc*.
**-ance**

**per·sis**|**t**' continue firmly (in doing sth, *esp.* in spite of warnings, *etc*); continue to exist. **-tent, -tence**

**per·son** (body or bodily presence of) individual human being

**per·son·al** private, relating or belonging to one's own or another's person: *my p. affair, p. hygiene, p. charms*; done in person; directed against a person

**per·son·al·i·ty** character of a person, including distinctive traits, abilities, characteristics, *etc*; person; *pl* (unfriendly, *etc*) personal remarks

**per·son·i·fy** represent (idea, *etc*) in human form; be typical example of. **person·ifica'tion**

**per·son·nel'** body of persons employed in factory, office, *etc*; department responsible for these people

**per·spec'tive** art of drawing objects so as to give impression of depth, true position, size, *etc*, way in which events, *etc* are viewed, *esp.* regarding their actual importance

**per·spire'** sweat. **perspira'·tion**

**per·suade'** get person to do or believe something by arguments, *etc*. **-sive**

**per·sua'sion** persuading; strong (religious) belief

**pert** saucy; trim and stylish; lively. **-ness**

**per·tain'** belong; have to do with; be appropriate

**per·ti·nent** relevant; to the point. **-nence**

**per·turb'** disturb greatly. **perturba'tion**

**pe·ruse'** read (carefully). **-sal**

**per·vade'** spread through every part of. **-sive**

**per·verse'** wrong; stubborn in being wrong

**per·vert'** *v* turn aside from proper use; lead astray from right opinion. **-sion**

**per·vert** *n* person who has turned away from what is accepted, *etc, esp.* sexually

**pes·si·mis·m** belief that the evils of life overbalance its good; tendency to take least hopeful view of things. **-mist, pessimis'tic**

**pest** insect or small animal which destroys crops, annoying or troublesome person

**pes'ter** annoy (with repeated demands)

**pes'ti·cide** (dangerous) substance used to kill pests

**pet** *n* tamed animal, *esp.* dog or cat, kept to play with and fondle; beloved person; *a* kept as pet; favorite; *v* stroke or fondle (sexually)

**pet'al** one of the *usu* colored leaf-like parts of flower

**pe·ti'tion** (make) formal (written) request (to authority)

**pet'ri·fy** paralyze with fright, *etc*; turn into stone. **petri·fac'tion**

**pet'rol** *UK* gasoline

**pe·tro'le·um** oily inflammable liquid found in upper strata of earth and distilled into gasoline, fuel oils, *etc*

**pet'ti·coat** underskirt or slip

**pet'ty** unimportant; minor; narrow-minded

**pet'u·lant** angrily impatient; irritable. **-lance**

**pew** bench in church

**pew'ter** (utensils of) dull gray alloy of tin and lead

**pha'lanx** (fā-) (*pl* **-lanxes**) body of troops; line of battle; (*pl* **-lan'ges** [-jēz]) bone in finger or toe

**phal'lus** image, *etc*, of male sexual organ. **-lic**

**phan'tom** ghost; form without substance or reality; illusion

**phar'ma·cy** science of preparation of medicines; place where medicines are sold or dispensed. **-cist. pharmaceu'tical**

**phase** stage of change or development

**phe·nom'e·non** (*pl* **-na**) any fact or event that can be observed; remarkable person or thing. **-nal**

**phi·lan'thro·py** love or good will towards all mankind; charitable act. **-pist, philanthrop'ic**

**phi·lat'e·list** stamp collector

**phil·o·soph'i·cal** of philosophy; wise; calm

**phi·los'o·phy** (any system concerned with) study of (ultimate) nature and meaning of life in all its aspects. **-pher, -phize** (*UK* **-phise**)

**phlegm** (flem) thick slimy substance given off in nose and throat; coolness or slowness of temperament. **phlegmat'ic**

**pho'bi·a** unreasonable fear or dislike

**phone** (make call using) telephone

**pho·net'ic** of or concerning sounds of speech; representing such sounds, *esp.* by special symbols, *etc*

**pho'net·ics** scientific study of spoken language

**pho'no·graph** record player

**phos'phate** chemical salt used as fertilizer

**phos·pho·res'|cent** giving off light without heat. **-cence**

**pho'to** see **photograph**

**pho'to·cop·y** (make) photographic copy of printed, *etc* material. **-ier**

**pho·to·e·lec'tric** of or using the change in electric current caused by light falling on a substance

**pho·to·gen'ic** very suitable for being photographed

**pho'to·graph** (make) picture

obtained by exposing film in a camera to light

**pho·tog·ra·phy** art, process or business of producing pictures or films. **-pher, photograph·ic**

**pho·to·syn·the·sis** method by which plants convert sun's energy into nourishment

**phrase** word, expression, *usu* without verb; short musical passage; *v* express in words; divide (music) into phrases

**phra·se·ol·o·gy** (frāzi-) style of expression in words

**phys·i·cal** of the body; matter or material things; of physics or natural forces

**phy·si·cian** (-zishen) medical doctor

**phys·i·cs** science of the properties of matter and energy. **-cist**

**phys·i·og·no·my** (art of judging character from) features of face

**phys·i·ol·o·gy** science of the processes and functions of living things. **physiolog·ical**

**phys·i·o·ther·a·py** treatment of disease by exercise, massage, *etc.* **-pist**

**phy·sique** (fizēk) bodily structure and appearance

**pi·a·n·o** (pianō) *mus* instrument with metal strings sounded by hammers operated from keyboard. **-nist**

**pick** *n* heavy tool with wooden handle attached to steel or iron bar with pointed ends; choice; best part (of); *v* choose (carefully): *p. one's partner, p. one's steps*; break fruit, *etc* off tree, *etc*; free (bone, *etc*) from adhering matter with fingers or teeth; remove unwanted pieces (from teeth, *etc*) using fingers or pointed stick; provoke (quarrel); rob: *p. pockets*; open (lock, *etc*) with wire, *etc* esp. for stealing; *US* pull (strings of musical instrument); **p. at** take food in small bits, as birds do; nag at; **p. out** select; see among others: *p. a person out in a crowd*; **p. up** take up (with fingers); get by chance or unintentionally: *p. up information, p. up a habit*; take along: *bus picks up passengers*; make casual acquaintance; regain (one's health); gather speed, become more lively, *etc.*

**pick·et** pointed stake for fence, *etc*; troop(s) on guard duty; person(s) posted by labor union to prevent strike-breaking

**pick·le** (preserve fish, vegetables, *etc* in) vinegar, *etc*; *usu pl* preserved cucumbers, *etc*

**pic·nic** (go on) pleasure trip for which food is taken to be eaten outdoors; the food taken

**pic·to·ri·al** of or in pictures

**pic'ture** (pikch*er*) painting, drawing, photograph, *etc*; image seen on television screen; any visible or mental reflection or impression: *p. in the mirror, p. in one's mind*; extreme likeness: *she is the p. of her mother*; motion picture

**pic·tur·esque'** like or fit to be a picture; striking. **-ness**

**pie** dish of fruit, meat, *etc*, baked in or between, or topped with, crust(s) of pastry

**piece** (pēs) limited and distinct amount of sth: *p. of cake*; definite quantity in which cloth, *etc*, is put up for sale; single item or part; example of workmanship, as a picture; (short) literary or musical composition; one of the parts which together form a whole or into which a thing is broken, torn, *etc*; figure in chess, *etc*; coin

**piece'meal** piece by piece; one part at a time

**pier** support for a bridge; structure built out into water and used as landing bridge, *etc*

**pierce** (of sharp instrument, pain, scream, *etc*) go into and through; make hole in; penetrate

**pi'e·ty** devotion to God and religion

**pig** heavy mammal with short legs, curly tail and thick hide, raised for its meat; untidy, greedy or sloppy person

**pi'geon** (pijen) bird with smooth (gray) feathers, plump body and short legs

**pi'geon·hole** small boxlike compartment in desk, *etc*

**pig'ment** natural coloring matter. **pigmenta'tion**

**pig'tail** braid of hair hanging from back of head

**pike** *hist* long stick with pointed metal head; large freshwater food fish

**pile** (heap up) mass of things, one upon the other in more or less orderly fashion; heap of wood on which dead body is burnt; apparatus of moderating substances and uranium, used to control atomic chain reaction; (pointed) beam driven into riverbed to support bridge, or used as support for wall, *etc*; soft fine hair, wool or fur

**piles** *pl* hemorrhoids

**pil'fer** steal, *esp*. small amounts

**pil'grim** person who travels to sacred place as act of devotion. **-age**

**pill** small rounded mass of medicinal substance

**pil'lage** plunder

**pil·lar** firm upright shaft as support; supporter

**pil·low** bag of cloth filled with feathers, *etc* (as support for head, *esp.* in bed); any similar support

**pi·lot** person who steers ship (in and out of harbor), flies aircraft, *etc*; guide

**pimp** (act as) one who sells sexual services of a prostitute

**pim·ple** small swelling on skin, *usu* filled with pus

**pin** small slender (pointed) piece of wood, metal, *etc*, for fastening, attaching, *etc*, things; badge, jewel, *etc*, with pointed bar for fastening it to clothing

**pin·cers** *pl* tool for gripping

**pinch** *v* press between tips of fingers, jaws of instrument, *etc*; squeeze painfully by being too tight; make (face) thin and drawn, as from sorrow; shrivel, as from cold; limit spending to (less than) what is necessary; *n* as much as can be taken up between tips of finger and thumb; painful squeeze

**pine** *n* (wood of) evergreen tree with needle-like leaves and woody fruit (pinecone); *v* long for eagerly; waste away from grief

**pine·ap·ple** (sweet yellow flesh of) large juicy fruit of a tropical plant

**pin·ion** *v* bind arms or legs; *n* wing; (flight) feather

**pink** *n* (of) pale red color; highest degree; *v* pierce slightly with sword, *etc*; cut saw-toothed edge in cloth, *etc*

**pink·ing shears** *pl* tailor's scissors with saw-toothed blades, used to keep cloth from raveling

**pin·na·cle** small tower on roof; peak; highest point

**pin·point** locate or identify (target, cause of sth, *etc*) with great accuracy

**pint** (-ī-) liquid or dry measure of capacity, equal to one half of a quart

**pi·o·neer** one of the first to settle unknown territory; person originating or advancing sth new

**pi·ous** religious; devoted to God

**pipe** hollow tube of metal, *etc*, for conducting water, gas, *etc* from one place to another; tube of wood, clay, *etc* with small bowl at one end for smoking tobacco; tube-shaped organ or passage in animal body; *mus* each sound-producing tube of organ; tube forming musical wind instrument

**pip·ing** pipes collectively; sound of pipes; shrill sound; tube of material for trimming edges of clothing, *etc*

**pi'quan|t** (pēk*ent*) pleasantly sharp; pleasantly exciting. **-cy**

**pique** (pēk) annoy; wound pride of; arouse

**pi'ra|te** sea robber; person illegally using another's (literary, *etc*) work. **-cy**

**pis·ta'chi·o** (-stash-) (tree with) small green nut

**pis'tol** small gun held and fired with one hand

**pis'ton** cylinder of metal, fitting closely within a tube in which it is moved up and down by pressure, causing connected parts to move

**pit** hole in ground; (covered) trap in ground; hole or shaft dug in ground for mining coal, obtaining minerals, *etc*; sunken area, *esp*. in workshop; part of theater where musicians sit; pockmark in skin, *etc*

**pitch** *v* set up, as tent; throw (ball, hay, *etc*); set voice or tone of musical instrument at particular level; (of land, *etc*) slope; fall heavily, *esp*. forward; (of ship) plunge so that bow and stern rise alternately; *n* toss or plunging; height, as of emotion; (degree of) slope; highness or lowness of a tone; dark sticky substance remaining after distillation of tar or petroleum

**pitch'er** large container for liquids, *usu* with handle and lip or spout

**pit'e·ous** arousing pity

**pit'fall** (pit used as a) trap

**pith** soft center of plants, *etc*; essential part or core

**pit'i·ful** causing, deserving pity

**pit'i·less** without pity; cruel

**pit'tance** small allowance or amount

**pit'|y** (feel) sorrow for others' suffering; regrettable fact. **-iable**

**piv'ot** point or pin on which sth turns; central point or person. **-al**

**plac'ard** poster; sign

**pla'cate** calm anger of

**place** particular part of space; part of space occupied by town, building, *etc*, or set aside for particular purpose; space or seat for person, as in a train; passage in book, *etc*; (proper, customary, *etc*) position, rank, *etc*: *everything is in its p., keep him in his p.*; proper time or moment; (high) office

**pla·ce'bo** (-sē-) simulated medicine without chemical value

**plac'id** (plasid) peaceful; quiet. **placid'ity**

**pla'gi·a·|rize**, *UK* **-rise** (plājierīz) steal another's words, ideas, *etc* and pass them off as one's own. **-rism**

**plague** any severe contagious disease; invasion of insects, rats, *etc*; nuisance

**plaid** (plad) (woolen) cloth with checked Scottish pattern

**plain** *a* clear to eye, ear or mind: *in p. sight of everybody, p. words*; downright or outspoken: *this is p. folly, the p. truth*; without elegance, decorations, special beauty, *etc*: *p. clothes, p. table, a p. face*; *n* flat stretch of country

**plain'tiff** one who brings suit in court of law

**plain'tive** expressing sorrow; sad

**plait** interweave three or more strands, as of hair, into rope; braid

**plan** (determine) course of action, arrangement, *etc*, to be followed in some undertaking; drawing showing top view or horizontal cut through building, *etc*; map

**plane** *a* flat; two-dimensional; *n* airplane; level surface; level (of development, ideas, *etc*); tool for smoothing wooden surface; *v* smooth off

**plan'et** heavenly body that revolves around sun. **-ary**

**plank** long heavy board; part of political, *etc*, program

**plank'ton** tiny forms of floating life in bodies of water

**plant** *n* living organism, *usu* rooted in soil and having leaves, such as vegetables, flowers, *etc*; the machines, tools, buildings, *etc*, necessary for carrying on industrial business; *v* put in ground for growth, as seeds, young trees, *etc*; set firmly in or on surface; *infml* hide (stolen goods, microphone, *etc*) so as to trap s.o.

**plan·ta'tion** large farm for cotton, tea, sugar *etc*; grove of planted trees

**plaque** ornamental flat piece of metal, *etc*, often as memorial; film on teeth in which bacteria breed

**plas'ma** colorless fluid part of blood containing blood cells; the fourth kind of matter, a gaslike substance found in space

**plas'ter** mixture of lime, sand, water, *etc*, for covering walls. *etc*, which hardens when drying; powdery white material, mixed with water, for making casts, statues, *etc*

**plas'tic** *n* any of a large group of synthetic substances that can be molded into any form; *a* made of plastic; easily molded; giving form. **plastic'ity**

**plas·tic sur'ge·ry** medical repair or reconstruction of ill-formed, damaged, *etc* body part using plastics

**plate** flat round dish from

which food is served or eaten; table articles of silver, *etc*; thin flat sheet of metal, as for engraving names on, printing from, *etc*; hard protective cover; thin layer of gold, *etc* over other metal; illustration in book; sheet of glass, metal, *etc*, covered with light-sensitive film, used in photography; shaped piece of metal, plastic, *etc* holding artificial teeth

**pla·teau'** elevated stretch of flat land; stable period, level, *etc* following rise, as in prices

**plat'form** raised flooring or surface, as for speaker in meeting-hall or alongside tracks in railway station; (statement of) principles and policy of political party, *esp.* US declaration made at party convention for nominating election candidates

**plat'i·num** heavy, whitish, very valuable metallic element of great softness

**plat'i·tude** commonplace remark. **platitu'dinous**

**plat'ter** large flat serving dish

**plau·si·ble** seeming reasonable or believable. **plausibil'ity**

**play** *n* dramatic piece to be performed by actors; exercise or any action done for amusement, sport, *etc*; action, conduct: *p. of fancy,*

*fair p.;* lively or brisk movement: *p. of water;* freedom of movement in space, as of part of machine; *v* act part in dramatic performance; amuse o.s. by games, *etc*; contend in game of football, *etc*; lay wager; use as in a game: *he played with words;* perform on musical instrument; cause (light, *etc*) to move over or across; **p. (up)on** exploit (another's weakness, *etc*); **p. up to** try to win favor of. **-er**

**play'house** theater

**play'thing** toy

**play'wright** writer of plays

**pla'za** public square; large shopping center

**plea** urgent request; *law* formal statement by accused in court proceedings

**plead** speak on behalf (party in court); beg of earnestly; bring as excuse

**pleas'ant** friendly; agreeable; (of weather) fine

**pleas'ant·ry** good-humored remark

**please** be agreeable to or satisfy others: *p. the public; we want to p. our customers;* find enjoyment in as: *I was much pleased by his coming;* like or wish: *do as you p.;* used as polite form of request or command: *could I have the butter, p.?, p. pass the butter.*

**pleas'ure**

**pleat** (make) fold in cloth

**pleb·is·cite** direct vote of the people on some matter of general importance

**pledge** thing given as security for loan, *etc*; promise; a toast

**ple·na·ry** full; complete; fully attended, as meeting

**plen·i·po·ten·ti·ar·y** (person) having full power to act, as ambassador, *etc*

**plen·ty** full or rich supply: *a time of great p.*

**pli·a·ble pli·ant** bending easily; yielding; easily influenced. **-bility, -ancy**

**pli·ers** (plī-) *pl* pincers with long jaws, used for bending wire, *etc*

**plight** (plīt) (sad) state or condition

**plod** walk heavily; work hard at

**plot** (small) piece of ground; story or plan of events in play, *etc*; (evil) secret plan

**plow, UK plough** (plou) farming implement for turning up soil; any instrument resembling this, as a snow p.

**pluck** *v* pull off; pick; *n infml* courage

**plug** sth for stopping up a hole; pronged device attached to cord of lamp, *etc*, which establishes contact when put in outlet for electric current

**plum** (tree bearing) sweet fleshy dark blue fruit with oblong stone; prize; (of) deep blue-red color

**plum·age** feathers of bird

**plumb** (plum) *n* ball of lead (on line) for testing depth of water or vertical line of wall; *a* vertical

**plumb·ing** (pluming) system of pipes, *etc*, for conveying water, liquid waste, *etc*, in building. **-er**

**plume** *n* large showy feather (worn as decoration); *v* clean and arrange feathers

**plump** *a* pleasantly rounded; well filled out with flesh; *v* **p. down** (let) fall heavily or suddenly; **p. for** speak in favour of; **p. up** make plump

**plun·der** take by force, *esp.* in war; rob; steal

**plunge** throw or force (into water, *etc*); dive; move or be thrown forward violently

**plu·ral** of or containing more than one

**plu·ral·is·m** (belief in) social structure embracing people of various races, religions, *etc*

**plu·ral·i·ty** state of being plural; majority

**plus** (symbol [+] signifying) with the addition of: *5 plus 2 is 7*

**plush(y)** *infml* stylish; expensive

**plu·to·ni·um** radioactive metal used to produce atomic energy

**ply'wood** board made of layers of wood glued together

**pneu·mat'ic** (nyū-) of or worked by air pressure

**pneu·mo'ni·a** (nyū-) serious inflammation of lungs

**poach** cook fish, shelled egg, *etc* in gently boiling liquid; hunt for game or fish illegally

**pock'et** small bag, *esp.* one sewn in garment, for carrying small articles; any similar hollow or pouch, as in earth

**pock'et·book** small (leather) case for papers, money, *etc*; *US* handbag; **pocket book** book small enough to fit in pocket

**pock'|mark** hollow or scar left on skin by smallpox, *etc*; sth like this. **-marked**

**pod** long seed vessel, as of peas, beans, *etc*

**po'di·um** raised platform for speaker, conductor, *etc*

**po'|em** (pōem, -im) composition in verse, *esp.* one characterized by elevated thought, beauty of form and content, *etc.* **-etry, -et, poet'ic(al)**

**po·grom'** organized killing of a group, *esp.* of Jews

**poi'gnan|t** (poin-) (painfully) sharp or touching. **-cy**

**point** *n* (mark made by) sharp end of implement, as dagger, pencil, needle, *etc*; something having position but neither length, width, *etc,* as intersection of two lines; definite position, as on scale, compass, *etc*; degree or stage in course of events, progress, *etc*; particular moment of time; important or essential part, as of problem, joke, *etc*; single item or part; feature; purpose or use; unit in counting scores of game, crediting (pupil) for work done, *etc*; unit in quoting prices, as on the stock exchange; mark (.) indicating end of sentence or, in figures, division of whole and fractional parts: *10.6*; *v* direct (finger, weapon, *etc*) at; have given direction: *compass points to the north, everything points to his guilt*; **p. out** draw attention to

**point'ed** tapering to a point; meant to be noticed: *a p. glance*; to the point; offensive: *a p. remark*

**point'er** hand on watch, scale, *etc*; long stick used to point out sth on map *etc*; hunting dog trained to point at game

**poise** composure; balance; manner of carrying body

**poi'son** (poizn) substance which can injure or kill living organism. **-ous**

**poke** thrust finger, stick, *etc* into sth; **p. fun at** make fun of s.o.

**po'ker** metal rod for stirring up fire; card game, *usu* played for money

**po'lar** of or near a pole of a magnet or the earth

**po·lar'i·ty** the state of having two opposite qualities or poles

**po'lar·ize**, *UK* **-ise** give polarity to; treat (light) so that it vibrates in a particular way

**pole** long slender piece of wood, *etc* used as support; end of earth's axis, magnet, *etc*

**po·lem'i·cal** attacking others' opinions

**po·lice'** (-lēs) department of government responsible for keeping law and order, seeking out and bringing criminals to justice, *etc*

**pol'i·cy** (wise) conduct of affairs; course of action of government, *etc*; document containing terms of insurance contract

**po·li·omy·e·li'tis** or **po'li·o** disease of spine causing paralysis, *esp.* in children

**pol'ish** (pol-) (substance used to) make surfaces smooth and glossy by rubbing

**po·lite'** showing or having good manners

**po·lit'i·cal** of public affairs or government; of politics

**pol·i·ti'cian** person active in politics; person who manipulates others to his advantage

**pol'i·tics** science of political government; political affairs or principles; activity to win advantage over others

**poll** questioning part of people to find out trends, *etc*; counting or casting of votes; *pl* place where votes are cast

**pol'len** fertilizing powder produced by male parts of flowers, *etc*

**pol·lut'ant** substance which pollutes

**pol·lute'** make soil, water, *etc* unclean or impure;: defile morally. **-tion**

**po·lyg'a·my** system of having more than one spouse at a time. **-mous**

**pol'y·es·ter** man-made fiber

**pol'y·glot** made up of or speaking many languages

**pol·y·syl·lab'ic** having many syllables

**pomp** showy or splendid display

**pomp'ous** self-important; showy. **pompos'ity**

**pond** small body of water

**pon'der** think over; weigh in mind

**pon'der·ous** heavy; dull. **-ness**

**pon·toon'** flat-bottomed boat used as support for temporary bridge; float on seaplane

**po'ny** small type of horse

**po'ny-tail** hair tied together at back of head and hanging down like pony's tail

**pool** *n* small (deep) body of water; puddle; swimming pool; collective stake in games of chance; common fund of people or things; cartel to fix prices and market shares; *US* game like billiards, *usu* played with 16 balls; *v* share or join in common fund

**poor** having little or no money; lacking something specified: *a country p. in coal*; of low or defective quality, construction *etc*; unfortunate

**pop** *v* make short explosive sound, as cork when pulled from bottle; come, go or move quickly or unexpectedly; *n* explosive sound; bubbling nonalcoholic drink; modern pop(ular) music

**pop'art** modern art showing objects of everyday life

**pop'corn** dried corn which bursts open when heated, *usu* served with salt and butter

**Pope** head of Roman Catholic church

**pop'lar** (light, soft wood of) tall slender tree

**pop'u·lace** the common people

**pop'u·lar** of the people: liked by many people. **popu·lar'ity** widespread; suited to needs, *etc* of most people. **-ize** (*UK* **-ise**)

**pop'u·late** inhabit; supply with inhabitants

**pop·u·la'tion** total number of people (or animals) living in a place

**pop'u·lous** inhabited by many people

**por'ce·lain** (objects made of) china, a fine earthenware with transparent glaze

**porch** covered approach to door of building; *US* veranda

**por'cu·pine** large rodent covered with long sharp quills

**por|e** *n* tiny opening in skin, leaf, *etc*. **-ous;** *v* **p. over** study deeply, as books; think deeply on

**pork** meat from pigs, used as food

**por·nog'ra·phy** (books, *etc* containing) explicit presentation of sex in order to arouse

**por'poise** (-pes) large blunt-snouted sea mammal

**port** (town possessing) place where ships can load and unload; left side of ship or plane when facing forward; sweet dessert wine

**port'a·ble** that can be carried

**por'tal** gate or stately door

**por·tend'** give sign or warning of; foreshadow

**por'tent** forewarning (of evil). **porten'tous**

**por'ter** one employed to carry baggage at airport, *etc*; doorkeeper

**port·fo'li·o** case for carrying papers; collection of drawings, stocks, *etc*; office and duties of minister of state

**port'hole** small (round) window in ship or plane

**por'ti·co** row of covered columns around (entrance of) building

**por'tion** part; share; amount enough for one person

**port'ly** (of men) corpulent; stout

**por'trai|t** (painted) picture of person. **-ture** vivid description

**por·tray'** make picture of, describe; act part in play, *etc*. **-al**

**pose** ask (difficult) question; put forward; take up or arrange in fixed attitude; **p. as** pretend to be

**po·si'tion** (-ish-) place (to be) occupied by thing or person in space; proper or correct place; situation with regard to circumstances; standing in society; job, employment; manner in which body is held: *standing p.*; attitude regarding problem, *etc*

**pos'i·tive** definite; helpful; convinced; marked by presence, not absence, of qualities; showing consent or agreement

**pos·ses|s'** own; influence strongly. **-sion**

**pos·ses'sive** of or showing possession or desire to possess. **-ness**

**pos'si·ble** that may or can be true, exist, happen, be done, *etc*. **possibil'ity**

**post** *n* strong piece of timber, metal, *etc*, used as support, for marking boundary or goal; position of employment, trust, *etc*; (permanent) military station, or body of troops occupying it; *UK* single delivery of letters; *UK* official system for conveying letters, *etc*; *UK* post office or letter box; *v* put (public notice, *etc*) on wall, *etc*; station as sentry, *etc*; mail (letters, *etc*); supply with full and up-to-date information

**post'age** charge for conveyance of letters, *etc* by mail, *usu* prepaid by means of **p. stamp**

**post'er** large printed picture, *etc* (posted in public place)

**pos·te'ri·or** coming later; situated behind

**pos·ter'i·ty** offspring; all generations following

**post·hu'mous** (-tyoo-) happening after one's death; born after death of father; published after death of author

**postmor'tem** (examination of body) done after death

**post·na'tal** existing or happening after birth

**post·pone'** put off till later. **-ment**

**post'script** addition to letter after signature

**pos'tu·late** v (-lāt) suggest idea as likely or true; n (-let) idea thought to be likely or true taken as basis of reasoning

**pos'ture** carriage of body; attitude

**pot** metal, earthenware, etc, container, usu round and deep; amount that it holds; small portable toilet for children; sum of bets at stake in card game, esp. poker; sl marihuana

**po'ta·ble** drinkable

**po·ta'to** (pl **-toes**) (plant with) starchy root, used as food

**po'ten|t** powerful; convincing. **-cy**

**po·ten'tial** a that can come into being or action; n possible power (of machine, country, etc). **potential'ity**

**po'tion** drink esp. dose of medicine or poison

**pot'ter** n maker of clay vessels. **-y**; v see **putter**

**pouch** small bag or pocket

**poul'try** chickens, etc kept for eggs and meat

**pounce** fall on suddenly and seize

**pound** v strike repeatedly and with force, as with fist or heavy instrument; crush by beating; walk heavily or vigorously; n unit of weight equal to 454 grams; UK unit of money (£) containing 100 pence; unit of money in other countries, as Egypt; enclosure for stray animals or for keeping goods seized as security

**pour** (pawr, pōr) cause liquid, grain, etc, to flow from container into, on(to) or from sth; flow forth, as rain from clouds

**pout** thrust out lips in displeasure; look sullen

**pov'er·ty** state of being poor; scarcity

**pow'der** n mass of fine dry particles; cosmetic or medicine in this form; v make into, cover or sprinkle with p.

**pow'er** ability to do or act, control or command others, etc; usu pl particular faculty of body or mind; political strength; physical force or bodily strength. **-ful, -less**; degree by which lens magnifies sth; written statement conferring legal authority; mechanical energy as distinguished from hand labor

**pox** disease marked by pustules on skin; syphilis

**prac'ti·ca·ble** that can be used or done. **practicabil'ity**

**prac'ti·cal** of or connected with ordinary activities or worldly affairs, rather than theory; useful or convenient; sensible

**prac'tice** (-tis) customary or usual way of acting, proceeding, *etc*; repeated exercise to gain perfection in art, skill, *etc*; actually doing sth, as opposed to theory; exercise of profession, *esp*. of law and medicine

**prac·ti'tion·er** person who works in a profession, *esp*. medicine

**prag·mat'ic** dealing with matters in practical terms

**prag'ma·tism** practical handling of affairs

**praise** (präz) express admiration of; mention in favorable manner

**pram** *UK* see **perambulator**

**prank** trick done in fun

**pray** beg or ask earnestly for; address o.s. to God in praise or need. **-er**

**preach** deliver sermon or proclaim the gospel. **-er**; give unwanted (moral) advice; ask others earnestly (to do, *etc*)

**pre'am·ble** introductory words, *esp*. of a law; introductory fact or event

**pre·car'i·ous** (dangerously) unstable. **-ness**

**pre·cau'tion** measure taken in advance to avoid harm or

guarantee good result. **-ary**

**pre·cede'** go before in time or importance. **preced'ence**

**prec'e·dent** former case, *etc* used as example for present or future action

**pre'cept** rule of action or conduct

**pre'cinct** (police, voting) district; *pl* area around a building, *etc*

**pre'cious** (preshes) of great value; beloved; affectedly refined (in speech, *etc*)

**prec'i·pice** cliff, *etc* with steep face; brink

**pre·cip'i·tate** *v* bring on suddenly; throw down; *a* headlong; hasty; rash

**pre·cip·i·ta'tion** act of precipitating; fall of rain, snow, *etc*

**pre·cise'** very exactly expressed; definite; careful in observing rules. **-sion**

**pre·clude'** prevent; make impossible. **-sion**

**pre·co'cious** developing unusually early. **-ty**

**pre·con·cep'tion** idea formed in advance without (enough) knowledge; prejudice. **-ceive**

**pre·cur'sor** forerunner

**pred'a·to·ry** of or disposed to robbery; preying on others; (of animal) feeding on other animals it kills

**pred'e·ces·sor** one that goes before; former holder of office or position

**pre·des'tine** settle beforehand, as if by God's will or fate. **predestina'tion**

**pre·dic'a·ment** unpleasant or dangerous situation

**pred'i·cate** state as true or existing; base statement or action on sth. **-ble**

**pre·dict'** foretell (future events). **-table, -tion**

**pre·dis·pose'** make inclined or subject to, *esp.* in advance. **predisposi'tion**

**pre·dom'i|nate** be the leading or main element; have controlling influence. **-nance, -nant**

**pre·em'i|nent** superior to or distinguished beyond others. **-nence**

**pre·fab'ri·cate** manufacture standard parts that can be put together later. **prefabrica'tion**

**pref'a|ce** introduction (to book, *etc*) **-tory**

**pre·fer'** like better. **pref'er·able, pref'erence;** put into higher position; promote. **-ment;** bring forward (charge, statement, *etc*)

**pre'fix** addition put before word to expand or change its meaning

**preg'nan|t** (of woman or female animal) carrying unborn child or young; rich or filled with (meaning, ideas, *etc*). **-cy**

**pre·his·tor'ic** of the period before written history

**prej'u·dice** *n* unfair or thoughtless opinion formed beforehand (without knowing facts); injury resulting from action or judgment of another; *v* influence unfairly; cause to have prejudice; have damaging effect on. **prejudic'ial**

**prej'u·diced** subject to prejudice; unfair

**pre·lim'i·nar·y** (sth) coming before or preparing main event, *etc*

**pre·ma·ture'** done or happening before proper time; born too early

**pre·med'i·tat·ed** planned with thought beforehand

**pre'mier** *a* first; foremost; *n* first minister of state in Britain, *etc*

**prem'ise** statement on which later one is based; *pl* house with grounds

**pre'mi·um** prize; extra payment; sum paid to buy insurance

**pre·mo·ni'tion** feeling that sth (unpleasant) is about to happen; forewarning

**pre·na'tal** existing or happening before birth

**pre·oc'cu|py** absorb one's entire attention. **-pied, preoccupa'tion**

**pre·or·dain'** determine beforehand

**pre·par|e'** make or get ready (for). **-atory, prepara'tion**

**pre·par'ed·ness** (state of) being prepared for sth

**pre·pon'der|ant** being of greater weight, importance, number, *etc.* **-ance**

**pre·pos'ter·ous** contrary to reason; absurd. **-ness**

**pre·req'ui·site** thing required as previous condition

**pre·rog'a·tive** special right or privilege

**pre|scribe'** lay down as rule; advise use of medicine. **-scription**

**pres'|ent** (preznt) *a* being at place, *etc* in question; here, there: *he was p. at the ceremony.* **-ence;** (of matter, problem, *etc*) existing or being dealt with just now; not belonging to past or future: *the p. value of the dollar;* **at p.** just now; **for the p.** for the time being; *n* the p. time, affairs, *etc;* gift

**pre·sent'** (prizent) *n* introduce, *esp.* formally or to superior; bring before the public: *we p. a new star;* make gift to or offer for acceptance, consideration, *etc;* (of idea, *etc*) suggest itself

**pre·sent'a·ble** suitable to be shown, *etc* in public

**pre·sen'ti·ment** feeling of sth (bad) about to happen

**pres'ent·ly** soon; *US* now

**pre·serve'** *v* keep safe or alive; keep in present state; keep from decaying; *n pl* fruit jam; area set apart for protection of wild animals. **-vative, preserva'tion**

**pre·side'** be in charge of meeting, *etc);* exercise control. **pres'ident. pres'idency**

**press** *v* bring (steady) force to bear upon by pushing down or squeezing; push against; squeeze (juice from fuit, *etc);* make flat, compact, *etc;* (of sorrows, *etc*) weigh heavily upon; (try to) make person do, accept, *etc;* call for speedy action: *time presses;* place emphasis on: *p. one's point; n* act of pressing; (building containing) machine for printing books, *etc;* trade of printing; news reporters or newspapers, *etc* in general; way in which events are reported: *good/bad p.;* machine or device for cutting, shaping, *etc* by means of pressure

**pres'sure** (amount of) force exerted upon one body by another in contact with it; trouble; strong influence

**pres'sur·ize,** *UK* **-ise** place under pressure; design to withstand pressure; maintain normal air pressure in plane, *etc*

**pres'tige** (-tēzh) reputation or influence due to success, rank, etc

**pre|sume'** take for granted; take the liberty of doing; **p. (up)on** take advantage (of person). **-sumption**

**pre·sump'tu·ous** arrogant; forward

**pre·sup·pose'** suppose beforehand; make necessary as cause. **presupposi'tion**

**pre|tend'** put forward false appearance; make believe; lay claim to. **-tense**

**pre·ten'tious** full of pretense; making an exaggerated outward show. **-ness**

**pre'text** excuse (to conceal true purpose or reason)

**pret|ty** (priti) charming; pleasing to eye or ear. **-tiness;** in or to some degree: *p. good*

**pret'zel** glazed salted cracker in shape of stick or loose knot

**pre·vail'** be widespread; win out or succeed; **p. (up)on** persuade. **prev'alent**

**pre·var'i·cate** not tell exact truth; lie

**pre·vent'** keep from doing or happening. **-tion, -tive**

**pre'view** (give) advance showing or description of film, book, etc

**pre'vi·ous** coming before in time

**prey** *n* animal hunted for food; victim; *v* **p. (up)on** hunt as prey; have troubling effect; victimize

**price** money for which thing is bought or sold; terms under which sth is done or for which it can be or is obtained. **-less**

**prick** make mark or tiny hole with pointed instrument; cause sharp stinging pain; **p. up one's ears** listen hard; (of dogs, etc) raise ears

**prick'le** small sharp thorn or spine; pricking sensation on skin

**prick'ly** full of prickles, tingling; irritating; hard to deal with

**pride** justified sense of one's position, duties, etc or just pleasure in one's own or another's deeds, etc, (exaggerated) opinion of one's qualities, etc

**priest** (-ē-) *f* **-ess** person authorized to perform religious rites. **-hood**

**prig** one irritatingly exact in observing correct behavior

**prim** very proper; prudish

**pri'ma·ry** earliest; first in order or importance; *n US* party vote to choose candidates for main election

**prime** first in time, quality or importance; fundamental

**prim'er** book for teaching children to read; small introductory book

**pri·me'val** of the earliest times of the world

**prim·i·tive** of the early times of the earth; not developed; original

**pri·mor'di·al** existing at or from the beginning of time

**prince** *f* **-cess** ruler of (small) state; member of royal family

**prin·ci·pal** *a* first in rank or importance; chief; *n* head of school; person for whom another acts as agent; sum lent or invested

**prin·ci·ple** rule of action or conduct; general law or truth; method of formation or operation

**print** produce (book, picture, *etc*) by applying inked types, plates, *etc*, to paper, cloth, *etc*; mark surface, *etc*, by pressing something on or into it; write in letters used in printing; (photography) make positive picture from negative

**print'er** person engaged in printing; machine for making copies, *esp.* from film; computer-guided machine for printing out computer data

**pri'or** earlier; preceding in time, order or importance

**pri·or'i·ty** state of being earlier or more important; right to be considered before others

**prism** (triangular) solid figure, *esp.* one of glass which separates light into its various colors

**pris'on** (prizn) public building where criminals or other persons are kept for punishment or to await trial. **-er**

**pris'tine** having original purity; undamaged

**pri'vate** (privit) belonging or relating to individual rather than community; personal; secret; not public: *keep the matter p.; p. entrance;* not holding public or official position; without the presence of others: *p. conversation;* withdrawn or secluded. **-cy; p. parts** outer sexual organs

**pri·va'tion** lack of comforts or necessities of life

**priv'i·lege** special right or benefit

**prize** reward given for victory, superior performance, *etc;* money, *etc,* (to be) won in lottery

**pro** *prep* in favor of; *n infml* (*pl* **pros**) professional athlete, *etc*

**prob'a·ble** reasonably likely or certain to happen, be true, *etc.* **prohabil'ity**

**pro'bate** *US law* action or process of proving a will valid

**pro·ba'tion** act or period of testing, *esp.* character, honesty, *etc*; *law* releasing prisoner on good behavior

**probe** *n* device for examining wound, *etc*; investigation; *v* search or examine closely

**prob'lem** question or matter that involves doubt or uncertainty, or is difficult to answer or settle; question put for solution, as in school. **problemat'ical**

**pro·ceed'** *v* go forward; go on; take (legal) action; originate from. **-dure**

**pro'ceeds** *n pl* sum obtained from sale, *etc*

**pro'cess** *n* course; method of operation; continuous action causing change: action at law; *v* subject to certain treatment

**pro·ces'sion** body of persons, *etc* moving along in orderly succession; parade

**pro·claim'** announce publicly (and officially). **proclama'tion**

**pro·cras'ti·nate** put off; delay. **procrastina'tion**

**pro·cre·ate** produce (young)

**pro·cure'** get by care or effort; bring about; provide sexual partner for. **-ment**

**prod** poke with pointed stick, *etc*; urge on

**prod'i·gy** person with extraordinary gifts; extraordinary thing

**pro·duce'** bring into existence; manufacture; bring

forth; bring forward. **-er, -tion, -tive, prod'uct**

**pro·fane'** not sacred; not respectful to religion. **-ity**

**pro·fess'** pretend; declare openly; declare faith in a religion. **-sion**

**pro·fes'sion·al** of or belonging to a profession; doing sth for payment; of a high standard

**pro·fes'sor** teacher of highest rank at university or college

**prof'fer** offer

**pro·fi'cient** expert; skilled. **-cy**

**pro'file** outline, *esp.* as seen from side; short biography, *esp.* for press or television

**prof'it** advantage; money gained in business. **-able**

**prof'li·gate** shamelessly immoral or extravagant (person)

**pro·found'** having great knowledge or insight; deep; of deep meaning; intense. **profun'dity**

**pro·fuse'** giving freely; extravagant; plentiful. **-sion**

**pro·gen'i·tor** ancestor

**prog'e·ny** offspring

**prog·no'sis** forecast, *esp.* of course of disease

**pro'gram** (supply computer with) list of coded instructions; *UK* **pro'gramme** plan to be followed; list giving piece(s) to be played, performers, *etc*, in musical, theatrical, *etc*, entertainment

**prog'ress** n forward movement; development

**pro·gres|s'** v move forward. **-sion**

**pro·gres'·sive** moving forward (step by step); favoring improvement or reform; modern

**pro·hib'it** forbid. **prohibi'tion**

**pro·jec|t'** v throw; stick out; plan; cause light, etc to fall on surface; portray o.s. to others; imagine that others share one's dreams, feelings, etc. **-tion, -tor**

**proj'ect** n plan

**pro·jec'tile** object fired from gun, etc

**pro·le·tar'i·|at** laboring and unpropertied class. **-an**

**pro·lif'ic** producing many offspring; richly fruitful

**pro'logue** (-log) speech, etc introducing play, etc; introductory event, etc

**pro·long'** make longer in time or space. **prolonga'tion**

**prom·e·nade'** walk, ride, etc taken for amusement; place for walking

**prom'i·|nent** standing out; easily seen; important; leading. **-nence**

**pro·mis'cu·ous** made up of mixed elements without order; careless of differences; having many sexual partners. **promiscu'ity**

**prom'ise** (-is) (give) assurance to another person that one will (not) do, give, etc, specified thing; (give rise to) expectation of future success, etc

**prom'on·to·ry** high point of land jutting out into sea

**pro·mo|te'** raise to higher position; help growth, etc of; aid in organizing (business, etc); make public in order to sell sth. **-tion**

**promp|t** done quickly or readily. **-titude;** v move to action; assist person in speaking by suggesting what he should say; give rise to

**prom'ul·gate** make known officially and formally; teach (doctrine) publicly

**prone** inclined to; lying face downwards

**prong** one of pointed ends of fork, electric plug, etc

**pro·nounce'** utter formally; declare to be; give opinion. **-ment;** say (words) in particular way. **pronuncia'tion**

**pro·nounced'** very marked

**proof** n facts, etc showing that sth is true; test for determining quality of manufactured goods, etc; trial copy of book, etc to be examined for errors; a resistant against

**prop** support; usu pl stage furniture, etc

**prop·a·gan'da** (misleading) information spread by organized plan. **-dist**

**prop'a·gate** reproduce by natural process, as plant or animal; hand down through offspring; spread (knowledge, *etc*)

**pro·pel'** drive forward. **-lant**

**pro·pel'ler** device with blades turned by engine to move ship or plane

**prop'er** suitable; correct or accurate; (of behavior, *etc*) being in agreement with accepted standards of society; relating or belonging exclusively or distinctly to person or thing; (of names, *etc*) designating individual person or thing

**prop'er·ty** sth owned, *esp.* land, *etc*; quality; characteristic

**proph'et** one who reveals will of God; one who foretells events. **prophet'ic**

**pro·phy·lac'tic** (sth) meant to prevent disease or harm

**pro·pi'tious** favorable

**pro·po'nent** one who puts forward or supports a cause, *etc*

**pro·por'tion** (comparative) part or relation; proper relation; *pl* dimensions. **-al, -ate**

**pro·pose'** put forward (for consideration); intend; put (person) forward for position; make offer of marriage. **-al, proposi'tion**

**pro·pri'e·tor** owner. **-tary**

**pro·pri'e·ty** fitness; rightness; correctness of behavior

**pro·pul'sion** act of driving or pushing forward; force that moves sth forward

**pro·sa'ic** like prose; dull; matter-of-fact

**prose** ordinary spoken or written language without verse

**pros'e·cu|te** follow up or go on with; take legal action against. **-tor, prosecu'tion**

**pros'pec|t** *n* view of landscape; possibility; outlook for the future; possible customer; *v UK* **pros·pect'** search district for gold, *etc.* **-tor**

**pro·spec'tive** expected; future

**pros'per** be successful; grow rich. **-ous, prosper'ity**

**pros'ti·tute** person who engages in sexual intercourse for money. **prostitu'tion**

**pros'trate** lying with face to ground; overcome; weakened or exhausted

**pro·tag'o·nist** leading character in play, *etc*

**pro·tect'** keep safe; guard or defend from harm, *etc.* **-tion, -tive**

**pro·té·gé**, *f* **-gée** one under the care and protection of another

**pro'tein** (-tēn) one of the organic compounds basic to all living organisms

**pro'test** *n* formal statement of objection or disapproval

**pro·test'** v make formal objection to; state solemnly

**pro'to·col** original draft of document, etc; rules of diplomatic ceremony

**pro'to·type** original model upon which others are based

**pro·trac|t'** lengthen in time. **-tion**

**pro·trac'tor** semicircular device for measuring angles

**pro·tru|de'** thrust forward; stick out. **-sion, -sive**

**proud** having or showing pride; having too high an opinion of o.s.; (of things) stately, splendid; (of achievements, etc) honorable

**prove** (prüv) (**proved, proved** or **prov'en**) show or test truth or genuineness of; demonstrate by action: *p. him a coward*; turn out: *he proved to be a failure*

**prov'erb** short saying in general use, expressing familiar truth, etc; wise saying. **prover'bial**

**pro·vide'** supply (means of support, etc); make preparations for; *law* require or lay down

**pro·vid'ed** on condition (that)

**prov'i·dence** divine care. **providen'tial**

**prov'i·dent** having foresight or care in planning for the future; thrifty

**prov'ince** division of country having local government; *pl* that part of country which lies outside chief city; sphere of action, learning, *etc.*

**provin'cial**

**pro·vi'sion** providing; clause in law or agreement; *pl* supply of food

**pro·vi'sion·al** for the time being

**pro·voke'** rouse (anger, *etc*); bring about. **provoca'tion, provoc'ative**

**prow** foremost part of ship

**prow'ess** skill; bravery

**prowl** wander around in search of prey or plunder

**prox·im'i·ty** nearness

**prox'y** person authorized to act, *esp.* to vote, for another; written power to act for another

**prud|e** person of excessive modesty. **-ery, -ish**

**pru|'dent** wise in practical affairs; wisely cautious. **-dence**

**prune** n dried plum; v cut away unnecessary branches of tree; remove or reduce unnecessary things

**pry** peer or ask with excessive curiosity; force open by leverage

**psalm** (sahm) sacred song

**pseu'do·nym** (syūdenim) false name used to conceal identity, *esp.* of author

**psy'che** (sīki) soul; mind

**psy·che·del'ic** (of drugs) ex-

**pulpit**

posing mental areas which are normally suppressed; (of art) producing similar effect through color, light, *etc*

**psy·chi'a·try** (sīkī-) study and treatment of diseases of the mind. **-trist**

**pry'chic** (sīkik) of the soul or mind; of supernatural forces

**psy·cho·a·nal'y·sis** (sīkō-) method of investigating (relations between) conscious and unconscious and treating neurosis. **psychoan'-alyst**

**psy·chol'o·gy** (sīkol-) science of the human mind. **-gist, psycholog'ical**

**psy'cho·path** (sīke-) mentally diseased person. **psycho-path'ic**

**psy·cho'|sis** (sīkō-) *pl* **-ses** severe mental disorder. **-tic**

**psy·cho·ther'a·|py** (sīkō-) treatment of mental disorders using psychology. **-pist**

**pu'ber·ty** earliest age at which person is capable of producing children

**pub'lic** of, belonging to, done for, *etc*, the people as a whole, or a state, *etc*; open to general use, enjoyment, knowledge, *etc*

**pub·lic'i·ty** public attention; business of making s.o. or sth generally known. **pub'-licize** (*UK* **-cise**)

**pub'lish** announce officially; make generally known; print

and bring out book, *etc*. **-er**

**puck** hard rubber disk used in ice hockey

**puck'er** gather into folds; wrinkle

**pud'ding** sweet dessert made with milk and eggs; dish of meat, sweets, *etc*, mixed with flour, *etc*, and boiled or steamed

**pud'dle** small body of (dirty) water

**puff** *v* pant; (cause smoke, *etc* to) come out in small amounts; **p. out** make larger (with air); blow out, as candle; **p. up** (cause to) swell; *n* short quick letting out of breath, as in running; blast of wind, *etc*; small pad for applying powder to face, *etc*; light pastry

**pug·na'cious** given to fighting; quarrelsome. **-ty**

**pull** take hold of sth and use force so as to draw it near, out of its base, tear it apart, *etc*; draw or move: *horse pulls the cart, train pulls out of the station*; damage by too much strain, as muscle; propel (boat) by moving oar

**pull'o·ver** sweater put on by pulling it over the head

**pul'mo·nar·y** of the lungs

**pulp** fleshy part of fruit, *etc*; soft, moist mass

**pul'pit** raised platform for preacher in church

**pul'sar** invisible star which gives off radio signals

**pul'sate** vibrate

**pulse** v beat; throb; n steady throbbing of arteries as blood is moved through them by contraction of heart; rhythmical beating, etc; radio, sound or electric vibration; (edible seeds of) plant of pea family

**pul'ver·ize** turn into powder by grinding, etc. **pulveriza'tion**

**pu'ma** large tawny-colored wild cat of N. and S. Amer.

**pump** (operate) machine for raising or transferring water or other liquids, compressing gases, etc; light shoe

**pump'kin** (vine with) round fleshy many-seeded fruit with deep-yellow rind

**pun** humorous play on words that sound alike or have two meanings

**punch** v strike, esp. with fist; make small hole through; press button (of time-clock, etc); n blow with fist; metal device for making holes; drink of wine or other spirits mixed with fruit juices, hot water, milk, etc

**punc'tu·al** exactly on time. **punctual'ity**

**punc'tu·ate** mark sentence with commas, etc to make meaning clear; interrupt (speech, etc) with cheers, etc

**punc'ture** (make) small hole by piercing

**pun'gent** tasting or smelling sharp; biting, as wit. **-cy**

**pun'ish** make (criminal, offender, etc) suffer loss, prison, etc, for thing done or omitted; treat roughly. **-ment**

**pu'ny** undersized and weak

**pup, pup'py** young dog

**pu'pa** form assumed by certain insects, as the silkworm, between larval and adult stage

**pu'pil** person, esp. child, who is being taught; small round opening in center of iris of eye which by contracting and expanding reacts to light falling on it

**pup'pet** doll moved by wires, etc; person controlled by outside influence

**pur'chase** v buy; n buying; thing bought

**pure** not mixed with anything else; free from imperfections: p. water, he speaks p. English; free of guilt; chaste; sheer, nothing but: p. nonsense; (of science, etc) strictly theoretical

**purge** clean thoroughly; cause to empty bowels; clear or rid of

**pu'ri·fy** make pure. **purifica'tion**

**pu'ri·tan** one who is extremely strict in religion or morals. **puritan'ical**

**pu'ri·ty** state of being pure

**pur'ple** color made by mixing blue and red

**pur'pose** aim; result or effect aimed at or intended. **-ful, -less; on p.** intentionally, not by accident

**purr** (make) low continuous murmuring sound, as of contented cat; similar sound, as of motor, *etc*

**purse** *n* small bag for carrying money in; woman's handbag; financial means; sum of money offered as prize or collected as a present; *v* draw together in wrinkles, as the lips

**purs'er** head steward on ship or plane who also keeps accounts

**pur·|sue'** chase; follow; seek after; carry on. **-suit**

**pus** substance produced in sores, wounds, *etc*

**push** press against something with force so as to move it away; (cause to) thrust out, forward, downward, *etc*: *a plant pushes new roots into the soil*; drive ahead or make one's way with force: *p. a matter through, p. through a crowd*; put pressure on; *infml* sell (illegal drugs)

**pus'tule** small pimple or blister

**put (put)** move (thing, *etc*) so as to place it in or out of certain position; cause to be

in certain state, order, *etc*: *p. the glass on a table, p. things in order*; drive or cause to do: *p. them to work*; attribute: *p. a wrong construction on his words*; place (question, matter, *etc*) before another for decision, acceptance, *etc*: *p. a question, I p. it to you*; express in words; place on as a charge: *p. a tax on tea*; take one's course: *the ship p. out to sea*; **p. across** establish (matter); do something successfully; **p. by** lay aside for future use; **p. down** suppress by force, as rebellion; take for: *I p. him down for a sailor*; attribute: *I p. it down to his youth*; write down; **p. off** delay doing; ask or cause to wait for later time, as by excuses, promises, *etc*; take off (clothes); (of boat) leave shore; **p. on** dress (o.s.) in; assume airs, *etc*; gain weight; **p. out** extinguish (fire); confuse; annoy; **p. up with** endure without complaining

**pu'tre·fy** make or become rotten. **putrefac'tion**

**pu'trid** rotten; stinking

**put'ter,** *UK* **pot'ter** move aimlessly; tinker about

**put'ty** (puti) dough-like kind of cement, used for stopping holes, fixing panes of glass in frame, *etc*

**puz'zle** toy or problem designed to amuse by testing patience, skill, *etc*; matter, question, *etc*, that puts one at a loss what to do or say, or that is hard to understand

**py·ja·mas** see **pajamas**

**pyr'a·mid** monumental stone structure, *usu* with square base and sloping triangular sides meeting in a point at top, as that built by ancient Egyptians

**py·ro·ma'ni·|a** unnatural desire to start fires. **-ac**

# Q

**q** seventeenth letter of English alphabet

**quack** fake doctor. **-ery;** (make) cry of duck

**quad'ran·gle** four-sided figure, as rectangle or square, *esp.* enclosed by walls or building. **quadran'gular**

**quad'ru·ped** four-footed animal

**quad'ru·ple** *a* consisting of four; fourfold; *v* multiply (number, *etc*) by four

**quag'mire** soft wet land

**quaint** (pleasingly) strange or old-fashioned. **-ness**

**quake** shake; shudder

**qual'i·|fy** describe as; limit or weaken effect of; make or be fit for or entitled to. **-fied, qualifica'tion**

**qual'i·ta·tive** concerned with quality

**qual'i·ty** degree of excellence; nature or characteristic

**qualm** (kwahm) sudden doubt or misgiving; scruple

**quan'da·ry** state of doubt; dilemma

**quan'ti·ta·tive** concerned with quantity

**quan'ti·ty** (measurable) amount

**quar'an·tine** (period of) enforced isolation for person, animal, *etc* with contagious disease

**quar'rel** (kwor-) (have) strong disagreement marked by angry feelings. **-some**

**quar'ry** object of chase; place where stone is dug from earth

**quart** (kwort) liquid or dry measure of capacity, equal to ¼ of a gallon

**quar'ter** (kwor-) one of the four equal parts into which thing is or can be divided; *US* and *CAN* (coin worth) 25 cents; fourth part of an hour or a year; region or district, *esp.* part of town inhabited by particular group of people; *pl* (military) lodgings. **-master;** mercy granted to enemy willing to surrender; source of information, *etc*: *we heard it from a high q.*

**quar'ter·ly** (magazine) appearing four times a year

**quar·tet'** (music for) group of four

**quash** make void; crush

**qua'ver** (of voice or sound) shake; tremble

**quay** (kē) paved landing place for (un)loading boats

**quea'|sy** causing or feeling nausea; ill at ease; over-scrupulous. **-siness**

**queen** wife of king; female monarch; most powerful piece in chess; playing card bearing picture of q.; fertile female in colony of bees, ants, etc; woman, place, etc superior in some way; sl male homosexual

**queer** strange or odd, esp. from customary form or view of society; faint or giddy. **-ness**

**quell** put an end to; overpower

**quench** put out (fire); satisfy (thirst)

**quer·u·lous** complaining. **-ness**

**que'ry** question

**quest** search

**ques·tion** (-schen) sentence which by its word order and meaning requests information, permission to do, etc; matter under or for discussion, investigation, etc; matter giving rise to uncertainty, difficulty or dispute, or re-quiring solution

**ques·tion·a·ble** doubtful; perhaps false, immoral, etc

**ques·tion mark** mark (?) put at end of sentence to indicate question

**ques·tion·naire'** (paper containing) set of questions for gathering statistics, etc

**queue** (kyū) pigtail; UK line of waiting persons, etc

**quib'ble** argue evasively or about small details

**quick** a done in short time or with only short interruptions; done, occurring, proceeding, moving, etc promptly or with speed; impatient or hasty: q. temper, q. tongue; full of liveliness or energy; prompt to do, learn, perceive, etc; n tender flesh below nails or skin; center of feeling: her words stung him to the q.

**quick'en** (cause to) become quicker; give (back) energy or vigor

**quick'sand** loose wet sand which yields to pressure and sucks in whatever touches it

**qui'et** (kwī-) making little or no noise; gentle; peaceful; moving gently or not at all: q. sea; (of manners) restrained; (of voice) gentle or low; (of colors) not bright

**quill** (hollow stem of) feather; hist pen made from this; spine of porcupine

**quilt** cover for bed with soft filling

**qui'nine** (kwĭnīn) substance found in bark of a tropical tree, used as tonic and to treat fevers; *esp.* malaria

**quint·es'sence** most essential part; perfect example

**quin·tet'** (music for) group of five

**quin'tu·ple** *a* consisting of five; fivefold; *v* multiply (number, *etc*) by five

**quip** (make) clever remark

**quirk** strange accident; peculiar habit

**quit** (**quit;** *UK* also **quitted**) stop (doing); leave (place, post of employment, *etc*)

**quite** completely, wholly: *q. wrong;* really, actually: *q. a. change; US* very: *q. small;* to considerable extent: *q. a lady*

**quiv'er** *n* case for arrows; *v* tremble

**quix·ot'ic** (kwiks-) idealistic but impractical

**quiz'zi·cal** odd; teasing

**quo'rum** number of members that must be present for a meeting to be held

**quo'ta** share of whole that each district, *etc* must give or be given

**quo·ta'tion** words of one person cited by another; act of quoting; price quoted

**quo·ta'tion mark** sign to show beginning (") and end (") of quotation

**quote** repeat words of others; mention as example; state price of (stocks)

**quo'tient** result obtained by dividing one number by another

# R

**r** eighteenth letter of English alphabet

**rab'bit** (fur of, meat from) small, long-eared burrowing animal

**rab'ble** disorderly crowd; mob

**rab'id** having rabies; furious; fanatical

**ra'bies** infectious virus disease causing madness and death in animals and humans

**rac·coon'** (fur of) small flesh-eating N. Amer. mammal with bushy tail, active at night

**ra|ce** contest of speed; (channel of) strong current of water; group of persons having common descent; tribe (believed to be) of same stock. **-cial**

**ra'cial·ism** racism. **-ist**

**rac'|is·m** belief that human abilities, *etc* are determined by race, thus resulting in natural dominance of a particular race; racial discrimination. **-ist**

**rack** n framework for holding fodder, keeping or displaying articles on, etc; hist instrument of torture by means of which body was stretched; v strain or shake violently: body racked by coughing, r. one's brain

**rack'e\t** confused and loud noise; illegal scheme for obtaining money by organized threats, etc. **-teer;** long-handled oval frame with usu nylon netting used in tennis, etc

**ra'cy** lively; of distinctive quality; risqué

**ra'dar** device for determining presence of airplanes, etc by radio waves reflected from them

**ra·di·al** of (or arranged like) rays moving out from a center; (of tires) having (steel) cords across edge of wheel

**ra'di·ant** giving off rays of light or heat; bright with joy, etc

**ra'di·ate** spread from central point; give off light or heat. **radia'tion**

**ra'di·a·tor** system of metal pipes through which hot water or steam runs, for heating; device for cooling engine in automobile

**rad'i·cal** of or going to the root; extreme; (person) desiring fundamental political change. **-ism**

**ra'di·o** system of wireless transmission of messages, musical or other programs, etc; apparatus for receiving broadcasts

**ra·di·o·ac'tive** giving off harmful rays due to the breaking up of atoms. **radioactiv'ity**

**ra·di·ol'o·gy** scientific study of X-rays and other forms of radiation and their use in medicine. **-gist**

**ra'di·o tel'e·scope** powerful radio receiver used in astronomy to observe and follow movement of stars

**rad'ish** (plant with) pungent root, usu eaten raw

**ra'di·um** radioactive metal used in radiology

**ra'di·us** (pl **-dii**) straight line from center of circle to circumference

**raft** floating platform of planks, rubber, etc used as boat or swimming pier; inflatable rubber boat for use in emergencies

**raft'er** timber forming part of framework for roof

**rag** torn or worn-out piece of woven, etc, material; pl old, worn-out clothes

**rage** (rāj) n violent anger; (object of) widespread temporary enthusiasm; v be in a rage; storm; move or spread violently

**rag'ged** old and torn; jagged or uneven; wearing frayed clothes

**raid** sudden attack by troops or search by police

**rail** n bar fixed horizontally as part of fence, barrier, etc, or as protection. **-ing**: one of pair of parallel steel bars on which wheels of train run; v complain bitterly or denounce strongly

**rail'road**, UK **rail'way** system of tracks on which trains are run for transportation of passengers, freight and mail

**rain** (send down) water falling in drops due to condensation of vapor in air. **-y**

**rain'bow** (-bō) arch of colors appearing in sky opposite the sun, caused by reflection of sun's rays in raindrops, mist, etc

**rain'drop** single drop of rain

**rain'fall** total rain falling in an area in a given time

**raise** (rāz) (cause to) move to higher or upright position; further growth of crops, cattle, etc; educate and look after one's child(ren); put in higher position; cause or put forward: r. a scene, r. a question; (of voice) make louder; collect, bring together: r. taxes, r. an army; make (prices, etc) higher; build;

end (blockade, etc

**rai'sin** (rāzn) sweet dried grape, used in baking, etc

**rake** n comblike gardening tool on long handle; v level soil, gather leaves, etc with rake; search through; sweep with (gun)fire, etc

**ral'ly** bring together (again); come together for joint action; revive or regain strength

**ram** n male sheep; machine for battering; v crash into; pack down tightly; squeeze into; force acceptance of

**ram'ble** go or talk aimlessly

**ram'i-fy** (cause to) spread out in branches. **ramifica'tion**

**ramp** sloping surface connecting two different levels of ground, etc

**ram'page** violent behavior

**ram'pant** widespread; unchecked (in growth); (in heraldry) rearing up on hind legs (esp. of lion)

**ram'shack-le** badly made; falling apart

**ran** see **run**

**ranch** (esp. US and CAN) large farm for breeding and raising cattle, etc. **-er**

**ran'cid** tasting or smelling of stale fat. **rancid'ity**

**ran'cor**, UK **-cour** bitter ill-will; hatred. **-ous**

**ran'dom** without plan, aim or pattern

**rang** see **ring**

**range** n limits between which variation is possible: *large r. of car models*; extent or scope of operation, action, *etc*: *within hearing r.*, *this gun has a long r.*; place for shooting practice; rank or class; line or series, as of mountains; reach of voice, capacities, *etc*; large stretch of grazing ground; large cooking stove; v place in row or line, or in particular position or group; wander over large area; vary within certain limits; stretch out in line or certain direction

**rank** n standing in society, military body, *etc*; place in scale of comparison; high standing: *a poet of r.*; (orderly) row or arrangement of things or persons; soldiers, *etc* drawn up in single line beside each other; *pl* ordinary soldiers; v arrange in order; have or assign standing; *a* growing richly or excessively; foul-smelling; indecent

**ran'sack** search thoroughly; plunder

**ran'som** (pay or collect) money for release of war prisoner, kidnaped victim, *etc*

**rant** talk loudly and pompously; scold

**rap** strike with quick or smart blow, as door; criticize; utter

(oath, *etc*) sharply; *US sl* chat

**ra·pa'cious** grasping; seizing what one wants. **-ty**

**rap|e** force person, *esp* woman, to submit to sexual intercourse. **-ist**

**rap'id** *a* speedy; quick; done in short time. **rapid'ity**; n *usu pl* rocky section of river with swift current

**ra'pi·er** straight slender sword

**rapt** wholly absorbed

**rap'tur|e** ecstasy. **-ous**

**rar|e** occurring or existing far apart in time or space; unusual; exceptional; unusually excellent, great, *etc*; not dense, as air or gases. **-ity**

**rare'ly** seldom

**rash** *a* overhasty; reckless. **-ness**; n breaking out of skin

**rasp** v scrape roughly; grate upon (nerves, *etc*); make grating sound; n rough file; grating sound

**rasp'ber·ry** (raz-) (shrub with) sweet red berry

**rat** long-tailed rodent resembling mouse, but larger in size; *infml* disloyal person

**rate** n numerical proportion between two quantities; relative speed, value or cost; price, *etc* fixed according to some standard: *freight/interest r.*; v estimate value of; deserve; rank

**rath·er** to some extent: *I r. like him*; more truly or accurately: *last night, or r. yesterday*; more readily or willingly: *I would r. go tomorrow*

**rat·i·fy** formally approve or make valid (what has been done by agent). **ratifica'tion**

**ra'tio** figure showing relationship between two quantities; proportion

**ra'tion** (limit to) fixed allowance of food, *etc*

**ra'tion·al** having reason; sensible

**ra'tion·al·is·m** doctrine that reason is highest authority in matters of belief or conduct, or is the foundation of knowledge. **-ist**

**ra'tion·al·ize**, *UK* **-ise** bring into line with reason; explain away by giving a reason; *esp. UK* improve efficiency (of business, *etc*) by reducing waste. **rationaliza'tion**

**rat'tle** *v* (cause to) give out quick succession of short sharp sounds, as by shaking, *etc*; talk rapidly; *infml* make or be made insecure or nervous; *n* baby's toy giving out rattling sound; set of horny rings on rattlesnake's tail

**rat'tle-snake** thick-bodied poisonous Amer. snake with rattle at end of tail

**rau'cous** hoarse; harsh--sounding

**rav'age** destroy; damage severely

**rave** talk wildly; speak delightedly of

**rav'el** make tangled; undo knitted fabric, *etc*

**ra'ven** bird of crow family with shiny black feathers

**rav'en·ous** very hungry

**ra·vine'** (-vēn) deep narrow valley

**rav'ish** fill with joy; rape

**rav'ish·ing** very beautiful or pleasing

**raw** (of food) not cooked; in natural state, not manufactured, diluted, *etc*: *r. silk*; inexperienced or unskilled; crude; (of skin) sore or exposing underlying flesh; (of weather) harsh

**ray** single narrow line of light; (straight) line in which radiant energy, *etc* is conveyed from source; any of (set of) lines spreading from or passing through a central point; large, flat-bodied sea fish

**ray'on** artificial silk made of cellulose

**raze** tear down; level to the ground

**ra'zor** sharp-edged instrument used in shaving

**reach** stretch out, as hand; extend in size, time, influence, *etc*, to: *his kingdom reached to the mountains*; arrive at (given point or object): *r. one's destination*; succeed in touching, grasp-

**reason**

ing, influencing, *etc*: *he could not r. the top, his complaints reached the king's ear*; give or take with outstretched hand: *r. for one's hat*; get in touch with: *he reached her by phone*

**re·act'** act in response to or against; undergo (chemical) change. **-tion**

**re·ac'tion·ar·y** (person) against social or political change

**read** *v* (rēd) (**read,** [red]) (be able to) take in and understand (sth written or printed); learn sth from paper, *etc*; say (written or printed words) aloud; make out meaning, *etc* by interpreting outward features; understand or interpret events, *etc* in certain way; (of thermometer, *etc*) register; study seriously by reading; have certain wording or allow given interpretation: *this may be read in several ways*; (of computer) copy or use data

**read'er** one who reads; proofreader; person evaluating manuscripts for publisher; *UK* university rank below professor; schoolbook, *esp.* for beginners in reading; device for scanning microfilm, *etc*

**re·ad·just'** adjust anew. **-ment**

**read'|y** (redi) fit for immedi-

ate use, action, *etc*: *breakfast is r.*; willing (to do, accept, *etc*); quick in understanding, speaking, *etc*: *a r. answer*; likely or about to do sth: *a flower r. to open*; immediately available: *r. cash*; within easy reach. **-iness**

**re'al** (rēel) existing as, or occurring in, fact; true; genuine; (of feelings, *etc*) sincere, not pretended. **real'ity**

**re·al es·tate** houses and land as property

**re'al·|is·m** regarding or dealing with things as they are in fact; interest in the real and practical; (of literature, *etc*) showing things as they are. **-ist, realis'tic**

**re'al·ize,** *UK* **-ise** understand clearly; make real; obtain as profit; convert into money. **realiza'tion**

**re'al·ly** in fact; truly; indeed

**realm** (relm) kingdom; special field or sphere

**re'al·ty** real estate. **-tor**

**reap** cut (grain); gather as reward, benefits, *etc*

**rear** *n* back part of anything, *v* bring up (children, *etc*); raise upright, as head; (of animal, *esp.* horse) rise up on back legs

**rear'most** farthest back to rear; last

**rear'ward** toward or at the rear

**rea'son** (rēzn) cause or motive: *his unhappiness was the r. for his behavior, I explained the r. of my absence*; mental powers of man, by which he draws conclusions from things observed, premises, *etc*; good sense or judgment; normal powers of mind; *v* think or argue logically; draw conclusions from facts, *etc*; bring (person) to do, believe, *etc*, by logical argument

**rea'son·a·ble** agreeing with reason and good judgment; moderate (in cost)

**re·as·sure'** give back confidence to. **-ance**

**re'bate** amount officially returned from sum paid

**re·bel'** *v* rise against established government, customs, *etc*. **-lion, -lious**

**reb'el** *n* one who rebels

**re·bound'** spring back after striking another body; recover after falling, as stock prices

**re·buff'** sharp refusal; snub

**re·buke'** (utter, *esp*. official) criticism

**re·but'** disprove. **-tal**

**re·cal'ci·trant** (-si-) stubbornly refusing to obey rules

**re·call'** call back event, *etc* to mind; remind one of; make (person) return; take back (promise, *etc*)

**re·cant'** publicly renounce former opinion

**re·ca·pit'u·late** state main points in brief summary

**re·cede'** go back or down, as flood; slant backward, as chin

**re·ceive'** (-sēv) take (sth offered or delivered) into one's hand or possession; have sth given or sent to one: *r. a present, r. orders*; meet with or suffer: *r. an insult*; entertain or greet (guests); admit into organization, *etc* as member; accept as true: *this principle is universally received*; take into the mind: *r. an impression*; (electronics) transform incoming signals into sound or picture. **recep'tion, recep'tive**

**re·ceiv'er** part of telephone held to ear

**re'cent** not long past; modern

**re·cep'ta·cle** container

**re·cep'tion·ist** person employed to welcome visitors, clients, *etc*

**re·cess'** pause between work periods or (*US*) school classes; hollow in wall, *etc*; withdrawn or secret place

**re·ces'sion** going or drawing back; temporary drop in business activity

**rec'i·pe** (-sipē) directions for preparing food, *etc*

**re·cip'i·ent** one who receives

**re·cip'ro·cal** felt or done in return; mutual. **-cate, reciproc'ity**

**re·cit'al** detailed statement of facts, *etc*; performance by one artist

**re·cite'** repeat aloud (poem, *etc*) from memory; tell in detail. **recita'tion**

**reck'less** careless; rash

**reck'on** figure out amount, number, *etc*; consider to be

**re·claim'** make (land) fit for cultivation; recover (useful substances) from waste; ask for return of; bring back to right ideas, *etc*

**re·cline'** lean back; rest

**re·cluse'** person living withdrawn from society

**rec'og·nize,** *UK* **-nise** realize or admit to be true, valid, *etc*; identify as known before. **-able, recogni'tion**

**re·coil'** draw or shrink back in fear, *etc*; spring back

**rec·ol·lect'** remember. **-tion**

**rec·om·mend'** praise or suggest as desirable; entrust to; make attractive; advise (to do). **recommenda'tion**

**rec'om·pense** repay, *esp.* for services; make good (injury or loss)

**rec'on·cile** make friendly or not opposed; settle (quarrel, *etc*); bring into agreement. **reconcilia'tion**

**re·con'nais·sance,** military, *etc* examination of area

**rec·on·noi'ter,** *UK* **-tre** examine region, *etc* and try to learn its conditions

**re·con·struct'** build again; make over (house, *etc*) by changing

**re·cord'** *v* set or write down in permanent form; tape sound, *etc* for reproduction. **-ing;** register

**rec'ord** *n* anything recorded; (official) written statement; report on person's past (accomplishments, *etc*); highest achievement in any field; disk with markings for reproducing sound

**re·cord'er** *mus* simple wind instrument; device for recording sound or pictures on (video)tape, or for playing tapes so recorded

**re·cord' play·er** device for converting markings on record into sound

**re·count'** tell in detail; count again

**re·coup'** get back (losses)

**re·course'** act of seeking help; person or thing one turns to for aid

**re·cov'er** get or win back; make good (losses); regain health, *etc*. **-y**

**rec·re·a'tion** (refreshment by means of) play, holiday, *etc*

**re·crim·i·na'tion** accusation brought in answer to accusation

**re·cruit'** new member (of armed forces, *etc*)

**rec'tan·gle** figure having

four sides and four right angles. **rectan'gular**

**rec'ti·fy** put right; adjust. **rectifica'tion**

**rec'ti·tude** moral uprightness

**rec'tor** clergyman; head of certain schools

**rec'tum** lowest part of large intestine

**re·cu'per·ate** recover from sickness or loss

**re·cur'** happen again, *esp.* of problem, difficulty, *etc*. **-rence, -rent**

**red** having the color of blood, cherries. **-den, -dish;** of the extreme political left; **R.** of or belonging to Soviet Union; **in(to)** or **out of the r.** in(to) or out of debt; **red-hand'ed** in the act of doing sth wrong: *caught him red-handed*

**re·deem'** buy back; fulfill (promise); pay (debt); make up for; save (soul). **re·demp'tion**

**red'head** person with red hair

**red'o·lent** having a strong smell; strongly suggestive of. **-lence**

**re·dou'ble** (-dubl) increase in amount or degree

**re·dress'** set right; make up for

**re·duce'** make smaller, lower, *etc;* change to other (simpler) form; lessen one's weight by diet, *etc.* **-tion**

**re·dun'dan|t** being in excess; unnecessary. **-cy**

**red'wood** (wood of) very tall California evergreen tree

**reed** (long straight stem of) marsh or water grass; vibrating piece of cane or metal set in mouth of some wind instruments as oboe or clarinet. **-y**

**reef** ridge of rocks or sand at or near surface of sea

**reek** give off smoke, unpleasant smell, *etc*

**reel** *n* roll on which thread, film, *etc* are wound; *v* wind on roll; stagger; turn round and round (dizzily); be shocked or confused

**re·fer'** mention; consult; direct attention to; hand over for consideration, decision, *etc.* **ref'erence**

**ref·er·ee'** (act as) umpire between opposing sides or in games

**ref·er·en'dum** submitting sth, as a proposed law, to popular vote

**re·fine'** bring to fine or pure state; make pure, elegant or cultured. **-ment**

**re·flect'** throw back (light, sound, *etc*). **-tor;** give back image of; bring credit or discredit on; think carefully. **-tion, -tive**

**re·flex'** (of) an automatic nervous response of the body

**re·for'est** replant with trees

**re·form'** (change so as to) become or make better, get rid of evils, *etc*. **reforma'tion**

**re·frac'to·ry** stubborn; difficult to manage

**re·frain'** *n* line or verse recurring at intervals in song or poem; *v* keep o.s. from (do-ing); not do

**re·frig'er·a|te** make or keep cold, *esp*. to preserve food. **-tor, refrigera'tion**

**ref'uge** shelter; place of protection from danger, storms, *etc*

**ref·u·gee'** one who flees to safety, *esp*. to a foreign country

**re·fund'** give back, *esp*. money

**re·fuse'** *v* turn down (request, *etc*); say that one will not do, grant, *etc*. **-al**

**ref'use** trash; rubbish

**re·fute'** prove (sth or s.o.) to be wrong. **refuta'tion**

**re'gal** of or like or fit for a king

**re·ga'li·a** *pl* emblems of office, *etc*

**re·gard'** *n* relation or connection: *with r. to his father*; attention or respect: *have r. for his feelings*; *pl* feelings of friendliness or respect: *give them my r.*; *v* consider (as); think highly of; look at; take into account

**re·gard'ing** concerning

**re·gard'less** in spite of everything; **r. of** not taking into consideration

**re·gen'er·ate** improve condition of; give new (better) form

**re'gen|t** one who rules when king is too young, ill, *etc*; university official. **-cy**

**re·gime'** (-zhēm) method of government; existing system of things

**reg'i·men|t** *n* army unit; *v* organize according to system. **regimen'tal**

**re'gion** district; area; section of human body. **-al**

**reg'is·ter** *n* (book with) official written record or list; device recording amount or quantity; *US v* set down in writing; enter (name, *etc*) in list; (shuttered) grill admitting flow of hot/cool air; make note of; show (effects, emotion, *etc*). **registra'tion**

**re·gres|s'** move backwards. **-sion, -sive**

**re·gret'** be sorry for; feel sense of loss. **-table**

**reg'u·lar** (of arrangement, shape, *etc*) following fixed principle; systematical; acting, done, recurring, *etc*, in uniform manner or at fixed times; habitual or customary; carried out in accordance with fixed (formal) rule, *etc*; properly qualified (for occupation, *etc*). **regu·lar'ity**

**reg'u·la|te** control by rule; adjust (machine, *etc*). **-tor, regula'tion**

**re·gur'gi·tate** (-ji-) cast up (food) again

**re·ha·bil'i·tate** return to good condition or reputation. **rehabilita'tion**

**re·hash'** put old material in new form without improving it

**re·hears|e** say over; practice (play, *etc*) for performance. **-al**

**reign** (rān) (period of) rule

**re·im·burse'** repay (person for expenses). **-ment**

**rein** leather strip for controlling horse; means of control

**re·in·car·na'tion** rebirth of soul in new body

**rein'deer** (rān-) large N. deer with branched antlers

**re·in·force'** strengthen by addition. **-ment**

**re·it'er·ate** say over again

**re·ject'** turn down or back; cast off. **-tion**

**re·joice'** (cause) to feel gladness or joy

**re·join'** join anew; reply

**re·join'der** (rude) reply

**re·ju've·nate** making young again. **rejuvena'tion**

**re·lapse'** (fall back into) worsened state after improvement

**re·la|te'** tell (story); bring in-

to connection; be connected with. **-tion**

**re·lat'ed** connected (by family)

**re·la'tion·ship** (friendly or family) connection

**rel'a·tive** *a* connected with; proportionate; not absolute. **relativ'ity;** *n* kinsman

**re·lax'** make or become looser, less strict, *etc*. **relaxa'tion**

**re·lay'** *n* group of workers, *etc* taking turns; electrical device for opening circuit; *v* carry forward (message, *etc*)

**re·lease'** turn loose; allow to be published; turn over to another

**rel'e·gate** send to lower position; transfer (matter for decision, *etc*)

**re·lent'** become less severe

**rel'e·vant** having to do with the matter at hand. **-vance, -vancy**

**re·li'a·ble** able to be trusted. **reliability**

**re·li'ance** trust; dependence

**rel'ic** sth remaining from past; sth venerated as belonging to holy person; *pl* dead body

**re·lief'** aid given to ease difficulty, pain, *etc*; person taking turn of duty; (method of) sculpture standing out from flat surface

**re·lieve'** lessen pain, *etc*; bring or be a relief; take or provide turn of duty

**re·li·¦gion** (-lijen) search for and recognition of superhuman power controlling the universe; system of faith in and worship of such power. **-gious**

**re·lin¦quish** give up; let go. **-ment**

**rel'ish** n enjoyment of food, etc; sth adding flavor; v enjoy

**re·luc'tant** unwilling. **-tance**

**re·ly'** depend on; put trust in

**re·main'** v continue to be in same place or state; stay behind; be left over. **-der;** n pl what is left over; dead body

**re·mark'** say; r. on notice

**re·mark'a·ble** worthy of special notice

**rem'e·dy** (provide) sth that cures or corrects. **reme'dial**

**re·mem'¦ber** recall by drawing on memory; keep or bear in mind; make present (to), esp. in one's last will; send greetings through another; r. me to him. **-brance**

**re·mind'** cause (o.s. or another) to remember. **-er**

**rem·i·nis'¦cence** remembering; remembered fact or event; feature that reminds. **-cent**

**re·miss'** careless of one's duty

**re·¦mit'** send (esp. money); refrain from carrying out (punishment, etc); pardon; give back; put off to future. **-mission**

**re·mit'tance** money sent

**rem'nant** small piece or part left over, esp. cloth; trace left over

**re·mon¦strate** complain; protest. **-strance**

**re·morse'** deep regret for wrongs done. **-ful**

**re·mote'** far away; out-of-the-way; connected some distance at a distance; slight; (of persons) withdrawn. **-ness**

**re·move'** take away; get rid of; take off. **-val**

**re·mu'ner·a¦te** pay (for work, trouble, etc). **-tive, remunera'tion**

**ren·ais·sance'**, **re·nas'-cence** new birth; revival, esp. in field of art, etc

**rend** (rent) tear apart

**ren'der** cause to be; pay (tribute to); depict; translate; perform, as service; give for consideration or inspection. **rendi'tion**

**ren'dez·vous** (rahndevū) agreement to meet at certain place; place of meeting

**ren'e·gade** one who deserts one cause for another

**re·new'** make new or effective again; begin again; make (store, etc) full again; get back (youth, vigor, etc). **-al**

**re·nounce'** give up formally; disown. **renuncia'tion**

**ren'o·vate** make over as if new. **renova'tion**

**re·nown'** fame. **-ed**

**rent** see **rend**

**rent** (make or receive) payment (at regular intervals) for use of property, *etc*. **-al;** a tear or slit

**re·pair'** mend; set right again. **rep'arable; r. to** go to

**rep·a·ra'tion** making amends; *usu pl* payment of damages, *esp*. by nation defeated in war

**re·pa'tri·ate** send (s.o.) back to native land

**re·pay'** (-paid) pay back; reward

**re·peal'** annul (law, decision, *etc*)

**re·peat'** say again; do, make, undergo, occur, *etc*, again

**re·pel'** drive back; be distasteful to. **-lent**

**re·pent'** feel regret or sorrow for sth one has (not) done. **-tance, -tant**

**re·per·cus'sion** serious after-effect; echo

**rep·e·ti'tion** (-tish-) act of repeating; sth repeated

**re·place'** return (sth) to former place; give back, as borrowed money; take the place of; find or provide a substitute. **-ment**

**re·plen'ish** fill up again. **-ment**

**re·plete'** filled; well-stocked

**rep'li·ca** close copy, *esp*. of art work

**re·ply'** (-plī) say, write or do as answer

**re·port'** (published) account of events, happenings, to provide information. **-er;** rumor; teacher's written opinion of pupil's work; loud noise, as of shot; *v* make r.; bring charge against; announce (one's) presence to superior, *etc*

**re·pose'** rest; lie; be based on; place (trust) in

**re·pos'i·tor·y** place where things are stored

**rep·re·hen'si·ble** deserving to be blamed

**rep·re·sent'** act for; be example of; stand for; describe as; portray. **-tative, representa'tion**

**re·press'** put down; check. **-sion, -sive**

**re·prieve'** delay (punishment); give temporary relief to

**rep'ri·mand** (express) severe formal reproof

**re·print'** print new copy of book, *etc*

**re'print** new printing of unaltered (book) text

**re·pris'al** injury, *etc* done in return, *esp*. in war

**re·proach'** blame; disgrace

**rep'ro·bate** (person who is) extremely immoral or sinful

**re·pro·duc'e** make copy of; produce again; produce offspring. **-tion, -tive**

**re·proof**¹ (expression of) blame

**re·prove**¹ scold; express disapproval

**rep·tile** cold-blooded scaly animal that lays eggs, as snake, lizard, *etc*. **reptil·ian**

**re·pub·li|c** state where power rests with citizens or their elected representatives. **-can**

**re·pu·di·ate** deny; disown. **repudia·tion**

**re·pug·nant** distasteful; offensive. **-nance**

**re·pulse**¹ drive back; refuse; turn down (advances, *etc*)

**re·pul·sion** disgust; dislike; force causing bodies, *etc* to repel each other. **-sive**

**rep·u·ta·ble** respectable; having a good reputation

**rep·u·ta·tion** what is generally said or believed about person or thing; state of being respectable

**re·quest**¹ ask(ing) for sth (to be given or allowed)

**re·qui·em** (music for) burial ceremony

**re·quire**¹ need; demand; make necessary; impose as condition. **-ment**

**req·ui·site** required; necessary

**req·ui·si·tion** (submit) official demand or order, *esp*. by military

**re·quite**¹ pay back in kind

**re·scind**¹ repeal; cancel by higher authority

**res·cue** save (from danger)

**re·search**¹ (make) careful inquiry into subject; (prepare) scientific study

**re·sem·ble** look or be like. **-blance**

**re·sent**¹ feel or show anger at insult, *etc*. **-ful**

**res·er·va·tion** feeling of doubt; limitation; booking of room in hotel, *etc*; district set aside for US Indian tribe

**re·serve**¹ *v* keep back for future use; set aside for particular use; *n* sth saved for future use; sth reserved, such as troops; place set aside for special use; self-restraint

**res·er·voir** (-vwahr) storage place, *esp*. for great amount of water; large supply (of facts, *etc*)

**re·side**¹ have one's home at; (of rights) rest in. **res·i·dence, res·i·dent**

**res·i·due** what is left over. **resid·ual**

**re·sign**¹ give up office, position, *etc*; accept (bad luck, *etc*) without resisting. **resignation**

**re·sil·i·ent** able to spring back to original form

**res·in** (rezin) sticky natural substance, *esp*. from fir and pine, used in medicine, *etc*; artificial substance used *esp*. in plastics. **-ous**

**re·sist'** struggle against; withstand. **-tance, -tant**

**res·o·lute** determined; firm of purpose

**re·solve'** break up into parts; clear up; decide to do. **resolu'tion**

**res'o·nant** echoing; continuing to sound. **-nance**

**re·sort'** v turn to (for aid); n place visited for health, etc

**re·sound'** echo; go on sounding

**re·source'** (usu pl) means or source of supply, aid etc; means of dealing with emergency; wealth (of a country)

**re·spect'** n esteem; consideration; detail; **with(out) r. to** with(out) regard to; v treat with consideration and high regard. **-ful**

**re·spect'a·ble** deserving respect; of good social standing. **respectabil'ity**

**re·spec'tive** particular; proper to each of a number

**re·spec'tive·ly** for each in the order mentioned

**res'pir·a·tor** device placed over nose and mouth to assist breathing

**re·spire'** breathe. **respira'tion**

**res'pite** interval of rest

**re·splen'|dent** shiningly bright; splendid. **-dence**

**re·spond'** give answer; act (as if) in answer. **-sponse**

**re·spon'si·ble** liable to answer for; reliable. **responsibil'ity**

**rest** v refresh by sleeping, relaxing, stopping work, etc; lie still. **-ful, -less;** (cause to) lie, be supported, etc: r. one's head on the table; (of burden, blame, etc) lie on; (of eyes, etc) be directed (at); n act, state or time of resting; (sign indicating) interval of silence between tones in music; thing serving as support: foot r.; part left behind or remaining; **for the r.** beyond what was mentioned

**res'tau·rant** place where meals are served to customers

**res·ti·tu'tion** giving back to proper owner; making good of injury; bringing back to original state

**re·store'** give back; bring back to original state, health, or use. **restora'tion**

**re·strain'** check; hold back; imprison. **-straint**

**re·strict'** limit. **-tion, -tive**

**re·sult'** (-zult) v arise or happen as consequence of former action, conditions, circumstances, etc; n that which results; value or quantity arrived at by calculation

**re·sume'** begin again; go on with; take again; sum up. **-sumption**

**ré·su·me'** (rezoomā) summary, (US) esp. one of past ca-

**reverend**

reer, *etc* when applying for job

**res·ur·rec|t'** raise from the dead; bring back into use, *etc*. **-tion**

**re·tail'** sell(ing) of goods in small quantities

**re·tain'** keep (in place); continue to have; not forget; engage services of by paying fee. **-er**

**re·tal'i·ate** return alike for like, *esp.* injury. **retalia'tion**

**re·tard'** make slow or late; hold back. **retarda'tion**

**re·ten'|tion** act or state of retaining. **-tive**

**ret'i·cent** not inclined to speak freely. **-cence**

**ret'i·na** membrane at back of eyeball which sends visual images to brain via the optic nerve

**ret'i·nue** body of attendants

**re·tire'** go away; go to bed; withdraw from active life. **-ment**; retreat (in battle)

**re·tir'ing** shy; withdrawn

**re·tort'** (make) quick, rude, witty, *etc* reply; glass container with long bent neck for heating chemicals

**re·touch'** improve (photograph, *etc*) by adding new touches

**re·trac|t'** draw back or in; take back (statement, *etc*). **-tion**

**re·treat'** *v* (troops) fall back; withdraw; *n* place of privacy or shelter

**re·trench'** reduce costs. **-ment**

**ret·ri·bu'tion** punishment (for evil). **retrib'utive, retrib'-utory**

**re·triev|e'** find and bring back; regain; rescue; set right. **-al**

**re·tro·ac'tive** operating backwards in time; existing now and applying to the past

**re·tro·spec'tive** looking backwards in time; retroactive

**re·turn'** *v* bring, come or go back to former state, place, *etc*; give back to (former) owner; say or do in reply to another's words or actions; render (verdict); yield (profits); *n* act of going, coming, sending or giving back; reply; *usu pl* profits from business, *etc*; official report

**re·un'ion** coming together again; gathering of old friends, *etc* after separation

**re·veal'** make known; show

**rev·e·la'tion** act of revealing; surprising disclosure; divine truth

**re·venge'** (-enj) sth done, said, *etc*, in reply to or as retaliation for insult, injury, injustice, *etc*. **-ful**

**rev'e·nue** income (of government from taxes, *etc*)

**re·vere'** regard with deep respect. **rev'erence**

**rev'er·end** (title of respect

for) clergyman: *the Rev. Smith*

**rev·er·ie** (state of) day-dreaming or deep thought

**re·verse|e¹** *a* opposite; contrary; backward; *v* turn in opposite direction; change (decision) to opposite; make (vehicle) travel backwards; in gear for moving (vehicle) backwards; rear side of; the contrary; bad luck. **-al, -ible**

**re·vert|t¹** return to former state; go back to (in thought). **-sion**

**re·view¹** *n* act of reviewing; general survey; (journal publishing) criticism of book, *etc*; *v* consider again; inspect (troops, *etc*); criticize (book, *etc*); survey (past)

**re·vile¹** call by bad names

**re·vi|se¹** alter; correct mistakes. **-sion**

**re·vive¹** come or bring back to life, use, *etc*. **-al**

**re·voke¹** withdraw; take back; cancel. **revoca·tion**

**re·volt¹** rise against authority; feel disgust at

**rev·o·lu·tion** act of turning in circle; complete change; overthrow of government by force. **-ary**

**re·volve¹** turn round; move in circle (around central point); think over

**re·volv·er** pistol with revolving bullet chamber which can be fired several times

without reloading

**re·ward¹** (sth given or received as) return for services, merit, *etc*; sum offered for tracing criminal, recovery of stolen goods, *etc*

**rhap·so|dy** musical composition or literary work showing intense emotion; enthusiastic or extravagant approval. **-dist, -dize** (*UK* **-dise**)

**Rhe·sus fac·tor, Rh fac·tor** substance in blood of most humans (Rh positive) which can produce extreme allergic reaction by contact with Rh negative blood

**rhet·o·ric** art of speaking or writing effectively or persuasively. **rhetor·ical**

**rheu·ma·tism** disease causing stiffness and pain in joints. **rheumat·ic**

**rhi·noc·er·os** (rinos-) (*pl* **-ros, -roses**) large thick-skinned powerful animal of Africa or Asia, with one or two upright horns on snout

**rhu·barb** (plant with) fleshy leafstalk, used as food

**rhyme** (verse, poem, *etc* marked by) agreement of sounds at end of lines or words, as *cat* and *hat*

**rhyth·|m** (ridhm) flow of regular beats or accents in music, verse, *etc*. **-mic(al)**

**rib** one of curved slender bones extending from spine

to breastbone; cut of meat containing such bone; curved piece of metal, *etc* used to support frame; raised ridge, as vein of leaf, *etc*

**rib'bon** band of fine woven material, as silk, for tying, as ornament, *etc*; anything similar to this in shape or use, as typewriter r.

**rice** (plant grown in warm wet climates with) seed used as food

**rich** having a lot of money, *etc*; yielding great supplies; expensive in style, material, *etc*; (of land) fertile; (of food) containing much butter, cream, *etc*; (of flavors) strong; (of color) deep; (of sounds) full. **-ness, -es**

**rick'ets** children's disease causing misshapen bones

**rick'et·y** weak; shaky

**rick'shaw** two-wheeled Asian passenger cart, drawn by hand or bicycle

**ric·o·chet'** (-shā) (of bullet, *etc*) skip at angle and rebound before hitting

**rid** (rid) free of sth unwanted, *etc*. **-dance**

**rid'dle** *n* puzzle; *v* pierce with many holes, as by gunfire

**ride** (rode, rid'den) sit on (animal) and cause (it) to move ahead; control horses; be carried in a vehicle; move along in any or in given way:

*instrument rides on an axis, the car rides smoothly*

**rid'er** person who rides; part added, *esp.* to bill of law, *etc*

**ridge** long narrow hilltop; mountain range; line (of roof) where two sloping surfaces meet; raised strip (of earth)

**rid'i·cule** make fun of

**ri·dic'u·lous** deserving to be laughed at; absurd

**rife** widespread; **r. with** full of

**riff'raff** low class of people

**ri'fle** *n* long gun with spiral grooves in barrel, fired from shoulder; *v* search and rob (all that can be found)

**rift** split; gap

**rig** fit with clothes or equipment; manage sth dishonestly

**right** *a* in accordance with what is good, true or just; free from error, or agreeing with standard or principle; in proper or satisfying state, position, *etc*: *he is all r.*, *set things in their r. place*; (of side of paper, cloth, *etc*) that which is used, shown, *etc*; of, at or to side turned towards the east when facing north, or, in person or animal, the side opposite to the heart; near, on or by this side; (of angles) formed by two lines meeting so that one line rises perfectly upright from other; *adv* towards the right: *turn r.*

*at the bridge*; properly or correctly: *he did it r.*; completely, or immediately: *the bullet went r. through, come r. away*; exactly: *r. here*; (in certain titles) very: *the r. reverend*; *n* that to which one is entitled on legal, moral, *etc*, grounds; that which is good or proper; body of politically conservative opinion. -**wing**

**right'eous** morally upright; honest. -**ness**

**rig'id** stiff; not bending; strict. **rigid'ity**

**rig'or**, *UK* -**our** firmness; harshness; hardship. -**ous**

**rim** (raised) outer edge or border, *esp.* of round object

**rind** (-ī-) bark of tree; thick outer layer of fruit, cheese, *etc*

**ring** *n* round band of metal, *etc*, *esp.* one of gold or silver worn on finger as ornament; anything of similar shape; persons or things arranged in circle; persons working together, often dishonestly; enclosed space for boxing, circus, *etc*; *v* encircle; put ring on (bird)

**ring** *v* (**rang, rung**) give forth clear, continuing sound, as a bell; cause (bell) to sound; sound bell for service, *etc*; be filled with (loud) sound; *esp. UK* call by telephone

**ring'lead·er** leader of a

group, *esp.* of troublemakers

**ring'worm** contagious skin disease

**rink** (building containing) surface of ice for skating, or smooth floor for roller skating

**rinse** wash by filling with water and shaking; remove soap, *etc* by putting in water

**ri'ot** noisy and disorderly behavior by large crowd; unrestrained display of color, *etc*

**rip** divide by tearing or cutting; split

**rip'-cord** cord pulled to open parachute

**ripe** fully grown or developed, so as to be ready for (eating, cutting, *etc*); advanced in years: *r. old age.* -**ness, rip'en**

**rip'ple** (cause to) form small waves; make sound like gently moving water

**rise** (rīz) (**rose, ris'en**) move to higher level or position; get up from kneeling, lying or sitting position; get out of bed; start opposition or revolt (against authority); ascend, as balloon, smoke, *etc*; extend upwards, as building, *etc*; appear, as sun above horizon; come into being or begin, as quarrel, *etc*; increase in force, as wind; come to surface; increase in price, value *etc*; (of feelings, *etc*) become stirred or more animated; (of dough) puff up, as by action of yeast; show oneself equal to demand, *etc*: r. *to the occasion*

**risk** (expose to) danger, possible loss, chance. **-y**

**ris|qué** (-kā) (of story, joke. *etc*) indecent

**rit|le** (set form of) religious or other ceremony. **-ual**

**ri'val** (be) one of two or more competing for s.o. or sth

**riv'er** large stream of water flowing into sea, lake or other stream

**riv'et** *n* metal bolt for joining metal plates; *v* fasten with rivets; hold (attention) firmly

**road** (paved) way over which man, animals and vehicles can travel

**roam** wander aimlessly

**roar** (make) loud deep full continuous sound, as of lion, thunder, *etc*; (utter) loud speech, laugh or shout

**roast** cook over open fire or in oven, as meat, or dry by heat, as coffee beans

**rob** take away (property) by force or violence; take away or withhold something unjustly. **-ber, -bery**

**robe** long loose flowing gown or wrap

**rob'in** small Eur. bird with red breast and throat; large N. Amer. thrush with dull red breast

**ro'bot** computer-driven machine able to do certain human tasks; efficient but insensitive person

**ro·bust'** strong; healthy; sturdy; sensible

**rock** *v* (cause to) move back and forth with swinging motion, as a cradle; shock; upset; *n* stony part of earth's crust; mass or piece of this; **on the rocks** failed; (of drinks) poured over ice; modern popular music with strong rhythm: *r. and roll*

**rock'er** one of curved bars on which cradle, *etc*, is mounted

**rock'et** *n* metal tube propelled by burning gases, used in space exploration, for driving jet airplanes or to carry (atomic) explosives; similar object of paper propelled by burning powder which explodes with shower of sparks (and loud noise), used as fireworks; *v* rise swiftly and suddenly; move very fast

**ro·co'co** *n* highly ornamental style popular in 18th century; *a* overly ornate

**rod** thin (metal) bar, as that on which curtain runs; fishing pole

**rode** see **ride**

**ro'dent** member of group of gnawing animals, such as rat, squirrel, *etc*

**rogu|e** (rōg) dishonest or

mischievous person. **-ery, -ish**

**role** (rōl) part in play; part in any action

**roll** v move by turning over and over, as ball or wheel; form (paper, yarn, etc) into cylinder or ball by winding round and round; turn round and round or from side to side; move with wavy motion, as sea; (of land) extend as in waves; (cause to) sound with deep continuous vibrating tone, as drums or thunder; (of ship) sway from side to side; walk with swaying steps; cast (dice); flatten out, as dough; (begin to) turn, as camera, etc; n paper, etc, rolled up; list of names, as of soldiers of a company; anything more or less cylindrical in shape; rolling sound or motion; small loaf of bread for one person

**roll'er** cylinder upon which sth is rolled along; small wheel at bottom of chair; rotating cylindrical body for rolling over sth to be flattened, inked, crushed, etc

**roll'er coast·er** amusement railway with great dips and narrow sharp curves

**roll'er skate** skate with four small wheels

**rol'lick·ing** noisily gay

**ro·man'ce** (medieval) tale of adventure or love; dreamy or emotional quality; love-affair, etc. **-tic; R. language** one developed from Latin, as French, Italian etc

**romp** play in lively manner, as children do

**roof** (cover with or be) structure forming upper outer covering of building, car etc

**room** (extent of) usable space. **-y;** part of house separated from rest by walls, floor and ceiling; opportunity for or to do: r. for doubt

**roost** bird's resting place, esp. in hen-house

**roost'er** esp. US male chicken

**root** (branched, bulbous, etc) part of plant which grows down into soil to absorb moisture and nourishment; base of tooth, hair etc; source or fundamental part

**rope** strong thick line made by twisting together strands of hemp, nylon, etc; pearls, etc, strung together in similar manner; pl fence around boxing ring

**rose** v see **rise**

**rose** n (thorny shrub with) showy, usu sweet-smelling red, white, pink or yellow flower; (of) pale to dark pink color

**rose'ma·ry** fragrant herb used in cooking

**ros'ter** list showing turns of duty, esp. of soldiers

**ros'trum** platform for public speaker, orchestra conductor, *etc*

**rot** (cause to) decay gradually by natural process; (cause to) go bad, as food, *etc*. **-ten**

**ro'tate** (cause to) turn round center or axis; (cause to) do sth in turn or alternately.
**ro'tary**

**ro'tor** part of machine which rotates; system of revolving blades in helicopter

**ro·tun'da** circular building

**rouge** (rūzh) red coloring substance for cheeks

**rough** (ruf) having an uneven surface due to breaks, irregularities, *etc*; (of cloth, *etc*) hairy. **-en**; done with or showing force or violence; unfeeling or lacking gentleness, politeness, *etc*; (of wheather, *etc*) stormy; not finished: *r. draft*

**rough'age** high-fiber food which stimulates the bowels

**round** *a* having or approaching circular, cylindrical or spherical form; (of face, body, *etc*) plump; complete; (of numbers) approximate, without smaller units; *adv* characterized by movement in circle: *the wheels went r.*; to or at every point of circle, or every member of a group, *etc*: *take the tray r.*; out from center in all directions; on or so as to enclose from all sides; *prep* around; throughout; *n* anything round; (single) stage of action, as in a contest; (ammunition for) single shot; regular trip to deliver or inspect sth; *v* go or make round

**rouse** wake from rest; stir up to activity or feeling

**rout** *n* utter confusion and defeat; *v* force out of hiding place, *etc*; put to flight

**route** (rūt) path or course to be traveled

**rou·tine'** (following or according to) course of regular or unchanging procedure

**rove** wander aimlessly

**row** (rou) *n* noisy quarrel

**row** (rō) *v* move (boat) by means of oars; *n* number of persons or things arranged in line

**row'dy** rough and noisy (person). **-ism**

**roy'al** of, like or worthy of a king

**roy'al·ty** royal persons; payment for use of copyright or patent

**rub** pass hand or object back and forth, or up and down, over surface so as to polish, clean,wear something off, make dry or warm, *etc*; slide or grate against; make into powder or soft mass, as by forcing through sieve

**rub'ber** elastic substance made from juice of tropical

plant or synthetically; *UK* piece of this used to rub out writing, *etc*

**rub'bish** waste matter

**rub'ble** broken stones or bricks

**ru'by** (gem having) rich red color

**ruck'sack** bag worn on the back, *usu* with metal frame, for carrying gear when hiking, climbing, *etc*

**rud'der** device for steering ship or plane

**rud'dy** of healthy red color; rosy; reddish. **-diness**

**rude** rough; very impolite; not carefully made; uneducated; violent. **-ness**

**ru'di·ments** basic beginning steps of an art or science. **rudimen'tary**

**rue'ful** expressing regret

**ruf'fi·an** cruel, brutal person

**ruf'fle** draw into wrinkles or folds; disturb; annoy

**rug** woollen, *etc* floor covering; large woollen coverlet

**rug'ged** rough; harsh; severe; sturdy

**ru'in** destruction; complete loss; *pl* remains of a building, *etc*

**rul|e** *n* (set of) ideas, thoughts, *etc*, intended to guide action, behavior, *etc*; accepted custom or standard; normal way of doing sth; government or supreme authority; straight strip of wood, metal, *etc*, used as guide in drawing lines: a ruler; *v* control (country, *etc*). **-er**; *law* deliver judgment in court

**rum** alcoholic liquor made from fermented sugar cane

**rum'ble** (make) low, heavy, rolling sound, as thunder

**ru'mi·nate** chew the cud; consider again and again

**rum'mage** (make) careful search by turning things over, *etc*

**ru'mor**, *UK* **-mour** common talk; story widely told but not necessarily true

**rump** rear end of animal

**rum'ple** make untidy; wrinkle

**run** *v* (**ran, run**) go by moving legs quickly; (cause to) move swiftly, as ship, car *etc*, or freely and continuously, as machine; operate or control, as business, *etc*; take part in race; try to be elected for government, *etc*, office; (of ship) sail or be driven (ashore, on rocks, *etc*); (of trains, *etc*) go regularly between places; (of liquid, river, *etc*) flow freely or in strong stream; (of colors in fabric, *etc*) melt and spread when made hot or wet; *esp. US* come undone, as fabric; have legal force for certain period, as contract; go by, as time; continue *esp.* for given period, as a play; (cause to) extend in particular direction: *the road runs to the north*; (cause to) appear in print, television, *etc*; meet with: *r. into trouble*; pass (successfully) through dangerous areas: *r. a blockade*; pass into given state: *the well ran dry*; stab (dagger, *etc*) through; have high body temperature: *r. a fever*; *n* act, manner or spell of running; distance covered by running; particular tendency or direction of something: *r. of events*; continuous course of some condition, *etc*: *r. of good luck*; usual or average kind; unusually strong demand: *a r. on rubber*; fixed route, as of railroad; fenced enclosure for animals; right to use freely; *esp. US* unravelled part of fabric

**run'down** *n infml* summary

**run-down** *a* dilapidated; not kept in good repair; tired out or in poor health

**rung** see **ring**

**run'-in** disagreement

**run-of-the-mill** *a* average

**runt** unusually small or weak animal or person

**run'way** (paved) strip of ground where planes take off and land

**rup'ture** (cause) a breaking apart or bursting; (cause o.s. to have) a hernia

**ru'ral** of the country or country life

**ruse** trick

**rush** *v* (cause to) move with speed, haste or violence; (of water, *etc*) pass or come quickly and with force; *n* sudden (violent) movement; sudden demand for sth; (hollow stem of) grass-like herb growing in wet places. **-y**; *pl* first prints made after shooting scene in motion picture

**rust** *n* reddish coating forming on iron, when exposed to (moist) air; (of) reddish-brown color; plant disease; *v* (cause to) form such coating; lose proper condition through disuse, *etc*. **-y**

**rus'tic** rural; made of rough timber, as furniture

**rus'tle** (cause to) make slight sound, as of dry leaves blown together by wind; *US* steal (cattle)

**rut** track in ground, *esp.* one made by wagon; regular and dull pattern (of life)

**ruth'less** pitiless

**rye** (rī) (grain of) a cereal grass; whiskey made from its seed

# S

**s** nineteenth letter of English alphabet

**sa·ber**, *UK* **-bre** sword with curved blade

**sa·ble** (valuable fur of) small northern animal; (of) very dark or black color

**sab·o·tage** (-tahzh) damage done to machinery, *etc* on purpose, as by strikers, enemy agents. **-teur**

**sac** baglike membrane in animals and plants

**sac·cha·rin** very sweet substance, used instead of sugar **sac·cha·rine** (excessively) sweet

**sack** large bag of heavy woven material. **-ing;** amount contained in a. s.; *esp. UK infml* **give s.o./get the s.** dismissal from job

**sac·ra·ment** solemn religious ceremony

**sa·cred** set apart in honor of, *esp.* of God; holy; for religious purposes. **-ness**

**sac·ri·fice** offering to a god; giving up sth valuable for more important; loss due to selling at low prices

**sac·ri·lege** disrespect of sth sacred. **sacrile·gious**

**sad** feeling or causing sorrow. **-den, -ness**

**sad·dle** leather seat for rider of horse, bicycle, *etc*; sth resembling this in shape

**sa·dism** (sexual) pleasure gained by causing pain or suffering. **-dist, sadis·tic**

**safe** *a* protected or free from danger, hurt, risk, *etc*; cautious in avoiding risks, *etc*. **-ty;** reliable; *n* steel box for storing money, valuables, *etc*

**safe·guard** (be or employ) sth which protects or defends from danger, *etc*

**sag** hang or bend downwards from weight or pressure; (of prices, demand *etc*) go down

**sa·ga** family, *etc* story covering long period

**sa·ga·cious** of keen judgment; wise. **-ty**

**sage** *a* wise. **-ness;** *n* wise person; herb with grayish-green leaves, used in cooking

**said** see **say**

**sail** *n* piece of canvas, *etc* stretched on mast(s) of boat to catch wind and cause boat to move; anything like s. in shape or function, as blade of windmill; *v* (cause to) travel on water by means of sails or engine power; glide through air

**sail·board** flat board with sail attached, used in windsurfing

**sail'boat**, UK **sail'ing boat** water vehicle moved by one or more sails, *esp.* as sport

**sail'or** person who works on ship, except officers; member of navy; person who sails

**saint** holy person

**sake: for my/his,** *etc* **sake** out of consideration for; **for the s. of** in the interest of; for some end or purpose

**sal'ad** cold dish of vegetables, meat, lettuce, *etc*, mixed with oil, lemon or vinegar, mayonnaise, *etc*

**sal'a·man·der** animal like lizard but with soft skin instead of scales

**sal'a·ry** fixed monthly sum paid by company, *etc* to employees. **-ried**

**sale** act of selling; **sales'|-man,** *f* **-woman;** selling of goods at reduced prices to clear stock; also *pl* amount sold

**sal'i·ent** standing out; most noticeable or important

**sa'line** of or containing salt; salty. **salin'ity**

**sa·li'va** fluid discharged by glands in mouth; spit

**sal'low** pale; sickly yellow in color. **-ness**

**sal'ly** lively or witty remark

**salm'on** (samen) sea fish, much valued as food, with orange-pink flesh; (of) this color

**sal'on** fashionable shop, *esp.*

one offering a service: *beauty s.*

**salt** (sawlt) *n* (white) crystalline substance, obtained by mining or by evaporating seawater, used to season and preserve food, *etc*. **-y;** *pl* (mixture of) mineral substances used as laxative, *etc*; compound for acid(s) with all or part of its hydrogen replaced by a metal; *v* add s. to food; preserve food with s.

**salt'cel·lar** small container for salt used at table

**salt'wa·ter** of or living in the sea

**sa·lu'bri·ous** healthful; pleasantly invigorating

**sal'u·tar·y** good for the health; bringing advantages in the future

**sa·lute'** greet with sign of respect. **saluta'tion**

**sal'vage** saving of wreckage, goods, *etc* of ship, property, *etc* (for payment)

**sal·va'tion** saving or rescue, *esp.* of a soul

**salve** (sav) *n* soothing ointment; *v* soothe

**sal'vo** shooting off of several guns at once; burst of cheers or shouts

**Sa·mar'i·tan, good S.** helpful and generous person

**same** being no other: *he is the s. person I saw yesterday;* alike, not different: *they are* *very much of the s. sort, the s. price*

**sam'ple** part of sth larger serving to show quality, nature, *etc*, of the whole; example

**san·a·to'ri·um** hospital, *esp.* for special diseases, as tuberculosis; health resort

**sanc'ti·fy** make sacred

**sanc'ti·mo·ny** outward pretense of holiness. **sanc'timo'nious**

**sanc'tion** formal approval of those in authority; penalty for breaking law, *etc; pl* (economic) action taken to force nation to comply with agreement, *etc*

**sanc'ti·ty** holiness; sacredness

**sanc'tu·a·ry** sacred place; place of shelter and protection

**sand** *n* tiny grains resulting from wearing down of rock by action of water and air, found on seashore, bottom of rivers, *etc; pl* area covered with s. **-y;** *v* polish or clean by rubbing with s.

**san'dal** light shoe consisting of sole held to foot by straps

**san'dal·wood** (Asian tree with) scented hardwood

**sand'pa·per** (rub with) rough paper covered with sand, *etc*

**sand'wich** *n* two slices of bread, *etc* with meat or other filling between them; *v* insert sth between two other things

**san|e** sound in mind. **-ity**

**sang** see **sing**

**san'guine** (sanggwin) cheerful; hopeful

**san'i·tar·y** of health or hygiene; clean; of or used in treating human waste

**san'i·ty** soundness of mind

**sank** see **sink**

**sap** *n* juice circulating in plants; *v* drain s. from tree, *etc*; exhaust strength, *etc* gradually

**sa'pi·ent** wise. **-ence**

**sap'ling** young tree

**sap'phire** (safir) (precious stone of) rich blue color

**sar'casm** keen or bitter words of (mocking) criticism. **sarcas'tic**

**sar·coph'a·gus** stone coffin

**sar·dine'** (-dēn) small young fish like herring, cured and canned in oil for food

**sar·don'ic** showing scorn and mockery

**sash** sliding wooden or metal frame into which glass of window, *etc* is set; long band of silk, *etc* worn round waist or across shoulder

**sat** see **sit**

**satch'el** small (leather) bag, *esp.* one for carrying books or tools

**sat'el·lite** heavenly body moving around larger one, *esp.* a planet; equipment in

339

**scab**

space to relay television, *etc* between continents

**sa'ti·ate** satisfy to or beyond fullness. **sati'ety**

**sat'in** glossy silk

**sat'ire** literary work making fun of human weaknesses or vices; biting wit used in this way. **-rize** (*UK* **-rise**), satir'ical

**sat'is·fy** meet or fulfill desires, expectations, demands, *etc*; supply what is needed; pay (debt); convince: *s. him of my innocence.* **satisfac'tory, satisfac'tion**

**sat'u·rate** soak or fill completely or to overflowing

**Sat'ur·day** sixth day of the week, between Friday and Sunday

**sat'yr** Greek god of the forest, half goat, half man; strongly sexed man

**sauce** liquid mixture of eggs, stock, seasoning, *etc*, served with food; *US* stewed (mashed) fruit, as apple s.

**sau'cer** small shallow plate for placing cup on

**sau'cy** impertinent

**sauer'kraut** (sourkrout) shredded pickled cabbage

**sau'na** (period spent in) room filled with steam

**saun'ter** walk in casual or leisurely way

**sau'sage** (sosij) minced seasoned meat stuffed into long tube of thin animal skin

**sau·té'** (-téed or -téd) fry quickly in hot fat

**sav'age** wild; untamed; cruel. **-ry**

**sa·vant'** learned person

**save** *v* come to aid of person or thing in danger, so as to protect from harm, *etc*; set apart for future use or emergency; avoid loss or consumption of: *the new motor saves gasoline, this will s. a lot of time*

**sav'ings** money saved (in bank)

**sav'ior**, *UK* **-iour** one who saves from danger; S. Jesus Christ

**sa'vor**, *UK* **-vour** *n* characteristic taste; *v* enjoy (taste of); **s. of** have flavor or quality of

**sa'vor·y**, *UK* **-vour-** pleasing to the taste

**saw** *n* tool having sharp toothed blade, for cutting wood, *etc*; *v* see **see**

**sax'o·phone** *mus* wind instrument consisting of brass tube, keys and clarinet reed

**say** *v* (**said**) utter (in words): *s. sth, s. what you mean*; repeat, as lesson; assume: *put it in, s., five days*; **that is to s.** in other words; *n* right or authority to decide

**scab** crust forming over sore while it is healing; form of infectious itching, mangy skin disease, *esp.* in animals. **-by**

**scab'bard** sheath for a sword

**scaf'fold** raised platform used in constructing, repairing, *etc* buildings; *esp. hist* platform for execution of criminals

**scald** burn with hot liquid or steam; heat (milk) almost to boiling point

**scal|e** *n* one of thin, hard plates covering lizards, fish, *etc*; any thin piece of similar form peeling from surface. **-iness, -y;** series of progressive steps or degrees in system for measuring or determining sth, as marks on thermometer; ratio between model of an object and actual object, as on a map; given size, degree, extent, *etc*: *he lives on a grand s.*; series of musical notes following each other at fixed intervals, *usu* 8 notes starting at given keynote: *C major*; *pl* instrument for weighing; *v* remove scales from; climb up or over sth (as if) by ladder

**scal'lop** *n* shellfish with two fluted shells having wavy rim; *esp. pl* series of curves as decorative edge; *v* cut in such a series

**scalp** (skin over) top of head

**scal'pel** surgeon's small straight knife

**scam'per** run in quick (playful) manner

**scan** examine closely; look at quickly, *usu* to find sth specific, as item in list, *etc*; read verse with emphasis on rhythm

**scan'dal** (action, *etc* that stirs up) general feeling of anger or malicious gossip. **-ous**

**scan'dal·ize**, *UK* **-ise** shock moral feelings of

**scan'ner** instrument used for scanning, as human body, *etc*

**scant** barely enough. **-y**

**scape'goat** one who is given blame for others

**scar** (cause to leave) mark after wound, *etc*, has healed

**scar|ce** not plentiful; rare. **-city**

**scare** make or become suddenly afraid; **s. up** *US infml* get, as money

**scarf** (*pl* **-s, scarves**) piece of silk, wool, *etc*, worn around neck, on head or over shoulders

**scar'let** (of) deep bright red

**scath'ing** harsh; bitter

**scat'ter** throw (things) or drive (persons, animals) in various directions

**scav'en·ger** (**-jer**) person who hunts for unwanted objects; animal that eats dead rotting flesh, *etc*

**sce·na'ri·o** detailed plot of film, *etc*; possible future course

**scene** (sēn) place where sth

occurs, *esp.* on the stage; view, as of landscape; outbreak of strong feeling or quarrel, *esp.* in public; division of play or film set in one place

**sce·ne·ry** (sē-) landscape or view. **-nic**; painted hangings, structures, *etc*, used on stage

**scent** (sent) *n* characteristic smell, *esp.* if agreeable; *UK* perfume; way of discovery or track; *v* smell; suspect; fill with odor

**scep·tic see skeptic**

**sched·ule** (sked-, *UK* shed-) printed list; timetable; plan of work

**scheme** (skēm) *n* systematic plan; plot; diagram; *v* make secret or dishonest plan

**schism** (sizm) split, *esp.* in a church group. **schismat·ic**

**schiz·o·phre·ni·a** (sk-) mental disorder with splitting of personality, *etc*. **schiz·oid**

**schol·ar** (sk-) learned person. **-ly**

**schol·ar·ship** learning; money allowance given to help student

**scho·las·tic** of schools or scholars; of scholasticism

**scho·las·ti·cism** leading Christian philosophy of Middle Ages

**school** (skūl) place where children are taught; (building of) department at univer-sity; followers of philosopher, system of thought, *etc*; large number of fish, *etc*, moving and feeding as a group

**sci·ence** (sī-) systematic knowledge of physical world; a branch of this knowledge, as physics; **s. fiction** story, *etc* set in imaginary landscape of the future

**sci·en·tif·ic** of science; done with great exactness; assisted by expert knowledge

**sci·en·tist** person engaged in science, as chemistry, biology, *etc*

**scin·til·late** (sin-) (seem to) give off sparks; sparkle

**sci·on** (sī-) offshoot of plant; (royal) descendant

**scis·sors** (siserz) *pl* two blades joined at middle and working so that edges cross each other, thereby cutting material between them

**scoff** show contempt by mocking words, *etc*

**scold** (skōld) criticize harshly

**scoop** *n* (amount contained in) small shorthandled shovel for taking up flour, coal, *etc*; *v* take up or hollow out (as if with s.; report (important) event before other newspapers, *etc*

**scoot·er** light vehicle with two small wheels and enclosed motor; child's toy vehicle

**scope** area or opportunity for action; extent covered by eye, subject, *etc*

**scorch** burn surface with great heat or flame

**score** *n* number of points won in game, *etc*; notch or mark; copy of musical composition giving all vocal and instrumental parts; set of twenty, as of years; *pl* a great number, *etc*; *v* win points in game, *etc*; record points won; achieve, as success; cut or mark; arrange music for

**scorn** (show) contempt. **-ful**

**scor·pi·on** tropical insect with long poisonous tail

**scot-free'** unhurt; unpunished

**scour** clean by rubbing with rough substance; search (area) swiftly or thoroughly

**scourge** (skurj) source of great suffering

**scout** look for s.o. or sth; examine (area) to gain information

**scowl** (make) angry frown

**scrab'ble** scratch or grope about for

**scrag'gy** lean and bony

**scram'ble** make one's way over rough ground by using one's hands and feet; struggle with others to get as much as possible of sth; cook eggs by mixing yolks and whites in pan; mix electric signals to form code;

throw things together in disorderly heap

**scrap** *n* small piece, as sth torn off or left over; pieces of old metal for remelting; *infml* fight; *pl* leftover bits of food; *v* throw away

**scrap|e** remove outer layer or sth sticking to surface by passing over object with sharp or rough instrument. **-er;** break skin by rubbing it on hard or rough surface; rub gratingly against sth else; get (money, *etc*) together with difficulty

**scratch** mark (surface, skin, *etc*) with sth sharp or rough, as with fingernail; dig or tear (as if) with claws or nails; rub (itching place on skin) with fingernails; remove (name) from list of competitors; draw across surface with grating noise, as pen; **from s.** from the beginning or from nothing; **come up to s.** reach required standard

**scrawl** write in hurried or scribbling way

**scraw'ny** thin and bony

**scream** give off loud sharp cry, as from pain or fear; laugh without restraint; utter words in loud violent voice

**screech** harsh shrill sound

**screen** *n* frame covered with cloth, netting, *etc*, serving as partition, to keep out insects, *etc*; sieve for grain, gravel, *etc*; anything that shelters, hides or protects: *a s. of secrecy*; surface onto which motion pictures are projected; glass display surface of television, computer, *etc*; *v* protect; sort out (by test, *etc*); show, as film

**screen'play** script of motion picture

**screw** narrow piece of metal with slotted head and spiral ridge leading towards pointed lower end, for fastening or attaching things; sth of spiral shape; device for propelling ship

**screw'driv·er** tool for turning screws

**scrib'ble** write carelessly or hastily; make meaningless marks with pencil, *etc*

**scrimp** skimp

**scrip** certificate entitling holder to stock, *etc*

**script** handwriting; imitation of handwriting in type; typewritten manuscript of play, *etc*

**scrip'ture** Bible; sacred book. **scrip'tural**

**script'writ·er** person who writes scripts, *esp.* for television, *etc*

**scroll** *n* roll of paper with writing on it; ornamental design resembling roll; *v* roll computer data across screen

**scrub** *v* clean by rubbing hard

with brush, cloth, *etc*; *n* low trees or bushes

**scruff** back of the neck

**scru'ple** doubt as to whether action is right or wrong. **-pulous**

**scru'ti·ny** close examination. **-nize** (*UK* **-nise**)

**scuff** walk with dragging feet; scrape (off) with feet

**scuf'fle** (engage in) disorderly struggle

**sculp'ture** art of making statues by carving, molding, *etc*; work produced in this way. **-tor**

**scum** dirty film that forms on surface of water; worst part (of society)

**scur'ri·lous** grossly abusive; using gross, coarse language. **scurril'ity**

**scur'ry** run hurriedly

**scur'vy** *n* disease due to lack of vitamin C; *a* low: mean

**scut'tle** *n* deep container for coal; *v* run hurriedly; sink (one's own) ship

**scythe** (sī-) tool for cutting grain or grass

**sea** (any of the parts of) body of salt water covering greater part of earth's surface; large heavy waves; large mass

**sea'board** (region along) coast of sea

**sea'food** (shell)fish from sea which can be eaten

**seal** *n* (fur of) sea mammal of

northern regions, feeding on fish; design or symbol impressed on piece of wax, or cut into stamp, *etc*, attached to or printed on document to show authenticity, finality, *etc*, or fixed to envelope, door, *etc*, so as to prevent unauthorized opening: substance used to make tight connection; *v* close or mark with s.; close envelope, *etc*, by means of gummy substance; close cans, *etc* by device which must be broken when opened

**sea' lev·el** average level of sea, used to measure heights on land

**seam** line where two edges, *esp.* of cloth, meet; thin layer of coal, *etc*

**seam'stress** woman who earns a living by sewing

**seam'y** showing seams; least pleasant; sordid

**sé'ance** meeting (*esp.* for spiritualistic purposes)

**sea'plane** airplane equipped with pontoons for landing on water

**sea'port** harbor town

**sear** burn, *esp.* on surface

**search** (surch) look or go through carefully in order to find sth; **s. warrant** document entitling police to s. premises for stolen goods, drugs, *etc*

**sea'sick·ness** nausea caused

by rolling of ship

**sea'son** (sēzn) *n* one of the four periods into which year is divided. **-al;** period of year marked by particular weather, events, *etc*, or one during which natural products are at their best or obtainable: *holiday s., asparagus s.* **-able;** *v* improve flavor of (food) by adding spices, salt, *etc*. **-ing;** make fit for use by special treatment, as wood

**seat** *n* place for sitting; part of chair, *etc* on which one sits; (part of garment covering) part of body on which one sits; place where government, firm, *etc*, resides permanently; *v* (cause to) sit down; afford sitting space. **-ing;** fix in particular place or place on supports; **s. belt** strap to hold person firmly in seat of car, plane, *etc*

**se-cede'** withdraw formally (from political group, *etc*). **-cession**

**se-clude'** stay or keep apart; withdraw into solitude. **-sion**

**sec'ond** (seknd) *a* next after first in time, space, degree, *etc*; another: *a s. cup of tea*; *n* sixtieth part of minute or time or degree of angle; one who aids or supports another; *v* support

**sec'ond·ar·y** next after primary in order, importance,

*etc*; depending on or derived from; of less importance

**sec'ond·hand'** having been used or owned previously; not obtained directly from source, as information, *etc*

**se'cre|t** (sē-) *a* done, kept, designed, *etc*, so as not to be noticed, known or understood by others; hidden; private. **-cy;** *n* sth hidden, concealed or not easily understood: *the s. of his behavior*

**sec're·tar·y** person who takes care of correspondence, records, *etc*. **secretar'iat;** head of government department; **S. of State** *US* foreign minister

**se·crete'** (of gland or plant organ) produce (liquid) substance; hide

**se'cre·tive** tending to keep things secret. **-ness**

**sect** group with (religious) belief other than that of majority. **secta'rian**

**sec'tion** part cut off; one of parts into which sth is divided

**sec'tor** part enclosed by two radii of a circle; area of business, *etc* activity: *finance s.*

**sec'u·lar** of worldly things; not religious. **-ism, -ize** (*UK* **-ise)**

**se·cure'** *a* safe; certain; *v* get hold of; make safe or certain; fasten

**se·cur'i·ty** safety; thing that

makes safe; thing given as pledge; *pl* stocks and bonds

**se|date'** *v* calm s.o. by using drugs. **-dation;** *a* calm; not lively. **-dateness**

**sed'a·tive** (drug) tending to soothe (pain, *etc*) or make sleepy

**sed'en·ta·ry** involving much sitting and little exercise

**sed'i·ment** matter which settles to bottom of a liquid

**se·di'|tion** action or language urging rebellion against government. **-tious**

**se·duce|'** lead astray from proper course, duty, *etc*; persuade s.o. to have sex with one; tempt. **-tion, -tive**

**see** (saw, seen) take in (appearance, outline, color, *etc*, of something) by means of the eyes; look at; understand: *I s. your point;* find out: *s. whether anything can be done;* make sure: *s. to it that he comes on time;* meet and talk to: *I saw him today;* accompany: *s. him to the door; n* area of power of (arch)bishop

**seed** part of plant, as grain of wheat, that has power of reproduction; beginning or cause of anything; *the s. of love;* offspring; fluid produced by reproductive organs of male; go to s. (of plant) produce s.; lose vigor, usefulness, *etc*

**seek** (**sought**) search; try to find or obtain; try to do: *s. to do the right thing*

**seem** create impression of; appear: *I s. to be lost, he seems to be working, his words s. to be true*

**seem'ing** pretended; apparent on surface but not real

**seem'ly** fitting; decent

**seep** ooze out; trickle

**se'er** one who has visions of future

**see'saw** *n* board balanced in middle so as to move up and down when children sit at opposite ends; *v* move up and down or back and forth

**seethe** bubble; boil; be angry or excited

**seg'ment** one of parts into which sth is or can be divided or cut

**seg're·gate** separate or set apart from the rest, *esp.* racial group. **segrega'tion**

**seis'mo·graph** instrument registering earthquakes

**seize** lay hold of suddenly or forcibly; take possession of by legal authority

**sei'zure** act of seizing; sudden attack, as of disease

**sel'dom** not often

**se·lect'** choose carefully; pick out **-tion. -tive**

**self** (*pl* **selves**) person or thing as an individual: *to your own s. be true*; one's nature: *one's better s.*

**self-as·sur|ed'** having (great) confidence in oneself. **-ance**

**self-cen'tered** selfish; concerned only with o.s.

**self-con'fi·dence** (strong) belief in one's own ability. **-dent**

**self-con'scious** overly aware of being observed, talked about, *etc*, by others

**self-con·tained'** not communicative; complete in itself

**self-con·trol'** ability to restrain one's emotions, *etc*

**self-de·fense'**, *UK* **-fence** act of defending one's person, *etc* against attack; *law* plea justifying use of force against another person

**self'-de·ter·mi·na'tion** right of nation to decide on its own form of government

**self-ev'i·dent** clear without having to be proved

**self-ex·plan'a·to·ry** needing no further explanation

**self-in'ter·est** regard for one's own advantage

**self'ish** only interested in or caring for o.s. **-ness**

**self'less** thinking only of others

**self-made'** having been successful in life through one's own efforts

**self-pi'ty** feeling (too) sorry for o.s.

**self-pos·ses|sed'** cool; in control of one's feelings. **-sion**

**send**

**self-pres·er·va'tion** (instinct for) protecting o.s. from harm or danger

**self-re·spect'** proper regard for one's own dignity or value

**self-right'eous** convinced of one's own moral quality or standards. **-ness**

**self'same** exactly the same

**self-sat'is·fied** too pleased with o.s.

**self-ser'vice** (having) system of serving o.s. and paying *usu* upon leaving (shop, *etc*)

**self-suf·fi'cient** able to supply one's own needs

**self-willed'** insisting stubbornly on one's own will

**sell** (**sold**) turn or make over (goods, property, *etc*) to another for money or other payment; deal in (given kind of goods); give up for money, as honor; betray: *s. one's country to the enemy*; (of goods) (cause to) find buyers. **-er**

**se·man'tics** study of meaning of words and signs

**sem'a·phore** code for signalling by person holding flag in each hand

**sem'blance** likeness; outward appearance

**se'men** (sē-) fluid containing male sperm

**se·mes'ter** *esp. US* one of two (18-week) terms of academic year

**sem·i·an'nu·al** occurring every half year

**sem'i·cir·cle** (shaped like) half of a circle

**sem'i·co·lon** punctuation mark (;) indicating separation between parts of sentence, having stronger value than comma

**sem·i·con·duc'tor** substance, as silicon, intermediate between insulator and conductor, which allows flow of electric current

**sem·i·de·tached'** (house) sharing one wall with another house

**sem·i·fi'nal** round, game, *etc*, immediately before final one. **-ist**

**sem'i·nal** (sem-) of, producing or containing semen or seed; original and influential: *a s. study*

**sem'i·nar** group (of advanced students)

**sem'i·nar·y** school training priests or ministers

**sem·i·pre'cious** (of gems) lower in value than precious stones

**sen'ate** upper branch of legislative body in some countries; governing body in university. **-tor**

**send** (**sent**) cause or order to go, be transported, conveyed, *etc*: *s. him to London, s. me a dozen eggs, s. a letter.* **-er**

**se'nile** (sē-) (showing the feebleness) of or caused by old age. **senil'ity**

**sen'ior** (person) higher in rank or older in age or standing. **senior'ity**

**sen·sa'tion** perception through the senses; physical or mental feeling; (cause of) state of excitement or interest. **-al**

**sen|se** (sens) *n* each of the special faculties by which physical objects or phenomena are perceived, *usu* sight, hearing, smell, taste and touch. **-sory;** ability to feel, understand, be aware, *etc*, of presence or nature of things: *s. of his nearness, s. of humor;* faculty of the mind for judging or appreciating things: *s. of one's duty;* ability to think or act reasonably; meaning of word, sentence, *etc; pl* sound mental faculties; *v* perceive; be or become (vaguely) aware of

**sense'less** foolish or meaningless; unconscious: *to be knocked s.*

**sen·si·bil'i·ty** capacity to feel; openness to emotional impressions

**sen'si·ble** having good sense; (keenly) aware of

**sen'si·|tive** very open to, or easily affected by, outward things. **-tize** (*UK* **-tise**),

**sensitiv'ity**

**sen'sor** device used to detect heat, light, *etc*

**sen'su·al** of physical sensation; inclined to gratify the senses, *esp.* sexually. **-ist, sensual'ity**

**sen'su·ous** pleasing to the senses; affecting the senses

**sen'tence** words arranged in specific grammatical order so as to form complete unit, statement, question, *etc;* (decision given by law court *esp.* one determining) punishment for convicted criminal

**sen·ten'tious** given to the use of maxims; fond of pompous moralizing. **-ness**

**sen'tient** (-shent) having power of perception or feeling

**sen'ti·ment** refined or tender emotion; thought influenced by feeling; opinion; meaning to be conveyed

**sen·ti·men'tal** influenced by feeling rather than reason; weakly emotional. **sentimental'ity**

**sen'ti·nel, sen'try** soldier stationed to keep guard

**sep'a·rate** *v* (-rāt) put, keep or live apart; go different ways; divide into parts; withdraw from; *a* (-ret) set apart from; individual; dissimilar. **separa'tion**

**Sep·tem'ber** ninth month of year

**sep'ul·cher,** UK **-chre** (-ker) burial place

**se'quel** (-kwel) what follows after or results; continuation of story *etc*

**se'quence** order in which things follow or happen; series without gaps; scene in film. **sequen'tial**

**se·ques'tered** set apart; secluded

**se'quin** (sē-) small shiny ornament sewn on clothing

**ser·e·nade'** piece of music played at night and outdoors, as by lover; piece of music for small group of instruments

**se·rene'** calm; clear. **-ity**

**serf** *hist* one whose services were attached to land and sold with it. **-dom**

**serge** durable twilled material

**ser'geant** (sahrjent) a military rank; police officer above common policeman

**se'ri·al** of or happening in a series. **-ize** (UK **-ise**)

**se'ries** number of things arranged or happening in order; set, as of coins, *etc*; television program, *etc* with several episodes

**se'ri·ous** grave or solemn; earnest; important; not easily solved, as problem, *etc*. **-ness**

**ser'mon** speech on religious or moral questions (*esp.* one delivered in church)

**ser'pen|t** (large) snake. **-tine**

**ser'rate, ser'ra·ted** having teeth like a saw

**se'rum** liquid made from blood containing immune bodies, used to fight disease; thin clear liquid part of blood, milk, *etc*

**serv'ant** person employed to do household work; person in the service of another

**serve** carry out duties of servant; distribute food, or wait, at table; offer food in given manner: *s. fish with tomato sauce*; help, as customer; go through period of military service, imprisonment, *etc*; carry out duties of an office: *s. as Secretary of State*; be of use (for given purpose); begin game of tennis, *etc* by striking ball; supply (person) continuously with something; treat in given manner: *s. him faithfully*; be suitable punishment: *serves him right*; make legal delivery of (court summons, *etc*); be enough for: *this recipe serves four*

**serv'ice** sth done for another or others, whether out of helpfulness or in supplying goods, activities, *etc*; system supplying the public with water, *etc*; employment as a servant, or in government, *etc*, office; also *pl* the armed forces of a country; (form prescribed for) public religious worship; set of dishes, etc: *tea/silver s.*; act of serving, as in tennis *etc*

**serv'ice·a·ble** useful; wearing well, as cloth

**serv'ile** of or like slaves; slavish. **servil'ity**

**serv'i·tude** slavery; forced labor

**ses'sion** (period of) meeting of court, legislature, *etc*; period devoted to some activity

**set** *v* (**set**) put in particular place, condition, *etc*: *s. the pot on the stove, s. one's affairs in order*; fix (value of sth) at certain amount; fix or appoint: *s. the date for the wedding*; assign, as task; fix in frame or mounting, as sails or gem; cause to sit; lay, as trap; put into proper state for use: *s. the clock*; put in or pass into fixed or settled state: *s. one's jaw, the jelly has s.*; (cause to) take particular direction or course: *s. the course of the ship*; fix for others to follow: *s. the fashion*; arrange wet hair; arrange printing type; put words to music; sink below horizon, as sun; **s. aside** save for future use; disregard; **s. down** put down (in writing); **s. in** begin; **s. off** start; cause to explode; make (colors, *etc*) appear stronger by contrast; **s. out** start (journey, *etc*); present; **s. to** begin (work); **s. up** start business; establish; put in position; *infml* cause innocent person to appear guilty; *n* number of things normally used or classed together; radio, *etc*, receiver; one round of match in tennis; scenery, *etc* used in theater or motion picture; persons of similar social type

**set'back** sth that checks progress

**set'ter** long-haired hunting dog

**set'tle** fix or agree upon (conditions, *etc*) definitely; pay bill, debt, *etc*; (cause to) take up residence, *esp.* in new country; (cause to) come to rest, permanent position, *etc*; (of dregs, sand *etc*) sink to bottom; terminate legal proceedings, argument, *etc*, by agreement. **-ment**

**sev'en** a number (7), one more than six

**sev'en·teen'** a number (17), one more than sixteen. **-teenth**

**sev'enth** next after sixth; being one of seven equal parts

**sev'en·ty** a number (70), seven times ten. **-tieth**

**sev'er** divide; cut or break off

**sev'er·al** more than two or three, but not many; separate, different: *on s. occasions, there are s. ways of doing this*

**se·ver|e**[1] harsh; strict; grave; difficult; without ornament. **-ity**

**sew (sewed, sewed** or **sewn)** (sō) fasten cloth, *etc*, together by passing thread through holes made with needle

**sew'age** waste matter carried in sewers

**sew'er** (syū-) large pipe for carrying off sewage

**sex** quality of being either male or female; males or females collectively; sexual intercourse; activity, *etc* connected with this. **-ual**

**sex'|is·m** treating members of one (*esp.* female) sex as if inferior, less intelligent, *etc*. **-ist**

**sex'tant** instrument for measuring angles between stars, used to plot course of ship, plane

**shab'by** showing long wear or use, as clothes; badly dressed; contemptible

**shack** small rough hut

**shack'le** device for fastening arms or legs together to prevent movement; sth that hinders

**shade** relative darkness caused by interception of (sun)light; area sheltered from sun; degree of bright-

ness, as in color; slight difference in degree: *his work is a s. better*; thing used for protection against light or heat: *lamp s.*

**shad'ow** shade, *esp.* dark figure cast on ground by body blocking rays of light; *pl* darkness setting in after sunset; dark area (sheltered from light, publicity, *etc*); person or thing, as dog, following another closely; ghost; trace: *without a s. of doubt*

**shad'y** of, in or producing shade; *infml* obscure and probably dishonest

**shaft** pole of spear, *etc*; ray of light, long stem; handle of tool; vertical passage, as in mine

**shag'gy** with rough and tangled hair or wool

**shake (shook, shak'en)** move quickly or violently up and down or to and fro, *esp.* so as to mix, free from adhering matter, *etc*; (cause to) tremble, as with cold; become unsteady; **s. hands** clasp hands in greeting

**shall (should)** auxiliary verb sometimes used in first person (*sing* and *pl*) to show future time: *I s. come tommorow*; in first person (*sing* and *pl*) to show question or offer: *s. I take care of it?*; used formally to show order, promise, law: *he s. be imprisoned for six months*

**shal'low** not deep; superficial. **-ness**

**sham** not genuine; pretended

**sham'ble** walk awkwardly

**sham'bles** (scene of) great disorder; mess

**shame** unpleasant feeling aroused by being or becoming aware of one's own or another's guilt, improper conduct, *etc*; (person or thing causing) disgrace or regret. **-ful, -less**

**shame'faced** ashamed; showing shame

**sham-poo'** (wash with) soaplike substance for cleaning hair, carpet *etc*

**sham'rock** three-leaved clover, used as national symbol of Ireland

**shank** part of tool between head and handle

**shan'ty** roughly-built hut

**shan'ty-town** (section of) town built of shanties where the poor live

**shape** *n* outline or outer surface of anything; phantom; form: *an idea took s. in his mind*; proper arrangement or order: *put everything into s.*; *v* give (definite or desired) form to; direct (events, policy, *etc*)

**shape'ly** well-formed

**share** part belonging to, given to or done by individual,

*esp.* one of a group; portion of ownership in stock company, *etc*

**shark** ferocious sea fish with sharp teeth; *infml* dishonest person who swindles money from others

**sharp** having cutting edge or fine point, as knife or needle. **-ener;** (of turn in road, *etc*) changing direction suddenly; (of sound) shrill; (of taste, odor *etc*) biting; (of pain) *etc*) violent or piercing; marked or clearly outlined, as contrast; quick to understand, see, *etc*; (of actions, speech *etc*) harsh or violent; (dishonestly) shrewd; higher than proper musical tone; punctually: *ten o'clock sharp*. **-en**

**shat'ter** break into pieces

**shave** remove hair from skin with razor; scrape away surface with sharp knife, *etc*; *infml* pass closely without or just barely touching: *the car just shaved the fence*

**shawl** piece of cloth worn around shoulders or over head by women

**she** (**her**) female person or animal already mentioned in talking, writing, *etc*; also applied to ship, country, moon, *etc*

**sheaf** (*pl* **sheaves**) bundle, *esp.* of stalks of grain tied together

**shear** v (**sheared, sheared** or **shorn**) cut with scissors, *etc*; cut off hair, wool, *etc*; strip; break off, as bolt *etc*; n pl large scissors; cutting tool

**sheath** close-fitting cover, *esp.* for blade, *etc*

**sheathe** put into a sheath; protect with covering layer

**shed** v (**shed**) (cause to) flow; give forth; let fall off, as leaves, hair, *etc*; n simple building used *esp.* for storing things

**sheen** brightness; luster

**sheep** (pl **sheep**) cud-chewing animal, bred for meat and wool

**sheep'ish** bashful. **-ness**

**sheer** unmixed; absolute; very steep; transparently thin

**sheet** large piece of linen, *etc*, spread on mattress and beneath blanket; broad thin layer, as of glass; square or oblong piece of paper; large mass, as of flame

**sheikh, sheik** (shēk, shāk) chief of Arab tribe, **-dom**

**shelf** (pl **shelves**) board of wood, *etc*, fixed horizontally to wall, inside closet, *etc* for storing dishes, books, *etc*; sth like a s., as sandbank under water

**shell** n hard outer covering of nuts, eggs, peas, *etc*; concave outer covering of oysters, lobsters, *etc*; case containing explosives, fired from cannon, rifle, *etc*; outward appearance: *he hid his feelings beneath a hard s.*; v remove from s.; bombard

**shel-lac'** kind of varnish

**shell'fish** water animal with shell, as lobster, used as food

**shel'ter** (provide) place of protection or safety

**shelve** place on shelf; put aside for later consideration; slope gradually

**shep'herd** (sheperd') (lead or guide like) person who watches over grazing sheep

**sher'iff** public officer responsible for enforcing law, *etc* in county

**shied** see **shy** v

**shield** piece of protective armor; protector

**shift** v move from one position to another; manage to get along; change gears of car while driving; n shifting; (work period of) group of workmen working in turn with others; simple loosely fitting dress

**shift'y** tricky; evasive

**shil'ling** UK former coin worth 12 pence or one twentieth of pound sterling

**shim'mer** gleam faintly; shine with wavering light

**shin** bony front part of leg between knee and ankle

**shine** (**shone**) give off or glow with light; be brilliant or extraordinary in some area; **(shined)** polish, as shoes

**shin'gle** thin board, *etc* to cover roof or walls of building; small signboard

**shin'gles** nervous disease causing painful blisters on skin

**ship** *n* large boat for ocean transportation; *v* transport (goods) by s., train, plane, *etc*. **-ment**

**ship'shape** in good order

**shirk** get out of or try to avoid (duty, work, *etc*)

**shirt** man's garment for upper part of body, with sleeves and collar; man's undergarment for upper part of body

**shiv'er** shake, as from cold or fear

**shoal** shallow place in sea; great number of fish swimming together

**shock** *n* sth that suddenly and deeply disturbs emotions or mind; acute bodily reaction to injury, bad news, *etc*; violent blow or impact, as one caused by colliding cars; tremor of earthquake, explosion, *etc*; effect on nerves when electric current passes through body; thick mass, as of hair; *v* cause violent terror, surprise, disgust, *etc*

**shod** see **shoe** *v*

**shod'dy** of inferior quality

**shoe** (shū) covering of leather, *etc* for foot, with stiff leather or rubber sole and supporting heel; metal plate nailed to under side of hoof of horse, *etc*; device for braking motion of wheel by friction; *v* **(shod)** fit with shoes

**shone** see **shine**

**shook** see **shake**

**shoot (shot)** discharge (bullets, arrows, *etc*) with force; (cause to) send out, as from gun; hit, kill or wound with bullet, *etc*; move swiftly; take picture with camera; *n* new branch or stem of plant; occasion for shooting, *esp*. animals

**shop** *UK* store. **-per-. -window. -keeper**; place where goods are manufactured, repairs carried out, *etc*; one's profession or trade, *esp*. as topic of conversation: *talk s.*

**shop'lift** steal goods from store. **-er**

**shore** land along sea, *etc*

**shorn** see **shear** *v*

**short** *a* having little extent in time, length or height; (of person) not tall; (of supplies, *etc*) not plentiful; scarce; failing to reach mark, goal, standard, *etc*; harsh, as speech; (of pastry, *etc*) containing much fat; **s. for** being an abbreviated form: *sub is s. for submarine*; *adv* suddenly: *he brought the horse*

**show**

up s.; not go quite as far as:
stop s. of murder; n pl loose
trousers stopping at
mid-thigh; **s. circuit** escaping
of current due to faulty
wire or circuit

**short'age** amount lacking;
scarcity

**short'com·ing** failure or defect

**short'en** make or become
shorter

**short'en·ing** fat used for
making pastry, etc

**short'hand** method of writing at great speed, using simple strokes, dots, etc, in place
of letters

**short'hand'ed** not having the
necessary number of workers

**short'sight'ed** unable to see
far; not looking far ahead in
making plans

**short'-tem'pered** getting angry easily

**shot** n act of shooting a rifle,
etc; attempt to hit mark, etc,
with bullet discharged from
firearm; one of number of
small balls of lead used in
shooting game; projectile
discharged from firearm;
person who shoots: he is a
very bad s.; attempt: have a s.
at it; injection of drug; short
drink of liquor; act of taking
a photograph; v see **shoot**; a
hit by bullet, etc; (of fabric)
woven so as to show many

colors

**should** past tense of **shall**
used to express duty, etc: you
s. go home; to qualify statement: I s. not think so; to
express uncertainty, etc: if he
s. come

**shoul'der** (shōl-) n part at top
of trunk of human or animal
body to which arm, wing or
foreleg is attached; anything
similar to this in shape or
position, as s. of garment;
US unpaved strip at side of
road: v push roughly with or
as with s.; carry on s.; take
on as burden: s. the responsibility

**shout** (give) loud strong call
(of joy, anger, etc)

**shove** (shuv) (give) rough or
forceful push

**shov'el** (shuvl) (use) tool
consisting of broad blade at
end of handle, for taking up
sand, coals, snow etc

**show** (shō) v (**showed,
shown** or **showed**) cause to
or let be seen; direct to: s.
him to the house; make clear,
explain or prove: s. him what
to do, s. his words to be false;
demonstrate (feeling) by
one's behavior: s. pity for
them; **s. off** overly display
one's abilities, etc; **s. up** appear; cause (another's faults,
etc) to be seen; n public exhibition; performance of play,
etc, on the stage

**show'case** glass container for displaying objects in museum, store, etc

**show'down** infml forced revelation of (another's) actual power, etc; final test

**show'er** (shou-) (pour down as) fall of rain, snow, etc lasting only for a short time; fall of sparks, etc; (use) bathing equipment consisting of upright pipe and perforated plate through which water flows from above

**show'y** striking; (too) colorful

**shrank** see shrink

**shrap'nel** pieces of metal scattered on explosion of bomb, etc

**shred** n (often pl) thin torn strip; smallest bit; v tear into thin strips. **-der**

**shrew** scolding woman. **-ish**

**shrewd** (shrōōd) smart in practical matters

**shriek** (make) loud sharp cry

**shrill** high-pitched and piercing in sound

**shrimp** long-tailed salt-water shellfish, valued for its meat

**shrine** case for sacred relics; place dedicated to (worship of) saint

**shrink** (shrank or shrunk, shrunk or shrunk'en) become smaller due to heat, moisture, etc, as cloth. **-age**; draw back, as in fear or disgust

**shriv'el** draw together into wrinkles; dry up; wither

**shroud** sheet in which dead person is wrapped; sth which covers or conceals

**shrub** woody plant smaller than tree. **-bery**

**shrug** raise shoulders in expression of doubt, indifference, contempt, etc

**shrunk('en)** see shrink

**shud'der** (feel) brief trembling, as from fear, cold etc

**shuf'fle** mix cards, etc; drag feet while walking; keep shifting one's position

**shun** keep away from (place, person, etc); take pains to avoid

**shunt** drive (train) to side track; move or turn aside

**shut** (shut) move (door, lid, etc) so as to stop an opening; let lids fall over eyes; keep from entering or leaving: s. him up in jail, s. out the wind; fold together, as umbrella; (of business, etc) (cause to) stop working; **s. down** (cause to) stop operating, esp. for longer period; **s. off** stop machine, etc by pressing button, etc; separate; **s. up** lock all windows, doors etc, of a house; infml stop talking

**shut'ter** (close using) movable cover for window, camera lens, etc

**shut'tle** n (vehicle for) usu

short trip back and forth on fixed route; spacecraft used more than once; part of loom moving quickly and carrying thread; *v* move quickly to and fro

**shy** *a* uneasy in company or easily embarrassed; (of animals) timid or easily startled; *v* draw back or start suddenly aside, as from fear, shock, *etc*

**Si·a·mese twins** twins joined together from birth at some part of their bodies

**sick** being affected by disease or illness; having uneasy upsetting feeling, *esp.* in the stomach. **-en, -ness**

**sick'le** short-handled tool with curved blade for cutting long grass, *etc*

**side** one of (flat) surfaces surrounding any solid object which is not round, *esp.* as distinguished from front, back, bottom and top; either surface of sheet of paper, cloth, *etc*; slope of hill; line bounding geometrical figure; (space next to) either half of human or animal body; part or direction considered as lying either right or left from or before or behind (assumed) line of division or center: *houses on either s. of the street;* one aspect: *hear his s. of the argument;* (members of) one of

two groups of opponents; line of descent: *relatives on my mother's side*

**side'board** table, *etc* at side of dining room for holding dishes, *etc*

**side'line** business, product, *etc* in addition to main one; also *pl* (space outside) line marking boundary at side of playing field

**side'step** step to side to avoid sth, as collision, blow, *etc;* avoid unwelcome question, *etc* by evasion

**side'walk** *US* walk for foot passengers at side of road

**side'ways** s, to from or at one side; with one side to the front: *stand s.*

**sid'ing** short side track along railway line

**siege** surrounding and cutting off of city by army to make it surrender

**si·er·ra** long irregular mountain chain

**si·es·ta** midday nap, *esp.* in hot countries

**sieve** (siv) (pass sth through) device for separating finer from coarser particles, *usu* having a bottom of wire mesh

**sift** put (sth dry, as flour) through sieve. **-er;** examine closely and critically (to separate sth out)

**sigh** (si) (take) deep audible breath, *esp.* as sign of weariness, sorrow, relief, *etc*

**sight** n act or power of seeing; sth seen or worth seeing, as landscape, or, pl, monuments, etc, of city; range within which person can see or object be seen: he is out of my s.; device on gun for finding exact direction of aim; **at|on s.** as soon as seen: shoot on s., pay the draft at s.; **by s.** recognition without knowing personally: she knew him by s.; v begin to see, esp. by coming near; observe star, etc, with optical instrument; aim (gun) by means of s.

**sight'ing** case of seeing sth or s.o.

**sign** n mark written, traced on surface, etc used to represent word, message, etc; movement of hand, head, etc, expressing order, wish, etc; public notice giving direction, warning, etc; sth which indicates presence or suggests future existence of a thing: signs of a storm coming up, a s. of love; v write one's name under letter, deed, etc, esp. so as to show validity or truthfulness of contents; employ by securing signature of: s. up an actor; speak with the deaf using special hand signals; **s. off** (in radio, etc) announce end of program or broadcasting time

**sig'nal** n (agreed-upon) sign meant to start action, give warning or message, esp. at a distance; direct occasion for some general action; electronic waves carrying sound, image, etc; v give s.; a unusual; noteworthy

**sig'na·to·ry** (of) party that has signed an agreement

**sig'na·ture** (-cher) one's name written by o.s.

**sig'net** official seal (in ring)

**sig·nif'i·cant** having a (special) meaning; important. **-cance**

**sig'ni·fy** be a sign of; mean; make known; be important. **significa'tion**

**si'lence** (sī-) n absence of (all) sound or noise; failure or refusal to make sth known; state of not speaking, writing, etc. **-lent;** v stop (another) from speaking by force or argument

**sil·hou·ette'** (silooet) (cause to appear as) dark outline, shape, shadow seen against light background

**sil'i·con** non-metallic element used in making computer chips, etc

**silk** (fabric made from) fine strong shining thread spun by larva of silkworm in making cocoon or nest. **-en, -y**

**sill** shelf of wood or stone at foot of door or, esp., window

**singular**

**sil'|ly** lacking sense or intelligence; foolish. **-liness**

**si'lo** (sī-) structure for storing green fodder, *etc*

**silt** soil, *etc* deposited by muddy water

**sil'ver** *n* valuable soft white metal, used to make coins, jewelry, tableware, *etc*; *a* made of or coated with s.; of the color of s.; denoting 25th anniversary: *s. wedding*. **-y**

**sim'i·an** (of or like) an ape or monkey

**sim'i·lar** like; resembling. **similar'ity**

**sim'i·le** (-lē) figure of speech comparing similar aspects of two otherwise unlike things

**sim'mer** boil gently; be on point of boiling

**sim'per** smile in silly artificial way

**sim'|ple** easy to understand or do, use, *etc*; consisting of only one element, part, *etc*; not ornamented, complicated, *etc*; not highly developed: *s. forms of animal life*; natural and unassuming in manner, appearance, *etc*; lacking learning or experience; common or ordinary; being exactly as stated: *it is simply folly to do this*. **-plify, simplic'ity**

**sim'ple·ton** foolish person

**sim'u·la|te** pretend to be, have or feel; act like; imitate given situation for training

purposes. **-tor**

**si·mul·ta'ne·ous** (sī-, si-) happening at the same time as. **simultane'ity**

**sin** (be guilty of) conduct which violates moral principles. **-ful, -fulness**

**since** *prep* between given time in past and now: *s. last week, s. Easter; conj* between given time in past and present: *many things have happened s. he left;* from then on (until now): *ever s. he came;* because: *he had to do it s. he had promised it; adv* before now: *this took place a long time s.*

**sin·cere'** honest; free from deceit; genuine. **-ity**

**sin'ew** tough tissue joining muscle to bone; strength. **-y**

**sing (sang, sung)** utter words or sounds by modulating the voice so that musical tones result; give forth melodious sound(s); praise in verse. **-er**

**singe** (-j) burn surface of; burn off hair

**sin'gle** *a* only one; separate; meant for or done by one person only; alone; unmarried; undivided; sincere: *s. devotion:; v* **s. out** choose

**sin'gle-mind'ed** having one purpose. **-ness**

**sin'gu·lar** of a single person or thing; unusual; strange; surprising. **singular'ity**

**sin·is·ter** wicked; evil-looking

**sink** v (**sank** or **sunk, sunk** or esp. a **sunk'en**) fall or come down to lower level or to bottom; (cause to) disappear beneath surface, as of water; go down below horizon; droop, as from weakness; pass into (sleep, etc); (of sound) become lower; decrease in number, value, etc; enter into: s. the knife into his body; become hollow, as cheeks; (of health) fail; lose confidence or hope; put (foundations, post, etc) into ground; make hole, shaft, etc in ground; n basin, esp. in kitchen, used for washing (dishes, etc)

**sin'u·ous** winding; with many curves. **sinuos'ity**

**si'nus** hollow, esp. in skull

**sip** drink little by little

**si'phon** (use) bent tube for drawing off liquids by means of air pressure

**sir** respectful form of address to man; **S.** title used before first name of knight or baronet or at beginning of letter

**sire** male parent

**si'ren** device giving loud warning sound

**sis'ter** daughter of same parents as person speaking or referred to; member of female religious community or organization

**sis'ter-in-law** sister of one's husband or wife; wife of one's brother

**sit** (**sat**) take or be in position in which lower part of trunk rests on ground, chair, etc thereby supporting rest of body; (of birds or animals) perch or rest on ground; rest or be situated (on base); act as model for artist, etc; meet officially, as court; (of birds) hatch eggs

**site** place where house, etc stood, stands or is to stand; location

**sit'-in** protest in which public place is occupied

**sit'u·at·ed** being at a certain place or in certain circumstances

**sit·u·a'tion** place occupied by sth; position or circumstances in which one finds o.s.; employment

**six** a number (6), five plus one

**six-'teen'** a number (16), one more than fifteen. **-teenth**

**sixth** next after fifth; being one of six equal parts

**six''ty** a number (60), six times ten. **-tieth**

**siz'a·ble,** UK **size-** rather large

**size** n (whole of) breadth, length, width, height or extent of anything; bigness; one of series of measures for garments; manufactured goods, etc; v **s. up** make estimate of (person, situation, *etc*)

**siz'zle** make sputtering sound as of frying fat

**skate** (move on) a steel blade attached to sole of shoe, used for, gliding over ice; (move on) a roller s.

**skein** (skān) thread or yarn wound in coil

**skel'e·ton** framework of the bones of body; supporting framework of building, *etc*; very thin person; outlines. **-tal**

**skep'tic**, *UK* **scep-** person who has doubting attitude; one who doubts truth of religion, *etc* **-cal, -cism**

**sketch** (make) simple or hasty outline with few details. **-y**; short play or essay

**skew'er** (fasten with) metal or wooden pin for holding meat while cooking

**ski** (skē) (move on) a slender plastic, *etc* board attached to special boot or shoe, used for gliding over snow

**skid** *n* act of skidding; plank or the like, *esp*. one of pair, on which sth may be rolled along; device preventing wheel from turning; runner under seaplane; *etc*; *v* (of wheel) slide along without turning

**skiff** small light boat

**skill** expertness; ability due to practice. **-ed, -ful**

**skil'let** pan with long handle, *esp*. for frying

**skim** remove surface layer from (liquid); pass over lightly; look over swiftly

**skimp** supply (food, *etc*) very stingily; be stingy

**skin** (remove) soft flexible outer covering of human or animal body; an animal skin as leather, *etc*; any outer covering, as of fruit; surface layer, as on liquid

**skin'graft** surgery to replace damaged with healthy s.

**skin'ny** (of body) very thin or lean

**skip** jump or lean lightly, *esp*. from one foot to the other; pass quickly from one subject, point *etc* to another, omitting what comes in between

**skir'mish** (conduct) unplanned fight or argument

**skirt** *n* woman's outer garment falling freely from waist; lower part of dress, coat, *etc*; also *pl* part of equipment as edge or guard; *v* go along or past edge of; avoid

**skulk** lie in hiding for evil reason; avoid duty; sneak

**skull** bony frame of head enclosing brain

**skunk** (skungk) small bushy-tailed N. Amer. mammal, black with white stripe.

which ejects repulsive smelling fluid when attacked

**sky** (*pl* **skies**) the region high above the earth, appearing to extend like a great dome from all points of the horizon

**sky'light** window in roof or ceiling

**sky'line** outline of buildings, mountains, *etc* seen against the sky

**sky'scrap·er** very tall building

**slab** broad flat piece of stone, *etc*; thick slice

**slack** (of rope, *etc*) loose; negligent; sluggish. **-en**

**slacks** *pl* loose trousers

**slag** waste matter from melting ore, *etc*

**slain** see **slay**

**slam** shut with loud noise: *s. the door*; push or throw down with force: *s. on the brakes*

**slan'der** (make) false and malicious statement or report about person. **-ous**

**slang** very colloquial, often impolite language, not used in formal speech or writing. **-y**

**slant** *v* be or place at an angle; report (news) so as to favor certain opinion, *etc*; *n* line, surface, *etc* diverging from horizontal or vertical plane; point of view; opinion or bias

**slap** strike with open hand or flat object; place sth carelessly or roughly

**slap'dash** hasty; careless

**slap'stick** low comedy with rough action

**slash** cut with sweeping motion or by great amount; whip

**slat** thin narrow board, *etc*

**slate** kind of fine-grained bluish-gray rock that splits easily into thin smooth plates, used to cover roofs or for writing on; *US* list of candidates offered for nomination

**slaugh'ter** (slawter) killing of animals for food; brutal killing, *esp.* of large numbers of persons

**slaugh'ter·house** place where animals are killed and prepared as meat

**slave** *n* person who is the property or completely in the control of another. **-ry;** *v* work hard, as if driven

**slay** (**slew, slain**) kill by violence

**slea'zy** cheap; disreputable

**sled** vehicle on runners, for travelling or transporting loads over snow

**sledge** heavy hammer

**sleek** smooth; shiny

**sleep** (**slept**) rest with closed eyes in a state where all conscious functions of the body and mind are stopped. **-less, -y**

**sleep'er** one who sleeps (in the stated way); railroad car with beds

**sleet** half frozen rain

**sleeve** part of garment that covers the arm; tube enclosing machine part; *UK* record cover

**sleigh** (slā) sled

**sleight of hand** (skill in) juggling tricks, magic *etc*

**slen'der** thin; slight; small

**slice** (cut) broad flat piece of sth (using knife)

**slick** smooth; sly; clever

**slide** *v* (**slid**) (cause to) glide over surface; pass along smoothly; pass gradually into given state, *etc*; **let things s.** let things take their own (negative) course; slip (sth) in or into; *n* act of sliding; smooth surface on which things or persons can s. down; small piece of framed film for projecting on screen; plate of glass, used to hold thin layer of tissue, *etc* for examination under microscope

**slight** (slīt) *a* small (in degree); frail; *v* neglect openly; *n* insult

**slim** slender; not thick

**slime** slippery thin-bodied matter, as watery secretion on wall, or mud, *etc*, *esp.* if offensive or disgusting

**sling** *v* (**slung**) throw with twirling motion; cause to

hang loosely: *s. a sack over one's shoulder*; *n* bandage hanging from shoulder to support injured arm; band, *etc* for lifting or supporting sth heavy; looped strap on rifle, *etc* for carrying it over shoulder; device for hurling stone, *etc*

**slink** (**slunk**) sneak; go secretly

**slip** *v* (cause to) pass or glide smoothly or quickly into, through, *etc*: *s. a letter over the threshold*; slide suddenly, as when losing one's footing; move or fall from position, one's grasp, *etc*: *the glass slipped from his fingers*; pass quickly, as time, or as thought from one's mind; make mistake due to carelessness; *n* act of slipping, mistake; woman's undergarment; small sheet of paper

**slip'per** light comfortable shoe, *usu* worn indoors

**slip'per·y** causing one to slip, as wet or icy ground; (of objects) hard to hold owing to smoothness, sliminess, *etc*

**slip'shod** careless; untidy

**slit** (slit) *v* cut open or apart, *esp.* by making long cut with knife; *n* long narrow opening

**slith'er** slide over surface, as snake does

**sliv'er** splinter; sharp piece of glass, *etc*

**slob'ber** let saliva run from mouth; be excessively sentimental

**slo'gan** phrase or cry used by party, group, *etc*; advertising phrase

**slop** *v* cause liquid to overflow; *n* (unappetizing) liquid food; *pl* kitchen refuse, fed to pigs

**slope** (of surface, *etc*) extend upward or downward at a slant

**slop'py** wet and muddy; untidy, as dress; careless, as speech; maudlin

**slot** long narrow groove or opening, for guiding or admitting sth, as coin

**sloth** laziness. **-ful;** slow-moving tree-dwelling mammal of S. and Cent. Amer.

**slouch** droop; sit, stand or walk with careless drooping posture

**slov'en·ly** untidy and careless in dress, *etc*. **-liness**

**slow** *a* not moving, acting, *etc* quickly; not thinking, understanding, *etc* quickly; (of, fire, heat *etc*) not burning or heating strongly; (of clock) not running at proper speed; *v* (cause to) move less quickly

**sludge** mud; sewage; mud-like deposit, as dirty oil in engine

**slug** kind of snail without shell; *esp. US infml* bullet

**slug'gish** moving slowly or with little energy. **-ness**

**sluice** device for changing level of water; drain

**slum** also *pl* poor, rundown, over-populated section of city

**slum'ber** sleep

**slump** fall suddenly and heavily; fall in price, *etc*

**slung** see **sling**

**slunk** see **slink**

**slur** speak unclearly; pass lightly over; insult

**slush** partly melted snow; silly sentimental writing

**slut** dirty or immoral woman

**sly** cunning; done in secret; mischievous. **-ness**

**smack** *v* strike, *esp.* with open hand; open and close mouth noisily, *esp.* as sign of enjoying one's food; loud kiss; hard blow; (slight) taste or suggestion of sth

**small** of (comparatively) little size, degree, value, *etc*; not big; slight; young: *s. child*; (of business, *etc*) carried on on a limited scale; not liberal or generous: *a s. mind*; early: *s. hours of the morning*

**small'pox** very contagious, formerly often fatal, disease marked by fever and pustules, *usu* leaving scars

**smart** *a* stylish; quick; *esp. US* clever; *v* cause or feel stinging pain

**smash** (cause to) break into pieces with loud noise; crash into; defeat or ruin utterly

**smat·ter·ing** slight superficial knowledge of subject

**smear** (smēr) rub oil, paint, dirt, *etc* over surface; make dirty; harm another's reputation by unfounded rumor

**smell** *n* the specific quality of a thing that is perceived by the nose; sense by which this quality is perceived; (bad) odor; *v* (**smelled** or **smelt**) have or use sense of s.; become aware of a s.; have (unpleasant) s.; suspect (presence of dishonesty, error, *etc*)

**smelt** melt ore to separate out metal

**smile** turn up ends of the mouth to express approval, amusement, affection, *etc* or scorn

**smirk** smile in affected or offensive way

**smite** (**smote**, **smit'ten**) strike with disease, misfortune, love, *etc*

**smock** loose overgarment

**smog** (*smoke + fog*) dark heavy air, *esp.* in cities, caused by fumes from industry and autos

**smoke** *n* visible vapor, mostly gray, blackish or brown, given off by burning substance, as coal, wood, *etc*; *v* give off s.; draw in and expel s. of cigarette, pipe *etc*; cure meat, *etc*, by exposing to s.; **s. out** drive out (insects, *etc*) from hiding by means of s.

**smooth** (smūdh) (of surfaces, objects, *etc*) even, free from roughness or irregularities, soft to the touch; free from lumps or grains, as sauce, honey, *etc*; (of road *etc*) having no holes, *etc*; (too) pleasant or polite: *s. manners*

**smol·der**, *UK* **smoul-** smoke or burn slowly without flame; (of feelings) exist without being shown outwardly

**smote** see smite

**smoth'er** kill by stopping breath of; kill fire with ashes; cover entirely; heap presents, *etc* on

**smudge** (make) dirty mark or smear; dense smoke to repel insects

**smug** self-satisfied (without cause)

**smug'gle** take goods into or out of country illegally

**snack** (eat) light meal

**snag** (catch on) rough projecting point or part, as stump of tree; obstacle; tear made by snagging

**snail** slow-moving, plant-eating animal with soft slimy body and hard shell

**snak|e** *n* slender limbless reptile with scaly skin, which may have poisonous bite;

move in twisting, winding manner. **-y**

**snap** *v* make sudden sharp sound, as of whip, teeth brought together, lock engaging, *etc*; break with sharp sound, as brittle twig; move with quick pecise motions of body; *s. to attention; infml* take photograph; utter (words, criticism, *etc*) quickly and sharply. **-pish**; seize or take up (sth) quickly; bite at suddenly; rub thumb and middle finger sharply together; *a* operating on spring catch; made or done suddenly or carelessly: *a s.* order

**snap'shot** photograph

**snare** trap for animals; lure; difficulties, *etc* in which one is caught

**snarl** *n* tangle, as of hair or traffic; *v* mix in confused mass; (of animals) growl angrily; express anger in ill-tempered words

**snatch** *v* seize sth suddenly or eagerly; grab; *n* act of snatching; *usu pl* brief period or bit or fragment of sth

**sneak** go in secretive or stealthy manner

**sneak'er** rubber-soled shoe, *usu* with canvas top, for sports

**sneer** smile in manner showing scorn; write or speak in manner expressing scorn

**sneeze** (snēz) expel breath

suddenly and involuntarily through nose and mouth, due to irritation of nostrils

**snick'er, UK snig'ger** (give) half-suppressed disrespectful laugh

**snide** mean; sneering

**sniff** draw in air through nose audibly, in order to smell; clear nose, *etc*; express scorn

**snif'fle** sniff repeatedly to keep nose from running

**snip** cut with scissors, *etc, esp.* by quick small strokes

**snipe** shoot at from hiding (at long range); make nasty remarks

**sniv'el** weep with sniffing sobs; sniffle

**snob** one who admires social rank, wealth, *etc* and dislikes people of lower social standing; one overproud of his superior knowledge or taste. **-bery, -bish**

**snoop** pry into others' affairs, *etc*. **-er, -y**

**snore** (breathe with) hoarse rattling sound while sleeping

**snor'kel** device for supplying fresh air to submarine or diver

**snort** force breath through nose with loud sound (to express anger, *etc*)

**snout** nose and jaws of animal; sth resembling this

**snow** (snō) (fall as) frozen water vapor in the form of white flakes. **-y**; snowfall; *sl* cocaine

**snow'ball** *n* ball rolled from snow; *v* grow rapidly; multiply

**snow'bound** cut off by heavy snow

**snow'fall** a fall of snow; amount of snow that falls in given period

**snub** treat with contempt

**snuff** *v* (*esp.* of animal) breathe in; put out (candle); *n* powdered tobacco

**snug** comfortable; close-fitting

**so** *adv* in the manner described, indicated, *etc*, or to given extent, degree, *etc*: *he can do it s., do not talk s. fast*; very: *you look s. pretty*; likewise: *he is coming, and s. am I*; indeed, certainly: *he found her very clever, and s. she is*; therefore: *the lecture was well planned and s. a success*; **or s.** about: *half a dozen or s.*; *conj* with result that: *I was sick, so I stayed home*; **s. as to** having the purpose of: *I came early s. as to catch the train*; **s. that** with the result that; in order that

**soak** (cause to) lie in water or other liquid so as to become wet through and through;; (of liquid) enter through pores or holes; become thoroughly wet, as from rain; **s. up** draw up liquid, as with sponge

**soap** (rub with) substance used for washing or cleaning, *usu* made by treating fat with alkali. **-y**

**soar** fly upward to great height; glide along (without flapping wings)

**sob** weep with convulsive gasps of breath

**so'ber** not drunk; quiet in manner; serious; free from excess; (of color) not bright. **sobri'ety**

**so'cia·ble** liking company; friendly, not formal

**so'cial** of the life and relations of people living in groups of society; of rank in society; living together in groups; outgoing; of private activity with friends; friendly

**so'cial·is·m** theory or practice of public ownership of means of production and distribution. **-ist**

**so·ci'e·ty** the people in terms of customs and organization of civilized nation; any social community; association based on common aim, interest, *etc*; the upper classes; company of others

**so·ci·ol'o·gy** scientific study of nature of human society or of social problems. **-gist**

**sock** short stocking reaching above the ankle; *infml* hard blow

**sock'et** hollow space for sth to fit into, as eye, electric plug, *etc*

**sod** upper layer of earth with grass and roots

**so'da** one of sodium compounds, used in baking, washing, *etc*; bubbling water, often mixed with fruit syrup, ice cream, *etc*

**so'do·|my** variant sexual intercourse, *esp.* between men or with animals. **-mite**

**so'fa** long upholstered seat with back and raised ends

**soft** yielding easily to pressure or touch; not hard; easily cut, changed in shape, *etc*; (of metal) of relatively low hardness, as lead; (of sound) low and pleasant; agreeable or comfortable; (of light and color) not glaring or harsh; (of climate, *etc*) gentle and mild; having compassion or gentleness; not strong or capable of great efforts; weak-willed; (of drug *etc*) less harmful; (of drinks) without alcohol; (of water) low in mineral salts, thus allowing soap to lather easily. **-en**

**soft'cop·y** information stored in computer memory or shown on screen, but not printed out

**soft'ware** program(s) containing instructions without which computer cannot be operated

**soft'wood** wood of evergreens, such as pine, *etc*

**sog'gy** soaked

**soil** *n* upper part of earth's surface, consisting of sand, clay, *etc*. and of remains of organic matter and living organisms; *v* make dirty or stain

**so'journ** (-jurn) stay or live at place for a while

**sol'ace** (sol-) comfort in sorrow; relief in distress

**so'lar** of, from or using the sun

**sold** see **sell**

**sol'der** (sod*er*) (join using) soft metal applied in melted state to harder metals

**sol'dier** (sōljer) one who serves in an army

**sole** *a* being the only one(s); exclusive; *n* bottom surface of foot or shoe; any of various flatfish, valued as food

**sol'emn** (solem) serious; grave; done in formal manner. **solem'nity**

**sol'em·nize** perform ceremony (*esp.* of marriage)

**so·lic'it** ask for earnestly, as help, orders for a business, *etc*; (*esp.* of woman) sell sexual favors. **solicita'tion**

**so·lic'i·tor** one who solicits business; *US* officer in charge of legal business of town; *UK* lawyer who prepares cases for barrister

**so·lic'i·|tous** eager to help; concerned. **-tude**

**sol'id** having length, breadth and thickness; having the inside completely filled; relatively hard or firm; not liquid; without gaps; of one substance or color; dependable. **solid'ify, solid'ity**

**sol·i·dar'i·ty** fellowship or holding together of those having same interests

**so·lil'o·quy** (-kwi) talking to o. s. (on stage) without or regardless of hearers; speech so made. **-quize**

**sol'ip·sism** theory that only the self exists or can be known

**sol'i·taire** game played by one person alone; precious stone set by itself

**sol'i·tar·y** (living) alone; done alone; being the only one. **-tude**

**so'lo** music, dance, etc performed by one person. **-ist**

**sol'stice** point in summer (longest day) or winter (shortest day) when sun is furthest from equator

**sol'u·ble** able to be (dis-)solved. **solubil'ity**

**so·lu'tion** act of (dis)solving; explanation; mixture of substance(s) with liquid

**solve** clear up; find answer to (puzzle, etc)

**sol'ven|t** able to pay all debts; having the power to dissolve. **-cy**

**som'ber,** UK **-bre;** grave; dark

**some** (sum) indicating certain unspecified (number of) persons or things: *s. of my friends, s. apples were rotten;* (considerable but) unspecified number, amount, degree, etc: *doing this involved s. difficulties;* being so to fullest extent: *that was s. rainstorm*

**some'bod·y** certain but unspecified person

**some'day** at an unspecified time in the future

**some'how** in unspecified, unknown, etc, way

**some'one** somebody

**some'place** US somewhere

**som'er·sault,** also US **som'er·set** forward roll in which person turns heels over head

**some'thing** certain but unspecified thing

**some'time** adv at some indefinite time in the future or in the past; a former: *a s. champion*

**some'times** on some occasions

**some'what** to some degree, extent, etc

**some'where** in, to, or at unspecified, unknown, etc. place; about: *he is s. around middle age*

**som·nam'bu·lism** walking in one's sleep. **somnambulis'tic**

**son** (sun) one's own or another's male child

**so·na'ta** muscial piece for one or two instruments

**so'nar** device using sound waves to detect underwater objects

**song** act of singing; piece of music for the voice; poem; musical sounds made by some birds; **for a s.** for very low price

**son'ic** of sound waves; **s. boom** explosive noise of plane traveling faster than speed of sound

**son'-in-law** husband of one's daugther

**son'net** 14-line poem with fixed rhyme scheme

**so·no'r|ous** giving out deep loud sound. **-ity**

**soon** not long after given or present time: *he will be here s.*; readily: *I would just as s. go now as later*; early: *he came too s.*

**soot** fine-grained black substance falling from smoke of coal, *etc.* **-y**

**soothe** make calm; quiet; relieve pain

**soph'ism** false argument (which seems reasonable but is not). **sophis'tical**

**so·phis'ti·cat·ed** worldly-wise; no longer simple

**soph'o·more** *US* second year high-school or university student

**sop'ping** soaked: *s. wet*

**so·pra'no** (woman or child with) highest voice range

**sor'did** mean; morally low. **-ness**

**sore** painfully sensitive, as open wound, inflamed muscles, *etc*; suffering or causing mental pain or sorrow, hardship, *etc*

**so·ror'i·ty** women's religious society; *US* girls' club at college

**sor'row** (sorō) mental pain or suffering caused by loss of loved ones, bad fortune, *etc*. **-ful**

**sor'ry** feeling or expressing sorrow, regret, pity, *etc*; miserable or shoddy: *he came to a s. end*

**sort** *n* kind, class, group, *etc.* of things marked by similar or special features; quality or nature of sth or s. o.; more or less adequate example: *a s. of argument*; **of sorts** of mediocre or doubtful kind; **out of sorts** not in good health, temper, *etc*; *v* arrange or separate according to class or kind

**sot** habitual drunkard. **-tish**

**souf·flé'** (sūflā) light baked dish made with stiffly beaten egg-white, cheese or fruit, *etc*

**sought** (sawt) see **seek**

**soul** spirit(ual part of man); emotional part of man's nature; *US* (of) black culture; best example

**soul'ful** expressing deep feeling

**sound** *n* sensation produced within the ear by vibrations in air caused by speaking, striking hard objects, music, *etc*; any articulated utterance, musical tone, *etc*; effect produced by spoken or other statement: *this has a strange s.*; broad passage of water; *v* make or (cause to) give off s.; create specific impression, as sth said or written; measure depth of water, *etc*, by letting down weighted line; measure distance by means of radio waves; (try to) find out views, *etc*, of person; *a* in good, healthy, undamaged, *etc*, condition; financially stable; well-founded or reliable: *s. judgment*; deep, as sleep; thorough: *a s. beating*

**sound'ing** measurement of depth (of ocean, *etc*); sampling of opinion, *etc*

**sound'proof** (make) unable to be penetrated by sound

**sound'track** record of music, speech and noises on motion picture film

**soup** (sūp) liquid food made by boiling vegetables, meat, *etc*, with stock

**sour** having the taste or smell characteristic of lemon juice, unripe apples, *etc*; having undergone fermentation, as milk; unpleasant in temper

**source** (sōrs) place where sth

originates; cause; s. o. or sth giving information

**south** towards or lying at the left of person facing the setting sun. **-ern**

**South Pole** southernmost point of earth

**sou·ve·nir'** something kept in memory of place, *etc*

**sov'er·eign** *n* ruler; king; *a* having supreme power

**so'vi·et** local or national council or parliament in Soviet Union

**sow** *v* (**sowed, sown** *or* **sowed**) (sō) scatter seeds in soil for growth; (try to) introduce: *s. suspicion*

**sow** *n* (sou) female of pig

**spa|ce** *n* the unlimited expanse, considered as having length, height and breadth and extending in all directions, in which physical objects are contained; particular portion of this having certain length, breadth and/or width, *esp.* as occupied by an object; universe beyond the earth's air; distance existing between two or more objects; blank left between written or printed words; extent or interval of time; *v* set at (given) intervals. **-cious**

**space'craft** vehicle able to travel beyond the earth's atmosphere

**spade** tool with broad blade

at end of wooden handle, used for digging; black leaflike figure on playing card; card with this figure

**span** *v* stretch across (a distance, a river, *etc*); *n* extent from end to end; period of time

**span'gle** thin glittering ornament sewn on clothing

**spank** strike (*esp.* child) with open hand (on buttocks)

**span'ner** UK wrench

**spar** box; fence with words

**spare** *a* scanty; kept in reserve; free, as time; *n* sth not required for ordinary use; reserve; *v* do without; not kill, hurt, *etc*

**spark** *n* small burning particle; small visible electrical charge caused by interrupted discharge of current; very small amount; *v* produce spark(s); cause (sth unpleasant); *esp.* US stimulate (to greater activity)

**spar'kle** give off sparks, or gleams of light; be brilliantly witty or lively

**spark** plug device in motor engine which ignites explosive gases by means of electric spark

**spar'row** small brownish-gray bird

**sparse** thinly scattered

**~r'tan** simple; severe; with~ury

sudden tightening of

muscles; sudden brief spell of activity, *etc.* **spasmod'ic**

**spat** see **spit**

**spa'tial** of or existing in space

**spat'ter** scatter in small drops or particles; splash with drops or small particles

**spat'u·la** broad flat blade for spreading, pressing, *etc*

**spawn** *v* give birth to (in large numbers); *n* eggs of fish, frogs, *etc*

**spay** remove ovaries of female animal

**speak** (spoke, spo'ken) utter words, *esp.* in communicating thoughts, *etc*; talk; deliver lecture, *etc* on particular subject; plead for or make statement on behalf of person or thing; (be able to) use given language: *s. Latin.* **-er**

**spear** (pierce with) long-handled, sharp-pointed weapon

**spe'cial** (speshl) of particular kind, type, *etc*; not general: *a s. type of paper, this word has a s. meaning;* having particular function, use, *etc*; exceptional, out of the ordinary: *s. favor, of s. importance*

**spe'cial·ize**, UK **-ise** pursue some particular line of work, study, *etc.* **-ist**

**spe'cies** (spēshēz) class of animal, *etc*; sort; kind

**spe·cif'ic** clearly expressed, definite; of species

**spec'i·fy** state exactly or in detail; state as condition. **specifica'tion**

**spec'i·men** part or individual taken as sample of whole

**spe'cious** seeming to be good or right, but not so in fact. **-ness**

**speck** very small bit, spot or stain

**spec'ta·cle** public show; object of public attention.

**spectac'ular, specta'tor;** *pl* eye-glasses

**spec'ter,** *UK* **-tre** ghost

**spec'tral** ghostlike; of a spectrum

**spec'tro·scope** instrument for examining spectrum of any source of light

**spec'trum** colors of rainbow produced when light is passed through prism; wide range, as of opinion

**spec'u·late** think or talk about sth without all the facts; invest in business with high risk

**speech** (spēch) power or manner of speaking. **-less;** that which is spoken, *esp.* lecture, public address, etc; language of particular people or group

**speed** *v* (sped or **speed'ed**) go or move quickly; drive too fast; *n* rate at which sth moves ahead; quick progress, motion, etc. **-y**

**spell** *v* (spelled or spelt)

write or name letters (of alphabet, word, etc) in their proper order; form word. **-ing;** signify: *the new law spells great changes for many; n* (words supposed to possess) magic charm; turn or short period of work, etc, *esp.* as done in relieving another; (short) period: *s. of cold weather, s. of coughing*

**spell'bound** enchanted; fascinated

**spend** (spent) pay out money, as for purchase; use time, thought, labor, etc (for or on sth): *s. time in completing a task;* pass (time) in given manner: *s. the winter in Florida*

**spend'thrift** wasteful or extravagant person

**sperm** male reproductive cell; liquid containing this

**spew** (spyū) vomit

**spher|e** any round figure, as ball, globe; planet or star; field of activity, operation, etc. **-ical**

**spice** vegetable substance of distinctive taste, as nutmeg, used to flavor food

**spi'der** (spī-) eight-legged insect which spins web to trap other insect

**spig'ot** plug to stop hole in cask; *US* faucet

**spike** large nail; pointed piece of metal, as on fence or on bottom of shoe; *pl* shoes for running, *etc*; flowers, grains, *etc* arranged closely together on upright axis

**spill** (spilled or spilt) cause to or (accidentally) let liquid, grain, *etc* run or fall from container; shed blood; (cause to) fall from horse or vehicle; *infml* disclose (secret) information (accidentally)

**spin** (spun) make thread (from flax, cotton, *etc*) by drawing out and twisting; (cause to) turn around or move rapidly, as a wheel; tell (story); have dizzy feeling

**spin·ach** (-ich) vegetable with dark-green juicy leaves boiled as food

**spin·al** of the spine; **s. column** spine, backbone; **s. cord** thick cord of nerves contained in s. column

**spin·dle** rounded rod in spinning and other machines

**spin·dly** tall and thin

**spin·e** backbone; thorn. **-y;** back of book's cover

**spin'-off** by-product

**spin·ster** unmarried woman, *esp.* elderly one

**spi·ral** *a* coiled; winding constantly about center (while approaching or receding from it); *n* sth coiled or winding; s. curve or movement, *esp.* upwards; *v* move in winding course; fall or *esp.* rise progressively

**spire** tall tapering structure, as church tower

**spir'it** *n* soul; person's mental or moral nature; non-material being; ghost; *pl* state of mind; courage; attitude; central meaning (as opposed to wording); *usu pl* strong alcohol; *v* bring (away) quickly and secretly

**spir'it·ed** lively; brisk; courageous

**spir'it·u·al** *a* of the soul or spirit; of religious things; *n* (black) religious song

**spir'it·u·al·is·m** belief in communication with spirits of the dead. **-tic**

**spit** *v* (spat or spit) eject liquid or saliva from mouth; sputter; utter (words, oath, *etc*) sharply and angrily; (spit'ted) impale or fix on pointed rod; *n* saliva; pointed thin rod on which meat is roasted over open fire

**spite** (be moved by) desire to hurt or annoy s.o.; ill will. **-ful; in s. of** without regard to; in defiance of

**spit'tle** saliva

**splash** make wet or dirty by throwing water, mud, *etc*, about; (of liquid) fall upon in mass of drops; walk noisily (through water, mud, *etc*); (of light) fall upon in patches

**spleen** organ of body producing certain changes in blood; bad temper

**splen'did** brilliant; glorious; excellent. **-dor** (*UK* **-dour**)

**splice** join together, as two pieces of rope, film, *etc*

**splint** thin piece of wood, *etc*, *esp.* one used to hold broken bone in place while it heals

**splin'ter** ([cause to] split off like) sharp thin piece of wood, stone, *etc*, broken off from main body

**split** *v* (**split**) (cause to) come apart lengthwise or between layers; break or burst open or into parts; divide into (equal) parts; (of persons) become divided into disagreeing or hostile groups; **s. hairs** make a fuss about petty details; *n* act of splitting or state of being split; crack or division (in surface); feat of spreading legs at right angles to body, *esp.* until legs touch floor at all points

**split-lev'el** (house) having floors built on different levels

**spoil** *v* (**spoiled** or **spoilt**) hurt or damage sth so that it can no longer be used, enjoyed, *etc*; injuriously affect character, *esp.* of children, by exaggerated kindness and indulgence; decay, as food. **-age**; *n pl* goods taken in war or stolen; profits

**spoke** *n* one of bars extending from center to rim of wheel; rung of ladder

**spoke, spo'ken** *v* see **speak**

**spokes' per·son** (also **spokesman, -wom·an**) one who speaks for others, *esp.* in public

**spon|ge** (spunj) *n* sea animal with porous body which is dried and used for cleaning, washing, *etc*, because it absorbs water readily; rubber, *etc* substance like s. **-gy;** *v* wipe off, out, up (as if) with s.; live off others by begging

**spon'sor** (act as) one who makes himself responsible for another; firm, *etc* which pays for show, broadcast, *etc* advertising its products

**spon·ta'ne·ous** impulsive; done without external influence; natural. **spontane'ity**

**spool** (wind onto) reel for yarn, tape, film, *etc*

**spoon** utensil consisting of small bowl on handle, used to take up or stir liquids or other soft food

**spoon'ful** amount held by a spoon

**spo·rad'ic** happening irregularly at intervals

**spore** walled single cell, such as that given off by ferns, *etc*, that is capable of individual development

**sport** pastime, *esp.* game for exercising athletic faculties, as football, tennis, golf, racing, fishing, *etc.* **-sman/ -swoman, -smanship;** generous person; playful spirit

**spot** *n* (roundish) mark on surface, either occurring naturally or produced by painting on or weaving in dots of different color, or by foreign matter, as dirt, ink, *etc.* **-less;** (particular) place: *this is the s. where he died;* particular part of one's body or feelings: *sore s.; UK* small quantity, as of food; **on the s.** immediately; at (given) place; forced to react; *v* stain or mark with spots; determine location of (s. o. or sth); recognize or single out, as person in a crowd

**spot'light** (round area of light cast by) lamp with bright narrow beam; public attention

**spouse** husband or wife

**spout** pipe or opening from which liquid is poured forth; jet of liquid

**sprain** twist (ankle, wrist, *etc*), so as to tear or stretch ligaments

**sprang** see **spring**

**sprawl** lie (carelessly) outstretched

**spray** twig with flowers, leaves or berries; water or other liquid blown through air in fine drops; (can, *etc* of) liquid, as paint, deodorant,

*etc* to be forced out in s. flying through air

**spread** (spred) *v* (**spread**) (cause to) extend over surface or to full width, as by flattening, smearing, *etc*, or by stretching out, as cloth; extend or distribute over region, *etc: the sea s. out before him, he s. the costs over several years;* cover or coat with sth, as butter; *n* action or degree of spreading; extent; covering for bed, *etc*; soft food for spreading on bread, as peanut butter; large article or advertisement in newspaper, *etc*

**spree** lively frolic

**sprig** small twig

**spright'ly** (sprīt-) lively; gay

**spring** *v* (**sprang** or **sprung, sprung**) rise or move suddenly, *esp.* through the air; proceed, as from source; move back suddenly into original position by elastic force; open or close (mechanically), as trap; produce, put forward, appear *etc* suddenly: *s. a leak, s. a surprise;* (of boards, *etc*) become warped; *n* act of springing; elastic coil or spiral of metal which resumes its original shape after being bent, *etc*; also *pl* place where water, *etc* bubbles out of the earth; first season of the year

**sprin'kle** scatter in drops

**sprin'kler** device for watering garden, *etc* or for putting out fires in buildings

**sprint** (make) short run at top speed

**sprout** begin to grow; put forth buds; grow quickly

**spruce** *n* (wood of) evergreen tree; *a* neat in dress and appearance

**spry** active; lively

**spun** see **spin**

**spur** *n* sharp-pointed instrument on rider's boot to urge on horse; incentive; side extension of railroad, mountains, *etc*; *v* urge on; incite; stimulate

**spu'ri·ous** not genuine; fraudulent

**spurn** reject; scorn

**spurt** *v* gush or pour forth suddenly; *n* short period of strong effort

**sput'ter** spit out or throw off small particles; speak excitedly

**spu'tum** saliva mixed with mucus

**spy** (act as) one who secretly watches actions of others, seeks to find out (military, *etc*) secrets, *esp.* from enemy

**squab'ble** (engage in) noisy petty quarrel

**squad** small team of soldiers, police, *etc*

**squad'ron** army, navy or air force unit

**squal'id** dirty and disgusting; miserable. **-or**

**squall** sudden violent gust of wind (and rain or snow)

**squan'der** spend money, *etc* wastefully

**square** *n* surface with four equal sides and four right angles; anything resembling this; (buildings around) open area in town, *etc*; instrument shaped like L or T, for drawing or testing right angles; a number multiplied by itself: $2^2 = 4$; *v* form into s. or rectangular shape

**squash** (skwosh) *v* press into flat or pulpy mass; squeeze into small space; suppress, as rumor, *etc*; *n* crowd; racket game played with ball on closed court; soft drink of crushed fruit; (vine with) gourdlike fruit used as vegetable

**squat** (-o-) *v* crouch on one's heels; settle in unoccupied buildings, *etc* without permission. **-ter**; *a* short and thick

**squawk** (give) loud sharp cry, as of parrot

**squeak** (make) shrill high sound, as unoiled hinge

**squeal** (utter) shrill cry, as in pain or fear

**squeam'ish** easily shocked or nauseated

**squeeze** (skwēz) press together from opposite sides, *esp.* to extract juice, toothpaste, *etc*; shake person's hand or hug person tightly; make one's way through narrow passage; make space for or fit in, *esp.* with difficulty

**squelch** crush; suppress; make or move with sucking sound, as through mud

**squid** sea animal with ten arms attached to soft body

**squint** look with partly closed eyes, as protection against bright light

**squirm** twist; wriggle

**squir'rel** small bushy-tailed gnawing animal, *usu* living in trees

**squirt** (skwurt) discharge liquid in stream through narrow opening

**stab** wound with pointed weapon

**sta'|ble** *a* fixed; steady; permanent; firm. **-bilize** (*UK* **-bilise**), **stabil'ity**; *n* also *pl* building where horses are kept

**stack** *n* large pile; chimney; *pl* part of library where books are stored; *v* make pile; cause planes to circle airport at different levels while waiting to land

**staff** employees of a business or teaching organization; group of assistants to a manager; rod or stick as aid in walking, as flagpole, *etc*

**stag** adult male deer

**stage** (stāj) raised platform, *esp.* one on which actors perform in theater; step in process, or particular period in development; section of rocket with its own engine

**stag'ger** walk or stand unsteadily; cause feeling of disbelief; arrange in overlapping order

**stag'|nate** cease to develop, as business; cease to flow, as water; become foul from standing. **-nant**

**staid** settled; steady; sober

**stain** (cause) spot on surface produced by dirt, coloring matter, *etc*; (make) spot of different color, as on wood; dye used for this

**stair** (stār) *usu pl* (one of) series of steps leading from one level to another. **-case**

**stake** pointed stick or post for driving into ground, *esp. hist* one to which person was tied for burning; money, *etc* bet in contest or game; share (of business, *etc*)

**stale** lacking freshness

**stale'mate** position in chess where no move can be made; deadlock

**stalk** *v* pursue game stealthily; walk in slow or stately manner; *n* stem of plant

**stall** compartment, as in stable, on marketplace for sale of goods, (*UK*) in theater for spectators, *etc*; *v* stop motion or progress (of); cause engine to fail

**stal'lion** adult male horse

**stal'wart** brave; strong

**stam'i·na** strength; power to endure hardship

**stam'mer** speak haltingly, with pauses or involuntary repetition of syllables

**stamp** *v* bring foot down with force; trample on; suppress: *s. out resistance*; *etc*; *n* act of stamping; impress mark, seal, *etc*, (on) as sign of approval, evidence of payment, *etc*; block or rubber seal engraved with words, official symbol, *etc*; impression made by this; distinctive mark or characteristic quality: *s. of genius*; small adhesive piece of paper printed with special design and affixed to envelope, document, *etc*, as sign of charge paid

**stam·pede'** (cause) sudden flight (of frightened animals)

**stanch**, *UK* **staunch** stop flow (of blood)

**stand** *v* (**stood**) be in or assume position in which feet are on the ground and body is upright; be of specified height: *s. five feet*; come to or remain in stationary position; (of things) (cause to) be in upright position; be situated, *esp.* on supporting surface; adopt certain position or course with re-

gard to person, problem, *etc*; be in specified position, state, *etc*: *he stands convicted of theft*; continue to be valid; (of water) be stagnant; endure without being affected, *etc*, or without complaining; *infml* dislike: *I can't s. him*; undergo: *s. trial*; **s. a chance** have a chance; **s. by** (be prepared to) aid; adhere to agreement, *etc*; wait in state of readiness; **s. out** project or be noticed easily; **s. to reason** be in accordance with reason; *n* act of standing or place where one stands; stopping of movement; position taken in resisting or aiding s.o.; point of view; place where witness testifies in court; raised platform for spectators; framework on which sth is placed for support or display

**stand'ard** approved model, level or rule. **-ize** (*UK* **-ise**); degree of excellence required; thing serving as basis for comparison; average quality; flag; upright support

**stand'ing** position; rank; length of existence, membership, *etc*

**stand'off** (in games) a tie or draw; point at which opposing views are held so strongly that no agreement is possible

**stand'point** point of view

**stand'still** state of no movement; stop(page)

**stank** see **stink**

**stan'za** division of a poem

**sta‖ple** n loop of iron or wire for fastening purposes. **-pler;** product in constant demand, as sugar; main product of a district; a basic; principally used

**star** heavenly body appearing at night as glittering point of light; figure with five or six points representing s. (as mark of honor, etc); famous person, esp. actor or actress; usu pl planet, etc thought to determine one's fate; asterisk; v (of film, etc) have or appear as main actor; mark with s.

**starch** white food substance contained in plants such as corn and potatoes; powder made from this for thickening foods, stiffening laundry, etc. **-y**

**stare** gaze fixedly, esp. with eyes wide open; be (unpleasantly) noticeable

**stark** bare; severe; utter; downright; absolutely (naked)

**start** (cause to) begin moving, doing, etc; set out on journey, new course, etc; do first part of work, etc; come suddenly into existence, activity, etc; become established, as

business; move suddenly or involuntarily, as when surprised

**star'tle** disturb suddenly; take by surprise; alarm

**starve** die of hunger; (cause to) suffer from lack of food. **starva'tion**

**state** n condition in which person or thing is at any given time, as determined by outward influences, inherent qualities, etc; (territory occupied by) people living in organized political community under one government; (often **S.**) smaller political or governing unit in a federal union, as in the US. **-hood;** v set forth one's views, facts, etc; specify

**state'ly** dignified; grand

**state'ment** sth which is (formally) stated; summary of financial account

**states'man** one skilled in managing affairs of a state, esp. foreign politics

**stat'ic** a fixed or not moving; (of electricity) at rest; n electricity which interferes with radio or television signals

**sta'tion** place where train, bus, etc stops regularly; building equipped for special function or activity, as for broadcasting, first aid, etc; police headquarters; place assigned to soldiers, sailors, *etc*, for military duty; position in society

**sta'tion·ar·y** not moving; having a fixed position

**sta'tion·er·y** writing paper and materials

**sta·tis'ti|cs** science dealing with collection and use of *esp.* numerical facts; the numerical facts themselves. **-cal, statisti'cian**

**stat'ue** figure of person, animal, *etc*, carved, molded, *etc*, from metal, *etc*

**stat·u·esque'** like a statue, *esp.* in dignity or beauty

**stat'ure** person's height; eminence or worth

**sta'tus** state of affairs; (social) standing; legal position

**stat'u|te** formal written law; rules of institute, as college. **-tory**

**staunch** *a* steadfast; loyal; *v* see **stanch**

**stay** *v* remain in certain place, position, *etc*, or during certain period of time; continue as specified: *s. happy*; delay (court proceedings, execution, *etc*); *n* act or period of staying; condition of being stayed; sth serving as support or prop

**stead'fast** firm; unwavering. **-ness**

**stead'y** (stedi) firmly fixed or supported; not easily upset; moving, proceeding, done, *etc*, regularly and in un-

changing manner; constant

**steak** (stāk) slice of beef for frying or broiling

**steal** (**stole, sto'len**) take away (another's possessions) secretly and unlawfully; take, win, do, by secret means; move (in or out) quietly and secretly

**stealth** (-e-) secret manner of acting. **-y**

**steam** water changed into vapor by boiling, widely used as source of mechanical power

**steam'er** ship propelled by steam; vessel for cooking with steam

**steed** *poet* horse

**steel** (harden, as) iron processed by melting with carbon, characterized by hardness, elasticity and great strength. **-y**

**steep** *a* sloping greatly; sudden (rise or fall). **-en;** *v* soak in liquid; pervade with

**stee'ple** high tower of church, *etc*

**stee'ple-chase** horse race or footrace across country, over obstacles, *etc*

**steer** *v* guide course of vehicle, *etc*; (cause to) take or follow certain course; *n* castrated male animal of cattle family

**stel'lar** *a* of or like stars

**stem** *n* main body of plant; long slender part of anything; stop flow of; originate from

**stench** strong bad smell

**sten·cil** (make copy using) thin patterned sheet of metal, *etc*; pattern made by pressing ink or paint through s.

**ste·nog·ra·phy** writing in shorthand. **-pher**

**step** *n* movement in which foot is lifted and set down again before or behind other foot, as in walking, running or dancing; distance covered by this movement; sound made by feet in walking, *etc*; manner of walking; measure taken in some course of action: *take steps to prevent this*; stage in progress or development: *the first s. of an experiment*; rung or board serving to support foot in moving from one level to another; *v* move by raising and lowering one foot after the other; tread

**step'|child** child of one's wife or husband from an earlier marriage. **-brother, -sister, -father, -mother, -parent, -daughter, -son**

**steppe** plain without trees, *esp.* in Russia

**ster·e·o** *n* record player, *etc* producing sound from two speakers; sound so produced; *a* (also **stereo-phon'ic**) using or producing sound from two sources

**ster·e·o·scope** instrument for viewing two slightly varying pictures of object at the same time, thus giving impression of depth. **stereoscop'ic**

**ster·e·o·type** (classify according to) set (incorrect) form

**ster·il|e** free from living germs; incapable of producing offspring; lacking imagination. **-ize** (*UK* **-ise**), **steril'ity**

**ster'ling** *n* money used in *UK*, based on pound; *a* genuine; of standard value, *etc*; of solid worth

**stern** *a* strict; without pity; *n* rear part of ship

**ste'roid** one of several powerful chemical compounds, including hormones

**steth'o·scope** instrument for listening to action of heart, lungs, *etc*

**ste've·dore** laborer who loads or unloads ship

**stew** (styū) cook vegetables, meat, *etc*, in their own juice over slow heat

**stew'ard**, *f* **-ess** attendant on plane, ship, *etc*

**stick** *n* branch of tree cut off and trimmed to desired length, used to make fires, as support in walking, in carpentry, *etc*; long slender mass of candy, *etc*; *v* (**stuck**) pierce with pointed instrument, as knife, needle; fasten to surface of sth by piercing or with paste, *etc.* **-y**; thrust into certain position: *s. one's head out of the window*; be brought to standstill or be prevented from progressing: *the car became stuck in the mud*; *the thought stuck in his mind*; remain faithful to promise, one's principles, *etc*; pursue matter at hand steadily: *s. to one's job*

**stick'er** adhesive label (with picture, *etc*)

**stiff** not bending or yielding; not capable of moving or behaving easily or freely: *a s. neck*; formal; hard to cope with or overcome: *(of wind, etc)* strong; *(of drinks)* containing much alcohol. **-en, -ness**

**sti'fle** smother

**stig'ma** mark of disgrace

**still** *a* (almost) entirely without motion or sound: *a s. night*; *(of voice)* soft and low. **-ness**; *adv* without motion: *sit s.*; until and during present or given time: *when he came, we were s. in the house*; in the future as now and before: *whatever may happen, she will s. be there*; nevertheless; even: *s. more to come*

**still'born** dead when born

**stilt** pole (with foot support) for raising user, building, *etc* from ground

**stilt'ed** pompous; bombastic. **-ness**

**stim'u·late** rouse to (stronger) action; cause reaction of (part of) body. **-lant**

**stim'u·lus** sth that causes activity or reaction

**sting (stung)** *(of bees, mosquitoes, etc)* wound by pricking with pointed organ through which venom is ejected; cause sharp pain when touched, as nettles; *(cause to)* feel sharp physical or mental pain

**stin'gy** (-ji) unwilling to give or spend money, *etc*

**stink (stank or stunk, stunk)** give off strong unpleasant or offensive smell

**sti'pend** fixed or regular pay

**stip'u·late** insist on as condition of agreement; fix or lay down in law, *etc*

**stir (stur)** move spoon, *etc*, around in liquid or any matter consisting of separate particles so as to mix; *(cause to)* move

**stir'rup** support attached to saddle for rider's foot

**stitch** (sew using) movement in which threaded needle passes through fabric twice so that loop of thread remains; sharp pain

**stock** the total of goods kept by store, *etc*, for supply to customers; provisions, *etc*, accumulated for future use; all of the cattle, sheep, *etc*, kept on a farm; group or class of animals or plants derived from one original type; raw material from which sth is made; broth made by boiling meat, *etc* in water; shares issued by business, corporation, *etc*, in return for capital. **-holder, -broker**

**stock·ade¹** pen or enclosure made with posts, *esp.* military prison

**stock ex·change** building in which shares, securities, *etc*, are bought and sold

**stock'ing** knitted woolen, silk, nylon, *etc*, covering for foot and leg

**stock'ly** thick, short and strongly built. **-iness**

**stock'yard** place where cattle, sheep, *etc*, are kept before slaughtering

**stodg'y** (of food) heavy; dull; uninteresting

**sto'|ic** person of great self-control, not given to complaining. **-ical, -icism**

**stoke** feed or stir up fire

**stole** *n* woman's wrap worn loosely over shoulders

**stole, sto'len** *v* see **steal**

**stol'id** not easily moved emotionally. **-ness**

**stom'ach** (stum*k*) (part of

body containing) saclike organ in which food is stored and digested, located between end of gullet and beginning of intestine

**ston|e** hard matter composed of mineral substances compressed by weight of earth's crust and occurring as pebbles, rock, *etc*; piece of this shaped or cut for particular purpose; gem, as ruby, sapphire, *etc*; *UK* unit of weight equal to 14 pounds

**stone-deaf¹** completely deaf

**stood** see **stand**

**stool** (wooden) seat without arms or back; small low bench for resting feet on, *etc*; solid waste passed from the body

**stoop** *v* bend head and shoulders forwards and down; lower o.s. to (do sth); *n US* and *CAN* raised platform in front of house, *esp.* one in front of door

**stop** *v* cease doing, moving, *etc*; put an end to or interrupt motion, operation, *etc* of sth: *s. the car*; prevent (person) from doing, saying, *etc*; block passage, *etc*, or fill up leak, hole, *etc*; interrupt journey and stay for short while at certain place, also **s. over**; *n* act of stopping or state of being stopped; place at which journey is interrupted, trains or other vehicles halt, *etc*; sth used to fill up opening, prevent passage, *etc*; *UK* dot as punctuation mark, *esp* a period

**stop'cock** valve to control flow of liquid through pipe

**stop'per** plug or cork for closing bottle, *etc*

**stor'age** (method of) storing of goods, *etc*; space where goods are stored

**store** *v* keep supply of sth for the future; place in storage; *n* stock or supply; *US* place where goods are kept for retail sale. **-keeper**; *UK* warehouse; degree of respect or esteem: *I set little s. by his abilities*

**stork** long-legged, long-necked and long-billed white wading bird with black-tipped wings

**storm** *n* violent disturbance of the atmosphere, marked by strong winds and often by rain, thunder, lightning or hail; violent attack on enemy's position; *v* (of wind, *etc*) blow with unusual force; speak with violent anger; attack with violence. **-y**

**sto'ry** (stōri) account of fictitious or true events; (*UK* **sto'rey**) one level of a building

**stout** fat or bulky; strong; brave. **-ness**

**stout'heart'ed** brave

**stove** (stōv) *esp. US* appara-

tus burning coal, wood, *etc*, used for cooking and heating

**stow** pack (goods) in right and convenient place

**stow'a·way** one who hides on ship, *etc* to get free passage

**strad'dle** stand or sit with a leg on either side of (horse, *etc*)

**strag'gle** stray from road or from main group

**straight** (strāt) (of line, road, *etc*) not curved or bent; extending constantly in same direction; (of course, *etc*) direct; (of speech) frank; (of conduct, *etc*) honest and reliable; (of reasoning, thoughts, *etc*) logical; in proper order: *s. accounts.* **-en**; (of liquor) undiluted

**straight'a·way** at once

**straight·for'ward**  direct; frank

**strain** *v* stretch tightly; exert to the utmost; *s. one's eyes to see something*; make strong physical or mental effort: *s. one's imagination*; damage or injure by overexertion, excessive tension, *etc*: *s. a. muscle*; distort (meaning of word, *etc*); put (too) great demands on one's own or another's strength, resources, *etc*; pass (liquid) through sieve, *etc*; *n* act of straining or state of being strained; also *pl* passage of music or poetry; spirit or tenor as expressed in talking, writing, *etc*; stock or breed of animals or plants; (hereditary) characteristic or tendency: *s. of insanity in the family*

**strained** unnatural; tense; passed through sieve, *etc*

**strain'er** sieve

**strait** *usu pl* narrow passage of water connecting two large bodies of water; *pl* situation of difficulty or need

**strait'jack·et**, also *US* **straight-** garment which confines arms, used to restrain mad persons; sth which restricts free movement

**strait-laced'**, also *US* **straight-** excessively strict in conduct, *etc*

**strand** *n* single piece of hair, wire, thread, *etc*, esp. as twisted to form rope, *etc*; shore, *v* drive (ship) onto shore; leave in helpless position, esp. without money

**strang|e** (strānj) unusual; not well known or familiar. **-er**

**stran'|gle** kill by squeezing windpipe; suppress. **-gler**

**strap** flexible strip of leather, *etc*, for fastening or holding things together

**strat'e|gy** art of directing large-scale (military) activities. **-gist**, **-gic**

**strat'o·sphere** outer layer of air around the earth with constant temperature

**straw** stems of grain, *etc*, cut and dried and used as fodder, bedding, *etc*; hollow drinking tube

**straw'ber·ry** (plant with) soft sweet red fruit

**stray** wander (away from right road, *etc*)

**streak** (strēk) *n* long narrow line, smear, band of color or light, *etc*, on surface; trace; short period (of luck, *etc*); *v* make streaks on; move very fast

**stream** body of water running in bed; flow of any liquid, esp. in large quantity

**stream'line** shaped to offer least resistance to motion; make more efficient

**street** (paved) road in village or town

**street'car** *US* public vehicle driven by electricity and running on rails

**strength** (quality of having or degree of) capacity of doing, moving, resisting, *etc*, through action of muscles; toughness, hardness or solidity of structure or material; bodily health; mental or moral firmness or courage; total number: *they were there in full s.*; effectiveness of argument, *etc*. **-en**

**stren'u·ous** marked by vigorous effort. **-ness**

**stress** pressure; emphasis; demand on energy; strain

**stretch** draw out or extend to greater or full length or size; reach or hold out, as the hand; (cause to) extend in space or time: *the bridge stretches across the river;* be elastic. **-y;** draw tight; strain to the utmost or beyond proper limits: *s. a. point;* lie down at full length: *s. out on the bed*

**stretch'er** framework for carrying sick or wounded

**strew (strewed, strewn** or **strewed)** scatter

**strick'en** troubled with illness, doubt, *etc*

**strict** governed by, or carefully observing, exact rules; exact. **-ness**

**stride (strode, strid'den)** walk with long steps

**strife** conflict; struggle

**strike (struck)** (cause to) come into forcible contact: *s. a. ball, s. a. person with one's hand, the ship struck the rocks;* cause emotional or physical reaction: *be struck dumb with surprise;* produce (sparks; *etc*) by friction; (of lightning) discharge electricity into object; (of match, *etc*) cause to light; (of light, sound) fall upon surface; find: *s. oil;* cancel; stop work in protest; produce sound by hitting against resonant surface: *the clock struck one;* arrive at bargain, agreement, *etc;* assume (pose, *etc*) suddenly and dramatically; lower flag in surrender or salute; stamp (coin); take given direction: *s. to the right;* enter upon (acquaintance, *etc*) casually

**strik'ing** noticeable; impressive; attractive

**string** *n* thread, *etc*, twisted together and used to tie up parcels, hold things together, *etc*; number of beads, pearls, *etc*, held together by cord running through holes in each of them; number of things or persons arranged in line or following closely one after another; taut piece of catgut, wire, *etc* stretched along length of violin, *etc*, which gives off sound; *pl* (players of) violins, cellos, violas, *etc* of an orchestra; *v* **(strung)** put together (on s.); supply with strings

**strin'gen|t** (-jent) strict, as rules, *etc*; requiring exact performance. **-cy**

**strip** *v* pull off or take away outer covering or clothes; take away (contents, equipment, *etc*); *n* narrow long piece of material, ground, *etc*

**stripe** long narow band on surface, differing in color, material, *etc*; band(s), *usu* V-shaped, on soldier's uniform, indicating rank, length of service, *etc*

**strive** (**strove, striv'en**) try hard; struggle (against)

**strode** see **stride**

**stroke** n act of striking; act of stroking; sudden strong attack, as of apoplexy; each of movements of legs and arms in swimming; (mark made by) single movement of pen or pencil; v pass hand over lightly

**stroll** walk leisurely

**strong** having or showing (great) mental or physical strength; not easily broken, torn, damaged, etc; healthy; powerful in influence, etc, or by quality, size, numbers, etc; intense, as smell, light, etc; (of voice) loud and clear; (of drinks, drugs, etc) containing large quantity of essential ingredients: s. coffee; (of contrast, likeness, etc) marked; firm or thorough: s. convictions

**strong'hold** heavily defended place or (cultural) position

**strove** see **strive**

**struck** see **strike**

**struc'tur·alism** method of study emphasizing structure rather than function

**struc'ture** manner in which house, etc is built; arrangement of parts; any system; any building. -al

**strug'gle** fight against opposing force; make strong determined efforts to overcome difficulties, obstacles, etc

**strung** see **string**

**strut** v walk in pompous or affected way; brace with s.; n strutting walk; crosspiece to strengthen structure of building, plane, etc

**strych'nine** highly poisonous drug

**stub** n projecting stump of tree; short piece remaining after larger part has been used, consumed, torn off, etc; v strike (one's toe) against something

**stub'ble** stumps of grain left in ground after crop is cut; short growth of beard

**stub'born** strong-willed; not easy to control; hard to move or change

**stub'by** short and thick

**stuc'co** plaster used for coating or ornamenting button

**stuck** see **stick**

**stud** horses, etc for breeding; nail with large head; ornamental button

**stu'dent** (styū-) one who studies, esp. at college, university, etc

**stu'di·o** workroom for artist, musician, etc; room specially equipped for broadcasting, shooting movies, etc

**stu'd|y** (studi) v acquire knowledge by reading, investigating, research, etc; examine or observe carefully;

think or reflect on a subject; *n* act or subject of studying; room set apart for reading and writing. **-dious**

**stuff** *n* material of which anything is made; unspecified material or matter; *v* fill by packing closely; stop up (hole, *etc*); line with padding; eat greedily

**stuff'ing** filling for sth; food mixture put into bird, *etc* before cooking

**stuf'fy** lacking fresh air; old-fashioned

**stum'ble** trip; make mistake; hesitate; come across by accident

**stump** base of tree in ground after main part is cut down; remaining end of sth worn down, broken or cut off, as tooth, limb, *etc*

**stun** make senseless, as by blow; daze or shock

**stung** see **sting**

**stunk** see **stink**

**stunt** *v* hinder growth of; *n* (dangerous) feat of skill; advertising device

**stu'pe·fy** astonish; stun

**stu·pen'dous** amazingly large or impressive

**stu'pid** (styū-) slow-witted; silly; boring. **stupid'ity**

**stu'por** dazed state, as caused by drugs, *etc*

**stur'·dy** strong; well-built; hardy. **-diness**

**stut'ter** speak with involun-

tary and spasmodic repetition of sounds

**sty** pen for pigs; filthy place; inflamed swelling on eyelid

**style** particular and characteristic way of writing, doing sth *etc*; superior quality or manner; kind, type; fashion (in dress)

**styl'ish** in keeping with the latest style; elegant

**sty'lus** needle with diamond, *etc* point, used to pick up sound from record

**styp'tic** (substance) able to stop bleeding

**sua|ve** (swäv) smoothly agreeable or polite. **-vity**

**sub·com·mit·tee** secondary committee

**sub·con'scious** (part of mind) not wholly conscious or below consciousness

**sub·di·vide'** divide again

**sub·due'** conquer; tame; (of color, sound *etc*) make less vivid or loud

**sub'ject** *n* theme or topic (to be) dealt with, discussed, considered, *etc*; any member of a state; person or animal used in experiment; *a* under the power of; liable or open to; dependent on

**sub·ject'** *v* bring under one's rule; expose to

**sub·jec'tive** determined by personal feelings, not objective; of the mind, imaginary. **subjectiv'ity**

**subjugate**

**sub'ju·gate** conquer; bring under complete control

**sub·let'** rent a rented property to s.o. else

**sub'li·mate** divert primitive impulse into acceptable behavior; purify

**sub·lime'** lofty; grand

**sub'ma·rine** *a* being, growing or used under water, *esp.* in the sea; *n* (war)ship operating under water

**sub·mer'ge** put completely under water. **-gence**

**sub·mer'si·ble** capable of being submerged. **-sion**

**sub·|mit'** yield; subject o.s. to; state for consideration. **-mission, -missive**

**sub·or'di·nate** (person) of a lower position or rank

**sub·poe'na** (-pē-) (issue) order commanding person to appear at court

**sub·|scribe'** sign one's name on document; enter one's name in list of contributors, promise to take and pay for. **-scriber, -scription; s. to** agree

**sub'se·quent** following

**sub·ser'vi·|ent** servile; subordinate. **-ence**

**sub·side'** sink to lower level; become less violent

**sub·sid'i·ar·y** (sth, *esp.* company) controlled by another; serving to help; secondary

**sub'si·|dy** money given as aid, usually by government

to private industry. **-dize** (*UK* **-dise**)

**sub·sist'** (continue to) exist; find means of living (*esp.* poorly). **-tence**

**sub·son'ic** at less than speed of sound

**sub'stance** matter; main part

**sub·stan'tial** having substance; of considerable value, *etc*; solid

**sub·stan'ti·ate** prove by giving evidence

**sub'sti·tute** (s.o. or sth) serving in place of. **substitu'tion**

**sub'ter·fuge** (-fyūj) trick

**sub·ter·ra'ne·an** underground

**sub'tle** (sutl) fine or delicate; requiring or showing mental sharpness; cunning. **-ty**

**sub·tract'** take away (part from whole). **-tion**

**sub'urb** outlying district of city. **subur'ban, subur'-banite**

**sub·vert'** overthrow, *esp.* government. **-sion, -sive**

**sub'way** *US* electric railway running underground

**suc·ceed'** reach desired result. **-cess;** follow (and take place of). **-cession, -cessive, -cessor**

**suc·cinct'** (suksingkt) briefly (but fully) expressed. **-ness**

**suc'cor,** *UK* **-cour** (give) help in time of need or danger

**suc'cu·|lent** (sukyūlent) juicy;

**sullen**

(of plants) juicy and fleshy.
**-lence**

**suc·cumb** (-kum) give way to superior force; die (as result of illness, *etc*)

**such** *a* of same kind, degree, character, *etc*, as that or those indicated: *s. mistakes are stupid;* so great, bad *etc*: *that was s. an insult; pron* being as stated, or the person or thing mentioned: *if s. is the case;* definite but not named: *if you do this, s. and s. will result; as s.* in itself: *food as s. doesn't interest him*

**suck** create partial vacuum by action of lips, pump, *etc*, thereby causing liquid to rise or flow; take up liquid, or air through surface, as plants do; extract juice from fruit with lips; roll about in mouth so as to dissolve, as candy; draw milk from breast or udder, as baby or calf does

**suck·le** nurse at the breast

**suc·tion** act or process of sucking

**sud·den** happening, done, coming, *etc*, quickly and unexpectedly

**suds** *pl* foam forming on soapy water

**sue** take action in court against; *s. for* ask or plead for sth

**suede** (swād) soft rough leather

**su·et** hard animal fat

**suf·fer** undergo (pain, change, *etc*); allow to do, happen, *etc*. **-ance**

**suf·fice** be enough. **-cient**

**suf·fo·cate** (cause to) die through lack of air

**suf·frage** right to vote

**suf·fuse** overspread with color or moisture, as tears

**sug·ar** (sh-) (sweeten food, *etc* with) sweet crystalline substance obtained from cane or beets. **-y**

**sug·gest** offer for consideration; evoke. **-tion**

**su·i·cide** (one committing) act of killing o.s.; action destroying one's interests. **suicid'al**

**suit** (sūt) *n* jacket with matching trousers or skirt, to be worn together; prosecution of claim, *etc*, in court of law; number of things of like kind, forming a set, as four divisions of playing cards; *v* make or be appropriate to or fitting for some thing, occasion, need, *etc*; be satisfactory. **-able**

**suit·case** flat rectangular leather, *etc*, bag for belongings during travel

**suite** (swēt) set, as of rooms in hotel

**sulk·y** sullenly ill-humored or resentful

**sul·len** showing ill humor by gloomy or angry silence

**sul'|try** (of weather) hot and damp; (of temper) passionate. **-triness**

**sum** n total amount of two or more numbers, quantities, etc, arrived at by multiplication, addition, division, etc; amount of money; summary; v **s. up** summarize

**sum'ma·ry** n brief account of main points; a brief; direct and prompt; law without delays of a formal trial. **-rize** (UK **-rise**), **summar'·ily**

**sum'mer** second and warmest season. **-y**

**sum'mit** highest point, degree, level, etc

**sum'mon** call, as with authority; call together

**sum'mons** (pl **sum'mon·ses**) call to do something; call by court, etc to appear

**sump'tu·ous** costly; splendid. **-ness**

**sun** n star around which the earth and other planets of our solar system revolve and from which they obtain light and warmth; v expose (o.s.) to sun. **-light, -ny**

**sun'burn** reddening of the skin due to over-exposure to sun's rays

**sun'dae** ice cream served with syrup, fruit, nuts, etc

**Sun'day** seventh day of week between Saturday and Monday

**sun'der** force apart

**sun'dries** pl various small items

**sun'dry** various; several

**sung** see **sing**

**sunk, sunk'en** see **sink**

**sun'rise** the rising of the sun above the horizon

**sun'roof** roof for sunning; part of car roof which can be opened for light and air

**sun'set** the dropping of the sun below the horizon

**sun'spot** dark patch appearing at times on surface of sun

**sun'tan** browning of skin by sun's rays

**su·perb'** excellent

**su·per·cil'i·ous** expressing contempt and haughtiness

**su·per·fi'cial** on the surface; outward; not deep (of character, knowledge, etc). **superficial'ity**

**su·per'flu·ous** more than enough; not needed. **superflu'ity**

**su·per·im·pose'** lay (sth) over sth else

**su·per·in·tend'** oversee and direct (work); inspect. **-ent**

**su·pe'ri·or** higher; better than average. **superior'ity**

**su·per'la·tive** of highest kind or degree

**su'per·mar·ket** large food store on self-service basis

**su·per·nat'u·ral** beyond the known laws of nature

**su·per·sede'** take place of in office, use, *etc*

**su·per·son'ic** greater than the speed of sound

**su·per·sti|tion** unreasoning belief in supernatural forces. **-tious**

**su'per·struc·ture** any structure built on a foundation or other structure

**su·per·vene'** happen as unexpected interruption

**su'per·vise** oversee and manage (work, etc). **super·vi'sion**

**sup'per** evening meal

**sup·plant'** take place of (by unfair means)

**sup'ple** flexible; bending easily; graceful. **-ness**

**sup'ple·ment** sth added to complete or enlarge). **supplemen'tary**

**sup'pli·ant** (person) humbly begging

**sup'pli·cate** beg or petition humbly. **-cant**

**sup·ply'** give (what is needed or lacking)

**sup·port'** give strength to; hold up (load); bear; take side of; provide with food, *etc*, needed for living. **-er**

**sup·pose'** require as condition; assume to be true; expect; think probable. **supposi'tion**

**sup·press|s'** put end to; hold back (smile, *etc*); withhold (book, news, *etc*) from being published; put down (revolt). **-sion, -sor**

**su·preme'** highest in power or authority; most excellent; greatest. **-acy**

**sur·charge'** (make) additional charge

**sure** (sh-) free from doubt; confident about facts, outcome, reliability of another, *etc*; certain (to happen); firm: *s. ground*; never disappointing, missing, erring, *etc*: *a s. shot*; **be s.** see to it that sth is done: *be s. that he gets it*

**sure'ty** guarantee; one who guarantees for another

**surf** (ride on) swell and foam of waves breaking on shore

**surf'board** board used to ride waves

**sur'face** outside part of an object; outward aspect

**surge** move up and down or to and fro, as waves, crowd, *etc*

**sur|ger·y** art of treating diseases, *etc* by operating with instruments; room where such operations are done. **-geon, -gical**

**sur'ly** rude or ill-tempered

**sur·mise'** guess; suppose

**sur·mount'** get to or be on top of; overcome

**sur'name** family name

**sur·pass'** outdo; be better than

**sur'plus** that which remains

beyond what is needed; excess of assets over liabilities

**sur·prise'** come upon or take unawares; amaze

**sur·ren'der** yield; give up

**sur'ro·gate** substitute; deputy officer

**sur·round'** be on all sides; form circle around

**sur'tax** extra tax

**sur·veil'lance** (survā́lens) watch kept over (person)

**sur·vey'** v inspect (closely); view sth as a whole; measure land; question people in a s.

**sur'vey** n general study; examination (of opinion); surveying

**sur·viv|e'** remain alive (after others or after event). **-al**

**sus·cep'ti·ble** able to be (easily) affected or influenced; admitting of. **susceptibil'ity**

**sus·pect'** v have doubts about; think person guilty without proof; guess

**sus'pect** n suspected person; a open to suspicion

**sus·pen|d'** hang; withhold (judgment) for a time; bar temporarily (from privilege, etc); stop operating temporarily. **-sion**

**sus·pense'** state of anxious uncertainty

**sus·pi'|cion** act of suspecting; slight trace. **-cious**

**sus·tain'** hold or bear up; un-

dergo (loss, etc); keep going or alive; uphold as true, valid, etc

**sus·te·nance** food; means of living

**su'ture** seam along which two things are joined, esp. stitched edge of a wound

**swab** mop; cotton pad for cleaning mouth, etc

**swag'ger** seam; walk with self-satisfied gait

**swal'low** (swolō) v let (food, drink, etc) pass down throat into stomach; envelop entirely; n act of swallowing; amount swallowed; small migratory bird with pointed wings and forked tail

**swam** see **swim**

**swamp** n piece of low, wet, spongy land; marsh. **-y;** v flood; overwhelm

**swan** (swon) large graceful water bird with long neck and white feathers

**swap,** UK **swop** (swop) exchange or trade one thing for another

**swarm** (sworm) large number of insects, birds or small animals flying or moving together; great number of persons

**swarth'y** dark-colored, esp. of skin

**swat** strike (insect) with hand or flat object

**swath** space covered by stroke of mowing machine

**sway** swing from side to side; influence

**swear** (swār) (**swore, sworn**) make statement on oath, *esp.* in court; promise solemnly (to do); use profane language in anger, *etc*

**sweat** (swet) (give off) watery fluid secreted by glands through pores of skin, as from heat, exercise, *etc*; (form) moisture on surface of object caused by differing inside and outside temperatures

**sweat'er** (swet-) knitted pullover

**sweat'shirt** heavy cotton sweater (worn *esp.* for exercise)

**sweat'shop** (swet-) place where workers are paid badly to work long hours under poor conditions

**sweep** (**swept**) clear away (dust, *etc*) by passing broom, brush, *etc*, over floor, *etc*; move (sth) along with steady, driving force: *the wind swept across the plains*

**sweep'ing** of or passing over wide range; generalizing: *a s. statement*

**sweet** having the taste characteristic of sugar, ripe fruit or honey. **-en;** pleasing to the senses; (of manner) pleasant, gentle

**sweet po·ta·to** (*pl* **-toes**) (tropical vine with) yel-low-pink root, used as vegetable

**swell** *v* (**swelled, swelled** or **swol'len**) (cause to) grow larger in volume, size, *etc*, as from absorption of water, inflammation, *etc*

**swel'ter** be oppressively hot

**swerve** change direction

**swift** very quick or rapid

**swill** *n* (partly) liquid garbage fed to pigs; *v* drink greedily or excessively; rinse

**swim** (**swam, swum**) move along in water by moving limbs, fins, or tail; be full of or surrounded by liquid; have sensation that everything is whirling: *the room swam before my eyes*

**swin'dle** cheat (*usu* out of money). **-dler**

**swine** full-grown pig

**swing** *v* (**swung**) (cause to) move back and forth from suspended position; cause sth attached to one side or at one point to move to and fro; move (sth) in curving or circular line; move through air from one level to another; influence, as opinion; walk lightly and rhythmically; *n* act or manner of swinging; action in full progress: *the meeting was in full s.;* free, swaying motion of the body, as in walking; seat suspended from above, on which one may s.

**swirl** whirl, *esp.* water

**swish** make, or move with, whispering motion, as rod cutting through air

**switch** *n* mechanism for breaking or establishing connection in system, as in electric circuit; device for changing direction of railway train by shifting tracks; slender shoot cut from tree, *esp.* one used in whipping; lashing movement; *v* whip; change (subject, direction, position, *etc*); turn on electric light or start operation of machine by means of s.

**swiv·el** (turn [as if] on) fastening device allowing sth, as chair, to swing around

**swol·len** see **swell**

**swoop** move down suddenly (to attack), as bird

**swop** see **swap**

**sword** (sōrd) weapon with straight or curved sharp pointed blade

**swore, sworn** see **swear**

**swum** see **swim**

**swung** see **swing**

**syl·la·ble** (part of) word containing vowel sound, often together with consonant(s). **syllab'ic**

**syl·la·bus** (*pl* **-buses** or **-bi**) program for course of study, *etc*

**sym·bi·o'sis** (*pl* **-ses**) interdependence of two different living things. **-otic**

**sym'bol** sign standing for something else; emblem. **-ism, -ize** (*UK* **-ise**), **symbol'ic**

**sym'me·try** (beauty resulting from) proper proportions; correspondence in size, *etc* of opposite parts. **symmet'rical**

**sym·pa·|thy** community of interests and feelings; sharing feelings of others; support; expression of sorrow for another's loss, *etc*. **-thize** (*UK* **-thise**), **sympathet'ic**

**sym·pho·ny** harmony of sounds; large composition for full orchestra. **symphon'ic**

**symp'tom** sign; change in body indicating disease. **symptoma'tic**

**syn'a·gogue** Jewish temple

**syn·chro·nize,** *UK* **-nise** (cause to) go on at same time and speed; add sound, foreign language, *etc* in time with action of movie. **-nous**

**syn'co·pate** place accents (in music) where they normally would not occur

**syn'di·cate** group of persons joined to carry out financial undertaking; business which sells stories, pictures to several newspapers

**syn'drome** set of (medical) symptoms characteristic of particular condition

**syn'o·nym** word having

(nearly) the same meaning as another. **synon'ymous**

**syn·op'sis** brief account

**syn'tax** (rules governing) way in which sentences are constructed in any language. **syntac'tical**

**syn'the·|sis** (sth resulting from) combination of parts into a whole. **-size** (*UK* -sise)

**syn'the·siz·er** musical instrument producing great variety of sounds electronically

**syn·thet'ic** artificially made or put together; not natural

or genuine

**syph'i·lis** (sif-) chronic contagious venereal disease

**sy·ringe'** (-inj) small hand pump for injecting liquids

**syr'up** (sir-) water or juice boiled with sugar; medicine in form of sweet liquid

**sys'tem** whole consisting of connected things or parts; set of principles; *etc*; method of doing, organization, *etc*. **systemat'ic**

**sys'tems a·nal'y·sis** examination of business, *etc* to establish how computers may best be used. **s. an'alyst**

# T

**t** twentieth letter of English alphabet

**tab** small piece of material, *esp*. one for identification, *etc*

**ta'ble** *n* piece of furniture with a flat top resting on legs or pillar, used for eating, writing, *etc*; flat elevated stretch of land, also **table-land**; smooth slab of wood or stone bearing an inscription; numbers, facts, references, *etc*, arranged in systematic order, *usu* in columns, as at end of book; *v* place sth on t. (for consideration); postpone discussion of (issue, motion, *etc*)

**ta'ble-spoon** large serving

spoon; amount held by t.

**tab'let** sheets of writing paper fastened together at one end; small flat slab bearing an inscription; small flat cake of medicine, a pill

**ta·boo'**, also *US* **ta·bu'** under a ban; prohibited by social custom; set apart as sacred

**tab'u·late** arrange in form of table, as figures. **-lar**

**ta·chom'e·ter** (-kom-) instrument for measuring speed of vehicle, *etc*

**tac'it** silent; understood without being stated

**tac'i·turn** inclined to silence

**tack** *n* small, sharp, flatheaded nail; long stitch used to fasten material together temporarily; *v* fasten by tack(s); fasten in temporary manner; sail a zigzag course against the wind; **t. on** attach (something) as addition or supplement, as to a legislative bill

**tack'le** *n* mechanism, *usu* consisting of ropes and pulley-blocks, for raising and lowering material, used *esp.* in building; equipment, *esp.* for fishing; *v* try to master, solve, *etc*, problem or work; (in football) seize an opponent, *usu* below hips

**tact** feeling for what is fitting, *esp.* of the right thing to do or say. **-ful**

**tac'tics** device or plan for achieving one's purpose. **-al**

**tad'pole** small black fishlike creature which develops into frog or toad

**taf'fe·ta** lightweight shiny silk or rayon fabric

**tag** *n* strip of paper, *etc* attached to sth and serving as label or mark; loop of material sewn on garment so that it can be hung up; well--known (trite) phrase; children's game in which one chases other players; *v* attach to; **t. along** join and follow

**tail** flexible extension of spine projecting from hindmost part of animal body; any-

thing like this in shape or position

**tail'light** red light mounted at back of vehicle for safety after dark

**tai'lor** one who makes outer garments, *esp.* for individual customers

**taint** *v* infect; corrupt; *n* touch of infection or corruption; touch of dishonor

**take** (**took, tak'en**) get into one's hands or possession, control, *etc*; conquer; accept, as advice, money, *etc*; carry with one: *t. this to the kitchen*; lead: *t. him to the door*; perform or undertake action: *t. a walk*; avail o.s. of or use sth: *t. a cab*; become infected: *t. a cold*; occupy or require: *this will t. some time*; write down (notes, *etc*); assume particular attitude towards sth: *t. it easy, t. exception*; make (photograph); understand: *I t. it that you are coming tonight*; introduce into the body: *t. medicine*; **t. after** be like (one's parent); **t. in** provide lodging; make clothing smaller; comprehend; deceive: *he was taken in by her promises*; **t. off** remove; set out on journey; (of airplane) leave ground; **t. on** hire (employees); assume (task, *etc*); **t. to** start doing, *esp.* habitually; feel (kindly) towards; **t. up**

**tape**

start sth, as a hobby; pursue a matter, *etc*; require space or time; continue

**take'off** start of a flight when plane, *etc* leaves ground; *infml* parody

**tale** story; lie; rumor

**tal'ent** special natural ability or gift (for music, *etc*)

**talk** speak, *esp.* to exchange ideas, *etc*; (be able to) express oneself in certain language; gossip

**talk'a·tive** fond of talking

**tall** of more than usual height; of specified height

**tal'low** hard melted animal fat, used for candles, *etc*

**tal'ly** *n* anything on which score or account is kept; ticket or label; *v* record; reckon up; agree with (*esp.* in number)

**tal'on** claw of bird of prey

**tame** (of animals) changed from wild state and adapted to live in human surroundings; gentle; lacking spirit or energy

**tam'per with** meddle with

**tam'pon** tubelike cotton mass, used to absorb blood, *etc*, *esp.* during woman's monthly period

**tan** *n* yellowish brown color; suntan; *v* change (skin) into leather. **-ner, -nery;** cause browning of skin, *esp.* by sunlight

**tan'dem** bicycle for two

persons; **in t.** in close co-operation

**tang** strong taste or smell

**tan'gent** (-jent) line touching a circle; sudden change from one course, thought, *etc* to another. **tangen'tial**

**tan'ge·rine** (-rēn) small sweet kind of orange

**tan'gi·ble** (-ji-) that can be touched; real; definite

**tan'gle** (cause to) become mixed in confused mass of intertwined strands

**tank** large container of wood, metal, *etc*, for storing liquids, gas, *etc*; armored military motor vehicle moving on caterpillar treads and armed with guns

**tank'er** ship, plane, *etc* for carrying liquid, *esp.* oil

**tan'ta·lize**, *UK* **-lise** tease

**tan'ta·mount** equal in value, meaning, *etc*

**tan'trum** fit of ill temper

**tap** *v* strike or knock with light blows; strike foot on floor with light repeated motion; make use of, as resources; draw off liquid (from cask by removing stopper); secretly or illegally intercept message by cutting into line of communication; *n* light blow; plug for stopping opening in cask; *esp.* *UK* faucet

**tape** long narrow strip of linen, *etc*, used for tying up

# taper

*etc*; strip stretched across

**ta'per** *v* grow gradually nar-

**tape' re·cord·er** see **record-er**

**tap'es·try** wall hanging of

**tap·i·o·ca** hard white grain

**tar** (cover with) dark sticky

**ta·ran'tu·la** large hairy, mild-

**tar'dy** moving slowly; late

**tare** weight allowance for

**tar'get** mark to shoot at;

**tar'iff** list of import (or ex-

**tar'nish** make dull, dim, or

**tar·pau'lin** (cover of) heavy

**tar'ry** stay in a place; delay

**tart** *n* small shell of pastry,

**tar'tan** Scottish woolen fabric

**task** piece of work to be done

**tas'sel** small hanging ornament

**taste** sensation produced on

*ern art*; ability to recognize

*etc*

**tat'ter** *usu pl* torn piece (hang-

**tat'tle** let out secrets; gossip

**tat·too'** drum signal; indelible

**taught** see **teach**

**taunt** mock; jeer at; tease

**taut** stretched tight; tense

**tau·tol'o·gy** needless repeti-

**tav'ern** place where liquor is

**taw'dry** showy and cheap

**taw'ny** (of) yellowish-brown

**tax** *n* money charged by gov-

**tax'i** *n* car with driver, hired

to convey passengers. Also **-cab;** *v* (of plane) move slowly on ground

**tea** dried leaves of Asian shrub; drink made with these

**teach** (**taught**) communicate knowledge, skill, *etc* by presenting information, demonstrating methods, *etc, esp.* to pupils. **-er**

**teak** (Asian tree with) valuable hard light brown wood

**team** group acting jointly, as in games. **-work;** two or more animals harnessed together to pull vehicle

**team'ster** person who drives truck

**tear** (tir) *n* drop of salty fluid secreted by eye glands, *esp.* as result of strong emotion, coughing, *etc.* **-ful**

**tear** (tār) *v* (**tore, torn**) pull apart by means of force, as paper or cloth; pull forcibly (off, out, from, *etc*); divide: *the family was torn by a quarrel*

**tease** (tēz) irritate, often for fun, with repeated questions, remarks, *etc*

**tea'spoon** small spoon for stirring tea or coffee, *etc;* amount held by t.

**teat** nipple on breast of female mammal through which milk passes

**tech'ni·cal** of useful or practical knowledge or skill; used

only in a particular trade, *etc;* of mechanical and industrial sciences. **techni'cian**

**tech·ni·cal'i·ty** technical nature; detail or rule of procedure of interest only to specialist

**tech·nique'** (-nēk) method or skill

**tech·nol'o·gy** (science dealing with) industrial and scientific methods or their practical use

**te'di·um** state of being boring. **-ous**

**teem** rain heavily; be full to point of overflowing with

**teen'ag·er** young person aged between 13 and 19

**teens** period of one's life between 13 and 19

**tee'ter** move unsteadily; seesaw

**teeth** *pl* of tooth

**teethe** grow teeth

**tee·to'tal·ler,** *UK* **-ler** person who drinks no alcohol

**tel'e·cast** (broadcast) television program

**tel·e·com·mu·ni·ca'tions** science of transmitting messages by telephone, telegraph, radio, television, *etc*

**tel'e·fax** electronic system permitting photographic transmission of messages, documents, *etc*

**tel'e·gram** (paper with) message sent by telegraph

**tel'e·graph** (apparatus used in) system of transmitting messages over distances by means of electrical impulses

**tel·e·ol·o·gy** view that objects or events are shaped by purpose which they serve

**te·lep'a·thy** direct communication between minds without use of senses

**tel'e·phone** (use) apparatus for sending speech over a distance by means of electrical impulses

**te·le·pho'to lens'** special camera lens for photographing distant objects

**tel'e·scope** *n* instrument for making distant object appear larger and nearer; *v* (cause to) become shorter in length or time

**tel'e·type**, *UK* **tel'e·print·er** telegraphic device for recording and transmitting typed message; message sent thus

**tel'e·vise** broadcast by television

**tel'e·vi·sion** transmitting of sound and images by radio waves; device for receiving such waves; programs broadcast in this way; business of producing such programs

**tell** (told) make known, explain, express (events, information, feelings, *etc*) in speech or writing; order

(s.o.) to do; make out or determine: *can you t. who is in the car*; have marked effect: *the tedious work was telling on his nerves*

**tell'er** one who handles and counts money in bank; one who counts votes in legislative body

**tell'ing** having force or effect; striking

**te·mer'i·ty** rash boldness

**tem'per** *n* state of mind or feelings; calmness of mind; passion; particular hardness given steel, *etc*; *v* moderate; tone down; treat (metal, *etc*) to give proper hardness, texture, *etc*

**tem'per·a·ment** person's natural physical and mental make-up

**tem'per·a·men'tal** having strongly-marked temperament; moody or sensitive

**tem'per·ance** self-control; moderate use of, or refraining from, alcoholic drinks

**tem'per·ate** moderate

**tem'per·a·ture** degree of hotness or coldness; degree of body heat above normal

**tem'pest** violent storm **tempes'tuous**

**tem'ple** place of worship; flat space on either side of forehead

**tem'po** speed or rhythm of music, work *etc*

**tem'po·ral** of time; worldly

**tem·po·rar·y** lasting or meant for a time only

**tem·po·rize**, UK **-rise** avoid making decision to win time

**tempt** try strength of will; try to persuade; try to lead into evil; attract. **tempta'tion**

**ten** a number (10), nine plus one

**ten'a·ble** (of belief, *etc*) able to be held or defended

**te·na'ci·ous** holding fast to course; stubborn. **-ty**

**ten'an|t** person who rents land, house, *etc* from another; occupant. **-cy**

**ten|d** be inclined to; tend toward. **-dency** take care of; look after

**ten·den'tious** (of writing, *etc*) meant to further certain idea, *etc*. **-ness**

**ten'der** *a* soft; delicate; sensitive; loving; *n* offer; auxiliary car or boat; *v* make formal offer

**ten'don** cord of tissue connecting muscle to bone

**ten'dril** slender outgrowth supporting climbing plant

**ten'e·ment** (cheap) house or apartment for renting

**ten'et** opinion, principle, or doctrine held as true

**ten'nis** ball game played on court by two (pairs of) people with rackets

**ten'or** general direction; general meaning (of document or speech); (man with) highest male voice range

**tense** stretched tight; feeling nervous strain. **-ness**

**ten'sile** of tension; capable of being stretched or drawn out

**ten'sion** state of being stretched or stretching; nervous state; voltage

**tent** portable (canvas) shelter, held up by pole(s)

**ten'ta·cle** long flexible feeler of animal

**ten'ta·tive** done as a trial or experiment; hesitant

**tenth** next after ninth; being one of ten equal parts

**ten'u·ous** thin; rarefied; not substantial; flimsy. **-ness**

**ten'ure** act, right or period of holding an office, land, *etc*

**tep'id** slightly warm. **-ness**

**term** (limited) period of time political office is held, contract is effective, organized instruction is given, or after which something must be done, paid, *etc*; *pl* conditions of agreement, contract, *etc*; *pl* relationship between persons: *they were on good terms*; word with particular meaning, *esp.* as used in certain field

**ter'mi·nal** *a* of or at the end; (of illness, *etc*) fatal; *n* passenger station of railway, bus, *etc*; point of connection in electrical circuit; computer workplace consisting of keyboard and screen, *usu* connected to large computer with many users

**ter'mi·nate** bring or come to an end; be at end of

**ter·mi·nol'o·gy** set of terms used in particular science, profession, *etc*

**ter'mi·nus** end of railroad, *etc* line

**ter'mite** (turmīt) ant-like insect feeding on wood

**ter'race** raised level strip of land; group of row houses; a balcony or outdoor living area, as a patio

**ter'ra cot'ta** hard unglazed earthenware for vases, *etc*

**ter·rain'** area of land, *esp.* with respect to its features

**ter·res'tri·al** of the earth; of or living on dry land

**ter'ri·ble** arousing great fear; awful; severe: *a t. storm*

**ter·rif'ic** *infml* excellent; very great

**ter'ri·fy** fill with fear. **-fied**

**ter'ri·to·ry** region or district; any land belonging to a state; field of thought, work, *etc.* **territo'rial**

**ter'ror** (act causing) sharp overpowering fear. **-ize** (*UK* **-ise**)

**ter'ror·|is·m** use of terror to govern or to obtain political ends. **-ist**

**terse** concise in speech or writing. **-ness**

**test** (apply) means or method of trying out or measuring

level, qualities, abilities or genuineness of anything

**tes'ta·ment** *law* a will; clear proof of sth: *a t. to their ability*. **testamen'tary**

**tes'ti·cle** male gland producing sperm

**tes'ti·fy** bear witness; make solemn declaration; (of things) be evidence of

**tes·ti·mo'ni·al** written document testifying to person's character, *etc*; gift, *etc* given person as token of admiration

**tes'ti·mo·ny** *law* formal statement under oath

**teth'er** rope, *etc* by which animal is fastened

**tex|t** actual or original wording of anything written or printed; main body of book as opposed to illustrations, notes, *etc*; subject or theme; textbook. **-tual**

**text'book** standard book for instruction in particular field

**tex'tile** woven fabric

**tex'tur|e** surface structure; characteristic weave. **-al**

**than** word used to introduce second member of comparison or a less acceptable choice: *she is prettier t. her sister, I'd rather read t. watch television*

**thank** express one's appreciation to s.o. for favor, gift, *etc*

**that** (*pl* **those**) word used to indicate person, thing, *etc*, pointed out, understood or mentioned, observed or named already or at the time: *t. is my automobile*, *t. was a good play*; to refer to sth further removed in time, place, *etc* or to show distinction: *at t. point of his career he had already been promoted, don't dig in this garden, dig in t. one*; also used as subject or object of relative clause or as *conj* to introduce statements, *etc*: *the house t. I bought recently, I know t. he will come*; also to such a degree: *t. much, t. high*

**thatch** (cover roof with) roof-covering of straw, rushes, *etc*

**thaw** melt, as snow

**the** the word used to refer to: person, thing, *etc*, already mentioned or under discussion: *t. king went to say, t. woman who came last night*; to refer to sth unique or outstanding: *t. class of vertebrates, he is t. actor for such parts*; also used correlatively to express in that degree, *etc*: *t. more we danced, t. happier we were*

**the·a·ter**, *UK* **-tre** (thēēter) building in which plays are performed or motion pictures presented; the art or field of drama, comedy, *etc*. **theat'rical**; room in which surgery is performed as demonstration for medical students; place of action: *t. of war*

**theft** act of stealing

**their** (dhār) word indicating possession by several persons: *t. house*

**theirs** belonging to them: *the house is t.*; of them: *t. is the best plan*

**the'ism** belief in one God

**them** objective case of they

**theme** subject of discussion; main subject in musical piece, literary work, *etc*

**them·selves'** reflexive form of they: *they did it t.*

**then** at that time: *we were happier t.*; soon afterward or next in order of time or place: *he came and t. told us the news*; in that case: *if you knew it, t. you should have said so*

**the·ol'o·gy** study of religion; particular body of religious beliefs. **theolo'gian**, **theolog'ical**

**the'o·rem** statement of sth to be proved; rule or law in mathematics, *etc*

**the·o·ret'i·cal** of or existing in theory; not practical

**the'o·ry** general principles offered to explain phenomena; proposed but unproven explanation; statement of principles of a science, art, *etc*. **-rize** (*UK* **-rise**)

**ther·a·peu'tic** of the curing of disease; curative

**ther·a·py** treatment of (mental) illness, *esp.* without drugs, *etc.* **-pist**

**there** (dhār) in, to, or at that place: *he stood t. for ten minutes;* also to introduce sentence in which verb precedes subject: *t. is nothing further to be said*

**there'a·bout(s)** about or near that place, amount, *etc*

**there·af'ter** after that

**there'by** as a result of that

**there'fore** as a result

**there·up·on'** immediately after that; in consequence of that

**ther'mal** of heat or temperature

**ther·mom'e·ter** (thermom-) instrument for measuring temperature

**ther'mos** (**bot·tle**) vacuum bottle designed to keep contents at desired temperature

**ther'mo·stat** automatic device for controlling temperature

**the·sau'rus** special kind of dictionary containing words grouped according to meaning

**these** *pl* of **this**

**the'sis** (*pl* **-ses**) statement made and supported by argument; long essay written to obtain university degree

**they** (dhā) (**them, their**) persons, things or animals already mentioned; people in general

**thick** of great or specified extent between opposite sides or surfaces; (of number of objects) set closely together; numerous or plentiful; filled or covered with: *the air is t. with smoke;* (of liquids) not thin and freely flowing; (of accent) obvious; (of voice) unclear. **-en, -ness**

**thick'et** dense growth of shrubbery, *etc*

**thief** (*pl* **thiev|es**) one who steals. **-ery, -ish**

**thigh** (thī) part of leg between hip and knee

**thim'ble** small metal cap placed on finger and used to push needle in sewing

**thin** having relatively small extent between opposite sides or surfaces; (of body) lean; (of number of objects) placed far apart; not abundant or plentiful; (of liquids) flowing easily; (of air) containing little oxygen; lacking solidity or substance

**thing** any material object that lacks life and consciousness; that which is or may be an object of thought; object, creature, *etc*, that is not or cannot be clearly described: *how much does that t. cost; pl* matters or affairs: *such t.*

*shouldn't be discussed; pl belongings: where are my t.?*

**think (thought)** form or have idea in the mind; bear in mind: *t. of what I told you;* remember: *I can't t. of his name;* believe, be of (specified) opinion: *I t. I'll be there by ten; I t. very much of his abilities;* turn (matter, *etc*) over in one's mind; form or have intention: *I'm thinking of going home*

**third** next after second; being one of three equal parts

**thirst** (feeling of dryness in mouth caused by) need of drink. **-y**

**thir·teen** a number (13), next after twelve. **-teenth**

**thir·ty** a number (30), three times ten. **-tieth**

**this** (*pl* **these**) word used to indicate person, thing, *etc*, held, observed, near to the speaker, *etc*: *t. is the man I want you to meet, look at t. flower;* to indicate one of two or more things or persons nearer in time, place, *etc*, or to show distinction: *t. store is nearer than that*

**thong** strip of leather

**thorn** sharp pointed projection on the branches or stems of various plants, as roses

**thorn·y** having thorns; difficult, as problem, *etc*

**thor·ough** (thurō) complete; fully done. **-ness**

**thor·ough·bred** (of animals) bred from the best stock

**thor·ough·fare** (main) public road; highway

**those** *pl* of **that**

**though** (dhō) in spite of the fact that; **as t.** as if

**thought** (thawt) *n* process or result of thinking; intention: *I had no t. of doing that;* consideration: *I'll give it some t., never had a t. for others.* **-ful, -less;** *v* see **think**

**thou·sand** (thouz-) a number (1000), ten times a hundred. **-sandth**

**thrash** thresh (grain); beat; **t. out** discuss thoroughly

**thread** (thred) *n* long thin cord of silk, cotton, plastic, *etc*, used in sewing or weaving fabric; twisted fibers, as of gold; spiral ridge of screw; *v* pass t. through eye of needle, hole in beads, *etc*; make one's way through narrow passage

**thread·bare** worn out; in poor condition; trite

**threat** declared intention to harm; any possible danger. **-en**

**three** a number (3), one more than two

**three-di·men·sion·al** having or appearing to have length, width and depth

**thresh** beat out grain (from stalks); thrash

**thresh'old** sill of a door; any point of entering or beginning

**threw** see **throw**

**thrift** economical management. **-y**

**thrill** (affect with) sudden wave of keen emotion

**thrive** (**throve** or **thrived**, **thriv'en** or **thrived**) prosper; grow rich; grow healthily

**throat** front of neck between chin and collarbones; passage from mouth to stomach or from mouth to lungs

**throb** (of heart, *etc*) beat regularly; vibrate

**throe** *usu pl* extreme pain

**throne** raised seat occupied by king, bishop, *etc*; also symbol of royal power

**throng** huge mass (of people)

**throt'tle** choke; strangle

**through** (thrū) *prep* in at one end, *etc* and out at the other: *t. a tunnel/pipe*; from end to end or side to side: *walk t. a house*; from beginning to end: *read t. a book*; by means of: *it was t. his aunt that she met him*; as a result of: *we lost it t. carelessness*; *US* up to and including: *Monday t. Friday*; *adv* in on one side and out on the other: *they let the boy t.*; having reached the end: *he is t. with his work*; making a connection: *we got t. by phone*; *it's hard to get t. to him*; thoroughly: *she was frozen t.*

**through-out'** *prep* in(to) or during every part; *adv* right through

**throve** see **thrive**

**throw** (**threw, thrown**) (thrō, thrū) cause sth held in hand to fly through air by means of muscular power; direct on surface or to particular point, as light, remark, *etc*; move switch, *etc*; roll dice

**thrush** small dull-colored migratory song bird

**thrust** (**thrust**) push with sudden or forceful movement; force o.s. on or through

**thud** dull sound, as that caused by fall of something heavy

**thug** ruffian; criminal

**thumb** (thum) short thick finger on inside of human hand, next to index finger

**thump** (strike with) heavy blow; (make) dull sound, as of heavy falling object

**thun'der** loud rumbling noise (following a discharge of lightning)

**Thurs'day** fourth day of the week, between Wednesday and Friday

**thus** in the way indicated; accordingly

**thwart** defeat plans of; prevent from happening

**tick** slight sharp repeated

**timer**

noise, as of clock; blood-sucking insect

**tick'et** printed paper or card entitling holder to admission, transport, *etc*; notice of fine for traffic violation; *US* list of candidates put forward by a political party

**tick'le** touch (person) lightly with fingers or soft object so as to cause tingling sensation

**tick'lish** sensitive to tickling; (of situation, *etc*) risky or difficult

**tide|** *n* periodic rise and fall of ocean. **-al**; trend; *v* t. **over** support through difficult period

**ti'|dy** (make) orderly or neat. **-diness**

**tie** *v* secure with cord, *etc*; fasten by drawing together and knotting ends; confine or limit; arrive at same score (as competitor); *n* necktie; anything which fastens or secures, acts as a bond or unites

**tie'-dye** dye cloth which has been knotted so as to color irregularly

**tier** row or rank, as of seats

**ti'ger** (tī-) large and powerful flesheating Asian animal of cat family with tawny fur and black stripes

**tight** (of rope, knot, *etc*) closely drawn or fastened; fixed firmly into place; fitting (too) closely; tense; (of situa-

tion, *etc*) difficult to manage. **-en**

**tights** *pl* close-fitting elastic garment covering legs and lower part of body

**tile** thin slab of baked clay, plastic, *etc*

**till** *prep, conj* until; *n* drawer in shop, bank, *etc* for holding money; *v* plow or cultivate land. **-er**

**til'ler** bar used to turn rudder

**tilt** (cause to) lean over, slope or slant; **at full t.** at full force

**tim'ber** wood for building; trees suitable for this

**tim'ber-line** see **treeline**

**tim'bre** (-ber) tone quality

**time** progress as divided into seconds, minutes, hours, days, *etc*; particular or limited portion or period of this in which events follow upon each other; any period in the history of the world; each occasion of a repeated action, *etc*: *he came for the third t.*; tempo; also used to indicate multiplication: *6 times 3 is 18*; **at times** occasionally; **in t.** in due course; **on t.** punctual(ly); (of purchases) to be paid for over a period of t.

**time'less** not affected by time; unending

**time'ly** occurring at a suitable time

**tim'er** person or device for measuring time elapsed, as

in race; device for starting or stopping process, machine, *etc* at some pre-set time

**time'ta·ble** schedule, *esp.* for public transportation

**tim'id, tim'o·rous** shy; easily frightened

**tin** soft silver-colored metallic element, used *esp.* to coat other metals with protective layer; *UK* can

**tinc'ture** solution of medicine in alcohol

**tin'der** matter that readily catches fire from a spark

**tine** prong of fork, comb, *etc*

**tinge** color slightly; add trace of (taste, feeling, *etc*)

**tin'gle** feel slight stinging sensation

**tink'er** *n* itinerant mender of pots, cell, *etc*; *v* repair or adjust sth without plan or in unskilled way

**tin'kle** ([cause to] give off) light ringing sound

**tin'sel** thin shiny metal strips, *etc*, as ornaments; sth brilliant but worthless

**tint** color weakened by mixture with white; delicate or pale color

**ti'ny** very small

**tip** *n* slender (pointed) end of finger, pencil, *etc*; gift of money for service performed; useful (private) information or advice; *v* furnish sth with end, cap, *etc*; (cause to) slant or lean over; overturn

or upset; give useful (secret) information to s.o.; grant t. to s.o., as waiter, *etc*

**tip'toe** move or walk on one's toes, *esp.* quietly

**ti'rade** (-räd) long scolding

**tire** *n UK* **tyre** (air-filled) hollow rubber tube placed around rim of wheel; *v* (cause to) become weary or exhausted, as from work

**tire'some** wearying; annoying

**tis'sue** (tishū) substance of which organ, cell, *etc*, is composed; thin paper (handkerchief); any fine woven fabric

**ti·tan'ic** of enormous strength or size

**tithe** tax (1/10 of income) to support church

**ti'tle** name of book, song, *etc*; name denoting office or rank; legal right to ownership. **-ular**

**to** word used to specify place, *etc*, which is to be or has been reached: *on his way t. the door, he came t. the house*; to express motion or direction: *from the mountains t. the sea*; point in time: *up t. the present day*; limit of movement or action: *the drill went down t. rockbottom*; contact with surface; *etc*: *fasten the lamp t. the wall*; result, aim, purpose, *etc*: *she realized t. her horror that she* *was too late, tear it t. pieces*; object of action, intention, *etc*: *give the present t. him, claim t. immunity*; adherence: *faithful to one's friends*; accompanying the infinitive: *t. go home*

**toad** tailless animal similar to frog, but living in water only when breeding

**toad'y** (behave as) person who is too friendly or obedient to one of higher rank

**toast** *n* bread browned on both sides by heating. **-er**; ceremonial act of drinking; *v* make brown by heat; drink to the health of

**to·bac'co** dried treated leaves of the t. plant, used for smoking, *etc*

**to·day'** (on) the present day; (in) the present

**tod'dle** walk with short tottering steps, as a child

**toe** one of the five digits in which human foot ends; part of shoe, *etc* covering these

**toe'nail** hard covering on upper tip of each toe

**to·geth'er** (-gedh-) in(to) one mass, body, contact, union, *etc*: *they came t. to discuss the matter, nail the boards t.*

**toil** work hard and long

**toi'let** water closet; *US* bathroom; **t. paper** thin soft paper used to clean o.s. after passing off waste matter

**to'ken** sign (of friendship, *etc*); keepsake; coin; metal disk used in place of money

**told** see **tell**

**tol'er·a·ble** bearable; fairly good

**tol'er·ate** allow to be or do; accept without complaining. **-ant**

**toll** *n* tax (for use of road, *etc*); anything taken or exacted; sound of ringing bell; *v* (cause to) ring slowly, as death bell

**to·ma'to** (*pl* **-toes**) (*US* -mā-, *UK* -mah-) (widely-grown plant with) fleshy red smoothskinned fruit used as vegetable

**tomb** (tūm) grave

**tom'boy** girl who likes rough sports, *etc*

**tomb'stone** gravestone

**to·mor'row** (-rō) (on) the day after today; (in) the future

**ton** unit of weight equal to 2,000 pounds avoirdupois in US and to 2,240 pounds avoirdupois in UK; unit for measuring volume of ship by its water displacement, equal to 35 cubic feet

**tone** quality of a sound with reference to its pitch, strength, *etc*; any sound given off by the human voice, birds, musical instruments, *etc*; variety or shade of color; prevailing quality of sth; proper firmness of muscles, *etc*

**tongs** *pl* instrument with movable arms hinged at one end, used for grasping and holding

**tongue** (tung) fleshy movable muscular organ in mouth, used for forming speech sounds, tasting, *etc*; ability to speak. **-tied;** language; anything resembling t. in shape or position, as strip of leather under shoe lacing

**ton'ic** invigorating; *mus* of or based on first note of scale of eight notes

**to·night** (on or during) night of the pressent day

**ton'nage** freight-carrying capacity of ship; freight charge per ton

**ton'sil** one of two small organs at back of tongue

**too** in addition: *I believe it, and my friend believes it, t.*: to an extent beyond the desirable, *etc: he ate t. much*; very: *I would be only t. happy to come*

**took** see **take**

**tool** any instrument used in performing mechanical operation, as a hammer, lathe, *etc*; *usu pl* sth required for one's job; person used by another for his own ends

**toot** (make) sound characteristic of horn

**tooth** (*pl* **teeth**) one of the hard white bodies rooted in the jawbone, used for biting off and chewing food, articulating speech and, in animals, as weapon of attack or defense; anything of similar shape or function, as projections on rim of saw, comb, *etc*

**tooth'ache** pain in the teeth

**tooth'brush** small long-handled brush for cleaning teeth

**tooth'paste** special substance for cleaning teeth

**top** highest or uppermost point, part or surface of anything; leading position or rank; best or choice part; lid of bottle, box, *etc*; woman's garment for upper part of body; highest part of plant above ground; child's spinning toy

**top'-heav·y** liable to fall because of too much weight at top; heavier at top than at bottom

**top'ic** subject of writing, discussion, *etc*

**top'i·cal** of or dealing with sth of local or present interest

**to·pog'ra·phy** (art of mapping out) details of a district, as height, location of rivers, *etc*. **topograph'ical**

**top'ple** (cause to) fall forward or over

**top'sy-tur'vy** upside down; in total confusion

**torch** burning piece of wood, *etc* used as light; *UK* flashlight

**tore, torn** see **tear**

**tor'e·a·dor** bullfighter

**tor·ment'** (inflict) great bodily pain or mental suffering; source causing this. **-or**

**tor·na'do** violent circular wind storm

**tor·pe'do** n explosive shell propelled through water; v attack ship with t.; destroy plan, etc

**tor'|por** temporary stopping or slowing of energy; mental sluggishness. **-pid**

**tor'rent** violent stream or rain. **torren'tial**

**tor'rid** extremely hot and dry

**tor'sion** act of twisting; state of being twisted

**tor'so** trunk of human body or statue; unfinished work

**tor'toise** (tortis) (land) turtle

**tor'tu·ous** full of twists and turns; indirect

**tor'ture** (expose to) severe bodily or mental pain, as punishment or to get information

**toss** throw or fling, as a ball; (cause to) roll or move with irregular motion: ship tossed by the waves, t. in one's bed; **t. a coin** decide or settle sth according to which way a coin falls after being thrown into the air

**to'tal** a of or making up a whole; complete; n sum of all items; v amount to; add up. **total'ity**

**to·tal·i·tar'i·an** of government which allows no opposition. **-ism**

**to'tem** (usu carved wooden) emblem of primitive tribes

**tot'ter** shake or walk as if about to fall

**touch** (tuch) meet at one or more points; put fingers on object or surface, so as to perceive its nature, texture, etc; caress; handle; leave visible (harmful) mark: hair touched with gray, leaves touched by frost; reach; (cause to) be affected with some feeling, as pity: she was touched by his misfortune; **t. up** improve by making small additions or changes: his work needs to be touched up; deal with or refer to: he touched on this subject

**touched** moved with emotion

**touch'ing** moving; pathetic

**touch'y** easily offended; sensitive; requiring tact or skillful handling

**tough** (tuf) not easily broken, torn, cut, etc. **-en;** hard to do, master, etc

**tou·pee'** (tūpā) artificial hair shaped to cover a bald spot

**tour** trip through country, etc; period of service, etc

**tour'na·ment** a series of contests of skill

**tour'ni·quet** (-ket) device for stopping flow of blood

**tow** pull along by rope, etc

**to·ward(s)** (tōerdz, tôrdz) in the direction of: *walk t. the shore;* near (in time): *they ate t. evening;* with regard to: *his attitude t. this problem;* in part payment: *the money went t. the boy's education*

**tow'el** (tou-) piece of cloth or paper used for wiping or drying sth. **-ling**

**tow'er** (tou-) tall, relatively narrow structure (rising from main building)

**town** (toun) great number of houses and other buildings, often densely populated; main business or shopping area

**tox'ic** of poison; poisonous

**toy** object, as doll, ball, *etc,* for children to play with; sth very small of its kind, *esp.* an animal: *t. poodle*

**trace** *v* draw; copy through transparent paper. **-ing;** follow track of; find signs of; *n* sign; mark; small amount; harness strap

**trac'er** chemical compound used in X-rays

**track** line of marks or footprints made by vehicle or animal in passing; rough road or path; course of movement; course made for particular purpose, as for racing; pair of parallel steel rails for railroad; band of tape for recording or already recorded; endless belt around wheels of vehicle, as bulldozer; sports connected with running: *t. and field*

**tract** large stretch of land; system of parts in body, as digestive t.

**trac'tion** act of pulling; friction of body on surface on which it moves

**trac'tor** large motor vehicle for pulling heavy loads

**trade** *n* exchange of goods for money or other commodities, as carried on within a country or between countries; business or any skilled work pursued to gain a livelihood; *v* buy and sell goods; exchange (goods). **-er**

**trade'mark** registered name, sign, *etc* to identify product's manufacturer; distinctive trait, *etc* by which a person can be recognized

**trade un'ion,** also *US* **labor union** or *UK* **trades union** association of workmen for protection of their interests. **-ist**

**tra·di'tion** beliefs or customs handed down from past. **-al**

**traf'fic** (the total of) people, vehicles, *etc,* in movement; trade in or transportation of goods, *etc;* buying and selling of forbidden goods

**trag'e·dy** drama of events leading to unhappy ending; terrible or sad event

**trag·|ic, -i·cal** of tragedy; sad
**trag·i·com'|e·dy** drama of mixed tragic and comic elements. **-ic**
**trail** (let) drag along the ground; draw or have floating along behind; follow the track of
**trail'er** vehicle drawn by another vehicle; *US* vehicle equipped as dwelling, *esp.* as used by tourists; small bits of a film, *etc* shown as advertisement
**train** *n* railroad engine and the cars pulled by it; line or series of moving persons, animals, *etc*; series of objects, events, thoughts, *etc*; part of gown trailing behind one; body of followers; *v* bring (person, animal) to desired state or standard by teaching, discipline, *etc*; cut or fasten plant to grow in certain way; point (camera, *etc*) at
**trait** (trāt, *UK usu* trā) specific quality, *esp.* of a person
**trai'tor** one who betrays trust, *esp.* of his country. **-ous**
**tram** *UK* streetcar
**tramp** *v* walk with heavy firm steps; walk steadily over long distance; travel on foot, living from occasional jobs; (of ship) travel between ports irregularly; *n* vagrant person; long walk; *US sl* lewd woman

**tram'ple** tread heavily upon; crush
**tram'po·line** canvas, *etc* stretched tautly over metal frame, used for jumping and tumbling
**trance** dazed state
**tran'quil** quiet; not excited
**trans·ac't'** carry on, *esp.* business. **-tion**
**tran·scen|d'** go beyond; surpass. **-dence, -dent**
**tran·scen·den'tal** beyond human experience or understanding
**tran·|scribe'** make (written or recorded) copy of. **-scription, tran'script**
**trans·fer'** (cause to) move from one place to another; hand over possession of; print or copy from one surface to another; change from one train, *etc* to another
**trans·fig'ure** change form or appearance of s.o. or sth, *esp.* to make beautiful or spiritual
**trans·form'** change completely in form, character, *etc*. **transforma'tion**
**trans·fu'sion** artificial replacement of lost blood or body fluids
**trans·gres|s'** go beyond limits allowed; break (law). **-sion**
**tran'sient** lasting or staying only for a short time
**trans'it** passage through or over

**tran·si·tion** passage; change from one state to another

**tran·si·to·ry** lasting only a short time

**trans·late'** express meaning in another language; change (ideas, *etc*) into another form

**trans·lu'|cent** permitting light to pass partially. **-cence, -cency**

**trans·mis·sion** act of transmitting; sth transmitted, as radio or television broadcast; parts of vehicle transferring power from engine to wheels

**trans·mit'** send from one place to another, as radio waves. **-ter**

**tran·som'** crossbeam; window over door

**trans·par'|ent** that can be seen through; clear. **-ence**

**tran·spire'** become known; happen

**trans·plant'** remove and reset (plant) in another soil, (person) in another place or (organ) in another body. **transplanta'tion**

**tràns·port'** carry from one place to another. **transporta'tion;** (cause to) be carried away with emotion

**trans·pose'** reverse position of (two or more things); change usual order of; *mus* change to different key

**trans·verse'** crosswise

**trans·ves'|tite** person who wears clothes of opposite sex (for sexual pleasure). **-tism**

**trap** device for catching animals, preventing escape of steam, gas *etc*, or for catching a person unawares

**tra·peze'** bar fixed at a height by cords and used by acrobats or gymnasts

**trap'pings** *pl* ornaments

**trash** worthless or waste matter

**trau·ma** shock due to wound, *etc*

**trav·el** go from one town, country, *etc*, to another. **-er** (*UK* **-ler**); proceed or move in any way; (of part of machine) move in fixed course; pass over distance

**trav·erse'** pass or lie across; consider entire scope of

**trav·es·ty** (make ridiculous by) exaggerated imitation

**trawl'er** fishing boat using large net dragged along sea bottom

**tray** flat broad wooden or metal board for carrying or displaying food, *etc*; lidless drawer inside trunk, *etc*

**treach'er·|ous** traitorous; not to be relied on. **-y**

**trea'cle** *UK* molasses

**tread** *v* (**trod, trod'den** or **trod**) set down one's foot, walk: *he trod over the marsh;* crush by walking on; *n* manner of or sound produced in stepping; upper surface of stairstep; heavy patterned part of tire, boot, *etc* touching ground

**trea'son** betrayal of trust; offense of betraying one's government. **-able, -ous**

**treas'ure** riches; store of money or valuables; very valuable object

**trea'**‖**su·ry** place where wealth, *esp.* public funds, is kept; department of government in charge of revenue. **-surer**

**treat** act towards (person) or handle (sth) in specified way; deal with or approach in particular manner: *t. the situation with great care;* try to relieve or cure disease medically. **-ment;** invite person to sth special or unexpected

**trea'tise** serious book or article on some subject

**trea'ty** agreement between nations

**tre'ble** *a* threefold; high-pitched; soprano; *v* multiply sth by 3, as profits, *etc*

**tree** plant with wooden trunk, *usu* growing tall, developing branches above the ground, and bearing either leaves or needles (and edible fruit); sth resembling this plant

**tree'line** altitude above which, or n. or s. latitude beyond which, trees do not grow

**trek** travel slowly, *esp.* over long distances

**trel'lis** frame with structure of crossed (wooden) strips, *esp.* as support for vines, *etc*

**trem'ble** shake, as with cold or fear; vibrate

**tre·men'dous** extraordinarily large, strong, *etc*

**trem'or** trembling

**trem'u·lous** shaking; fearful; unsteady. **-ness**

**trench** long ditch, *esp.* as shelter from enemy fire

**tren'chant** cutting; sharp

**trend** general direction or inclination; fashion

**trep·i·da'tion** anxiety; fear

**tres'pass** enter private property without owner's permission; offend (against law, duty)

**tres'tle** supporting framework, *esp.* for railroad over river, *etc*

**tri'al** judicial examination by court; test; method or manner of testing sth

**tri'an·gle** figure with three sides and three angles; sth resembling this figure. **trian'gular**

**tribe** social group of common stock and with one chief. **-al**

**trib·u·la'tion** suffering

**tri·bu'nal** court of justice; people appointed to deal with particular question

**trib·u·tar·y** (stream, etc) flowing into larger body (of water); (person, nation) paying tribute

**trib'ute** sth done, said or offered as mark of respect; sum paid by state, etc to another as price for peace, etc

**trick** means of or device for deceiving; prank played for fun; clever skillful feat, as done by magician. **-ery**

**trick'le** flow in drops or small thin stream

**tri'cy·cle** vehicle with one wheel in front and two in back used by small children

**tri'fle** n unimportant thing or fact; small amount; kind of dessert; v treat without proper seriousness; play idly with

**trig'ger** device for releasing spring, etc

**trig·o·nom'e·try** branch of mathematics dealing with relations of sides and angles of triangles

**trill** (give forth) vibrating sound, as in singing

**tril'lion** US one million millions

**tril'o·gy** group of three related literary compositions

**trim** make neat or orderly by cutting off projecting parts, etc; fasten ornaments on. **-ming**; free of what is unnecessary: t. a budget

**trin'i·ty** group of three

**trin'ket** small ornament; toy

**tri'o** group of three; musical composition for three

**trip** v (cause to) catch one's foot on projection, or make false step so that one falls; make mistake; walk lightly; release, as switch, etc; n (short) journey; act of tripping; sl period of visions caused by drugs, as LSD

**tripe** stomach of ox as food

**tri'ple** (make) three times as great, etc; having three parts

**trip'let** one of three babies born at the same time to the same mother

**trip'li·cate** made in three copies; tripled

**tri'pod** support resting on three legs, as for camera

**trite** (of phrases, etc) commonplace or worn out

**tri'umph** (achieve) state of being victorious or successful; (exult over) great success or achievement. **trium'phant**

**triv'i·al** of little importance; shallow. **trivial'ity**

**trod, trod'den** see tread

**trol'ley** streetcar; small truck running on tracks

**trom·bon'e** mus large brass wind instrument with sliding tube which is moved to change note. **-ist**

**troop** n body of (moving) persons, etc; pl soldiers; v come together or move in group

**tro'phy** anything taken or awarded for victory

**trop'i|cs** *pl* hot regions near equator. **-cal**

**trot** run at moderate speed

**trou'ble** (trubl) disturb or upset person's mind; worry; cause to undergo inconvenience, pain, extra work, *etc*; cause bodily pain: *he was troubled by a headache*; annoy; agitate: *troubled waters*. **-some**

**trou'ble·mak·er** person who (un)consciously causes difficulty for others

**trou'ble·shoot·er** person who locates and repairs defects in machinery, *etc*; mediator in disputes

**trough** (trof) long narrow container for animal food, *etc*; channel for carrying rain away

**trounce** beat severely

**troupe** (trūp) company of actors, *etc*

**trou'sers** *pl* (trouzerz) two-legged outer garment covering body from waist *usu* to ankles

**trous·seau'** (trūsō) bride's outfit of linen, clothes, *etc*

**trout** *a usu* freshwater food fish of salmon family

**trow'el** tool with flat blade for spreading mortar, *etc*; garden tool for light digging

**tru'an|t** one who stays away from shool, *etc* without

leave. **-cy**

**truce** (agreement for) temporary stop in fighting, *etc*

**truck**, *UK* **lor'ry** heavy motor vehicle for transporting goods *etc*; *US* fruits and vegetables raised for sale

**truc'u·lent** aggressive; bad-tempered. **-lence**

**trudge** walk tiredly and heavily

**true** (trū) in accordance with actual facts or reality; genuine; (of persons, character, *etc*) sincere, non-deceiving; loyal; exact or accurate: *the ship held t. to its course*; deserving its name: *t. genius*

**tru'ism** self-evident truth

**trump** *n* card of suit declared to rank higher than the others; *v* beat (by playing t.); **t. up** invent, as false charges against s.o.

**trum'pet** *mus* tubelike brass wind instrument widening at the end and having clear powerful tone. **-er;** sth resembling t.; (make) loud cry of elephant

**trun'cheon** policeman's club

**trun'dle** (cause to) roll along (heavily)

**trunk** main body of tree; large box with hinged lid for carrying clothes during trip; long flexible tubelike nose of elephant; main part of human or animal body, without the head and limbs; telephone line between two main exchanges; *US* lidded compartment at back of auto for transporting objects (*UK* **boot**); *pl* shorts worn for swimming, *etc*

**truss** *v* fasten; bind; *n* supporting framework or belt

**trust** *n* belief or confidence in another's reliability, honesty, *etc*, in outcome of events, or in cause; *sth* or *s.o.* placed under another's care, management or guard; number of companies, *etc* which have combined to control prices and exclude competition; *v* believe in; rely on; entrust to. **-ful, -ing, -worthy**

**trus·tee'** person who manages property in trust for another. **-ship**

**truth** (trūth) that which is true or conforms to reality or principles of logic, *etc*; honesty. **-ful, -fulness**

**try** make effort to do *sth*; experiment to find out nature, establish truth, *etc*; test quality, value, *etc*; examine and decide a law case; melt (fat) to get oil; expose to suffering, painful experience, *etc*

**tsar** see **czar**

**tub** wide round (wooden) vessel; *infml* bathtub; amount held by t.

**tu·ba** (tū-) *mus* very large low-pitched wind instrument

**tube** hollow round body of metal, glass, *etc*, for conveying or storing liquids; short flexible cylinder of metal, *etc*, for toothpaste, paint, *etc*; any hollow rounded organ or part; *UK infml* subway

**tu·ber·cu·lo'sis**, also **TB** infectious disease attacking *esp.* the lungs. **tuber'cular**

**tu'bu·lar** tube-shaped

**tuck** put into narrow space; turn blanket under edges of mattress; draw up in folds, as material; draw one's legs under oneself

**Tues'day** (tūzdi) second day of the week, between Monday and Wednesday

**tuft** small bunch of threads, feathers, *etc*

**tug** pull violently (at); move by pulling along

**tu·i'tion** (fee for) teaching

**tu'lip** (tū-) (bulb plant with) colorful cuplike flower

**tulle** (tūl) fine silk or nylon net material

**tum'ble** (cause to) fall (down or over) suddenly, as by losing balance; perform leaps, springs *etc*, in acrobatic performance; move hastily

**tum'bler** large drinking glass; part of lock mechanism; acrobat

**tu'mor,** *UK* **-mour** unnatural growth in body

**tu'mult** uproar; confusion; vi-

olent disorder or excitement.
**tumul'tuous**

**tu'na** (tū-) (flesh of) large saltwater food fish

**tun'dra** mossy treeless plain
in arctic regions

**tune** *n mus* series of sounds
forming a (simple) melody.
**-ful;** state of being in harmony or proper pitch; *v* bring
instrument to proper pitch;
adjust engine; set radio, *etc*
to receive particular station

**tu'nic** loose (sleeveless)
blouse or coat

**tun'nel** (build) underground
passage

**tur'ban** scarf wound around
head, as worn by Moslems

**tur'bid** muddy; unclear

**tur'bine** wheel in engine, *etc*
driven by water, steam, *etc*

**tur'bu·lent** disordered; dis-
turbed; uncontrolled. **-lence**

**tu·reen'** deep covered dish
for soup

**turf** (piece of) grassy soil;
racetrack

**tur'gid** (-jid) unnaturally
swollen; pompous (as style)

**tur'key** (flesh of) large do-
mesticated game bird, much
valued as food

**tur'moil** state of excitement
or disorder

**turn** *v* (cause to) move around
center or axis; fold over from
one side to another as pages;
bring under or inner parts to
surface: *t. up the soil;* (cause

to) change course or direction; aim in particular direction; change nature or appearance of: *t. wine into vinegar, the weather turned cold;*
(cause to) become sour, as
milk; reach or pass (certain
age, *etc*): *he has just turned
fifty;* direct (thought, attention, *etc*) towards; bend or
twist; (cause to) be affected
with nausea or giddiness:
*her stomach turned at the sight of
blood;* **t. off** stop current,
flow of water, *etc*, by throwing switch, tightening faucet,
*etc;* **t. on** cause water or electric current to flow; **t. over**
think over, consider; transfer management of affairs,
*etc;* sell goods worth specified amount; *n* act of turning
or state of being turned;
bend in road; action execut-
ed in order by each of a
group: *it is my t.*

**turn'coat** one who changes
his party or principles

**tur'nip** (plant with) fleshy
yellowish root, used as vegetable

**turn'o·ver** rate at which sth is
sold; amount of business
done in a given period; rate
of fluctuation, *esp.* in a company's workers; small cres-
cent-shaped fruit pastry

**turn'pike** *US* toll highway

**turn'stile** gate with four arms
revolving on a post, turned

to admit one person at a time

**turn'ta·ble** revolving platform for playing records or for turning locomotives around

**tur'pen·tine** oil made from tree gum, used to thin or remove paint, *etc*

**tur'quoise** bluish green (gem)

**tur'ret** small tower

**tur'tle** reptile whose body is enclosed in hard round shell

**tusk** long pointed tooth, as of elephant

**tus'sle** struggle roughly

**tu'te·lage** guardianship

**tu'tor** (private) teacher. **tuto'rial**

**tux·e·do** *US* dinner jacket

**twang** ([cause to] make) sharp ringing metallic sound; (of voice) nasal tone

**tweak** twist or pull sharply; pinch

**tweed** rough woolen cloth

**twee'zérs** *pl* small pincers for pulling out hairs, *etc*

**twelfth** next after eleventh; one of twelve equal parts

**twelve** a number (12), eleven plus one

**twen'|ty** a number (20), two times ten. **-tieth**

**twice** two times

**twid'dle one's thumbs** move thumbs around each other for lack of sth better to do

**twig** small shoot or branch

**twi'light** (twī-) period sepa-

rating day and night; light in sky just after sunset or just before sunrise; period of decline

**twin** one of two children born at the same time to the same mother; either of two closely related or similar people or objects

**twine** *v* twist (strands) together; wind around; *n* string made from several strands twisted together

**twinge** (twinj) sharp sudden pain

**twin'kle** shine with quick gleams; sparkle

**twirl** (cause to) turn round and round; spin

**twist** wind two or more strands or threads together; (cause to) assume different shape, *esp.* due to force; change original meaning of words, *etc*; turn in different direction or in spiral course: *the road twisted along the coastline*

**twitch** move (part of body) suddenly and involuntarily

**twit'ter** utter small sounds, as bird

**two** (tū) a number (2), one more than one

**two'-faced** false; insincere

**two'-tone** having two colors or shades of color

**ty-coon'** businessman of great wealth

**type** *n* kind, class, *etc*, distinguished from others by particular characteristics; person, thing, *etc*, embodying characteristics of its class, or serving as standard, *etc*. **typ'ical**; piece of metal on which letter is cut in relief, used in printing; *v* write using typewriter or computer; establish the t. of

**type'writ·er** machine for producing printed letters on paper by means of levers operated by pressure of fingers on keys

**ty'phoid (fe'ver)** infectious

disease causing intestinal inflammation and often death

**ty·phoon'** violent windstorm, *esp.* near or on sea

**ty'phus** infectious fever causing red spots, great weakness, *etc*

**typ'i·fy** be typical specimen of; serve as symbol of

**ty·pog'ra·phy** art of printing; appearance of printed matter. **-pher, typograph'ic(al)**

**ty'rant** absolute and cruel ruler. **-ny, -nize** (*UK* **-nise**)

**tyre** *see* **tire**

# U

**u** twenty-first letter of Englisch alphabet

**u·biq'ui·tous** encountered everywhere

**ud'der** milk-containing gland of cow, *etc*

**UFO** *Unidentified Flying Object*, often thought to be from outer space

**ug'ly** not pleasing to sight or sound; very unattractive; nasty or threatening: *u. wound*

**ul'cer** open sore forming pus, *etc*. **-ate, -ous**

**ul·te'ri·or** intentionally kept concealed

**ul'ti·mate** furthest; last; beyond which no other is possible; fundamental

**ul·ti·ma'tum** (-mā-) final

statement of terms *usu* accompanied by some kind of threat

**ul'tra** extreme; going beyond what is ordinary

**ul·tra·ma·rine'** deep blue (of) color

**ul·tra·son'ic** beyond the upper limit of human hearing

**ul·tra·vi'o·let** of or using invisible rays of spectrum beyond violet

**um'ber** (of) dark brown color

**um·bil'i·cal cord** feeding tube connecting unborn child with mother

**um'brage: take u.** take offense; feel insulted

**um·brel'la** round piece of silk, *etc* stretched over folding metal rods attached to central rod with handle, used as protection from rain; sth offering protection

**um'pire** (act as) person chosen to enforce rules of game, arbitrate dispute, *etc*

**un·a·bridged'** not shortened or cut, as book, film, *etc*

**un·ac·count'a·ble** difficult to explain or understand

**un·ad·vised'** without advice; rash

**un·af·fect'ed** not affected; sincere; simple

**u·nan'i·mous** in complete agreement. **unanim'ity**

**un·as·sum'ing** modest

**un·a·vail'ing** having no effect; useless

**un·a·ware'** without knowledge or consciousness of

**un·a·wares'** unexpectedly

**un·bal'anced** lacking balance; mentally unstable

**un·bend'** (-bent) (cause to) become straight; relax from formality

**un·bend'ing** inflexible

**un·bri'dled** uncontrolled

**un·called'-for** unnecessary

**un·can'ny** mysterious; arousing superstition

**un'cle** brother of one's father or mother or husband of one's aunt

**un·com'fort·a·ble** not comfortable; embarrassed

**un·con'scion·a·ble** (-shen-) unreasonable; excessive

**un·con'scious** *a* without

consciousness; unaware; unintentional; *n* that part of one's mental life or of one's thoughts, fears, *etc*, of which one is not consciously aware

**un·cork'** remove cork from bottle, *etc*

**un·couth'** lacking good manners; clumsy; (of language) rude

**unc'tu·ous** fawning; insincere

**un·cut'** unabridged; (of gems) not yet cut and polished

**un·daunt'ed** fearless; not discouraged

**un'der** in or to position below or lower than rest; below or beneath the surface of; subject to control, authority, *etc*, of, or to restrictions, rules, *etc*: he studied *u.* Newman; according to: *u. the provisions of the law*; exposed to: *u. the surgeon's knife*; bearing weight of: *he groaned u. the burden*; inferior to, less than: *his income is u. a 1000 dollars, u. age*; **u. way** in or into transport

**un·der·act'** act (part in play) with restraint

**un'der·arm** of or for the armpit; with arm below level of the shoulder

**un'der·brush** bushes and small trees in forest

**un'der·car·riage** supporting framework (of vehicle); landing gear of airplane

**undoing**

un'der·clothes see **underwear**

un·der·cov'er secret; not public

un'der·cur'rent current moving below surface; hidden climate of opinion

un'der·dog the weaker person, team, etc

un'der·done not thoroughly cooked

un·der·es'ti·mate attach too little value or importance to

un·der·foot' beneath one's feet; in the way

un'der·ground a secret; not generally accepted; below the earth's surface; n UK subway; secret political group working against government

un·der·go' (-went, -gone) go through; suffer

un·der·grad'u·ate student who has not yet graduated

un'der·hand, -hand·ed not open; dishonorable

un'der·line' draw line under; emphasize

un·der·mine' make tunnel under; wear away foundation; harm secretly

un·der·neath' (directly) below surface or object

un'der·pass' road, etc under railway or another road

un·der·rate' underestimate

un·der·score' underline

un'der·shirt (sleeveless) garment worn over upper body

beneath clothing

un·der·stand' (-stood) take in or grasp the meaning, nature, etc of; infer (from previous information): I u. he is coming tonight; be versed in or able to deal with: u. physics; be tacitly expected or accepted: his help is understood. **-able**

un·der·stand'ing n insight; intelligence; power of rational and abstract thought; agreement or thing agreed upon: the contract was based on this u.; a sympathetic

un'der·stud·y person who learns a role, so as to replace usual actor in emergency

un·der·take' (-took, -tak'en) enter upon (task); promise to do; take responsibility for

un'der·tak·er person who manages funerals

un'der·tow backward flow of waves breaking on beach

un'der·wear garments worn next to skin beneath clothing

un·der·went' see **undergo**

un'der·world criminal elements of society; myth. the home of the dead

un·der·write' (-wrote, -writ'ten) sign; agree to pay costs of; guarantee sale

un·di·vid'ed complete

un·do'ing reversing of what has been done; cause of destruction

**un·dress'** remove (one's) clothes

**un·due'** excessive

**un·du·late** move in waves; look like waves

**un·du'ly** more than proper

**un·earth'** dig out of earth; discover (secret, *etc*)

**un·earth'ly** supernaturally strange

**un·eas'y** anxious; uncomfortable

**un·e·quiv'o·cal** clear; plain

**un·faith'ful** engaging in sex with s.o. other than one's partner. **-ness**

**un·fledged'** not developed

**un·found'ed** baseless

**un·gain'ly** clumsy; awkward

**un'guent** ointment for burns, *etc*

**un·hinge'** take from the hinges; unsettle (mentally)

**u'ni·corn** mythical horselike animal with single horn in middle of forehead

**u'ni·form** *a* not varying in form or character; conforming to the same rule. **uni·form'ity;** *n* particular kind of dress worn by all members of a group, as policemen

**u'ni·fy** join together; make one or uniform. **unifica'tion**

**u·ni·lat'er·al** of or done by one side only; one-sided

**un·in·hab'i·ta·ble** not fit to be lived in

**un·in·hib'it·ed** lacking inhibitions

**un'ion** being united (in marriage, business, *etc*); agreement; coupling for pipes; see **trade union**

**u·nique'** (-nēk) being without like or equal; alone in kind or excellence. **-ness**

**u'ni·sex** worn, used, *etc* by both male and female

**u'ni·son** agreement; *mus* singing, *etc* the same note

**u'nit** individual part of larger whole; quantity chosen as standard; the number one

**u·nite'** join together; (cause to) become one. **u'nity**

**u·ni·ver'sal** of, done by or affecting all. **universal'ity**

**u'ni·verse** all existing things; the whole of creation

**u·ni·ver'si·ty** institution of higher learning, empowered to confer degrees in law, the arts, *etc*

**un·kempt'** uncombed; untidy

**un·less'** if not

**un·let'tered** not educated

**un·like'ly** improbable

**un·looked'-for** not foreseen or expected

**un·man'ner·ly** not polite

**un·mis·tak'a·ble** clear

**un·nat'u·ral** contrary to nature; artificial

**un·nerve'** take away (one's) courage, strength, *etc*

**un·ob·tru'sive** not striking; not easily noticed. **-ness**

**un·prec'e·dent·ed** for which there is no past example

**un·pre·ten'tious** not showy; simple

**un·quote'** word used to show end of quotation

**un·rav'el** separate threads of; solve or lay open, as riddle, plot etc

**un·re·lent'ing** without pity; not relaxing in speed, etc

**un·re·mit'ting** not stopping; not growing weaker

**un·rest'** lack of calm; uneasiness; dissatisfaction

**un·ru'ly** not obeying; difficult to manage. **-liness**

**un·scathed'** (-skādhd) unharmed

**un·scru'pu·lous** dishonest; without principle. **-ness**

**un·seem'ly** not proper. **-liness**

**un·set'tle** disturb; upset

**un·set'tled** changing (often); not yet decided; (of bills, etc) not paid; having no permanent inhabitants

**un·sight'ly** ugly. **-liness**

**un·spar'ing** very generous

**un·sta'ble** lacking firmness or balance; fickle; lacking mental steadiness

**un·strung'** nervously tired or anxious; having the strings loose

**un·think'ing** thoughtless

**un·til'** up to the time, point, degree, etc of: stay u. tomorrow, he hit him u. he was unconscious

**un·time'ly** premature; happening at the wrong time

**un·tir'ing** without stopping or giving up

**un·told'** not told; too many to be counted

**un·to'ward** difficult to manage; awkward; unlucky

**un·var'nished** plain; direct

**un·war'rant·ed** done without authority

**un·wield'ly** clumsy; unmanageably bulky. **-iness**

**un·wit'ting** not knowing; not intentional. **-ly**

**un·wont'ed** unusual

**up** adv to or in a high or higher position, place, rank, degree, etc; to or in an erect position: stand u.; to or at equal position with something followed, competed with, etc: catch u. with him; being capable of dealing with or mastering: he is u. to the situation, be u. to someone's tricks; in(to) activity or action: take the matter u.; into view, etc: he turned u. today; into proper condition, etc: tidy u.; to state of conclusion, termination, etc: the candle was burnt u.; prep to higher point: he went u. the stairs; at or in higher part: he lives u. the street; to or at the source: sail u. the river

**up·braid'** scold; reproach

**up·bring·ing** (manner of) raising and educating children

**up·date**' bring up to date

**up·end**' set on end, as a cask

**up·heav·al** sudden (violent) change

**up·hold**' (-held) support; confirm

**up·hol·ster** provide furniture with stuffing, covering, *etc*. **-er, -y**

**up·keep** process or cost of supporting

**up·on**' on

**up·per** higher in place, position, *etc*

**up·per·most** highest in place, rank, *etc*

**up·right** erect; pointing or raised directly upward; honest or just

**up·ris·ing** revolt

**up·roar** violent or noisy disturbance. **uproar·ious**

**up·root**' tear up by roots; get rid of

**up·set**' (-set) cause to fall over; defeat; create disorder; trouble (the mind); make ill

**up·shot** outcome

**up·side down** with top and bottom inverted; in(to) great disorder

**up·stairs**' (to, at, in) part of house above ground floor

**up·stand·ing** erect; straightforward; honest

**up·start** person who has risen suddenly from low social position

**up'·-to-date**' modern; including latest facts, *etc: an u. summary*

**up·ward** toward a higher place or position

**u·ra·ni·um** heavy radioactive metallic element, used as source of atomic energy

**ur·ban** of a city or town

**ur·bane** polite; refined in manner. **urban·ity**

**urge** press s.o. to do or accept; try to persuade; drive or press forward

**ur·gent** urging; calling for immediate attention. **-cy**

**u·ri·nal** vessel or building for urinating

**u·rine** fluid waste material from kidneys. **-nate**

**urn** large vase with foot, *esp.* to hold ashes of the dead; large container, *usu* with tap, for making and serving coffee or tea

**us** objective case of we

**us·age** customary practice or use (of language); manner of treatment

**use** *v* (yūz) employ, occupy o.s. with, avail o.s. of, *etc: u. a towel, u. the bus to get to work*; consume, *esp.* habitually: *he uses drugs*; exploit (person): *he used him for selfish purposes*; **used** + *infinitive* to indicate sth that happened regularly in the past: *he used to play golf, I used to wait for her every morning*; **used** + *present participle to*

**vacuum cleaner**

indicate being accustomed to sth through experience, *etc*: *he was used to going hungry, I'm used to her complaining*; **u. up** expend, bring to an end, *etc*: *we must u. up this meat, u. up this piece of soap*; *n* (yūs) state or method of using or being used; function; usefulness. **-er**

**used** secondhand

**use'ful** of use; helpful; effective. **-ness**

**ush'er** *n* one who seats people in theater, church, *etc*; *v* bring (in[to], out, *etc*): *he ushered him into the room, the sun ushers in the dawn*

**u'su·al** (yūzh-) commonly or customarily met with, done or occurring

**u·surp'** take and hold wrongfully, *esp.* office, position, *etc*. **usurpa'tion**

**u'su·ry** lending of money at illegally high rate of interest. **-rer, usu'rious**

**u·ten'sil** instrument, *esp.* for household use

**u'ter·us** womb, the organ in female where young are nourished by birth

**u·til·i·tar'i·an** of, based on or aiming at usefulness. **-ism**

**u·til'i·ty** usefulness; useful thing; *pl* public services, such as electricity

**u'ti·lize**, *UK* **-lise** make use of. **utiliza'tion**

**ut'most** of the greatest, highest, *etc* degree; extreme

**u·to'pi·an** (of plans, *etc*) ideal but impractical. **-ism**

**ut'ter** *a* complete; total. **-ly**; *v* express in words; make audible sound, as cry. **-ance**

**u'vu·la** soft lobe of flesh hanging at back of mouth

# V

**v** twenty-second letter of the English alphabet

**va'can|t** empty; not occupied; disinterested; empty-headed. **-cy**

**va·cate** go away from so as to leave empty

**va·ca'tion** scheduled period away from work, school, *etc*, used for traveling, recreation, *etc*

**vac'ci·nate** inject weakened disease germs (vaccine) to protect against infection

**vac'il·late** waver in opinion, *etc*

**vac'u·ous** empty; stupid. **-ness**

**vac'u·um** *n* space (almost) entirely empty of air; void; state of isolation or loss; *v* clean, using v. cleaner

**vac'u·um clean·er** electric appliance which sucks up dirt, used for cleaning carpets, drapes, *etc*

**va·gi·na** canal in females that leads from the vulva to the uterus and serves both for sexual intercourse and as birth canal

**va·grant** person with no fixed home or means of support. **-cy**

**vague** not clear; not clearly expressed, felt, *etc*. **-ness**

**vain** useless; having too high an opinion of o.s.

**vale** valley

**val·e·dic·to·ry** bidding farewell, as a speech

**val·en·tine** (card, *etc* sent on St. Valentine's Day, Feb. 14, to) one's love

**val·et** personal manservant; hotel, *etc* employee who performs services, as pressing clothes, *etc*

**val·iant** (-yent) brave

**val·id** founded on truth or fact; having legal force. **-date, valid·ity**

**va·lise** small traveling bag

**val·ley** low area between hills

**val·or**, *UK* **-our** personal bravery

**val·u·a·ble** (sth) of great value

**val·u·a·tion** estimate of worth

**val·ue** (valyū) that quality of a thing for which it is held in regard or considered useful, desirable, *etc*: *the v. of having loyal friends*; amount of money for which thing can be bought or sold; fair re-

turn for money paid; *pl* standards or principles

**valve** doorlike device controlling flow of liquid, *etc*

**vam·pire** night-wandering bloodsucking ghost

**van** covered (delivery) truck

**va·na·di·um** hard metallic element, used *esp.* to strengthen steel

**van·dal** person who purposely ruins property of others, *etc*. **-ism, -ize** (*UK* **-ise**)

**vane** device showing direction of wind; blade of propeller, windmill, *etc*

**van·guard** body of troops marching in front; those leading in development, opinion, *etc*

**va·nil·la** (tropical plant whose pod yields) substance used in flavoring, making perfume, *etc*

**van·ish** disappear; pass from existence

**van·i·ty** quality of being vain or conceited; futility

**van·quish** overcome; conquer

**vap·id** dull; uninteresting

**va·por**, *UK* **-pour** fine particles of moisture in air; gaseous form of normally solid or liquid substance. **-ize** (*UK* **-ise**)

**var·i·a·ble** *a* that can be changed; likely to change; *n* sth that can vary in number or quality. **variabil'ity**

**var'i·ance** disagreement; lack of harmony; **at v.** not in agreement or harmony with

**var'i·ant** different (form, as of word)

**var·i·a'tion** (degree of) change from former or normal condition, *etc*, *pl mus* set of short pieces based on same melody

**var'i·cose** (of veins) abnormally swollen

**va·ri'e·ty** state of being varied or different; many-sidedness; a collection of different things

**var'i·ous** of differing kinds, many

**var'nish** (apply) resinous solution, *etc* which produces hard, transparent glossy coating, *esp*. on wood

**var'y** change; make different; differ from

**vase** (vās, *UK* vahz) container for flowers

**vas·ec'to·my** *med* surgical cutting of sperm ducts in order to make a man sterile

**Vas'e·line** TM petroleum jelly, used in dressings, ointments, *etc*

**vast** very great in number, size, *etc*. **-ness**

**vat** large tub or cask for holding liquids

**vault** *n* arched roof; underground room for storage or burial; *v* leap; jump over

**vaunt** boast; brag

**veal** flesh of calf used as food

**veer** change direction

**veg'e·ta·ble** (vej-) *n* (part of) plant grown for food and eaten with main part of meal; *a* of, made from or growing like plant

**veg·e·tar'i·an** (of or for) person who lives only on vegetables, plant products, *etc*. **-ism**

**veg'e·tate** grow like plant; lead dull inactive life

**veg·e·ta'tion** plants collectively; particular plant life: *tropical v.*

**ve'he·ment** showing or caused by strong feeling; forceful. **-mence**

**ve'hi·cle** carrier for people, goods, etc. **vehic'ular**; sth used as means to convey, support, exhibit sth else

**veil** (vāl) (wear) transparent piece of material to cover (esp. woman's) face; (cover with) sth that conceals or hides

**vein** (vān) one of the tube-shaped vessels which convey blood back to the heart; rib in insect's wing or plant leaf; clearly defined layer of coal, ore, *etc*

**ve·loc'i·ty** (rate of) speed

**vel'vet** soft (silk, *etc*) fabric with thick short hairs. **-y**

**vend** sell (small wares) **-or**

**vend'ing ma·chine** coin--operated machine dispensing cigarettes, *etc*

**ve·neer'** thin layer of fine wood glued over cheaper wood; superficial polish of manner, *etc*

**ven·er·a|te** regard with deep respect. **-ble**

**ve·ne're·al** of or arising from sexual intercourse

**venge'ance** punishment in return for wrong

**venge'ful** filled with a desire for revenge

**ven'i·son** flesh of deer used as food

**ven'om** poison, as of snakes, bees, *etc*. **-ous**

**vent** *n* small opening; outlet; *v* give expression or outlet to (feelings *etc*)

**ven'ti·la|te** cause fresh air to move through. **-tor**; discuss freely and openly

**ven·tril'o|quis·m** art of speaking so that voice appears to come from some source other than speaker's mouth. **-quist**

**ven'ture** take risk; dare to do or go; put forward (opinion). **-some**

**ve·ran'da** roofed platform attached to house, open on three sides

**ver'bal** of words; spoken, not written. **-ize** (*UK* **-ise**)

**ver·ba'tim** repeated exactly word for word

**ver·bos|e'** wordy. **-ity**

**ver'dict** decision of jury; opinion

**verge** *n* extreme edge or border; *v* **v. (up)on** border on

**ver'i·fy** confirm; check accuracy of. **verifica'tion**

**ver'i·ta·ble** real; rightly so called. **-bly**

**ver'min** destructive small animals, as rats, fleas, *etc*

**ver·nac'u·lar** *a* native to a particular place; *n* language actually spoken as opposed to official language; colloquial language

**ver'sa·tile** many-sided; having many uses. **versatil'ity**

**verse** poetry; a line of poetry; stanza; division of the Bible

**versed** skilled; learned

**ver'sion** translation; description from one point of view (as contrasted with another); adaptation

**ver'sus** against, as in legal actions or contests

**ver'te·bra** (*pl* **-brae**) one of the bones forming the backbone. **-bral**

**ver'te·brate** (animal) having a backbone

**ver'ti·cal** at right angles to ground, *etc*; upright

**ver'y** *adv* to a high degree: *he is a v. good writer*; especially: *v. few apples*; *a* being such in the full sense of the word: *the v. essence of spring*, was the *v. flippancy of this remark which made him angry*; even: *they hated his v. name*; identical: *the v. man whom I saw yesterday*

**ves'sel** ship, *esp.* a large one; blood tube or canal; container

**vest** *n* short sleeveless garment (worn under man's jacket); *UK* undershirt; *v* **v. in** give power or authority to; give right or control to

**ves'ti·bule** entrance hall

**ves'tige** trace of something no longer existent

**vest'ment** official or ceremonial garment

**vet'er·an** *n* former soldier; *a* having long experience

**vet'er·i·nar·y** of the medical care of animals. **veterinar'ian**

**ve'to** *n* (*pl* **ve'toes**) right (of one branch of government) to reject measures decided on by another; *v* prohibit

**vex** irritate; make angry. **vexa'tion, vexa'tious**

**vi'a** by way of

**vi'a·ble** capable of living or developing; able to be done or used

**vi'a·duct** bridge carrying road, railway over valley, *etc*

**vi'al** small bottle. Also **phi'al**

**vi'brant** vibrating; throbbing with energy; exciting; resounding. **-cy**

**vi'bra·phone** *mus* instrument consisting of frame with metal bars which vibrate when struck

**vi'brate** quiver; tremble; thrill (with emotion). **vibra'·tion**

**vi'bra·tor** device producing vibrations, *esp.* one used to massage the body

**vic'ar** Anglican priest. **-age**

**vice** immoral or wicked habit; fault; see also **vise**

**vi·ce ver'sa** (vīsi vurse) in reversed order

**vi·cin'i·ty** nearness; neighborhood

**vi'cious** (vishes) evil; cruel; of ugly disposition; **v. circle** chain (of events) in which solution of one problem creates new problem (which makes first one worse). **-ness**

**vi·cis'si·tude** *usu pl* constant changes in one's life or fortunes

**vic'tim** sufferer of injury, evil deed, *etc*; one sacrificed in religious rite. **-ize** (*UK* **-ise**)

**vic'to|r** winner in battle or contest. **-ry, victo'rious**

**vid'e·o** *a* of or related to broadcast or reception of television; *n* videotape recording

**vid'e·o re·cor·der** machine for taping and playing back television images

**vid'e·o·cas·sette** magnetic tape used to record picture and sound, as of television broadcast, for later replaying

**vie** compete with

**view** (vyū) (range of) sight; examination by eye; way of seeing sth or s.o.; thing seen, as a landscape; opinion: *what is your v. on this matter?*; **in v. of** considering; **with a v. to** with the aim of: *with a v. to bettering himself*

**vig'il** (vij-) period of watchful attention, *esp.* at night

**vig'ilant** on guard; watchful. **-lance**

**vig'or**, UK **-our** strength; energy. **-ous**

**vile** evil; disgusting

**vil'ify** speak evil of. **vilifica'tion**

**vil'la** country residence

**vil'lage** (vilij) small group of houses covering small area, less than a town

**vil'lain** evil character in novel, film, *etc*

**vim** force; energy

**vin'ai-grette** (salad) dressing of oil and vinegar

**vin'dicate** clear person of suspicion; justify

**vin-dic'tive** revengeful. **-ness**

**vine** plant with winding woody stem, *esp.* one bearing grapes; climbing or trailing plant, as ivy

**vin'egar** (viniger) sour liquid made by fermenting fruit juice, used to preserve or prepare food. **-y**

**vine'yard** plantation of grapevines

**vin'tage** *n* grape harvest; fine wine from grapes gathered in one season; *a* of high quality; classic

**vi'ola** *mus* stringed instrument larger and deeper in tone than violin

**vi'olate** break (law, promise, *etc*); disturb rudely; rape

**vi'olent** involving force; wild or uncontrolled; severe; caused by outside force. **-lence**

**vi'olet** (vī-) (small plant with) blue, purple, yellow or white flower; (of) bluish-purple color

**vi-o-lin'** (vī-) *mus* four-stringed instrument played with a bow. **-ist**

**vi'per** poisonous snake

**vi'ral** of or caused by a virus

**vir'gin** *n* person, *esp.* woman, who has had no sexual intercourse; *a* pure; unused. **-al, virgin'ity**

**vir'ile** manly; strong and forceful. **viril'ity**

**vir'tual** being such in practice though not in name

**vir'tue** moral goodness; good quality; advantage. **-ous**

**vir-tu-o'so** person with great (performing) skill, *esp.* in music. **-ity**

**vir'ulent** poisonous; dangerous; intensely hostile. **-lence**

**vi'rus** especially small type of disease-causing germ

**vi'sa** official stamp on passport permitting person to enter, pass through or leave country

**vis'age** face

**vis'cous** (of liquids) thick; sticky. **viscos'ity**

**vise**, *UK* **vice** tool with movable metal jaws for holding object firmly

**vis·i·bil'i·ty** conditions of light, *etc* as affecting range and clarity of vision; being visible

**vis'i·ble** that can be seen

**vi'sion** sight; act or power of seeing; mental image; sight seen in dream, *etc*; power of imagination

**vi'sion·ar·y** endowed with vision; imaginary; not practical

**vis'it** go to see or inspect; stay with; **v. on** afflict with suffering; *etc.* **-or**, **visita'tion**

**vi'sor** movable piece above car window to protect against light; front piece of cap, *etc* projecting over eyes

**vis'ta** view

**vis'u·al** of sight or the eyes

**vis'u·al·ize**, *UK* **-ise** form mental picture of. **visualiza'tion**

**vi'tal** of, affecting or essential to life; very important; full of life. **vital'ity**

**vi'ta·min** (vī-) any of a number of substances necessary for health but not supplying energy

**vit'ri·ol** sulfuric acid; severe criticism, *etc.* **vitriol'ic**

**vi·va'cious** lively. **-ty**

**viv'id** strikingly bright, as color; full of life; clearly to be seen; distinct

**viv·i·sec'tion** operating, *etc* on living animals for medical research

**vix'en** female fox; quarrelsome woman

**vo·cab'u·lar·y** all the words of a language; stock of words used by person, group, *etc*; list of words

**vo'cal** of, by or for the voice; (loudly) talkative

**vo'cal cords** thin bands of membrane in throat which produce sound when air passes over them

**vo'cal·ist** singer

**vo·ca'tion** occupation or profession. **-al**

**vo·cif'er·ate** shout. **-ous**

**vod'ka** strong colorless (Russian) alcoholic drink

**vogue** (vōg) fashion at a particular time

**voice** (ability to make) sound(s) uttered through the mouth, *esp.* in speaking, singing, *etc*; characteristic quality of such utterance: *a low v.*; expression in words: *give v. to one's opinions*

**void** *a* empty; without legal effect; *n* outer space; feeling of loss

**vol'a·tile** evaporating rapid-

**ly; lively; (dangerously) changeable**

**vol·ca·n|o** mountain with opening through which molten rock, gases, *etc*, are thrown up with explosive force due to pressure beneath earth's crust. **-ic**

**vo·li·tion** act of willing or choosing

**vol·ley** discharge of a number of shots at one time; playing a ball before it hits the ground

**vol·ley·ball** team game in which ball is struck with the hands over a high net

**vol·u·ble** talkative

**vol·ume** (large) book; amount of space enclosed by the three dimensions; amount; (degree of) loudness of sound

**vo·lu·mi·nous** large; filling many books

**vol·un·tar·y** done of one's own free will (without pay); controlled by the will

**vol·un·teer** offer (one's services) freely without pay

**vo·lup·tu·ous** of or given to sensuous or sensual pleasures. **-ness**

**vom·it** spit out (contents of stomach through mouth)

**voo·doo** witchcraft

**vo·ra·cious** greedy (in eating). **-ness**

**vor·tex** whirlpool; whirlwind; moving circular mass

**vote** (provide) formal expression of one's will, *esp*. in politics. **-er**

**vouch for** guarantee

**vouch·er** document proving truth of claimed expenditure; prepaid ticket, *etc*

**vouch·safe** give as favor

**vow** (give) solemn (religious) promise

**voy·age** long (sea) trip. **-er**

**voy·eur** person who gains sexual pleasure from observing sexual organs or acts of others. **-ism**

**vul·gar** crude; lacking good manners or taste; common. **-ize** (*UK* **-ise**), **vulgar'ity**

**vul·ner·a·ble** that may be (easily) wounded; not safe from attack. **vulnerabil'ity**

**vul·ture** (vulch*er*) large bird with naked head and neck which feeds on dead animals; person who profits from misfortune of others

**vul·va** outer female sex organs

# W

**w** twenty-third letter of English alphabet

**wad** (wod) small ball of cotton, paper, *etc*, for stuffing opening; roll of paper money

**wad'dle** walk with short steps while swaying from side to side, as duck

**wade** walk through sth that offers resistance, as water, mud, *etc*

**wa'fer** thin crisp cake

**waf'fle** (wofl) batter cake baked in hinged metal shell

**waft** (cause to) move smoothly (as if) on wind or water

**wag** move repeatedly from side to side or up and down: *the dog wagged its tail, wagging tongues*

**wage** *n pl* pay received for work; *v* carry on (war)

**wa'ger** (place) a bet

**wag'on**, *UK* **-gon** four-wheeled (horse-drawn) vehicle for carrying heavy loads

**waif** homeless child

**wail** (utter) long mournful cry (of pain, grief, *etc*)

**wain'scot** wooden paneling

**waist** (part of garment covering) narrow part of human body below ribs and above hips

**wait** remain without acting, moving, *etc* in expectation of sth or until specified or indefinite time has passed: *I'm waiting for the train, you must w. your turn*; (of thing) be provided or in readiness: *there is 500 dollars waiting for you*; **w. on** serve person(s), as at table (*UK* **w. at**). **-er, -ress** wait for; attend or care for s.o., *esp.* superior: *w. on the Prime Minister*

**waiv'e** give up (right or privilege). **-er**

**wake** *v* (**woke** or **waked**, **waked** or **wok'en**) (cause to) become roused from sleep or inactive state; *n* grieving watch over corpse before burial; track left by moving object, as ship in water

**wak'en** (cause to) wake

**walk** (wawk) *v* (cause to) move along by lifting and setting down feet alternately, *esp.* at relatively slow pace, as for exercise or pleasure; go on foot; *n* (act of or place for) moving on foot; distance to be walked; **w. of life** one's occupation or profession

**walk'er** person who walks; metal device to support *esp.* baby or lame person while walking

**walk·ie-talk·ie** two-way portable radio for sending and receiving signals

**walk'man** *TM* small portable stereo recorder with earphones

**wall** upright solid structure higher and longer than it is thick, made of stone, brick, glass, *etc* and serving to enclose; protection, division, *etc*, as one of sides of room or building; anything which suggests a wall: *his argument met with a w. of distrust*

**wal'let** flat leather case for bills and papers

**wal'low** roll in mud, *etc*

**wall'pa·per** decorative paper for covering the walls of a room

**wal'nut** (wawl-) (tree with) edible nut; valuable hardwood of this tree

**wal'rus** (wawl-, wol-) large sea mammal with long tusks, related to seals

**waltz** (wawlts) (music for) ballroom dance for couples

**wand** (wond) slender stick

**wan'der** (won-) go about without definite aim or purpose. **-er;** move or pass idly or aimlessly: *his eyes wandered about the room;* (of thoughts, *etc*) stray from subject

**wane** become smaller in size or brightness, as moon; lose power, *etc*

**want** have need or desire for or to do; be lacking, fall short of or be without: *the project wants money*

**wan'ton** (won-) done without reason or justification; loose in sexual behavior; playful; wild. **-ness**

**war** (wawr) quarrel carried out (between nations) by armed force; any struggle or conflict of interests. **-fare, -rior**

**war'ble** sing with constant trills, like bird

**ward** person, *esp.* minor, under care of guardian; administrative division of city; separate part of hospital, *usu* for similar treatment: *cancer w.*. **w. off** turn aside, as blow, *etc*

**ward'en** officer in charge of prison; official supervising specific area: *game w., traffic w.; UK* college or school official

**ward'robe** large cupboard for clothes; (person's) stock of clothes

**ware** *pl* goods, merchandise. **ware'house**

**warm** characterized by or giving off moderate heat; (of climate) having relatively high average temperature; having sensation of increased body temperature, as produced by exercise, heavy clothing, *etc;* (of color) tending toward red, orange or yellow; showing or characterized by strong lively feelings, sympathy, *etc*. **warmth**

**warm-blood'ed** having high body temperature not affected by outside conditions

**warn** give notice of or put on guard against danger, possible harm, *etc*; caution against sth forbidden, dangerous, *etc*. **-ing**

**warp** (cause to) bend or twist out of shape

**war'rant** *n* authorization; justification; *v* authorize; justify; guarantee

**war'ran-ty** manufacturer's written guarantee

**wart** small hard growth on skin

**war'ly** watchful; cautious; careful. **-iness**

**was** see **be**

**wash** (wosh) make clean, *esp*. using water and soap. **-able**; (of waves, *etc*) flow over or against shore, cliff, *etc*; (cause to) be carried or moved by force of water: *he was washed overboard*; carry away by action of water: *the flood washed away houses and barns*

**wash'ing ma-chine**, also *US* **wash'er** large electrical appliance for washing clothes

**wasp** (wosp) fierce yellow and black stinging insect. **-ish**

**waste** *v* spend, use up, employ without purpose or definite end: *w. money*. **-ful**; (cause to) be in bad, damaged or severely unhealthy condition; **w. away** be consumed: *the patient was wasting away from cancer, his resources wasted away*; *n* act of wasting or state of being wasted; also *pl* tract of uncultivated (wild and barren) land; sth of no value or use

**watch** (woch) *v* look out for sth or sone (at) attentively; be careful to avoid danger, damage, *etc*: *w. your step*; stay awake for special purpose; *n* small timepiece, *usu* worn on wrist; act of watching; period of time allotted to watching, *esp*. on ship

**wa'ter** (wawter) the colorless tasteless odorless mixture of oxygen and hydrogen in liquid state, turned to steam by heat and ice by cold, which constitutes rain, tears, *etc*; a liquid solution or preparation, as mineral w.

**wa'ter bird** bird that swims or wades in water

**wa'ter clos-et** seatlike porcelain apparatus for carrying off bodily waste by flushing it down waste pipe with water

**wa'ter-course** stream of water, as a river

**wa'ter-fall** stream of water

falling down over crest of cliff, *etc*

**wa·ter·front** section of land or town facing body of water, *esp.* when used as port or landing

**wa·ter·logged** so filled with water as to barely float

**wa·ter·mel·on** large round many-seeded melon with smooth green rind and soft edible red flesh

**wa·ter·proof** not permitting water to pass through

**wa·ter·shed** elevated land between two river systems; critical turning point

**wa·ter ski·ing** sport in which person on skis is pulled over the water by a boat

**wa·ter·tight** waterproof; sealed so that water cannot pass through; (of argument, *etc*) allowing no disagreement

**wa·ter·way** channel for boats, as canal, part of lake, *etc*

**watt** (wot) unit of electrical power. **-age**

**wave** *v* (cause to) move in alternating swells and depressions, as a flag in the wind; (cause to) move alternately in opposite directions; *w. one's handkerchief in farewell*; (cause to) have curved appearance, as hair; *n* arched ridge caused on surface of water by wind or current; act of waving; arching

curve in a surface or line; temporary increase in sth, as emotion, *etc*: *w. of anger, w. of bankruptcies*; curve in the hair; vibration caused by light, sound or electrical power

**wa·ver** flicker; be unsteady; show doubt or indecision

**wax** *n* soft substance secreted by bees and used for candles; similar substance made from fats, oils, *etc*. **-y**; *v* cover with wax, as floor, *etc*; grow in size, as moon; increase

**way** passage for walking, riding, *etc*; anything along or through which one may pass: *doorway*; direction: *look this w.*; distance (to be) covered in space or time: *this money will go a long w.*; manner: *that's his w. of doing things*; means or plan of doing or accomplishing sth: *this would be a good w. to do it*; one's course in (life): *make one's w.*; respect: *in many ways, this is a good argument*; condition: *things are in a bad w.*; *pl* habits: *they have strange ways of behaving*; **by the w.** incidentally; **by w. of** by the route of; **under w.** in progress

**way·lay** (**-laid**) lie in wait for

**way·ward** self-willed; turning away from what is right or proper; changing irregularly. **-ness**

**weed**

**we** (wē) **(us, our)** pronoun used when speaker or writer refers to himself and at least one other person or to people in general

**weak** easily broken, torn or damaged; lacking strength, number, intensity, *etc*; lacking bodily vigor or energy, as from sickness or age; lacking character or determination; lacking power or effectiveness; lacking ability or skill; below average; (of food) mixed with (too) much water; (of sound) low. **-en, -ness**

**wealth** (welth) large amount of financial or other valuable possessions; large or abundant store or supply of: *a w. of ideas*

**wean** accustom child to food other than milk from mother's breast

**weap'on** instrument for use in fighting, as gun

**wear (wore, worn)** (wār) have on one's body as covering, ornament, *etc*: *w. heavy clothes, w. a ruby necklace*; have given expression: *w. a look of self-confidence*; damage or deteriorate by use: *w. a hole in one's clothes*

**wea'ri·some** tiring; dull

**wea'r|y** (make) tired (through work, suffering, *etc*). **-iness**

**wea'sel** small nimble flesheating animal

**weath'er** (wedh-) *n* condition of atmosphere with regard to wind, rain, sunshine, warmth, *etc*; *v* become discolored, worn away, *etc*, by exposure; succeed in coming through storm, *etc*, as ship

**weath'er·man** meteorologist, a person who predicts weather; person on television, *etc* who reads weather prediction

**weav|e (wove, wo'ven)** make fabric by interlacing thread, strips, *etc*, so as to form close network. **-er**; combine various strands; work into whole; move in zigzag course

**web** woven fabric; thin network spun by spider; skin between toes of certain animals, *esp*. swimming birds

**wed'ding** marriage ceremony, *usu* followed by social gathering

**wedge** V-shaped piece of wood or metal, used to split wood, widen opening, maintain distance between two parts, *etc*; sth shaped like this: *w. of pie*

**wed'lock** state of marriage

**Wednes'day** (wenzdi) third day of the week, between Tuesday and Thursday

**wee** very **tiny**

**weed** *n* wild plant, *esp*. one

harmful to other plants by hindering their growth; v root out weeds; **w. out** sort out and remove undesirable parts

**week** period of 7 days from Monday through Sunday; any period of 7 days

**week'day** day exept Sunday and usu also Saturday

**week'end** Saturday and Sunday (plus Friday after working hours)

**week'ly** a (happening) once a week; n magazine appearing each week

**weep (wept)** show emotion by crying tears; give off drops of liquid

**weigh** (wā) have certain weight: the boxes w. 2 pounds each; determine weight of by means of scale, etc; consider value, importance, etc (of) in order to form opinion or choice; have value or importance: this weighs heavily in her favor; raise (anchor)

**weight** (wāt) (amount of) heaviness esp. as measured on scale; system of units for measuring this, as divided into pounds, ounces, etc; importance, measure of influence or effectiveness, etc: his word carries great w.; pressure or burden: the w. of unhappiness. **-less, -y**

**weird** mysterious; supernatural; infml strange or odd. **-ness**

**wel'come** n (word expressing) kindly greeting or warm reception; v greet warmly; receive or accept gladly: I w. this change; a gladly received; agreeable (as visitor); willingly allowed

**weld** unite metals by hammering, etc when hot. **-er;** join firmly together

**wel'fare** well-being; state of health and prosperity; money, etc granted (by state) to needy persons

**well** adv (**better, best**) in satisfactory or favorable manner or condition: the work is w. done, he works w.; with justice or reason: you may w. ask why I came; thoroughly: this is w. thought out; to a considerable extent: w. over 200 dollars; **as w.** also: you can ask them to come as w.; with equal reason or justification: I might as w. stay at home as go out; **as w. as** in addition to (being): it was cold as w. as rainy; interj used to express surprise, agreement, doubt, etc: w., here you are, w., I don't really know; a (**better, best**) in good health: he doesn't look w.; n hole drilled in earth for water or oil; spring; v (start to) flow, as water, tears, etc

**well-be'ing** personal (physical) comfort

**well'-nigh** (-ni) almost

443

**when**

**well-to-do'** prosperous

**welt** ridge on skin (due to blow)

**wel'ter** chaotic mass

**went** see **go**

**were** see **be**

**were'wolf** (*pl* **-wolves**) person in stories who changes into wolf

**west** toward or lying in the direction of the setting sun. **-ern, -a**

**west'ern** story, *esp.* a film, about cowboys, *etc*

**wet** *a* covered with or consisting of liquid, as water; moist; (of weather) rainy; *v* (**wet** or **wet'ted**) make or become wet. **-ness**

**whale** very large sea mammal with fishlike body, valued for blubber and flesh

**wharf** (hw-) platform beside which boats are anchored for unloading

**what** (hwot) word used to ask for specific information: *w. is your age?*, *w. will this cost?*; to inquire into nature, class, origin, *etc.* of thing or person: *w. kind of a man is he?*; to ask for importance, value, *etc*: *w. is that to me?*; to express surprise, indignation, *etc*: *w. a day!*, *w. do you think you are doing?*; to indicate the thing(s) that: *this is w. I think of it, it is hard to say w. happened then*; the kind of person or thing that:

*he has just w. it takes to be successful*; anything that: *do w. you want*

**what-ev'er** any amount or degree: *w. I have is yours*; anything: *w. you say will not change my mind*; regardless of: *do it, w. the others may say*

**wheat** (the grain of) widely cultivated cereal grass, used for making flour

**wheel** round frame with spokes or solid disk, turning on axis and thereby moving vehicles, machinery, *etc*; round object connected to gears, rudder, *etc* and used for steering cars, ships, *etc*; circular movement

**wheel'bar-row** small cart with wheel at front, two legs at back and two handles for pushing it

**wheel'chair** chair with large wheels which are *usu* turned by hand, used *esp.* by people who cannot walk

**wheeze** (make) whistling or rasping sound due to difficulty in breathing

**when** *adv, conj* at what time: *w. is he coming?*; at the time that: *w. London was built*; at any time: *I always feel tired w. I'm hungry*; whereas: *you are dancing w. you should be studying*; considering that: *you needn't worry w. you're doing so well*

**when·ev·er** *adv, conj* at whatever time or occasion; any/every time that

**where** in or to what place: *w. is he?, w. did they go?*; in what state, position, *etc*: *w. would you be without him?*; from what place or source: *w. did you hear that?*; in, to or at any or given place: *he went to w. they were sitting*

**where·a·bouts** place where s.o. or sth is

**where·as** but; in view of the fact that

**where·by** by what or which

**where·up·on** as a result of which; upon or after which

**where·with·al** means, *esp*. money, to do something

**whet** (hwet) sharpen

**wheth·er** (hwedh-) word introducing the first of two or more alternatives: *I don't know w. to go or stay*; if ... or not: *see w. he has come*

**whet·stone** stone for sharpening tool edges

**which** word asking for choice from number of things implied or indicated: *w. book do you want?*, or for specification: *w. one of you will go?*; used to introduce relative clause referring to thing or animal already mentioned: *the horse w. won last year's race*

**whiff** (hw-) slight puff of air, smoke, odor, *etc*

**while** *n* period of time: *a long w.*; **in a w.** soon; **once in a w.** from time to time; *conj* (also *UK* **whilst**) during the time that: *he came w. I was away, wait w. I eat*; although: *w. talented, she has no chance to get the job*; whereas: *he worked, w. his brother played*; *v* **w. away** (time) pass time, *esp*. pleasantly

**whim** (hw-) odd or fanciful notion or desire

**whim·per** (hwim-) (utter) low feeble cry, as of frightened animal

**whim·si·cal** given to odd notions

**whine** (hwīn) cry in low complaining tone

**whin·ny** (make) sound of horse

**whip** *n* strip of leather attached to handle, used to drive on animals, *etc*; official who ensures discipline, regular attendance, *etc* of party members; (sweet) food made with whipped cream, *etc*; *v* beat or strike with quick repeated blows, *esp*. with something slender and flexible; move, pull, jerk, *etc*, quickly and suddenly; beat (eggs, cream, *etc*) into light fluffy mass

**whir,** *UK* **whirr** (make) buzzing sound, as of beating wings, spinning wheel, *etc*

**whirl** (hw-) spin rapidly

**whirl'pool** circular current of water in river, *etc*; **w. bath** special tub in which jets of water create circular current

**whirl'wind** tall funnel of whirling air moving across land at high speeds

**whisk** *n* small brush; device for beating eggs, *etc*; *v* brush; move rapidly; beat, *esp.* with w.

**whisk'er** *usu pl* hair growing on side of man's face; one of the long bristles growing near mouth of cat, rat, *etc*

**whis'key,** UK **-ky** (glass of) alcoholic liquor made from grain

**whis'per** speak in hushed voice without vibrating vocal cords; make soft rustling sound, as leaves; pass on (information, rumor)

**whis'tle** produce clear shrill sound by forcing breath through contracted lips; produce similar sound by breathing into or forcing steam through wooden or metal tube or other device; pass with whizzing sound, as bullet

**white** of the color of snow or common salt; of or concerning light-skinned race; (of skin) pale, as from sickness or fear; (of wine) yellowish, as opposed to red

**white'wash** mixture for whit-

ening walls, *etc*; anything used to cover or hide faults

**whit'tle** (hw-) cut off bits with a knife; reduce gradually

**who** (hū) (**whom, whose**) what person(s): *w. is at the door?*; what sort of person, with regard to rank, nature, *etc*: *I told them w. he was*; also used to introduce relative clause, referring to person already mentioned: *the friend w. gave me this book*

**who-ev'er** whatever person(s): *w. may come*

**whole** (hōl) comprising the full amount, number, extent, *etc*: *the w. class was there, I could see the w. country stretching before me*; undivided: *he swallowed the w. capsule*; undamaged or uninjured: *the vase fell to the ground but remained w.*; denoting a thing complete in itself: *you must consider this matter as a w.*

**whole'sale** *n* the sale of goods in large quantities, *esp.* for resale in shops; *a* on a large scale (at low prices)

**whole'some** (hōlsem) favorable to health; morally good. **-ness**

**whom** (hūm) objective case of who

**whoop'ing cough** infectious (childhood) disease marked by fits of violent coughing

**whore** (hōr) prostitute

**whose** (hūz) word indicating possession by person or thing spoken of: *the man w. house burnt down, a problem w. impact is enormous*; or asking for possessor of: *w. book is this?*

**why** (hwī) for what reason, purpose or on what basis: *w. did you act that way?*; the cause or reason for which: *that is w.* I refused to give

**wick** strip of material in candle, *etc* which burns

**wick'ed** evil; morally bad; mischievous. **-ness**

**wick'er** thin branches of willow, *etc* woven together to make baskets, furniture, *etc*

**wid|e** having great or specified extent from side to side; (of area, *etc*) stretching over a great distance; of great range, extensive: *w. knowledge*; fully open: *looked at him with w. eyes*; not tight: *a w. skirt*; **-en, width; w. of the mark** at some distance from point aimed at

**wide'spread** widely distributed; occurring often

**wid'ow** woman whose husband has died

**wid'ow·er** man whose wife has died

**wield** manage or handle (broom, weapon, *etc*); exercise (power, *etc*)

**wife** (*pl* **wives**) a married woman

**wig** artificial head of hair

**wig'gle** move with short irregular movements from side to side; squirm. **-gly**

**wig'wam** (-wom) hut or tent of native Americans

**wild** (wīld) living or existing in natural state, not tamed or cultivated: *w. duck, w rose*; characterized by unrestrained force, violence, passion, *etc*: *w. storms, w. anger*; far off the mark: *a w. throw/guess*

**wild'cat** *n* naturally wild cat, larger and fiercer than house cat; fierce-tempered person; *a* reckless; unofficial (*esp.* of strikes); *v* drill for oil in unproven areas

**wil'der·ness** (uncultivated or uninhabited) wild region

**wild-goose' chase** futile or foolish search

**wild'life** living things, *esp.* animals, fish, *etc* in their natural surroundings

**wild oats', sow one's w. o.** live wildly while young before settling down

**wild rice'** (edible grain of) a N. Amer. marsh grass

**wile** *usu pl* trick; guile

**will** *v* (**would** [wood]) (am, is, are) about or going to do: *I w. have dinner now*; willing or intending to do: *I w. come tomorrow*; expected or supposed to do: *I trust that he w.*

*do what I say*; sure to do: *he w. insist on having his way*; accustomed to do: *he w. sit there for hours listening to the radio*

**will** *n* faculty of deciding on one's course of action; control exercised over one's feelings, wishes, *etc*. **-power;** determined intention: *have the w. to accomplish one's aims*; action as determined by one's wishes, discretion, *etc*; *he wandered at w. amongst the forest*; one's attitude toward another: *ill w.*; legal (written) declaration stating how one's property should be divided after death; *v* give or receive (property, *etc*) according to a w.; (try to) effect by willpower

**will'ful,** UK **wil-** intentional; perversely obstinate. **-ness**

**will'ing** ready (to do sth); given or done freely

**wil'low** (long flexible branches or wood of) tree with spear-shaped leaves, *usu* growing near water

**wil'low·y** gracefully slender

**wilt** become limp and drooping, like flower

**wi'ily** cunning; sly. **-iness**

**wimp** *infml* weak person

**win** (**won**) succeed in gaining by effort: obtain as result of successful competition, *etc*: *w. a prize, w. a game*; succeed

in gaining by effort: *w. fame, w. someone's approval*. **-ner**

**wince** shrink or start back, as from pain

**winch** (pull or lift using) machine with drum(s) around which rope or chain can be wound; crank

**wind** (wind) *n* current of air caused by natural forces. **-y;** any current or stream of air; (power of) breathing; *mus* (players of) any of the instruments sounded by means of breath; empty talk; **get w. of** suspect; *v* (**wind'ed**) be out of breath from exercise, *etc*: *he was winded from running*; detect by smell

**wind** (wīnd) *v* (**wound** [wound]) (cause to) turn around and around (sth): *w. a handle, w. thread around a spool*; tighten (spring of watch, *etc*) for operation by turning; move in spiral or circular course: *the road wound up the hill*; **w. up** bring into state of tension: *his nerves were wound up*; conclude: *he wound up by quoting his predecessor*

**wind'fall** unexpected profit or gain

**wind'mill** mill, water pump, *etc* worked by wind turning wheel equipped with sails or vanes; sth resembling w.

**win'dow** (windō) (glass-covered) opening in wall or roof

to admit light and air; glass or frame of w.; area for displaying goods visible from outside shop; sth like a w.

**win·dow dress·ing** artful display of goods in shop window; sth intended to produce good (but erroneous) impression

**win·dow-shop** look at goods in shop windows without buying. **-per**

**wind'shield**, UK **-screen** glass in car, *etc* in front of driver

**wind'surf·ing** sport of riding on sailboards. **-er**

**wine** fermented grape juice, produced in many varieties; fermented juice of other fruit: *blackberry w.*

**wing** *n* movable limb with which birds, insects, *etc* fly; flat horizontal surface projecting from body of airplane; part of building projecting from main building; political group with opinions differing from main body; space at either side of theater stage; *v* fly (as if) with wings; wound superficially with bullet

**wink** close and open eyes in rapid succession; open and close one eye quickly, *usu* as signal

**win·|ter** fourth and coldest season. **-try**

**wipe** clean or dry (surface,

*etc*) by rubbing with cloth, hand, *etc*; **w. out** destroy: *the enemy was wiped out*

**wire** (piece of) threadlike metal, used to fasten things together, convey electricity, *etc*

**wire'less** without wires; operated by electromagnetic waves, as radio set

**wir'|y** of or like wire; lean and tough. **-iness**

**wis'dom** being wise; quality of having experience and knowledge

**wise** marked by judgment and the power to discern what is right, reasonable, *etc*

**wish** want (to do, have, be, *etc*) or long for: *I w. to see him, I w. I could go home*; express hope, greeting, *etc*: *w. s.o. well*

**wish'y-wash·y** (morally) weak

**wisp** small bit of straw, hair, *etc*

**wist'ful** thoughtful; having vague sad longings. **-ness**

**wit** (person with) keen (verbal) humor. **-ty**; also *pl* mental ability. **-less**

**witch** woman practicing (black) magic; ugly old woman. **-ery**

**witch'craft** (black) magic

**witch'-hunt** pursuit and persecution of persons with unpopular (political) views

**with** accompanied by or accompanying: *serve fish w. a white sauce*, *I'll go w. you*; having or characterized by: *a person w. a great future*; in given relation to: *talk w. friends*, *in love with s.o.*; by means of or using: *sprinkle the flowers w. his work*; including: *w. John, we'll be six*; against: *a race w. the clock*; in favor of: *we are w. him on this point*; correspondingly to: *the army grew stronger w. every victory*; in regard to: *be dissatisfied w. his work*; owing to: *die w. hunger*; in the same direction: *sail w. the tide*

**with·draw'** (**-drew, -drawn**) take back or away; move back. **-al**

**with·er** make or become dry or shrunken

**with·hold'** (**-held**) keep back

**with·in'** in or to the inner side or part; on the inside; not beyond: *w. view*; in the course of: *w. the next ten days*;: inside the limits of: *w. reason*

**with·out'** not with: *they came w. him*: in the absence of: *w. Mary we can't proceed*; free from: *w. further charges*

**with·stand'** (**-stood**) stand up to or hold out against

**wit'ness** one who is present and sees a thing (and testifies to it in court or by signature)

**wit'ti·cism** clever remark

**wives** pl of **wife**

**wiz'ard** man with magic powers; person with unusual talents. **-ry**

**wob'ble** waver or rock from side to side. **-bly**

**woe** deep sorrow; *usu pl* problem. **-ful**

**woe·be·gone** looking sad

**woke, wok'en** see **wake**

**wolf** (pl **wolves**) (woolf, -vz) large wild flesh-eating animal of dog family

**wom'an** (pl **wom'en**) (woomen, wimin) adult human female. **-hood, -ly**

**womb** (wūm) organ in female mammals where young develop till birth

**won** see **win**

**won'der** (wun-) v be affected with surprise or astonishment, as at sth extraordinary; be curious to know or find out; doubt: *I w. if he will do it*; n (sth causing) feeling of awe

**won'der·ful** very good or admirable

**wont** (wunt) a accustomed (to do); n habit; custom

**woo** seek love of; seek to win or persuade

**wood** hard fibrous substance beneath the bark of trees. **-en, -y;** also pl large group of trees growing together, but smaller than forest. **-ed, -y**

**wood'cut** (print made from) design cut in block of wood

**wood'peck·er** colorful bird with a long sharp bill for making holes in tree bark in search of insects

**wood'wind** (player or) one of the wind instruments: flutes, clarinets, oboes or bassoons

**wool** soft thick hair of sheep, *etc*; yarn or cloth made from this. **-en** (*UK* **-len**), **-ly**

**word** any of the meaningful combinations of sounds or its representation in written form which make up a language and are used to designate object, idea, action, *etc*; also *pl* speech or talk; sth expressed or uttered: *gave him a w. of praise*; *pl* text of a song, *etc*; news: *I just had w. from him*; promise: *I give you my w. on it*. **-ing**, **-less**, **-y**

**word'pro·cess·or** small computer for writing, editing and storing texts

**wore** see **wear**

**work** *n* action or effort taken to do, make, *etc*, sth *esp*. for pay and as means of livelihood; task or sth to be done or made; thing made, done, accomplished, *etc*: *a good piece of w.*; *a w. of art*; *usu pl* fortifications; bridge, road, building, *etc*, *esp*. one erected under public management; *pl* place where sth is manufactured, processed, *etc*: *iron works*; *pl* operating parts of machinery or other mechanical apparatus; *v* do w., *esp*. as one employed; (of machine, *etc*) be in operation; manage, exploit by w.: *w. a mine*; (of plans, *etc*) have effect or desired result; bring about: *w. miracles*; move, be agitated: *the horse worked loose, his face worked with emotion*; treat, handle, *etc*: *w. dough, w. iron*; (of liquid) ferment. **-er**, **-man**

**work·a·hol·ic** *infml* person addicted to work

**work'shop** place where repairs, *etc* are done; meeting to discuss and study some special subject: *drama w.*

**work'sta·tion** desk, *etc* in office with a personal computer which is *usu* connected to large central computer

**world** the entire universe; the earth; particular part of the earth: *Old W.*; state of the earth at particular time, or with regard to particular class or group of mankind: *the w. of the Incas*; mankind in general; any particular sphere of activities, *etc*: *the w. of politics/fashion*; vast number or extent: *a w. of troubles*

**world'wide** throughout the world

**worm** small spineless, limbless creeping animal, *esp*. earthworm. **-y**; spiral ridge on a screw

**worn** see **wear**

**wor'ri·some** causing worry

**wor'ry** (wuri) (cause to) feel uneasy, troubled, anxious

**wors|e** bad in greater degree; of lower quality; in poorer health or condition. **-en**

**wor'ship** service or honor paid to God; adoration

**worst** bad in greatest degree; of lowest quality; most inferior or unsatisfactory

**wor'sted** (woostid) (cloth made from) woolen yarn

**worth** having specified value, *esp.* in terms of money; deserving consideration, attention, *etc: a plan w. our notice*; owning property equal to stated amount: *he is w. a million dollars.* **-less**

**worth·while** being worth the time, money, *etc* expended

**would** see **will**

**wound** (wünd) *n* injury by cut, blow, *etc*; hurt done to feelings; *v* cause a w.

**wound** (wound) see **wind** *v*

**wove, wo'ven** see **weave**

**wran'gle** (have) noisy argument

**wrap** (rap) enclose or cause to be covered entirely by sth folded around. **-per, -ping(s)**

**wrath** (rath, rawth) fierce anger. **-ful**

**wreak** (rēk) carry out (revenge, *etc*)

**wreath** flowers, *etc* wound into circle

**wreck** ship, building, *etc*, that has been destroyed; ruin. **-age**

**wrench** *n* (*UK* **span'ner**) tool for turning nut or bolt; *v* twist suddenly or forcibly, *esp.* a joint of the body

**wrest** twist or turn; take away by force

**wres'tle** (resl) fight by trying to hold or throw opponent to the ground, *usu* as sport. **-tler**

**wretch** very unlucky or unhappy person; person of low character

**wretch'ed** miserable; of poor quality; mean. **-ness.**

**wring** (**wrung**) (r-) twist (wet clothes) forcibly, so as to squeeze out water; clasp (one's own or another's) hand(s); twist violently, so as to break: *w. a chicken's neck*; extract (secret) by force or persuasion

**wrin'kle** (r-) (form) small ridge or line on surface (of brow, cloth, *etc*), caused by contraction, folding *etc*

**wrist** (r-) joint connecting forearm and hand

**wrist'watch** watch attached to metal, *etc* band and worn around the wrist

**writ** (rit) formal written order by court, *etc*

**writ|e** (**wrote, writ'ten**) (rīt, rōt) trace letter(s), word(s), *etc*, on surface, *esp.* with pen or pencil; express thoughts, information, *etc*, in this manner; compose and send letter; produce literary work: *he writes for a living*. **-er:** put (program) data into computer; **w. off** cancel, as debt, *etc*; accept as lost

**writhe** twist or roll about (as if) in sharp pain, *etc*

**writ'ing** handwriting; sth written; *pl* author's works

**wrong** (r-) not in accordance with what is true or correct; not proper; out of order or in unsatisfactory condition; not suitable; (of side of clothes) under or inner

**wrong·head'ed** stubbornly mistaken

**wrote** see **write**

**wrought** (rawt) shaped by working: *w. iron*; made

**wrung** see **wring**

**wry** crooked, *esp*. of facial expression; mockingly humorous

# X

**x** twenty-fourth letter of English alphabet

**xen·o·pho**|**bi·a** (zen-) fear and dislike of foreigners or anything foreign. **-bic**

**xe'rox** (zē-) *TM n* (photocopy made by) special reproduction process; *v* make such a copy

**X'-ray** *n* (photograph made using) extremely short radio rays which penetrate solids, used for detection and treatment of diseases; *v* make such a photograph

**xy'lo·phone** *mus* instrument with wooden bars of varying lengths which are struck with small hammers

# Y

**y** twenty-fifth letter of English alphabet

**yak** large long-haired Asian ox

**yacht** (yot) light fast boat used for racing, trips, *etc*

**yard** unit of linear measure in English-speaking countries, equal to 3 feet or 36 inches; enclosed piece of ground, *esp.* one attached to building or one used for particular purpose, as a dockyard

**yarn** thread spun or twisted together; long story

**yawn** open mouth wide and inhale, *esp.* when tired or bored; (of chasm, *etc*) open wide

**year** (yir) period in which the

earth revolves once around the sun; period of 365 or 366 days, from January 1 to December 31, divided into twelve months; any period of twelve calendar months: *a y. from now*; *pl* (old) age

**yearn** long for. **-ing**

**yeast** yellowish sticky substance of tiny fungus cells, used as leavening for dough or in fermentation, *esp.* in brewing beer

**yell** cry out; scream

**yel'low** of the color of lemons or butter; having y. skin; (of newspaper, *etc*) printing sensational or scandalous reports; *sl* cowardly

**yelp** (give) short sharp cry of pain, *etc*

**yes** word used to express affirmation or consent: *y., he is coming, y., you can go now*; compliance with order or request; *y., I will do it*

**yes'ter·day** (on) the day before today; a short time ago

**yet** *adv* up to the present or a particular time: *don't go y.*; so far: *I have not y. done it*; still: *there is y. time*; even: *a y. stronger effort*; nevertheless: *the wind is strong y. warm*; *conj* but

**yew** (wood of) evergreen tree with small red berries

**yield** give forth, as fruit, results, *etc*; give up; give way

**yo'ga** Hindu system of meditation to free the self; system of exercises used in y.

**yo'gi** follower of yoga

**yo'gurt**, also **-ghurt** thickened fermented milk (with fruit)

**yoke** wooden crosspiece for joining two animals pulling wagon, *etc*

**yolk** (yōk) yellow part of egg

**you** (yū) *sing* and *pl* (**you, your**) the person(s) spoken to: *y. should be glad, he saw y. there*; anyone, one: *y. have to be careful with money*

**young** (yung) in the early stage of life or development; inexperienced; of, for or like young people. **-ster**

**your** (yoor) belonging or pertaining to the person(s) spoken to: *y. book*

**your·self'** (*pl* **-selves**) emphatic or reflexive form of **you**: *you are coming y., did you wash y.?*

**youth** (yūth) state of being young. **-ful**; period during which one is young; the young: *the y. of the country*; male teenager

**yule** Christmas festival. **-tide**

# Z

**z** (*US* zē, *UK* zed) twenty-sixth letter of English alphabet

**za'ny** comically absurd (person)

**zeal** eagerness in pursuit of sth or in support of person or cause. **-ous**

**zeal'ot** fanatic

**ze'bra** (zē-) wild horselike African animal with black and white stripes

**ze'nith** point directly overhead; highest point or state

**ze'ro** the figure O; nothing; point between plus and minus on a graduated scale, as on thermometer; lowest point

**zest** interesting flavor; keen enjoyment or interest

**zig'zag** (move in) line or course marked by sharp alternate right and left turns like letter Z

**zinc** bluish-white metallic element, used to coat iron, *etc*

**zip** close zipper; move very quickly

**zip'per,** *UK* **zip** or **zip fas'ten·er** fastening device made of two flexible toothed bands which can be interlocked by means of sliding piece pulled along them

**zith'er** *mus* flat horizontal instrument with 30–40 strings, played by plucking

**zo'di·ac** imaginary belt in space with all the positions of sun, moon and planets as known in ancient times and divided into twelve equal parts, the signs of the zodiac

**zom'bie** dead person said to be brought to life by witchcraft

**zon|e** division of earth distinguished from others by climate, *etc*; any area marked by special features, as time z. **-al**

**zo·ol'o·gy** scientific study of animals, their history, *etc*. **-gist, zoolog'ical**

**zoom** climb steeply with airplane; give off continuous humming sound; (of camera) move quickly from distant to close-up view using a special z. lens

**zuc·chi'ni** (-kē-) (plant with) green vegetable resembling cucumber

# The 50 states of the USA

| state | state postal abbreviation | capital |
|-------|---------------------------|---------|
| Alabama | AL | Montgomery |
| Alaska | AK | Juneau |
| Arizona | AZ | Phoenix |
| Arkansas | AR | Little Rock |
| California | CA | Sacramento |
| Colorado | CO | Denver |
| Connecticut | CT | Hartford |
| Delaware | DE | Dover |
| Florida | FL | Tallahassee |
| Georgia | GA | Atlanta |
| Hawaii | HI | Honolulu |
| Idaho | ID | Boise |
| Illinois | IL | Springfield |
| Indiana | IN | Indianapolis |
| Iowa | IA | Des Moines |
| Kansas | KS | Topeka |
| Kentucky | KY | Frankfort |
| Louisiana | LA | Baton Rouge |
| Maine | ME | Augusta |
| Maryland | MD | Annapolis |
| Massachusetts | MA | Boston |
| Michigan | MI | Lansing |
| Minnesota | MN | St. Paul |
| Mississippi | MS | Jackson |
| Missouri | MO | Jefferson City |
| Montana | MT | Helena |
| Nebraska | NE | Lincoln |
| Nevada | NV | Carson City |
| New Hampshire | NH | Concord |

| state | state postal abbreviation | capital |
|---|---|---|
| New Jersey | NJ | Trenton |
| New Mexico | NM | Santa Fe |
| New York | NY | Albany |
| North Carolina | NC | Raleigh |
| North Dakota | ND | Bismarck |
| Oklahoma | OK | Oklahoma City |
| Ohio | OH | Columbus |
| Oregon | OR | Salem |
| Pennsylvania | PA | Harrisburg |
| Rhode Island | RI | Providence |
| South Carolina | SC | Columbia |
| South Dakota | SD | Pierre |
| Tennessee | TN | Nashville |
| Texas | TX | Austin |
| Utah | UT | Salt Lake City |
| Vermont | VT | Montpelier |
| Virginia | VA | Richmond |
| Washington | WA | Olympia |
| West Virginia | WV | Charleston |
| Wisconsin | WI | Madison |
| Wyoming | WY | Cheyenne |

| state | population (,000) | rank | area sq miles | rank |
|---|---|---|---|---|
| Alabama | 4,118 | 22 | 51,705 | 29 |
| Alaska | 527 | 49 | 591,000 | 1 |
| Arizona | 3,556 | 24 | 114,000 | 6 |
| Arkansas | 2,406 | 33 | 53,178 | 27 |
| California | 29,063 | 1 | 158,706 | 3 |
| Colorado | 3,317 | 26 | 104,091 | 8 |
| Connecticut | 3,329 | 27 | 5,018 | 48 |
| Delaware | 673 | 46 | 2,045 | 49 |
| Florida | 12,671 | 4 | 58,664 | 22 |
| Georgia | 6,436 | 11 | 58,910 | 21 |
| Hawaii | 1,112 | 39 | 6,471 | 47 |
| Idaho | 1,014 | 42 | 83,564 | 13 |
| Illinois | 11,658 | 66 | 56,345 | 24 |
| Indiana | 5,593 | 14 | 36,185 | 38 |
| Iowa | 2,840 | 29 | 56,275 | 25 |
| Kansas | 2,513 | 32 | 82,277 | 14 |
| Kentucky | 3,727 | 23 | 40,410 | 37 |
| Louisiana | 4,382 | 20 | 47,753 | 31 |
| Maine | 1,222 | 38 | 33,265 | 39 |
| Maryland | 4,695 | 19 | 10,460 | 42 |
| Massachusetts | 5,913 | 13 | 8,284 | 45 |
| Michigan | 9,273 | 8 | 58,527 | 23 |
| Minnesota | 4,353 | 21 | 84,402 | 12 |
| Mississippi | 2,621 | 31 | 47,689 | 32 |
| Missouri | 5,159 | 15 | 69,697 | 19 |
| Montana | 806 | 44 | 147,046 | 4 |
| Nebraska | 1,611 | 36 | 77,355 | 15 |
| Nevada | 1,111 | 40 | 110,561 | 7 |
| New Hampshire | 1,107 | 41 | 9,279 | 44 |
| New Jersey | 7,736 | 9 | 7,787 | 46 |
| New Mexico | 1,528 | 37 | 121,593 | 5 |
| New York | 17,950 | 2 | 49,108 | 30 |
| North Carolina | 6,571 | 10 | 52,669 | 28 |
| North Dakota | 660 | 47 | 70,702 | 17 |
| Oklahoma | 3,224 | 28 | 41,330 | 35 |
| Ohio | 10,907 | 7 | 69,919 | 18 |

| state | population (,000) | rank | area sq miles | rank |
|---|---|---|---|---|
| Oregon | 2,820 | 30 | 97,073 | 10 |
| Pennsylvania | 12,040 | 5 | 45,308 | 33 |
| Rhode Island | 998 | 43 | 1,212 | 50 |
| South Carolina | 3,512 | 25 | 31,113 | 40 |
| South Dakota | 715 | 45 | 77,116 | 16 |
| Tennessee | 4,940 | 16 | 42,114 | 34 |
| Texas | 16,991 | 3 | 266,807 | 2 |
| Utah | 1,707 | 35 | 84,899 | 11 |
| Vermont | 567 | 48 | 9,614 | 43 |
| Virginia | 6,098 | 12 | 40,767 | 36 |
| Washington | 4,761 | 18 | 68,139 | 20 |
| West Virginia | 1,857 | 34 | 24,232 | 41 |
| Wisconsin | 4,867 | 17 | 56,153 | 26 |
| Wyoming | 475 | 50 | 97,809 | 9 |

*From: The World Almanac and Book of Facts 1990, New York 1990.

| state | nickname |
|-------|----------|
| Alabama | The Heart of Dixie |
| Alaska | The Last Frontier |
| Arizona | The Grand Canyon State |
| Arkansas | The Land of Opportunity |
| California | The Golden State |
| Colorado | The Centennial State |
| Connecticut | The Constitution State |
| Delaware | The First State |
| Florida | The Sunshine State |
| Georgia | The Empire State of the South |
| Hawaii | The Aloha State |
| Idaho | The Gem State |
| Illinois | The Prairie State |
| Indiana | The Hoosier State |
| Iowa | The Hawkeye State |
| Kansas | The Sunflower State |
| Kentucky | The Bluegrass State |
| Louisiana | The Pelican State |
| Maine | The Pine Tree State |
| Maryland | The Old Line State |
| Massachusetts | The Bay State |
| Michigan | The Wolverine State |
| Minnesota | The North Star State |
| Mississippi | The Magnolia State |
| Missouri | The Show Me State |
| Montana | The Treasure State |
| Nebraska | The Cornhusker State |
| Nevada | The Silver State |
| New Hampshire | The Granite State |
| New Jersey | The Garden State |
| New Mexico | The Land of Enchantment |
| New York | The Empire State |
| North Carolina | The Tar Heel State |
| North Dakota | The Sioux State |
| Oklahoma | The Sooner State |
| Ohio | The Buckeye State |
| Oregon | The Beaver State |

| state | nickname |
|-------|----------|
| Pennsylvania | The Keystone State |
| Rhode Island | Little Rhody |
| South Carolina | The Palmetto State |
| South Dakota | The Coyote State |
| Tennessee | The Volunteer State |
| Texas | The Lone Star State |
| Utah | The Beehive State |
| Vermont | The Green Mountain State |
| Virginia | The Old Dominion |
| Washington | The Evergreen State |
| West Virginia | The Mountain State |
| Wisconsin | The Badger State |
| Wyoming | The Equality State |

# Tables of Measures and Weights

## 1. Linear Measures

1 inch (in.) = 2.54 cm

1 foot (ft.) = 12 inches = 30.48 cm

1 yard (yd.) = 3 feet = 91.44 cm

## 2. Distance and Surveyors' Measures

1 link (li., l.) = 7.92 inches = 20.12 cm

1 rod (rd.), pole *or* perch (p.) = 25 links = 5.03 m

1 chain (ch.) = 4 rods = 20.12 m

1 furlong (fur.) = 10 chains = 201.17 m

1 (statute) mile (mi.) = 8 furlongs = 1609.34 m

## 3. Nautical Measures

1 fathom (fm.) = 6 feet = 1.83 m

1 cable('s) length = 100 fathoms = 183 m; *US* 120 fathoms = 219 m

1 nautical mile (n. m.) = 10 cables' length = 1852 m

## 4. Square Measures

1 square inch (sq. in.) = 6.45 cm²

1 square foot (sq. ft.) = 144 square inches = 929.03 cm²

1 square yard (sq. yd.) = 9 square feet = 0.836 m²

1 square rod (sq. rd.) = 30.25 square yards = 25.29 m²

1 rood (ro.) = 40 square rods = 10.12 ares

1 acre (a.) = 4 roods = 40.47 ares

1 square mile (sq. mi.) = 640 acres = 2.59 km²

## 5. Cubic Measures

1 cubic inch (cu. in.) = 16.387 cm³

1 cubic foot (cu. ft.) = 1728 cubic inches = 0.028 m³

1 cubic yard (cu. yd.) = 27 cubic feet = 0.765 m³

1 register ton (reg. tn.) = 100 cubic feet = 2.832 m³

## 6. British Measures of Capacity

### Dry and Liquid Measures

1 British *or* Imperial gill (gi., gl.) = 0.142 l

1 British *or* Imperial pint (pt.) = 4 gills = 0.568 l

1 British *or* Imperial quart (qt.) = 2 Imp. pints = 1.136 l

1 British *or* Imp. gallon (Imp. gal.) = 4 Imp. quarts = 4.546 l

### Dry Measures

1 British *or* Imperial peck (pk.) = 2 Imp. gallons = 9.092 l

1 Brit. *or* Imp. bushel (bu., bsh.) = 4 Imp. pecks = 36.36 l

1 Brit. *or* Imperial quarter (qr.) 8 Imp. bushels = 290.94 l

### Liquid Measure

1 Brit. *or* Imp. barrel (bbl., bl.) = 36 Imp. gallons = 1.636 hl.

## 7. U.S. Measures of Capacity

### Dry Measures

1 U.S. dry pint = 0.550 l

1 U.S. dry quart = 2 dry pints = 1.1 l

1 U.S. peck = 8 dry quarts = 8.81 l

1 U.S. bushel = 4 pecks = 35.24 l

### Liquid Measures

1 U.S. liquid gill = 0.118 l

1 U.S. liquid pint = 4 gills = 0.473 l

1 U.S. liquid quart = 2 liquid pints = 0.946 l

1 U.S. gallon = 4 liquid quarts = 3.785 l

1 U.S. barrel = 31 ½ gallons = 119 l

1 U.S. barrel petroleum = 42 gallons = 158.97 l

## 8. Apothecaries' Fluid Measures

1 minim (min., m.) = 0.0006 dl

1 fluid drachm, *US* dram (dr. fl.) = 60 minims = 0.0355 dl

1 fluid ounce (oz. fl.) = 8 fluid dra(ch)ms = 0.284 dl

1 pint (pt.) = 20 fluid ounces = 0.568 l; *US* 16 fluid ounces = 0.473 l

## 9. Avoirdupois Weight

1 grain (gr.) = 0.0648 g

1 drachm, *US* dram (dr. av.) = 27.34 grains = 1.77 g

1 ounce (oz. av.) = 16 dra(ch)ms = 28.35 g

1 pound (lb. av.) = 16 ounces = 0.453 kg

1 stone (st.) = 14 pounds = 6.35 kg

1 quarter (qr.) = 28 pounds = 12.7 kg; *US* 25 pounds = 11.34 kg

1 hundredweight (cwt.) =

112 pounds = 50.8 kg (*a.* long hundredweight: cwt. l.); *US* 100 pounds = 45.36 kg (*a.* short hundredweight: cwt. sh.)

1 ton (tn., t.) = 2240 pounds (= 20 cwt. l.) = 1016 kg (*a.* long ton: tn. l.); *US* 2000 pounds (= 20 cwt. sh.) = 907.18 kg (*a.* short ton: tn. sh.)